THE CINEMA OF ISOLATION

the

a history

cinema

of physical disability

of

in the movies

isolation

martin f. norden

rutgers university press
new brunswick, new jersey

Library of Congress Cataloging-in-Publication Data

Norden, Martin F., 1951–
    The cinema of isolation : a history of physical disability in the
movies / Martin F. Norden.
        p.   cm.
    Includes bibliographical references and indexes.
    ISBN 0-8135-2103-3 (cloth) — ISBN 0-8135-2104-1 (pbk.)
    1. Handicapped in motion pictures.   I. Title.
PN1995.9.H34N67   1994
791.43´6520816 — dc20   93-44547
                                                              CIP
British Cataloging-in-Publication information available

for my family, who understood

contents

preface and acknowledgments

Every history is an act of interpretation laden with biases, and this one is no exception. What I have tried to do in the following pages, written with an admitted slant that will become evident rather quickly, is examine the ways that the mainstream movie industry has depicted the physically disabled experience and explore possible reasons for its fascination with the topic. Despite Joseph Stubbins's blunt declaration that "the toughest item on the agenda of disability is that modern America has no need for most disabled persons" (and in complete contrast to media scholars Keith Byrd and Randolph Pipes's ingenuous finding that "disability is not totally ignored by the film industry"), mainstream filmmakers have constructed hundreds upon hundreds of cinematic portraits of disabled characters for predominantly able-bodied audiences since the earliest years of the medium, and it is worth asking how and why. Following a general "reveal and resist" approach to media imagery, this book focuses on the American commercial (a.k.a. "Hollywood") cinema while also paying attention to a number of international films that have conspicuously worked their way into the American scene. *The Cinema of Isolation* is by no means comprehensive, but I do believe the films I have chosen to discuss are characteristic of their time and reflect the industry's general trends as they relate to physical disability issues.[1]

Conceived as a study aimed at covering almost one hundred years' worth of representative films and their linkages with changes in the mainstream movie industry and U.S. society at large, *The Cinema of Isolation* in some ways follows what feminist film theorists Mary Ann Doane, Patricia Mellencamp, and Linda Williams have labeled the "image of" approach. This sociologically minded framework, particularly useful for dealing with a relatively large quantity of films and charting associated historical trends, has served as the basis for a number of important works that have examined the portrayal of women and minorities in mainstream movies. "It is important to recognize the value of such studies," wrote Doane *et al.*, "both as a point of departure for students first encountering the subject and for historians and sociologists who seek more detailed information about the relation of stereotypical images to the epochs that produce them." Robert Allen and Douglas Gomery offered a similar perspective in their pioneering work on film historiography, *Film History: Theory and Practice*. "Examining how various social groups within society have been depicted in the films of a particular era has formed the focus of a significant body of film historical research," they wrote. "At issue is not how an individual film represents a particular ethnic or demographic group, but whether there is a pattern of screen images among films, if these images change over time, and how this change comes about."[2]

While the "image of" approach is helpful in establishing and investigating correlations among films and historical circumstances, I do think it is both appropriate and necessary to modify it to accommodate other concerns: notably, commodification issues and the construction of spectator positions. The mutually causal relationship of movies and society is also mutually reflective; movies demonstrate aspects of the society that produced them, but just as importantly society mirrors the values of its movies in various ways. (Disabled Vietnam veteran Ron Kovic's early gung-ho view of war, shaped to an important extent by World War II action films such as 1943's *Guadalcanal Diary* and 1949's *Sands of Iwo Jima*, is perhaps the most famous and tragic example, particularly in its implications for an entire society.) Following this line of thinking, or at least the latter portion thereof, some postmodern theorists have argued that the visual media that dominate our high-tech age, movies very much included, position audience members primarily as consumers. From this perspective, physical disability in the movies is not simply a reflection of societal values; it's also a politically charged commodity that moviemakers are asking audiences to "buy." This observation leads to a series of questions concerning disability-related films that this book will attempt to address: What are moviemakers trying to position spectators into believing? What exactly are their movies trying to "sell" and for what purpose, and to what extent does reading these movies "against the grain" reveal the strategies for representing this minority group?[3]

Related to these issues are generative energies behind the films that their makers may only dimly be aware of, if at all, that have also shaped the ways that spectators receive the productions: namely, the deepseated psychosexual forces that have helped form the paternalistic, phallocentric society in which we live as reflected in both its surface structures (e.g., rituals, languages, films) and in the very mechanisms for seeing. Though *The Cinema of Isolation* is primarily an investigation of culturally dominant movie images created within the overlapping historical contexts of U.S. mainstream society, the movie industry, and individual practitioners within that industry (an opinionated investigation consistent, I think, with E. Ann Kaplan's call "for Cultural Studies scholars to address the issue of a text's aesthetic/moral/intellectual 'quality'"),[4] I have tried to expand it to include such concerns.

Within the scope of this study, I have attempted to account for the fluctuating relationship between mainstream American society and its physically disabled minority, how the movie industry's evolving portrait of people with physical disabilities has reflected and contributed to that relationship, the major movie-industry people responsible for this imagery, and a sense of the form (especially as it relates to issues of audience positioning), content, and general popularity of the films themselves. This is a huge agenda, and of necessity I have opted for breadth over depth in the belief that a wide-ranging study would provide a much-needed contextual backdrop for future, more narrowly focused studies of individual films, the conditions that allowed for their construction, and the spectator positions they invite. I do hope, immodestly so, that this historical overview will serve as a major frame of reference against which other researchers could confirm or dispute the findings and interpretations I have offered here.

The Cinema of Isolation is for anyone interested in such topics as the ever-changing concerns and lifestyles of people with physical disabilities (particularly as portrayed in mainstream media), the relationship of film and society, movies as political commodities, and media stereotyping. Readers interested in the process by which directors, screenwriters, studio executives, actors, and others in the industry contribute to the construction of movies will also find this book of value (those engaged in directorial studies, for example, will learn that such auteurs as D. W. Griffith, Alfred Hitchcock, and Frank Capra share the limelight with such lesser knowns as John Cromwell, Tod Browning, and Fred Zinnemann in the "pantheon" of movie directors who have drawn repeatedly from the world of physical disability in the name of movie entertainment), and I have made an extra effort to identify physically disabled people within and outside the movie industry who have had an impact on the imagery. Finally, *The Cinema of Isolation* would prove useful for moviemakers planning to incorporate, or even build entire films around, one or more physically disabled characters. It could serve as a guide for designing such characters and surrounding narrative contexts, albeit from a general "how not to do it" perspective.

One need only read the Rehabilitation Act of 1973 and the Americans with Disabilities Act of 1990 to recognize the wide range of disabling circumstances. In fact, the acts' definitions are so broad that they proved an untenable basis on which to build a single book. To keep the focus of *The Cinema of Isolation* at least somewhat manageable, I have limited my discussions primarily to movies that present at least one person with a severe visual, auditory, or orthopedic impairment (I use this latter catch-all term in reference to disabling conditions related to muscles and bones—paralysis, amputation, musculo-skeletal deformations—without regard to its "corrective" connotations) or cerebral palsy or epilepsy.[5] This book does not examine the movie depictions of people with other disabling phenomena, such as diseases, mental disabilities, or temporary injuries, though on this latter point it does address the longstanding moviemaker interest in facile cures for what would ordinarily be permanent physical disabilities. In addition, it does not investigate the disabled experience as represented in documentary films and television programming. These worthy topics I leave to other researchers in the hope they will find *The Cinema of Isolation* a suitable foundation on which to build their own studies.[6]

In the course of writing this book, I have tried to maintain a sensitivity to language issues. Terms such as "handicapped," "invalid," and "wheelchair-bound" have long been out of favor, and, except for their occasional appearance in direct quotations and titles of books, articles, and films, they find no forum here. I am also aware that the phrase "a person with a physical disability" is not the same as "a physically disabled person"; the latter identifies the person primarily in terms of the disability while the former treats the disability as one of the person's attributes. I confess to using the "physically disabled person" type of wording from time to time, but only out of a desire to avoid unwieldy sentences and with no invidious intent.[7]

I anticipate that some readers might find my general use of the "physical disability" and "physically disabled" terms too reductionistic or restricting. For instance, many people with deafness regard themselves as a distinct cultural minority in and of itself with its own norms, language, and literature. In addition, some people that I treat here as physically disabled may not necessarily perceive themselves as such. Consider, for example, Amy Hamburger's finding in a so-called "Cleveland Cripple Survey" of 1918: "Some were amazed that they should be considered cripples, even though they were without an arm or leg, or perhaps seriously crippled as a result of infantile paralysis. They had never considered themselves handicapped in any sense."[8]

Without trying to deny the uniqueness of the deaf culture or the importance of self-assessment, I believe a case can be made for examining the movie treatment of people with various physical impairments intermingled in one volume and indeed regarding them as people with physical disabilities. In basic terms, this book is about mainstream *perceptions* of society's largest minority as reflected in the movies, and one of the prime perceptions is "You're different because one or more of your physical attributes doesn't work properly, and that difference makes me uncomfortable but intrigues me at the same time." The bigotry arising from this general sentiment is something to which all members of this minority, regardless of their self-perception, have been exposed in varying degrees. In the belief that awareness of our society's ableist heritage is a key ingredient in the struggle for social change, I find it well worth examining the various forms this prejudice has historically assumed in one of the most pervasive and influential of the media arts, the movies.[9]

I would like to thank the people who have contributed to the years-long process of researching and writing this book. Mark Bail, Sharon Butts, Susan Hill, Lisa Letizio, and Laurie Weisman helped me gather library materials during the project's early going, while Jeff Klenotic and Logan Bickford provided similar assistance during its latter stages. The archivists with whom I worked, especially Charles Silver of the Museum of Modern Art Film Department and Leith G. Johnson of the Wesleyan University Cinema Archives, expertly guided me through various research mazes, and the staff members of the New York Public Library at Lincoln Center handled my many requests with a commendable degree of patience and precision. Terry Geesken and Mary Corliss of MOMA's Film Stills Archive, Ray Routhier of the late and lamented "Good Old Days," and the crew at Jerry Ohlinger's Movie Material Store on Manhattan's 14th Street (a mere stone's throw from D. W. Griffith's old stomping grounds) helped streamline the photo selection process. Paul Appleby, Director of Disability Services at the University of Massachusetts/Amherst, offered useful and supportive commentary on an early draft of the manuscript, as did filmmakers Laurie Block and John Crowley of Straight Ahead Pictures and Joseph Shapiro, senior editor at *U.S. News & World Report*. I am grateful to Stuart Mitchner for his many insights and impressive copyediting skills, and I would like to acknowledge the general support of the UMass Communication Department, particularly Maddy Cahill, Jarice Hanson, Hermann Stelzner, and Dick Stromgren. A tip of the hat to the ever-gracious John Michael Hayes, and special thanks to my editor, Leslie Mitchner, whose unwavering commitment, encouragement, and good cheer helped make this book a reality. And to my long-suffering family, Kim, Toby, and Erika, words cannot express . . .

THE CINEMA OF ISOLATION

introduction / politics, movies, and physical disability

Anyone remotely aware of the mainstream movie industry's penchant for constructing warped social imagery should not be surprised to learn that this divisive behavior has extended as much to the depiction of people with physical disabilities as it has to other repressed social subgroups. As film historians Leonard Quart and Albert Auster have argued, "Hollywood, hardly noted for its realistic screen treatment of racial and ethnic minorities and women, has not been any more sensitive or illuminating in its portrayal of the disabled."[1] As powerful cultural tools, the movies have played a major role in perpetuating mainstream society's regard for people with disabilities, and more often than not the images borne in those movies have differed sharply from the realities of the physically disabled experience.

The general thesis guiding this book is simple: most movies have tended to isolate disabled characters from their able-bodied peers as well as from each other. This phenomenon, suggested in the title of this study, is reflected not only in the typical storylines of the films but also to a large extent in the ways that filmmakers have visualized the characters interacting in their environments; they have often used the basic tools of their trade—framing, editing, sound, lighting, set-design elements (e.g., fences, windows, staircase bannisters)—to suggest a physical or symbolic separation of disabled characters from the rest of society. Audience positioning within the films becomes a critical issue, for more often than not moviemakers photograph and edit their works to reflect an able-bodied point of view. (Given that the very apparatus of the movie medium—its basic technology—was designed with mainstream audiences in mind and despite such innovations as captioning and descriptive visual services continues to exclude numerous members of the disabled community, this is hardly a surprising phenomenon.)[2] By encouraging audience members to perceive the world depicted in the movies, and by implication the world in general, from this perspective and thus associate themselves with able-bodied characters, this strategy has a two-fold effect: it enhances the disabled characters' isolation and "Otherness" by reducing them to objectifications of pity, fear, scorn, etc.—in short, objects of spectacle—as a means of pandering to the needs of the able-bodied majority, and it contributes to a sense of isolation and self-loathing among audience members with disabilities.[3]

Moviemakers' general tendency to isolate disabled characters is consistent with the way that mainstream society has treated its disabled population for centuries. As Andrew Grant and Frank Bowe have noted, "Prior to [the late 1960s and early 1970s], being disabled almost assured social, educational and occupational isolation." The process of mainstreaming—bringing disabled people out of institutions and into the mainstream of society, allowing them and able-bodied people to learn from each other—has by its very nature weakened the trend toward isolation, but unfortunately it has done little to vitiate the moviemaker tendency to characterize disabled people as isolated individuals. Paul Longmore's 1985 article on disability and film did not directly address the effects of mainstreaming on moviemaker attitudes, but it is clear from its general tone that little has changed: "The disabled person is excluded because of the fear and contempt of the nondisabled majority. Still, even when the handicapped character is presented sympathetically as a victim of bigotry, it remains clear that severe disability makes social integration impossible. While viewers are urged to pity [such a character], we are let off the hook by being shown that disability or bias or both must forever ostracize severely disabled persons from society."[4]

Why isolation? Why has it occurred in society and the movies, and why is it such a powerful course of action? Philosopher John McDermott provided a lead toward answering these questions in a 1981 essay titled "Isolation as Starvation," in which he argued that such a deprivation is critically detrimental to the human condition and explicitly linked it to mainstream society's treatment of its disabled minority:

> It is important to notice that the most severe difficulty encountered by a human being is that of isolation from the flow of events. This isolation prevents the making of relations and prevents recoveries and consequently growth. Periodic alienation enhances the rhythm of our transactions with nature and the world of experience, but isolation drops us out and away from the very leads and implications which the flow of experience harbors for our needs. The historical isolation of the handicapped from the flow of events resulted in precisely this devolutionary situation, wherein the actual handicap became a minor and subsidiary problem in comparison to being cut off from the avenues and possibilities of future experience.[5]

Regardless of the manner by which it has been enacted (unquestioningly, intuitively, consciously, conspiratorially, etc.), the strategy of isolating disabled people reflects a political agenda of sizable proportions. Mainstream society has long followed a divide-and-quarantine approach to controlling minorities, and, since movies have always played such a conspicuous role in this agenda, it might prove helpful to examine the general topic of political issues and their linkage with movies at this juncture. Briefly put, a majority society will do whatever it can to maintain itself in power, and its practice of keeping minorities such as physically disabled people "in their place" and dependent by defining the issues represents a significant part of its self-continuance. Specialists in the rehabilitation field, an area dominated by able-bodied people, have certainly exhibited this perspective, as Joseph Stubbins has argued: "[Rehabilitation] professionals define the problems, the agenda, and the social reality of disabled persons in ways that serve their own interests more closely than those of their clients." The movie industry, so intertwined with other institutions of the dominant culture, has likewise demonstrated this point of view. Its products constitute an important mode of discourse by which the culture perpetuates itself and its perspectives, and they operate on several levels in service to it. Not only do they frequently deal explicitly with contemporaneous social concerns (the films of the 1940s and 1950s that examined the lives of disabled World War II veterans are obvious examples), but more significantly they also contain submerged ideological perspectives, or what Gerald Mast and Bruce Kawin have called "the unspoken, assumed cultural values of films—values that seem so obviously true for that culture that they are accepted as inevitable, normal, and natural rather than as constructs of the culture itself." These values, which typically go undetected and unquestioned by mainstream audiences, often assume the form of stereotyped images that, though sheer repetition, eventually take on a ring of truth in that society.[6]

In the case of people with physical disabilities, the movie industry has perpetuated or initiated a number of stereotypes over the years as a part of the general practice of isolation—stereotypes so durable and pervasive that they have become mainstream society's perception of disabled people and have obscured if not outright supplanted disabled people's perception of themselves. As the following chapters of this book will reveal, its more common representations include extraordinary (and often initially embittered) individuals whose lonely struggles against incredible odds make for what it considers heart-warming stories of courage and triumph, violence-prone beasts just asking to be destroyed, comic characters who inadvertently cause trouble for themselves or others, saintly sages who possess the gift of second sight, and sweet young things whose goodness and innocence are sufficient currency for a one-way ticket out of isolation in the form of a miraculous cure.

Such images are often far removed from the actual experiences and lifestyles of people with disabilities. After examining hundreds of disability-related film and television dramas, Lauri Klobas concluded that "an immense chasm exists between disabled people and their screen counterparts." It is a view shared by John Schuchman, a Gallaudet University professor immersed in deaf-related issues all his life: "The deaf characters I have seen on movie screens and on television bear little resemblance to the deaf people or community that I knew as a boy or that I know today as a professional in daily contact with deaf people." According to Klobas, the discrepancies between real-life disabled people and their movie portrayals are traceable to mainstream society's reluctance to recognize disabled people as a minority group suffering from discrimination:

The "cultural" chasm between real-life and screen disability can be graphically defined by looking at disability not as a physical/personal problem, but as one of human rights. A simplistic parallel argument would be to state that the reason black Americans did not vote in previous decades, could not use all public bathrooms, and had to sit at the back of the bus was because they had not "accepted" the reality they were black. Their anger resulted from not "overcoming" their race. Obviously, this was never the case and it sounds ludicrous to state the same. However, it is happening to the nation's disabled citizens. Their social problems and individual idiosyncrasies are ignored, while easy emotional stories of "bitterness," "overcoming," and "courage" abound.[7]

Appraising the situation in similar terms, Paul Longmore has noted that the able-bodied majority views disability as "primarily a problem of emotional coping, of personal acceptance. It is not a problem of social stigma and discrimination. It is a matter of individuals overcoming not only the physical impairments of their own bodies but, more importantly, the emotional consequences of such impairments. [The films] convey the message that success or failure in living with a disability results almost solely from the emotional choices, courage, and character of the individual."[8]

The people immediately responsible for this and other messages are of course the able-bodied folk who continue to dominate the movie industry. They and their associates in allied fields have long ascribed significant dramatic and commercial potential to disability-related issues ("The natural tragedy of blindness overtaking a person provides a splendid theme for dramatic situations, whether in fiction, plays or pictures," wrote a movie reviewer for the trade journal *Variety* in 1925, while sixty-odd years later a *Premiere* writer began an article on Oscar-nominated disabled-character performances by noting that "the showier the affliction, the better the chances are for a statuette"), and the attitudes toward disabled people as expressed in the resulting films have ranged from mildly insulting to overwhelmingly hostile. A handful of old-line Hollywood directors have had physical impairments themselves, most notably, John Ford, Raoul Walsh, André de Toth, Nicholas Ray, Tay Garnett, and William Wyler, but little of their work—Wyler's *The Best Years of Our Lives* (1946), Ray's *On Dangerous Ground* (1951), Ford's *The Wings of Eagles* (1957), maybe a few others—suggests any sensitivity to disability issues. Occasionally, people with disabilities act as advisors on a film, but ultimately the authorship of the movie rests with one or more able-bodied people. This is not to say the able-bodied can't have insights into the physically disabled experience, but far more often than not they warp the images to fit preconceived notions. The resulting films often have only the most tenuous connection to the world of people with physical disabilities.[9]

Though members of the movie industry are obviously the front-line cultivators of these images, it would hardly be appropriate to suggest that they have been operating independently of longstanding mainstream values. Though movies are intimately tied to the twentieth century, they are informed to a large extent by negative attitudes toward physically disabled people that predate the cinema by centuries and have found their way into a variety of cultural expressions. They are certainly present in our language ("She's blind to that situation," "Their proposal fell on deaf ears," "That's a lame excuse," "He doesn't have a leg to stand on," etc.), for instance, as well as in the rules and regulations that have helped shape our society. In her analysis of pre-twentieth century laws and public policy statements, Claire Liachowitz concluded that "the cultural practice of translating physical abnormality into social inferiority is so deeply rooted as to have had an almost certain impact on both the formulation and implementation of later public policy."[10] These same deeply ingrained attitudes toward people with physical disabilities have also served as the movie industry's basis for such characters that populate its films.

Consider, for example, a typical moviemaker use of disability: to suggest some element of a person's character, a tradition that carries back to the earliest days of the medium. "A screenplay, remember, is a story told with pictures," wrote Syd Field, the dean of screenwriting teachers. "Pictures, or images, reveal aspects of character. In Robert Rossen's classic film *The Hustler*, a physical defect symbolizes an aspect of character. The girl played by Piper Laurie is a cripple; she walks with a limp. She is also an emotional cripple; she drinks too much, has no sense of aim or purpose in life. The physical limp underscores her emotional qualities—*visually*." Field's prime justification for admonishing screenwriters to continue this contemptible tendency is its sheer longevity: "Physical handicap—as an aspect of characterization—is a theatrical convention that extends far back into the past. One thinks of *Richard III*." If Field's beliefs are anywhere near the industry norm, there is little mystery why such images continue to find their way into the movies.[11]

Field's comments reflect one of the major components of the general strategy of isolation—the positioning of physically disabled people as Others through the exploitation of their appearances—and it may well be the key to understanding why moviemakers create physically disabled characters at all. George Henderson and Willie V. Bryan suggested that "throughout history, people without disabilities have had a paradoxical repulsion-attraction for those with disabilities," an observation that echoes the work of philosopher and socio-cultural critic Leslie Fiedler. In his *Freaks: Myths and Images of the Secret Self*, Fiedler argued that members of mainstream society are fascinated by people with genetic disorders (e.g., dwarfs, giants, hermaphrodites, Siamese twins) because the latter, simultaneously Others and mirrors of the self, are akin to mythic icons that reflect the former's dreams and fears. Though Fiedler distinguished people with genetic disorders from those with other disabilities, a number of his generalizations have particular relevance here.[12]

Chief among them is his observation that "human Freaks have, in fact, been manufactured for ritual aesthetic and commercial purposes ever since history began." Members of mainstream society have always had a strong desire to gaze upon human anomalies, and others are all too willing to offer glimpses of them for the right price. And, although Fiedler was referring in the above quote to people who have been intentionally deformed ("the binding of feet by the

Chinese, the stretching of the lower lip among the Ubangis"), it's an idea that applies to moviemaking as well; moviemakers have quite literally manufactured disabled characters in the name of commercial gain. The people responsible for *The Hunchback of Notre Dame*, a 1939 film notable for its freakshow qualities, were so conscious of mainstream society's fascination with deformity and ugliness that even as they went about constructing one of moviedom's most famous disabled characters they had no less a personage than King Louis XI acknowledge the topic. "The ugly is very appealing to man," said the monarch during the film's infamous fools' day festival sequence. "One shrinks from the ugly and wants to look at it. There's a devilish fascination in it. We extract pleasure from horror." Fiedler has rightly pointed out that movies have usurped the inglorious function of carnival sideshows, which despite occasional revivals have been in decline since the advent of movies: "Human curiosities [have], for most Americans, passed inevitably from the platform and the pit to the screen, flesh becoming shadow." If we agree with Linda Williams's assertion that "there is not that much difference between an object of desire and an object of horror as far as the male look is concerned," an observation that implies a hierarchy of seeing in which the investigating gaze, the desiring gaze, and other variations on the look can co-exist, we begin to draw near to an understanding of the gratifications that able-bodied spectators—male ones, at any rate—seem to enjoy.[13]

Underlying this commodification of physical disability are forces that may help explain its captivating qualities for mainstream moviemakers and audiences alike. Sigmund Freud, who had been writing about disability issues at least as early as 1893 and began articulating the concept of a castration complex shortly thereafter, wrote an article called "The Uncanny" (1919) in which he ascribed a symbolic dimension to disability. Appearing at a time when the world was pondering the disabling effects of war on countless numbers of soldiers and civilians, Freud's essay equated the fear of becoming disabled with castration anxiety. "A study of dreams, phantasies and myths has taught us that anxiety about one's eyes, the fear of going blind, is often enough a substitute for the dread of being castrated," he wrote, suggesting further that the castration complex "is what first gives the idea of losing other organs its intense colouring."[14] Intuitively recognizing the disempowering quality of disability to which Freud alluded, moviemakers have often exploited it in the name of maintaining patriarchal order in several conspicuous ways: by continuing to weaken female figures who from a Freudian perspective are already "castrated," and by creating cautionary tales in which symbolically castrated male figures who seek revenge against patriarchal authorities are often punished further for their Oedipal crimes. Needless to say, such strategies and resulting fetishizations are a significant concern of this book.

Before turning to the actual history of movie portrayals of people with physical disabilities, I think it worthwhile to offer a sketch of mainstream society's attitudes toward disabled people prior to the twentieth century. Such an overview should provide a foundation of understanding for the disability-related movies that have followed.

In their book *Psychosocial Aspects of Disability*, Henderson and Bryan have noted that people with disabilities were considered expendable in ancient societies for several reasons: they failed to contribute to the needs of the community, and they harbored evil *mana* or spirits who caused the disabling condition as a result of the individual's failure to appease the spirits:

> Mana encapsulates the primitive belief in a powerful, invisible, all-pervading force at work in the universe, which could cripple and kill at will. Thus, mental illnesses and physical afflictions were generally viewed as the work of evil mana, or spirits. If, after considerable coaxing, the spirits did not leave a possessed body, this was believed to be indisputable evidence that the individual was being punished. In order to prevent contamination, people possessed with evil spirits were to be either avoided or killed.[15]

People who experienced war-related disabilities were usually exempt from such despicable treatment. In ancient Athens, disabled soldiers received pensions while their Roman counterparts shared in the distribution of such items as food, money, and land grants. By the time of the Middle Ages, however, most disabled war veterans were reduced to roadside begging. If governments were no longer supporting them, they at least experienced a general exemption from mendicancy laws.[16]

Such profoundly ambivalent attitudes toward people with physical disabilities found expression in other forms. Fiedler noted that disabled people have been exhibited for the edification and amusement of audiences ranging from royalty to peasantry since antiquity and in later years often enjoyed church sponsorship (presumably to show agog spectators the results of God's displeasure). In addition, many ancient works of literature contain sections that equate physical perfection with spiritual goodness and disability and illness with evil or punishment for evil. The Bible, a major defining text for Western civilization, includes numerous passages that suggest a linkage of disease and disability with punishment from God, as Nancy Weinberg and Carol Sebian have observed: "In the Old Testament, God admonished people to obey all his commandments or he would inflict them with blindness (Deut. 27:27). The New Testament restates this same sentiment—that physical illness and disability are punishments for some religious transgression. Jesus, upon healing a man said, 'See, you are well! sin no more, that nothing worse befall you' (John 5:14). In another instance of healing he said to a man with palsy, 'My son; your sins are forgiven' (Matt. 9:2). These teachings imply that the sick and disabled deserve to suffer as a punishment for having sinned." Weinberg and Sebian also underscored "the biblical tradition of giving alms to the disabled but not accepting disabled persons as equals"—a view that has changed little over the centuries.[17]

Such perspectives on disability are deepseated and continue to exert a powerful influence. As Henderson and Bryan further noted:

> Many of the ancient myths and stereotypes of people with disabilities still exist. Although few persons currently subscribe to abandoning or killing people with disabilities, many do associate disabilities with sin and the Devil. They either consciously or subconsciously think that *disability* is a synonym of *bad*. More often than not, *able-bodied* is associated with *good*, i.e., Christ and the angels, cleanliness, and virtue. None of the great artists ever created images of angels with disabilities. Conversely, persons with disabilities have been associated through the ages with all that is bad.[18]

Nowhere in literature are evil and disability so inextricably fused as in Shakespeare's infamous Richard Crookback, a character whose disability-informed identity is superseded only by his unremitting evil. Scholars have long been aware of the discrepancy between Richard's historical personage

Filmmakers have followed the lead of playwrights, novelists, and other writers of earlier times by frequently raising fears of disability, as in this interrogation scene from the Cold-War thriller The Girl in the Kremlin. *Copyright © 1957 Universal Pictures Co.*

and Shakespeare's treatment of him. Marchette Chute's assessment is typical: "Shakespeare's portrait of Richard does not have much resemblance to the real King Richard of history, any more than his portrait of a peasant witch has much to do with the real Joan of Arc. But it was the portrait he found in the only history books that were available to him, and he had no reason to question it. Moreover, it gave him the opportunity to show a complete villain in action and he made the most of it." [19] The Bard introduced the treacherous character in *Henry VI, Part 2* and cranked up his wickedness in *Henry VI, Part 3* by having him slay King Henry to end the play. The words he utters over the dead monarch—"Then, since the heavens have shaped my body so, let hell make crook'd my mind to answer it"—not only set the stage for his consummate villainy in *Richard III* but have also served as a longstanding reminder of the disability-evil linkage.

Even as Shakespeare's villainous hunchback initially trod the boards, however, members of the able-bodied majority had begun moving away from the strategy of routinely disposing of its disabled minority and toward a more paternalistic perspective. Legal decrees such as the Elizabethan English Poor Laws of the late sixteenth and early seventeenth centuries helped protect disabled people, even to the point of offering financial assistance, while a number of Western societies began acting on the newfound view that people with disabilities, particularly deafness, were educable and could actually become contributing members of society. As Richard Scotch has noted, education for people with physical disabilities had progressed to the institutional stage by the 1700s; facilities such as the Paris-based Institution Nationale, the place where Louis Braille developed the tactile form of printing that bears his name, were established during this time. [20]

These positive efforts were greatly hampered by the woeful levels of medical expertise, however, which remained inadequate until well into the nineteenth century. As Jeffrey Klenotic has pointed out, "Any advances in the treatment of disabled persons brought on by the humanist and empiricist turns taken during the Renaissance were restricted by a lack of extant medical knowledge and facilities—a fact that severely limited the reach and quality of the era's goals for rehabilitation of the handicapped." [21]

By the nineteenth century, as medical knowledge and procedures were undergoing strong reforms (including the establishment of special hospitals for people with disabilities), various governmental and nongovernmental entities explored other means of improving the lot of disabled people, particularly those injured in war. By the 1800s, Western societies such as Great Britain, France, and the United States had developed disability pension plans well beyond their primitive beginnings in the sixteenth and seventeenth centuries and had also begun establishing homes and other services for disabled veterans. In addition, the early decades witnessed the founding of private educational facilities dedicated to the needs of Americans with disabilities, including a Baltimore-based school for visually impaired people in 1812, Thomas Hopkins Gallaudet's school for deaf people in Hartford in 1817, and the Perkins Institute/Massachusetts School for the Blind in 1823. By the latter part of the century, charitable organizations such as the Salvation Army, which commenced its work in Great Britain in 1878 and shortly thereafter formed a branch in the United States, and the American Red Cross, appearing in 1881, began making their important contributions as well.[22]

Significant as these advances were, mainstream society continued to perceive people with physical disabilities as freakish and socially peripheral. Fiedler suggested that its interest in human "curiosities" such as those exhibited in the Barnum and Bailey circus peaked during the Victorian era, and its perception of their marginality found ample expression in the literary works of the day. In his study of nineteenth-century literature, Leonard Kriegel concluded that "the disabled, at best, served merely an ornamental function in the literature of early America." In support of this contention, Kriegel noted that the image that dominated American narrative writing during the nineteenth century and the first half of the twentieth was the individual male, healthy in mind and body, who carves a sense of self out of a chaotic environment. A pure spirit and a strong body were such requisite traits that they became inseparable. As Kriegel put it, "Physical

Tiny Tim of A Christmas Carol *remains one of the most durable literary characters to have influenced the Cinema of Isolation.* Scrooge, *a 1970 British musical directed by Ronald Neame, is among the countless moving-image adaptations of Dickens's novel.*

health and moral virtue were virtually synonymous during the nineteenth century in American writing." Such a literary preoccupation left little room in which physically disabled people could participate. "If the wilderness allowed ordinary men the opportunity to be heroic, to confront their inner selves and the external wilderness at one and the same time, what did it offer the crippled and the disabled?" queried Kriegel. "What the wilderness demanded as it offered itself for conquest, the cripple lacked."[23]

The few fictional characters with disabilities of the time, represented in the literary output of several Western societies, could be placed in two broad categories: what Kriegel has identified as the "demonic cripple" and the "charity cripple." Captain Ahab of Melville's *Moby Dick* is a particularly vivid example of the former type—an obsessed male who will not rest until he has had revenge on the entity he holds responsible for his disability—while the latter is strongly represented in Victorian-era literary works such as Dickens's *A Christmas Carol* (that crutch-bearing cherub, Tiny Tim) and the d'Ennery-Cormon stage hit *Les Deux Orphelines* (the blind ingénue Louise). These images did little to alleviate the sense of social marginality that has historically clung to people with physical disabilities; if anything, they encouraged audiences to continue regarding disabled people mainly in terms of fear or pity and served for better or worse as the foundation for many a disability-related film.

The historical tendencies outlined above have led to numerous socio-cultural influences still very much at work in our society. Disability-rights activist Marsha Saxton provided this insightful mid–1980s overview, which, despite the subsequent passage and implementation of the Americans with Disabilities Act (ADA), remains a reasonably accurate assessment of the current state of affairs:

> We, especially in the U.S., live in a culture obsessed with health and well-being. We value rugged self-reliance, athletic prowess, and rigid standards of beauty. We incessantly pursue eternal youth, and the treatment of our elders attests to an ingrained denial, fear and even hate of our own aging and accompanying physical limitation. The disabled person in our society is the target of attitudes and behaviors from the able-bodied world, ranging from gawking to avoidance, pity to resentment, or from vastly lower expectations to awe. Along with these attitudes disabled persons confront a variety of tangible barriers: architectural inaccessibility, lack of sign language interpreters for deaf people, insufficient taped or brailled materials for blind persons. In addition, disabled persons confront less tangible barriers: discrimination in employment, second-class education, and restricted opportunities for full participation in the life of the community.[24]

Related to these factors are mainstream society's need to maintain its integrity by personifying what Kaoru Yamamoto has termed "evil, intangible dangers" and its strong tendency to bestow a sense of deviance on certain groups such as disabled people in pursuit of that desire. As Yamamoto further observed, "Deviance is not inherent in any particular pattern of behavior or physical attribute. Society determines whether some individuals should be regarded as different by selecting certain facets of their being and then attaching to these facets degrading labels and interpretations. . . . The singled-out individuals personify the kinds of experience that fall beyond the boundary of the accepted group norm. In this sense, they preserve stability in society by embodying otherwise formless dangers." Such timeworn constructs remain a conspicuous part of majority consciousness.[25]

Even today, most members of mainstream society seldom perceive people with disabilities as minority-group members subject to alternating rounds of bigotry, paternalism, and indifference, in part because the latter lack an ethnic heritage and identity common to other oppressed groups. Irving Kenneth Zola, who has written extensively on disability issues, has made this point clear: "While most minority groups grow up in some special subculture and, thus, form a series of norms and expectations, the physically handicapped are not similarly prepared. Born for the most part into normal families, we are socialized into that world. The world of sickness is one we enter only later—poorly prepared, and with all the prejudices of the normal. We think of ourselves in the shadows of the external world. The very vocabulary we use to describe ourselves is borrowed from that society. We are *de*-formed, *dis*-eased, *dis*-abled, *dis*-ordered, *ab*-normal, and most telling of all, an *in*-valid." Majority members are more inclined to regard them simply as hard-luck individuals who accept their "fate" only after a long personal struggle. As Nancy Weinberg has observed, "The general public tends to believe that people with physical disabilities have suffered a terrible tragedy and are forever bitter about their misfortune," a view often at odds with the way disabled people themselves feel about their disabilities and adapt to them.[26]

Such narrow perspectives are born from ignorance and misunderstanding (social scientists have long known that most able-bodied people tend to avoid interactions with disabled people because they are uncertain how to behave in their presence)[27] and nourished by the fear that a disabling circumstance may occur to anyone at any time. As Paul Longmore has noted, the movie representations of people with physical disabilities often reflect these concerns: "Disability happens around us more often than we generally recognize or care to notice, and we harbor unspoken anxieties about the possibility of disablement, to us or to someone close to us. What we fear, we often stigmatize and shun and sometimes seek to destroy. Popular entertainments depicting disabled characters allude to these fears and prejudices, or address them obliquely or fragmentarily, seeking to reassure us about ourselves."[28]

Such limited perspectives are not as immutable as they might appear. In another article, Weinberg suggested that continued intermingling of disabled and able-bodied people has the general effect of minimizing differences as perceived by the latter group. "As contact between able bodied and disabled is intensified, the stereotype of the disabled as different diminishes," Weinberg wrote. "There is a positive relationship between contact and perceived similarity: as contact increases, perceived similarity increases." We need to keep making progress in this area, and advancements in social policy—most notably, the passage of the ADA in 1990, which extended basic civil rights protection to the nation's forty-three million disabled citizens—will aid and abet our work. If we don't, the ancient stereotypes will continue to guide mainstream society's perception and treatment of its disabled minority in life as well as in the movies.[29]

1 / emergence of an impoverished image

Like all movies produced during those quaintly optimistic and sentimental years before World War I, the first films of physical disability had a distinctly cosmopolitan quality. Moviegoers lining up at their neighborhood nickelodeons to marvel at (or complain about) the latest "living pictures" were about as likely to see films produced by Pathé Frères, Gaumont, Méliès, Urban, Society Italian Cines, the Great Northern Film Company, and other European companies as those bearing U.S. tradenames such as Edison, Biograph, Lubin, Vitagraph, Selig, and Imp. Modification of foreign-language films for domestic consumption was a simple enough affair; there were no soundtracks to alter, so those who dealt in imported films, legally or otherwise, needed merely to replace the title-cards and perhaps trim, rearrange, or delete a few scenes for good measure. The monumental tragedy that was World War I completely changed the face of the worldwide movie industry, forcing European production to a virtual standstill while making the United States the undisputed heavyweight of movie production, but before that time the cinema had an international flavor seldom matched in the decades that followed. Out of that melting pot of films that greeted the earliest filmgoers emerged the beginnings of the Cinema of Isolation.

Even as the first motion pictures flickered across European and American screens, filmmakers were turning to the world of physical disability issues for exploitable material. One subject area they found fertile with possibility was a major social concern on both sides of the Atlantic: beggars, especially those with fake disabilities. The *New York Times* noted in November 1895 that the City Hall Park area of New York City had "become thoroughly infested with tramps and beggars" many of whom had mastered "all the ingenuousness, plausibility, pseudo-frankness, persistency, and cunning for which the beggars of London, and especially of Paris, are notorious."[1] In 1896, the same year that Koster & Bial's Music Hall in New York, equipped with one of Thomas Edison's Vitascopes, showed movies to paying audiences for the first time, police in that city launched a major crackdown on beggars pretending to be disabled after learning that their law-enforcement colleagues in Boston had recently arrested three beggars with bogus disabilities and saw each of them sentenced to a year's imprisonment at hard labor.

Mainstream filmmakers, who never have been known for resisting the temptation to profit from current social phenomena, did not wait long to take advantage of this one. On a humid August day in 1898, a New York audience viewed what may well have been the first storytelling film with a disability theme: Thomas Edison's *Fake Beggar*, a movie about fifty seconds long that ushered in one of the more contemptible trends in the Cinema of Isolation—disability as a source of humor. Film catalogist Kemp R. Niver describes the brief film this way:

> The establishing scene is of a legless beggar leading a man with a sign on his chest reading "Help the Blind." They stop near the camera and, as the film progresses, several people pass by and drop coins in the blind man's cup. One passer-by drops a coin that hits the sidewalk instead of the cup and a policeman standing nearby notices that the blind man reaches out and picks it up. The policeman attempts to arrest the blind man and takes hold of his coat, but the blind man wriggles out of it and runs down the street with the policeman in close pursuit.[2]

Though it may perhaps be tempting to read this film as an oblique commentary on Edison's work ethic (the prolific inventor, who had experienced significant hearing loss as a youth, was living proof that a disability did not have to lead to a life of poverty and beggary), historians agree that Edison had only minimal interest in the craft of filmmaking and none whatsoever in directing. Constantly at work on other projects and embroiled in patent-infringement lawsuits against rival movie companies throughout that year, the "Wizard of Menlo Park" was more than content to let the cast and crew work out the details. The film that emerged mainly reflected the camera operator's (and *de facto* director's) perception that he could fashion an amusing moment based on a current social issue and fit it within the technologically determined time limitations of the medium, which back then were better measured in seconds than minutes.[3]

Other filmmakers wasted little time exploring comparable themes. Later that same August, James Williamson directed *The Fraudulent Beggars*, a minute-long British comedy that showed a constable giving chase after discovering a "blind" beggar reading a story from the funny papers to his supposedly deaf associate. In 1900, Cecil Hepworth created a film in a similar vein with *The Beggar's Deceit*, fifty seconds' worth of humor about a mendicant who "miraculously" regains the use of his legs and leads a portly police officer on a merry chase after the latter character discovers the former's fraudulence. Around the same time Philadelphia's Sigmund "Pop" Lubin, never hesitant to model his films after others' successes, oversaw his company's production of the minute-long *The Fraudulent Beggar*, about a policeman who chases a sham blind man only to trip over a crutch the faker had left behind. The Alpha Trading Company's Arthur Cooper jumped on the bandwagon with *Blind Man's Bluff* (1903), a meditation eighty seconds in length on a seemingly blind and one-legged beggar. The highlight of this travesty occurs when the beggar, after seeing that a coin given him is bogus, strikes the supposed patron with his wooden leg in retaliation. The simple formula involving the first gratuitous use of disability was now well established.[4]

As movies began expanding in length and complexity circa 1903 to that multi-shot narrative unit known as the one-reeler, companies made certain the fake beggar hitched a ride. In 1905, the Lubin company returned to the idea behind its successful *Fraudulent Beggar* by creating *The Fake Blind Man*, which with a running time of about seven minutes was a much longer movie. Unlike the earlier fake-beggar films, which typically consisted of one run of the camera and had a single soul—almost always a hapless policeman—give chase, *The Fake Blind Man* features a sizable crowd that seems to get larger with every shot. Two years later, the Chicago-based Selig Polyscope Company produced *One of the Finest*, a film that thematically went a step further than the previous films; it turned the issue of police crackdowns on beggars into a travesty as well. Filmed near the company's headquarters on Peck Court, an alley in the heart of the Windy City's tenderloin district, the comedy featured two able-bodied tramps masquerading as a policeman and a disabled mendicant in a scheme to fleece sympathetic onlookers. As an announcement in *Moving Picture World*, a trade journal of the time, described it: "The fraud policeman pretends to savagely assault the blind man and beat him brutally about the head, just as a kindly-looking old lady arrives in sight. She of course remonstrates and gives the supposed blind man a handsome present, which the two divide as soon as she is out of sight." As with several other fake-beggar films, *One of the Finest* did not explicitly show the triumph of justice; the film ends with a shot of "our unscrupulous friend [i.e., the tramp who had stolen a policeman's uniform to begin the film] counting his ill-gotten gains with a smile of unmitigated slyness and audacity."[5]

Corresponding closely to philosopher-*cum*-cinéphile Henri Bergson's turn-of-the-century dictum that "any incident is comic that calls our attention to the physical in a person, when it is the moral side that is concerned," these first films said to audiences that physical disabilities were acceptable subjects for humor as long as the characters weren't really disabled. Though it may be tempting to regard these brief films as relatively innocuous, they nevertheless reveal a deeply rooted prejudice against people with physical disabilities and represent a not-so-veiled assault against them. To some people of the day, beggars with feigned disabilities weren't that different from those with real ones. New York City Police Chief Peter Conlin, who led the 1896 crackdown on sham disabled beggars and soon thereafter authorized the arrest of beggars who truly were disabled, saw little distinction. "The law is clear about such mendicants who pretend to be deaf or dumb or afflicted in any way, and there is no reason why they should not be sent to prison," said the chief. "There are a number of beggars who are really afflicted or deformed, and who thrust their deformities forward to the public gaze, much to the disgust of ladies. They are impudent and persistent, and will be attended to also. If the Magistrates enforce the penalties of the law against these persistent beggars, as they have done in Boston, this source of annoyance will soon cease." No less an opinion leader than the *New York Times* editorial board likewise obscured the difference among the two sets of beggars while applauding Boston's successful prosecution of the three fakers: "This vigorous action will undoubtedly tend to diminish the visible supply in Massachusetts of blind persons, hopeless cripples, wrecks of the civil war, and the like," it suggested, also noting with resentment that the police heretofore did not usually enforce vagrancy and beggary laws against truly disabled people. "Even when, as in several authentic cases, a blind or disabled beggar manages by diligence and frugality to amass much more money by begging than he could hope to acquire by labor if he were able-bodied," grumbled the *Times*, "his incapacity to labor is regarded as an excuse."[6]

Simply put, beggars were perceived as public nuisances or worse who deserved to be prosecuted for their actions, and it mattered little if their disabilities were real or faked. The movies' insistence on representing all disabled mendicants as fakers who often eluded the long arm of the law not only reinforced doubts about police efficacy (Mack Sennett, who was to plumb the depths of police ineptitude in his Keystone Kops movies, once wrote that police officers were high on the list of "characters whom the public wants to see roughly handled") but also deepened the fears of those who perceived beggars that way.[7]

The issue of audience positioning within these films further illustrates the "Otherness" status that the filmmakers conferred on beggars. Following the stylistic norms of the day, these movies used mostly fixed-perspective shots that revealed not only the mendicants in full figure but also their immediate environment (busy city sidewalks, in most cases). Through such visualizations, they presented the fake beggars in much the same way as average moviegoers would encounter them on the street: hand outstretched, at some remove, objectified. As viewers gazed at the screen beggars and detected signs of their fraudulence moments thereafter, they shared not only the police officers' general perspective but also their frustrating inability to effect a meaningful change.

It is somehow fitting that the first round of disability-related movies should traffic in fakery, for in a sense subterfuge would characterize the movie industry's philosophy and modus operandi for years to come. Not only would physically disabled characters be typically played by able-bodied actors in subsequent films—a type of fraudulence akin to white actors performing in blackface—but their concerns and lifestyles as presented in the movies would take on an unreal quality as well. These new levels of misrepresentation would soon define the essence of the Cinema of Isolation.

Just as the New York City police eventually expanded their crackdown on beggars to include those with real disabilities, filmmakers who exploited disability-related issues, sensing little if any resistance, no longer restricted themselves to characters with phony disabilities. At the forefront of this trend was a company remembered today as one of the most significant and influential of the period: the American Mutoscope and Biograph Company, better known by the truncated "Biograph" label it officially adopted in mid–1909. Founded around 1896 by Elias B. Koopman, Henry N. Marvin, Herman Casler, and William Kennedy Laurie Dickson, the corporation manufactured peep shows and movie projectors—"Mutoscopes" and "Biographs," respectively—as well as short films that would run on its machines. Though the New York-based company photographed many of its productions in a makeshift rooftop studio atop its Broadway office building to take maximum advantage of the sunlight, it often sent its camera operators on the road in search of unusual subjects.

Among the filmmakers' stops in 1902 was Washington, D.C., where they photographed fourteen brief films at various educational institutions. One of the single-shot affairs was called *Deaf Mute Girl Reciting "Star Spangled Banner,"* also known as *A Deaf Mute Recitation.* Produced at a time when many films were not much more than simple recordings of unvarnished stage acts, this film of about seventy-five seconds presented a full-figure shot of a young woman wearing a dark floor-length dress who stands in front of a giant Old Glory motif and uses American Sign Language to perform the lyrics of the national anthem.

The patriotic dimension of the film was nothing new for the Biograph. Terry Ramsaye, one of cinema's first historians, noted that *Major McKinley at Home*, a Biograph film shown during the company's first public movie exhibition in 1896, "closed with a handsome view of the Stars and Stripes, waving vigorously." In a way, the presence of the young deaf woman wasn't new, either. "Anything that smacked of novelty, fame or near-fame was material for the Mutoscope," opined Ramsaye, and there is little question as to which of three descriptors the Biograph folks had in mind when they persuaded the woman to perform before their camera. Presumably filmed in a Gallaudet classroom (a Biograph film catalog noted that the woman performed the national anthem "in sign language as taught at Gallaudet Institute"), *Deaf Mute Girl* exhibited a dualism that soon became a hallmark of the Cinema of Isolation; it encouraged the audience's participation (designed to be accompanied by an appropriate musical score but containing no explanatory title-cards, the film invited audiences familiar with the lyrics to "fill in the blanks") but simultaneously pandered to its desire for freakish entertainment.[8]

Though *Deaf Mute Girl* was neither comedic nor narrative, its treatment of a disabled person as a human novelty was an idea reborn years later in Biograph slapstick comedies. The person initially responsible for placing characters with physical disabilities in such films was the company's first full-time director, a conscript from the stage named Wallace "Old Man" McCutcheon. Remembered by Biograph actress Linda Arvidson as a good-natured and generous fellow, McCutcheon earned his nickname as a result of having fathered eight children, several of whom assisted him at the studio. No doubt accustomed to bedlam around the house, McCutcheon cultivated a talent for orchestrating chaos before his camera at a time when slapstick was fast becoming the narrative mode of choice in the movies. According to historian Ramsaye, a McCutcheon-directed film of 1904 called *Personal*, about an amorous Frenchman who makes the mistake of advertising in a New York newspaper to find romance, "derived its action largely from an ensuing chase involving citizens, policemen, workmen and a general wild miscellany" and "may be considered a landmark as being first to present the chase idea in full bloom." Photographed by a then-obscure cinematographer named G. W. "Billy" Bitzer, *Personal* and other McCutcheon films revealed the director's growing familiarity with the rules of slapstick comedies, including reasonably close matching of action among the shots, in-depth compositions that often showed pursuers and pursued in the same frame, and occasional shots that highlighted comic bits of business involving individual pursuers.[9]

The latter was well-illustrated in McCutcheon's *The Lost Child* (1904), about a stranger chased by townspeople who erroneously believe him guilty of kidnapping a child. In this film that a Biograph promotional writer proudly proclaimed "founded on fact," the unfortunate had among his pursuers "a crusty old gentleman . . . in an invalid's chair" and "a one-legged boy hopping along on crutches," both of whom manage to dodge all sorts of obstacles that come their way.[10] Another of McCutcheon's rules was to make a social outsider the focus of the pandemonium: a person from another country, a tramp, an escapee from an insane asylum, and so on. Though the "Old Man" was to move on shortly to the archrival Edison company, the Biograph directors who took his place didn't take long to build on his legacy; they quickly perceived the comic possibilities of placing people with disabilities at the center of such chaotic movies.

The Biograph company was by 1907 ensconced in its new studios at 11 E. 14th Street in lower Manhattan, and one of the films produced there that year was *Mrs. Smithers' Boarding-School.* Based partially on a half-minute Biograph effort of at least five years before called *The Nearsighted School Teacher*, it featured the idea of a bunch of girls playing pranks on a visually impaired professor. During the course of the film, the girls fill the old gent's hat with ashes, nail his shoes to the floor, and trick him into proposing marriage to a pupil dressed as Mrs. Smithers. A description in *Moving Picture World* summarizes the film's supposed high point this way: "The entire class pounce [sic] upon him, tie a rope about him, and pull him up to the ceiling, screaming and helpless. Mrs. Smithers comes to the rescue and puts an end to their hilarity."[11]

Believing it had not crossed the boundaries of good taste (after all, the professor wasn't blind, the studio heads might have argued), Biograph used *Mrs. Smithers' Boarding-School* as a springboard for another comedy that year, one that involved people with the "invisible" disability of deafness. By the turn of the century, it had become common for deaf organizations such as the New York-based Deaf Mutes' Union League and Fanwood Quad to hold annual parties, a fact that the studio could not resist exploiting in *The Deaf-Mutes' Ball*. In this movie, also known as *The Deaf-Mutes' Masquerade*, two deaf men attend a masquerade party dressed as a polar bear and an Italian bear-trainer, become drunk, and inadvertently start causing problems as they head home. A summary in *MPW* reveals how the characters' deafness was used ever so unsubtly for comedic purposes: "On the way they become separated, and the human bear, bereft of his powers of communication in sign language—being securely fastened up in his costume, with his hands encased in the claws—terrorizes the town." As the townspeople and the police keep their distance, the "human bear" enters a saloon for one more drink. After he scares the barkeeper and a few patrons, the police apprehend him and take him to a zoo in Central Park. They are about to toss him into a bear pit "when his chum rushes up and in sign language explains matters, thus saving him from an awful fate." Fortunately, but improbably, the police just happened to understand sign language.[12] With these films, Biograph developed both strains of an early and particularly durable stereotype we might call the "Comic Misadventurer": a disabled person victimized by one or more able-bodied people, and a disabled person whose impairment leads to trouble, whether self-directed, other-directed, or both. All in the name of comedy, of course.

Biograph certainly wasn't alone in its use of slapstick humor to trivialize issues of physical disability. Perhaps inspired by *Mrs. Smithers*, filmmakers for Urban and Lubin furthered the idea of gratuitous humor at the expense of a person who saw with less than perfect vision by producing *The Near-Sighted Cyclist* (1907) and *Near-Sighted Mary* (1909). Both comedies featured people who generate problem after problem for all concerned because of their impaired vision. Harry and Herbert Miles, one-time Biograph exhibitors remembered in the film history books for establishing the world's first film exchange in 1902, were also responsible for something called *The Invalid's Adventure* (1907). Modeled after McCutcheon's *The Lost Child* and other Biograph films, the film shows what can happen when a wheelchair-using man "is seized with a mad desire to do a little exploiting on his own account," to use a contemporary description. He escapes from his attendant, and a wild chase ensues "with any number of ludicrous and highly amusing accidents en route, in each of which the invalid manages to retain his equilibrium." He eventually falls into a stream and almost drowns before local townspeople rescue him.[13]

The comic idea of a person with an impairment outmaneuvering able-bodied people also informs Gaumont's *The Legless Runner* (1907). The title character, who uses a low wagon and specially prepared pieces of wood to propel himself around town, enters a saloon, buys a bottle of wine, and departs without paying. A summary published in *MPW* breathlessly describes his escape and the bizarre pursuit that follows:

> In his haste he rushes down a steep pathway of steps, knocking over others who are coming up. Falling in a heap at the bottom, he gathers himself together and flees. An officer tries to stop him, but is bowled over. Hastily rushing to the barracks, he orders out a sergeant and squad of infantry who in obeying orders get themselves mixed up in trying to capture the man, who leads them on a merry dance up the side of a house and off the roof, up hill and down dale, eluding them at every point. He is seen making his way in the distance, and the soldiers deploy in the valley hoping to cut off his chance of escape as he comes down a rapid incline. The better to do this, they bring barrels, and get into them to hide. In his rapid descent he trundles the barrels and

soldiers down the hillside into the river, into which he falls himself, and is rescued by the soldiers, who have difficulty in putting him into his wagon. They tie his hands and push him along over the difficult places through which they have to retrace their steps, until they reach the barracks, where they hand their prisoner over to the guard.[14]

In addition to developing this concept guaranteed to elicit guffaws from ableist audiences, Gaumont also found it necessary to share with the world its enlightened views on the subject of physically disabled people and marriage. In *Two Ladies and a Beggar* (1909), a film which also kept alive the fake-disability beggar image that had haunted the Cinema of Isolation for years, a beggar pretending to have no legs uses a low cart as his perch for seeking alms. Two good-hearted elderly women decide to take him under their wing and provide him with all kinds of aid. The mendicant is delighted at first, but things quickly get out of hand; the ladies alter his trousers to a more suitable length for a legless person, and they also throw out all his full-sized furniture and replace it with cut-down items. The beggar's breaking point occurs when the women bring in a truly legless young woman with the hope of arranging a marriage for their ward. The message the moviemakers hammered home is unmistakable: a physically disabled woman is far less than prime marriage material. In this instance, the beggar, on seeing the young woman, drops his facade and escapes in high-energy fashion by literally jumping through the ceiling to end another ableist comedy.

Men with physical disabilities who wanted to marry faced fewer obstacles, but the kind of treatment they received in the movies took on an all-too-familiar tone. Indeed, *The Cripple's Marriage* (1909), billed as a comedy about the nuptials of "a cripple minus his legs, and a tall spinster," proved an even greater demonstration of ableist insensitivity. Gaumont's summary of *The Cripple's Marriage* as published in *MPW* is short on details but does suggest the movie's considerable gratuitous humor: "The wedding march, the court room scene, the supper and the return to the new home are all features bound to create boundless hilarity." An *MPW* review of the film, just as vague on the details, described *The Cripple's Marriage* as "a comedy from the Gaumont Co. which contains sufficient absurdities and unexpected situations to keep everybody who sees it laughing."[15]

Another supposedly humorous idea—the disappearance or theft of a prosthesis—served as the main concept for several films. In Essanay's *Don't Pull My Leg* (1908), a man steals an artificial leg from a prosthetics store and is immediately chased by the store owner. The humor here arises out of the pandemonium resulting from the merchant's belief that every person he meets is wearing the artificial leg. He pulls a man off a horse, painters off a scaffold, people off wagons, etc., before finally recovering his prized prosthesis. Lubin presented *A Cork Leg Legacy* a year later, about a wealthy one-legged woman who dies and leaves only her cork leg to her husband. He's furious and tosses the leg out a window, and a passing tramp picks it up. The husband later learns, however, that the leg contains a

$100,000 check and tries to find the tramp. The latter character, meanwhile, has been trying to sell the leg to every one-legged person he meets but, getting no taker, ends up throwing the leg away. The husband manages to track him down and they go to the dump and finally retrieve the check.

Moviemaker assaults on physically impaired people in the name of humor took other forms. The title character of Lux's *The Electrified Humpback* (1909) buys an electric device to help ease the discomfort of his impairment, but the Comic Misadventurer later angrily tears it off and demands a refund after it gives shocks to him and everyone he encounters. More in keeping with an obscure belief about people with severely distorted spines—that they are living good-luck charms—was Pathé's *The Hunchback Brings Luck* (1908), in which an able-bodied "Mr. Hardup," besieged by creditors, jumps out of his apartment window and lands atop a hunchbacked man selling lottery tickets. In a token of gratitude for breaking his fall, Hardup buys the fellow's last ticket. The next day, after learning that he won the lottery, Hardup puts an ad in the newspaper seeking the impaired man who saved both his life and his bank account. According to a write-up in *MPW*, "A hundred cripples answer the ad, but they all return empty handed, and Mr. Hardup is despairing of ever finding his benefactor when the original hunchback makes his appearance, and soon after he is seen departing, handsomely rewarded by our now wealthy citizen." In this rare example of a movie that features multiple numbers of physically disabled people, the filmmakers used superstitious nonsense as an excuse to create comedy at disabled people's expense: first, by having a huge number of them chase the able-bodied protagonist en masse in classic slapstick fashion and, second, by having the latter character turn on them at film's end. According to an *MPW* review of *The Hunchback Brings Luck*, "the long chase [of Hardup by the disabled characters] which follows is funny. He finds the one of whom he purchased his ticket and rewards him, and the rest are driven away."[16] Like *A Cork Leg Legacy*, *The Hunchback Brings Luck* pivots on the concept of an able-bodied person acquiring considerable wealth by way of a disabled person. Not so coincidentally, it's an idea that also sums up the relationship of mainstream filmmakers and the physically disabled characters they put on display.

As a general rule, movie companies for decades have followed the insensitive practice of using able-bodied performers to play disabled movie characters. The negative attitudes of movie professionals toward disabled performers, or even the possibility of hiring such performers, during the early days of the medium are well-illustrated by the comments of an anonymous French producer, appalled that one of his directors, Robert Péguy, wanted to use shots that showed his actors from the waist up as opposed to the full-figure shots that were the norm back then. "Are you crazy?" he cried. "What are all these individuals of whom one sees only the upper half? Audiences are going to think that we have hired a lot of cripples!"[17] In their never-ending quest to provide novelty to their mainstream audiences, however, several companies—most notably, the premiere French film companies of Pathé and Gaumont—recruited performers with amputated limbs for comedies and other films that depended on the "shock" effect of their appearance. Frederick Talbot's account of the making of a Gaumont one-reeler made around 1904 called *The Automobile Accident* offers a graphic illustration of insensitivity to performers with physical disabilities. In this trick-effect film "which created a sensation when it appeared," according to Talbot, an able-bodied workman is on his way home and, having had too much to drink, decides to lie down in the middle of a road for a nap. In short order, a taxi appears and drives over the sleeping man's legs, bloodlessly amputating them. Talbot summarized the film's trick-effect conclusion: "The shock awakes the man rudely, and he is surprised to find his lower limbs scattered across the roadway. The chauffeur is horrified by the unfortunate accident; but his fare, on the contrary, a doctor, is not much perturbed. He descends from his carriage, picks up the dismembered limbs, replaces them in position, assists the afflicted man to his feet, and after shaking hands each proceeds on his separate way, the workman resuming his journey as if nothing had happened."

To pull off this effect, the filmmakers edited in footage of a legless actor, dressed to resemble the lead actor, whose prop limbs were swept away by the taxi's wheels. Though the same actor presumably went on to play the title roles in Gaumont's *The Cripple's Marriage* and *The Legless Runner* noted above, Talbot's commentary clearly suggests that people with disabilities were rarely allowed the opportunity to act in films: "The legless cripple is, of course, the key to the whole situation. The great difficulty was to find such a luckless individual, and, when he had been discovered, to bribe him to participate in a picture play. Probably the unfortunate had never before found his misfortune so profitable to him." Talbot also refers to "the neat and skilful manner in which the change from the actor to the cripple, and back from the cripple to the actor, is effected," implying that, as far as moviemakers of the day were concerned, physically disabled people and actors were mutually exclusive groups of people.[18]

The Pathé Frères Company had among its ranks an exceptionally agile performer sans one leg. One of his first films for Pathé was *The One-Legged Man* (1908), which told the tale of a sleeping fellow whose wooden leg is stolen. The character immediately awakens and, after pinching a crutch from a dozing old man to aid him in his chase, proves more proficient at pursuit than any of the able-bodied characters who appear in the film. As a report in *MPW* described the action: "At one point two policemen join in the chase and they follow the thief over walls, down hills and around corners, the one-legged man always traveling faster than the others. Crossing a meadow, the fugitive attempts to leap a ditch, but falls in and has to scramble out, as do the others. But the one-legged man clears the ditch in one leap. The thief is finally run down near the course of a stream, but makes a high dive and gains the water; but the cripple is upon him, and reaching the opposite shore, holds him until help arrives." The tenuousness of this alleged

A disabled actor and his able-bodied lookalike take direction in The Automobile Accident, *a turn-of-the-century comedy. This Gaumont effort was one of many early films whose appeal hinged on the physical difference of its disabled performer.*

comedy was not lost on the reviewer for the trade journal *Variety*, who wrote that its comic quality "does not become visible. It's not humorous to watch a one-legged man hobble about."[19]

Pathé knew a novelty when it saw one, however, and in January 1910 the French concern released a five-minute film called *Story of a Leg* starring the same actor. This time, he played a fellow equipped with a cork prosthesis who goes to a local park for his daily constitutional. He later falls asleep on a park bench, and several prankish boys tie his artificial leg to the bench and then tickle him with a straw. He awakens and starts to chase after them, but then notices to his chagrin that he left his prosthesis behind. Embarrassed, he retrieves the leg and hops home. His wife becomes enraged for some inexplicable reason and tosses the prosthesis out a window, where it's found by a ragpicker. The latter character later gives the cork leg to a legless beggar, who according to a description in *MPW* "fastens it on to one of his stumps and jumps up as good as new and travels as quickly on that one leg without crutch or cane, as most men do on two." The anonymous star of the film, who played not only the lead character but also the beggar after he attached the prosthesis, impressed the reviewer for *MPW*: "The one-legged fellow seen in this picture is a wonder much more nimble than many men possessing both limbs."[20]

He must have also impressed his bosses, for a few months later he appeared again before the Pathé cameras, this time with another disabled performer in a circus routine; the resulting four-minute film, *One-Legged Acrobats*, is another vivid example of the freakshow fascination some filmmakers had with disabled people. Reviewers were sharply divided on the film's merits. *MPW* had nothing but praise for the film: "A couple of expert acrobats, with only one pair of legs between them, give a highly diverting variety turn, including balancing, jumping onto tables and various other feats, all executed with agility and precision. The performance, which winds up with a comical dance and a quick march movement, is both good and amusing." *Variety*, however, offered a far different interpretation: "This film fails to disclose anything startling unless it can be called a novelty to see two men hop around the stage on one foot aided by crutches, occasionally jumping over a stationary object. An attempt at comedy falls away short. The picture fails to show a single redeeming feature."[21]

These films represent the worst type of exploitation, in that the only kind of movies in which disabled actors could find work were those that paid undue attention to their disabilities. These performers were well aware of the general public's fascination with human "defects" and, sad to say, were forced by economic necessity to contribute to that interest in the unusual. For example, a New York-area man, unemployed as a result of a railroad accident, wrote the following letter to the Kalem Company in 1913:

I am sending you a drawing of my right hand, which has two fingers missing. Could you use me or my hand in any scenario? I have been a railroad brakeman for seven years and can be useful to you in a railroad scenario or maybe you can use my hand in some Sherlock Holmes plays or anything you may suggest, as the public is always looking for something new.

A Kalem executive passed the letter along to Epes Winthrop Sargent of *MPW*, who published it in his "The Photoplaywright" column. Sargent's reaction to the letter, while not optimistic about the brakeman's chances, was consistent with the movie industry's typical view of disabled performers—that their only value was in their unsettling appearance: "We used to have a one-legged man who wanted to be an actor. Perhaps a script could use both of these starts [i.e., startling people], but we are afraid that the chance of selling a story written around a fingerless hand is too slight."[22]

The victimization of disabled characters—and disabled actors—so readily evident in the slapstick comedies was also a *sine qua non* for the earliest dramatic films. The latter productions, representing a trend that would eventually over-shadow the comedic movies, initially manifested a heavily downbeat quality. A 1907 *Variety* article on nickelodeons made passing reference to a specific movie image—"the angel rises from the brave little hero-cripple's corpse"—as if it were relatively common, the image (or at least variations on it) no doubt epito-mizing the tragic conclusions of so many pre–1908 disability dramas.[23]

Characters with blindness made their first appearances in such movies. In vivid contrast to treatments of most other characters with physical disabilities, filmmakers initially portrayed people with severe visual impairments as poverty-stricken social outcasts who often died by the end of the story. An illustration of this "Tragic Victim" trend may be found in the form of the 1907 Urban–Eclipse film, *The Faithful Dog; or, True to the End*. This movie tells the tale of a blind beggar and his dog, who assists his master by wearing a tin cup around his neck and sitting up on his hind legs. After yet another day of begging, the duo returns home to the beggar's tenement. During the night, however, the mendicant devel-ops a coughing fit. He calls for his dog, writes out a note to a doctor, and sends the dog on his way. Despite performing this and other critical errands, the dog is un-able to save the beggar's life. As a description in *MPW* put it, the film ends as "the poor, faithful canine dies in sorrow on the grave of his master."[24]

Another tearjerker was *His Daughter's Voice* (1907), a film directed by Urban's W. R. Booth and designed to be shown in loose synchronization with a recording of the song, "Daddy." The story centers on a young sighted woman who sings in the streets for a living and her elderly blind father who accompanies her on the violin. One day, a passerby is so impressed by their performance that he asks them to visit his establishment to make a "talking machine record." They are paid for their efforts, a fact not unnoticed by a drunkard who assaults them after they leave the studio. He swings his bottle at the old man, but the daughter, jump-ing in to protect her father, takes the full brunt of the hit and collapses on the sidewalk. While some bystanders carry her off and others chase the drunk, the old man is left to fend for himself until a boy helps him find his way home. The street violinist visits his daughter frequently in the hospital, but she later dies from her injury. After the funeral, the broken-hearted father returns to the place where he and his daughter made the recording, and the movie concludes on a note of pure tragedy: "Left alone in the room, he listens to the reproduction of his daughter's voice, even plays a few strains on his violin to accompany her as he was wont to do, but his grief and the added burden of life weigh upon him heavily; he collapses under the strain and with visions of his transfigured daughter floating before him [which the filmmakers accomplished by superimposing her image over that of the recording machine] he expires." A hit with audiences, *His Daughter's Voice* proved the inspiration for several imitative tragedies featuring blind violin-playing paupers.[25]

With the implication that mainstream society as represented by specific able-bodied individuals bears responsibility for the victimization, these modestly exploratory tales were not that far off the mark in their attempts to show the typical economic circumstances of physically disabled citizens at that time. One of the unfortunate byproducts of the industrial age was the sharp increase in the number of disabling accidents on the job. Businesses were rarely held accountable for the mishaps, and, with the concepts of disability pensions and rehabilitation programs still years away, many of these newly disabled folk had little choice but to beg for alms. As Charlene DeLoach and her associates have noted, "many people incurred high medical expenses and, at the same time, lost their ability to work and earn an income. These people were quickly impoverished and had little assistance on which they could depend." Except for the federal government's long-standing policy of offering pensions or shelter to disabled war veterans and a 1908 workers' compensation law that affected only federal employees, no government entity on any level in the U.S. provided assistance to people with physical disabilities. As Red Cross executive Howard Heydon noted, disabled folk had to struggle against poverty with minimal support: "Up to 1911 in this country when the first financial liability was placed by law upon the employer, there had never been any general recognition of a social obligation to the [nonmilitary] injured. If the person had sufficient perseverance or intelligence or both to overcome the physical handicap, he succeeded, while on the other hand if he lacked those qualities, he failed. There is no half way average."[26]

Moviemakers further reflected the times by centering their "films of despair" on those disabled persons who suffered the brunt of economic misfortune and discrimination: people with blindness. "There are many types of handicaps which result in economic and social troubles," wrote James Bordley, a U.S. medical corps officer during World War I, "but I think I can aptly term the blind as the Ishmaelites of this century. They have been driven out of community life, out of industry, prevented from owning their own homes and maintaining them, and for decades they have cried out for a chance and the answer has always been 'Charity.' What could be more conducive to idleness, to melancholy and to despair than to know that your brother must be your keeper?"[27] Yet in their haste to provide weepy melodrama for their audiences, these filmmakers posed the unsubtle suggestion that death inevitably follows despair, that no alternative to the misery exists. These films never hinted that the perpetrator of the hardships—mainstream society—could or should do something to ease the economic and discriminatory treatment of people with disabilities. Instead, the films followed an easy emotional and intellectual out by "mercifully" killing off the disabled characters.

Not all dramas turned their disabled characters into Tragic Victims, however; several of them featured individuals who overcame their victimization by striking back at the able-bodied people tormenting them and their families. An example may be found in the form of *The Paralytic's Vengeance* (1908), a film imported by George Kleine from the Paris-based Raleigh & Robert company in which an artisan ekes out a living while providing for his wife and her paralyzed father. A game warden finds the wife attractive, but after she rejects his advances he starts a campaign of intimidation against the family. After insulting the family members, he arrests the husband for poaching and then goes to their home to gloat. During a struggle with the wife, the game warden falls over a table near the father, who according to a description in *MPW* "seizes the opportunity to clutch his throat and strangle him, thus ending the persecution to which his family has been subjected." Pathé's *The Sailor's Sweetheart* (1908) told a comparable story of a young woman who lives with her disabled mother and dates a sailor. Things come to a boil when a wealthy nogoodnik has his ruffians beat up her boyfriend while he forces his attentions on the heroine "as the helpless mother looks on, powerless to give assistance. All at once, however, the invalid seems possessed with supernatural strength, and grabbing the fiend by the throat forces him to the floor, never loosening her hold until he lies dead at her feet."[28]

As commendable as it might otherwise be to show physically disabled characters taking decisive action and breaking out of their victimization, these films, by virtue of the fact their disabled characters actually kill the able-bodied tormentors, unfortunately demonstrated what media scholar Paul Longmore has identified as a common ableist prejudice: "Disabled people resent the nondisabled and would, if they could, destroy them."[29] Though such films were relatively scarce during the period preceding World War I, they would return—with a vengeance—during the decade following it.

A rare example of an early film depicting a heroic disabled person in which victimization and vengeance are refreshingly absent (or at least largely subdued) is Pathé's *The Little Cripple* (1908). One of the first films to use disability in a more or less incidental way and an embryonic version of the "Civilian Superstar" films that would enjoy popularity from the late 1930s through the 1950s and beyond, *The Little Cripple* centers on two boyhood friends, one of whom has no legs. The mother of the other boy runs the local tavern, and one evening she decides to let one of her patrons sleep off his drunkenness in her bar. Later that night, two criminals break into the tavern and kill the mother after she tries to stop them from robbing the place. Believing the still-dozing drunkard will take the fall for their actions, the crooks abduct her son with the plan of dumping the boy's unconscious body into a river. Unfortunately for them, they're seen by the legless boy. An account in *MPW* picks up the story: "Waiting only to throw off the wooden stumps which serve him as limbs, the little fellow dives into the water and is soon swimming desperately after the boat, unobserved. When in midstream the robbers drop the boy over into the water, and turn back to shore. Of course, the legless swimmer rescues his friend, but when the men reach the shore the police are waiting and after a fierce fight they are captured." The boy identifies them as the killers, thereby helping set free the innocent drunkard whom the police had arrested, and "the last picture shows the tavern boy thanking his rescuer." The reviewer for *Variety* noted that "the firm of Pathé has turned out another notably excellent film . . . The picture runs to an uncommon length [i.e., about fifteen minutes, when many films were about seven to ten minutes], is divided into many scenes, but throughout its story is connected and well told. The beholder finds interest, and the film should be popular in general exhibition."[30]

Another rare disabled-hero film, *The Empty Sleeve; or, Memories of Bygone Days* (1909), featured a different tack: the protagonist becomes disabled as a result of heroism. This Vitagraph film, which took the unusual step of centering on a disabled veteran of the Civil War, begins by depicting an elderly Union veteran and his wife as they chance upon a romantic spot of their youth. They flashback to 1861, when the veteran was a young cavalry officer. He leads his unit in a charge up a hill and silences a Confederate battery but loses an arm in the process. A young nurse attends to him, and, when he's later discharged, she accompanies him to his parents' home where they eventually marry. They flashforward back to the present where they meet a company of veterans on the march. The veteran leads them again, but this time to a grandstand where he makes a Decoration Day speech.

While *The Little Cripple* and *The Empty Sleeve* are noteworthy for showing their protagonists in other than helpless or vengeful situations, they did conveniently gloss over the economic circumstances that undoubtedly held back their real-life counterparts. The title character of *The Little Cripple* seems to exist without any means of support (and finds his heroism devalued after receiving a mere handshake for his deeds), while the former cavalry officer, perhaps the movie industry's first of many constructions of what I call the "Noble Warrior" stereotype, represents a completely sentimentalized view of a disabled war hero. With its suggestion that the loss of a limb was tantamount to a badge of honor, *The Empty Sleeve* gave little indication of the hardships facing most disabled Civil War vets. The federal government did pay them pensions at ever-increasing rates, but the amounts remained modest; at the time *The Empty Sleeve* appeared, a severely disabled veteran (e.g., one who had lost both hands in the war) would receive only $100 a month along with the option of a new prosthesis or a cash substitute every three years. Others received proportionally less. Compounding the vets' economic difficulties was the fact that the federal government's commitment seldom extended beyond simple financial support, as Red Cross official Curtis Lakeman noted: "No concerted systematic effort was made by the government to restore the wounded veterans of the Civil War to earning capacity. The legless or armless veteran became a common and pitiful spectacle of our daily life. Only those of sufficient strength of character and will power fought out their own problems and made their way in spite of such handicaps."[31]

The romanticization evident in *The Empty Sleeve* and other early films was one part of a general trend among the portrayals of physically disabled people in movie dramas. Just as mainstream society was responding ever so sluggishly to the needs of disabled people (mainly in the form of workers' compensation laws that assisted people disabled by industrial accidents), moviemakers began shifting away from tragic portrayals to ones in which disabled people, still impoverished, were eventually "rescued" by some benevolent able-bodied sorts. In Pathé's *A Blind Woman's Story* (1908), for example, an able-bodied artist is so taken by an indigent blind woman and her dog that he insists on painting their portrait in his studio and paying them a modest sitting fee. Later at home, the elderly woman is mistreated by her son who is, according to an account published in *MPW*, "brutality and vice personified." To pay for his booze, the son takes the few dimes the painter had given her and even sells her dog to one of his unsavory acquaintances. The canine manages to escape and reunite with its mistress, but the woman later loses her grip on the animal and tumbles down a cliff. The dog, remembering the painter's kindness, goes for help and brings back a rescue party. The painter and his wife, "appalled by such misery, take the old woman and her faithful dog to their home, and the last picture shows the young couple and the once poor beggar woman now enjoying happiness." A *MPW* review underscored the positiveness of *A Blind Woman's Story*'s conclusion and also noted the film's difference: "It is a simple enough story, and its chief attraction lies in its ending, which shows the woman and her dog cared for and made comfortable. In this the picture is better than some which are rather disposed to leave the person they are depicting in trouble."[32] Or dead.

"Feel good" movies such as *A Blind Woman's Story*, which helped perpetuate the dominant mainstream belief that people with physical disabilities are helpless and must depend on others, appealed to a cinema-going public that wanted to think something was being done to ease the plight of destitute people with physical disabilities, if only on a grassroots level. These films almost always portrayed the aid-givers as concerned relatives, acquaintances, or passers-by (people with whom able-bodied audience members could readily identify, of course), an approach that reflected an exceedingly old-fashioned way of thinking. Not only did they fail to acknowledge, let alone advocate, the emerging concept of governmental assistance to people with physical disabilities, but they even ignored the important work conducted on behalf of disabled people by charitable organizations.

A number of these institutions were well-established at the time these movies appeared—the U.S. branch of the Salvation Army had been founded in 1879, the American Red Cross two years later, and Goodwill Industries in 1902—but moviemakers effectively devalued their contributions by paying minimal if any attention to them. Instead, moviemakers expressed their regressive views on disability issues by borrowing heavily from cultural phenomena that predated the rise of charitable and governmental assistance. In short, it was the time of the "film d'art."

The year 1908 was a watershed for the international film community in a number of respects. Some of the most powerful movie companies—among them, Edison, Pathé Frères, Biograph, Selig, Lubin, and, by way of the Kleine film importing company, Gaumont and Urban—hoped to place a chokehold on the ever-expanding American movie industry by forming the Edison-Pathé combine. This "combination of interests among the manufacturers," to use a phrase of the day, reorganized itself the following year as the far more familiar Motion Picture Patents Company. The MPPC, otherwise known simply as "the Trust," aimed at dominating the movie industry through monopolistic business practices.

On another front, moviemakers by that year had overcome many of the technological challenges posed by the young medium, but their works now faced widespread condemnation—if not outright calls for censorship—by civic and religious groups upset by what they perceived to be scandalous subject matter. In the hope that upgrading the status of the movies would stave off further economic turmoil, filmmakers in France, Great Britain, Italy, and the United States turned to the idea of producing high-brow movies based on masterworks of the stage and printed page.[33] As film historians Maurice Bardèche and Robert Brasillach poetically put it, "The cinema was bidding farewell to tents and circuses in order to woo a buskined Muse." A French journal of the time trumpeted the arrival of moviedom's "new era of accurate settings, of admirable reconstructions of history, of adaptations from the masterpieces which are the glory of our race and of our language," but historians Bardèche and Brasillach offered a very different commentary on the film d'art, applicable not only to the French cinema of the day but to the other high-minded films as well: "Now that the film had mastered its technical problems, it began to look upon art just as a nouveau riche might. Ten years of horrors were to result."[34]

Whatever the movie companies' motivations for creating such works—to raise the prestige of movies, to fend off censorship, to attract new audiences, to preserve a cultural heritage (and in a very cost-effective way, since many of the tried-and-true tales they appropriated were in the public domain and thus free of restrictions)—their drive to bring art to the masses commencing in 1908 had far-reaching consequences for the Cinema of Isolation. In particular, a number of their movies succeeded in reviving stereotypic images of physically disabled people that were to echo throughout the mainstream cinema for decades.

A most disturbing trend ushered in by the film d'art movement was the rise of dramatic films that represented physically disabled people as objectifications of evil. Tapping one of the most deeply entrenched beliefs about disabled people—"Deformity of the body is a sure sign of deformity of the soul," in Joanmarie Kalter's words—these films treated physical disabilities solely as parts that represent the whole, with the whole simply consisting of unrelenting villainy.[35]

Virtually unknown during the first dozen years of the cinema, the disabled-villain image burst onto the movie scene in 1908 when Vitagraph, flush with film d'art fever, offered up perhaps the first cinematic incarnation of Shakespeare's infamous "lump of foul deformity," Richard Crookback, in *Richard III*. Produced by J. Stuart Blackton at Vitagraph's Brooklyn studio, the one-reel film starred renowned Broadway actor Maurice Costello, "Vitagraph Girl" Florence Turner, and future movie magnate Thomas Ince. The movie was the brain child of William V. Ranous, an erstwhile actor who had made a name playing villainous roles in Shakespearean and other plays (*Richard III* doubtless among them) for various stock companies before turning to movie acting and directing. Aware that other moviemakers had been dabbling with excerpts from the Bard's plays as early as 1899, Ranous believed it possible to render complete Shakespearean stories on film, albeit in a highly compressed way, and convinced Blackton to allow him to direct a series of films based on Shakespearean texts and, for good measure, Biblical stories as well. The resulting "High Art Films," as Vitagraph billed them, represent the initial attempts of the cinema world to tell full Shakespearean stories. Limited to one reel each, however, the Ranous films offered only the barest outline of the original texts. Unless accompanied by the likes of W. Stephen Bush, a lecturer who often contracted with theaters in the New York and Philadelphia areas to provide running commentaries on such "prestigious" films, they often left audiences—even those familiar with the stories—more mystified than enlightened.[36]

Not much better than its American predecessor was a British two-reel *Richard III* created two years later by the Co-operative Cinematograph Company and starring Frank Benson. Whatever advantages it held over the Ranous film in length were more than overwhelmed by its primitive formal aspects, typified by static camerawork, full-figure shots, painted backdrops, theatrical stagings (e.g., characters entering and exiting the frame from left and right, as they would on stage), actors overgesticulating before the lone camera spectator, and a plethora of title cards that often functioned merely as billboards for ensuing scenes. Neither of these filmic renderings of Shakespeare's play may be said to further the art of cinema (Rachael Low begins her analysis of the Benson version by stating that "it would probably not be unfair to say that *Richard III* represents the pre–1914 stage adaptations at their worst" and quite rightly identifies the film as "a series of incomprehensible happenings linked only by the presence of Richard, black-shrouded, chin-stroking and prone to violent arm-swinging argument"). Nevertheless, Shakespeare's "rudely stamp'd" king, rivalled only by Robert Louis Stevenson's Long

John Silver as the earliest of moviedom's disabled villains, set the stage for a long line of evil characters, especially ones with severely distorted spines.[37]

Another prime image re-introduced by the international film d'art movement was a fixture of Victorian melodrama: the "Sweet Innocent," a type akin to what Leonard Kriegel in his study of nineteenth-century literature has identified as the "charity cripple."[38] Invariably a child or young unmarried woman, the Sweet Innocent anchored the opposite end of the stereotype spectrum and was an embodiment of the deeply ingrained mainstream belief that disabled people must depend on others for their every need. Filmmakers usually showed the character, who occasionally lucked into wealth but was far more often a destitute figure, as "perfect" in every way except for the disability; respectful, humble, gentle, cheerful, godly, pure, and exceptionally pitiable are adjectives that come readily to mind. Typically, the Sweet Innocent was far more reactive than proactive and seemed to bring out the protectiveness of every good-hearted able-bodied person who came his or her way.

The primary literary antecedent for the child variant of the Sweet Innocent is Tiny Tim of Charles Dickens's famous 1843 work, *A Christmas Carol*, and filmmakers on both sides of the puddle lost little time bringing the crutch-using Cratchit urchin to the screen; a fragmentary 1901 British version directed by W. R. Booth and produced by Robert Paul was followed in due course by adaptations created by Essanay in 1908, an anonymous Italian company and Edison in 1910, another American concern in 1912, the Zenith Film Company in 1913, the Fenning London Film Company in 1914, and Universal in 1916. Recognizing Tim's appeal, other companies created movies that featured disabled children, each with a poignant tale to tell. Consider, for example, the title character of Lubin's *The Blind Boy* (1908). After his father's death, a boy blind since birth learns that his father has willed him his entire estate while cutting off the boy's no-account older brother without a cent. The elder son, angered by his father's action, steals the will and alters it. He also abducts his brother and, as Lubin described it, holds him captive in "an old rookery where he is shamefully treated, but manages to escape. In his sightless condition he stumbles along an unfamiliar path, eventually falling over a precipice." He is rescued by a local fisherman, who helps him notify the police. The film's happy ending: "The officers finally track [the older brother] and his wicked associates to a low groggery, where they are led off handcuffed. The poor little blind orphan is providentially protected and restored to his home and position."[39]

Providential protection also played a prominent role in Vitagraph's 1909 film, *A Maker of Diamonds*. The title character, an indigent fellow who lives with his wife and partially paralyzed daughter, discovers a way to manufacture diamonds in his makeshift basement laboratory. A local diamond dealer, fearful of the economic consequences, eventually destroys the lab, but the family members had fortunately had the foresight to set aside a number of diamonds for them to become rich.

The Sweet Innocent of Edison's *A Street Waif's Christmas* (1908), a young boy named Ronald, also avoids the severe economic difficulties so often associated with the early images of physically disabled people (an account in *MPW* characterized him as "a crippled child of wealthy parents")[40] but his heavy dependence on able-bodied types is all too apparent; not only is he completely beholden to his parents (and will remain so, by implication) but he also owes a major debt of gratitude to a little girl named Marie, the title character, who rescues him from an out-of-control team of horses. Though from opposite ends of the socio-economic spectrum, the children become friends, and, since the holiday season is upon them, they start thinking about what they would like to receive for Christmas. Ronald asks Santa for a sister, while the selfless Marie, wandering the streets, asks Santa to grant whatever Ronald wishes for and then collapses from hunger into a snowbank. Both children have their requests fulfilled in classic

The Cratchits wonder at Scrooge's benevolence in Carl Laemmle's 1916 version of A Christmas Carol *known as* The Right to Be Happy *(a.k.a.* Marley's Ghost*), produced under Universal's Bluebird Photoplays label. Adapted by E. J. Clawson and directed by Rupert Julian, the latter of whom also starred as Scrooge, it featured John Cook and Claire McDowell as Mr. and Mrs. Cratchit and Francis Lee (second from right) as Tiny Tim. Courtesy Museum of Modern Art/Film Stills Archive.*

Christmas fairytale fashion when Ronald's father rescues her and, with his wife, eventually adopts her.

The youthful Sweet Innocent's adult counterpart—the ingénue, or unworldly maiden—also had a literary forerunner: Louise of the 1874 play *Les Deux Orphelines* by Adolphe Philippe d'Ennery and Eugène Cormon. Though not nearly as well-known to modern audiences as *A Christmas Carol*, the d'Ennery-Cormon melodrama was a solid stage hit (one reviewer hyperbolized that it "has been acclaimed with triumphant success in every civilized country under the sun as one of the most successful and heart-stirring dramas ever staged")[41] and moviemakers found it a most serviceable commodity for perpetuating beliefs about physically disabled people. Its story about two young women raised as sisters, one of whom is blind, and the mishaps that befall them in and around Paris provided the foundation for at least seven silent movie adaptations.

The first two American film versions of *Les Deux Orphelines* each bore the anglicized title *The Two Orphans*, and, adding to the confusion, both were produced by the same entity: the Selig Polyscope Company. Selig's first, a one-reeler that ran about a quarter of an hour, appeared in 1908. Though details of the film are sketchy (an account of *The Two Orphans* published in *Moving Picture World* skimped on some of the adaptation's particulars because "the story of the play is too well known to necessitate any extended description"), it is possible to glean some sense of the film's treatment of its disabled characters from the summary in *MPW*. Discussions of the first and third acts of this six-act film are reproduced below:

Act I. opens with a beautiful view of the River Seine in the background and shows the arrival of the blind girl and her sister. They encounter an old hag who makes her living by begging and worse practices, and who has two sons, one a cripple who makes a poor living as a scissors grinder, the other a vagabond who lives on what he can steal. . . .

Act III., a street in Paris during a severe snow storm. The hag is seen compelling the girl to beg from passersby. Whatever money is obtained in this way is at once appropriated by her taskmistress, who departs with her youngest son, leaving the cripple and the blind girl together, between whom an affecting scene takes place, each offering words of comfort for the other's affliction.

By film's end, the sighted sister, having been falsely arrested and released, traces her sister back to the hag's house. They're happily reunited, but the hag and her thieving son appear. The brothers fight while the hag tries to restrain the sisters, but gendarmes eventually arrive to break up the hostilities. The final sentence of the *MPW* description is vague on details but suggests something of an upbeat ending: "The hag and her villainous son are placed under arrest and the other characters are made happy as is their due."[42]

The appearance of a "Série d'Art" production of *Les Deux Orphelines* (1910) directed by Pathé's Albert Capellani failed to dampen Selig's enthusiasm for this particular movie vehicle. Working closely with Kate Claxton, the actress who starred as Louise in numerous theatrical productions of *The Two Orphans* dating back to its 1875 New York premiere, Selig's Otis Turner produced a second, three-reel version in 1911 featuring two of its most bankable stars: Kathlyn Williams as Henriette and Winnifred Greenwood as Louise. *Moving Picture World* was effusive in its praise for the film's detailed settings and costumes. James S. McQuade of *MPW* called it a "massive production" and "a triumph for the Selig Polyscope Company and will go down in moving picture history as one of the big successes scored by the silent drama. It illustrates in a remarkable manner how the moving picture can convey the story and plot of a drama, the motives governing the various characters—their loves and hatreds, their crimes and follies—all so convincingly that the spectator's mind is held in thrall." Though the film may have been much more lavish than its predecessor, its treatment of its disabled characters was distressingly the same, at least as filtered through the ableist critical perspectives of the day. McQuade considered Greenwood's groping and stumbling to be "a pretty bit of realistic acting" while further noting that "Pierre, [the] crippled brother, is pathetically sustained by James O. Burrell."[43]

Many of the early movies featuring Sweet Innocents or other disabled beneficiaries of able-bodied largesse concluded simply by showing the disabled characters embarking on a new life shielded from financial worries and/or the machinations of evil able-bodied characters by the romantic or familial love that surrounds them. They were classic manifestations of mainstream society's need to create and then "service" a charity-worthy underclass to enhance its sense of superiority, a paternalistic attitude that also found expression in at least one incipient documentary of the time, Edison's four-scene *The Rescue, Care and Education of Blind Babies* (1912). For some critics, audiences, and filmmakers, however, the films didn't go far enough in resolving the disabled characters' pitiable circumstances. They believed that the promise of a harmonious life wasn't enough of a reward for these characters, that there was something morally repellent (or at least morally ambiguous) about implying that "good" people might live the rest of their lives with a disability. Lurking beneath this view was the deeply held ableist notion that people seldom win high social-approval ratings as long as they have some physical impairment. As social scientist Teresa E. Levitin has suggested, "In a society that values physical health and attractiveness, [people with physical disabilities] are less than fully acceptable," even ones who have demonstrated their prosocial qualities.[44] As long as they bear disabilities, they are Others.

Audiences and reviewers responded much more favorably to a set of films that initially paralleled the former group of dramatic films but offered a far different narrative resolution: the reward of a miracle cure for the "good" characters. Even

Kate Claxton's **Two Orphans** Selig's Immortal Masterpiece

Produced in Three Reels by Special Arrangement with Miss Kate Claxton (Sole Owner of the Copyright). Staged under Miss Claxton's personal supervision, by Mr. Otis Turner at the Selig Studios, Chicago, U.S.A. All Moving Picture Rights Reserved.

CAST

CHEVALIER MAURICE De VAUDREY ....T. J Carrigan
COUNT DE LINIERES, Minister of Police.......................Charles Clary
PICARD, Valet to the Chevalier ...... Miles McCarthy
JAQUES FROCHARD, An Outlaw . Leighton Stark

PIERRE FROCHARD, The Cripple, His Brother ...... James O'Burrell
MARQUIS DE PREALES............. Rex Rosselli
DOCTOR .... Frank Weed
LA FLEUR..................... Will Stowell
ANTOINE............ Tom I. Comberford
OFFICER OF THE GUARD.... Louis Pierce

HENRIETTE | The Two | ...... Kathlyn Williams
LOUISE | Orphans | ...... Winnifred Greenwood
MARIANNE, An Outcast........ Adrienne Krowell
LA FROCHARD, The Hag...... Lillian Leighton
MADAM GIRARD .... Vera Hamilton
COUNTESS DE LINIERES...... Myrtle Stedman

ENSEMBLE:—Parisioners, Gentlemen and Ladies of the French Nobility, Gendarmes, Soldiers, Peasants, Prisoners, Nuns, etc.

SECOND REEL

THE COUNT DE LINIERES, now Minister of Police, discovers that there is in existence secret archives containing the histories of noble families. The Countess tells the Chevalier of her early marriage and baby Louise. The Count overhears enough to make him suspicious. The Chevalier tears out the incriminating page and burns it.

The Chevalier, deeply in love with Henriette, arouses the King's displeasure by proposing to the girl. She refuses him and he renews his search for Louise.

Meantime, poor Louise, clad only in rags, is forced to sing on the snow covered streets, by Frochard. Pierre attempts to aid Louise but is rebuffed by Jaques.

The Countess pleads with Henriette not to marry the Chevalier. Henriette hears the voice of her blind sister in the street below, and attempts to rush to her, but is arrested. Louise is dragged away by Frochard.

Miss Kathlyn Williams **SELIG** Miss Winnifred Greenwood

A handbill for the second reel of Selig's The Two Orphans *(1911). By releasing the movie one reel per day over a three-day period, Otis Turner was able to develop a longer narrative format while avoiding the wrath of the one- and two-reel minded Motion Picture Patents Company.*

more of a denial of the disabled experience than the fake-disability strategy, the facile remedy fleetingly appeared in *Passion Play*, a multipart film on the life of Jesus Christ made before the turn of the century, but didn't make a major comeback until moviemakers renewed their interest in projects with a religious bent about ten years later. "Biblical subjects seem popular with all manufacturers [i.e., film producers] just now," noted an *MPW* commentator in mid–1909, and with those subjects came a strong sense of divine intervention and miracle cures. In Gaumont's *The Blind Man of Jerusalem* (1909), for instance, the wealthy title character encounters none other than Christ himself and has his vision restored. The newly sighted man keeps his cure hidden from his household and, seeing how his servants steal from him and even his own daughter betrays him, he leaves his home in despair. He accidently meets Christ again, this time on his way to Calvary, and "the sight of the suffering Saviour teaches him to forgive his offenders." A *MPW* reviewer noted that "the most moving scenes, the two climaxes, first when Christ restores the sight of the blind man, and the second when the former blind man watches Christ pass, bearing his cross on the way to crucifixion, are so impressive they are not soon forgotten."[45]

In films set in other than biblical times, the divine intervention took a more indirect route. In Vitagraph's 1908 *Stricken Blind* (alternately titled *To Forgive Is Divine*), two señoritas, Margaret and Angela, vie for the attention of the local gallant, Juan. Juan favors Margaret and gives her a betrothal ring, an act that angers Angela so much that she hires an old hag to render Margaret sightless by pouring a poisonous liquid into the latter's wash basin. The moviemakers conformed the newly blinded Margaret's behavior to conventional mainstream beliefs by having her want to release Juan from his marriage vow but he will have none of it. While the whole town prays for Margaret's recovery, Juan swears his undying love for Margaret and later rejects Angela's advances. Angela's guilty conscience eventually gets the best of her and, in front of the whole town, she prostrates herself in front of Margaret and confesses her culpability. According to an account in *MPW*, Margaret then "crosses herself, walks over to her rival, raises her and kisses her in token of forgiveness. As she does so, her blindness vanishes, and amid great rejoicing, Margaret rushes into Juan's arms."[46]

Appearing at a time when mainstream society offered little beyond basic charity to its physically disabled population and the faith-healing philosophy of Mary Baker Eddy's Christian Science Church was on the rise, movies that featured the concept of a God-delivered cure represented a major shift in moviemaker attitudes toward disability. In a very short period of time, filmmakers working with noncomedic victimization themes moved from tragedy to general able-bodied helpfulness to the ultimate in paternalistic attitudes, curability. By dodging the long-term implications of permanent disability in favor of facile cures, the movie industry, consciously or not, was pursuing an ableist agenda of enormous proportions. The moviemaker most responsible for this "curable romantic" trend created more than a dozen disability-related films while working for the Biograph and several more after he had left that company's employ: the legendary David Wark Griffith.

The state of the Biograph company and its films prior to Griffith's ascendancy as its premiere writer-director was less than auspicious. The quality of Biograph films had dropped markedly after the departure of "Old Man" McCutcheon and the company's move to 11 E. 14th Street in 1906 and had affected movie sales; according to Iris Barry, the number of prints of each film the Biograph sold at that time dwindled to as low as twenty. Terry Ramsaye noted that Biograph films "were openly called 'rotten' on the market" by 1907, and those who offered that assessment doubtless had been downwind of such disability comedies as *Mrs. Smithers' Boarding-School* and *The Deaf-Mutes' Ball*. McCutcheon came back to the Biograph in January 1908 after several years at Edison, but his new films did little to reverse the company's fortunes. As suggested by Benjamin B. Hampton, audiences by then had become bored with the general kind of fare the "Old Man" provided: "Action films were satisfying for awhile, and then the most active minds in audiences grew restless with repeated pursuits, and with comedies built on the crudest of antique structures. . . . They wanted something different, and unless that something could be discovered and supplied many of them would cease to be customers of the little show-shops. The movie-makers blundered along until they discovered that romance was the recipe to sell more tickets at the box-office." Anything that smacked of romance in McCutcheon's slapstick films was strictly incidental to the riotous action, but the focus of Biograph films was soon to change. In failing health since early 1908, McCutcheon left the company by July of that year and was replaced as its primary director by Griffith, a courtly Kentuckian whom the studio had hired as an actor several months earlier. Initially reluctant to direct films, Griffith quickly demonstrated his virtuosity behind the camera and at the editing bench, and concomitantly began developing sentimental story ideas and romanticized characterizations far removed from those of his Biograph predecessors. He had discovered Hampton's "recipe."[47]

Actually, Griffith began experimenting with it years before he first set foot into the dingy domain of the Biograph. A play he completed in 1906 called *A Fool and a Girl*, which, though a flop, provided Griffith with an entrée into the world of filmmaking, offers strong sense of the philosophy that was to shape his movies. Set in a landscape of the lower classes, *A Fool and a Girl* centers on a youthful dreamer named Albert Holly, a character not unlike his creator, and Effie "Freshie" Tucker, a young woman described by Griffith as "full of good nature and sparkling with life—with a sweet, fresh beauty." Albert's declaration of love for this prototypical Griffith movie heroine contains several indications of things to come: "I have been as blind as death all my life. . . . Yes, blind. I never saw anything until I came to look at all things with you. You took away the blindness from my eyes and everything was sweet. You! You! YOU! I knew, of course, there was a God. They made me kneel down to Him when I was that high, and pray to

Him—but I never really knew Him—but tonight, when I was with you, I felt that you were on one side and that on the other there was some mysterious, undreamed of God's arm around me, and that he was leading us on, on over the hills—over the hills."[48]

In just a few lines of dialogue, Griffith suggested some of the conservative values that would eventually make his movies famous the world over: in this instance, a syrupy mix of sentimental romance, religious faith, and an oblique perspective on disability. Albert is only talking about figurative blindness, of course, but Griffith saw little distinction between it and its literal counterpart once he started making movies. He lived in a society in which, just as today, the phrase "I see" meant "I understand," and he no doubt believed the reversal of that sentiment was also true; a person who literally cannot see is also unlikely to understand. In his desire to emphasize visuals over words, Griffith found no better way to telegraph a person's ignorance or misunderstanding of some situation to the audience than to make the character literally blind. Griffith's oft-quoted paraphrase of Joseph Conrad—"The task I'm trying to achieve above all, is to make you see"—thus takes on a particular resonance; en route to opening the audience's eyes, as it were, he would occasionally create characters literally and figuratively blind to some situation.

Griffith wasted little time developing this idea. About a month after he started directing movies for the Biograph, he created *The Man and the Woman* (1908), a

David Wark Griffith, writer-director extraordinaire and creator of more than a dozen disability-related melodramas for the Biograph.

one-reeler that had among its characters a stereotype reflecting both ableist and ageist agendas: an "Elderly Dupe" in the form of a mother blind in several senses to the morally questionable activities of one of her sons. As Biograph publicist Lee "Doc" Dougherty put it: "John has succeeded in keeping [his brother's transgressions] from his dear mother, whose blindness is almost a blessing, for a mother would rather her eyes be sightless than to view the indiscretions of her loved ones." By the end of the brief film, however, the Dupe's goodness and spirituality reform the wayward youth: "The blind mother, like a ministering angel, appears and Tom's heart is at last softened."[49] Griffith's equation of ignorance with literal blindness, a classic if incredibly simplistic expression of ability-related prejudice, received significant support from a technical limitation of the medium: the lack of spoken dialogue, which lent credence to the notion that withholding information from a blind person is relatively easy.

In all, Griffith directed at least fourteen films for the Biograph that dealt with physical disability, mostly on a gratuitous level. They ranged from primitive references (1909's *In a Hempen Bag* featured a gardener about to dispose of a cat in a bag, unaware, because of his deafness, that it actually contains an infant) to relatively sustained levels of stereotyping. *The Roué's Heart*, one of many films that Griffith wrote and directed in 1909, serves well as an example of the latter tendency.

A twelve-minute film photographed by longtime Griffith cinematographer Billy Bitzer at Biograph's Manhattan studio, the film amply demonstrated a prime truism of Sweet Innocent films: the inevitable romance that develops between the Sweet Innocent and her benefactor is initially founded on the strong feelings of pity that the character seems to evoke automatically. Set in Renaissance times, *The Roué's Heart* centers on the wealthy and bored Monsieur Flamant (Harry Solter), who discovers a sculpture and insists on meeting its creator. He encounters the sculptress (Marion Leonard) and, as Dougherty noted, "at once falls passionately in love with her as only a man of his type can, but when he learns that she is totally blind, his feelings change to one of deepest pity, which is, we know, the kindling of pure love." An *MPW* reviewer put it somewhat differently: "He finds she is blind, and her purity prevents his carrying out his evil designs."[50]

As with other films of that vintage (most notably, Gaumont's *Two Ladies and a Beggar* and *The Cripple's Marriage*), *The Roué's Heart* underscored the supposed incompatibility of physical disability and marriage. This time, however, the disabled person herself arrives at this conclusion, as noted in Dougherty's description in *MPW*: "He arranges with her to sit for a bust of himself and when it is finished he declares his love for her but she realizes her condition and rejects it, although she has by intuition come to love him deeply. As he leaves the studio crestfallen she sinks down and for the first time feels the enormity of her affliction, sobbing she cries: 'Oh! God, how I love him, and yet it must not be.'" Spectators caught up in this film (one reviewer observed "the audience sits almost breathless through some of the scenes, notably the one where she rejects his first offer of marriage") need not have worried, for Griffith as the ableist perpetrator of this film made certain this disabled person's silly fears were unfounded. One of her young models witnesses her self-torture and informs the roué, who "rushes back to the studio to set aside the sculptress' compunction and claim her as his own." While the film commendably shows a disabled person to be self-sufficient as far as making a living is concerned, it still exhibits a very strong sense of an able-bodied type "rescuing" that person. In addition, it contains the repugnant message that disabled people themselves think they are not marriage material. It remains chiefly notable today as a kind of testing ground for Griffith, who in 1921 went on to create the most famous Sweet Innocent film of the silent era, *Orphans of the Storm*.[51]

At 755 feet, *The Roué's Heart* was short by one-reel standards, so Griffith added a brief comedy to bring the total footage close to the usual thousand-foot length. The filler was a truly tasteless four-minute affair called *The Wooden Leg*, about two able-bodied people who exploit another person's disability to achieve marital bliss. *The Roué's Heart* and *The Wooden Leg* made for an exceptionally disconcerting double-bill of disability films.

Photographed in February of that year by Arthur Marvin, brother of Biograph co-owner Henry Marvin, and Billy Bitzer (why this tiny film needed two cinematographers is anyone's guess), *The Wooden Leg* tells the story of Harry and Claire (David Miles and Florence Lawrence) who want to marry. Her father (John R. Cumpson) will have none of it, however, having already arranged his daughter's marriage to a "wealthy old fossil." The couple is nearly bankrupt of ideas when Harry encounters a one-legged tramp (Mack Sennett) and comes up with a plan absolutely reeking of ableism; he suggests that Claire pretend to wear the hobo's wooden leg to scare off the would-be suitor. Sad to say, the plan works; when the elderly swain "sees the tip of the wooden leg protruding from underneath the flounce of her skirt he turns and 'beats it' with such dispatch that he knocks Papa over when he tries to detain him." A *Moving Picture World* review was essentially neutral on the film ("It develops some amusing situations, but is not especially interesting") but made no note of the film's prejudicial views.[52] Griffith's gratuitous use of disability in this film is a bit surprising in light of the fact that several members of his own immediate family had orthopedic impairments; a childhood bout with malaria had left his brother with an impaired use of a leg, while his father, a Confederate colonel, had been severely injured in the shoulder and leg during the Civil War. The film's romance certainly marks *The Wooden Leg* as a Griffith product, and like *The Roué's Heart* it underscores the supposed incongruity of a disabled woman and marriage, but its comedic aspects make it something of an anomaly for him. Though Griffith is credited as the film's writer and director, it probably owes a great deal of its concept to Mack Sennett, the actor who played the tramp and who harbored moviemaking ambitions quite different from Griffith's. Sennett often peppered his mentor with questions about the filmmaking process and, according to historians Kalton Lahue and

Terry Brewer, "was anxious to discuss his theories on the possibilities of screen comedy, a topic which left Griffith completely unmoved."[53]

More to Griffith's melodramatic tastes was *The Violin Maker of Cremona* (1909), featuring Griffith regular David Miles as Filippo, the disabled title character. Memorable today mainly as Mary Pickford's first major vehicle, *Violin Maker* was another film that gave a thumbs down to a romantic relationship between differently abled people and underscored the importance of the disabled character "nobly" withdrawing from it. This film, based on François Coppée's one-act play, presents the ever so slightly contrived premise of an annual violin-making contest with a gold chain and, this year, the hand in marriage of the contest sponsor's daughter Giannina (Pickford) as the prizes. Secretly in love with the runner-up Sandro (Owen Moore), Giannina recoils when the orthopedically impaired Filippo wins the contest. Seeing her despair, Filippo intentionally breaks his violin and thereby allows his rival to claim the "prizes." The final shot of the film, described by publicist Dougherty as depicting Filippo "alone in his room, crushed and dejected, yet contented in the thought that he has made her happy" and praised by the reviewer for *The New York Dramatic Mirror* as "art in its highest sense," is formally most unusual, even for Griffith, and strongly reinforces the ableist notion that disabled people should be kept isolated. Kemp Niver described it this way: "At this point, Griffith reaches into his theatrical past to come up with a kind of mood lighting to help the actor, David Miles, who is the only person in the room, convince the audience that he is reconciled to the lonely fate he has so nobly chosen for himself. The actor is given a full 58 seconds, including a 19-second fade to black, to cover the action that ends the last scene of the picture."[54] Lest anyone miss his perspective, Griffith painted an even bleaker picture of unrequited love in *The Faded Lillies* [sic], released a mere ten days after *Violin Maker* and again starring David Miles, this time as a musician with a distorted spine who turns suicidal upon learning that the able-bodied woman of his dreams has deceived him.

Like other filmmakers, Griffith eventually gravitated toward the concept of curable disabilities. Later that year, he wrote and directed *The Light That Came*, a film described by Robert Henderson as "a reworking of the Cinderella story" and one of the first films to employ the facile cure in other than a religious context. Photographed by Billy Bitzer, *The Light That Came* is about a working-class young woman with a scarred face named Grace (Ruth Hart) who ordinarily does drudge work at home while her vivacious sisters (Marion Leonard and Mary Pickford) enjoy themselves at fancy East Side parties. One evening, however, Grace attends such an event at her mother's encouragement and meets a kindred spirit in the form of Carl Wagner (Owen Moore), the party's musical entertainer and another of moviedom's poor blind violinists. The two become sweethearts and soon announce their engagement, but a bit of "good news-bad news" jolts their relationship; a doctor examining Carl states that an operation could restore the musician's sight, but the expense of bringing in the proper eye specialist

BIOGRAPH
TRADE MARK — TRADE MARK

FILMS

RELEASED NOVEMBER 8, 1909.

THE RESTORATION

A Doctor's Plan to Retrieve a Shattered Mind.

The world's history would contain many blank pages if it were not for the frequent occasions of misconstruction of intent. How many commendable deeds have been misconstrued and made the genesis of woe. Wrong impressions, converted ideas and hallucinations have formed the greater part of the causes of calamity, and there is no stronger ideological force than jealousy, and jealousy thrives most in the fagged brain. Henry Morley was suffering from what seemed to be an attack of hypochondriasis. He was low spirited, irresolute of purpose, and in fact on the verge of nervous collapse. His wife becomes solicitous and urges outdoor exercise, such as hunting, driving and the like. Mrs. Morley's cousin Alice is spending the Summer with them. Alice and her sweetheart Jack Dudley indulge in a lovers' quarrel, and Mrs. Morley volunteers to patch it up. Morley misconstrues the intent of their meeting, and entering the drawing-room in the evening after the couple had made up, sees Jack enfolding Alice in his arms. Thinking it his wife he sends Jack reeling to the floor with a blow of his whip handle. Realising his mistake, his mind is unbalanced. Jack is only stunned and the doctor, in order to restore Morley's reason, has Jack and Alice re-enact the scene, with successful results.

LENGTH, 964 FEET.

RELEASED NOVEMBER 11, 1909.

THE LIGHT THAT CAME

Romance of a Blind Musician.

We, of course, assume that being most unfortunate over whose sight fate has drawn the mantle of darkness, and it is reasonable so to do, but Divine Providence is sure to compensate those so afflicted with ameliorating gifts that help them bear their ills with fortitude, and not only that, their powers of discernment are far more acute than those endowed with sight. There is the sight of the soul, which sees farther than the eyes. This may be called intuition; but whatever it may be, it is a rare gift. Carl Wagner was bereft of his sight and in order that he might earn a livelihood he learned music, and played violin for the dancing at many of the East Side balls. One of the affairs is attended by Grace, Vivian and Daisy, three sisters. Vivian and Daisy are rather pretty girls and are the center of attraction. Grace, however, has a disfiguring scar on her face, which makes her a wall-flower throughout the evening. At the close of the entertainment, she meets Carl, and a sympathy, which ripens to love, springs up. They become sweethearts, and later become engaged. A friend of the family declares his belief that Carl's sight can be restored, and Grace is moved to help him with her savings. On second thought she realises that when he sees her as she is, she will lose his love. This she struggles against, and when the cure is effected, she finds her fears were groundless, for the heart has seen farther than the eyes could have.

LENGTH, 998 FEET.

A Full Description of these Subjects will be Found on Another Page

---

Release days of Biograph Subjects—MONDAY and THURSDAY

Get on Our Mail List and Keep Posted. Write for Our Descriptive Circulars

BIOGRAPH COMPANY

Licensee of the Motion Picture Patents Co.

11 EAST 14th STREET :: NEW YORK

GEORGE KLEINE, Selling Agent for Chicago (52 State St., Chicago, Ill.).

A Biograph advertisement for an early Griffith film of disability, The Light That Came *(1909), as published in the trade journal* Moving Picture World.

would be very high. The near-destitute Carl is more despairing than ever, but Grace, who has built up some savings over the years, is willing to bankroll the operation. She is afraid Carl will go running after taking one gander at her countenance, however, but eventually puts up the money for the surgery. After the successful operation, the musician, far from being repelled, allays Grace's fears by reaffirming his love for her.

If the *Moving Picture World* review of the film is any indication, *The Light That Came* struck a responsive chord with audiences weary of seeing people with physical disabilities in slapstick comedies and maudlin dramas. "A certain delicious and soothing tenderness pervades this film, which casts a hallowed influence over the audience and holds them in an impressive silence which lasts as long as the picture remains with them," wrote the reviewer, who continued:

> The development of character in this picture is so natural and is accomplished with so little effort that one seems to feel the story as it is illustrated. Living [i.e., theatrical] characters could not make it plainer and in places the silent drama seems even more impressive than spoken lines could make it. The imagination is stimulated and enables one to appreciate more fully the dramatic situations which are inherent in the picture. In some respects this is the greatest film of the week. Its suggestiveness is so strong that one does not forget it easily and it will serve as a basis of comparison for many days to come.

The reviewer's words were prescient, for, as Lauri Klobas has noted, *The Light That Came* set the standard for other films and television programs dealing with disability issues for years.[55]

Though never abandoning his interest in characters with permanent disabilities, Griffith continued making movies that explored curable disability themes. *A Flash of Light* (1910) told the strange tale of a chemist (Charles H. West, one of Griffith's favorite actors), blinded and deafened by a lab explosion, who undergoes a successful double operation only to be accidently reblinded by his estranged wife. West also starred as an impoverished troubadour in *The Blind Princess and the Poet* (1911), a costumer straight out of storybookland about a royal daughter (Blanche Sweet) whose vision and awareness are restored by the magic of his true-love kiss. Its fairytale quality made it so popular with audiences that it was re-released in 1916, years after Griffith's departure.

Griffith continued to refine his filmmaking skills while at the Biograph, and as a part of that process he experimented with his characters' acts of looking as a means of tying shots together. He learned that alternating shots of observer and observed made for a more fluid and unified narrative, and this discovery eventually evolved into a major structuring principle for his works and countless narrative films by others who followed his lead. In her landmark essay on visual pleasure, Laura Mulvey stated bluntly that "it is the place of the look that defines cinema,"[56] and Griffith was one of the first filmmakers to recognize that truism. He learned that he could significantly empower a character by having him or her wield the gaze, a lesson that had profound ramifications for the Cinema of Isolation, particularly regarding the portrayal of visually impaired characters. By following this strategy, filmmakers such as Griffith systematically excluded blind characters from privileged positions in film; they manipulated the formal aspects of the medium to perpetuate longstanding beliefs about the powerlessness and marginality of blind people. Typically endowed with the time-worn theatrical convention of the blank stare, visually impaired characters lacked the power so deeply at the heart of narrative cinema and thus found themselves reduced to objects of spectacle for the sighted characters and the audience. It's a visual narrative strategy that has changed little.

Joyce Jesionowski's analysis of *Through Darkened Vales* (1911), one of Griffith's last disability-related Biograph movies, illustrates this principle. This film, about two young people named Grace and Dave (Sweet and West, again) who go blind, concludes with a sequence that alternates shots of the following subjects: Grace, her vision recently restored as a result of Dave's sacrifice, seated in her room looking rightward out a window, and the sightless Dave, carrying a load of brooms on his shoulder, wandering leftward across a road and toward her home. As the sequence progresses, the shots change from long to medium, and, although the ones of Dave are not specifically from Grace's perspective, it is clear she is in the privileged position while he represents the powerless object of the gaze. She is the one with the power of the look, and she is the one who resolves the sequence by rushing into the cinematic space that he had exclusively occupied up to that point.[57]

Anyone who has studied the early history of cinema cannot help but note the conspicuousness of certain recurring company names—Biograph, Pathé, Vitagraph, Edison, Lubin, Selig, Essanay, Urban, Gaumont—during this period of the Cinema of Isolation. In short, members or associates of the conservative Motion Picture Patents Company, a.k.a. "the Trust," were at the forefront of movie companies that created disparaging or fantasy-filled movies of people with physical disabilities. The highly restrictive trade practices of the film world's first monopoly are well-documented and need no elaboration here. Suffice it to say that the MPPC firms' anti-progressive tendencies extended well beyond patents, licenses, and frequent lawsuit threats to include the content of the films themselves, as these and other films so amply demonstrated.[58]

It would be a mistake to assume, however, that the MPPC companies were out of touch with audience tastes when it came to disability issues. Reflecting the conservative spirit of the times, audiences and reviewers welcomed the new trend of people being cured of their disabilities as presented in Gaumont's *The Blind Man of Jerusalem*, Vitagraph's *Stricken Blind*, and other MPPC films while turning away from movies, many of which were produced by independent companies, that featured young people with permanent disabilities who live out their lives in squalor.

An illustration of this point may be found in a 1909 report offered by an anonymous *Moving Picture World* writer who visited a Bronx nickelodeon and reviewed its offerings. Among the films the reviewer saw that day at "Nicoland" was *The Blind Foundling* (1909), produced by the independent Great Northern Film Company, about a Sweet Innocent, sightless since birth, who lives a life full of hard knocks before she is reunited with her mother. Though suggesting the film "is a very fine piece of photography and stage craft," the reviewer also offered comments that reveal a sense of the mainstream views of the day:

> Now, I beg to protest in the most emphatic manner possible against the exhibition on the silent [screen] of physical deformities or defects. They are not pleasant to contemplate in real life; they are positively repellent to most minds on the [screen]. This girl becomes a waitress amongst dissolute men, two of whom fight a duel; then she is decoyed by criminals, beaten, turned adrift, and the door is open for suggestion that even a worse fate than this befalls her. I submit that this is not a pleasant theme to show ladies and children, and those around me at Nicoland the other day evidently had the same opinion. The picture had a very depressing effect. I hope my good friends of the Great Northern Film Company will take this stricture in the best part and not send out such sombre subjects in future.[59]

A similar backlash occurred over *United by Misfortune* (1909), a film produced by the Independent, a company whose very name proclaimed nonalignment with the MPPC. This movie was about a man injured in a tree-trimming accident who is brought to the same hospital as his estranged daughter, a Sweet Innocent blinded in an explosion. Though their bittersweet reunion ended the film on a hopeful note, the *MPW* reviewer in so many words found the happiness of the film's ending compromised by the permanence of the Sweet Innocent's blindness. "The photography is good and the staging could scarcely be improved," wrote the reviewer, "but the story is not to be recommended. It is too depressing. It doesn't amuse, and that should be the primary requisite of a motion picture."[60]

As the Trust's economic clout waned during the early-to-mid 1910s and movies concomitantly began expanding to multi-reel lengths, the independent film companies that continued to challenge the Motion Picture Patents Company and eventually saw its demise demonstrated that moviedom's first cartel had no monopoly on regressive imagery. Acting on a desire to exploit growing public awareness of disability issues but mindful of the negative reactions to such fare as *The Blind Foundling* and *United by Misfortune*, many of these upstart companies would pursue an agenda ever more sharply at odds with the realities of physical disability.

The films discussed in this chapter, admittedly only a small fraction of the total movie output prior to the rise of the feature film, nevertheless represent reasonably clear trends related to physical disability. Through its constructions, the movie industry essentially denied the existence of people with physical disabilities at first by focusing on beggars with fake impairments. When it finally got around to portraying people with actual disabilities, it devalued them further by treating them mainly as human novelties (and often used disabled actors recruited solely for their appearance to flesh them out) or victims whose deaths are imminent. With the rise of the film d'art, filmmakers began experimenting with images based on famous literary works and developed types that for the most part represented either consummate villainy or consummate innocence—a dichotomy based rather conspicuously on gender. The industry's infantilization of women and villainization of men through disability, presented in only rudimentary form during the medium's earliest stages, would undergo significant development during and immediately after the years that marked the carnage of World War I.

2 / the misbegotten multi-reelers

On a brisk March afternoon in 1912, a mild-mannered and exceedingly patient fellow named Adolph Zukor waited nearly three hours in the offices of the Motion Picture Patents Company for a special audience. The willingness of "Creepy," as the soft-spoken but icy-eyed Zukor was sometimes called, to wait so long was understandable; he and partners Edwin S. Porter and Joseph Engel had recently formed the Famous Players Film Company, a company dedicated to recording "famous players in famous plays" on film, and the fledgling concern had just spent $18,000 to acquire the U. S. distribution rights to a French film d'art known alternately as *Les Amours de la Reine Élisabeth* and *Élisabeth Reine d'Angleterre*. Zukor now sought a license from the MPPC to show it but knew he would run into opposition; directed the previous year by Louis Mercanton for the Eclipse company and starring the most famous player of the period, Sarah Bernhardt, the film ran a then-lengthy four reels and the Trust had heretofore approved of only one- and two-reel films. He had the support of some Trust executives, most notably, Biograph bigwig Henry Marvin, and after some bickering the Trust grudgingly conceded Zukor a license to exhibit the film. Despite its relative artlessness, the now-retitled *Queen Elizabeth* was a hit with audiences and made a lot of money for "Creepy" and his partners. Though the next three years were marked by considerable opposition to multi-reel films from established filmmakers and distributors, both Trust-aligned and independent (mainly because of increased production costs and the necessity of developing more complex storylines), *Queen Elizabeth* holds the distinction of opening up the feature-film era in the United States. That its star happened to have been disabled—Bernhardt was unable to walk without support because of an ever-worsening leg injury that resulted from a 1905 theater accident—was an aspect of the film that went largely unnoticed.[1]

As the film industry ever so sluggishly embraced the multi-reel or feature-length format during the early 1910s, the cultivators of the Cinema of Isolation began sending out mixed signals. Several signs suggested the movie image of physically disabled people might actually be improving. Primary among them was the decline in the number of disability comedies, as more and more moviemakers, under the international film d'art movement's spell of high-mindedness, eventually recognized the tastelessness of mixing disability and farce. Moviemakers who clung to the one- and two-reel formats did occasionally revive the combination; for example, a young Mack Sennett protégé named Charles Chaplin wrote and directed a one-reeler in 1914 called *His New Profession*, in which his Tramp persona stirs up what critic Uno Asplund has termed "disagreeably sadistic humour" while pushing the wheelchair of a crotchety old man. As this and later chapters will reveal, however, the tendency of using humor to trivialize disability issues that had proven so strong during the first dozen years or so of the medium only sporadically appeared in subsequent movies.[2]

Another positive indication came from Famous Players, then awash in proceeds from the exhibition of *Queen Elizabeth*. Its success had allowed Adolph Zukor and his associates to continue making movies themselves, and, in line with the Bernhardt film, many of the productions were longer than the standard one and two reels still advocated by the fast-fading MPPC. Among the first was a crime mystery featuring a detective who happened to use a wheelchair.

The movie, *Chelsea 7750* (1913), was written and directed by J. Searle Dawley, an Edwin Porter recruit whose 300-odd films for the Edison and Rex companies included such disability-related fare as *A Christmas Carol* (1910) and *Treasure Island* (1911) and who also held the distinction of introducing D. W. Griffith to the world of filmmaking by hiring him to play the lead in *Rescued from an Eagle's Nest* back in 1907. *Chelsea 7750* was a four-reel feature that followed the activities of a sleuth named Kirby (Henry E. Dixey, one of Famous Players'

The divine Sarah Bernhardt in a histrionic moment from the French film d'art later anglicized as Queen Elizabeth *by Adolph Zukor and friends. Courtesy Museum of Modern Art/Film Stills Archive.*

"famous players" starring in his first movie) who becomes partially paralyzed during the course of the film. The villain of the piece, the head of a counterfeiting ring named Grimble (House Peters), abducts the detective's daughter Kate (Laura Sawyer) in retaliation for Kirby's role in his son's imprisonment years before. En route to a happy ending, the sleuth uses his considerable mental agility not only to save himself—at one point, he eludes Grimble's thugs by setting fire to his own lodgings in the hope that firemen will rescue him, which they do—but also to save his daughter. Like the title character of the previous decade's *The Little Cripple*, Kirby represents an early version of the Civilian Superstar: a resourceful, adaptive, and courageous individual who happens to have a disability. "It is true that many peace-time cripples have lived out their lives heroically and successfully and are holding positions of responsibility," wrote a disability survey administrator during the 1910s, and Kirby was a welcome if all-too-rare cinematic embodiment of that truth during the silent-film era.[3]

The appearance of *Chelsea 7750* and the drop-off of slapstick comedies were encouraging but ultimately misleading signs during the first years of the feature-film era. Dawley and Famous Players vitiated the good intentions expressed in *Chelsea 7750* almost as quickly as they created them when they followed up with a four-reel sequel about a month later. Also written and directed by Dawley, *An Hour Before Dawn* (1913) changed the focus of the storyline developed in *Chelsea 7750* by concentrating on Kate in her profession as a detective following her father's semi-retirement. *Chelsea 7750* and *An Hour Before Dawn* were actually continuations of a "Kate Kirby" film series that Dawley had established for Edison, but the writer-director opted to stress father over daughter in the former feature due to the involvement of Dixey, a somewhat tarnished but still prominent luminary of the legitimate stage. Dixey returned to his Broadway environs immediately after completing work on *Chelsea 7750*, however, and, with a not-so-famous player now assuming the role of the wheelchair-using father, Dawley returned to the series' original premise. Though the new film continued to generate interest in risk-taking young women—the Kate Kirby movies soon began sharing screen time with other alliteratively titled film serials such as *The Perils of Pauline*, *The Mysteries of Myra*, and *The Exploits of Elaine*—it also had the unfortunate effect of shoving its Civilian Superstar into a background role and eventual oblivion.[4]

As for the comedies, their rapid decline belied the resiliency of the freakshow mentality that had guided them. Indeed, the undue fascination with the appearance of people with disabilities soon began reappearing in several forms, the most unsettling of which were representations of mainstream fears.

The ever-growing movie trend of casting characters with orthopedic impairments as villains, a stereotype so entrenched in the mythology of many cultures, took firm root in the movies during the early–to–mid–1910s. In 1912, an obscure little concern called the Sterling Camera and Film Company produced what may well have been the world's first feature film centering on a disabled character: yet another telling of the Richard III tale, this one a lavish four-reeler by M. B. Dudley and James Keene (trade advertisements laden with stills from the film trumpeted its "100 big scenes," cast of 1,000, and 200 horses) and copyrighted under the bloated title, *Mr. Frederick Warde in Shakespeare's Masterpiece, "The Life and Death of King Richard III."* Due perhaps to fears of the Trust's reaction to it, the film did not receive widespread attention until the following year. Once it did, however, other disabled movie evildoers madly proliferated in its wake.[5]

Filmmakers showed little restraint in associating a variety of disabilities with villainous behavior. A criminal known simply if disparagingly by his appendages served as the title character of Herbert Blaché's *Hook and Hand* (1914), for example, while a paralyzed man (played by prolific director-to-be Edward Sloman) vows vengeance on the son of the man he holds responsible for his disability in Universal's 1914 serialized *The Trey O'Hearts.* Moviemakers found Richard Crookback such a conspicuous and compelling figure, however, that they made males with severely distorted spines, so-called "hunchbacks," the most prominent by far of the different types of disabled villains. Easily the most maligned of disabled film characters, people with such orthopedic impairments have almost always been objectified in the movies as embodiments of villainy or, at the very least, obsessive behavior. They were among the first movie representations of a stereotype we might call the "Obsessive Avenger": an egomaniacal sort, almost always an adult male, who does not rest until he has had his revenge on those he holds responsible for his disablement and/or violating his moral code in some other way.

Even as the trade papers abounded with promotions for the Sterling *Richard III,* the Kalem Company released a two-reeler simply entitled *The Hunchback* (1913). It starred Tom Moore as "Humpty" Johnson, described by an *MPW* reviewer as "a degenerate cripple, whose mind is even more deformed than his body, [who forces] Marie, a wholesome, lovable girl into a marriage with him." The moviemakers, Moore very much included, endowed him with a classic mix of fascinating and repellent qualities, as the reviewer's comments make clear: "Moore gives a wonderful performance as the hunchback. While this splendid Kalem performer makes the cripple absolutely repulsive, he also contrives to arouse a sense of pity for the unfortunate man. One feels that the hunchback's tigerish nature is due to the constant illusions [sic] to his deformity. And this feeling of pity remains with the observer even when the cripple is seen committing a murder in a way which shocks to the very core."[6]

In the tradition of this film and D. W. Griffith's *The Faded Lillies,* filmmakers working during the initial years of the feature-film era tended to design such characters as outcasts who worshipped some able-bodied woman from afar and then invariably lost control of their emotions after an able-bodied male rival appears on the scene. The message was clear: theirs was a "forbidden love" (the ability-related equivalent of miscegenation seldom found approval on the screen during this time),[7] and their inability to accept that social norm inevitably brought out their "beastly" nature and often led to their deaths.

A director responsible for several of these films was a Cleveland-born recruit from the worlds of theater and opera named Oscar Apfel. A one-time associate of J. Searle Dawley (they jointly directed *Aïda* for Edison in 1911), Apfel migrated to the Jesse L. Lasky Feature Play Company, where he developed the concept of a vengeful hunchback in a 1914 film he directed called *The Circus Man*. This film tells of the odd relationship between a hunchbacked circus performer named Ernie Cronk (that his last name is a phonetic spelling of the German *krank*, which means "sick," was probably no coincidence) and an able-bodied fellow who hides out with Ernie's circus after being falsely accused of murder. Even though the latter character saved his life, Ernie is extremely jealous of the handsome young man attracted to the circus owner's daughter and informs the police as to his whereabouts.

The Circus Man was one of a core of Apfel films that impressed William Fox, a major figure in the early film industry who had recently helped smash the MPPC and was now in the process of consolidating his various film enterprises into the Fox Film Corporation. Fox found Apfel the perfect candidate to co-write and direct *The Broken Law* (1915), a convoluted tale of Romany Gypsies and their conflicts with outsiders. At the film's climax, one of the Gypsies, a hunch-backed fellow named Gorgiko, slays a nobleman who had seduced an Esmeralda-like woman in his camp and then commits suicide. Fox was so pleased with Apfel's film that he not only re-released it four years later but also used it as a testing ground for a far more familiar tale of Gypsies and disability: Victor Hugo's *Notre-Dame de Paris*, better known to modern audiences as *The Hunchback of Notre Dame*. Retitled *The Darling of Paris* to draw attention to the charms of its red-hot star, Theda Bara, and piloted by the "Bara director," J. Gordon Edwards, Fox's adaptation of the Hugo novel hit the screens a little more than a year after *The Broken Law*'s premiere.[8]

The movies of Apfel and Fox were certainly not the only constructions that devalued people with such orthopedic impairments. Jealousy also surfaces in the Life Photo Film's *The Ordeal* (1914), a film set during the Franco–Prussian War, in which a hunchbacked man loses his girlfriend to an able-bodied suitor and in revenge tells the swain's war-veteran father that his son refused to enlist in the army to fight the Prussians. With India as its setting, Universal's *The Gates of Doom* (1917) reveals the story of Agatha, a young woman of British and Indian descent, who, with the help of an opportunistic hunchback named Jang Sahib, rescues her mother from a harem. Sahib demands that Agatha marry him and she agrees, but she later strangles him on the day they were to be married. The movies devalue a disabled person's life once again, as a friend of Agatha's late father rescues her just as she was to be executed for Sahib's death. *The Butterfly* (1915), *Man and His Angel* (1916), and *The Path of Happiness* (1916) were among the

other movies of the time that featured men with distorted spines who pursue revenge schemes as an antidote for their unrequited love.[9]

Such films are not difficult to interpret on a psychoanalytic level as re-
enactments of that defining structure for classic narrative, the Oedipal scenario:
the disabled male, who never resolved his Oedipal crisis as a child because of
psychological problems emblemized by his disability, is doomed to repeat it with
the Mother and Father surrogates that he encounters—the able-bodied woman
and man—with less than gratifying if not downright calamitous results. Viewed
from this perspective, these films are particularly distressing in that they treat the
characters' disabled status as the equivalent of deep psychological disturbances
and provide little by way of resolution other than death.

As ominous as these movies and attitudes were, they weren't the worst of the
trend; the right combination of social conditions, directorial authority, and actor
ability to make Obsessive Avenger films hugely popular at the box office was still
several years away. In the mean time, moviegoers' attention was increasingly
diverted by the escalating events in Europe that had among their many consequences a profound effect on issues of physical disability and their portrayal in
the movies.

Most Americans responded to the outbreak of hostilities in August 1914 by
following President Woodrow Wilson's proclamation of neutrality. "I Didn't
Raise My Boy to Be a Soldier," the title of a popular 1915 song written by Tin Pan
Alley's Alfred Bryan and Al Piantadosi, seemed to sum up the national sentiment.
The American movie industry knew that neutrality was not the same thing as dis-
interest, however, and it cultivated an audience fascination with war-related topics
within a month after the conflict began by releasing numerous films that incorporated military footage and by even reviving old films that had anything to do with
war in general. It also made certain a steady diet of wartime newsreels and propaganda films created by both sides of the European conflict found its way into theaters to satisfy its information-hungry audiences.

What movie patrons saw, however, came increasingly under the control of
military censors who greatly limited the war-related topics that could be presented in theaters. "The great European war is the first war in which the cinematograph has played an important part," wrote *Motion Picture Supplement*
correspondent Charles Doran in 1915, "and would have played a still more important one had the Moving Picture men not been restricted by the military
censorship, which, in most cases, meant seizure of films likely to be of real interest to a foreign public." Soldiers disabled by the conflict were high on the list of
forbidden subjects, as the censors believed that newsreels bearing such images
might undermine civilian support of the war effort. As Doran explained, "To permit these films to be shown to the public, it is feared, might cast a gloom over the
land and send such a horror of the cruelties and devastation of war home to the
non-combatants as to cause public demonstration against further levies of men

and taxes to continue hostilities. The censors in Berlin, and for that matter Paris and London as well, know all this, and they guard well against the possibility of the cinematograph awakening in the public mind anything that might discourage military fervor and enthusiasm." The American Red Cross picked up some of the slack by forming a film bureau to educate the public about the war and raise capital for its overseas operations. Its films tended to consist of foreign and domestic newsreel snippets bearing images of disabled soldiers, among other subjects, and it soon began distributing movies produced by the primary source of American-made films containing war footage, the U.S. Army Signal Corps. Unfortunately, the films were typically shown in Red Cross meeting places, not in theaters, and failed to reach large audiences until well into 1918, the last year of the war, when the Committee on Public Information formed a Division of Pictures that offered a more efficient distribution of war films than that provided by the Red Cross.[10]

Thus, the newsreels most Americans saw glorified the war through images of pomp and pageantry, military drills, and leaders on horseback, while showing little of its staggering toll of deaths and permanent injuries. Newspaper accounts of the conflict somewhat counterbalanced their romanticized representations, however, and as Americans began reading news stories about German brutality their attitudes toward neutrality changed dramatically. When a German submarine sunk the British ship *Lusitania* in May 1915, killing more than 1,100 people (including 128 U.S. citizens), many Americans started arguing in favor of war preparedness against the Germans. They also exhibited a concern for the massive number of wounded soldiers, whose stories, despite the efforts of the military censors, were finding their way to the public. Frank Gilbreth, who spoke before the American Society of Mechanical Engineers in 1915 after visiting numerous hospitals in Europe, said that "no one who has not actually seen hundreds of wounded soldiers writhing in agony in the freight cars or the hospitals can fully realize the conditions that exist, but the pictures and accounts from the front have been so vivid that the whole world has been aroused to a concrete expression of sympathy and efforts to alleviate the immediate suffering."[11]

Eager to profit from the turnabout of opinions, the American movie industry began producing movies that urged war preparedness, the most famous of which was J. Stuart Blackton's opus about a mythical country's invasion of New York City, *The Battle Cry of Peace* (1915). As a means of capitalizing on the growing concern for disabled soldiers, moviemakers also began including such characters in their casts. An early example was a movie inspired by the lyrics of "I Didn't Raise My Boy to Be a Soldier" (indeed, this was its working title) but whose new label reflected the recent reversal of sentiments: *I'm Glad My Boy Grew Up to Be a Soldier*, directed by Frank Beal and peopled with such Selig stock-company actors as Guy Oliver, Eugenie Besserer, and Harry Mestayer. In the planning stages in July 1915, and released late that year, *I'm Glad My Boy* was a mass of unsubtleties about two characters named "Warrington" and "Archer" who go off to war, the former of whom is killed while the latter loses an arm. Following in the tradition of that early cinematic Noble Warrior, the cavalry officer of 1909's *The Empty Sleeve*, Archer unfortunately doesn't have much of a role after returning stateside; he's mainly reduced to acting as a messenger, informing Warrington's wife and young son of their loved one's battlefield heroism. In a strangely prescient narrative twist, the movie depicts a new war breaking out years later, and the son, now an adult, follows in his father's footsteps by enlisting. Archer's daughter, a Red Cross nurse (named "Mercy," of course), tells Mrs. Warrington her son was killed in battle, but Mrs. W., patriotic soul that she is, harbors no bitterness and proudly stands by the philosophy summed up in the film's title.

As national prowar sentiment mounted, the movie industry stepped up production of movies sympathetic to the war effort. Despite the relative harmony of the industry and the federal government on this score, it became increasingly evident that the two institutions held differing perspectives on the topic of disabled soldiers.

The government's position was a blend of paternalism and pragmatism. Even before it entered the conflict in April 1917, it had begun making plans for the massive number of permanently injured soldiers that would return and within several months after that date passed the War Risk Insurance Act, which provided a fixed monthly income for disabled soldiers and sailors regardless of their later earning ability as rehabilitated veterans. The government realized early on, however, that pensions alone would not prove a cost-effective means of compensating the country's injured veterans. After considering the information gathered by an ad hoc group called the Committee on Vocational Training for Disabled Soldiers, both Congressional houses unanimously passed the Veterans' Rehabilitation Act (also known as the Smith–Sears Act) in June 1918. This piece of legislation completely changed the federal government's responsibility to its disabled veterans, which heretofore had been limited mainly to the provision of shelter or pensions. Though the responsibility of physical rehabilitation remained with the Office of the Surgeon General of the Army and the Bureau of Medicine and Surgery of the Navy, a newly constituted Board of Vocational Education was now in charge of job training and placement of injured veterans.[12]

While the federal government pursued such progressive goals during the war, the American movie industry remained mired in old-fashioned views. "All the war pictures had been glamorous—fellows with shiny boots, epaulettes and medals and beautiful costumes," remembered Hollywood director King Vidor, who years later would pilot a de-romanticized treatment of the war called *The Big Parade* (1925). Exhibiting little awareness of the government's new role in the lives of its disabled veterans, the wartime movies led by the bellwether *I'm Glad My Boy Grew Up to Be a Soldier* subscribed to the pre–WW I glorified notions of battlefield heroism and were hopelessly naïve in their treatment of disability issues. Films such as *For Valour* (1917), *Too Fat to Fight* (1918), and *Eyes of the Soul* (1919) all had disabled veterans at their centers, and like *I'm Glad My Boy* they represented disabilities as not much more than noble badges of personal sacrifice on behalf of the greater "good."[13]

The person at the forefront of the industry's prowar sentiments, Vitagraph's J. Stuart Blackton, was also a significant contributor to the early incarnation of the Noble Warrior; the British native had not only overseen the production of *The Empty Sleeve* the previous decade but also created *Womanhood, the Glory of the Nation* (1917), a follow-up to *The Battle Cry of Peace* that had among its minor characters a soldier blinded during the conflict. Blackton, who shortly after completing *Womanhood* severed his link with Vitagraph to become an independent producer, once again sensed changes in the wind and turned his wartime enthusiasm to a new purpose: the creation of *Dawn* (1919), a movie that reflected his belief in the worthiness of the recently passed Veterans' Rehabilitation Act. Aware of changing audience tastes (most notably, the sharply declining interest in war-related subjects), however, Blackton hedged his bets by centering the film not on a disabled veteran but on a disabled civilian; *Dawn* examines the situation of an artist going blind as a long-delayed result of a childhood fall from a tree, and, after disentangling several misunderstandings with those around him, he not only marries the wealthy woman of his dreams but also becomes the head of a vocational school for blinded veterans.

One of the exceedingly few films to acknowledge the federal government's new relationship with its injured veterans,[14] *Dawn* also reflected the latest development in mainstream society's relationship with its disabled population; the returning disabled veteran was now directing attention on the world of all physically disabled people. The growth of industrial accident boards and outbreaks of infantile paralysis during the war years certainly contributed to the public's awareness of general disability issues, but as Amy Hamburger, Associate Director of the Cleveland Cripple Survey, observed in 1918, "The community has not been aroused until the present time, to take any active steps in carrying out a constructive program, thus indicating their recognition of the significance of this group in community life. Now, because of the war, the care of the returned crippled soldier forces the community to immediate action." In 1920, President Wilson signed into law the Vocational Rehabilitation Act (a.k.a. the Smith–Fess Act), which extended the job-related services of the Smith–Sears Act to all people with physical disabilities, not just veterans. In addition, forty-five states and territories had enacted workers' compensation programs during the period from 1910 to 1921, while in 1917 industrialist Jeremiah Milbank founded what became known as the Institute for the Crippled and Disabled, a private organization that began offering job training to disabled vets and quickly extended its services to disabled civilians.[15]

The movie industry likewise expressed a strong interest in assimilating physically disabled people, civilians and veterans alike, into the mainstream of American society, but as a general rule it rarely presented such characters as healthy in mind and body with steady-state impairments. In a denial of gargantuan proportions, the industry entrenched itself ever more deeply in beliefs of the past and churned out highly sentimentalized movies with traditional happy endings, many of which featured characters healed of their disabilities. Articles occasionally surfaced in the press about people cured of their impairments (blindness, usually) but there was hardly a correlation between them and the high rate of corrective operations in WW I–era films, to say nothing of the stories' veracity. Some medical experts were moved to complain about the films (in 1915, an optometrist challenged the procedure by which a teenager, blind since birth, has her vision restored in a Biograph film called *A Bit of Driftwood*, for example), but their opinions had little effect; within the context of the cataclysmic conflict and the immediate postwar period, the trend toward romanticization that had begun innocently enough with such films as *Stricken Blind* and *The Light That Came* the previous decade suddenly became the industry's premiere way of representing physical disability issues. "Raising of false hopes is one of the unkindnesses to be guarded against in all work with the handicapped," warned an administrator at the Boston School of Social Work in 1918. "The temptation is great." Unfortunately, it was a temptation to which moviemakers frequently succumbed.[16]

Aware that audiences craved consolation and inspiration during those troubled times, the movie industry initially pursued a general strategy that attempted to minimize the carnage of World War I and create the impression that a greater "good" will prevail over any emergent chaos. With their fabricated optimism and idealism, the movies served as a major refuge for audiences disillusioned by the war and weary of other concerns. Consider, for example, the observations of historians Allan Nevins and Henry Steele Commager on typical films and audiences of the day:

> It was from the movies that the rising generation got many of its ideas about life, usually romantic and often highly misleading. To many the moving pictures offered an escape from drab reality into the never-never world of romance, where wickedness was always punished and virtue always rewarded, where all women were beautiful and all men handsome and acrobatic, where riches brought happiness and poverty contentment, and where all stories had a happy ending.[17]

Movies that portrayed people cured of what would ordinarily be permanent physical disabilities were a striking part of this trend and were also the most significant development in the Cinema of Isolation during the 1910s and 1920s, clearly overshadowing the first wave of veteran and villain depictions. Information culled from the two American Film Institute feature-film catalogs that cover this period suggests a powerful curability trend, one that grew even stronger during the 1920s. From 1912 to 1930, a time-frame that includes a handful of disability-related feature films made before the war and, at the opposite end, the earliest sound films, the industry produced approximately 430 feature films with disability themes. Of that number, about 150, or 35 percent, had their disabled characters eventually gain or regain the use of their sight, hearing, legs, etc., through corrective operations, God's will, or sheer good fortune (such as a serendipitous bonk on the head). The 1920s were particularly curability-minded; more than ninety out of the approximately 200 disability films produced during that decade—almost half—featured characters cured of their disabilities.[18] Without question, filmmakers viewed the prospect of a permanent disability, particularly for people not villainous or elderly, as an increasingly ill-fitting component in their movies' narrative structure.

Before the war provided the climate that allowed such films to prosper, feature films with curability themes drew scant attention. *Quincy Adams Sawyer* (1912), a four-reeler produced by a little-known concern called the Puritan Special Features Company and arguably the film that ushered in the curability tradition among feature-length productions, is a case in point. Based on Justin Adams's 1902 play of the same name, which Adams in turn had adapted from a 1900 novel by Charles Felton Pidgin, *Quincy Adams Sawyer* had among its minor characters a sweet young woman named Alice Pettingill cured of her blindness by film's end. Appearing in December 1912, however, the film preceded the outbreak of WW I by a year and a half and, judging from the limited number of newspaper and magazine citations in the AFI catalog, came and went with hardly any notice.[19] By the time another company had remade the film ten years later, the situation had changed considerably. In the midst of Hollywood's curable-disability craze, director Clarence Badger and screenwriter Bernard McConville elevated Pettingill to leading-character status and entrusted the part to an actress long familiar to audiences in such roles: Blanche Sweet, who had begun essaying curable Sweet Innocents—"Sweet" Innocents, indeed—while a teenager in such movies as Griffith's *The Blind Princess and the Poet* and *Through Darkened Vales*.

Blindness was by far the most curable of movie disabilities, and one of the first wartime feature films to deal with the topic had a decidedly familiar ring. Envious of Selig's success with its film versions of the old d'Ennery–Cormon potboiler *Les Deux Orphelines*, William Fox decided to have a go himself. He authorized Herbert Brenon, a Dublin-born writer-director who specialized in adapting literary material to the screen and described by film historian Terry Ramsaye as "one of the motion picture's most spectacular and volatile personalities,"[20] to forge ahead, and the result was the fourth moving-image telling of *The Two Orphans*. Filmed on the company's open-air set in Jersey City and in Quebec, this 1915 movie hewed closely to the d'Ennery–Cormon play. True to the movie industry's curable romantic trend then underway, however, it made explicit what the play and presumably the Selig films only implied: the cure of Louise's blindness.

Aside from its romanticized treatment of disability, the Fox–Brenon *Two Orphans* is memorable today chiefly for two reasons, the first of which is its casting; not only did it star Theda Bara, better remembered for her "vamp" portrayals, as the sighted sister Henriette, but it also featured Brenon himself as Mother Frochard's disabled son, Pierre. A seasoned theatrical performer who occasionally acted in his own films, Brenon had recently recovered from a major accident (he was seriously injured by an exploding studio tank the previous year), and perhaps the circumstances surrounding his temporary disablement had led him to identify with this particular character, the last role he would play before the camera. Unfortunately, the importance that Brenon ascribed to the part by playing it himself (not to mention the sheer significance of a director casting himself as a disabled character) was completely lost on Fox's public relations department. In pre-release publicity, it merely resorted to insulting language by referring to Brenon's character as "the cripple who loves Louise with the blind worship of an inferior being."[21]

The Two Orphans is also remembered for the legal and financial complications surrounding it. Though Fox's flacks claimed the movie "differs radically from the stage version in power, life and color,"[22] their transparent statement failed to deter Kate Claxton, the actress who played Louise in countless theatrical incarnations of *The Two Orphans* and held a proprietary interest in it. She claimed Fox and Brenon had made the film without her permission and, in concert with Selig, sued Fox's company for $100,000 in 1915. Though he actually paid only a small fraction of that amount to Claxton in settlement and even went on to re-release the film successfully in 1918, Fox learned an important lesson that was to serve him well years later.

With *The Two Orphans* and *The Broken Law* in the can and such projects as *The Darling of Paris* and *Treasure Island* still to come, Fox was in many respects a pivotal player in the development of the Cinema of Isolation during the mid–1910s. Though a variety of directors, writers, actors, and other production personnel contributed to the "steady flow of unpretentious, sentimental, and folksy pictures," as one-time Fox publicity chief Glen Allvine once characterized the early productions, the movies unmistakably bore the imprint of Fox's authority.[23] As Fox told Upton Sinclair:

> I was acquainted with every story that was selected by my companies. I read every story they ever produced. I made suggestions in the majority of the stories produced by our companies. In the early years I wrote most of the scenarios. No picture ever produced by the Fox Film Corporation was permitted to be viewed by the general public, until every title it contained had been approved and passed by me, and I don't remember a single picture ever made by the company that the titles contained therein were not corrected, edited and rewritten by me.[24]

It is well worth noting that Fox himself was disabled—an incompetent surgeon left him with a virtually functionless left arm after he had broken it in a fall from a truck as a youth—but whatever sympathies he harbored for disabled people while developing these films were eclipsed by his overwhelming drive to turn a profit. An opportunistic workaholic who as a teenager in the 1890s was not above initiating a "fake blind man" scheme to raise quick cash, Fox relied heavily on public-domain material for his movies' subject matter as a cost-cutting measure during his salad days as a producer. *The Two Orphans*, *The Broken Law*, *The Darling of Paris*, and *Treasure Island* were among the many Fox films based on literary vehicles from the 1800s, and it's certainly arguable that their disability-related aspects, informed by their antecedents' antiquated perspectives on disability, were incidental to his desire to hold down costs. Always interested in enhancing the box-office potential of his films, however, Fox often tinkered with the stories to make them conform to the general "happy ending" trend sweeping the American movie industry. *The Two Orphans* explicitly showed Louise in a cured state, for example, and even his studio's version of *The Hunchback of Notre Dame* contained a curability theme. Movie reviewers, well aware of the liberties Fox and others were taking with literary works of an earlier age, criticized the final act of *The Darling of Paris* in which, in the words of historian Gertrude Jobes, "a surgeon performs an operation on Quasimodo and straightens him out so he can marry Esmeralda."[25] In brief, money—whether preserving it or creating more of it—was the main factor that guided Fox's decisions.

A vivid illustration of Fox's business acumen occurred when he learned another filmmaker was planning a lavish remake of *Les Deux Orphelines*. Remembering the legal maneuverings of his old foe Kate Claxton, Fox moved with uncommon haste to acquire the French and British rights to the story and eventually extracted a tidy fee of $85,000 in exchange for his permission to exhibit the film in those countries. He was less than awed by the venerable figure he had outfoxed, so to speak: that grand old master of the Cinema of Isolation, D. W. Griffith.

William Fox, whose own impairment did not prevent him from producing a number of rather questionable disability movies during the 1910s. Courtesy Museum of Modern Art/Film Stills Archive.

The film was of course *Orphans of the Storm* (1921), a Dickensian-like saga written, produced, and directed by Griffith and the best-remembered Sweet Innocent feature of the silent era. By this time Griffith had gained international renown as a result of such films as *The Birth of a Nation* (1915), *Intolerance* (1916), and *Broken Blossoms* (1919), and, with bankers and venture capitalists now making millions of dollars available to movie companies old and new during the prosperous postwar period, he was in a position to do something about the meddlesome studio executives that had been the bane of his professional life. He incorporated as "D. W. Griffith, Inc." in 1920, a year after building a fourteen-acre studio complex on a peninsula near Mamaroneck, N.Y., and co-founding a movie distribution company, United Artists, with Charles Chaplin, Mary Pickford, and Douglas Fairbanks. One of the first projects he chose to develop as an independent movie producer was a story particularly close to his heart; one of the first plays he had attended after his family had moved to Louisville in the late 1800s was Claxton's roadshow production of *The Two Orphans*, and it had impressed him deeply. Now up to his neck in debt (he borrowed two million dollars from two New York banks late in 1921 to keep his company afloat), he gambled hundreds of thousands of dollars on the belief that a ready market existed for yet another telling of the d'Ennery-Cormon tale.

With *Orphans of the Storm*, renamed from *The Two Orphans* at the last minute at a cost of more than $25,000 to distinguish it from other films bearing that title,[26] Griffith fused his sentimentalized view of disability issues made prominent in such earlier films as *The Roué's Heart* and *The Light That Came* with the story structure that worked so well for him in his famous epic, *The Birth of a Nation*: a melodrama of personal struggles played out against the historical backdrop of a nation divided by war. As he had done in two Biograph one-reelers, *Nursing a Viper* (1909) and *The Oath and the Man* (1910), Griffith used the French Revolution—the "storm" suggested in the title—as the historical context. Replete with period costumes, ornate settings (including replicas of the Notre Dame cathedral and the Bastille), and a cast of hundreds, not to mention dramatic ironies and coincidences galore, the resulting film mingled fictional characters with historical personages, several of whom—the revolutionary figures Danton and Robespierre—play pivotal roles in Griffith's story.

Orphans of the Storm is such a well-known film that only the barest outline need be offered here. The film tells the tale of Henriette and Louise (Lillian and Dorothy Gish, respectively), two young women raised as sisters by a commoner family during the years prior to the French Revolution. After a brief prologue that explains how they came together (which includes a title card indicating that a plague has killed Henriette's parents and left Louise blind), the young women embark on a fateful trip to Paris to visit an optical surgeon. The remainder of the film chronicles the misadventures that arise from their separation before and during the French Revolution, culminating in yet another variation on the narrative-*cum*-editing device that made Griffith famous: the last-minute rescue. Griffith interspersed shots of Danton and his followers galloping to the execution site at an increasingly breathless rate with shots of Henriette and her beloved Chevalier being led to the guillotine until Danton arrives in the nick of time to save them. Louise, who with the help of Pierre has escaped from the clutches of Mother Frochard, is in the crowd, and Danton gallantly reunites the sisters. The movie ends with Henriette and Louise living in bliss with the Chevalier and Pierre after a doctor had miraculously restored Louise's eyesight.[27]

In retrospect, it should not be surprising that Griffith, in a position to select his own material without having to seek studio approval, should have chosen to make *Orphans of the Storm*. The story not only lent itself to the epic sweep of which he was so fond but also afforded him the chance to explore once again his favorite character type: the Sweet Innocent. "Griffith was indeed possessed by an image of the female innocent," according to biographer Martin Williams. "She was a main subject of his films. She was also his muse. She was the guardian of his inner being. She was his Beatrice who guided his sensibilities through the world of artistic images. She was the focal point through which he saw human existence

Dorothy and Lillian Gish as Louise and Henriette in the most famous of the many silent-screen adaptations of Les Deux Orphelines, *D. W. Griffith's* Orphans of the Storm *(1921).*

and human aspirations, through which he assessed human virtue and human vice."[28] If Griffith was fascinated by the general ingénue type, he found a blind one absolutely irresistible—the pinnacle of purity, as far as he was concerned—and used *Orphans of the Storm* as an extended forum for propagating his disability views to a mostly receptive audience.

Most notably, Griffith designed the character of Louise to be exceptionally childlike, helpless, and dependent. Henriette, by far the more aggressive and proactive of the orphans, takes on a parental role for her blind sister, while the latter spends most of her time reacting in ineffectual ways to the various forms of adversity that surround her. Her blindness—conveyed mainly through the theatrical conventions of the blank stare and attendant groping—enhances her innocent, virginal qualities, and Griffith wasted little time bludgeoning the audience with what he perceived was an appropriate metaphor. An early title card proclaims, "Since Louise's blindness Henriette has cared for her with a love overwhelming as that of a mother for her helpless baby." Via other title cards, the audience learns that Henriette calls Louise "Miss Baby" and describes her to others as "Blind—so helpless—like taking care of a baby." Although both Gishes played ingénues in *Orphans of the Storm*, it's clear Griffith constructed the characters with two distinct levels of ingenuousness in mind.

Financed with a $340,000 loan from the New York-based Central Union Trust Company, *Orphans of the Storm* did respectable box office but was not the financial smash Griffith needed to keep alive his dream of independent moviemaking. Indeed, it turned out to be an unexpected money drain. Kate Claxton, who belatedly submitted the Selig *Two Orphans* three-reeler to the U.S. copyright office in 1916 following her imbroglio with William Fox, waved her registration form in front of Griffith's nose and suckered him into paying her $5,000 for the rights to *The Two Orphans*. (She had conveniently neglected to tell him the copyright to the American adaptation of the play had expired in 1917.) In addition to that amount and the $85,000 he forked over to Fox, Griffith purchased the rights to Robert Stark's German film based on *Les Deux Orphelines* to keep it from competing with his film in American theaters. He was unable, however, to halt distribution of an Italian-made *Two Orphans* that circulated widely in Europe and was distributed in the U.S. by the First National Company during *Orphans of the Storm*'s premiere in the hope of capitalizing on the massive hype surrounding the Griffith film. (First National, a company for which Griffith had directed several films to help finance his dream of independent filmmaking, certainly demonstrated little deference to its former director on this score. Indeed, it tried to sell theaters on the Italian film by referring to it with considerable chutzpah as "the production with a million dollars' worth of publicity behind it.") In addition to these woes, the "roadshow" presentational style that had served Griffith so well in the past failed him here; guided by the increasingly questionable management skills of Griffith's brother Albert, the film lost money through its initial release to big-city theaters and advance ticket sales.[29]

The financial tribulations that surrounded *Orphans of the Storm* seriously damaged Griffith's independent-filmmaking aspirations and signaled a major downturn in his career. When it became clear *Orphans* was not going to be the box-office bonanza Griffith needed, his banks started making stronger demands in connection with new loans (including approval of his films' subject matter and the right to call in their loans if they were not satisfied with the resulting films), and within a few years he was forced to sell his Mamaroneck studio and return to directorial servitude. Let there be no question about it: *Orphans of the Storm* and the longstanding perspective on disability it embodied did strike a responsive chord with audiences and critics. Griffith's financial overextensions and general fiscal mismanagement were the main factors that brought about his failure as an independent filmmaker, not audience rejection of the film and its message. "While realism was apparently encroaching on the romantic idealism heretofore demanded by the movie public, audiences by the millions would pour into theaters to see a film based on a theme that had been pronounced hopelessly old-fashioned," wrote Benjamin Hampton of the postwar period, and *Orphans of the Storm* serves as a solid example of that truth. Though Griffith was to make at least one more movie with a disability theme, the creator of so many sentimental dramas, increasingly encumbered by financial concerns, was fast fading as a major force in the Cinema of Isolation.[30]

Though Griffith had gotten in over his head with *Orphans of the Storm*, other filmmakers with lesser ambitions found solid financial success working with curable disability themes. One was a former Griffith protégée who developed several vehicles for herself that featured characters cured of paralysis: the Canadian-born actress turned "America's Sweetheart," Mary Pickford. The superstar performer, whose first major film role was opposite a disabled character in Griffith's *The Violin Maker of Cremona*, had formed her own production company by 1916 and was constantly on the lookout for movie projects that might enable her to break out of her little-girl movie image. One of her more successful efforts was a 1918 film set in Britain called *Stella Maris*. Adapted by Frances Marion from the novel by William J. Locke and directed by one-time Pickford co-star (and yet another former Griffith employee) Marshall "Mickey" Neilan, the film featured Pickford in two roles: the Sweet Innocent named in the title, a paralyzed young woman shielded from life's cruelties by her wealthy aunt and uncle; and Unity Blake, a poverty-stricken orphan. The common denominator in their lives is journalist John Risca (Conway Tearle), one of Stella's favorite visitors and also the husband of Louise (Marcia Manon), a cruel woman who hires Unity as their servant. Louise later faces a lengthy stay in prison for abusing the young Cockney woman, and, while the kindly John makes amends by adopting Unity, Stella emerges from a successful operation that cured her paralysis to learn that the world outside her room is not all sweetness and light. She learns that John is married and tries to break off the relationship but eventually an unexpected source helps her solve her dilemma. Frederick James Smith, a reviewer for *Motion Picture Classic*, summarized the film's conclusion: "Little Unity loves Risca in her own pathetic way, and, when she realizes that the man's drunkard wife stands in the way of his happiness, she kills the woman and herself. Thus the way is opened for Risca to marry Stella, now able to walk thru an operation and coming face to face with the sordid things of life for the first time."[31]

Critics were united in their praise for the film and particularly for Pickford's dual performance. "I have never seen her in a more satisfying performance, true to life and to art, dramatic rather than theatric," raved *MPW*'s Louis Reeves Harrison. "Even as quiet little Stella Maris, whose happenings are not those of intense action, she succeeds in affecting the heart and the mind of the spectator by some exquisite portrayals of character. She seems to have become transformed by her own experience and study to a creature of finer spiritual force." Harrison's enthusiasm for *Stella Maris* was matched by *MPC*'s Smith, who referred to the film as "the greatest effort of the Pickford career. Why? Because she is permitted to get away from curls and cupid-bow lips to a character role with pathos and humor." *Photoplay*'s Randolph Bartlett wrote that Neilan "made it exquisitely beautiful when opportunity offered, as well as sordid and relentlessly gripping when the theme was in minor key. The supporting cast is in perfect tune . . . *Stella Maris* should prove a turning point in the history of America's favorite star." Though critical response has remained undimmed over the years (in 1968, Kevin Brownlow referred to the film as "an honest and brilliant production"), the fact remains that *Stella Maris* matched the ongoing curable romantic trend in every respect.[32]

Pickford herself was quite pleased with the film as well but, realizing the moviegoing public was far more willing to part with its money to see her play her patented poor little girl character, she and Frances Marion developed another project designed solely to cash in on the producer-star's classic form. "We proceeded with the dull routine of making a picture we both thought nauseating, *Pollyanna*, the Glad Girl," remembered Marion many years later. "I hated writing it, Mary hated playing it, yet we managed to edge in some funny little scenes in spite of our indifference." Directed by Paul Powell and released with much fanfare by United Artists in 1920, *Pollyanna* closely followed Eleanor Porter's 1912 novel about an eternally optimistic preadolescent who spreads goodness and cheer wherever she goes. (After she arrives to live with her Aunt Polly, another youth proclaims that "it'll be more fun here now, with that kid 'round, than movin'-picture shows.") Near the end of the film, a car strikes Pollyanna as she tries to rescue a child, and it appears she will be paralyzed permanently. Audiences need not have worried, however; her Aunt Polly (Katherine Griffith) renews a long neglected relationship with the town doctor, who performs the requisite undisabling operation. Featuring a rather ripe example of the curable Sweet Innocent—Pickford at 27 was playing a character less than half her age—*Pollyanna* revealed little of its creators' distaste and cynicism; highly touted by religious leaders and the National Board of Review of Motion Pictures for its inexorably wholesome qualities, *Pollyanna* is perhaps best remembered today as "one of the most unrelievedly sentimental . . . of all the Mary Pickford vehicles," in the words of historian William K. Everson.[33]

Blindness and paralysis accounted for the vast majority of curable disabilities during this period of the Cinema of Isolation; films that centered on a person with corrected deafness were comparatively rare. Among the few was *The Silent Voice* (1915) starring Francis X. Bushman as a well-to-do musician who, becoming deaf, turns cynical and cuts himself off from the rest of society. He eventually does good deeds (most notably, he helps a young man with tuberculosis), however, and fate later rewards him with a corrective operation. No less facile a cure occurs in *Rimrock Jones* (1918), in which a western lass journeys to New York to have her deafness corrected, and there discovers that a Wall Street magnate plans to take over a copper mine owned by her boyfriend, the title character (Wallace Reid). *The Big Little Person* (1919) starred Mae Murray as Arathea Manning, a school teacher who becomes aurally impaired after a bout with scarlet fever. Her

An astute businessperson, Mary Pickford often produced her own starring vehicles. In this scene from 1920's Pollyanna, *Pickford as the ringletted title character is about to demonstrate the results of her operation to Aunt Polly (Katherine Griffith) and a gaggle of supportive onlookers. Courtesy Museum of Modern Art/Film Stills Archive.*

fiancé (a relative unknown named Rudolph Valentino) detects a growing romantic relationship between her and the man who invented a hearing-aid device called an auriphone, and he destroys her engagement ring. She faints on seeing this act, hits her head, and later learns she doesn't need the device; the accident has caused her hearing to return.

Deaf, blind, or paralyzed civilians weren't the only figures to be returned to majority status, however; several WW I disabled vet films couldn't resist the temptation to have their vets undergo miracle cures. *The Dark Silence* (1916) features a young man who joins the army in despair after a lover jilts him. The woman realizes the error of her ways and joins the Red Cross to be near him. He's blinded in battle and, unbeknownst to him, his ex-lover now tends to him as his nurse. They fall in love, and, after the woman arranges an operation for him to restore his sight, the man realizes the strength of her love. In a similar vein, *The Belgian* (1918) tells the story of a young sculptor who is blinded in the war and nursed back to health by his former lover. When his eyesight is restored, so too is his love for her.

A trio of 1920 films featured a somewhat different focus: a wayward doctor who undergoes a reformation and then, duly restored to a prominent position within the paternalistic power structure, performs a corrective operation. *When Dawn Came* tells the story of a physician who turns to drugs, alcohol, and atheism after a woman jilts him but who, after a priest sets him straight, meets and falls in love with a blind woman and restores her sight. The title character of *The Scoffer*, a doctor embittered after five years of wrongful imprisonment, initially refuses to operate on a disabled boy but relents after being touched by the goodness of a local townswoman. In *The Daughter Pays*, a fellow marries and then torments the daughter of a former lover. Eventually recognizing the cruelty of his vengeful actions, the man partially atones for his sins by curing his wife's orthopedically impaired sister. Appearing at a time when disability issues had moved to the fore in postwar society, these films like so many others of their vintage were mainly odes to patriarchal authority.

Performers with physical disabilities continued to appear in movies during the middle stages of the silent period, but except for Helen Keller, who played herself in the final episode of her own 1919 film biography, *Deliverance*,[34] they found themselves subject to the same type of mainstream mentality that guided the creation of the movie stereotypes. For example, moviemakers expressed their interest in curability not only in the strategies already noted but also in a far more oblique way through some of their casting decisions; they occasionally asked disabled actors to mask their disabilities and attempt to "pass" for able-bodied people before the camera. Through the moviemakers' careful staging, photography, editing, and costuming, the actors suddenly found themselves "cured" of their disabilities, if only on screen and in service to an able-bodied agenda.

Several of these actors were proven screen commodities prior to their disablement and found they were in a position to continue their careers in the medium. Sarah Bernhardt, the stage actress who had made her movie debut in a Shakespearean snippet, *Le Duel d'Hamlet*, in 1900, suffered a severe knee injury in a 1905 theater accident. Despite intense pain, she went on to star in such movies as *Tosca* (1908), *La Dame aux Camélias* (1911), the previously noted *Queen Elizabeth*, and a movie that she also wrote called *Adrienne Lecouvreur* (1913). Anxious to lead her adoring fans into thinking her disablement was minor, Bernhardt also appeared in *Sarah Bernhardt at Home* (1912), a two-reel documentary that showed her playing tennis among other activities. The injury never improved, however (she could not bend her knee by 1914), and in 1915 a surgeon amputated her leg. That action, however, did not prevent the 71-year-old trouper from starring in a pair of wartime flagwavers called *Jeanne Doré* (1915) and *Mères françaises* (1917), the latter anglicized as *Mothers of France* for its American and British exhibition that year, as well as the incomplete *La Voyante* (1923). Typically clad in floor-length dresses, she would try to rely as inconspicuously as possible on objects and people for support. Observers were quite divided on her performances. Louis Verneuil, a playwright and friend who worked extensively with Bernhardt in her later years, said "she was so prodigiously clever, with so much skill and grace at the same time, that nobody in the audience could suspect the incredible effort she had to make in order to seem as if she were walking in normal fashion." This view sharply differed from Terry Ramsaye's, who offered this assessment of Bernhardt in *Mères françaises*: "In this picture, Bernhardt, crippled and enfeebled, a sad relic of herself as the personification of Gallic emotion, sat through her scenes in a chair."[35]

In early 1920, Harold Lloyd, famous for his "Lonesome Luke" character and other comic portrayals in scores of films, was involved in an incident that thrust him into the minority of film actors with physical disabilities. Lloyd, who had recently signed with Hal Roach to produce a series of two-reel comedies for Pathé, was posing for publicity pictures when a bomb he thought was a prop detonated in his right hand, causing the partial paralysis of the hand along with the loss of his thumb and forefinger. Despite this accident, Lloyd acted in more than two dozen other movies before retiring from the screen in 1947. Wearing either a lifelike rubber glove or merely a pair of ordinary gloves, he continued to perform many of his own stunts and, if anything, was determined to take on even greater risks. In 1921, he inaugurated a series of films that historians Gerald Mast and Bruce Kawin have aptly labeled Lloyd's "high-rise comedies of thrills" in which the actor placed himself in precarious positions high atop skyscrapers. In *High and Dizzy* (1921), for example, he pursues a sleepwalking woman on a building ledge high above real city streets before becoming trapped out on the ledge himself. In *Safety Last* (1923), his most famous film, the image of Lloyd dangling from the clock face of a skyscraper has become an indelible part of the iconography of the American silent film. As the hapless Lloyd character struggles to maintain his grip in this and so many other films of the 1920s, our knowledge that he had only the partial use of his right hand adds to our sense of the apparent riskiness of the shuddery stunts.[36]

Actors who were disabled prior to embarking on a Hollywood career met with limited success. In his study of deaf culture and the Hollywood movie industry, John Schuchman identified five deaf actors who appeared in minor roles in movies during the silent era, two of whom—Granville Redmond and Emerson Romero—played supporting characters with some regularity. Redmond had become friends with Charles Chaplin and played nondisabled characters in a number of his films including *A Dog's Life* (1918), *A Day's Pleasure* (1919), *The Kid* (1921), *A Woman of Paris* (1923), and that holdover from the silent era, *City Lights* (1931). Redmond also appeared with Douglas Fairbanks in *The Three Musketeers* (1921) and in a pair of vehicles for the comedian Raymond Griffith, *He's a Prince* (1925) and *You'd Be Surprised* (1926). The latter film presented Redmond in an able-bodied role brimming with irony: a coroner's assistant who

A begloved and beloved Harold Lloyd in a typical predicament from Never Weaken *(1921), one of his "high-rise comedies of thrills" of the early 1920s.*

masquerades as a deaf valet. It was as close as Redmond would come to playing a deaf person on screen. As for Romero, a Cuban who adopted the professional name of Tommie Albert, he appeared in comedy shorts of the 1920s including *Beach Nuts*, *The Cat's Meow*, *Great Guns*, *Henpecked in Morocco*, and *Sappy Days* typically playing baby-faced, able-bodied characters in the Harry Langdon tradition. Except for Redmond's brief participation in *City Lights* (he played one of the platform dignitaries during the statue-unveiling ceremony that opens the film), the movie careers of both men ended with the coming of sound.[37]

Though filmmakers were now asking physically disabled performers to pass with increasing frequency, they continued to subject those actors who couldn't or wouldn't to the same kind of freakshow mentality that had guided much of the industry during its primitive days. Movies were still without synchronous sound, of course, and filmmakers, maintaining their preference for performers' appearances over lengthy title cards, had by the mid–1920s cultivated something of a cottage industry involving actors whose exteriors were less than perfect. "The real plutocrats of the movies seek the freaks!" proclaimed Barrett Kiesling, a *New York Times* reporter who arrived at that realization after meeting with directors, actors, and casting agents on the general topic summarized in the title of his 1925 article, "Lucrative Ugliness." He noted further that "good looks are a 40–to–1 gamble in motion pictures, but a cauliflower ear spells a steady job." The most prominent director he interviewed, Cecil B. De Mille, underscored the movie industry's reliance on observable attributes ("Without words, the movies must tell their story either in action or human appearance," he said) and offered this sage bit of insight to would-be actors: "If I were starting in pictures I would prefer a good case of St. Vitus's Dance to a perfect Grecian profile. The affliction is much more salable!"[38]

One of Hollywood's premiere directors during the mid-to-late silent film era had so strong an interest in actors who possessed less than physical perfection that it bordered on the obsessive: the Irish émigré Rex Ingram. A filmmaker who enjoyed enormous respect and admiration from his peers (Erich von Stroheim once referred to him as "the world's greatest director"), Ingram began by working as an actor, set designer, scriptwriter, and general utility person for such studios as Edison, Vitagraph, and Fox before embarking on a directing career for Carl Laemmle's Universal company in 1916 at the age of 23. Though most of the ten films he directed for that studio are now inaccessible, they were, in the words of his biographer, Liam O'Leary, "distinguished by a fine pictorial sense, relentless pursuit of atmosphere and the use of deformed actors, especially dwarfs and hunchbacks." (For example, O'Leary noted that critics assailed the beginning of his 1917 film, *The Reward of the Faithless*, "for its vivid depiction of an underworld inhabited by dwarfs, cripples, drunkards and degenerates.") Laemmle fired him the very next year after repeated run-ins, one of which may have had something to do with the young director's casting proclivities. As O'Leary observed, "legend had it that he was sacked by Carl Laemmle because he had put every hunchback and dwarf in Hollywood on Universal's payroll." (His movies were not the only Universal productions to present such characters, however; others were 1916's *The Path of Happiness* and *The Heritage of Hate* and 1917's *The Gates of Doom*.) After migrating to Metro in 1920, Ingram continued recruiting hunchbacked and short-stature performers (principally, a Syrian actor named Tufei Fatella who after immigrating to the U.S. in 1911 used the screen name John George) to play minor characters in such films as *The Prisoner of Zenda* (1922), *Trifling Women* (1922), *Where the Pavement Ends* (1923), *Scaramouche* (1923), *Mare Nostrum* (1925), and *The Magician* (1926). The rationale guiding Ingram's casting decisions is obscure at best, but superstitious belief seemed to play a prominent role. According to O'Leary, Ingram maintained a decade-long obsession with such performers in part because he believed they would bring him luck.[39]

To sum up: while some WW I–era filmmakers cultivated the idea of evil disabled characters and others treated the disabilities of veterans as not much more than badges of honor, a greater number initially responded to the carnage of the Great War by picking up on ideas expressed in such early films as *Stricken Blind*, *The Blind Man of Jerusalem*, and *The Light That Came* and developing them into feature-length productions. Many of these new, longer films managed to out-sentimentalize their Victorian–era literary forebears by explicitly showing formerly disabled characters in a cured state. (It is worth noting that Dickens only implied a cure for Tiny Tim at the end of *A Christmas Carol* with vague references to Scrooge's newly found benevolence and the boy's survival, while d'Ennery and Cormon concluded *Les Deux Orphelines* by merely having a doctor state his willingness to operate on Louise.) Moviemakers took the suggestions offered by these and other nineteenth-century authors, unsubtle to begin with, and gave them the ham-handed treatment in the movies.

The curability movies generally followed the mainstream psychological beliefs of the time, in that the characters once cured were basically the same as they had been before the disabling incident. As psychologist Franklin Shontz has noted:

Before serious study of the psychological aspects of physical disability began in the late 1940s, the fundamental cause of psychological disturbance in persons with disabilities seemed obvious. Common sense supported the belief that the primary source of distress in reactions to illness or to disability was the illness or disability itself. If a person with paraplegia had psychological problems, the evident cause of the problems was the spinal cord injury and the logical solution was to restore neural functioning. Failing that, alternatives were devised to help the person bypass or overcome the effects of his condition by providing therapy and necessary equipment such as braces, a wheelchair, and similar devices. It followed that, once a disability was removed or circumvented, its associated psychological disturbances should have disappeared along with it.[40]

With one basic exception—the cured character often sees something (a problematic relationship, usually) in a new way—movies of the World War I era generally subscribed to this view by showing their newly cured characters unaffected by their disabled experiences. Though this naïve attitude remained in effect until the post–World War II era as Shontz has suggested, it did undergo a major modification during the latter phase of the silent-film era as the Cinema of Isolation settled into a more downbeat phase and filmmakers began paying attention, however limited or hurtful, to the lingering consequences of disablement.

3 / man of a thousand disabilities and his brethren

The sentimental optimism of the restored-to-able-bodiedness Sweet Innocent and other curable romantics dominated the Cinema of Isolation during the middle portion of the silent film era, but for most people the mind-numbing devastation of the World War all but destroyed the romanticized notions of war and war-related issues. Movie companies, clinging to now-outdated formulas, continued to churn out films of curability but their time was limited; the overall number of such films declined significantly from the peak period of 1917–1922. More importantly, their optimistic values, shaky even during their heyday, rang hollow during much of the 1920s. The grim outlook on physical disability issues that characterized the latter stages of the decade found expression in a range of movies, most notably ones that featured Lon Chaney, a major Hollywood star known as the "Man of a Thousand Faces" at the height of his career.

Historians have often characterized the years following the Great War as an era of high spirits, low morality, and unmitigated prosperity, laced with a strong dose of cynicism. Arthur Lennig offered this colorful characterization of America's postwar social and moral upheavals:

> People variously blamed it on the war, the anarchists, the League of Nations, the automobile, and the movies. But, whatever the cause, the revolution occurred. The good old days of high morals and low skirts, of calling cards and cutaway coats and afternoon teas vanished. Victorian mannerisms and concepts of women as "Dear Little Ones," in short, the whole tradition of Puritanism, dissolved in a wispy cloud of a woman's cigarette and in the strong breath of bootleg booze. The young maiden smelling of rose petals and blushing at the slightest hint of reality soon reeked of perfume and talked of Freudian repressions and phallic symbolism. America entered the twentieth century late, but it entered it with a vengeance.
>
> The shock of the war, the let-down after the peace treaty, the problems of "How're you gonna keep them down on the farm," the loss of the pioneer spirit, and Harding's "normalcy" had their effect. The postwar theme came to be "Let's live it up." Jazz and bathtub gin bestowed danger and drama on the simple act of drinking and dancing. Everyone, it seemed, was having a helluva good time. And the drive to have as much fun as possible—"you're only young once"—caught on.[1]

Audience interest in war films dropped off markedly after the armistice on November 11, 1918, and was replaced by a "broadening of tastes," according to Benjamin Hampton, that "became so unpredictable that producers had nothing substantial upon which to base analyses or guesses." Saddled with a backlog of war films still being shot or already in the can and suffering from the economic throes of consolidation (many smaller producing and distributing firms and theaters went under or were absorbed by larger rivals during this time), Hollywood went into a temporary state of shock. A revamping of popular prewar formulas marked its relatively quick recovery, as Hampton's assessment of the period makes clear:

The inevitable candy-sweet pretty girls and collar-advertisement heroes of an earlier day were losing their popularity. Girls with charm, or the indefinable quality of sex appeal, could win a large following even though they did not qualify as pretty, and heroes might be "homely" and yet satisfy the romantic longings of ticket buyers. Battling male stars now might safely present dirty faces and torn clothing; no longer was it necessary for the hero at the conclusion of a knock-down-and-drag-out encounter with two dozen villains in a western drinking hell [sic] to appear in his close-ups as though he had just left his valet. It even became possible occasionally to modify the happy ending.[2]

An example of this period, particularly as it relates to physical disability issues, is *Tol'able David* (1921), a product of the Inspiration Pictures Company that Henry King, Charles Duell, and Richard Barthelmess founded that year. Produced by Duell, directed and co-written by King, and starring Barthelmess in the title role, this tale of country folks beset by a family of villainous hillbillies has a number of qualities that suggest moviemaking values of an earlier age. Filmed amid bucolic Virginia hills only a few miles from where King grew up, *Tol'able David* is replete with incidents from the director's own rural upbringing and reflects a longing for a pre-industrial world that was the domain of D. W. Griffith.[3] (Indeed, Griffith had started work on the *Tol'able David* adaptation and some of his contributions remained in the final production.) A distinct difference between it and some of Griffith's later fare emerges, however, when the young man who drives the all-important mail hack, Allen Kinemon (Warner Richmond), is struck on the back of the neck with a rock by one of the hillbillies. Unlike earlier films, in which young "good" people who experienced disabling accidents inevitably receive cures, Allen is permanently paralyzed from the neck down.

Such a change should have provided King and his collaborators with the perfect forum to explore the issues confronting newly disabled people, such as those faced by so many WW I veterans, but unfortunately their interests lay elsewhere. They showed precious little of Allen's life as a disabled person, opting instead to treat the subject mainly as a plotting device; Allen's younger brother, David, eventually uses the disablement as an excuse to seek revenge on the hillbilly and the latter's family and thus prove himself a "man." (From a psychoanalytic perspective, Allen and David could be viewed as two halves of the same male figure who seeks to avenge the paternalistic hillbilly's symbolic act of castration and remasculinize himself in the process.) As Walter Coppedge has noted, cinematographer Henry Cronjager did create some haunting and evocative images of Allen and his family after the disabling accident,[4] but they are used mainly to establish and support a sense of intense grief and have little to do with the character's new day-to-day life as a disabled person. A doctor's pronouncement via a title card that "Allen is helpless for the rest of his life" epitomizes the filmmakers' regard for Allen. He's not much more than another rendering of the Tragic Victim image and is quickly forgotten as David and his revenge schemes take center stage.

As for war-related topics, moviemakers were all too aware of their audiences' lack of interest in them during the immediate postwar years but gradually realized that box-office potential existed in movies produced from the general "war is terrible" perspective that had swept the country. Metro's Rex Ingram took time off from his obsession with performers of short stature and distorted spines to direct an early example called *The Four Horsemen of the Apocalypse* (1921), produced and adapted by June Mathis from the enormously successful novel by Vicente Blasco-Ibáñez. At once a classic re-enactment of the Oedipal triangle—dashing Julio Desnoyers (Rudolph Valentino, in the role that made him a star) has an affair with Marguerite Laurier (Alice Terry), the wife of a much older man—and a graphic depiction of World War horrors, *Horsemen* proved an immediate financial success. "Keeping the war in mind seems to take an effort that even our losses do not help us to achieve," wrote a *Literary Digest* reviewer, "but a moving picture may. Ibáñez's novel of *The Four Horsemen*, read probably in all the four corners of our land, has entered upon its film life, and, so says the New York *World*, 'will be seen by the whole world with a wringing of hearts and a resolute determination that wars must cease to be.'"[5]

A psychoanalytic reading of this movie suggests a different use of male disability than that found in most earlier feature films, in that the disabled figure—Marguerite's husband, blinded in the war—represents the Father, not the child. (An alternative viewing, one that places the husband in the role of the child, adds a subtextual legitimization to the romance of Julio and Marguerite but is not entirely satisfactory due to the advanced age of the character, the source of his disablement, and his relatively minor role in the film.) The filmmakers used his disability mainly to continue the old blindness-equals-ignorance belief (an embodiment of the Elderly Dupe and Noble Warrior stereotypes, Marguerite's husband is somehow unaware that the woman ministering to him is his own estranged wife), however, making its psychoanalytic dimension tangential to other concerns. Of more interest, I think, is the fact that *Horsemen* breached the gap between the older, romanticized view of war and the more sobering depictions of it. As Martyn Auty has observed, *Horsemen* examined "how the experience of war could be related to romance and escapism without compromising the seriousness of the events depicted."[6]

Filmmakers and other mass-culture practitioners of the day tuned into this spirit and commenced a warfare de-glorification process that continued well into the 1930s. Two years after he had "gone independent" and established his own movie production company, Samuel Goldwyn authorized George Fitzmaurice to direct *The Dark Angel* (1925) shortly after the former had viewed a production of H. N. Trevelyan's similarly titled wartime play in London. *The Dark Angel*, about a romantic triangle that included among its members a blinded WW I veteran, was written for the screen by Frances Marion, who by virtue of her work on *Stella Maris*, *Pollyanna*, and many other films had risen to the top of the screenwriting profession. "She had more muscle than most women in Hollywood," said Gloria Swanson, "because she was a gold mine of ideas—ideas that could become stories that could become scripts that could become films that could save careers, lives, and corporations." An incredibly prolific writer—she wrote the screenplays for eleven Hollywood movies released in 1925 alone—Marion doubtless had ideas of her own when she went to work on the *Dark Angel* adaptation; descendant and namesake of a Revolutionary War general (and no doubt steeped in tales of his exploits as a child), Marion had been one of the first women correspondents to report from the WW I battlefields and drew on her war-related experiences while writing the script.[7]

Set in Great Britain, *The Dark Angel* starred Ronald Colman as Captain Alan Trent, Vilma Banky as Kitty Vane, and Wyndham Standing as Captain Gerald Shannon. Alan and Kitty are romantically entwined but, after Alan goes off to fight in the Great War and is blinded, he seeks unilaterally to end the relationship. Following a sadly durable tradition that began in the cinema with such entries as *Stricken Blind* and *The Violin Maker of Cremona*, *The Dark Angel* has Alan so afraid of being a burden on his fiancée that he pretends to have been killed in the war and then goes off to live in an isolated part of the country to pursue a career as a writer of children's books. Shannon, who has been courting Kitty after Alan's presumed death, discovers his friend and, knowing that the latter was Kitty's first love, tells her as to his whereabouts. At an arranged meeting, the disabled vet tries to withdraw from the relationship once again by pretending to be sighted and telling her he no longer loves her, but Kitty sees through the charade and the film ends with the former lovers reunited.

The Dark Angel is best remembered as a love story, but Goldwyn, Marion, and Fitzmaurice vitiated the play's sentimental quality with conspicuous antiwar touches. "One of these has the troops coming back from war," noted a *Variety* reviewer, "and when brought to a halt, the bereaved parents are shown sadly looking into the depleted ranks. Slowly figures of the dead soldiers arise, resplendent in white uniforms. This effect is corking, as is the phantom of the dark angel, Death, flying over the battlefields and then into the quiet English home of Kitty."[8]

Though a critical and financial triumph that helped legitimize Goldwyn's status as a major producer of serious films,[9] *The Dark Angel* was overshadowed by the work of the person at the center of antiwar narratives during the mid–1920s:

Laurence Stallings, a New York *World* journalist and Marine veteran who had lost a leg at Belleau Wood. The year 1924 was auspicious for him; not only did he publish *Plumes*, a semiautobiographical novel about a severely injured veteran who questions his sense of patriotism, but he also saw his play *What Price Glory?*, co-written with Maxwell Anderson, make a splash on Broadway with its rough-and-tumble characters, irreverent humor, and antiwar stance. An appreciative audience member was a young man named Irving Thalberg, the *wunderkind* MGM production head who had been in New York scouting out material for future films. Recalling the popularity of Metro's war-related *Horsemen*, the 25-year-old Thalberg tried to buy the play's movie rights from Stallings and Anderson. Having been beaten to the punch by the ever-competitive William Fox, whose company in due course would produce *What Price Glory?* as a movie in 1926, Thalberg approached Stallings about developing another idea for a wartime film. The latter readily agreed and even accompanied Thalberg on a crosscountry train trip back to Los Angeles. By the time they arrived on the west coast, they had already developed the movie's basic premise and characters. Under Thalberg's supervision, Stallings and MGM scriptwriter Harry Behn worked out the details of the screenplay for the project that Stallings had labeled *The Big Parade*.

The subsequent film, produced concurrently with *The Dark Angel* during the summer of 1925 and released with it during September of that year, was the most conspicuous of the Hollywood products to de-romanticize the World War.[10] Set in 1917, *The Big Parade* tells the story of Jim Apperson, a wealthy man's son engaged to be married who casts everything aside after catching war fever. He enlists and is stationed near the French town of Champillon where he cultivates a warm and loving relationship with a woman named Melisande. He's later sent to the front, where during the course of a battle he loses a leg. Jim returns home after the war only to discover that changes in himself and those around him have made it difficult if not impossible to pick up where he left off before the war. With his mother's encouragement, he returns to France and resumes his relationship with Melisande to conclude the story.

Despite Jim's privileged background, King Vidor, the Texas native who directed *The Big Parade*, originally envisioned the character as "just the ordinary guy," a suggestion borne out somewhat in the character's last name (from Vidor's viewpoint, "Apperson" was simply "a person"). Consistent with this perspective, the director at first wanted an unknown in the lead role and resisted the studio's suggestion of John Gilbert, a debonair Fox star on the rise. According to Gilbert, Vidor didn't want him in particular because he seemed too sophisticated for the part and had developed a reputation for being hard to handle. Thalberg prevailed, however, and Gilbert landed his first major role in an MGM film. Paired with frequent co-star Renée Adorée (they had appeared together in at least three films before *The Big Parade* and made four more after it), Gilbert gave a finely tuned, multi-layered performance as Jim Apperson that helped the film become a huge box-office hit.[11]

One of the first films to reflect a sobering perspective on wartime disability was The Big Parade *(1925), directed by King Vidor from a story by disabled WW I veteran Laurence Stallings. Here Melisande (Renée Adorée) and Jim Apperson (John Gilbert) share a pensive moment shortly before his disablement.*

As a means of accentuating its story's downbeat and ironic qualities, the film foreshadows the loss of Jim's leg through close-ups of his feet stamping in time to military music as a parade of new recruits passes by early in the film and, after Jim's enlistment, a close-up of his left boot as he polishes it. Innocuous activities in and of themselves, they take on a weighty quality through Vidor's rendering of them in such detail. In addition, the film employs a series of unusually composed shots of Jim reading a letter from his American fiancée; the shots show only his legs as he lies in a cart, in contrast to the utterly routine long and medium shots of Melisande intercut with them. Shortly thereafter, when Jim's unit is called to action at the front, he throws various things down to Melisande even as his truck pulls away. The final thing he throws her is one of his boots. She clutches it to her chest and collapses to her knees, a lonely figure, as the scene fades out.

The reunion of Jim with his family after his disablement is a poignant and tension-charged affair that reflects more than any other scene the bittersweet sentiments of the period. After the veteran and his mother embrace, the film offers a tight close-up of the latter with scenes from Jim's childhood superimposed over her face. The fleeting scenes end with a medium shot of his legs as they currently look: one whole, the other amputated at the knee. This bit of pathos, or bathos, from the mother's perspective is followed by Jim's brother Harry telling him he looks great, to which the latter hotly responds, "Don't try to kid me! I know what I look like!" Not long thereafter, Jim leaves his family and their values behind in a final act of rejection and returns to France to be with Melisande, who arguably must now embody the symbolically incestuous roles of Jim's maternal nurturer and sexual partner.

Though *The Big Parade* is obscure on issues relating to Jim's new life as a disabled person (it makes no explicit mention of financial or rehabilitative concerns and ends simply with Jim and Melisande's initial encounter after the war), it remains a sensitive and insightful look at how war-related trauma physical as well as mental can change a person's life. An early Noble Warrior film to bestow something beyond "badge of honor" status to a war injury, it was also one of the first major features to break away from the ancient stereotypes that had been plaguing—and unfortunately continue to plague—the Cinema of Isolation. Not only was its powerful story written originally for the screen (up to that time, so many had been adapted from ableist literary/theatrical material of earlier periods) but it was also one of the first films developed by a physically disabled person who put much of his own experience into the lead character. *The Big Parade* also became one of the biggest money-makers of the silent era (it ran for two years at New York's Astor Theater and commanded ticket prices comparable to those for Broadway productions), its immense popularity suggesting that audiences had considerably broadened their tastes; they were now quite willing to see films that offered not only war-related themes but also fresh perspectives on disability issues.[12]

The following year moviegoers witnessed a unique twist on the theme of war and disability—an able-bodied veteran seeks out a disabled civilian—in *The*

Strong Man (1926), Frank Capra's first feature-length film as sole director and a major vehicle for silent-screen comic Harry Langdon. Described by Capra as having "a fine Langdon 'story line' with superb routines and gags tailor-made to suit his unique pantomimic talents," [13] *The Strong Man* stars Langdon as Paul Bergot, a bean-shooting Belgian soldier who between battles corresponds with an American Sweet Innocent named Mary Brown (Priscilla Bonner) who is blind. His capture by a German soldier interrupts their communication, but as soon as the war ends Paul makes plans to track down his soulmate. He gets his chance when he his erstwhile German captor, a professional weight-lifter with whom he has become friends, wants to start a circus act in the United States. Arriving in America, Paul experiences several comedic misadventures before finally finding Mary in Cloverdale, a small town infested by a gang of bootleggers. Paul and Mary want to marry but run into opposition from Mary's father, Parson Brown, who is also at the forefront of the town's battle against the bootleggers. After Paul heroically drives the gang out of town, the parson acquiesces on their marriage plans.

While most critics praised the comedic qualities of *The Strong Man* (participants in the annual Film Critics Poll voted it one of the ten best films of 1926), a number questioned the propriety of placing a person with a disability in the middle of a film loaded with physical-comedy bits. "It is perhaps in bad taste to have a sightless heroine in a broad farce, even though the girl's optimism is pointed out," wrote Mordaunt Hall of the *New York Times*, a view shared by *The New Yorker*'s Oliver Claxton: "In an endeavor to gild the lily of Mr. Langdon's wistfulness the Hollywood merry-andrews have injected a blind girl into the story, and blindness is too terrible a thing to make successful foil for comedy." [14]

The key to Mary's presence in this film is an understanding of the comedic persona that Langdon had cultivated during the years prior to *The Strong Man*: "The man-child whose only ally was God," as Capra described it. In most of his films, the baby-faced Langdon played an innocent, helpless, and rather stupid creature eternally victimized by others. So timid was his character that the mere prospect of a sexual encounter turned him to jelly. Such an image had the potential for conflicting directly with the character he was to play in *The Strong Man*: a war veteran who routs a gang of criminals to demonstrate the depth of his love for the woman he wants to marry. In their desire to minimize any possible disparity among these images, the film's authors turned the object of Paul's affections into what they perceived was the ultimate in childlike purity—a blind Sweet Innocent—thus placing her on relatively equal ground with Paul. By pairing this all-too-familiar image of physically disabled people with the renowned Langdon persona, the authors signaled to their audiences that little if any sexual attraction would occur between hero and heroine. Though the same kind of ableism that informs *The Strong Man* unfortunately mars critic Kathleen Walker's own writing about the film, her analysis of the film's perverse qualities cuts to the heart of the issue: "Preferring the abstract notion of romantic love [to anything of a sexual nature], Paul can have a successful—though perhaps unfulfilled—relationship with Mary Brown because, like him, she is physically helpless and morally pure. But the element of perversion surfaces again, especially in the last shot, where we see the blind girl leading this borderline hebephrenic around town. It would be hard to find a more unlikely successful couple."[15]

More downbeat than their predecessors—modestly so, perhaps, in the case of *The Strong Man*—the new war-related movies occupied a kind of middle ground within the Cinema of Isolation during the 1920s. Not nearly as sugary as the Sweet Innocent films (though a surprising number of them did carry curability themes), they blanched in comparison to another trend of the 1920s: a dramatic resurgence of movies featuring the Obsessive Avenger. Bush-league versions of this character type had popped up in silent features ever since Frederick Warde overgesticulated his way through the Sterling *Richard III* of 1912, but in this new sardonic age the Obsessive Avenger dominated the Cinema of Isolation and enjoyed an incredible popularity with audiences. Two men in particular shared the credit for developing this image: director Tod Browning and actor Lon Chaney, the latter often participating in his movies' production and direction decisions. Together or separately, Browning and Chaney accounted for well over a dozen high-profile films with disability themes during the late silent and early sound eras, many of which featured such a character in a lead role.

After an early peripatetic show business career that included stints as a circus clown, contortionist, sideshow barker, and vaudeville comedian, Charles Albert "Tod" Browning turned to the world of movies in 1913 and found work as an actor in a number of comedies produced by the Biograph. While there he encountered the company's most prominent director, D. W. Griffith, who took a shine to the newcomer even as he made plans to depart the restrictive-minded company for greener pastures.

Seven years Griffith's junior, Browning could not help but see himself reflected in the famed director. Both were native Kentuckians (Browning was born in Louisville while Griffith was raised there after having been born on a farm about twenty miles away) and both had made the plunge into cinema as actors while in their early thirties. Impressed that a person from his neck of the woods had reached world-class prominence through film writing and directing, Browning began making career moves that paralleled Griffith's own. Within two years of his arrival in Hollywood, he had significantly cut back on his acting career and was hard at work writing and directing movies of his own. Reacting favorably to the younger man's 1915 directorial output, Griffith recruited Browning as an assistant director on his elephantine *Intolerance* and also cast him as a minor character in that film's modern story.

Inspired by his mentor's love of melodramatic conventions and zeal for the creative process, Browning did not take long to begin dabbling in the cinema of physical disability. In 1917, he directed a five-reeler for Metro called *The Jury of Fate*, about a pair of French-Canadian twins named Jeanne and Jacques Labordie and their rivalry for the love of their blind father Henri. After Jacques, Henri's favorite, drowns in a canoeing accident, Jeanne decides to shield her father from the dreadful news by masquerading as her dead brother and telling the Elderly Dupe it was Jeanne who died. (This being a silent film, of course, Browning conveniently skirted the issue of different-sounding voices.) In 1919, he co-wrote and directed a Universal picture called *Bonnie, Bonnie Lassie*, about a young Scots woman named Alisa Graeme who visits and enchants her grandfather's well-to-do American friend, Jeremiah Wishart, who happens to use a wheelchair.

Both films feature the concept of a disabled parental figure trying to arrange a marriage for a young able-bodied woman (Jeanne learns after her father died that he had promised her to the son of a friend in Montreal, while Jeremiah tries several times to marry Alisa off to one of his nephews), but the topic of arranged marriages was common and in neither case is the disabled person the main character. (Indeed, the working title of *Bonnie, Bonnie Lassie* was *Auld Jeremiah*, based on Henry Rowland's short story of the same name, but Browning and co-scenarist Violet Clark, under pressure from Universal to emphasize the young woman, changed it to reflect the main characters' repositioning.) More of interest is Browning's unwillingness to go along with the dominant curability trend—a refusal that was to characterize all his many films of disability—and his use of an obscured relationship between a disabled father and an able-bodied adult child in *The Jury of Fate*. Though Browning presented the latter in only rudimentary form, he was strongly influenced by Finis Fox's original story and the adapted script by June Mathis (who herself would construct a similar relationship several years later in *The Four Horsemen of the Apocalypse*) and would frequently return to this narrative premise in his mature works.

Though the melodramatic qualities of these early Browning films suggest something of the Griffith philosophy (indeed, Griffith examined the idea of a person misrepresenting a brother to a blind parent in his own first film of disability, *The Man and the Woman*), it became apparent within several years that the two filmmakers held vastly differing perspectives on various topics, including physical disability issues. As previously noted, Griffith held a deep respect for mainstream conservative values, especially those reflected in literary and theatrical works of the nineteenth century, and clung to them even after the experiences of the World War made them hopelessly passé. Browning, on the other hand, was more of a square peg who never felt entirely comfortable with these sentimental values. A runaway as a teenager, he joined a circus to find an outlet for his need to perform and also to be around the physically unusual people that had so intrigued him as a youth. Like the throngs of able-bodied gawkers who attended the sideshows, Browning found his co-workers both fascinating and repellent, and he fancied they possessed emotions as extreme as their appearance. He kept the imaginary stories he spun for them under wraps during his first few years as a filmmaker and instead dutifully turned out films with tried-and-true storylines the movie executives expected of him, but things would soon change dramatically.

Chafing under the studio-imposed yoke of conventionality, Browning went on a drinking binge that lasted on and off from 1923 to 1925. This part of Browning's life, which he characterized as a time when he tried to drink up "all the bad liquor in the world," was a crucible from which he emerged determined to pursue ideas based on the haunting circus and sideshow images of his youth.[16] His big chance came when he and writer Waldemar Young, a former newspaperman from Utah who had labored briefly on the *Bonnie, Bonnie Lassie* script, discovered a novel by a kindred spirit named Clarence Aaron "Tod" Robbins about a trio of refugees from a sideshow—a ventriloquist, a midget, and a strong man—who affect various disguises while pursuing criminal activities. Browning and Young began approaching production executives about the idea of adapting it into a movie. After running into repeated rejection—the concept was too oddball for popular tastes, the execs claimed—they proposed the project to Browning's old boss, Irving Thalberg, now head of production at MGM. Ever alert for vehicles for one of his pet stars, Thalberg agreed to the idea and began developing it by purchasing the rights to the tale and allowing the Kentuckian to direct from Young's adapted script. Thalberg's sense of audience tastes was impeccable; critics placed the resulting film—*The Unholy Three* (1925), which raked in more than two million at the box office—alongside his *The Big Parade* as among the best movies that year. He knew the success of the film hinged on the actor who played the ventriloquist/gang leader, and the person he had in mind was to become Browning's most significant collaborator in this new phase of his filmmaking career: a chameleon in human form named Lon Chaney.

Born on April Fool's Day, 1883, in Colorado Springs, Alonzo Chaney was one of four hearing children born to profoundly deaf parents (his father Frank lost his hearing at age three; his mother Clara was deaf from birth). He learned to communicate with his parents through gestures and facial expressions, skills which he later parlayed into an enormously successful career as a silent-film actor. After several undistinguished years as a backstage opera-house assistant and a touring musical-comedy performer, Chaney moved to Hollywood and commenced a movie acting career filled with highly diverse roles. Chaney, the legendary Man of a Thousand Faces, is best remembered for his portrayal of characters who were physically disabled or so pretended as a part of a nefarious scheme.

Chaney began essaying such roles the very first year he broke into the movies: 1913, with Universal. Indeed, the second effort for which he received billing—*The Sea Urchin* (1913), a short film produced by Universal's Powers subsidiary—presented him as an orthopedically impaired fisherman in love with an able-bodied woman who in turn adores an able-bodied man. One in a long line of disability dramas so conspicuously based on the Oedipal scenario, *The Sea Urchin* proved pivotal for Chaney, as the actor himself acknowledged: "My first work was with Allen Curtis, at Universal, in a regular slapstick comedy. Then I played a strong character role, a hunchback fisherman, one of those rough exteriors but with a heart of gold, in a story written by Jeanie Macpherson. Tho only a two-reeler, it went big, while I made the discovery that the screen was more interesting than the stage."[17]

Hewing closely to prevailing movie-industry perspectives, *The Sea Urchin* showed its disabled character plotting revenge but then risking his life by rescuing his beloved from drowning. The grateful woman now consents to marriage, but the fisherman, seeing how happy she is with his rival, follows the all-too-familiar pattern of "nobly" withdrawing from the relationship. After playing a villainous blind character in a Universal "Rex" two-reeler late the following year (*Her Escape*, about a gangster, recently blinded in a fight, who tries to get his wholesome sister to steal money from her miner husband but manages instead to kill himself by falling down a staircase while chasing her), Chaney played another hunchbacked fisherman in *Star of the Sea* in early 1915. In this film, whose title (an allusion to starfish), like that of *The Sea Urchin*, contributed to the dehumanization of its disabled character, Tomasco the fisherman had hoped to marry a sculptor's model, who of course loves the sculptor. In a revenge scheme that has Oedipal crisis written all over it, Tomasco and one of the sculptor's jilted lovers plan to smash his prized statue—titled "Madonna and Child," no less—but are overcome by the statue's spirituality and relent.[18]

By 1919 Chaney was a veteran of more than one hundred films, mostly one- and two-reelers, but was little known outside the industry when he landed a role that propelled him to worldwide attention: "the Frog" in *The Miracle Man*. The film's story began its life in 1914 as a serialized novel by Frank L. Packard and was adapted into a less-than-memorable play later that year by George M. Cohan. George Loane Tucker, a director who made movies on both sides of the Atlantic for such companies as Imp, Reliance-Majestic, and Goldwyn, and had dealt with disability in Universal's very first feature, 1913's *Traffic in Souls*, eventually acquired the screen rights.[19] Produced under the auspices of Isaac Wolper's struggling young Mayflower Photoplay Corporation, *The Miracle Man* was hailed by such diverse organizations as the Boston-based Christian Science Church for its embodiment of Mary Baker Eddy's teachings and the *New York Times* as one of the most important films of the year.[20] It told the story of four crooks who encounter an elderly faith-healer known simply as "the Patriarch." Believing the deaf and visually impaired Patriarch an easy dupe, the crooks concoct a bogus faith-healing scheme in the hope of fleecing his gullible followers. The plan calls for the Frog, an able-bodied member of the gang, to contort his limbs and go about the city begging, stealing, and generally acting spitefully to everyone he meets. After the twisted fellow becomes a familiar figure to the locals, he would then allow the Patriarch to "heal" him in both body and spirit. The crooks hope the effect would induce bystanders into contributing to the Patriarch's cause—proceeds that would eventually find their way into the criminals' pockets.

The "healing" scene remains one of the most powerful in the canon of Chaney films: the Frog painfully dragging himself up to the Patriarch and then experiencing the "miracle" by slowly unbending his limbs and finally standing upright. The dramatic "healing" has a greater effect than the criminal intended; one of the crowd's onlookers, a Sweet Innocent who uses a wheelchair, is so overwhelmed by what she experiences that, in classic curable romantic fashion, she rises from her vehicle and walks. The crooks reap the financial benefits of this and other healings but, touched by the Patriarch's decency and the strength of his faith, they one by one come under his influence and eventually renounce their evil ways.

Tucker knew the role of the Frog, called "the Flopper" in the novel, would require a performer with considerable physical dexterity and had difficulty finding such a person. Chaney, who initially intended to model the Frog after his *Sea Urchin* and *Star of the Sea* characters during the audition ("I planned to be a cripple, have a withered hand and a hump on my back," said he, "but when I discovered that I had to unfold *twice* before the camera, these three infirmities were, of course, impossible"), changed strategies to enhance his chances of winning the role.[21] Said Chaney of the director:

> He wanted a professional contortionist, but the five he had already tried out in the part couldn't act it. When Tucker described the part to me I knew my whole future rested on my getting it. Tucker explained that the first scene he would shoot would be the one where the fake cripple unwound himself in front of his pals. If I could do that, I got the job. I went home to try to think it out. I'm not a contortionist, of course. It would have been easier lots of times in my subsequent work if I had been. While I was sitting, pondering over that part I unconsciously did a trick I've done since childhood. I crossed my legs, then double crossed them, wrapping my left foot around my right ankle. I caught sight of myself in the mirror and jumped up to try walking that way. I found I could do it with a little practice. Then I rushed out to buy the right clothes.
>
> When I came to the studio on the test day Tucker was already behind the camera. He gave me one glance and called "Camera!" I flopped down, dragging myself forward along the floor, my eyes rolling, my face twitching and my legs wrapping tighter and tighter around each other. Tucker didn't speak and the sweat rolled off me. Finally I heard a single whispered word from him. "God," Tucker said. I wanted to say that, too, but not for the same reason.[22]

Despite Chaney's uncertainties after the audition ("I thought I was out," he told Tod Browning after Tucker said he'd think it over), Tucker did indeed cast him in the pivotal role and the film went on to be a huge success, earning millions on its $120,000 production cost and leading the publisher Grosset & Dunlap to reprint Packard's novel, now laden with photographs from the film, shortly thereafter.[23]

Chaney's work in *The Miracle Man* quickly gained the attention of other Hollywood directors, one of whom was Maurice Tourneur, a French émigré known as much for his lush visual style as his talent for selecting bankable subjects. (Years later—1933, to be precise—he would direct a sound remake of that hoary commercial vehicle, *Les Deux Orphelines,* in his native country.) "Making pictures is a commercial business, the same as making soap and, to be successful, one must make a commodity that will sell," he declared in 1920 and, recognizing that Chaney's presence would enhance the marketability of his own commodities, cast him in several films that year, including a remake of Robert Louis Stevenson's *Treasure Island* for Paramount-Artcraft. Chaney played two roles in this six-reel feature, one of whom was the blind pirate Pew. In the novel, Pew is a short-lived and thoroughly unpleasant character. ("I never saw in my life a more dreadful looking figure," Jim Hawkins says of him, and uses such adjectives as "cruel," "cold," and "ugly" to characterize him further.) Aided by Tourneur's direction and Jules Furthman's script, Chaney retained all of the unsavoriness of Stevenson's stereotype while giving the character a greater prominence than the novelist had originally envisioned.[24]

The conspicuousness of Chaney's Pew is related in large measure to the actor's obsession with developing startling make-up effects, which he treated as an arcane art. Not content to simply cover his face with a visor similar to the green shade that obscured Pew's eyes and nose in the novel, Chaney went to the extent of covering his eyes with bits of the translucent white membrane found in eggshells to achieve a look of blindness. Working with uneven false teeth, bristly

Sans opaque eye coverings, Lon Chaney as the blind pirate Pew poses with Treasure Island *director Maurice Tourneur and co-star Shirley Mason in 1920.*

eyebrows, and a stringy wig, Chaney managed to exaggerate an already grotesque stereotype. His work here and in many other films epitomized the general Hollywood tendency to turn its disability-related movies into sideshows—a tendency that would continue for decades.

In November 1920, several months after he completed *Treasure Island*, Chaney created another vivid character with a disability: Blizzard in *The Penalty*. Blizzard, a San Francisco underworld czar, lost both his legs as a child when a surgeon decided to amputate them after the boy was injured in a traffic accident. The film implies that Blizzard's corrupt and bitter nature stems largely from his longstanding belief that society, as represented by the surgeon, Dr. Ferris, needlessly victimized him. Blaming Ferris for his disability, Blizzard plots a most contrived form of revenge. He arranges a meeting with Rose, the surgeon's daughter, and their ensuing relationship takes some odd turns; in a bit of symbolic heavy-handedness, she sculpts a bust of Satan using him as a model at one point. Blizzard eventually holds her hostage and demands that the surgeon graft the legs of Rose's fiancé Wilmont onto his stumps. At the point of the actual operation, however, the doctor performs surgery on the legless man's brain; by removing a blood clot, Ferris somehow restores Blizzard's moral equilibrium. Although Blizzard is now cured of his evil ways, he must still pay the penalty for his wicked former life; a former crony bumps him off to end the film.

In light of *The Penalty*'s many contrivances, it is tempting to conclude that it offers no more than a hopelessly gratuitous treatment of its disabled character. After all, so many of the plot's twists and turns depend on Blizzard's one-dimensional attitude toward his disability and the people he believes responsible for it, and like *Treasure Island*, it exhibits a pronounced freakshow quality. Chaney, who modeled his character partially after his second wife's legless ex-husband, went to considerable pains to achieve the look of a man without legs; he bent his lower legs up against his thighs, strapped them into place with a leather harness, and walked about on leather-protected knees with the aide of a pair of short crutches. The resulting effect was so startling that it prompted *MPW*'s Jacob Smith to give this marketing advice to theater owners showing *The Penalty*: "Play on Lon Chaney and his hit in *The Miracle Man*. Work on the legless stuff and tell that he has two perfectly good legs, which he gets away with in some mysterious fashion other than taking them off!"[25]

What helps elevate *The Penalty* beyond the level of simple exploitation is the strength of Chaney's acting, which transcends the plot limitations, the flatly written characters, and even his own startling appearance. A reviewer for the *New York Times* detected a more resonant characterization beneath Chaney's exterior both in this film and *The Miracle Man*, and underscored the audience members' ability to recognize it as more of an incidental treatment:

When they first saw *The Miracle Man*, some were struck at first by Chaney's ability to make himself seem a hopeless cripple, but before the picture was finished they forgot his stunt as such and their interest was all in the person he seemed to be. Likewise, when Chaney appears in *The Penalty* with both of his legs apparently sawed off above the knees, some will exclaim "How in the world can he do that?", but after they have followed his acting a while, and felt the force of his presence on the screen, they will take it as just a part of his role that his legs are missing. And, as a matter of fact, his physical appearance is one of the least persuasive things about his performance, because, in several side views, the outline of his legs strapped up behind him is evident. But in all that he does, the man he is supposed to be is present.[26]

The Penalty was the first collaboration of Chaney and Goldwyn director Wallace Worsley, and it proved an auspicious pairing. After working together and separately on several other film projects (including *Flesh and Blood*, a 1922 knock-off of *The Miracle Man* in which Chaney played another crook who assumes the guise of a disabled beggar), Chaney and Worsley created *A Blind Bargain* (1922), a Goldwyn film in which the actor played two roles: mad Dr. Lamb and a man made hunchbacked as a result of one of the doctor's experiments. The story centers around a destitute fellow who agrees to undergo one of Lamb's vaguely explained experiments in return for much-needed money to help with his mother's medical expenses. After Lamb restrains him, the young man is horrified to learn that the doctor is trying to prove humans evolved from apes by "de-evolving" several human subjects into ape-like humanoids through glandular transplants. Before Lamb can carry out his latest experiment, however, one of his "failures" (Chaney as the hunchback noted above) exacts revenge on the doctor by releasing a caged ape-man, who dispatches the doctor to end the film.

After playing what may well have been his only curable romantic character— a reformed gangster healed of his paralysis as a result of the San Francisco earthquake, in Lambert Hillyer's *The Shock* (1923)—Chaney discovered that his minor role as *A Blind Bargain*'s vengeful hunchback was in effect preparatory work for his very next collaboration with Worsley: *The Hunchback of Notre Dame* (1923), yet another adaptation of Victor Hugo's classic tale of misunderstood passions, *Notre-Dame de Paris*, to make it to the screen. It was Chaney who recommended Worsley as director to Universal production head Irving Thalberg, who had conceived the project with Chaney in mind as Quasimodo and had already authorized construction of the massive sets at the Universal City studio complex but hadn't yet settled on a director who could bring out the bellringer's sympathetic qualities. "I want the audience to slowly grow to love this repulsive beast of a man," Thalberg said in a none-too-subtle perspective on the disabled character, and after viewing a print of *The Penalty* at Chaney's request he found the director he believed could pull it off.[27]

With Worsley lined up as director, Chaney threw himself into the Quasimodo characterization and took pains, literally, to achieve a certain look. Here, as with *The Miracle Man* and *The Penalty*, he put himself through extreme discomfort; every day for about three months, Chaney wore forty pounds' worth of molded rubber on his chest and back, held in place by a thirty-pound harness not unlike the equipment worn by football players. The combined weight and restrictive quality of this outfit, over which he wore a rubber suit festooned with tufts of animal hair ("He looks like a piece of moth-eaten upholstery with the stuffing bursting through," commented an *Exceptional Photoplays* critic), prevented him from standing upright. Chaney was able to work in front of Worsley's camera for only short time periods because of the obvious painfulness and the fact that his perspiration would spoil his make-up. And what make-up it was. Chaney used modeling putty to exaggerate his cheekbones and nose and, as he did with Pew in *Treasure Island*, wore a coating of egg membrane to simulate blindness, uneven false teeth, and an unkempt wig. In the words of Tay Garnett, then on the *Hunchback* set as a reporter for *Photoplayer's Weekly*, the actor's make-up was "so grotesque that even the jaded extras avoided looking at him."[28]

Worsley and writers Perley Poore Sheehan and Edward Lowe wasted little time underscoring Quasimodo's difference and isolation from the other Parisians. The movie begins with long shots and extreme long shots of people prancing about in the courtyard opposite the Notre Dame cathedral on the Festival of Fools day. A long shot of Notre Dame eventually irises in on an almost imperceptible figure amid the ornate architecture. A closer shot revealing Quasimodo watching the activity below is followed by a title card that reads: "Deaf—half-blind—shut off from his fellow-men by his deformities, the bells were the only voice of his groping soul." The filmmakers also stressed his isolation by exploiting the auditory losses of both Quasimodo and another character: a hard-of-hearing judge. The two misunderstand each other during a hearing (more appropriately, a mishearing) and, thinking Quasimodo is making fun of his diminished ability, the judge orders the bellringer flogged.

Worsley and his writers also underscored the bellringer's vengeful qualities but in doing so changed the target of his enmity. Hoping to head off criticism from religious organizations offended by Hugo's venal Dom Claude Frollo, the filmmakers greatly expanded the role of Claude's younger brother Jehan and attributed to him the archdeacon's morally repellent qualities. A far cry from Hugo's fresh fellow with a "laughing, scampish face, whose beams had so often lifted the gloom from the sombre countenance of the priest," Jehan (Brandon Hurst) is now a worldly miscreant with an eye for Esmeralda (Patsy Ruth Miller). He orders Quasimodo to abduct the Gypsy woman and then allows him to take the fall after Phoebus and his men break things up. As a title card makes clear, "In Quasimodo's soul was born a bitter hatred for his betrayer." Later, after the bellringer has successfully fended off Clopin the beggar-king (Ernest Torrence) and his "troops" from Notre Dame, he stumbles into a room where Jehan is trying to coerce Esmeralda. His moral code suffering several violations, he and Jehan fight it out with predictable results; he eventually tosses Jehan off the top of the cathedral before dying of his injuries.

Audiences loved *Hunchback* and paid ticket prices as high as $1.65 (at a time when the norm was closer to fifty cents) to see Chaney contort his way through the title role. Critics generally praised his performance but came down hard on the film for deviating from the original narrative ("A gorgeous and vigorously acted medieval spectacle," remarked playwright Robert E. Sherwood, then a critic for *Life*, "but try to find Victor Hugo"). To Worsley's credit, he did follow Hugo's lead by photographing and editing a considerable amount of the film from Quasimodo's perspective. It's one of the first feature films of physical disability to replicate a disabled person's point of view, though to be sure the director never allowed this strategy to go on too long without positioning the audience, often through title cards, to treat Quasimodo primarily as an object of spectacle. For example, a medium shot of Quasimodo enjoying the bells and then looking down into the courtyard is followed by an extreme long shot from his point of view showing people, antlike, in the courtyard. We then cut back to a medium shot of Quasimodo who yells at them, followed by a title card that reads: "To the townspeople he was an inhuman freak, a monstrous joke of Nature—and for their jeers he gave them scorn and bitter hate."[29]

Other aspects of Worsley's decision to endow Quasimodo with the power of the look strongly suggest additional dimensions of an ableist agenda. The parts of

Clopin and Quasimodo (Ernest Torrence, Lon Chaney) demonstrate their mutual respect in The Hunchback of Notre Dame *(1923). Lending a hand is Nigel De Brulier as the ascetic Dom Claude.*

the movie that the director did present from the bellringer's perspective often reinforce the film's general theme of isolation—in the example noted above, the objective shots are of Quasimodo high up in his Notre Dame perch and the subjective ones of the townspeople as tiny dots far below—and, more disturbingly, they reflect the same kind of masochistic tendency that filmmakers of the time typically reserved for female figures (vamps in particular) on whom they bestowed the gaze. In a variation on Mary Ann Doane's observation that "the woman's exercise of an active investigating gaze can only be simultaneous with her own victimization," Quasimodo, too, is punished for what he sees since like the women he is a perceived threat to the patriarchal order. Together, these factors effectively reduce Quasimodo's look to a travesty of the "power gaze" wielded by able-bodied males in the movies.[30]

By the time Universal released *The Hunchback of Notre Dame* in September 1923, Thalberg had already departed the studio to become production head at Louis B. Mayer Productions. The company became part of the Metro-Goldwyn-Mayer film studio the following year, and one of Thalberg's first acts as production head of the new concern was to sign Chaney to a long-term contract. After the actor completed a final film for Universal (it turned out to be the memorable *Phantom of the Opera*), Chaney entered what was to be the last phase of his career. He acted in eighteen films for MGM and remained with the studio until his death in 1930. He was one of the first residents of Hollywood's fabled "Home of the Stars."

Even before he lured Chaney to his new studio, Thalberg had already taken steps, wittingly or not, to make MGM the premiere Hollywood studio for developing movies with physical disability themes, a position it held well into the 1940s. Thalberg, who himself bore a disability (he had a congenital heart deformity so severe that doctors predicted he wouldn't live past 30), had also hired writer-director Tod Browning, a fellow who, having directed Chaney in *The Wicked Darling* (1919) and *Outside the Law* (1921) while at Universal, was amply aware of the actor's talents. Thalberg found Browning's emerging penchant for revenge-driven melodrama and Chaney's protean performing skills well-matched, for Browning directed nearly half of Chaney's MGM films, several of which featured Chaney as a character with a physical disability.

Browning and Chaney's professional regard for one another was curious, to say the least. Browning, who had encouraged Chaney to leap into the part of Frog after having seen the theatrical incarnation of *The Miracle Man* and had admired the actor's work as the vengeful man with no legs in *The Penalty*, saw him as the perfect facilitator for his art. Said he of Chaney in a 1928 interview, "I'm particularly lucky in carrying out my ideas by having an artist like Lon to take on guises and disguises of the most grotesque nature. . . . He will do anything, permit almost anything to be done to him, for the sake of his pictures. When we're getting ready to discuss a new story, he'll amble into my office and say, 'Well, what's it going to be this time, boss?' I'll say 'This time a leg comes off, or an arm, or a nose'—whatever it may be. Lon will sit there a minute, scratching the back of his neck. 'Hmmm,' he'll say. 'That'll be pretty hard to do. But we'll do it.'" Chaney, on the other hand, was rather indifferent about Browning. "I've had good directors," said he that same year. "Tod Browning and I have worked so much together he's called the Chaney director. I like his work. I think Victor Seastrom [Sjöström] and Benjamin Christensen are great directors. Their values are finer. But I don't really worry over who they hand me."[31]

If their admiration for one another's talents was somewhat less than mutual, Browning and Chaney nevertheless functioned well as a filmmaking team under Thalberg's guidance. Their first effort to exhibit a major disability theme— 1926's *The Blackbird*, which Waldemar Young adapted from one of Browning's own literary efforts—contains echoes from Chaney's breakthrough film, *The Miracle Man*. Chaney played Dan Tate, an able-bodied thug nicknamed "the Blackbird" who treats the Limehouse slums as his criminal empire. To elude the police, Tate hides out in a missionhouse and assumes an identity physically and spiritually far removed from the vicious Blackbird: his brother, "the Bishop," a gentle and good-hearted clergyman whose entire side is paralyzed and severely contorted. (The role, one of the most taxing of Chaney's career, required him to keep the muscles and joints on one side of his body perfectly rigid for minutes on end.) The main story of *The Blackbird* revolves around Tate's desire to break up an affair between Madame Fifi (Renée Adorée), a nightclub singer, and West End Bertie (Owen Moore), a dapper, well-to-do crook and Tate's rival for Fifi's affections. Tate's plan to wreck the relationship goes dreadfully awry, however, when the police enter the missionhouse after he is alone with Fifi and another woman. *New York Times* reviewer Mordaunt Hall described Tate's actions: "He leaps into an adjoining room and pretends to be struggling and fighting with his crippled brother while he is merely changing his Blackbird clothes for those of the 'Bishop.' He falls in his haste and is so badly hurt that they send for a doctor. Knowing that he has shammed as the 'Bishop' he wants no physician to reveal his trickery, and therefore when the man of medicine appears, despite the fact that he is torn with intense physical agony, he lies as if asleep on the bed."[32] His back broken, his muscles and limbs locked, Tate remains unrepentant to the end. "I'm foolin' em, I'm foolin' em, I'm foolin' em," the dying crook chortles to himself. Browning thus set the stage for the film's final irony when the poor people whom the Bishop has helped at the missionhouse come across Tate's twisted body and say, "God will be good to you, Bishop, because you were good to us."

Eager to capitalize on the box-office success of *The Blackbird*, Browning and Chaney followed up with another gangster tale, this one set in Singapore. *The Road to Mandalay* (1926) features Chaney as a one-time sea captain named "Singapore Joe" who now runs a whorehouse and who tries to sabotage the impending marriage of his daughter (Lois Moran) to an underworld crony nicknamed "the Admiral" (Owen Moore). Clashes with rival criminals have left Joe with deep facial scars and the use of only one eye, and he believes himself—not to mention his questionable career—so repellent to his daughter that he withholds his identity from her. Though Joe maintains his distance (in one poignant scene, he pauses outside a gift shop where she works and achingly stares at her through a display window filled with religious paraphernalia), his overriding concern has always been for her welfare; for years he had been sending money to his brother, a priest named James (Henry B. Walthall), to help raise her, and now he wants to prevent her from marrying one of his criminal cohorts. After Joe talks his brother out of performing the wedding, several of his underlings abduct the Admiral. Sensing her father behind the disruption, the daughter travels to his whorehouse to confront him but instead encounters an Asian named English Charlie Wing (Kamiyama Sojin), who tries to rape her. Joe intervenes in the assault and is fatally stabbed.

At least one critic was annoyed by the film's emphasis on Chaney's grotesque make-up at the expense of his acting. Mordaunt Hall complained that "in this current effort he has covered one of his eyes so that it seems to have a cataract, and this undeniably painstaking disguise is to be blamed for much of his posing. It is obvious in many of the scenes that he does not wish the audience to forget his blind eye." Yet Stuart Rosenthal, a modern critic, saw in Chaney's physiognomy something far different: a considerable range of emotions that helps propel the film's final scenes. "As Singapore Joe jubilantly prepares a practical joke for the oily Charlie Wing, his face undergoes a transition from mischievousness to amazement to anger ending in threatening hostility when he finds his daughter in the room with his brother and the 'Admiral.' This sets the tone for the film's final

Writer-director Tod Browning, a major figure in the Cinema of Isolation. The prospect of creating yet another revenge-driven disability drama no doubt lent that certain gleam to his eye.

movement which culminates with the Oriental's harrowing sexual advance and Joe's death. Everything preceding this moment is a treatment of a frustrated romance—in effect, a family quarrel. Chaney's face is used structurally in this case as a visual pivot to redirect the mood."[33]

Browning was foremost among his generation of moving-image artists in his ability to wring drama out of obscured relationships between parents and their adult children. *The Road to Mandalay* is one of several examples of Browning's work in which a father refuses to reveal his identity to his child or discovers to his inevitable chagrin that he is indeed the parent of a person he had hitherto spent a good deal of time manipulating. *The Show* (1927), which Browning directed the next year from a script by Waldemar Young as a follow-up to *Mandalay*, follows a similar pattern, even to the point of featuring a visually impaired father.

Set against a carnival background in Budapest, *The Show* featured a trio of MGM stars: Lionel Barrymore as "the Greek," Renée Adorée as "Salome," and John Gilbert as "Cock Robin." In the Palace of Illusions sideshow, they perform a re-enactment of the story of Salome and John the Baptist several times a day, in which the Greek appears to behead Cock Robin. Offstage, the Greek is in love with Salome, who in turn is smitten by the callous and cavalier Cock Robin. The animosity between the Greek and Cock Robin grows so strong that at one point the former "accidently" tries to use a real axe on the latter during their act. Salome happens to live with an elderly blind veteran (Edward Connelly) whose son has been imprisoned and sentenced to death. To keep the old man's spirits up, Salome has been writing and reading letters to him while pretending they have been written by his son. One day, while Salome hides Cock Robin from the police, the Elderly Dupe mistakes the sideshow performer for his own son. Cock Robin maintains the illusion at Salome's request and later learns after the old man has died that he was Salome's father. Touched by her goodness, Cock Robin finally returns her love.

Though overshadowed by the many Browning–Chaney productions and dismissed by its star (John Gilbert described it as "nothing whatever to be proud of"),[34] *The Show* is interesting in that it offers another installment of Browning's "obscured familial relationship" theme and presents a father whose disability plays a special role. (If we combine his functions with those of the Greek, we have in effect constructed one corner of the Oedipal triangle: a disabled Father figure similar to the one in *The Four Horsemen of the Apocalypse*.) In addition, *The Show* was one of the first Browning films to use a carnival or circus setting as a backdrop for a story involving a disabled person. Circus life became a major motif in Browning's later work; it is a background he used for his most famous disability film, *Freaks* (1932), as well as his very next film, *The Unknown* (1927).

Yet another three-way collaboration involving Browning, Chaney, and Young— the latter, clearly the director's favorite writer, once again adapted a Browning story—*The Unknown* starred Chaney as Alonzo (the actor's real first name!), a circus performer billed as "The Armless Wonder." His speciality is a bizarre act in which he throws knives at Estrellita (Joan Crawford) with his toes. Unbeknownst to everyone save Alonzo's assistant, a hunchbacked dwarf named Cojo (Rex Ingram's protégé, John George), Alonzo really does have arms but keeps them tightly strapped to his sides when in public. He even has a double thumb on his left hand, an anomaly that becomes a major plotting device in the film.

Alonzo is completely smitten by Estrellita, but the highly neurotic woman has a pronounced fear of being handled by any man. A title card reads, "Estrellita wishes God has taken the arms from all men." During an argument, Alonzo kills Estrellita's father, the circus owner. Estrellita sees the murder but can identify the killer only on the basis of the fact that he has a double thumb. To avoid identification and at the same time to cement his relationship with Estrellita, Alonzo takes the extreme step of blackmailing a doctor into amputating his arms. Unfortunately for him, the woman overcomes her neurosis and falls in love with Malabar, the circus strongman whose speciality is restraining two horses galloping on treadmills, one with each arm. The now truly armless Alonzo becomes completely unhinged and plots a strange form of revenge; during one of Malabar's performances, he tries to jam the treadmills with the hope that the horses will yank the strongman's arms from their sockets. Alonzo's plot fatally backfires, however, after he slips and falls under the pounding horse hooves.

From a Freudian perspective, it is almost impossible not to read Estrellita's fear of male arms, Alonzo's self-disablement, and the latter's attempted mutilation of Malabar as thinly disguised sexual symbolism. Like so many other disability-related films, the disabling acts in *The Unknown* may be likened to a form of disempowerment or symbolic castration. Indeed, Stuart Rosenthal in his book on Browning suggests that Alonzo is a very physical and virile man, and that his decision to amputate his arms is a form of self-castration in order to win the affections of the sex-shy Estrellita.[35] The newly disempowered Alonzo, shocked to learn that Estrellita has overcome her sexual hangups, now seeks to "castrate" his rival, the type of man that she earlier had found repugnant.

If Chaney, Browning, and Young were aware of the deeper psychosexual aspects of their film, they didn't express them in public. Chaney viewed the film mainly as his latest attempt to instill redeeming qualities into people he regarded as the dregs of society. "I've tried to show that the lowliest people frequently have the highest ideals," said he. "In the lower depths when life hasn't been too pleasant for me I've always that gentleness of feeling, that compassion of an under dog for a fellow sufferer. *The Hunchback* was an example of it. So was *The Unknown*." Browning likewise minimized any subtext: "When I am working on a story for Chaney, I never think of the plot. That follows of itself after you have conceived a characterization. For instance, on *The Unknown* I started first only with the idea of an armless man. 'Let's see,' I thought to myself. 'What are the most startling situations for such a deformity?' The final plot, which concerned a circus performer who used his feet as he would his hands, who loved and lost the girl, and eventually attempted a terrible crime with his toes, grew out of that reasoning. The same applies to *The Road to Mandalay*. The nucleus idea was merely that of a man of such revolting hideousness that he was ashamed to reveal himself to his daughter. It is possible to get two or three plots and treatments out of such a situation."[36]

A certain attitude about disability is detectable in Browning's comments above as well as in his films. As Rosenthal noted of Browning and his concerns: "He is inevitably attracted to situations of moral and sexual frustration. In this, as well as in his preoccupation with interchangeable guilt, interchangeable personalities and patterns of human repulsion and attraction, he coincides remarkably with [French filmmaker Claude] Chabrol. What sets Browning apart is his abnormal fascination with the deformed creatures who populate his films—a fascination that is not always entirely intellectual, and one in which he takes extreme delight."[37]

Yet another example that illustrates Browning's attraction to so-called "deformed creatures" is *West of Zanzibar* (1928), co-written by Young from the Broadway play *Kongo* by Chester De Vonde and Kilbourne Gordon. Chaney played a professional magician named Phroso ("Flint," in some prints of the film) who becomes paralyzed from the waist down after his wife's lover, a cad named

"Dead Legs" reacts to the news that the young woman he thought was his rival's daughter is instead his own in Tod Browning's West of Zanzibar *(1928), a film that starred Lon Chaney, Lionel Barrymore, and Mary Nolan.*

Crane (Lionel Barrymore), pushes him off a balcony. His desire to seek revenge on the lover is only heightened later after he finds his wife dead alongside a little girl. Thinking Crane is the girl's father, Phroso (now called "Dead Legs" in the film) devises a most sinister, and certainly contrived, form of revenge: he abducts her, raises her to young adulthood, and then plans to have the young woman murdered while Crane watches. The plan backfires after Dead Legs learns that the young woman is his own daughter, however, and he dies after saving her from his hired killers. *West of Zanzibar* is a particularly vivid illustration of Browning's penchant for creating disabled characters with strong and conflicting emotions brewing beneath the surface, as Rosenthal has noted: "Physical disfiguration for Browning is a sign of teeming internal chaos and by no means denotes a pure or sympathetic creature. In Browning's films real suffering brings out the dangerous qualities in a man. Whatever good deed he may eventually do is the result of his initial strength of character and in spite of the externally imposed suffering which forces men like Dead Legs . . . into new and deeper guilt."[38]

Critics of the period appreciated Chaney's performing skills but were generally disdainful of the films themselves and their preposterous narrative twists. "The whole idea is wildly improbable," wrote J. S. Dickerson of *The Penalty*, a view shared by Welford Beaton in his review of *The Unknown*: "The idea itself is ridiculous, if we are to take the picture seriously, which I presume is what Browning would like us to do. . . . It is unbelievable that a man would do such a fool thing, therefore the whole story is unconvincing and uninteresting." Although the films did not enjoy much critical success, audiences were fascinated by the concept of physically disabled characters whose vengeful efforts tragically backfire and they flocked to the theaters that showed such movies. "They are so formularized, so interchangeable in plot and characters, that their popular success is hard to explain," wrote historian William K. Everson. "One can only attribute it to the incredible pantomimic performances of Lon Chaney, who certainly salvaged them all from their mediocrity, and to the fact that they were all so short and inexpensive that they could hardly help but make money. For the most part, they were cruel, perverse, excessively morbid tales. One alone might seem strong meat, with Browning's penchant for ironical climaxes quite striking; but seen collectively, they are a clichéd group."[39]

If we take a broader perspective, however, other possibilities for the films' popularity begin to emerge. Chaney's breakthrough film, *The Miracle Man*, appeared the same year that Americans witnessed wave after wave of returning battle-weary doughboys, many now disabled. In the face of a renewed social awareness of disability issues, Browning, Chaney, and their collaborators may have based their subsequent films on a perception that physically disabled males, veterans and civilians alike, were embittered as a result of society's contributions to and maintenance of their disabled status. (It's worth noting that by 1920—the same year of Chaney's *The Penalty*—it had become clear that the Veterans' Rehabilitation Act was failing to serve all but a small minority of disabled veterans and it augured poorly for the Smith–Fess Act, a similar piece of legislation that Woodrow Wilson signed into law that year that authorized a vocational rehabilitation program for physically disabled civilians.) As portrayed in the Chaney–Browning movies, they were physically and psychically wounded animals—threats to the patriarchal order that needed punishment.

This observation in itself doesn't explain the films' popularity, but audiences may well have been riveted by the primal messages offered on the films' subtextual level. The movies of Chaney and Browning differed from earlier Obsessive Avenger entries such as *The Circus Man*, *The Broken Law*, and *The Ordeal* in that they often included the act of disablement within their narrative contexts. (In the older films, the characters' disabling conditions—distorted spines, usually—existed prior to the start of the films.) They may well have forced the spectators on an unconscious level into regarding the newly disabled characters as post-Oedipal aberrations. In other words, audiences may have perceived the figures as renegades who had violated the Law of the Father by refusing to repress their desire for the Mother, were disempowered, and then sought revenge as a means of regaining the phallus. Though moviemakers and audiences may not have been wholly conscious of it, they were creating and receiving "sexual outlaws"—types who succumbed to tantalizingly forbidden desires and who, despite the retribution they inevitably received (or perhaps because of it), would be difficult to top in terms of sheer fascination.

Though Lon Chaney's portrayals of physically disabled people overwhelmed the Cinema of Isolation during the 1920s, he certainly was not alone in bringing such characters to life. The hulking Scots actor Ernest Torrence, who in at least two films— *Tol' able David* and *The Hunchback of Notre Dame*—played an able-bodied miscreant who benefited from another's disability, appeared as a disabled character himself, one of the most famous, in 1924. That was the year that Herbert Brenon, late of Fox's *The Two Orphans*, directed *Peter Pan* for Paramount. With a script by Willis Goldbeck (a Rex Ingram discovery who later garnered some notoriety as the principal scriptwriter for Tod Browning's *Freaks*) based on James M. Barrie's children's play of the same name, Brenon's film starred Torrence as Captain Hook, the pirate chief out to avenge the loss of his hand, and Betty Bronson as the title character and focus of Hook's wrath.

Barrie, who was decidedly whimsical on the subject of Hook's villainy ("The man is not wholly evil," he wrote, "he has a Thesaurus in his cabin, and is no mean performer on the flute"), had been wooed for years by moviemakers, notably Mary Pickford, to lend his talents to their projects. In 1920, the 60-year-old Barrie wrote a *Scenario for a Proposed Film of Peter Pan*, a movie script of sorts that carried a cinematic sense, suggested material that might be cut from the play, and served as a distinct source of pleasure for the playwright. "I am entertaining myself successfully by going over the *P. Pan* film scenario again and putting in new things," he wrote. "One could go on doing this till doom cracks, and then put in the crack." The powers-that-were at Paramount borrowed some of the scenario's ideas but for reasons not entirely clear decided to design the film along traditional theatrical lines, including the look of the film. James Wong Howe's cinematography generally consists of long shots with virtually no camera movement, and he and Brenon kept cinematic-based special effects to a minimum. It was a quality that did not go unnoticed by the Scots playwright: "I saw the *P. Pan* piece of film today with all the cuts I had made in it carried out, and I thought decidedly more favourably of it, but so far it is only repeating what is done on the stage, and the only reason for a film should be that it does the things the stage can't do."[40]

Despite *Peter Pan*'s generally theatrical quality, Brenon did represent part of it from his disabled character's perspective, just as Wallace Worsley had done the year before with *The Hunchback of Notre Dame*. During a key scene in which Hook tries to poison Peter Pan, Brenon endowed Hook with the "power of the look" by alternating close-ups and medium shots of him as he looks toward Pan with longer shots of Pan asleep. Just as Worsley had used this strategy in service to an ableist agenda (in that case, by enhancing Quasimodo's isolation), however, so too did Brenon. His decision to fragment Hook's body cinematically through a series of close shots afforded him the perfect opportunity to accentuate the very object Barrie used to define the villain's identity. As Jacqueline Rose has noted, the captain's infamous prosthesis is the first and last sign of him in the scene and serves as the basis for in her words "a visual-verbal pun on Hook as name and as object."[41] Though Barrie is certainly the main person responsible for developing the Hook persona, Brenon's accentuation of Hook's prosthesis—repeated in the Disney *Peter Pan* (1953) and Steven Spielberg's *Hook* (1991)—has no counterpart in this scene from Barrie's play. In addition, the director made certain that the evildoer eventually receives punishment for looking, just as Worsley had done with Quasimodo.

Hook wasn't the only seafarer to serve as a model for filmdom's Obsessive Avenger. Another important literary antecedent was Captain Ahab of *Moby Dick*, and this character too found his way to the screen during the mid–1920s. The person mainly responsible was the celebrated theater star John Barrymore, who while riding the crest of his popularity signed a major three-film deal with Warner Bros. in the spring of 1925. Warners wanted the first of the "super-pictures" to be *Don Juan*, but that early Vitaphone film would have to wait; the matinee idol, whose extraordinary contractual agreement gave him the right to approve the subject matter of the three films, insisted the initial movie be an adaptation of *Moby Dick*. Barrymore, who had a first edition of Melville's 1851 work among his cherished possessions, called Ahab a "dream role" and eagerly sought to bring the novel to the screen: "This book appeals to me and always has. It has an especial appeal now, for in the last few years, both on the stage and on the screen, I have played so many scented, bepuffed, bewigged and ringletted characters— princes and kings, and the like—that I revel in the rough and almost demoniacal character, such as Captain Ahab becomes in the last half of the picture after his leg has been amputated by Moby Dick, the white whale."[42]

It is surely no exaggeration to note that the "Great Profile" delighted in any opportunity to play characters in great pain and characters with disabilities. It was as if Barrymore wanted to prove to audiences he was no mere "star" but a consummate actor who could handle the tormented parts associated with Lon Chaney in the moviegoing public's mind. One of his favorite stage roles was Shakespeare's Richard Crookback, a character that he played to much acclaim in a Broadway production of *Richard III* in 1920. He collapsed from the physical and psychological demands of the part after only a month but nevertheless relished the opportunity to have played it: "I rather believe it was the first genuine acting I ever managed to achieve, and perhaps my own best. It was the first time I ever actually got *inside* the character I was playing. I mean I thought I *was* the character, and in my dreams I *knew* that I was he."[43] For Barrymore, the role of Ahab represented a return to precisely that kind of intensive acting experience.

Despite the anticipated success of a project involving Barrymore's talents, the studio was concerned that a faithful rendering of Melville's novel would alienate a significant number of audience members. "What we are going to do for a love interest, I don't quite know," wrote Barrymore. "He might fall in love with the whale. I am sure, however, Hollywood will find a way."[44] Indeed, it did; production head Jack Warner assigned the script to Bess Meredyth, a screenwriter with some experience designing Obsessive Avengers (she wrote the scripts for Universal's 1914 serialized film about a vengeful paralyzed man called *The Trey O'Hearts*), and she promptly invented a love triangle for the production, now titled *The Sea Beast*. She turned the screenplay over to director Millard Webb, a native Kentukian who like Meredyth had broken into the business as an extra in D. W. Griffith movies, and in his hands the triangle took on a prominence equal to Ahab's ongoing obsession with the white whale.

Barrymore leaped whole-heartedly into the production and used his considerable clout to influence many aspects of the film. Exercising his right to choose the actress opposite him, he with Webb dutifully by his side viewed countless screen tests of potential co-stars before eventually settling on 20-year-old Dolores Costello, by coincidence the daughter of the Broadway actor who had starred in Vitagraph's *Richard III* back in 1908, Maurice Costello. Barrymore bombarded Meredyth with story and characterization ideas, many of which she diplomatically deflected. He helped supervise the construction of costumes and settings. An avid deep-sea fisherman, he even tried to talk Warners into corralling a real whale with whom he could do battle (the studio demurred, citing the expense and the risk to its star).

Filmed along the San Pedro waterfront and the Catalina Islands, *The Sea Beast* starred Barrymore as Ahab Ceeley, a New Bedford-based whaler whose long-simmering conflict with his half-brother Derek (George O'Hara) over the beautiful Esther (Dolores Costello) comes to a boil when Derek pushes Ahab overboard during a whaling expedition and the giant white whale named Moby Dick rips off the latter's leg. Back on land, Derek tricks his disabled half-brother into thinking that Esther does not love him, a ruse that sends Ahab back to sea where he pursues Moby Dick with the intent of exacting revenge on the whale. (At this point, there may be some question as to whom the title of the film refers. A more appropriate label might have been *Sea Beasts*.) Another of Meredyth's inventions—and one that further separates *The Sea Beast* from Melville's novel as well as the other Obsessive Avenger films—was a happy ending; after learning of Derek's treachery and taking his revenge, Ahab settles down to a relatively harmonious life with his adoring Esther.

Though Meredyth's romantic subplot was highly questionable to Melville purists and its conclusion rather subversive on a psychoanalytic level (Ahab's vengeful quest to do in the paternalistic representations of Derek and the whale, far from tragically backfiring, is rousingly successful and leads to a situation tantamount to a "mother and child reunion"), Warner Bros. hardly regarded *The Sea Beast* as an affront to mainstream patriarchal values; indeed, the studio decided to

Profile in isolation: the legendary John Barrymore as Captain Ahab in The Sea Beast *(1926), the first of several Warner Bros. films based on Herman Melville's* Moby Dick.

"road-show" the production since it sensed a hit in the offing. It rented major theaters to exhibit the film and charged a then-hefty $2 ticket price, and the strategy paid off; *The Sea Beast* was among Warners' biggest money-makers that year. Audiences adored it, as did critics unconcerned with *The Sea Beast*'s faithfulness to Melville's novel. Calling it "eminently satisfying" and "a classic," a *Photoplay* reviewer waxed effusive: "The outstanding feature of the film play is the exquisite love story of Ahab and Esther, beautifully played by John Barrymore and Dolores Costello. The flowering of their romance, the sweet agony of their partings when Ahab goes to sea, the anguish caused by the misunderstanding that separates the lovers—are some of the most poignant moments ever pictured on the screen." The romance and the implication that a relatively tranquil life awaits its disabled character represented a significant departure from earlier Avenger films and the classic Browning–Chaney collaborations to follow, though Barrymore as the major force behind the film seemed far more interested in revealing, and reveling in, his character's anguish. As the *Photoplay* reviewer noted of Barrymore's performance, "his agony is almost too realistic in the scene wherein the sailors cauterize the bloody stump of the leg torn off by the sea beast. It's too gruesome for sensitive souls." The critic for the *National Board of Review Magazine* likewise found it overheated: "His screen work frequently shows a tendency towards exaggeration and an indulgence in virtuosity for its own sake. His registration of pain when his lacerated leg is being seared with hot irons is certainly overdone as regards artistic effect." Nevertheless, as Barrymore moved on to the more "scented" and "bepuffed" roles expected of him, he longed to repeat the experience. During the early years of the sound-film era, he was to find that chance.[45]

Meanwhile, his brother Lionel took a turn himself as a disabled character in yet another entry in the Obsessive Avenger tradition. Like *The Sea Beast*, *Drums of Love* (1928) lacked the hard-edged contours of the Browning–Chaney films, but unlike the former film it was directed by a person well-versed in the Cinema of Isolation: a close friend of the Barrymores named D. W. Griffith. The disappointing box-office returns of *Orphans of the Storm* and other financial setbacks had forced Griffith to sell his Mamaroneck studio in 1925, and by the late 1920s he was in the employ of the new head of United Artists, Joseph Schenck.[46] One of his first directing projects for Schenck was an adaptation of the famous Italian tragedy, *Francesca da Rimini*, penned by Griffith's one-time publicity agent, Gerrit Lloyd. Griffith was no doubt impressed by the melodrama's pedigree (*Francesca da Rimini* has been the source of inspiration for countless artistic works) and was quite familiar with one of its offspring: George Henry Boker's 1853 theatrical adaptation, widely revived during the late nineteenth century. With Schenck's promise of artistic and financial freedom and the chance to work again with one of his favorite actors, Griffith plunged into the work.[47]

Perhaps wishing to avoid running afoul of copyright laws, Lloyd and Griffith transplanted the famous Italian story to Portugeuse South America and titled their film *Drums of Love* but otherwise remained reasonably faithful to Boker's play. They told the tale of the Duke Cathos de Alvia (Barrymore), an eighteenth-century nobleman about to enter an arranged marriage to the daughter of a political rival. Unbeknownst to his betrothed, Princess Emanuella (Mary Philbin), he is much older than she and has a distorted spine. (Barrymore even wore glued animal hair on the backs of his hands as the filmmakers' way of enhancing the Duke's "repulsive" qualities and reinforcing the association of such characters with beasts made prominent in earlier Chaney fare such as *A Blind Bargain* and *The Hunchback of Notre Dame*.) The Duke sends his handsome younger brother, Count Leonardo (Valentino lookalike Don Alvarado) to meet her, and it doesn't take long for sparks to fly among the two young people. While the Duke is off at war, Emanuella and Leonardo engage in surreptitious lovemaking. They're observed by the vindictive court jester Bopi (Tully Marshall) who later informs the Duke of their indiscretions. The original ending of *Drums of Love* more or less follows the conclusion established in the many tellings of the Francesca da Rimini story: his moral code violated, the Duke murders the young lovers before expiring himself.

Somewhat reminiscent of *The Four Horsemen of the Apocalypse* and *The Show* in its positioning of a disabled male as a duped Father figure, *Drums of Love* premiered in New York in January 1928 and inspired only lukewarm praise. Its poor reception is traceable in part to the film's tragic ending, made incongruous by Lloyd and Griffith's conception of Cathos (which they based heavily on Boker's "Lanciotto" character) and the way Barrymore fleshed it out. In previous tellings of the Francesca da Rimini story, Lanciotto was a simple embodiment of villainy, but in Boker's hands the character became more more complex and sympathetic. Ordinarily, such development would be a positive thing, but, in his eagerness to create a character of Shakespearean proportions, Boker introduced so many conflicting elements that, according to his biographer, Lanciotto became "unintelligible" and confounded the story's traditionally tragic ending. Lloyd and Griffith unfortunately reproduced this flaw in their film, and Barrymore's performance as the cuckolded Cathos, wonderfully sensitive and touching on its own terms, only accentuated it as did the rather flat portrayals rendered by Philbin and Alvarado. As Richard Schickel put it, "It is perhaps not so much the death of the lovers, an uninteresting couple throughout, that disturbed audiences, but the fact that it is Barrymore's duke who having won their hearts must now yield to the dictates of 'honor' and put them to death. One does not want him to do so, and does not totally believe him capable of the act."[48]

Believing surgery would improve the film's chances with subsequent reviewers and audiences, Griffith recalled the cast and crew and shot a new ending the following month. This new ending, which Griffith grafted onto the film for its general release in March, also has traces of the Obsessive Avenger tale: Bopi taunts the Duke about the unredressed moral code violations, and the two of them mortally wound one another. The dying Cathos forgives Emanuella and Leonardo, thereby allowing the young lovers to pursue their romance unimpeded. Though this strange ending is in some ways more consistent with the characterizations that preceded it, it's still offensive; not only does it maintain the idea of yet another tragic disabled character, but now it also features the idea of a wronged disabled person who, far from receiving justice for the moral transgression against him, dies while the transgressors prosper. To put it another way, yet another disabled character bites the dust in the name of able-bodied bliss. That the new ending did nothing to improve the film's standing with critics and audiences indicated among other things that audiences were at last growing weary of such fare.

A discussion of the late silent film era would not be complete without some acknowledgment of a movie that, while obscure on its own terms, set the stage for a new round of films that featured disabled characters with villainous and/or obsessive qualities: *The Magician* (1926), Rex Ingram's last disability-related film. Adapted from a 1908 Somerset Maugham novel and filmed at Ingram's tiny production facility on the French Riviera (seeking an escape from Louis Mayer, Irving Thalberg, and the restrictive corporate mentality they represented to him, Ingram had moved to Nice in 1924 where he nevertheless continued to make movies for MGM), *The Magician* starred the distinguished German actor Paul Wegener as Oliver Haddo, the title character, whom Ingram and Maugham before him based to a large extent on the high priest of occultism, Aleister Crowley. Akin to Mary Shelley's Dr. Frankenstein, the castle-dwelling Haddo needs a virgin's heart to revivify a corpse and abducts a young woman (Alice Terry) on the eve of her wedding for that purpose. He hypnotizes her but is foiled by her fiancé (Ivan Petrovitch) before he can carry out his designs. Assisting Haddo throughout much of this sinister tale is an evil, and doomed, hunchbacked dwarf, played in broken-toothed and matted-hair splendor by Henry Wilson, Ingram's then-current living good-luck charm. Though the film received mostly negative reviews and performed poorly at the box office (critics and audiences expecting something more in line with Ingram's tradition of romanticized tales were put off by the film's grisly implications), it did set in motion a trend that resounded throughout the 1930s and beyond. As William K. Everson has argued, *The Magician* "was probably Hollywood's first full-blooded essay in the 'mad doctor' school and contained the ingredients of many a later horror film." With the awareness that Maugham's novel contains no reference to any laboratory assistant, disabled or otherwise (Ingram invented the character for the film, presumably to give work to his friend Wilson and to capitalize on audience fascination with figures such as Lon Chaney's Quasimodo), *The Magician* may well be the first in a long line of movies to present a minor male character with an orthopedic impairment who obediently serves his insane master.[49]

If a message can be distilled from the amalgam of silent-era movies that stretched from 1912 to the late 1920s, it is this: moviemakers would have their audiences believe that helplessness and dependency on able-bodied people were the norms for physically disabled people, and that if they weren't cured, or at the very least kept dependent, they were dangerous deviants. If in the movies disabled characters showed their worthiness through some combination of good deeds, innocence, spirituality, and a general long-suffering life, and weren't elderly, they would probably return to the mainstream world—their ultimate "reward," as it were—through a cure. Significantly, it's an action not of their own making; doctors, representing able-bodied society, would in classic paternalistic fashion administer the cure, though occasionally a happy accident or the greatest paternalistic figure of them all—God—would be its cause. The movie industry's emphasis on passivity over self-direction took a considerably darker form as well. Its practitioners never hesitated to show what disabled characters would receive if they strayed from their socially sanctioned roles to become self-reliant action-takers, especially embittered and vengeful ones: punishment, usually by death. Filmmakers distinctly found something objectionable about people with steady-state disabilities; in the majority of their movies, they found they either had to cure and reabsorb the characters into mainstream society, or kill them.

Evil hunchbacks ready to commit unspeakable crimes became common in silent-era films. Separated from his charges by a winding staircase, Oliver Haddo's laboratory assistant (Henry Wilson) keeps a wary eye on the distressed hero (Ivan Petrovitch) and his ever-grateful heroine (Alice Terry) in Rex Ingram's The Magician *(1926).*

Cure or kill. Stark words, these, but they basically summarize the not-so-hidden philosophy of mainstream society toward its physically disabled minority as reflected in its silent-era films, particularly the feature-length ones. This philosophy, though unsettling, is not that surprising in view of the fact that it has guided majority actions on numerous other occasions. As Roland Barthes observed in his seminal *Mythologies*, a "petit-bourgeois" society typically acts on its fear of Others by neutralizing them in one of two ways: transforming them into parts of itself or condemning them. "Any otherness is reduced to sameness," he wrote, "because the Other is a scandal which threatens [petit-bourgeois] existence." (Indeed, Robin Wood's extension of Barthes's views corresponds even more closely to this "cure or kill" philosophy. Bourgeois society deals with Otherness, he argued, "either by rejecting *and if possible annihilating it*, or by rendering it safe and assimilating it, converting it as far as possible into a replica of itself" [my emphasis].)[50]

Interestingly, the films from this period bore a distinctly differing message from the one pushed during the same years by rehabilitation professionals. These leaders in the field insisted disabled soldiers and civilians could conquer their disabilities, re-enter the workplace, and become useful citizens again, *if* they had the right attitude. Perhaps recognizing government sluggishness and general ineptitude on such issues, the rehab professionals kept stressing self-reliance as the key to a successful life. This perspective, which represented an incredibly lopsided way of dealing with disability issues (particularly in its lack of regard for the discrimination inevitably directed toward people with physical disabilities), did contain the positive message that people should take charge of their own lives. As we have observed, however, it was a concept the movie industry found untenable.

This apparent discrepancy among the agendas of two mainstream institutions can best be explained in terms of what we might call the lag phenomenon. By virtue of the fact that the movie industry typically takes months, years, even decades in some cases to readjust its thinking and create movies that mirror majority sentiments, the movies cannot help but trail behind current mainstream views. Molly Haskell's view is apt:

> Sociologists like to think of movies as a mirror of society, but of course the record they provide is really a historical document, since in the time it takes to get a picture packaged, produced, and released, the society whose portrait it offers has acquired new wrinkles and character lines. The lag time has traditionally been a function not just of the logistics of moviemaking but of the natural conservatism of the moneymen in charge, ombudsmen of the "mass audience" who responded to cultural stimuli less quickly than novelist, essayists, aestheticians.[51]

Even as the U.S. government was making plans for the massive number of disabled veterans, for example, the movie industry was for the most part still cranking out highly sentimentalized productions. An even greater industrial lag occurred after the general message of self-reliance. It took a second war some two dozen years later to provide the climate for the movie industry to catch up, but when it did—as Chapter Five will make clear—it pushed the message with a vengeance.

As questionable as these images are today, filmmakers back then continued to find them a most serviceable means of keeping the physically disabled minority in its place. As the industry matured into a full-fledged oligopoly guided by an ever-expanding conservative philosophy, the prospects for enlightened imagery were bleak.

4 / golden-age freakshows

Even as the emerging technology of synchronous sound promised new artistic and commercial possibilities for filmmakers, economic forces were at work that assured a continuation of conservative trends that developed during the immediate post–World War I period. As a result of ever-increasing competition for moviegoers' dollars and the new high costs of making and showing films, the Hollywood consolidation process continued apace; many smaller businesses that had survived the deflationary effects of the early 1920s were either absorbed by rival concerns or simply died off. Fewer studios were making movies, and those that did—MGM, Paramount, Warner Bros., Fox, Radio–Keith–Orpheum (RKO), and to a lesser extent such companies as Universal, Columbia, Goldwyn, and Disney—expanded rapidly.

As a part of this industrial solidification, the movie companies became increasingly dependent on Wall Street investors and bankers during the period following the 1929 stock-market crash. "Talkies" and the conversion of theaters to exhibit them (including Warners' short-lived strategy of equipping theaters with headphones to aid aurally and visually impaired audience members)[1] were expensive propositions and forced the movie corporations to incur huge debts. Well aware that large audiences were flocking to the talkies, however, financiers and bankers were quite willing to put money into these attractive investment vehicles in exchange for a hefty share of the profits and the ability to exert a strong influence over the companies and their films.[2] It should thus come as no surprise to learn that the movie industry, already a conservative institution, would continue its tendency toward regressive story structures and characterizations. Able-bodied and disabled characters now had voices, but their utterances became increasingly subject to the approval of the conservative forces representing finance capital. Though the movie representations of people with physical disabilities were to change generally for the better during the World War II era, the images the industry had been cultivating for decades found continued expression during the years of Hollywood's so-called "Golden Age" leading up to that time.

"During the decade following the Armistice we wished to forget the war and all that pertained to it," wrote *The Film Spectator*'s Welford Beaton in 1930, "but we have passed through that mental stage, and are willing to face the thing as it was." Influenced by the instantaneous worldwide acclaim that greeted *All Quiet on the Western Front*, Erich Maria Remarque's 1929 antiwar novel about German youths caught up in the glory of war only to die one by one, members of the movie industry capitalized on the revival of interest in the World War by creating a surge of pacifist-minded war movies during the early 1930s. Building on the

legacy of *The Four Horsemen of the Apocalypse*, *The Big Parade*, and other silent-era antiwar films, they constructed *Journey's End* (1930), *The Dawn Patrol* (1930), *The Last Flight* (1931), *Beyond Victory* (1931), and *The Eagle and the Hawk* (1933), among others. As a means of reinforcing their productions' pacifist themes, the moviemakers often portrayed soldiers disabled by the war as living, and often dying, testaments to the absurdity of the conflict.[3]

Leading the pack was Universal's recently anointed production head Carl Laemmle, Jr., known within the industry as "Junior Laemmle." He had announced his studio's plans to focus on prestigious, big-budgeted films, and one of the first projects the 22-year-old would supervise was ambitious indeed: an adaptation of Remarque's *All Quiet on the Western Front* at a cost of $1.2 million. With the

The Cinema of Isolation in transition as personified by Junior Laemmle (center) and D. W. Griffith (right). Posing with theater magnate Sid Grauman in 1928, Griffith had just suffered through the ill-fated Drums of Love *and was on his way toward oblivion after twenty years of filmmaking, while Laemmle would soon be crowned Universal production head by his father and oversee such successful movies as* All Quiet on the Western Front *and* Frankenstein. *Courtesy Museum of Modern Art/Film Stills Archive.*

assent of his father, he recruited theater notables Maxwell Anderson (author of *What Price, Glory?*) and George Abbott to write the script and chose as director Lewis Milestone, a Russian-born WW I veteran who had honed his moviemaking skills as an assistant director on U.S. Signal Corps training films during the war and as an editor on many Hollywood movies (such as *The Sea Beast*) during the 1920s. Shooting *All Quiet* entirely on the Universal City backlot, Laemmle and Milestone populated its battle scenes with two thousand extras, many of whom were actual veterans, and daringly filled the speaking roles with mostly no-name actors. After Remarque declined an offer to play the autobiographical figure of Paul Baumer himself, the producer-director team assigned the central role to a relative unknown: Lew Ayres, a 20-year-old who later figured in a number of other disability-related movies.

Influenced by *The Big Parade* and its use of boot imagery, the *All Quiet* moviemakers made the footwear a recurring motif as a means of dealing with am-putation issues. While the young German soldiers, appropriately, are at "boot camp" early in the film, Franz Kemmerich (Ben Alexander) proudly shows off his imported boots to Mueller (Russell Gleason), one of his comrades, claiming they are the best pair in the army. Later, one of the film's most compelling moments occurs when Kemmerich's friends visit him in a makeshift hospital after he has lost a leg in battle. (It's a moment that incidentally is revealed to the audience from the other soldiers' perspective; after Kemmerich notes that "every toe in my right foot hurts," the camera, reflecting an able-bodied view, tilts down from an upper-body shot of him in bed to his blanket-draped legs.) Mueller momentarily finds Kemmerich's boots under the bed and shows them to the others, all of whom fondle their fine leather. Mueller holds the soles of the boots to his own to check their size and then says, "I was was just thinking. If you're not going to be using these, Franz, why don't you leave them with us? What good are they to you? I can use them. My boots give me blister after blister." Shortly before dying, Kemmerich tells Paul in private to give Mueller the boots. The latter eagerly tries them on and exclaims "My boots!" even as Paul in some anguish says "I saw him die." What follows are several close-ups of the boots as Mueller wears them into battle. He's killed, but the boots end up on the feet of another soldier; photographed from the legs down, it is only a matter of seconds before he too is killed.

All Quiet on the Western Front was a financial hit for the Laemmles and won all kinds of awards, including Oscars for Best Picture and Best Director, and criti-cal accolades aplenty. "No more terrific picture of war has been made . . . a huge and superb canvas," raved *Cinema*'s James Hamilton, for instance, while *The Film Spectator*'s Beaton simply called it "the greatest motion picture ever made." Despite the emotional resonance of *All Quiet* and other antiwar films, however, the realities of the Great Depression were hitting home and the industry had al-ready begun moving away from such relentlessly depressing fare. As Hollywood began gravitating toward more escapist material, the poignant and exceptionally downbeat treatment of disability provided by the war films was overshadowed by a renewed interest in one of the more troubling legacies of the late silent cinema.[4]

After having proven its Vitaphone sound-on-disk system was for the time a commercially viable process, Warners released a compendium of filmed vaudeville and theatrical bits directed by John Adolfi called *The Show of Shows* in late 1929. One segment, filmed in Technicolor, featured a solid performance by John Barrymore, late of such hits as *Don Juan* and *The Sea Beast*. Critics were struck by Barrymore's handling of his first movie speaking role. For example, the *New York Times'* Mordaunt Hall wrote that "the most compelling stretch [in *The Show of Shows*] is that given over to John Barrymore's magnificent delivery. . . . It impressed one with the marvelous control of his facial features and with his ability to deal out the full effect of the role."[5] The character he played, however, was distressingly familiar: a black-armored, hunchbacked Richard toting a bloody head, no less, in a soliloquy from *Henry VI, Part Three*.

This familiarity also extended to one of the first full-length talking films to feature a disability theme: Warners' *Moby Dick* (1930). Buoyed by the success of *The Sea Beast* four years before, the studio decided to remake the film as a talkie with John Barrymore once again starring as Ahab Ceeley. As he did in the former film, Barrymore initially played the New Bedford-based whaler as a roguish ladies' man whose flair for shipboard acrobatics rivaled that of Douglas Fairbanks. After his disabling run-in with Moby Dick, however, his only concern is to hunt down the giant whale, even calling on Lucifer to help him in his quest.

Apart from the obvious attempt to capitalize on *The Sea Beast* and the prominence of its star, *Moby Dick* seemed mainly an excuse for Barrymore to reprise a favorite role and embellish it through the new technology of synchronous sound. As a Barrymore biographer noted, "John, as always, relished any opportunity to simulate physical suffering, insanity, death throes, whatever required him to deform his body and uglify his face, and moviegoers were chilled to the marrow by Ahab's screams of agony as he endured the cauterization of his severed leg. 'Give them more torture,' said John. 'The public loves torture.' "[6]

On the surface, a comparison of *Moby Dick* with *The Sea Beast* suggests that the Obsessive Avenger had run its course. *Moby Dick* does maintain the love triangle that Bess Meredyth had developed for the prior movie, but the new writer-director team of J. Grubb Alexander and Lloyd Bacon greatly modified the character of Derek and in so doing contributed to the winding-down of vengeful activity so closely associated with the earlier Obsessive Avenger films. In *The Sea Beast*, Ahab directed his vengeful efforts in relatively equal measure toward Moby Dick and Derek, the latter of whom shoved Ahab overboard and into the whale's path. In *Moby Dick*, however, Derek is a wimpy landlubber who has nothing to do with Ahab's leg injury but who does raise his ire as a result of the misinformation he had been purveying. Though, like its predecessor, *Moby Dick* ends with Ahab surviving his double-pronged quest and settling down to a serene life with his beloved, Ahab's revenge against his brother has a far more incidental and attenuated quality than in the silent film.

This aspect of *Moby Dick* was only one of several factors to suggest the Obsessive Avenger might be on the wane. Alcohol-related problems began forcing Barrymore's career into a downward spiral and, though he continued making movies throughout the 1930s (his last was in 1941, a year before his death), he seldom returned to the physical and psychological challenges posed by playing Obsessive Avengers and related characters. Lon Chaney was also wearing down under health concerns, one of which was directly connected to the taxing nature of many of his screen characterizations. "I can't play these crippled roles any more," he said shortly after *The Unknown*. "That trouble with my spine is worse every time I do one, and it's beginning to worry me."[7] Only a month after completing a remake of *The Unholy Three* (1930), his only sound film, Chaney succumbed to throat cancer and other complications.

Despite Chaney's death and Barrymore's declining involvement, the Obsessive Avenger and related disabled villains lived on during the 1930s, notably as a result of a sharply rising interest in horror movies. Robert Bogdan and his colleagues have observed that "from the first horror films to modern-day renderings, physical and mental disabilities have been shown to connote murder, violence, and danger,"[8] and nowhere is this tendency more evident than in Universal Pictures' Frankenstein movie series, commencing with *Frankenstein* in 1931. Launched by Junior Laemmle with the first two installments handled by newly hired British director James Whale, this cycle of films extended well into the following decade and offered a veritable sideshow of disability-related stereotypes. Most notably, it continued the tradition Universal and other Hollywood studios cultivated during the silent-feature years by ascribing villainous or obsessive attributes to characters with twisted spines.

The character so treated in *Frankenstein* is Fritz (Dwight Frye), a scruffy fellow who aids Dr. Henry Frankenstein (Colin Clive) by robbing graves and stealing bodies still dangling on the gallows. Bluntly put, Frankenstein treats his assistant like a dog. He frequently calls his assistant a fool and orders him about, yet Fritz faithfully and eagerly follows the doctor's orders to the letter. Fritz can only take so much abuse, however, and away from his master he vents his frustrations on Frankenstein's creation, the Monster (Boris Karloff). In one scene, Fritz enters a dungeon-like room and orders the chained and growling Monster to be quiet. Like an animal trainer showing authority to his charges, Fritz cracks a whip at the Monster's feet. Frankenstein comes in and, in a tone of voice more sad than angry, rebukes his assistant: "Oh, come away, Fritz. Leave it alone, leave it alone." After Frankenstein takes the coiled whip and exits, Fritz, who earlier had learned by accident that the Monster fears fire, begins terrorizing the Monster with a torch.

Big mistake. In the very next scene, a distant scream distracts Frankenstein and his mentor Dr. Waldman from their reading. They go downstairs to investigate and find the body of Fritz hanging from the rafters, his shadow falling starkly on a nearby wall. (Whale had filmed a scene that actually showed the Monster killing Fritz, but it fell victim to the censors.) The filmmakers heaped further scorn on the pathetic Fritz by having him die in the same manner as many of those whose bodies he stole in service to his master. When we learn of his death, we feel no remorse but are instead left with the sense that one vicious animal has just killed another, more contemptible one.

Whale and scenarists Peggy Webling, Garrett Fort, and Francis Edward Faragoh got the idea for Fritz from Richard Brinsley Peake's 1823 theatrical adaptation of Mary Shelley's novel called *Presumption; or, the Fate of Frankenstein* (the book contains no such character) but were clearly following their own agenda in developing him; the Peake Fritz, a chatty bit of able-bodied comic relief, bears little resemblance to the spiteful assistant played by Dwight Frye. Using Haddo's assistant in *The Magician* instead as their primary model, the filmmakers seldom allowed their creation to rise to the level of a full-fledged human being. They dehumanized him at every turn and did not hesitate to endow him with gratuitous villainy. There is no mistaking their message; in the tradition of the hunchbacked villains of the silent film era, his twisted body is symbolic of a twisted mind—in his case, a mind that readily accedes to the most ghoulish requests and takes a sado-masochistic delight in terrorization.[9]

The filmmakers even made Fritz bear the brunt of the responsibility for the Monster's violent behavior. Robert Florey, a French cinéphile who contributed to the *Frankenstein* script and was originally slated to direct, was the person who dreamed up the infamous scene in which Fritz breaks into a medical-school classroom, finds and then drops the "normal" brain Frankenstein wanted, and takes one marked "abnormal" instead. That bit of business along with the sadistic streak that the filmmakers ascribed to him set the stage for the ensuing turmoil. "Fritz's cruelty in torturing him begat cruelty in the Monster," said Whale while discussing the film's narrative strategy, "and the rest was merely devising the types of murders and how to commit them."[10]

Its questionable perspective on disability issues notwithstanding, *Frankenstein* brought in five million during its first run—more than seventeen times its production cost—and went on to earn much more. Its success sent other Hollywood executives scrambling to develop their own horror movies. As the genre that had enjoyed a long history in the European cinema now started coming into its own in Hollywood films, one of the unfortunate upshots was a renewed interest in associating physical disability with villainous behavior.

In a conspicuous departure from his studio's gangster films and newfound interest in musicals, Warners' Hal Wallis produced his own horror film featuring a cerebral type messing about with corpses: *Mystery of the Wax Museum* (1933). With the bulk of its story set in New York City that year (the contemporary setting was one of the few things that marked it as a Warners film), *Mystery* followed *Frankenstein*'s lead by placing a disabled person among the mad lead character's assistants: in this case, a prelingual deaf person named Hugo (Matthew Betz).

Director Michael Curtiz, who had recently created his own version of the Obsessive Avenger by way of Warners' German-language version of *Moby Dick* called *Dämon des Meeres* (1931), kept Hugo's screen time to just a few minutes and limited him to two main functions: serving as a suspect in the grisly deeds (could he be the mysterious figure who steals bodies from the morgue?) and adding to the generally creepy atmosphere of the film. Denying him the use of sign language, the filmmakers had him "communicate" with unintelligible vocalizations, and they occasionally (and, within the context of the established setting, inexplicably) illuminated his face with a light source from underneath, a tactic that accentuated the actor's already craggy features. Both strategies had the effect of reducing him to a strange and sinister beast whose sole purpose was to provide transient shock value.

More significant than *Frankenstein*'s influence on Warner Bros. was its impact on one of Universal's erstwhile executives. Envious of his former studio's smash hit, MGM's Irving Thalberg turned to one of his long-time directors and allegedly told him, "I want something that out-horrors *Frankenstein*." [11] The director, whose tastes in film subjects often gravitated toward the horrific and who late in his career had contributed at least two bona fide genre entries—*London After Midnight* (1927) and *Dracula* (1931)—responded all too eagerly by creating an entire colony of Obsessive Avengers in one of the most disturbing films ever made: the notorious *Freaks* (1932), directed by Tod Browning.

Browning, who had based his *The Unholy Three* on a like-titled novel by Tod Robbins in 1925, turned to his namesake once again for source material. This time, he followed a suggestion by Harry Earles (a short-statured actor who had co-starred with Lon Chaney in both the silent and sound versions of *The Unholy Three*) and read a short story called "Spurs" Robbins had published in a 1923 issue of *Munsey's Magazine*. The director could not help but be intrigued by the tale—a circus dwarf named Jacques Courbé turns vindictive after able-bodied co-workers try to bilk him out of an inheritance—and soon began working out the narrative details with scenarists Willis Goldbeck and Leon Gordon. Browning then assembled a group of real-life mentally and physically disabled people from around the world to play major and minor roles in his films as sideshow freaks (for example, one recruit was a limbless performer from New Guinea named Randian, known professionally by such monikers as the "Living Torso," the "Snake Man," and the "Caterpillar Man") and took evident delight in working with them. "There was a certain glee in the way Tod Browning went about making this picture that made us think of him as Count Dracula on Stage Ten," wrote Budd Schulberg, who in 1932 was a teenaged observer on the MGM lot. "Those freaks were all over the set and it sent shivers through us to look at them. But he enjoyed it too much." The unsettling film that resulted alternates between cloying sentimentality and outrageous exploitation. [12]

In pre-release publicity, MGM clearly sought to "out-horror" the competition. It billed the film as a "thrillingly gruesome tale" and referred to the disabled performers with such phrases as "creatures of the abyss," "strange children of the shadows," and "nightmare shapes in the dark." The headline of one of its essays, "More Sideshow Attractions in *Freaks* Than in Combined Circuses of Entire World," hyperbolically summed up the company's approach to marketing the film. One of its ads was pure Browning: "Grim pranks of nature—living in a world apart—yet as human as any of us, moved by the same love, jealousy and hatred! Here at last is their real drama."[13]

Freaks focuses on Hans (Earles), a midget who loves an able-bodied trapeze artist named Cleopatra (Olga Baclanova). His love is unrequited until she learns that he stands to inherit a sizable fortune. Cleopatra marries the short-statured performer, whereupon she and her lover—Hercules, the circus strong man (Henry Victor)—plan to poison the hapless Hans. When the other "freaks" learn that the pair of able-bodied circus performers has manipulated and nearly murdered one of their own, they do not hesitate to exact a cold-blooded revenge; in a nightmarish sequence replete with thunder and lightning, the title characters slay Hercules and mutilate Cleopatra to such an extent that she becomes a "freak," too: a grotesque "chicken woman." As a carny barker sagely observes near the beginning of *Freaks*, "You offend one and you offend them all!"[14]

The revenge scene was the most conspicuous deviation from Robbins's work, both in terms of the number of assailants involved and the extent of their retribution. In the short story, only Courbé with the help of his trained dog exacts any retaliation and significantly it does not entail permanent disfigurement. Browning and his writers transferred Courbé's spiteful quality to an entire community of disabled performers (though very much a victim, Harry Earles's Hans is relatively benign compared to his *Freaks* peers and Courbé) and unlike Robbins's vengeful dwarf the title characters resort to mutilation to disempower an able-bodied tormentor. The revenge scene thus takes on a chilling, contradictory quality (consider the twists: members of a traditionally disempowered minority use their collective force to disempower a majority member—to turn her into one of them, in effect—leading one to wonder if she is truly disempowered or empowered in a new way) and, in a noteworthy departure from Browning's previous work, the director did not show his Obsessive Avengers receiving any form of punishment for their actions. Their revenge-taking has led most critics over the years to denounce it as a significant miscalculation by Browning and his scenarists. John Brosnan represented the views of many when he wrote:

> This retaliation by the freaks, though partly justified, is a major flaw in the picture. Up to then Browning had effectively presented them as basically "normal" people, despite their physical handicaps . . . and much more likeable than the two physically perfect people. But by resorting finally to the popular image of circus freaks as being strange and sinister creatures he destroyed all his previous good work, laying himself open, at the same time, to the charge of exploitation—though to be fair to Browning the idea for the story came from the midget, Harry Earles, himself.[15]

The unsettling qualities of the revenge scene were heightened by the way Browning had cinematographer Merritt Gerstad photograph it. Though the darkness of the scene (it's at night and only occasionally lit by lightning) and overriding noise of the storm make seeing or hearing things difficult, Browning had Gerstad film much of it from the disabled characters' perspectives as they crawl through the mud. Once again, a decision to have characters with physical disabilities share the power of the look with their able-bodied counterparts—demonstrated in such earlier fare as *The Hunchback of Notre Dame* and *Peter Pan*—hardly suggests a sense of fair play; the principal times the disabled characters are endowed with the look are either when they are in relatively helpless positions (as reflected chiefly in the lovesick gaze of Hans and the heartsick gaze of his one-time fiancée, Frieda, played by Earles's short-statured sister Daisy) or murderously bearing down on the able-bodied miscreants.

Had it not been for Browning's reputation as a creator of money-making films for MGM during the 1920s, the studio higher-ups would never have allowed him to make *Freaks*. His patron was unquestionably Irving Thalberg, who desperately wanted the studio to have a competitive horror film and who, according to MGM

"Here's looking at you!" The title characters of Tod Browning's Freaks *(1932) wield the power of the gaze during Hans and Cleo's wedding feast.*

story editor Samuel Marx, "was an innovator. He was not averse to trying things that Louis B. Mayer didn't even want to try, and they had quarrels about [*Freaks*]." King Vidor, whom Thalberg had authorized to direct *The Big Parade* and *Hallelujah* (1929), the latter a rare film with an all-black cast, echoed these sentiments: "[Thalberg] says, 'Well, I think MGM is making enough pictures, enough money, they can afford an experimental film every once in a while. It'll do something for the studio and it'll do something for the whole industry.' So that was a pretty good attitude for a top production executive." Thalberg lent Browning solid support during the making of *Freaks* and foiled efforts by distressed MGM employees and executives, an appalled Mayer among them, to shut down the film in mid-production. Recalled Marx:

> Suddenly, we who were sitting in the commissary having lunch would find "Zip the What-Is-It" sitting at the next table or the Siamese twins who were linked together, and half the studio would empty when they would walk in because the appetites went out. And so [MGM producer] Harry Rapf, who was a great moral figure, got a bunch of us together and we went in and complained to Irving about the freaks, and he laughed at that. He said, "You know, we're making all kinds of movies. Forget it! I'm going to make this picture. Tod Browning is a fine director, he knows what he's doing," and the picture was made.[16]

As a compromise to keep the film going, Thalberg did agree to make the studio canteen off-limits to the disabled performers—to isolate them, in effect—but that didn't stop other MGM employees from voicing their displeasure, and using dehumanizing language in the process, about having to work with Browning's troupe. Said one of the *Freaks* editors: "It was bad enough to see them during the day when you went down on the set, but when you had to look at it [sic] on the movieola for eighteen hours a day, it drove you up the walls."[17]

Significant among *Freaks*' many ramifications was its contribution to the undoing of Thalberg's career. He had told the Rapf delegation that "if it's a mistake, I'll take the blame," and his words came back to haunt him after the film detonated in theaters during the summer of 1932. His congenitally deformed heart already weakened by rheumatic fever and the stresses of a high-profile job, Thalberg suffered a major heart attack in late 1932 and spent an extended period of time abroad recovering from it. When he returned to the west coast the following year, he found that Louis Mayer—the *Freaks* fiasco among his considerations—had reduced Thalberg's role at the studio from vice president in charge of production to simply that of a producer. Though Thalberg was to create a string of quality films for MGM up until the time of his death in 1936 at the age of 37 (including the 1935 Oscar winner for Best Picture, *Mutiny on the Bounty*), he unwisely chose a revamping of *Freaks* as one of his first come-back projects. After adding a new prologue (a sociologically minded affair still attached to most prints of *Freaks* available today) and rechristening the movie *Nature's Mistakes*, he used a positive comment by the Hearst papers' Louella Parsons as the cornerstone for a new marketing campaign. Unfortunately for all concerned, however, the reinvented film sank about as quickly as Thalberg's executive authority at MGM. One can't help but think he had *Freaks* and his subsequent tinkering with it in mind when he wrote in late 1933 that "a bad picture, or even a fairly good picture which is not so good as it should be, may do the company which puts it out many times as much harm as the cost of the picture itself. So, knowing all this, usually from bitter experience, the intelligent producer will go on experimenting—which in pictures means going on spending—until he believes in his own mind that he has made the best possible product." [18]

Freaks was a disaster at the box office and a heavy blow to MGM's reputation, but for reasons that surpass understanding the studio allowed Browning to continue making movies. MGM did keep him away from its late 1932 reworking of

The three males in this 1933 photo contributed significantly to the Cinema of Isolation during the 1930s and 1940s: Irving Thalberg (right), who oversaw numerous disability-related films during his tenure as MGM's production head; Louis Mayer (left), MGM vice-president and general manager; and Sam Wood (second from left), who during the 1940s would direct such disability dramas as Kings Row *and* The Stratton Story. *Courtesy Museum of Modern Art/Film Stills Archive.*

West of Zanzibar called *Kongo* (directed by the unheralded William Cowan, it starred Walter Huston as the wheelchair-using "Dead Legs," a role he had first essayed on Broadway), but Browning took advantage of the vicissitudes surrounding Thalberg's departure and convinced other MGM executives he could revert to his old box-office form, especially in the horror genre.

After directing two more films, one of which was *Mark of the Vampire* (1935), Browning returned to the Obsessive Avenger theme with *The Devil-Doll* (1936). His writers, bearing provocative credentials, included *Frankenstein* scenarist Garrett Fort; Guy Endore, who had developed a reputation for horror writing as a result of his work on the previous year's *Mark of the Vampire, Mad Love,* and *The Raven;* and, quite unexpectedly, Erich von Stroheim. Using Abraham Merritt's novel *Burn Witch Burn!* as their basis, Browning and his writers developed the story of Paul Levond (Lionel Barrymore), a Parisian banker wrongly convicted of embezzlement and murder. He escapes from the Ile du Diable with an old scientist named Marcel (Henry B. Walthall), who prior to his incarceration had been experimenting with a method of reducing humans to doll size and commanding them to do his will. They link up with Marcel's crutch-using wife, Malita (Rafaela Ottiano), a saucer-eyed woman with perpetually raised eyebrows who has maintained the laboratory in her husband's absence. Intrigued by the possibilities of tiny humans, Lavond moves to Paris with Malita to continue their work after Marcel dies of a heart attack, and there they set up a toy store as the front for their experiments. Using the guise of an old woman, Lavond orders the "dolls" to seek revenge on the three bankers who framed him.

Though his actions and subsequent guilt make the able-bodied Lavond the figure who most closely resembles Lon Chaney's disabled characters of the Browning silents, the orthopedically and morally impaired Malita offers him stiff competition. A rare female Obsessive Avenger, Malita (dare we translate her name as "bad little one"?) shares a distinct quality with *Peter Pan*'s Captain Hook, *Frankenstein*'s Fritz, and so many other characters within the Cinema of Isolation: she bears a disability that quickly takes on negative symbolic overtones. It does not take the audience long to learn she and her husband are insane, but Browning pushes her characterization one step further; she is not only crazy but malevolent as well. She plans to avenge Marcel's death by maniacally insisting on carrying out their plans to shrink the entire world's population, with or without Lavond's cooperation. When Lavond refuses to put up with her obsession, she orders one of the dolls to stab him with a tiny poisoned stiletto. Lavond eludes the miniaturized assassin and says to her, "Why, you poor insane wretch! I should destroy you with all the rest of this horror!" He starts wrecking the lab, and in response Malita threatens to throw a vial of explosive fluid at him. Lavond tries to stop her but she indeed throws the bottle and blows up the lab. He escapes but she does not.

Not content to malign disabled people through only one character, Browning and his writers turned *The Devil-Doll* into a compendium of impairment-related stereotypes. The evil Malita shares significant screen time with a range of figures, including Lavond's saintly blind mother (Lucy Beaumont), who offers to serve as a mediator for Lavond and his estranged daughter; a mentally disabled Sweet Innocent named Lachna (Grace Ford), a young blonde woman described as "an inbred peasant half-wit" by her employer Malita; and a variation on the Tragic Victim image in the form of Emil Coulvet (Robert Greig), one of Lavond's former banking colleagues. (The latter becomes totally immobilized after one of Lavond's dolls stabs him with a poisoned knife, and the attending doctor makes the filmmakers' ableist views clear: "He'll never be able to tell us [what happened]. He'll be hopelessly paralyzed for the rest of his life. A brilliant mind imprisoned in a useless body.") Inexplicably eager to follow up *Freaks* with another film that featured multiple disabled characters but wishing to avoid the enormous backlash that greeted the earlier film, Browning took the more traditional route of recruiting able-bodied actors to play them.

Perhaps *The Devil-Doll*'s depiction of bankers as villainous, vindictive, and victimized proved too much for MGM (which like any other studio depended heavily on the banking industry for its survival), for Browning was to make only

Rafaela Ottiano and Lionel Barrymore in a stare-down from The Devil-Doll *(1936), Tod Browning's penultimate film. The obscure Ottiano played a character type seldom constructed in the movies: a female Obsessive Avenger.*

one more movie before exiting the Hollywood scene. No Irving Thalberg or other sympathetic executives to shield him anymore, Browning was only 57 at the time MGM set him out to pasture. Settling down to a relatively affluent retirement in Santa Monica, the man who had spent two decades cultivating the darker reaches of the Cinema of Isolation lived there in obscurity until his death at age 80. The year he died, 1962, almost perfectly coincided with a renewed interest in the movie that had unravelled his career; *Freaks* saw its thirty-year British ban rescinded, became a somewhat respected film in Europe (indeed, it played at the Cannes Film Festival in 1962, though unfortunately representing the "horror" category), and engendered numerous debates in the United States following its re-release early that decade.

Even as Browning's moviemaking career began winding down in the mid–1930s, a fellow Louisville native who had also joined MGM around 1925, Hunt Stromberg, was at work constructing several physically disabled villains for a film whose story had been filmed at least four times before: *Treasure Island* (1934), based on Robert Louis Stevenson's 1881–82 serialized novel. With a screenplay by John Lee Mahin, direction by Victor Fleming (the latter, yet another in a very long list of filmmakers who apprenticed under D. W. Griffith, would put dozens of short-stature singers and dancers through their paces in MGM's 1939 *The Wizard of Oz*), and boasting the talents of three cinematographers, *Treasure Island* closely followed Stevenson's narrative details. As might be expected, the proximity extended to reproducing the novel's disability-villainy linkages, which Stromberg and crew enhanced through various moviemaking strategies.

The chief evildoer is of course the lying, thieving, and thoroughly treacherous Long John Silver, played in the MGM film by long-time contract actor Wallace Beery. The film introduces Silver in classic objectified fashion, shortly after the youthful Jim Hawkins (played by 12-year-old Jackie Cooper) has excitedly boarded Squire Trelawney's ship *Hispaniola*. The boy finds a cannon and pretends to fire it. He looks through a small opening in the boat near the cannon to see the lower half of a man standing on the pier. The man's right leg is missing at the knee and he bears a crutch under his right arm. Fleming's camera, representing Jim's perspective, then tilts to reveal the entire person. The man, Silver, peers back at the camera and in a rough voice says, "Well, sonny, was you aimin' to blow the other leg off?"

This objectifying technique contributed to a decidedly mixed characterization of Stevenson's famous villain. In both the novel and the movie, Silver is unquestionably a cold-blooded killer; he thinks nothing of murdering other crewmen, such as the unsuspecting fellow whom he knifes after knocking him down with his crutch. By the end of the film, however, he comes across as a huggable rogue. This latter quality, clearly the image MGM's publicity department sought to develop in its advertisements for the film, was largely the result of Stromberg's decision to cast Wallace Beery, a major if unconventional star, in the role. According to Ephraim Katz, Beery's "gross physique, gravel voice, rubbery face, crooked mouth, and mischievous twinkle added up to a most unlikely hero per-sonality; yet he became one of the most popular performers of his time, often playing a lovable slob [and] was particularly adept at playing opposite young-sters."[19] By pairing Beery with Jackie Cooper, Stromberg hoped to recapture the special chemistry that had worked so well between the performers in such movies as *The Champ* (1931) and *The Bowery* (1933).

Among Stevenson's minor characters was a blind pirate named Pew, a hateful creation made prominent in a 1920 movie version of *Treasure Island* by an actor on the rise named Lon Chaney. As played in the new film by William V. Mong, Pew exhibits little of the moviemakers' ambivalence toward Silver; they pre-sented him simply as a repulsive, manipulative villain. Toothless, with long stringy hair, dressed in ragged clothes, Pew initially objectifies himself as a poor blind man "who has lost the precious sight of his eyes in the gracious defense of his native country, England" as a means of gaining the confidence of anyone who will tell him where he is. After Jim informs him he's at the Admiral Benbow Inn, the sweet-sounding Pew grabs the boy's arm and immediately changes his tune. He demands to see Billy Bones and threatens to break his arm if he doesn't. Later blaming Jim for finding no treasure in Bones's room, Pew calls the youth a "little sneaking brat. I should have torn his arm off. I should have put his eyes out." Pew meets an untimely end after a coach knocks him down moments thereafter with the vehicle's occupant, ironically a physician, remaining almost completely oblivi-ous to the fatal trauma his coach has just rendered. It wasn't enough to increase the number of horses that collided with Pew (only one does in the novel); the filmmakers couldn't resist turning the situation into Grand Guignol by inserting a shot that explicitly shows the coach's wheels rolling over the screaming pirate. Expiring in a graphic fashion to the concern of absolutely no one in the film, Pew, unlike Silver, is in no uncertain terms a vivid objectification of able-bodied fears.

The year 1934 also witnessed the development of another seafaring MGM movie with a disability theme: *Mutiny on the Bounty*, released the following year. The main force behind the movie was the independent director Frank Lloyd, a Glasgow native who on his own had acquired the rights to the first of Charles Nordhoff and James Norman Hall's *Bounty* trilogy—*Mutiny on the Bounty*, first published in 1932—as well as the proposed sequels, *Men Against the Sea* and *Pitcairn's Island*, which began appearing on bookstore shelves two years later. Lloyd approached Irving Thalberg in 1934 with the idea of making the film at MGM with the proviso that he be allowed to direct, and Thalberg, on the lookout for projects that would enhance his standing at the studio (and also help people forget his *Freaks* debacle), jumped at the opportunity. He could not, however, wholly shake off the old *Freaks* mentality. "People are fascinated with cruelty, and that's why *Mutiny* will have appeal," he declared.[20]

While John Farrow, Talbot Jennings, Jules Furthman (who under the pseud-onym of Stephen Fox had written the screenplay for 1920's *Treasure Island*), and Carey Wilson worked on various versions of the script, Thalberg began mulling over casting possibilities and other production details. The original plans called

for the role of Bligh to go to Wallace Beery, then appearing in *Treasure Island*, but Thalberg wanted an authentic Briton to play the imperious captain and chose instead his close associate Charles Laughton. The other principal roles—Fletcher Christian and Roger Byam—went respectively to Clark Gable and Franchot Tone. Thalberg and Lloyd began filming in early 1935 on MGM's backlot and at such locations as Catalina Island, the Santa Barbara straits, and Tahiti, and the final film, produced at a cost of around $1.9 million, was released in November of that year.[21]

Though *Mutiny on the Bounty* is best remembered for its examination of the horrors of British naval life during the 1700s, it did have among its secondary characters a comic-relief ship's doctor with a disability. An alcoholic nicknamed "Bacchus," the surgeon (Dudley Digges) is sans a leg and delights in weaving fanciful tales as to how he lost it. In one version, it occurred while fighting against the French near Jamaica; in another, it was at the hands of a drunken Spanish bull-fighter off Trinidad. (At one point Captain Bligh tells him, "Surgeon, you would have made an excellent historian. You have a profound contempt for facts." The medico elicits Bligh's only laugh in the entire film when he responds, "I don't despise facts, sir; I'm indifferent to them.") He's a generous and much-liked figure among the crew, though his good will takes curious turns at times. After Bligh orders Roger Byam back up into a masthead during a raging storm, for example, the surgeon gives the midshipman his jacket, booze bottle, and the following cheery send-off: "You're a plucky youngster. If necessary, I'd be happy to cut off *your* leg anytime." His eventual death as a result of the captain's cruelty (grievously ill, the surgeon collapses after Bligh insists he attend a flogging) affects each man on board and provides a major turning point in the film's story.

Though the surgeon represents still another victim of able-bodied intolerance, there is a commendable aspect to his representation. Unlike the vast majority of other movies that portrayed characters with physical disabilities up to that time, *Mutiny on the Bounty* dwells very little on the appearance of surgeon's amputated leg. Though the doctor frequently talks about his loss, usually from a humorous perspective (his suggestion that some other person "did the trick for me" by amputating his leg becomes a virtual repetend in the film), Lloyd had his cinematographer Arthur Edeson photograph Digges almost exclusively from the knees up. Whether this was a conscious decision to downplay the disability or merely a means of accommodating an aging and decidedly non-Chaneyesque actor, *Mutiny on the Bounty* was one of MGM's first 1930s movies to suggest a winding-down of its preoccupation with freakish imagery.

Though advertisements for MGM's Treasure Island *(1934) downplayed Long John Silver's disability, the movie itself reflected quite a different approach.*

The idea of mixing humor and physical disability during the decade was certainly not unique to *Mutiny on the Bounty*. Indeed, it had gotten its start early in the sound-film era with a literal holdover from the previous period: Charles Chaplin's *City Lights* (1931). One of a handful of 1930s films that kept alive the curable Sweet Innocent stereotype and arguably Chaplin's best-remembered picture, *City Lights* centers on his familiar Tramp character, smitten by an impoverished young blind woman who has mistaken him for a wealthy man and his series of comic misadventures while trying to raise money for a sight-restoring operation.

Chaplin, who produced, directed, wrote, and edited the film and composed its musical score, had begun work on *City Lights* in 1928, a time when many moviemakers were converting their in-progress silent films to partial talkies or abandoning them in favor of making "100 percent talking films." He stopped production for several months to assess his options and eventually concluded that the new technology would ruin the universality of the Tramp character he had spent fifteen years cultivating. When he resumed work on the film, he had decided to keep the film essentially in a silent form. "My screen character remains speechless from choice," he declared. "*City Lights* is synchronized [to a musical score] and certain sound effects are part of the comedy, but it is a non-dialogue picture because I preferred that it be that."[22] Everyone within his orbit thought him out of touch with the times, but he persevered.

The film's much-discussed main storyline involving the Tramp and the blind woman who sells flowers needs little detailing here,[23] but it's worth observing that it had its roots in a maudlin tale Tod Browning of all people might have found promising. Wrote Chaplin,

> It evolved from a story of a clown who, through an accident at the circus, has lost his sight. He has a little daughter, a sick, nervous child, and when he returns from the hospital the doctor warns him that he must hide his blindness from her until she is well and strong enough to understand, as the shock might be too much for her. His stumblings and bumpings into things make the little girl laugh joyously.

However aware he was of the story's proximity to Browning's oeuvre (the circus setting, the misrepresentation between a disabled father and his child), Chaplin didn't take long to bring it in line with his growing sentimentality. As he noted of the original story, "That was too 'icky.' However, the blindness of the clown was transferred to the flower girl in *City Lights*."[24]

Chaplin defined the nameless young woman simply in terms of her disability (she's "A Blind Girl" in the credits) and conceived her along classic Sweet Innocent lines. He referred to the role as "a spiritual part" and noted that one of his challenges in casting it "was to find a girl who could look blind without detracting from her beauty. So many applicants looked upward, showing the whites of their eyes, which was too distressing."[25] Not only did Chaplin insist the helpless and pure "Blind Girl" be pleasurable to look at, but he also disempowered the already-sightless character further by stripping her of a mind's eye approximation of the gaze. As the 1983 documentary *Unknown Chaplin* makes clear, Chaplin had shot test footage of himself as a medal-bedecked prince in an attempt to represent the woman's mental image of her benefactor, but he decided it strayed too far from the message he wanted to convey and did not include it in the final film. Several moments in the film suggest an interest in mimicking the look of the "look"—an early close-up of the woman shows her wistfully "gazing" out a window after hearing a young couple leaving her apartment building, for example—but in general Chaplin deprived her of the power associated with it until the end of the film when, her sight restored (and also, by implication, her sexuality), she takes on a soubrette's assertiveness and shortly thereafter participates in perhaps the most famous and poignant exchange of glances in the history of world cinema.

The filmmaker assigned the role of the young woman to a 20-year-old from Chicago with little acting experience named Virginia Cherrill. "To my surprise

Played by Virginia Cherrill, the blind flower-seller of Charles Chaplin's City Lights *(1931) is one of cinema's most famous Sweet Innocents. Courtesy Movie Star News.*

she had the faculty of looking blind," wrote Chaplin. "I instructed her to look at me but to look inwardly and not to see me, and she could do it." Chaplin had initially hoped her untrained quality would translate on screen as a lack of worldliness, a quality critical to the type of character he wanted to construct. He later found the unskilled actress difficult to work with, however, and fired her about a year into production only to rehire her after realizing how much refilming would be required (but not before shooting test footage of Georgia Hale, his co-star from 1925's *The Gold Rush*, in the role). Cherrill later speculated the reason Chaplin had become so unhappy with her was that he had difficulty separating her from the character she played, and that as a divorced "society girl," she bore little similarity to the ingénue he was trying to create. "Perhaps he saw me as the blind girl and not as me," she stated, "and for this reason didn't like me."[26]

Ultimately, it mattered little to audiences that Cherrill didn't play Galatea to Chaplin's Pygmalion offscreen. Caught up in Chaplin's sentimental romance of two down-and-outers, they made *City Lights* an unqualified hit (the movie raked in a profit of five million during its first run alone). It also went over well with reviewers, but a few dissenting voices could be heard among the critical hosannas. Writing of the film several months after it opened, Francis Fergusson stated in no uncertain terms that "Chaplin uses some of the dead trappings of the movies—he has not completely vitalized his medium. His music, though extraordinarily well related to the changing moods and rhythms of the pantomime, is trite movie music; his blind girl, though very good of her kind, is a film ingénue." George Jean Nathan likewise found the film's pathos overwrought, tracing its key element—"the blindness which imagines it beholds beauty and, with the return of vision, finds to its own and another's heartache only the commonplace and the sadly ugly"—to sentimental literary and theatrical works of an earlier era. Even Chaplin himself was somewhat disconcerted by the film's old-fashioned quality: "I was depressed by the remark of a young critic who said that *City Lights* was very good, but that it verged on the sentimental, and that in my future films I should try to approximate realism. I found myself agreeing with him." Despite the film's regressive form and content, the fact remains that *City Lights* struck a major chord with audiences, its age-old paternalistic attitude toward disabled characters playing no small part.[27]

Among other things, Chaplin's film signaled the acceptability—at least to mainstream filmmakers and audiences—of returning to the old combination of disability and humor. Paramount's Norman Z. McLeod, a World War I veteran who quickly gravitated toward comedy after entering the movie industry in 1919, directed W. C. Fields in *It's a Gift* (1934), a remake of Fields' silent *It's the Old Army Game* (1926). Based on a story Fields himself had written under the pseudonym "Charles Bogle," *It's a Gift* concerns a New Jersey grocer named Harold Bissonette (Fields) and his plans to buy an orange grove in California. Entirely incidental to this main narrative, if it can be called that, are the destructive tendencies of an elderly blind and hard-of-hearing customer named Muckle (Charles Sellon). On-screen for only a few minutes, Muckle mucks things up in short order by demolishing the store's front-door window pane, boxes full of glassware, and a light-bulb display. Oblivious to the chaos he has caused and generally treated like a child (Bissonette frequently asks him to sit down while calling him "honey"), Muckle is not much more than a throwback to the Comic Misadventurers of the pre–1910s cinema.

Another Paramount comedy, although one far removed from the slapstick of *It's a Gift*, was *Hands Across the Table* (1935). Directed by Mitchell Leisen, who had begun rivaling newly appointed Paramount production chief Ernst Lubitsch as the studio's premiere director of romantic comedies, *Hands Across the Table* focuses on two Depression-era golddiggers—a manicurist named Reggi Allen (Carole Lombard) and the dashing but recently impoverished Theodore Drew III (Fred MacMurray)—who fall in love amid comic misrepresentations and misunderstandings while pursuing separate quests to find well-heeled mates. Theodore's romantic rival is Allen Macklyn (Ralph Bellamy), a wealthy ex-pilot who uses a wheelchair after having sustained injuries in an airplane crash several years before. Despite their inexplicably overlapping names, Reggi and Allen do not a couple make in this film. Allen is thoroughly enamored of Reggi and plans to propose marriage, but Reggi, who had eagerly sought out the tycoon before discovering his disabled status, perceives him strictly as her best friend. Indeed, the *New York Times* reviewer, André Sennwald, didn't even regard Allen as one of Reggi's romantic interests; he merely referred to the character as "a crippled aviator who plays confidant to the girl."[28]

Sennwald can hardly be blamed for arriving at that interpretation, since the movie positions the spectators into treating Allen as less than a "real man" during the character's very first scene. They learn he uses a wheelchair, and are encouraged to objectify him, through a series of shots informed by the style that Hollywood filmmakers usually reserved for female figures: (1) a panning shot that shifts from a medium shot of Reggi entering Allen's apartment to a long shot of him seated at work, his back to the camera and his wheelchair pulled in under his desk enough to make it look like an ordinary executive chair; (2) a close-up of Reggi's face, full of anticipation; (3) a long shot of Allen turning toward her and moving away from the desk, revealing his wheelchair; (4) a medium shot of Allen as he looks at her; (5) a close-up of Reggi, her slightly slackening face and follow-up weak smile saying it all. Both she and the audience have recognized his "femininized" qualities; he has been duly fetishized as an Other. Among the comedy's other problematic elements are the inappropriate design of Allen's art-deco wheelchair (movie analyst Lauri Klobas characterized it as a "monstrosity of a chair that further disabled Macklyn"), financial and mobility questions (the movie shows the affluent Allen only in his high-rise apartment, isolated from the rest of the world), and the message that disabled people should sacrifice their happiness and withdraw from romantic relationships with able-bodied people.[29]

Comedy of a decidedly different sort appeared that same year as a result of Junior Laemmle's plans for a sequel to one of his studio's box-office bonanzas. Laemmle, who had resigned as Universal production head in late 1934 ("I didn't need to work so damned hard," said he. "It just wasn't worth it"), did supervise several films during 1935, and the first was a project he had envisioned several years before: a follow-up to *Frankenstein*. He immediately encountered a "whale" of a problem, however; the original director wanted nothing to do with the new project. Said James Whale of Laemmle and other Universal executives:

> They're always like that. If they score a hit with a picture they always want to do it again. They've got a perfectly sound commercial reason. *Frankenstein* was a gold-mine at the box office, and a sequel is bound to win, however rotten it is. They've had a script made for a sequel, and it stinks to heaven. In any case, I squeezed the idea dry on the original picture, and I never want to work on it again.[30]

Junior would not be denied, however. Badly needing another hit to help counterbalance Universal's fast-sinking fortunes (despite the windfalls of *All Quiet on the Western Front* and *Frankenstein*, the effects of the Depression and Laemmle's 1929 decision to concentrate on expensive features forced his company into a loss position during much of his tenure as production chief), he dangled sufficient financial incentives before Whale and finally got him to agree to direct. Believing it would be a mistake to follow up *Frankenstein* with a similarly handled story, however, Whale decided to infuse the sequel, *Bride of Frankenstein*, with grotesque humor relating mostly to marginalized sexuality. The resulting film was and is a curious blend of attributes, as Whale's biographer, James Curtis, has suggested: "Those looking for an exciting, well-paced monster movie are not disappointed. But adults and the more sophisticated can enjoy *Bride* as not so much a horror show as a whimsical fantasy and an exciting piece of cinema. *Bride* is frequently hilariously funny. What distinguishes it from a lot of other such films is that the humor is entirely intentional."[31]

One of the first tasks facing Whale and scenarists William Hurlbut and John Balderston was to build a new story from the ashes of *Frankenstein*'s conclusion: the Monster's fiery end in an old windmill. Despite the seeming definitiveness of this scene, the filmmakers revived the storyline by showing that the Monster had avoided a barbecued fate by falling into the windmill's conveniently flooded cellar. While Hurlbut and Balderston worked out the ensuing details, Whale helped ensure a continuity among the films by hiring Colin Clive and Boris Karloff to reprise their roles as Frankenstein and the Monster, respectively.

The director also wanted to use Dwight Frye again as a grave-robbing assistant but ran into a distinct problem: the Monster had killed Fritz in the first film. Whale and his writers solved the issue by creating a substitute character for him to play named "Karl" (an oblique reference to the Laemmles, perhaps) and, no longer needing an embodiment of disability and evil to explain the Monster's violent behavior, designed him as an able-bodied character. Frye did not play the squirrelly Fritz and Karl with much variation (both characters display a willingness to commit crimes—necrophilous deeds, in particular—on Frankenstein's behalf), but there are some ableist-based differences worth noting. Though Whale and his first set of screenwriters showed Frankenstein threatening Fritz with beatings and actually using the whip on him, he and his new team spared Karl such treatment. Instead, Frankenstein and his colleague Dr. Pretorius (Ernst Thesiger) offer Karl cash rewards to carry out unsavory deeds such as fetching a fresh female corpse. In so doing, the filmmakers implied that the disabled Fritz is much more dependent than Karl on his mentors. In a related difference, the unabused Karl does not act nearly as spiteful toward the Monster as Fritz. Again, since Whale had already demonstrated Fritz's contribution to the Monster's violent behavior, he and his scenarists saw no need to repeat themselves, at least on this point, by having a second Frankenstein assistant take out his frustrations on the Monster.

More conspicuous than Whale, Hurlbut, and Balderston's handling of this new Dwight Frye role was their development of a stereotype whose heyday ran from the mid–1930s to the mid–1940s: the "Saintly Sage," a pious older person with a disability (almost always blindness) who serves as a voice of reason and conscience in a chaotic world. Almost exclusively a supporting character, the Saintly Sage is sensible, charitable, and above all wise. Without the slightest trace of bitterness, the Cassandra-like Sage freely dispenses his/her wisdom to the surrounding able-bodied protagonists, who ignore it at their peril. Like its Sweet Innocent cousin, the Saintly Sage type exhibits a high degree of spirituality and a concomitant lack of sexuality. The Sage lacks the requirement of youth to qualify for the miracle cure so often bestowed on the Sweet Innocent, but as a recompense of sorts filmmakers usually endow the Sage with the ability to "see" (i.e., understand) things that sighted people do not.

The movie industry's reinforcement of the stereotypic "second sight" abilities of blind people is traceable at least as far back as 1909 with the appearance of D. W. Griffith's *The Light That Came*. In an advertisement for the film, the Biograph company made its views known:

We, of course, assume that being most unfortunate over whose sight Fate has drawn the mantle of darkness, and it is reasonable so to do, but Divine Providence is sure to compensate those so afflicted with ameliorating gifts that help them bear their ills with fortitude, and not only that, their powers of discernment are far more acute than those endowed with sight. There is the sight of the soul, which sees farther than the eyes. This may be called intuition; but whatever it may be, it is a rare gift.[32]

Heir to the Elderly Dupe (this latter stereotype, also based on ageist and ableist views, was limited largely to the silent-film era),[33] the Saintly Sage appeared in films as otherwise disparate as *The Devil-Doll* (Lavond's mother, noted above), *Heidi* (1937), *Saboteur* (1942), and *The Enchanted Cottage* (1945) but found its fullest expression in *Bride of Frankenstein*, one of the first sound-era films to feature such a character. It took the form of a nameless blind hermit, played by the Scots actor O. P. Heggie, who befriends the Frankenstein monster. Eyes alight with a mystic glow, his bearded visage often turned heavenward, the hermit looks as if he just stepped out of a Bible story. As the lonely fellow offers a profoundly felt prayer of thanks for the gift of a friend, Whale accentuated the moment by offering a solo organ rendition of "Ave Maria" in the background and allowing a crucifix, hanging prominently on a nearby wall, to glow a few seconds after everything else has faded out of the shot.

In the next scene, we learn the hermit has been sharing his food, drink, and lodging with the Monster and even begun a modest socialization program for him. His humane treatment leads to a strong irony later in the film when a hunter (John Carradine), startled at the sight of the Monster living with the hermit, asks incredulously, "Good heavens, man, can't you see?" Though sightless, the hermit does "see"; he is the only character in the entire film who understands the Monster will behave as a human being if so treated. We are never quite certain of the filmmakers' regard for their Saintly Sage (he is an exceptionally overwrought

A blind hermit (O. P. Heggie) lights up a cigar, unaware of the distress he thereby causes for the Monster (Boris Karloff) in 1935's **Bride of Frankenstein,** *directed by James Whale.*

character in his bathos and piety, qualities that led Mel Brooks to satirize him mercilessly almost forty years later in *Young Frankenstein*), but in a film replete with quirky humor and fey figures, many of whom are prone to violence at a moment's notice, *Bride*'s hermit comes across as one of the very few representations of stability, thoughtfulness, and peace in the entire film.

The rise of the Saintly Sage during the latter part of the decade and the early part of the next coincided roughly with the decline of its stereotypic relative, the Sweet Innocent. Chaplin's reversionary *City Lights*, which had also lit the way for Hollywood's return to various disability-humor combinations, kept the image alive and inspired other filmmakers to return, however briefly, to themes of curability.

The juvenile version of the curable Sweet Innocent made a fleeting comeback during the 1930s, most notably in a pair of films based on a Dickens classic: *Scrooge* (1935), produced by Great Britain's Twickenham studios, and MGM's *A Christmas Carol*, a film originally scheduled for production by David O. Selznick in 1935 but not completed until 1938 by Joseph Mankiewicz.[34] Both movies featured that Innocent's Innocent, Tiny Tim. Though the miserly Ebenezer Scrooge tends to call more attention to himself in *Scrooge* than in *A Christmas Carol* (an unsurprising development, given the film's title and the fact that Seymour Hicks, who played Scrooge not only in this film but in a like-titled silent film twenty-two years before, was one of the film's writers), the makers of both films presented Tiny Tim as a poor, lovable waif whose angelic tones and cherubic manner would make him a shoo-in for an opening the Vienna Boys' Choir. MGM director Edwin Marin made certain to objectify Tim through a series of shots early in *A Christmas Carol* by cutting from a close-up of Scrooge's smiling nephew Fred as he lowers his eyes from Tim's face to a shot of the boy's braced right foot, and both films stressed Tim's pitiable and spiritual qualities ("He told me coming home that he hoped that the people in the church saw him because he was a cripple," his father notes to his mother in *Scrooge*, "and if it might be pleasant for them to remember, upon a Christmas day, who made lame beggars walk and blind men to see"). Perhaps sensing that Depression-era audiences would identify strongly with such a character, the filmmakers used the disability as a literal representation of the economic disabilities visited on just about everyone back then.

The Christmas season and its promise of otherworldly rewards also provided a major context for *Heidi* (1937), one of Darryl Zanuck's contributions to the freakshow mania that had engulfed the movie industry. Zanuck, a one-time Warners screenwriter who worked his way up to become production executive under Jack Warner, had broken away from that studio in 1933 to form his own, Twentieth Century Pictures, with Joseph Schenck. Two years later, he and Schenck merged their company with the old Fox outfit to create Twentieth Century–Fox, with Zanuck serving as head of production and Schenck chairman of the board. (William Fox, an important figure in the Cinema of Isolation during the WW I era, had sold controlling interest in his firm to bankers in 1930 after the stock-market crash of 1929 compounded by government antitrust suits almost sank the company.) Formed at a most unpropitious time, Twentieth Century-Fox held a precarious position during much of the Depression and survived it mostly through the strong popularity of its Shirley Temple films. A comparative late-comer to the Cinema of Isolation, the studio quickly emulated its rivals by turning out several movies with disability themes. The stand-out, if it may be called that, featured Zanuck's biggest star in the lead.[35]

Adapted by Walter Ferris and Julien Josephson from Johanna Spyri's famed tale and directed by Allan Dwan—the latter well into his third decade as a movie director—*Heidi* follows the fortunes of its young orphaned title character, played with overdone if characteristic spunk and poutiness by the nine-year-old Temple. Near the beginning of the film, her callous Aunt Dete (Mady Christians) dumps the moppet on her Alps-dwelling grandfather (Jean Hersholt), a recluse feared by the townspeople living at the foot of his mountain home. Lest any audience member should worry, the filmmakers quickly trotted out a Saintly Sage in the form of the elderly Anna (Helen Westley, whose character is actually identified in the credits not as "Anna" but "Blind Anna"), who serves as a veritable fount of expository information on the mysterious grandfather's positive qualities. As with Saintly Sages before and after, her comments carry a strong ring of truth.

Heidi's Aunt Dete is as mercenary as she is uncaring, for she later complicates matters by abducting her curly-topped niece to Frankfurt and "selling" her to the wealthy Herr Sesemann (Sidney Blackmer) as a companion for his wheelchair-using and often isolated daughter Klara, played by Marcia Mae Jones. (Sesemann, a widower, is often out of the country on business.) Heidi resists at first, but she later succumbs and provides Klara with many a merry moment. While there she meets and clashes with Fraülein Rottenmeier (Mary Nash), Klara's humorless governess who Sesemann had hired shortly after Klara injured her back and who more than lives up to the first two syllables of her last name.

Though marred by alternating rounds of under- and overacting, *Heidi* is notable as one of the first sound-era films to show an able-bodied character consciously trying to keep a disabled person—a child, no less—"in her place" for financial gain. (Silent-era moviemakers frequently explored that concept, of course, through the Mother Frochard/Louise relationship in the many adaptations of *Les Deux Orphelines*.) The odious Fraülein Rottenmeier is forever telling Klara things like "Remember what a sick little girl you are," mainly because it's in her interests to keep her dependent; as a tension-charged exchange between Dete and the Fraülein makes clear, she's out of a job if Klara ever walks. As for her malleable charge, Klara's privileged background sets her off from her fellow Sweet Innocents in *City Lights*, *Scrooge*, and *A Christmas Carol*, but like them she is completely guileless, naïve, and trusting—qualities enhanced, if that's the right word, by Jones's flat and uninvolving performance. As Klara confides to Heidi in all bland sincerity, "Fraülein says perhaps I'll never walk again."

Though commendable for its explicit recognition of able-bodied exploitation and relatively balanced in its representation of character gazes, *Heidi* otherwise deals with issues of physical disability in a simplistic and facile way. The ever-optimistic Heidi encourages Klara to try walking, and by the end of the film the other characters and the audience learn that Heidi has been her therapist, working with her every day up to that climactic moment on Christmas Day when, as a gift to her father, Klara walks a few halting steps. As a part of this revelatory process, the movie equates the continuance of a disabling circumstance with a lack of will power (Heidi says on several occasions that Klara could walk if she truly wanted to) and significantly never shows any "therapy" beyond the abortive first attempts.

Its superficial treatment is traceable not only to the original Spyri text but also to a curability drama that Allan Dwan produced and directed in 1920 called *The Scoffer*, about a recalcitrant physician who eventually softens and performs an undisabling operation on a young boy. Following the lead of this earlier film, Dwan centered *Heidi* on an able-bodied person who initially rebels at the notion of having to "service" a disabled child (though in this case the child is ironically older than the main character) but warms up to the calling and helps the youth return to the ranks of the able-bodied. By not only revisiting the topic of curable disabilities but also having a child lead the way back to able-bodiedness, Dwan, who publicly acknowledged his love of happy endings, forced *Heidi* into a level of bathos that verges on parody. Its strong popularity notwithstanding (a major vehicle for Shirley Temple, it helped make her the number one Hollywood box-office draw during the mid–1930s), *Heidi* signaled a declining Hollywood interest in curability themes but only after several other studios explored variations on them.[36]

The traditional Sweet Innocents of *City Lights, Scrooge, A Christmas Carol,* and *Heidi* weren't the only movie characters of the Golden Age to have cures bestowed upon them. A one-time assistant director to Tod Browning named Pandro Berman had been anointed head of production at RKO in early 1934 and one of his first acts was to hire John Cromwell to direct the curability-minded *Of Human Bondage* from a screenplay by Lester Cohen. Based on the novel published by W. Somerset Maugham in 1915, a time when curable themes were becoming a norm in feature films, *Of Human Bondage* is about a medical student and would-be artist named Philip Carey (Leslie Howard) who happens to have a club foot and who happens to be infatuated with—or, to use his phrase, "bound up" to—a lowlife Cockney waitress, Mildred Rogers (Bette Davis). Though the film was not the hit Berman had hoped for (according to studio insider Betty Lasky, the film performed in less than spectacular fashion because "Howard's perfect performance played too forcefully on female heartstrings. The female audience could not forgive the crippled Carey . . . for taking back the despicable Mildred so many times"),[37] *Of Human Bondage* is notable for an adult male playing essentially a

Sweet Innocent role—the delicately featured Howard looks exceptionally doe-eyed throughout much of the movie—and its rather self-conscious handling of his disability.

The heavy-handedness is evident in several respects. In a bit of body fragmentation seldom found in nondisability-related films, *Of Human Bondage* employs shots of people's feet, especially Carey's, in several scenes, starting with a "defining moment" that juxtaposes one of the protagonist's statements—"I have my limitations"—with a shot of his feet that plainly reveals his club foot and special shoe. Composer Max Steiner, whom RKO executives called on to write a new score after preview audiences snickered in the wrong places, added insult to injury by designing a musical motif for Carey that mimics his uneven walking rhythm.[38]

As if these questionable tactics weren't enough, Cromwell and Cohen subjected Carey to several humiliating encounters with ableists, and then couldn't resist throwing in a blame-the-victim piece of business by having a "friend" tell him he's too sensitive about his foot. Following Maugham's lead, they also ascribed a symbolic quality to Carey's disability by associating his limping with his infatuation with the sordid Mildred. After he finally reaches the point of no return in his relationship with her (she has just snarled at him: "D'you know what you are, you gimpy-legged monster? A cripple! A cripple!! A CRIPPLE!!!"), he frees himself of this particular "human bondage" and coincidentally undergoes an operation that cures his foot. Carey then notes to his new paramour that he was "limping through life" during his time with Mildred, but now "that's all over. I'm not limping anymore. My life's all right."

Despite such problematic qualities, it's worth noting that Cromwell remained true to the stylistic and masculinist norms of the day by having cinematographer Henry Gerrard photograph much of the movie from Carey's perspective. As a sympathetic male with a non-ocular disability—a rare combination in those days—Carey is by turns an object to be gazed at and the wielder of the look. It's a potent combination that has the effect of pulling all the audience's identification tendencies toward him.

A film of similar vintage that employed a notably different visual strategy—one that tended to minimize differences among its able-bodied and disabled characters—but strongly reflected ableist assumptions just the same was Universal's *Magnificent Obsession* (1935). Adapted from the Lloyd C. Douglas bestseller by the wife-and-husband team of Sarah Y. Mason and Victor Heerman along with George O'Neil, *Magnificent Obsession* revolves around millionaire playboy Bobby Merrick (Robert Taylor) who indirectly causes two major accidents in the life of a wealthy doctor's wife, Helen Hudson (Irene Dunne): a specially equipped rescue boat, busy tending the drunken Merrick who had fallen overboard during a boating accident, was unable to get to her drowning husband in time; and she herself is struck by a car and blinded after trying to get away from him. Learning of a mysterious "power of infinite goodness" that had guided Helen's late husband, Bobby dedicates his life to her, even to the point of falling in love with her and becoming a brain surgeon so that he might be able to to restore her vision, which he does.

Piloting this spiritual and sentimental affair was John Stahl, who had come to the studio in 1930 after producing a line of shoestring-budgeted films for the Tiffany company and, with James Whale, had become one of the Laemmles' primary directors. Stahl's emerging reputation as a "woman's film" director was borne out not only in the film's storyline (though Stahl was not credited as a screenwriter on this tale of suffering womanhood, he and his scriptwriters extensively rewrote the film on the set)[39] but also its general look. There are few close-ups and very little sense of the customary subjective-objective crosscutting designed to encourage identification with a particular character (the male lead, usually). Instead, Stahl had cinematographer John Mescall, who had also photographed *Bride of Frankenstein* that year, use a highly mobile camera to visualize the film primarily through medium and medium-long shots. The results often show two or more actors at once, typically from the knees up. The equally pretty and glamorous leads are often shown in the same shot and as a result Helen is seldom the pleasurable or pitiable object of Bobby's gaze. The principals come across instead as visual feasts for the audience to consume.

Though *Magnificent Obsession* is formally a most even-handed affair, its cinematography and editing belie the film's various messages. For example, the filmmakers followed the novel's lead by having Helen speak self-demeaning dialogue to maintain her isolation after Bobby has just proposed marriage. Consider the following exchange, overlaid with Franz Waxman's drippy violin music, that Stahl and Mescall rendered through a single medium shot showing the characters in profile:

HELEN: "Marry you? No, I couldn't."

BOBBY: "But why not, my dear? There's nothing to prevent it now."

HELEN: "How can you say that? A blind woman who must be led around by the hand."

BOBBY: "No, that's not true, Helen. Besides, what difference does it make, when I want to hold you by the hand, forever?"

HELEN: "What difference, when everywhere we'd go there'd be glances and whispers? I wouldn't mind for myself, but for you I couldn't bear it. I couldn't have you pitied because of me. I love you too much."

BOBBY: "But, darling, if you love me that's all that matters."

HELEN: "No use, Bob. You're in the world. I'm out of it."

In addition to this distressing perspective that harkens back to the days of D. W. Griffith's *The Roué's Heart* and beyond, *Magnificent Obsession*, like *Heidi*, *Hands Across the Table*, and many other Depression-era films designed as fantasies for financially strapped audiences, employs great wealth as a context. The widow of a well-to-do doctor, Helen later tells Bobby her father's copper mine shares will give her an income for the rest of her life. The newly disabled Helen is thus able to continue her highly privileged lifestyle amid opulent settings, the economic problems inevitably faced by her real-life counterparts hardly a concern.

More disturbing than the economic fantasyland the filmmakers constructed for Helen was the rock-hard ableist belief at the center of the film: the so-called "magnificent obsession." Reduced to its essentials, it refers to a desire on the part of physicians, newly infused with a God-like power, to perform unselfish deeds. As the movie presents it, the most unselfish deed of all—the very pinnacle of quasi-Godliness—is to perform corrective operations. In other words, the movie champions the notion that able-bodied doctors should act like divine surrogates to cure people of their disabilities—to convert them, in effect, with missionary zeal. Quite bluntly, the film reflects the zenith in paternalistic attitudes toward people with physical disabilities. Though the performers play their roles in a sincere and straightforward fashion, the movie is so exaggerated in its values that, like *Heidi*, it borders on parody. (Indeed, a number of latter-day critics have commented on its comedic qualities, though the intentionality of all its humor remains moot.)[40] With the realities of the physically disabled experience finally starting to sink in, filmmakers only occasionally returned to such themes in subsequent decades.

As the movie industry entered the late 1930s, it was ill-prepared for the tumultuous times that lay ahead. Though the industry had matured into a vertically integrated monopoly with a relatively low number of companies controlling movie production, distribution, and exhibition, it nevertheless was wracked by aftershocks from the Depression and years of overspending (to say nothing of the Roosevelt administration's anti-trust suit launched against the eight major Hollywood companies in 1938). Pummeled on all sides by economic forces, it showed little inclination to experiment with progressive depictions of disabled people or any other oppressed group for that matter. In the belief that pumping more money into its productions—borrowed money, in most cases—would be the prime means of turning its fortunes around, it clung ever more tenaciously to the idea of creating extravaganzas based heavily on works, and images, of the past.

Such economic forces played a distinct role in the eventual revival of one of filmdom's most conspicuous Obsessive Avengers: Quasimodo, a role made famous in 1923 by Lon Chaney. The Universal Pictures Corp. had fallen victim to hard times after years of losses, and in 1936 Laemmle *père et fils* surrendered majority control of their studio to J. Cheever Cowdin, president of the Standard Capital Corporation. Ousted as a result, Junior Laemmle began making the rounds in Hollywood as an independent producer and briefly latched on to MGM in 1937. Remembering his old studio's most successful silent-era film, Laemmle worked to convince MGM executives to buy the rights to *The Hunchback of Notre Dame* in the hope he could create a showcase for the combined talents of actor Paul Muni and director William Dieterle, the team responsible for creating several prestigious biographies for Warner Bros. To his delight the studio did make the purchase, but he later learned it did so mainly out of deference to the late Irving Thalberg. (The youthful executive who had produced Chaney's *Hunchback* for Universal in 1923 and sought to remake the film at MGM had died of pneumonia the previous year.) MGM's interest in the project waned almost as quickly as Laemmle's influence at the studio—he was out the door about two months later—and it resold the rights to one of its smaller rivals. It was thus at RKO that that formidable Avenger, Quasimodo, was reborn in modified form.

The climate was right for a company like RKO to take on the big-budget production that *Hunchback* would most likely be. The former head of Paramount sales, George Schaefer, took over as RKO president in 1938 and early the next year announced that his studio would stress big-budget films ("A" films, in industry parlance) over low-cost programmers (the "B" films). The very next week, RKO production head Pandro Berman reported that the biggest picture on his studio's forty-film production schedule that year would be *The Hunchback of Notre Dame*, to be directed by William Dieterle, late of Warner Bros. The studio at one point toyed with the idea of having Lon Chaney, Jr. (né Creighton Chaney) play the role made famous by his father but eventually assigned it to an actor who had been craving it ever since Thalberg discussed the possibility with him in 1934: Charles Laughton, star of MGM's *Mutiny on the Bounty* and portrayer of another Avenger, Captain Hook, in a 1936 London Palladium staging of *Peter Pan*. With a distinguished supporting case that included Maureen O'Hara as Esmeralda, Cedric Hardwicke as Jean Frollo (evidently "Jehan," the name Hugo used in the original 1831 text, didn't seem French enough for RKO), Thomas Mitchell as Clopin, Edmond O'Brien as Gringoire, and Harry Davenport as King Louis XI, filming began on an elaborate set built on RKO's Encino backlot that imitated Notre Dame square at a cost of $250,000.

One of RKO's biggest stars, Laughton wielded considerable influence at the studio (he got Berman to hire his 19-year-old Irish protégée Maureen O'Hara, for example) and was responsible in large measure for the film's freakshow qualities. He had screened and rescreened the Universal *Hunchback* to prepare himself for the role of the bellringer and, entranced by Lon Chaney's performance and general "look," insisted on grotesque make-up for himself and demanded the studio hire Warners' Perc Westmore of the peerless Westmore family of Hollywood make-up designers to create it to his satisfaction. (Jack Warner willingly loaned out his prized artist to RKO for a fee of $10,000.) Laughton and Westmore frequently clashed over details of the make-up design for months but eventually agreed on the overall effect, which to say the least was startling; Westmore's make-up made Laughton look as if half his head were melting, and the actor accentuated the effect by letting his mouth hang open, revealing missing teeth and a protruding tongue, and wildly flicking his "good" eye back and forth. As a means of tantalizing the audience, Dieterle initially presented highly fragmented glimpses of him during the film's fools' festival and then, at the supreme moment, had him pop his head out of a window-like opening in a tight close-up designed to shock both the fools' day onlookers and the movie audience.[41]

Despite Laughton's jolting appearance, which did not go unnoticed by the critics (when the film opened in New York's Radio City Music Hall in late 1939, *New York Times* critic Frank Nugent was moved to remark that "the Music Hall is the last place in the world where we should expect to find a freak show, but *The Hunchback of Notre Dame* is that and little more"), the character he played represented a change in the movie industry's Obsessive Avenger. Strongly influenced by the rise of right-wing extremism in Europe and the outbreak of World War II, the filmmakers altered the relationship of Quasimodo and his mentor by cranking up the fascistic qualities of the worldly Frollo and turning the bellringer into more of a Christ-like martyr than any character Chaney ever played. Dieterle viewed Quasimodo as one of innumerable victims of tyranny, as his comments on the flogging scene suggest: "When Laughton acted that scene, enduring the terrible torture, he was not the poor crippled creature expecting compassion from the mob, but rather oppressed and enslaved mankind, suffering the most awful injustice." As Nazi tanks rolled through Poland during the making of this film, there was little doubt as to the German expatriate's frame of reference.[42]

Several factors were at work here. To avoid running afoul of the Production Code Administration in their handling of Victor Hugo's immoral Dom Claude Frollo, Dieterle and screenwriters Sonya Levien and Bruno Frank followed the same basic strategy of Wallace Worsley and his Universal colleagues sixteen years before by ascribing Dom Claude's malignant qualities to his younger brother, Jean, played with consummate guile in the new movie by Cedric Hardwicke. In the Universal film, the villainous Jehan tries to pin the blame for Phoebus's murder on Quasimodo, an act that sparks the latter's obsession, but in the RKO film Jean tries to incriminate the Gypsy Esmeralda whom he sees as coming "from an evil race." This action throws Quasimodo into a self-sacrificial mode; recalling the woman's kindness (she was the only one to have given him water after his flogging), he bursts into the courtroom and claims he did it. As in the silent film, the bellringer does eventually take revenge on the evildoer by tossing him from the heights of the cathedral after a struggle, but the creators of this new film went out of their way to suggest he was merely instrumental in doing so. While sadly watching Quasimodo's whipping, Dom Claude observes that "if his punishment seems unjust, there is a higher power who watches [pause] and avenges." Ascribing an antifascistic quality to his vengeful actions and attributing them to God's will, Dieterle, Levien, and Frank—unlike their Universal counterparts and indeed Hugo himself—saw no need to dispose of him; they returned instead to the basic theme of isolation by having Quasimodo sit by a Notre Dame gargoyle after the forces of rightist tyranny have been defeated, watch Esmeralda ride off with the poet Gringoire, and wonder aloud why he wasn't made of stone.[43]

At about the time RKO was first putting together its plans for *The Hunchback of Notre Dame*, executives at Universal were taking a closer look at some of their studio's profitable productions of the Laemmle era. After catching wind of the huge profits rolling up for a Los Angeles movie theater showing a triple feature of early-30s horror films—*Frankenstein*, *Dracula*, and *Son of Kong* (1933)—during the summer of 1938, the reorganized studio gleefully re-released *Frankenstein* on a double bill with *Dracula* across the country early that fall to enormous financial returns. Cowdin's Universal management team of president Nathan Blumberg and production head Cliff Work needed no further prompting and began developing a project designed to capitalize on these successes. Refusing to go with James Whale, who by this time was commanding fees that were rising in inverse proportion to his tractability, Blumberg and Work signed a multi-picture deal with journeyman producer-director Rowland V. Lee.

In late 1938, Lee began work on *Son of Frankenstein*, which turned out to be yet another movie featuring a villainous character with a disability. In this film as well as the follow-up *Ghost of Frankenstein* (1942) this most serviceable type of character is Ygor, an evil shepherd who cheated the gallows but emerged with a contorted body as the result of a broken neck. Created by Lee to give work to his friend Bela Lugosi (playing him in both films, Lugosi said of the character, "God, he was cute!"), Ygor learns in the earlier film that the Monster (Boris Karloff, for the third time) survived the *Bride of Frankenstein*-ending explosion that obliterated Frankenstein's castle and befriends him with an intent that has Obsessive Avenger written all over it; he plans to use him as a means of wreaking revenge on the jurors who sentenced him to death. Believing Frankenstein's son Wolf (Basil Rathbone) intends to kill the Monster to restore honor to the family name, Ygor tries to dispatch him but instead winds up on the receiving end of a shotgun blast administered by Frankenstein *fils* himself. A vengeful Monster abducts Wolf's son, but Wolf rescues his son and sends the Monster to a presumed death in a sulphur pit. Significantly aiding him in his quest was Inspector Krogh (Lionel Atwill, who had played *Mystery of the Wax Museum*'s mad lead character back in 1933), the town's one-armed police chief who has a vengeful streak himself; at one point he notes to Wolf that the Monster had yanked his arm from its socket when he was a mere child. "One doesn't easily forget, Herr Baron, an arm torn out by the roots!" he says. In *Ghost of Frankenstein*, directed for Universal by Erle C. Kenton, the now bullet-ridden Ygor blackmails yet another Frankenstein son, Ludwig (Cedric Hardwicke), into transplanting his brain into the body of the Monster, with disastrous results; mismatched blood types render him blind ("What good is a brain without eyes to see?" he rages) and lead to his death moments thereafter.[44]

Though Fritz and Ygor represent disabled characters at their worst, some notable differences do exist between them. As played by the redoubtable Bela Lugosi in both films, Ygor is far craftier and more intelligent than Fritz, and the extent to which he carries out vengeance is much more pronounced. Fritz is content merely to swing a torch or a whip at the Frankenstein monster, but Ygor develops a full-blown plot to do in the people he holds responsible for his condition and almost succeeds in carrying it off. The degree of dependence on able-bodied members of society is also a major difference; Fritz is entirely dependent on Dr. Frankenstein for his livelihood, while Ygor operates quite independently of the Frankenstein offspring, turning to them only when he needs their scientific expertise or tries to do them in. Appearing at a time when the news media were full of accounts of fascist actions overseas, Ygor and his more calculating form of evil in some ways reflected the spirit of the times; the rather low-level form of villainy that Fritz represented in 1931, on the other hand, seemed quite out of place by the end of the decade.[45]

Blumberg and Work put the combined talents of Lee, Karloff, and Rathbone into service again in 1939 with a return visit to that hunchback's hunchback, Richard Crookback, in Universal's answer to Warners' swashbuckling movies of the late 1930s. Produced and directed by Rowland Lee and written by Robert N. Lee, *The Tower of London* starred Rathbone as Richard and Karloff as his devoted (and club-footed) executioner, Mord. The Lees did not hesitate to accentuate their characters' disabilities, but they did so mainly through dialogue. As Richard notes to Mord, "Crookback and Dragfoot. Misfits, eh? Well, what we lack in physical perfection we make up here [points to forehead], eh?," while the wily Anne Neville says, "It'll take more than his misshapen genius to prevail against me." To the filmmakers' credit, they tended not to dwell on the disabilities of Richard and Mord through their visualizations. True to the Obsessive Avenger tradition, however, Richard with Mord as his instrument lie, torture, and murder

A classic example of "a twisted mind in a twisted body" : Bela Lugosi as the evil shepherd Ygor of Son of Frankenstein *(1939) and* Ghost of Frankenstein *(1942).*

to achieve their ends before biting the dust—in this case, the dust of Bosworth Field—courtesy of Henry Tudor and his minions.[46]

Hollywood's construction of freakshow aberrations and other limited characterizations reached a peak of sorts with *The Hunchback of Notre Dame*, the *Frankenstein* sequels, and *The Tower of London*, as well as such money-making vehicles involving short-stature characters as Disney's *Snow White and the Seven Dwarfs* (1938) and MGM's *The Wizard of Oz* (1939). Even *The Terror of Tiny Town* (1938), independent producer Jed Buell's exploitative musical western employing a cast made up entirely of small-stature actors, turned a profit. In some ways these films corresponded with commonly held views of disabled people, as Meinhardt Raabe, an actor of short stature who played *Oz*'s Munchkin coroner, discovered when he tried to find an accounting job after the movie. "Prejudice was very outspoken at that time," he remembered. "The chief accountant at a major corporation didn't even look at my resumé. He said: 'You have no business here. You belong in a carnival!'" Though the tendency of majority society and its filmmakers to perceive disabled people as freakish continued into the 1940s and indeed has never quite disappeared, some signs suggested changing interests and concerns. *New York Times* critic Frank Nugent spoke for a generation of filmgoers when he opined that Laughton's Quasimodo belonged "back in the simpler days of the movies; he's a bit too coarse for our tastes now." Some significant developments in rehabilitative care for people with physical disabilities had developed during the 1930s (most notably, a movement focusing on professional counseling and psychotherapy, and another advocating self-help on a grassroots level), and Hollywood moviemakers began recognizing these phenomena albeit in their typically sluggish and oblique way.[47]

Their acknowledgment initially took the form of compelling characterizations of soldiers disabled by war. One of the first such treatments to emerge during the latter stages of Hollywood's sideshow era was Samuel Goldwyn's production of *The Dark Angel* (1935), a remake of his similarly titled 1925 film. Co-written by Lillian Hellman and directed by Sidney Franklin, *The Dark Angel* presented Fredric March as the WW I veteran who competes with another (Herbert Marshall) for the affections of their childhood sweetheart (Merle Oberon) and who develops severe self-doubts after being blinded in the war only to have them allayed by his friends. In 1939, William Wellman produced and directed *The Light That Failed*, an adaptation of Kipling's novel, for Paramount. Having admired Ronald Colman's work as the blinded vet in Goldwyn's silent-era *The Dark Angel*, Wellman recruited the British actor to play Dickie Heldar, an artist who eventually goes blind after wartime service in the Sudan and lives a relatively mobile and independent life with friends and associates. Though the films do contain ruinous messages—*The Dark Angel* has its blinded vet conducting ruses to make his fiancée think he's dead and, failing that, that he can see, while Heldar turns suicidal—they otherwise have a strong ring of truth and sensitivity, and one cannot help but think the WW I veterans who helped construct the films—among them, March, Marshall (who lost a leg in the war), Wellman, and Colman—made the difference.[48]

Such films were hard to find amid Hollywood's Golden-Age freakshows, but, as Frank Nugent and those who shared his views would soon discover, more progressive depictions of physically disabled people were on the way. The rising tide of World War II began exerting a strong influence on the movie industry, and it wasn't long before the Cinema of Isolation, led ironically by the studio that had created the most damage during the 1920s and 30s, began spinning off in a new direction.

5 / the road to rehabilitation

Though Universal had given it a run with such films as *All Quiet on the Western Front*, the *Frankenstein* cycle, *The Tower of London*, and *Magnificent Obsession*, Metro-Goldwyn-Mayer emerged from the 1930s as the premiere film company to deal with themes of physical disability. It was a distinction hardly worth trumpeting. Under the guidance and philosophy of Irving Thalberg, MGM had built a solid reputation for creating lavish entertainments, but unfortunately a number of them were designed at the expense of characters with physical impairments.

After Thalberg died in 1936 and the remaining films bearing the mark of his influence were completed, MGM entered a new phase of disability-related movie-making quite unlike the one it was leaving behind; the studio's films now featured intelligent, resourceful, and strong-willed individuals who treated their disabilities in a relatively incidental way. If MGM was trying to atone for its Thalberg-era excesses, it was doing so at a time when the world for very understandable reasons was paying renewed attention to issues of physical disability. Beginning in the late 1930s, MGM's construction of disabled civilians—"Civilian Superstars" who harkened back to the heroes of the singular *The Little Cripple* and *Chelsea 7750*—coincided with the events that led up to World War II as well as the war itself, and the resulting films, along with the prototypical *The Dark Angel* and *The Light That Failed*, paved the way for the entire industry's return to the topic of disabled war veterans during the mid-1940s. Leading this surge of improved depictions was a charismatic actor and one-time director who defined the new image in life as well as the cinema.

The movie career of Lionel Barrymore stretched from the early 1910s through 1953, the year before his death. Elder brother of John Barrymore, he was a favorite actor of the two directors who did the most to shape the Cinema of Isolation up to that time, D. W. Griffith and Tod Browning, and occasionally appeared in their movies of physical disability. Joining the MGM stable of stars in 1926, he like his colleague Lon Chaney remained associated with the studio the rest of his life. "His loyalty to me never wanes," he said simply of Louis Mayer, "and that is why I remain loyal to him."[1]

Barrymore faced a major turning point in 1938 after an accident aggravated the ever-worsening arthritis in his legs. Despite extreme discomfort (during the making of that year's *You Can't Take It with You*, director Frank Capra noted that Barrymore, whose "body was a mess," needed hourly shots to ease the arthritic pain),[2] Barrymore did not slow down his acting career. Indeed, rival studios took his disablement as a sign they might be able to weaken MGM's grip on his services as a performer. Consider, for example, the words of independent producer David O. Selznick:

The only reason we were able to get [a possible loan-out of] Lionel Barrymore is that he is now unfortunately crippled to such an extent (and I am sorry to say that I understand it is probably permanent) that he is unable to walk, and such appearances as the poor fellow is able to make in the future are going to have to be in a wheel chair . . . which naturally limits the number of things he can do, thereby making him more available than he was a few months ago when MGM was keeping him busy fifty-two weeks a year.[3]

Though MGM continued to keep him busy, Barrymore did increase his work outside the studio, acting in films for Warners, Selznick's various enterprises, and Liberty Films, the latter an independent firm established by directorial luminaries Capra, William Wyler, and George Stevens after World War II. Anchoring one end of his post-disablement roles was the misanthropic tightwad Henry Potter who makes life miserable for the hearing-impaired George Bailey (James Stewart) and everyone else in the Capra-directed *It's a Wonderful Life* (1946). "No one else would do," wrote Capra, who had his writers specify Potter's wheelchair-using status in their script.[4] At the other was the role of James Temple, the victimized Florida hotel owner who along with his daughter-in-law (Lauren Bacall) and his late son's commanding officer (Humphrey Bogart) are held captive by gangsters during a hurricane in *Key Largo* (1948), the John Huston–Richard Brooks adaptation of Maxwell Anderson's play. In all, Barrymore would go on to play roles of considerable variety and depth in more than three dozen movies after he began using a wheelchair in 1938.

The moviemakers with whom Barrymore worked pursued several strategies to accommodate his impaired mobility. An early idea came from Barrymore himself when he suggested his character in *You Can't Take It with You*, Grandpa Vanderhof, wear a cast and use crutches. Though Capra later downplayed Barrymore's disabled status in publicity material (the actor appeared in nine photographs in a promotional brochure for the film, none of which showed him using crutches), he and his screenwriter Robert Riskin modified the character easily enough by having Grandpa state early in the film that he sprained his leg after taking up his granddaughter's challenge to slide down a bannister. Such an alteration affected Riskin's original conception of the character only minimally: "There's nothing peculiar about him. Just a man of sixty. On the street you wouldn't give him a second glance." A far more common tactic was to have Barrymore perform while using his wheelchair, a solution elegant if radical in its simplicity.[5]

The idea surfaced during the planning stages for a low-budget MGM series in which Barrymore would be participating: the "Dr. Kildare" film cycle of the 1930s and 1940s. Basking in the success of their "Andy Hardy" series, B-film producer Joe Cohn and writer-turned-executive-producer Carey Wilson had been casting about for a new series idea—preferably one that captured the spirit of the father-son relationship that had worked so well in the prior series—when Wilson came across a magazine article called "Whiskey Sour." Written by Max Brand (né

Henrik Faust), it told the story of an idealistic doctor fresh from medical school and his crusty mentor. Wilson and Cohn contacted Brand, and together they began developing storylines that were eventually turned into scripts by Harry Ruskin and the ever-resilient Willis Goldbeck, the former protégé of Rex Ingram, Herbert Brenon, and Tod Browning who later directed several Kildare installments himself.

Cohn and Wilson chose as main director Harold S. "Harry" Bucquet, a Briton who had labored in obscurity for years as an assistant director before piloting several "Crime Does Not Pay" short subjects that MGM had begun producing in 1935. The Kildare medical series represented Bucquet's first opportunity to direct feature films, and, his Christian Science convictions notwithstanding, he eagerly accepted the assignment. For the pivotal role of the stern yet supportive Dr. Gillespie he wanted Barrymore, who was his own "Gillespie" in a way; thirteen years Bucquet's senior, Barrymore directed several movies during the late 1920s and early 1930s and often employed Bucquet's services as an assistant.

With Lew Ayres of *All Quiet on the Western Front* fame slated to play the title character, Bucquet was about to begin work on the first of the Kildare series when the producers discovered Barrymore had started using a wheelchair. The studio front office at first wanted Barrymore off the project but, with strong support from the actor, Bucquet prevailed. "Harry did a lot for me," Barrymore said. "I'll play that part for him if I have to do it in a wheel chair." Having no desire to deprive themselves of Barrymore's formidable talents, Wilson, Ruskin, and Goldbeck duly modified Gillespie, and thus was born one of filmdom's most memorable characters with a physical disability. Barrymore co-starred in all fifteen of the Kildare films, commencing with *Young Dr. Kildare* in 1938 and concluding with 1947's *Dark Delusion*, and remains best remembered for his portrayal of the series' cantankerous diagnostician.[6]

Barrymore was as colorful on the Kildare set as on the screen. "He was the most caustic person I've ever known," remembered Ayres. "He was in his wheelchair, and he would be wheeled into the center of the room, and he could hold court, and he could talk back to anybody." At times he appeared to relish using the device, according to Ayres: "He also said, 'There's a marvelous thing about being in a wheelchair: I don't have to light any lady's cigarette, I don't have to take my hat off, I don't have to do anything, really. . . . I don't even have to push the wheelchair.'" In between filming sessions, Barrymore as a self-acknowledged "wheelchair salesman" fielded countless letters from disabled people worldwide who admired his movie work and wanted to know more about the type of chair he used.[7]

The series was hardly perfect in its rendering of Gillespie and his use of the chair. It rarely showed the doctor's life outside the hospital and the accessibility and prejudicial problems he might thus encounter, for example, and the filmmakers occasionally had the other characters acknowledge his use of a wheelchair with varying degrees of insensitivity. In *The Secret of Dr. Kildare* (1939), for instance, a hospital administrator refers to Gillespie as "an inspiration to the whole medical profession" but in the same breath notes that "his legs are hopelessly crippled," while in that same year's *Calling Dr. Kildare*, the title character devalues other people with disabilities by praising Gillespie as "the greatest diagnostician in the world today. Why, if anyone else couldn't walk, they—they'd fold up and quit. He's pushed his way right up the top in a wheelchair." The filmmakers kept such slams to a minimum, however, and generally handled Gillespie's use of a wheelchair in a low-key, unobtrusive way.

In addition to the Kildare series, a pair of 1940 MGM films likewise took the incidental route by focusing on the life of Thomas Edison, who had lived with severe hearing loss throughout his adult life ("You will have to speak louder," he told J. Stuart Blackton, then a reporter for the New York *Evening World*, in 1896, "I am stone deaf ")[8] and who had died in 1931 at the age of 84. Directed by Norman Taurog and starring Mickey Rooney, an exuberant 20-year-old who had recently eclipsed Shirley Temple as Hollywood's biggest star, *Young Tom Edison* centered on the inventor's youthful escapades and demonstrated how his ebullience and ingenuity went largely unaffected by an injury that permanently damaged his hearing. (The film shows a railroad conductor pulling him up by his head onto a moving train, leading the boy to note matter-of-factly that "something snapped in my ear," and later boxing the youth hard on the ears for accidently starting a fire on board).

Despite Rooney's popularity and the movie's generally high production values, *Young Tom Edison* did not do well at the box office, leading some at the studio to wonder about the potential of its planned follow-up. Their fears were allayed several months later by the respectable financial returns of the Clarence Brown-directed *Edison, the Man*, a film featuring Spencer Tracy in the title role

Amid varied roles in a movie career that spanned more than four decades, crotchety Dr. Leonard Gillespie of MGM's "Dr. Kildare" series was Lionel Barrymore's most famous character as well as his personal favorite. Barrymore poses here with frequent co-star Lew Ayres.

and dwelling mostly on the great inventor's struggle to perfect the light bulb. Both films took the highly sentimentalized route (portraying Edison as a lover of milk and apple pie, they showed nothing of the inventor's penchant for launching patent-infringement lawsuits and attempts to monopolize the early movie industry) and were guilty of grossly minimizing his disability and others' reactions to it. After the accident and brief medical follow-up in *Young Tom Edison*, the filmmakers did little beyond having the Edison character occasionally cup his hand to his ear and say "Hmm?" or "Beg pardon?" By the second half of *Edison, the Man*, there's no reference to his hearing loss at all. On the positive side, the films, like those of the Kildare series, did not define the character primarily in terms of his disability and showed that intelligence, strength of character, and resourcefulness are far more significant than the loss of a physical function.

One of the scriptwriters for *Young Tom Edison* and story contributors for *Edison, the Man* was a 35-year-old from New Jersey named Isadore "Dore" Schary. Wishing to extol the virtues of a prominent figure who had lived and worked in the Garden State for many years, Schary contributed significantly to the films' romanticized and heroized treatment of their lead character. A close associate of Spencer Tracy (they appeared together in a 1930 Broadway production of *The Last Mile*, and he later wrote the screenplays for such Tracy vehicles as 1937's *The Big City* and 1938's *Boys Town*), Schary believed the MGM star would be the perfect person to embody the heroic qualities he was trying to convey and pressed Brown and producer John Considine for his casting as the mature Edison. (Tracy, whose teenaged son John had been born profoundly deaf, readily agreed to the role and went through extensive preparation for it.)[9] Largely as a result of Schary's work on these films, Louis Mayer appointed him the executive producer of the studio's B-film unit—the division that oversaw the Kildare series, among other productions—the following year. During the subsequent movie-executive career that would span more than two decades, Schary, a well-known Rooseveltian dedicated to liberal causes, would return repeatedly to the concept of treating characters with physical disabilities as heroes. He was already on his way toward becoming a major figure in the Cinema of Isolation during World War II and the postwar era.

An early film that came within his purview was *Eyes in the Night* (1942), the first of two MGM entries based on novels by Baynard Kendrick featuring a visually impaired detective. Kendrick, who served in World War I with the First Canadian Battalion, first encountered veterans blinded during the war while in Europe. He was so inspired by the men and their abilities (such as one fellow's skill at detailing the military careers of others by running his fingers over their insignia) that after the war he wrote several novels featuring a blind shamus named Duncan Maclain who made efficient use of his other senses to solve crimes. Among the appreciative readers of Kendrick's mystery novels was Edward Arnold, a Hollywood actor whose own father had been blind for the last twenty-five years of his life. Intrigued by the novelist's treatment of the impaired protagonist, Arnold approached a receptive Schary about making several movies based on his books.

One of the results was the modestly budgeted *Eyes in the Night* (1942), adapted from Kendrick's 1941 novel *The Odor of Violets*. Directed by an up and coming 35-year-old named Fred Zinnemann and starring Arnold as Maclain, it details the actions of the detective and his trusty seeing-eye dog Friday as they use their combined abilities (including judo moves, punches, and dog bites) to solve a murder and also break up a Nazi spy ring in Connecticut. By the time its sequel—*The Hidden Eye*, directed by Richard Whorf and again starring Arnold—appeared in 1945, Schary had already departed MGM to work for David Selznick's Vanguard company. While there, he would find yet another opportunity to heroize a physically disabled person.[10]

MGM was not alone in its interest in constructing charismatic and intelligent civilian characters with physical disabilities. The Warner Bros. studio shared that interest, but its two main disability-related films of the time—*The Sea Wolf* (1941) and *Kings Row* (1941)—lapsed into melodramatic conventions and exhibited a starker quality than MGM's.

The Sea Wolf was the latest in Warners' string of highly popular seafaring movies, and the studio had not hesitated assigning its directing chores to the man who had helmed most of them: the Hungarian émigré Michael Curtiz. Brought over from Europe by Harry Warner too late to participate in *The Sea Beast*, Curtiz nevertheless went on to direct the German-language version of *Moby Dick* (1931), *Captain Blood* (1935), and *The Sea Hawk* (1940) and had demonstrated his versatility in other ways, such as directing the studio's rare excursion into horror, *Mystery of the Wax Museum*. With Curtiz, the studio assured itself of another slickly crafted tale of the high seas.

Edward Arnold, who convinced MGM to allow him to star as blind sleuth Duncan Maclain in Eyes in the Night *(1942) and* The Hidden Eye *(1945).*

A holdover from Hollywood's freakshow era (it initially went into development during the mid-1930s), *The Sea Wolf* was also the latest in a long line of movie adaptations based on Jack London's 1904 novel. His tale of a domineering ship's captain whose intermittent blindness becomes permanent had been a favorite of filmmakers for decades (Hobart Bosworth's 1913 production, in which London himself played a small role, competed with a Balboa Amusement version and was followed by others produced by Famous Players-Lasky in 1920, Ralph W. Ince in 1926, and Fox in 1930), and this latest incarnation gained added resonance in the wake of recent world events. In earlier movie versions as well as the novel, Wolf Larsen is by turns charming and brutal, his strong philosophical streak frequently tempered by bouts of cruelty. As represented by Curtiz and screenwriter Robert Rossen in the Warners film, he does share with MGM's Gillespie, Edison, and Maclain figures a high degree of intelligence and strength of character, but other forces were at work that modified him significantly; the Warner Bros. powers-that-were perceived the iron-fisted captain who goes blind as the perfect symbol for the fascism that had engulfed the world and decided to downplay his gentler, philosophical side. The movie's star, Edward G. Robinson, frankly described Larsen as "a Nazi in everything but name," a result of production head Hal Wallis's decision to coarsen the character. As Wallis wrote to the film's producer, Henry Blanke: "Let's at all times keep Eddie in character. Keep him hard, tough, and don't let him become too much of an intellectual." Audiences evidently agreed with this approach, for they made *The Sea Wolf* one of the most popular films that year.[11]

Another 1941 Warners production, one equally vivid in its use of physical disability, is a film remembered for its melodramatic abundance: *Kings Row*, based

"A Nazi in everything but name":
Wolf Larsen (Edward G. Robinson)
in the midst of another blind spell
in Warner Bros.' The Sea Wolf.
Copyright © 1941 Vitagraph Inc.

on Henry Bellamann's similarly titled novel which graphically contrasted the pleasures and horrors of small-town life in a midwestern community during the 1890s. After the studio had acquired the rights to the quirky book, the film's associate producer, Wolfgang Reinhardt, was quick to express his concerns about its unsavory qualities to Wallis:

> I prefer not to kid myself or you regarding the enormous difficulties that a screening of this best seller will undoubtedly offer. As far as plot is concerned, the material in *Kings Row* is for the most part either censurable or too gruesome and depressing to be used. The hero finding out that his girl has been carrying on incestuous relations with her father, a sadistic doctor who amputates legs and disfigures people willfully, a host of moronic or otherwise mentally diseased characters, the background of a lunatic asylum, people dying from cancer, suicides—these are the principal elements of the story.[12]

Reinhardt's reservations were right on target; as correspondence from the period reveals, the studio had to do backflips to get Casey Robinson's adapted script past the movie industry's self-regulatory organization, the Production Code Administration. As orchestrated by freelance director Sam Wood, the resulting movie was considerably diluted, but, abetted by the superb cinematography and musical score supplied respectively by James Wong Howe and Erich Wolfgang Korngold, it reached the level of what *Time* movie critic James Agee called "potent, artful cinema" despite its "difficult and ugly" central narrative.[13]

Kings Row revolves around Parris Mitchell, Randy Monaghan, Drake McHugh, and Cassandra Tower (Robert Cummings, Ann Sheridan, Ronald Reagan, and Betty Field), childhood chums who grow up to face major conflicts with their elders. A major turning point occurs after the devil-may-care Drake, reduced to poverty by a crooked bank president, gets a nighttime job at the local railyard. As he waves to a passing train while carrying a coffee pot, a stack of heavy tiles suddenly collapses behind him, simultaneously pushing him under the train wheels and partially burying him. A close-up of the coffee pot sliced in two by the wheels effectively symbolizes Drake's fate.

Shocked when he awakens to discover his legs have been amputated (he screams "Where's the rest of me?," the now-famous line that became the title of Ronald Reagan's 1965 autobiography), Drake becomes an embittered soul. His friend Parris, about to take a job at a prestigious psychiatric school in Vienna, writes a letter to Randy and through voice-over narration indicates his concern about Drake's "ghastly, terrible tragedy" and its psychological effects: "The psychic injuries strike at his pride, his initiative, and we shall have to save them if we're to save Drake." He further notes that Drake must find a job or something else outside himself to enhance his self-reliance: "The helpless invalid complex must be avoided at all costs."

With Parris's encouragement and financial backing, Randy convinces Drake to enter the real estate business. The twosome meet with success, but Drake's attempts at humor ("Not bad for a girl and an old cripple piled up in bed," he jokes to Parris in reference to their good fortune) mask psychological problems; he refuses to use a wheelchair, rarely goes downstairs, and wants Randy to promise they'll never move out of that house. In order to shock him out of his depression, Parris tells Drake there's a strong possibility the double amputation may have been unnecessary; the surgeon, Dr. Henry Gordon (Charles Coburn), may well have performed it solely for revenge on Drake, who once was engaged to his daughter. After being informed of this, Drake breaks into defiant, almost hysterical laughter and then says, "That's a hot one. Where did Gordon think I lived, in my legs? Did he think those things were Drake McHugh?" As the film draws to a close, Drake says to Randy with mounting enthusiasm, "What was it you wanted, honey? To build a house? We'll move into it in broad daylight. And we'll invite the folks in, too. For Pete's sake, let's give a party. I feel swell!"

The rapid and facile way by which Drake moves from self-pity to an almost manic level of glee mainly represented the studio's desire to impose something of a happy ending on a series of relentlessly morbid tales. Ronald Reagan clearly did not share his character's "Where did Gordon think I lived" kind of optimism. While discussing his difficulties preparing for and playing the critical moment when Drake discovers the loss of his legs—"the most challenging acting problem in my career," he called it—Reagan dismissed Drake as "only half a man" and suggested that "a whole actor would find such a scene difficult; giving it the necessary dramatic impact as half an actor was murderous." An impaired person himself (he sustained permanent damage to his auditory nerve after someone fired a pistol close to his right ear during a 1930s moviemaking session), Reagan nevertheless did consult with wheelchair-using people as well as physicians and psychologists to gain a better sense of how to play his character's post-disablement scenes.[14]

Though notably weak on some rehabilitation issues, *Kings Row* remains an important film in several respects. It was one of the first films to deal in a reasonably sensitive way with the psychological aspects of physical disability and to suggest that romance and careers for physically disabled people did not have to be what so many prior movies had passed off as unthinkable. Such attributes were soon to become norms within the Cinema of Isolation.

The Civilian Superstar image that MGM and, to a lesser extent, Warner Bros. began cultivating shortly before America's entry into World War II represented a major step away from the Obsessive Avenger stereotype that the industry had constructed so often to suggest a male with a disability. Appearing at a time when newspapers were once again filling with stories about people permanently maimed as a result of war, the films bearing this image reflected a predominantly conservative sensibility (Dore Schary's participation to the contrary, many of the filmmakers were dyed-in-the-wool conservatives, such as Sam Wood, Norman Taurog, Clarence Brown, Charles Coburn, Casey Robinson, even Lionel Barrymore, and included reactionary-in-the-making Ronald Reagan). True to that spirit, they celebrated the individual who relies heavily on his intelligence and sheer strength of character to see him through. Though often ignoring such important issues as rehabilitation, access, and prejudice, these movies nevertheless represented the most positive image of physically disabled males up to that point in the sound era. And they were only a beginning.

By the time the U.S. entered the war in late 1941, the American movie industry was once again in turmoil. As a result of the escalating hostilities in Europe and Asia during the late 1930s, the dominant Hollywood companies had witnessed massive shrinkages in their overseas revenues and had come under attack from congressional isolationists for creating movie propaganda on behalf of markets the studios wanted to protect, principally Great Britain.[15] In addition to the troubled foreign operations, which accounted for a sizable portion of their total earnings, they now faced the prospect of losing some of their most bankable actors, directors, writers, and other studio personnel to military service. The list of Hollywood denizens whose services the studios temporarily lost to the war effort would eventually include such prominent figures as Clark Gable, Henry Fonda, Robert Montgomery, Victor Mature, Glenn Ford, Tyrone Power, James Stewart, Ronald Reagan, Douglas Fairbanks, Jr., William Holden, Jack Warner, Darryl Zanuck, Frank Capra, John Ford, John Huston, John Sturges, George Stevens, and William Wyler. In all, about one-sixth of Hollywood's workforce of 240,000 would go on active duty at some point during the war.[16]

Despite these setbacks, the studios would soon discover they had embarked on one of their most prosperous periods ever. Americans' personal earnings rose steadily and, with consumer goods becoming scarcer by the day, civilians took their newfound disposable income and turned to the movies in record numbers. The revenue generated by domestic movie consumption not only erased the studios' formidable overseas losses but also made the five year period starting with 1942 and ending with 1946 the most profitable ever for the industry. Amid the action-packed war dramas and patriotic-tinged escapist fare that saturated theater screens during that time, films of physical disability began playing a noteworthy part.

One of the first moviemakers to experiment with disability issues within the context of the new conflict was Alfred Hitchcock. Brought over to the United States by independent producer David O. Selznick to direct the Oscar-winning *Rebecca* (1940), the Briton quickly gravitated toward wartime material but from a highly idiosyncratic direction. Having linked comedy with war-related disability issues at least once before (his 1936 British film *Secret Agent* featured a touch of slapstick involving a one-armed WW I veteran struggling with an empty coffin),

Hitchcock gave vent to his bizarre sense of humor once again through several early–1940s movies with physical disability themes.

Produced by *Mutiny on the Bounty*'s Frank Lloyd for Universal and written by Peter Viertel, Joan Harrison, and Dorothy Parker, *Saboteur* (1942) follows the exploits of Barry Kane (Robert Cummings, just coming off *Kings Row*), a youthful paragon of honesty and virtue forced into flight after being accused of torching the military aircraft plant where he works. In a scene reminiscent of *Bride of Frankenstein*, the refugee stumbles on an isolated cabin in the woods and there meets an overwrought character in the form an elderly, music-loving Saintly Sage. Though the Sage gently mocks Barry's lack of musical prowess, his blindness proves no detriment to detecting the hero's good qualities ("I can see intangible things: for example, innocence") and he encourages his skeptical niece Patricia (Priscilla Lane) to help Barry find the real saboteur.

Hitchcock's disability perspective took a sharp turn after Barry and Patricia stow away on a bus after their car has broken down; they soon learn the vehicle is occupied by the "freaks" of a traveling circus. The latter characters—a fat woman, a bearded woman, a thin man, Siamese twins, among others—are generally sympathetic to the fugitives except for their leader, a fascist-minded fellow of short stature called "the Major" (Billy Curtis) who wants them thrown out of the circus caravan. Populated mostly by able-bodied actors and quite different in spirit from the unsettling *Freaks* ten years before ("I remember people roaring with laughter throughout that whole scene," François Truffaut told Hitchcock, a reaction far removed from the ones usually elicited by the Browning work), this episode was largely the work of humorist Dorothy Parker but nevertheless contained touches unmistakably Hitchcock's.[17]

The director's comic sense turned considerably darker in *Lifeboat*, a movie launched in 1943. Written by Jo Swerling from a short story by John Steinbeck and produced by Kenneth Macgowan for Twentieth Century–Fox,[18] this famous film centers on a group of Allied civilians sharing a rescue boat with a German surgeon named Willy (Walter Slezak) whom they later learn is the Nazi U-boat officer who sunk their freighter. Among the characters is a seaman named Gus (William Bendix), whose leg was severely injured during the torpedoing and who, in a classic bit of Hitchcockian irony, had been a champion jitterbug dancer back in the states. His leg develops gangrene, and several of his fellow survivors tell him the leg must come off. He initially refuses, believing his dance-loving girlfriend will leave him when he returns: "What good's a hepcat with one gam missing?" he queries. "If my leg goes, Rosie goes." The others convince him his condition is life-threatening, however, and he relents.

Mindful of the Production Code Administration's warnings on portraying surgical operations, Hitchcock followed a strategy that harkened back to *The Big Parade* and *All Quiet on the Western Front*: while Willy works on the leg offscreen, a passenger takes Gus's boot and tosses it toward the camera, which tilts down to "look" at it in close-up before the shot fades out. During the period following the leg removal, however, the director couldn't resist echoing the literal fragmentation of Gus's body with a bit of cinematic fragmentation that reflected his characteristically perverse sense of humor; shortly after offering a close-up of two other passengers' feet as they play footsie with one another, he presented a medium shot of Gus sitting by the edge of the boat facing left unaware of the twosome's wiggling feet that appear in the lower right-hand part of the frame behind him. Hitchcock followed his ironic view of the world through to the end by having Willy, who saved Gus's life through the operation, push the seaman overboard to his death after the latter observes him hoarding fresh water. When the other passengers learn what has happened, they savagely assault Willy, one of them using Gus's boot to beat him.[19]

As movies focusing on the Allied effort continued flooding theaters, a number of filmmakers began constructing portrayals of injured military men. Appearing at a time when the federal government modified the rehabilitation legislation passed during the WW I era to include physical restorative services,[20] the initial movies—*Song of Russia* (1943), *Thirty Seconds Over Tokyo* (1944), *Since You Went Away* (1944), and *The Enchanted Cottage* (1945), among them—were heavy with sentiment and patriotism and, in a classic example of lag, didn't go terribly far in exploring the vets' post-disablement lives. Nevertheless they did endow their disabled characters with an aura of acceptability and formed the basis for a trend that would flourish during the first few years of the postwar era. The so-called "Noble Warrior" had returned.

The first of the MGM entries, *Song of Russia*, is best remembered for its pre–Cold War sympathetic views of the Russians. Directed by one-time St. Petersburg resident Gregory Ratoff and scripted by Paul Jarrico and Richard Collins, it tells the story of an American conductor named John Meredith (*Magnificent Obsession*'s Robert Taylor) who marries a Russian musician (Susan Peters) in the midst of the war. A brief scene that contributed strongly to its pro-Russian views consists of a nighttime encounter between Meredith and a Russian soldier (Konstantine Shayne) out on patrol despite having lost a leg. Meredith asks him why he's still on active duty, and the soldier, super-patriotic soul that he is, responds by noting his two good arms and eyes, and ability to shoot. Meredith concludes their conversation by saying he finds the soldier so inspirational that he wishes more light would illuminate his face so he could see "what courage looks like." Taking up only a few minutes of screen time, this embodiment of total dedication to defending Mother Russia wasn't much different from the disabled soldiers of the early World War I movies that depicted missing limbs or blindness as little more than badges of honor.

Screenwriter Dalton Trumbo and director Mervyn LeRoy created a more extended example of the Noble Warrior for MGM the following year in a tribute to America's Chinese allies sanctioned by the Office of War Information. Unlike

Song of Russia, whose patently absurd storyline was not lost on even the most rabid of pro-Allied movie critics, *Thirty Seconds Over Tokyo* was based on an actual event: an air raid on April 18, 1942, masterminded by Lt. Col. James H. Doolittle (played by in the movie by Spencer Tracy, late of *Edison, the Man*), in which sixteen American B-25s bombed Tokyo and other cities, inflicting minimal damage on their targets but generating untold morale-boosting value. Trumbo worked specifically from a 1943 bestselling account of the raid by Ted Lawson, a pilot whose plane, the "Ruptured Duck," ran out of fuel and went down in Japanese-occupied China after the raid. One of America's first badly wounded military men to return to the states during WW II, Lawson included a number of touching details about his disablement that Trumbo and LeRoy heightened in their film.[21]

Disability issues soon surface after the Ruptured Duck crash-lands; Lawson (Van Johnson) is severely injured and learns after Chinese partisans rescue him that he must have a gangrenous leg amputated. A U.S. military physician performs the surgery but with rapidly weakening anaesthesia, and Lawson passes out. (In one of several heavy-handed moments in this film, an ensuing dream sequence shows an able-bodied Lawson chatting happily on the phone to his wife while two other men are cutting down a tree in the distance behind him. The tree falls, and the sequence blurs out.) After the operation, a member of the Chinese resistance offers him the gift of a pair of silk slippers, to their mutual embarrassment. The most poignant moment in the movie, based on another incident in Lawson's book, is the scene in which the wheelchair-using veteran first sees his wife Ellen (Phyllis Thaxter) after the mission; though he has repeatedly vowed to avoid her until after he has received an artificial leg, he is overcome by the sight of her (Ellen, by the way, is a suitably adoring military spouse by WW II Hollywood standards, exhibiting no misgivings whatsoever) and tries to stand only to fall to the floor.

Despite its pronounced manipulative qualities and money-making success, *Thirty Seconds Over Tokyo* proved no match for a film produced by David Selznick that same year. After gaining international acclaim for the back-to-back successes of *Gone With the Wind* (1939) and *Rebecca*, Selznick had been on the prowl for a worthy follow-up, preferably one with a war-related theme. He considered possibilities ranging from a sequel to *A Star Is Born* to a movie based on Adolf Hitler's *Mein Kampf* before settling on an adaptation of Margaret Buell Wilder's *Since You Went Away*, a three-hanky novel serialized in the *Ladies' Home Journal* about the women of a well-to-do family awaiting the return of the male head-of-household from war overseas. Selznick purchased the rights to the book and selected as director John Cromwell, who had demonstrated an aptitude for such sentimentalized material in *Of Human Bondage* a decade before. The cast members would eventually include Claudette Colbert as Anne Hilton, Jennifer Jones and Shirley Temple as her daughters Jane and Bridget, and, in a bit role that made no reference to his disability, Lionel Barrymore as Reverend Jamieson.

Selznick, who wrote the screenplay for *Since You Went Away* himself, took pains to make the movie more relevant to average moviegoers by making the family less upscale than Wilder depicted it and updating the story to 1943. "We are including episodes dealing with food rationing and other typical, timely problems," he wrote, and one such "problem" he and Cromwell developed into a subplot was the premise of working with injured vets on the homefront.[22] Wanting to do something for the war effort, Jane pressures her mother into letting her become a nurse's aide. Anne agrees, and soon Jane is helping disabled veterans with their rehabilitation. The women later encounter Emily Hawkins (Agnes Moorehead), a stuffy blue-blood who thinks it's "a revolting idea" for Jane to work as a nurse's aide:

> EMILY: "I simply feel that well-brought-up young girls shouldn't be permitted to have such intimate contact with all sorts of . . ."
> JANE: "All sorts of boys who've lost their arms and legs? They're young, too—lots of them. But they weren't too young for that, Mrs. Hawkins, and I don't think breeding entered into it, either."

This sharply worded conflict among able-bodied types is only one small part of *Since You Went Away* (Selznick characterized the movie as "a jigsaw puzzle [with] literally more than a dozen major story threads to pursue to some kind of a conclusion") but it did help establish what many perceived as the "proper" mainstream attitude toward disabled vets. It's important to point out *Since You Went Away* is primarily about the Hilton women and told almost exclusively from their perspective. Though Selznick and Cromwell treated the vets—played by actual disabled veterans—with great sympathy, they gave them very limited screen time and ultimately reduced them to pitiable objects for the Hiltons and the audience. The noteworthy first instance of this strategy occurs more than halfway into the film when Anne, traveling in a train's crowded dining car, sits next to a sailor and overhears a bit of his conversation with a businessman. A conductor blocks the camera's view of the sailor, but as the latter begins to speak ("Oh, I'm in no hurry. I've got plenty of time from now on") the camera mimics Anne's look as it pans to the sailor and then tilts down to reveal his missing arm. *Since You Went Away* went on to become an overwhelming success, due no doubt to its timely subject matter and excessive sentimentality abetted by Selznick's marketing acumen (while designing the film's promotional campaign, Selznick consulted pollster George Gallup "as to how great an extent I should advertise myself in connection with the film" and learned that about two out of three moviegoers knew who he was). One can only assume the film's paternalistic attitudes and objectifying qualities contributed to that popularity.[23]

As for John Cromwell, he found his directorial services in greater demand as a result of his work on *Since You Went Away*. Immediately after completing the Selznick film, he returned to his home studio, RKO, where producer Harriet

Parsons, daughter of famed critic-*cum*-gossip Louella Parsons, assigned him to direct another highly sentimental movie, *The Enchanted Cottage*. The newly hired Parsons set the project in motion in 1943 when she came across Arthur Wing Pinero's 1922 play of the same name among the studio's undeveloped properties. She put together a treatment that impressed current RKO production head Charles Koerner but to her chagrin he turned the project over to writer-turned-producer Dudley Nichols with the hope of getting the great French cinéaste Jean Renoir to direct. Only after her mother's long-time rival Hedda Hopper published a strongly worded rebuke to RKO did Parsons regain control over the project, and she and Cromwell eventually brought it to the screen in April 1945.

Audiences hardly found *The Enchanted Cottage* a ground-breaking film. Pinero's play, a maudlin affair about a disabled WW I veteran, had first been adapted in 1924 by Inspiration Pictures, the same company responsible for 1921's *Tol'able David*, as a vehicle for company co-owner and resident star Richard Barthelmess. In attempting to update the story for modern audiences, screenwriters DeWitt Bodeen and Herman Mankiewicz set the bulk of the story in 1941 and turned the embittered Oliver Bashforth character (renamed a less aggressive sounding "Oliver Bradford" and played by Robert Young) into a WW II combat flyer shot down over Java who returns home with an injured arm and a badly scarred face. He's eventually delivered out of his depression by a rather plain young woman named Laura Pennington (Dorothy McGuire), piano-playing WW I veteran John Hillgrove (Herbert Marshall) blinded after going down in flames over the Argonne, and the magical spell exerted by the title building that enables its occupants to see beauty beneath the surface.

Although Parsons and crew changed dates and references in *The Enchanted Cottage* to suggest a modern story, the resulting film had little to do with the realities of WW II, especially the rehabilitation programs then underway. *New York Times* critic Bosley Crowther claimed the movie "contemporizes the subject in peculiarly obsolete terms. . . . It is hard to believe that a depressed veteran's entire recuperation would be allowed to devolve upon a frustrated girl, an intuitive blind man, and a honeymoon cottage possessing charm." Among the film's hoarier aspects was the type of character represented by John Hillgrove. With lines such as "In place of these two eyes that are gone, I have a hundred invisible ones that see things as they really are" and "Sometimes I feel that it was before the Argonne that I was blind and that it's only now that I see," Hillgrove is a rather ripe example of the Saintly Sage, and Marshall, who had been cultivating the image off-screen as well as on, played it to the hilt.[24]

One of the few salient aspects of *The Enchanted Cottage* was the fact that the actor who played its Saintly Sage had actually been disabled as a result of WW I service. Born in London in 1890, Marshall had lost a leg while fighting in the Great War but maintained an active career as a stage and movie actor from the 1920s all the way up to 1965, the year before his death. At the time of *The Enchanted Cottage*, he had been an RKO contract player for about nine years, having been recruited to lend his considerable marquee value to that studio's growing list of "A" films. He typically played suave, urbane leading men with mature appeal, but unlike his great contemporary Lionel Barrymore he usually hid his disability from the camera. (Indeed, Marshall and Barrymore appeared together in David Selznick's *Duel in the Sun* in 1946, the former passing for an able-bodied person and the latter using a wheelchair.) *The Enchanted Cottage* was a rare film in which Marshall played a physically disabled character though ironically the disability was different from his own.

By turns mawkish and hawkish, the wartime disability films eventually found themselves drowned out by the jubilation that swept the nation following V-J Day in August 1945. In their place were movies that repositioned the disabled-vet characters, giving them greater prominence and focusing specifically on rehabilitation and post-rehabilitation issues. The first wave of these latter films, initiated during the final stages of the war but released after it, were among the first entries in Hollywood's great age of social consciousness, when many filmmakers tempered their liberal sentiments with the realization that issues such as the "veteran problem," racism, anti-Semitism, alcohol abuse, and malignant social institutions were for the time hot box-office material.

One of the first films to place the concerns of a disabled vet at center stage was *Pride of the Marines* (1945), written by Albert Maltz and directed by Delmer Daves for Warner Bros. In development since 1943 and scheduled to coincide with the third anniversary of the Marine assault on Guadalcanal, a major turning point in the war's Pacific theater,[25] *Pride of the Marines* was released in August 1945 and told the story of a real-life soldier named Al Schmid (played by John

Herbert Marshall, debonair RKO star who, despite a severe war injury, typically played able-bodied characters in plays and movies from the 1920s until well into the 1960s.

Garfield), an average kind of guy who enlists in the Marines after Pearl Harbor, is blinded by a Japanese grenade at Guadalcanal, and returns to the U.S. an embittered man before family and friends convince him to shuck his self-imposed isolation. Much of the movie's impetus was provided by Warners producer Jerry Wald, famous for turning newspaper and magazine articles into timely movies (he first learned of Schmid from a *Life* story) and who, according to *New York Times* reporter Thomas Pryor, "produced more and better war movies than any other individual" in Hollywood.[26]

Pride of the Marines contains a number of commendable points. A veritable paean to teamwork, it argues that an individual can't make it in this world alone, that retreating into a shell won't work. It also addresses the issue of discrimination that invariably comes blind people's way by having Al's Jewish friend Lee Diamond (Dane Clark) draw parallels to the kind of prejudice he has faced:

> Sure, there'll be guys who won't hire you even when they know you can handle a job. There's guys that won't hire me because my name is Diamond instead of Jones. 'Cause I celebrate Passover instead of Easter. Do you see what I mean? You and me, we need the same kind of a world; we need a country to live in where nobody gets booted around for any reason.

Despite the filmmakers' good intentions, they presented and empowered the blind Al in problematic ways. For Lauri Klobas, the aspect "most annoying about the portrayal was the actor's wooden stare and unmoving head. Two minutes after having the grenade tossed in his face, he stopped moving his head in the direction of sounds."[27] They did endow Al with the power of the look in a dream sequence, but it is a nightmarish, punishing affair filled with solarized imagery, locomotive montages, and music played in reverse, the highlights of which are Al operating a machine gun one bullet at a time synchronized to "stop it, stop it, stop it" and later seeing a double of himself as a blind civilian.

In addition to these questionable strategies, the moviemakers made little effort to have Al partake of the rehabilitation services available to recently blinded vets. Like Oliver in *The Enchanted Cottage*, Al basically goes it alone and, as the movie suggests, is himself responsible for his isolation from family and friends. As Dana Polan put it in his trenchant analysis of the film, "Al's blindness is finally not so much a problem; the problem is the way Al reacts to that blindness as something he feels sets him apart from other people. . . . Al wrongly internalizes his blindness as an ultimate problem and not as the minor setback that the film argues it is." Al is quick to deny his blindness at every turn ("Don't call me blind," he tells Lee. "I don't see so good yet, that's all. Don't you ever call me blind again") and while doing so remains "blind" to other things: his heroism (he insists he was an ordinary guy whose blindness now makes him less than ordinary), his love for hometown girlfriend Ruth (Eleanor Parker) and vice versa, and his dependency on other members of society in general. After receiving emotional bombardments from Lee, Ruth, and his nurse Virginia (Rosemary DeCamp), Al finally sees the light not only figuratively but literally as well; at the end of the film, his sight starts to come back. It's as if he's being rewarded for these realizations through the restoration of his sight. Klobas summed it up best when she wrote that "*Pride of the Marines* was more of a wartime morale picture built upon a real-life hero than an honest depiction of a man facing a life with a visual limitation."[28]

The production of disabled-vet films continued apace with *Till the End of Time* (1946), an RKO movie co-created with David Selznick's Vanguard company. Written by Allen Rivkin from the Niven Busch novel *They Dream of Home* and directed by Edward Dmytryk,[29] the film was produced by Dore Schary, who had allied with Selznick three years earlier following a dispute with MGM and had become known for encouraging screenwriters and directors to explore socially relevant material. *Till the End of Time*, which sports a later narrative point of attack than *Pride of the Marines* (unlike the latter, its vets are already back on U.S. soil at the start), follows the intertwined tales of three former Marines: all-American boy Cliff Harper (Guy Madison), a cowboy gambler with a plate in his head named Bill Tabeshaw (Robert Mitchum), and an ex-boxer who lost both legs in the war, Perry Kincheloe (Bill Williams). The film focuses primarily on the able-bodied Cliff—indeed, he is in almost every scene—and dwells at length on his relationship with Pat Ruscomb (Dorothy McGuire). When it finally gets around to dealing with the minor character Perry, the audience discovers him to be an embittered 21-year-old who refuses to wear his prostheses and who pours his energies into training his younger brother for the pugilistic life. (When questioned on this latter issue, he responds, "Why not? Got no life of my own left.") Considered "a problem" by several characters, Perry hesitates to break out of his shell of self-pity when Harper phones him to help with Bill, who's been experiencing severe headaches stemming from his war injury. He's stirred to action only after his mother alludes to the post-disablement successes of Franklin Roosevelt, not coincidentally an inspirational figure for producer Schary. Viewed from his mother's perspective, Perry emerges triumphant from his bedroom wearing his military dress uniform and both prostheses, and walking with two canes. For the first time in the film, Dmytryk positioned his camera to look up at him from a slightly low angle, bestowing a certain heroic quality on the vet as he walks toward it. Perry later demonstrates he's lost none of his talent for fisticuffs by landing haymakers on several neo-fascists during a bar fight.

Though hailed by *Variety* as "an achievement for Dore Schary from a production standpoint," *Till the End of Time* was seriously hampered by a low budget and mediocre acting by its pretty-boy lead. Its most memorable aspect had nothing to do with Perry or even veteran issues in general: the film's score and particularly its title song, based on Chopin's Polonaise in A-flat Major. Selznick himself thought it "a bad picture; but largely because of the song, it rolled up a very, very big gross."[30]

RKO, which released *Till the End of Time* in July 1946, ironically began competing with itself several months later when it distributed *The Best Years of Our Lives*, the most famous of the postwar films to include disabled-vet issues among its concerns. *Best Years* began its own life as the brain child of independent producer Sam Goldwyn, a fixture of the movie industry ever since he and brother-in-law Jesse Lasky formed a forerunner to Paramount back in 1913. Goldwyn, who had dealt with issues facing disabled WW I veterans in *The Dark Angel* (1925) and its 1935 sound remake, had been casting about for movie ideas in mid–1944 when a thought occurred to him: with fifteen million war-weary veterans sooner or later returning to the United States, an examination of America and its values during the anticipated postwar era might strike a responsive chord with audiences. He paid MacKinlay Kantor $12,500 to develop a fifty-page screen treatment, believing his credentials as a journalist, Air Corps veteran, and novelist whose works celebrated mainstream American values would make him a suitable candidate for such an assignment. Unbeknownst to him, however, Kantor possessed an independent streak that had made him unpopular with other moviemakers (Hitchcock cashiered him after he labored a mere two weeks on the *Lifeboat* screenplay), and when the writer returned to Goldwyn months later the project he submitted was far removed from what the producer expected: a 434-page manuscript written in blank verse about a trio of veterans learning to adjust to new stateside roles. Eventually published as a novel, *Glory for Me* was strong enough to stand on its own merits (it was eventually touted by the Literary Guild) but was hardly in a form Goldwyn could use. After Kantor's follow-up attempt at

Dore Schary (right), here chatting with Guy Madison on the set of Till the End of Time, *was an executive whose movies often presented relatively progressive depictions of people with physical disabilities. Courtesy Museum of Modern Art/Film Stills Archive.*

a screenplay proved a failure, Goldwyn hired Robert E. Sherwood, the multiple award-winning playwright, FDR confidant, and former associate director of the Office of War Information, to create a script based on the novel. Goldwyn assigned the directorial duties to the Alsatian-born William Wyler, who as a lieutenant colonel in the U.S. Air Forces had just returned from active duty.

Sherwood and Wyler began serious work on the screenplay in December 1945. They maintained Kantor's key concept of three veterans returning to their home town after the war but puzzled over how they might portray the disabled vet as Kantor drew him in the novel: a soldier whose battlefield injury left him spastic. Wyler, himself a disabled veteran (awarded an Air Medal for participating in five bombing missions over Germany, he endured significant hearing loss while serving in Great Britain, France, and Italy as chief of the Special Photographic Unit of the 8th and 12th Air Forces), wanted to include a severely injured character in the movie but both he and Sherwood found Kantor's particular construction problematic. According to the director, it "would always seem as though it was acted." [31]

His head abuzz with possible treatments of the character, Wyler took time off from the script to attend a war bond rally in Hollywood. While there he saw a film of about twenty-five minutes that the U.S. Army Signal Corps had produced under the direction of the Veterans Administration. Originally designed to facilitate the rehabilitation process, *Diary of a Sergeant* featured a paratrooper named Harold Russell who had lost both his hands during a demolition accident while on maneuvers in North Carolina. It closely paralleled Russell's own experiences, even to the extent of having the character hold Russell's rank and pinning his accident on the same date as Russell's: June 6, 1944—by coincidence, D-Day. Though Russell did not speak in the film (the film's makers used an offscreen narrator to reveal the character's thoughts to circumvent Russell's thick Boston-area accent), *Diary* showed him essentially playing himself as his character moved from early self-doubts to learn how to use artificial hands and eventually embark on a post-rehabilitative life full of promise.

Russell's performance so impressed Wyler that he borrowed a copy of *Diary* from the rally organizers and showed it to Goldwyn. Knowing from experience about disabled characters played by able-bodied actors (a relative and one-time underling of Carl Laemmle, he had assisted on the Lon Chaney production of *The Hunchback of Notre Dame* while in his early 20s), Wyler insisted Russell would be perfect in the role. "No matter how good a performance an actor gave of a man without hands, an audience could reassure itself by saying, 'It's only a movie,'" he wrote. "With Russell playing Homer, no such reassurance was possible." The very next day, Goldwyn's office contacted Russell and persuaded him to come to Hollywood to test for the film. Goldwyn, Wyler, and Sherwood had found their disabled vet. [32]

Goldwyn's peers in the industry were quick to question his decision. Recalled Russell: "The 'professionals,' whoever the hell they are, told Sam: 'This thing will never go. With all your good intentions, you just can't show an amputee in a motion picture. This movie is not good box office.'" Perhaps in response to this criticism, Goldwyn had his flacks soft-peddle Russell's disabled status in pre-release publicity. A two-page *Time* advertisement, part of which was designed to resemble a news story, noted Russell's participation in the yet-unreleased film but made no mention of his disability: "Harold Russell, a onetime Army sergeant, had appeared before a movie camera only once before—in an Army Signal Corps film. However, Harold Russell is as American as apple pie and Mr. Goldwyn felt somehow that he would be unforgettable." Yet if Goldwyn harbored any doubts he never let them be known to the cast and crew.[33]

Eschewing acting school at Wyler's request, Russell fleshed out the role of Homer Parrish, a sailor who had lost his hands as a result of a fire on board his attacked ship. In the company of fellow veterans Al Stephenson (Fredric March,

Harold Russell (left) played Homer Parrish, one of three World War II veterans who find the road to readjustment a bit rocky in The Best Years of Our Lives *(1946), produced by Sam Goldwyn. Though Fredric March (right) and Dana Andrews (center) played able-bodied characters in this film, March had coincidentally essayed a disabled World War I vet in Goldwyn's* The Dark Angel *in 1935 while Andrews would play a veteran blinded after his war service in 1947's* Night Song.

who played the blinded WW I vet in Goldwyn's 1935 production of *The Dark Angel*) and Fred Derry (Dana Andrews), all three of whom are homeward bound to the fictional Boone City, he shows dexterity in lighting a match and tells them he can do such things as dial a telephone and drive a car. In the presence of his family and that of his girlfriend Wilma Cameron (Cathy O'Donnell), however, Homer becomes quite awkward as they often stare at his hooks or turn away from him. Wilma later tells him her parents want to send her away from Boone City in the hope the young people will forget each other, and Homer, reflecting a classic bit of ableism, offers to withdraw from the relationship. He even goes to the extent of showing her how "helpless" he becomes after taking off his prostheses before going to bed.

Though the film's bedtime-preparation scene is misleading in an important respect—Russell was indeed able to put his prostheses on by himself, an ability his screen counterpart lacked—Wyler perceived it as the major turning point in Homer's story and one that required a certain deftness of touch to avoid raising Production Code Administration hackles and sensationalizing Russell's appearance. As he explained,

> I had to decide whether or not I could do such a scene on the screen. There were delicate problems in bringing a boy and girl to a bedroom at night, with the boy getting into his pyjama top, revealing his leather harness which enabled him to work his hooks, and finally, taking the harness off. After discussions with Bob [Sherwood], we solved the problems, and felt we could play the scene without the slightest suggestion of indelicacy, and without presenting Homer's hooks in a shocking or horrifying manner. As a matter of fact, we felt we could do quite the opposite, and make it a moving and tender love scene. Wilma meets the test squarely, makes Homer see that she doesn't mind the hooks, and what she feels for him is not pity, but love.[34]

To the director's credit, the film seldom follows the usual Hollywood pattern of showing its disabled person from an able-bodied perspective through subjective-objective crosscutting. Wyler encouraged his cinematographer Gregg Toland to use his celebrated deep-focus photographic techniques to show Homer and others in the same shot, often through triangular compositions (i.e., three characters in each shot given relatively equal weight). People in the movie do stare often at Homer's prostheses, but Wyler and Toland's visual strategies rarely prompt the audience to identify with them—or with Homer, for that matter. Though Homer, Al, and Fred are clearly its main foci, the film has the rather refreshing effect of encouraging audiences to contemplate the characters instead of alternately identifying with them or objectifying them.

Despite some negative criticism over the years (chiefly for its avoidance of social issues insoluble beyond the individual level)[35] and the few flaws noted above, *The Best Years of Our Lives*, with its stress on abilities and its acknowledgment of the discrimination that inevitably comes disabled people's way, is one of the most forthright, sensitive, and honest depictions of the physically disabled experience in movie history. *Best Years* was also a major box-office success and won seven Academy Awards: Best Picture, Director, Screenplay, Actor (Fredric March), Supporting Actor (Harold Russell), Musical Score, and Editing. The Academy also awarded a special second Oscar to Russell "for bringing hope and courage to his fellow veterans" and another to Goldwyn in the form of the Irving Thalberg Memorial Award for his "consistently high quality of production" over the years.[36]

Despite the various limitations of *Pride of the Marines, Till the End of Time*, and *The Best Years of Our Lives*—modest ones, in the case of the latter—these films mirrored postwar concerns in a number of respects. For starters, they captured the sense of disorientation experienced by many veterans, regardless of ability level. Dmytryk's assessment of his own film suggests this quality: "It had to do with lonesomeness; it had to do with the people who came back and suddenly found themselves with nothing to do. They had been used to doing a certain kind of thing for four years and now they didn't know what the hell they were doing. They were nowhere. They were in a lost world, you know, which can be psychologically certainly very, very disorienting, and not too many people were paying attention to that, and it was something worth talking about."[37]

Veterans with disabilities faced additional issues, a number of which also found their way into the movies. George K. Pratt, an M.D. who served as a psychiatric examiner in the U.S. military during the war, wrote in 1944 that one of the most distressing adjustment problems facing disabled veterans was "their doubt of acceptance by the family. No matter how securely they felt entrenched in the love of parents or wife before the injury, they cannot wholly rid themselves of the horrid fear that perhaps these persons will now find them repulsive and that as a consequence their affections may cool. Such handicapped men may also feel this way about their first meeting with former friends and employers."[38] The first round of post–WW II movies featuring disabled vets clearly reflected such concerns.

Conceived while the war was still being fought, *Pride of the Marines, The Best Years of Our Lives*, and *Till the End of Time* are understandably obscure on postwar job-related prospects for their disabled vets, but the general reassurances that Al, Homer, and Perry received were consistent with American postwar society's favorable treatment of its injured veterans. "As never before, the disabled veteran looking for opportunity has both public and private facilities that were not dreamed of only a few years ago," wrote Charles Hurd in 1946. "The government naturally is at the center of this activity [with its pension plans, rehabilitation assistance, and half-billion dollars' worth of new V.A. hospitals], but there is hardly a community or an industry that is not cooperating in the top priority of the veterans' program: giving the disabled the break they have earned."[39]

An outstanding example of this trend was a program offered to disabled veterans (and to disabled civilians shortly thereafter) by the University of Illinois at Champaign–Urbana in 1948. Its services included educational support, wheelchair-accessible housing and transportation, training in daily living activities, and peer counseling. Although its admission policy differed from that typically followed by the Independent Living centers and programs that developed during the early 1970s (it denied admission to those potential students unable to live on a day-to-day basis without assistance), the University of Illinois program was an early model for the IL movement.

Significant as such developments were, they were largely obscured by an undertow of uncertainties that pulled at the nation during the immediate postwar period. The optimism and high spirits that marked the end of the war quickly gave way to a complex of concerns: among them, the growing tensions of the Cold War and life in the atomic age, the crisis of leadership among Western societies, the shift in the domestic economy, veterans' readjustment problems, the continuing revelations of the Nazi death camps, and memories of the worldwide theater of destruction that had just culminated in the carnage of Hiroshima and Nagasaki.

A number of historians have interpreted the postwar years as an age when mass-media practitioners and other opinion leaders, faced with issues overwhelming in their enormity and intricacy, moved away from the causes of social problems that had been their prewar focus (best illustrated by a trilogy of films directed by Frank Capra—*Mr. Deeds Goes to Town*, *Mr. Smith Goes to Washington*, and *Meet John Doe*—that examined the corrupting influences of Big Government and Big Business) to the victims. The Cinema of Isolation illustrated this "age of the victim" in two distinct ways. *Pride of the Marines*, *The Best Years of Our Lives*, and *Till the End of Time*, early examples of what Edward Dmytryk called "a type of film in which a character overcomes a mental obstacle in order to conquer a physical handicap resulting from fate or misfortune," reflect the victimization that occurs when a person's life is shattered by a disabling accident. Other movies, made by people eager to represent the moral uncertainties of the period, represented victimization of a chillingly different sort: characters who had come to terms with their disabilities long before the story begins but who now find themselves threatened or tormented by able-bodied forces.[40]

In the years immediately following the war, a number of filmmakers began exploring the darker aspects of human behavior through what has since become known as film noir. So labeled by latter-day French critics, film noir is a genre-transcending type of movie that frequently offers a bleak, despairing view of life. Typically awash in night scenes and deep shadows, representatives of film noir are stylistically as dark as their nihilistic central characters who maneuver their way through a world by turns uncaring and hostile. Filmmakers preoccupied with such concerns occasionally crossed them with disability themes, leading to highly unsettling results.

The most infamous of the films noir to depict a physically disabled person as a victim of able-bodied designs is one that ironically affords very little screen time to that person: *Kiss of Death* (1947). Written by Ben Hecht and Charles Lederer and directed by Henry Hathaway for Twentieth Century–Fox, this gangland tale centering on a criminal who tries to go straight (Victor Mature) contains a sequence involving a psychotic killer named Tommy Udo (an eyebrowless Richard Widmark) who verbally harasses a wheelchair-using mother of a "squealer" he's been assigned to find. The final images of the sequence remain as shocking as they were in 1947; after calling the woman a "lying old hag" and binding her to her chair with a lamp cord, Udo wheels her out of the apartment and shoves her down a long flight of stairs. Fox production head Darryl Zanuck, who liked the film but hated its title (he believed it would lead audiences to think it was a horror film—a freakshowish genre temporarily out of vogue in Hollywood), clashed with Hathaway during the movie's production over this sequence's violent conclusion. The director, however, had little difficulty justifying the brutality. "Darryl forbade me to shoot it," he recalled, "but when he saw it in the picture he changed his mind. The point was that it would make the audience realize the depths of which Widmark was capable when he later threatened to get back at Victor Mature through his family."[41]

A more extended example of the trend, *The Lady from Shanghai* (1948), featured the acting, writing, directing, and producing talents of the fabled Orson Welles. Known as a "genius" whose films seldom made money, Welles had finally scored a modest financial hit with *The Stranger* (1946), a movie he both starred in and directed. Using a connection to Columbia Pictures provided by his wife Rita Hayworth, a major Hollywood star then under contract to appear in one more film for the studio, Welles approached Columbia production chief Harry Cohn to take on his next project and cited *The Stranger* as proof of his ability to create moneymaking movies. The proposed production, which would star Hayworth and Welles, was an adaptation of a Sherwood King novel called *If I Die Before I Wake*, a work to which Cohn already owned the screen rights. Needing another hit from Hayworth before her departure and believing Welles capable of delivering, Cohn assented to the project and authorized Welles to begin filming, which he did in late 1946.[42]

Recalling *Drums of Love* and other silent era works that positioned disabled males as duped Father figures, the resulting *The Lady from Shanghai* focuses on a highly charged triangle consisting of Arthur Bannister (Everett Sloane), a brilliant criminal lawyer who walks with canes and leg braces; his much younger wife, Elsa Bannister (Hayworth); and Michael "Black Irish" O'Hara (Welles), a roving young seaman whom Elsa lures into a murder plot against her husband. Welles insisted that Arthur be disabled (Everett Sloane complained about the painful braces before filming began and tried to get out of wearing them, to no avail), and he did so presumably to enhance the character's sense of vulnerability and suggest his presumed impotence. With these important exceptions, however, Welles didn't make a big deal of the lawyer's disability. He accentuated Arthur's impaired use of his legs on only a handful of occasions, mainly at the film's beginning and end. He introduced Arthur on a note of high irony by having a car attendant tell Michael the glamorous Elsa is married to a world-famous attorney and conclude with "Gee, some guys have all the luck." The film then dissolves from Michael's profile to the film's first view of Arthur: an objectifying shot of his legs as he walks with braces. At the end of the film, Elsa and Michael encounter each other in an amusement park's hall of mirrors after it has become clear Elsa wants the seaman to take the fall for her husband's planned murder. A pair of hands holding two canes momentarily emerge from the shadows; it's Arthur, of course, who says he knows about Elsa's plans. In one of Welles' justly famous set-pieces, wife and husband shoot it out—mirrors shattering all about them—and mortally wound one another, leaving Michael the sole survivor of a particularly messy ménage à trois.

Welles completed *The Lady from Shanghai* by early 1947, but Cohn, concerned about the image of his star and appalled by the general murkiness of the movie's narrative ("I'll give $1,000 to anyone who can explain the story to me," he said),[43] began tinkering with the film and held up its release for about a year. When it finally appeared as the second half of a double bill with virtually no publicity, *The Lady from Shanghai* thudded at the box office. Generally well-regarded by latter-day film noir aficionados and much acclaimed for its visual pyrotechnics, it vanished from theaters in 1948 almost as abruptly as it appeared, leaving contemporary audiences scant opportunity to consider its disabled paternalistic character.

While Welles was putting what he thought were the finishing touches on his soon-to-be shanghaied film, the studio that had severed relations with him earlier in the decade—RKO—was preparing a film with a remarkably similar-sounding premise: a youngish fellow who knows his way around a boat meets and is mesmerized by a mysterious beautiful woman married to a brilliant older man with a physical disability. In particular, *The Woman on the Beach* (1947), directed and co-written by Jean Renoir during the latter stages of his "American period," focused on a psychologically disturbed Coast Guard officer named Scott Burnett (Robert Ryan) and his relationships with Peggy Butler (Joan Bennett), an enigmatic woman who lives on a beach that he routinely patrols, and her husband Tod (Charles Bickford), a famous painter recently blinded.

Unlike the Welles film, however, *The Woman on the Beach* detours in a most unproductive direction: smitten by the woman, the officer spends an inordinate amount of time and energy trying to determine if her husband—who has behaved snappishly toward her but in a friendly manner toward him—is faking his blindness as a part of some scheme. To plant doubts in the minds of the audience, Renoir often photographed and edited Tod and Scott's exchanges through the classic Hollywood style of alternating close-ups, a tactic that gives Tod a simulation of the gaze. Renoir even took the virtually unprecedented step of having a character acknowledge the socially constructed nature of disability (when Scott asks if his cane is helpful, Tod replies, "Not really. People always expect a blind man to carry a cane and I hate to disappoint them"), but he did so mainly to sow further doubts about the character's lack of visual acuity. Though the movie is strong in its noirish qualities—the dark and brooding lead character, the photogenic woman ambiguous underneath her flashy trappings, the claustrophobic sense that permeates the film—it ultimately deviates from the genre in that none of the characters has committed any premeditated criminal activity; it's all in the head of the lead character. The audience eventually learns Tod is indeed blind—Peggy had caused her husband's sightlessness when she had thrown a glass at him and achieved an effect greater than intended—and Scott has needlessly tormented him with his various "tests," some of them life-threatening.

Preview audiences reacted badly to this "much ado about nothing" film, sending Renoir back to the editing bench and even leading him to recall the principal cast members. "I was the first to advise cuts and changes. I asked for a writer as collaborator, so as not to be alone," he said. "I reshot numerous scenes, being very prudent. About one-third of the film, essentially the scenes between Joan Bennett and Robert Ryan, and I put out a film that was neither flesh nor fish, that had lost its raison-d'être. I'd let myself be too influenced by the Santa Barbara preview."[44] Renoir's extensive reshooting and re-editing resulted in a highly fragmented movie only seventy-one minutes long and barely better than the original. It remains a humiliating conclusion to his American sojourn.

The Woman on the Beach was one of at least three films with physical disability themes RKO released that year. Another that illustrated the postwar sense of victimization but from a non-noir angle was *Night Song* (1947), a contrivance-laden affair about a fur- and jewel-bedecked socialite who falls in love with an embittered blind pianist. Created by the same people mainly responsible for *The Enchanted Cottage*—principally producer Harriet Parsons, director John Cromwell, and story adaptor DeWitt Bodeen—*Night Song* more than matched their earlier film in its sentimentalized perspectives. Not only was it a variation on the impoverished blind musician type of movie popular during the early 1900s, but it also featured an element becoming rapidly outmoded in the Cinema of Isolation: the miracle cure.

Though the filmmakers created *Night Song* during World War II's aftermath, they curiously declined to explore the situation of a veteran disabled by the war; they went out of their way to indicate that Dan Evans (Dana Andrews, one of the stars of *The Best Years of Our Lives*) had come through the war without a scratch but had lost his vision in a freak accident shortly after returning stateside. Soured on life as a result, Dan squanders his concerto-writing talents in favor of playing in a San Francisco dive. Recognizing his prodigious musical talents but receiving his scorn, Cathy Mallory (Merle Oberon), who no doubt had just come out of a theater showing *Magnificent Obsession*, weaves a fanciful fabrication; she pretends to be a relatively destitute blind person as a means of getting close to him (in the tradition of so many other hoodwinked blind characters, Dan doesn't recognize her voice) and, after she learns he needs $5,000 for an eye operation but won't take charity, she also invents a bogus music-composition contest for him to win: first prize, $5,000 and a performance in Carnegie Hall. After Dan undergoes surgery—a quick and complete success, of course—the audience's disbelief, which has been suspended precariously throughout the movie, comes crashing down when Artur Rubenstein and Eugene Ormandy, playing themselves in the film, just happen to like his "award-winning" music and perform it in Carnegie Hall with the New York Philharmonic. Moviegoers couldn't help but gag on the extent of Dan's good fortune: the love of a beautiful woman who uses her big bucks to intervene, a vision-restoring operation, the sight of his name next to Mozart and Beethoven's on a Carnegie Hall billboard, and his composition performed by world-class musicians on a national radio broadcast.

Night Song's laughable situations reveal only part of the filmmakers' ableist bias. Another, darker aspect was their equation of blindness with death when they had Dan's friend Chick Morgan (Hoagy Carmichael) describe the pianist's post-surgery behavior to Cathy: "You see, the guy was blind. He was in a big black grave as big as this world, and he suddenly came to life and things fell in place again." In addition, the filmmakers photographed much of *Night Song* from Cathy's perspective and had Dan serve as the object of her gaze in many of the movie's pre-surgery portions. Their decision to empower the Oberon character was not surprising in some respects—the film was produced by a woman, its director had long been known for incorporating female perspectives in his films, and its cinematographer, Lucien Ballard, happened to be married to Oberon—but an unfortunate upshot was the all-too-typical objectification of a physically disabled character. (Indeed, even Dan refers to himself in objectified terms: "I'm Exhibit A around here," he says sardonically. "I'm the blind piano player.") All this changes once the operation restores Dan's sight. Not only does he become a far more likable character, but the filmmakers began filming a few scenes from the newly empowered Dan's perspective. By the end of the film, he is her equal in the gaze-sharing department.

Hopelessly dated in its perspectives, *Night Song* wasn't the worst of the 1947 RKO films to deal with disability. A mere sixty minutes long, *Dick Tracy's Dilemma* was one of a series of quickly made, low-budgeted films based on Chester Gould's famous comic strip character and an unfortunate throwback to the days of *Richard III* and *Hook and Hand*. Not specifically a noir (its title character, played by Ralph Byrd, is far too much of a clean-cut, honest character with a specific sense of right and wrong for the film to qualify fully), this crime drama nevertheless is suffused with such noir-like qualities as harshly lit urban night scenes and a littering of seedy characters devoid of any sense of morality. The prime example of the latter is Steve Michel (Jack Lambert), a member of a fur-thievery gang. A hulking, grungy brute, he is yet another villainous character defined almost exclusively by disabilities; bearing a conspicuous limp and a hook for a right hand, Michel is known by one and all as "the Claw."

Within moments after the movie introduces him, Michel uses his prosthesis to no good purpose; he conks a fur warehouse's nightwatchman on the head with it several times, splitting his skull. An associate later berates him for escalating their criminal activity to include homicide: "All because of you and that itchy hangnail. You can't use your brains, can ya? 'Stead of your brains, you gotta use that hunk of steel like, like some stupid animal." His nemesis Tracy later learns he incurred both limb injuries while engaged in hijacking and bootlegging during Prohibition ("A Coast Guard cutter rammed him and he lost his right hand and crippled his right leg," the gumshoe notes) and later tracks him to an electrical substation, where the villain meets his end in classic ableist-fetishized fashion; hook raised to strike the hero, he accidently touches it to the electrical apparatus and electrocutes himself. In the midst of all the postwar movies with victimized or victimized/heroized treatments of their physically disabled characters, *Dick Tracy's Dilemma* with its vicious, cartoon-like qualities was a most atypical embodiment of disability issues for its time. Sadly, it foreshadowed the return to such simplistic and hateful images during the 1950s and 1960s.

Steve Michel, alias "The Claw" (Jack Lambert), up to no good in Dick Tracy's Dilemma *(1947), an RKO programmer directed by John Rawlins.*

United by a generally bleak perspective on disability (alleviated somewhat in *Night Song* through its heavily contrived optimism), this trio of RKO movies appeared at a time when the studio had just experienced a turnover at the top. Dore Schary, who had suitably impressed RKO with his handling of *Till the End of Time* and other films, had become the company's top production executive on January 1, 1947 following the death of Charles Koerner and found he had inherited a number of projects containing physical disability themes. Dark-minded in their outlook, *The Woman on the Beach*, *Night Song*, and *Dick Tracy's Dilemma* had little to do with the production chief's philosophy, though perhaps he found ex-soldier Dan Evans's heroic return to the world of classical music somewhat to his liking. It would be several years before the progressive Schary, working as a hands-on producer, returned to making movies that more closely paralleled his personal views.

While Schary oversaw the production of RKO's disability fare with skepticism that year, his rivals at Warners were in the process of creating the most famous disabled-civilian-as-victim film of the period. Jerry Wald, who had produced *Pride of the Marines* for the studio in 1945 and would soon oversee *Key Largo*, saw dollar signs in another tale of disability: a play written by Elmer Harris called *Johnny Belinda*. Set in a remote fishing community in Nova Scotia, the play centered on a young hearing-impaired woman whom the entire town believes is retarded. A newly arrived physician senses her intelligence and teaches her sign language, but no sooner does she break out of her isolation than a local lowlife rapes and impregnates her and later tries to kidnap her baby, the title character. In mid–1946, Wald worked to convince production head Jack Warner and the latter's executive assistant Steve Trilling to buy the rights to the Harris work: "I can't stress to you enough the great box-office picture there is in this material. . . . Why nobody has purchased this property before this is somewhat beyond my powers of comprehension. In a very slick fashion, you are dealing with the most primitive emotional subject in the world—an unwed mother who is having her child taken away. The mother, in order to defend her child, kills the man who is attempting to do this. . . . [It also has] the sensational characterization of a deaf and dumb girl."[45]

Agreeing with the producer's assessment, Warner and Trilling acquired the rights and gave him the go-ahead. Wald then hired Irmgard Von Cube and Allen Vincent to work closely with him on developing a script. After the trio finished the screenplay about a year later, Wald recruited Jean Negulesco, a Romanian native who had been directing movies for Warner Bros. since the early 1940s and whose eagerness to participate was immediate. "Jerry Wald gave me a copy of *Johnny Belinda* to read this morning," he wrote to Trilling in mid–1947. "I read it very carefully and I must say it's one of the most exciting, human and colorful scripts I have read in a long time. I am terribly enthusiastic about the possibility of doing it, because I know I could make a good job of it."[46]

With Negulesco slated to direct, Wald and Warner went about casting the film. On Warner's decision, they chose Lew Ayres, late of the "Dr. Kildare" series, over a mumbling young actor from the New York stage named Marlon Brando to play the part of the intervening, paternalistic Dr. Robert Richardson. Charles Bickford, who played the blind painter in *Woman on the Beach*, was selected as the young woman's father, Mac MacDonald. They assigned the main role of Belinda Mac-Donald to Jane Wyman, a Warners contract player since the mid-1930s whose stock in trade up to that point had been playing "dumb bunnies," in her words, but who was starting to make a name for herself as a result of strong performances in *The Lost Weekend* (1945) and *The Yearling* (1946). Never mind that at 34 she was about twice the age of her character; Wald thought the baby-faced Wyman a most suitable actress to play *Johnny Belinda*'s unadorned Sweet Innocent, modified for postwar audiences.

To add authenticity to her characterization, Wyman learned sign language and spent a considerable amount of time working with deaf people to gain a sense of their perspective. It was a very practical consideration, though, that helped her

Accustomed to medical roles, Lew Ayres (center) as Dr. Robert Richardson awaits the results of Belinda MacDonald's audiological tests in Johnny Belinda *(1948). Jane Wyman co-starred.*

learn to behave like a deaf person: "Though I had studied with the deaf for six months nothing seemed to work until I plugged my ears with wax." Her months of hard work eventually paid off in a stunning wordless performance full of subtlety and power, and, unlike many other Hollywood movies before and since that have featured deaf characters, *Johnny Belinda* (1948) allowed audiences unfamiliar with sign language to appreciate its expressive beauty while still participating fully in the characters' conversations; as John Schuchman has observed, the movie was one of the first to have a hearing and speaking character serve as a translator. The most trenchant illustration of this strategy occurs during a wake for Belinda's father, killed by the same guy who had raped his daughter; the camera lingers on Belinda's face and hands as she recites the Lord's Prayer through sign language while offscreen Richardson speaks the words and a chorus of voices joins in.[47]

As far as Jack Warner was concerned, however, the movie wasn't clear enough. Immediately after Wald and Negulesco screened what they believed was the final version of *Johnny Belinda* for Warner, the production chief threw a bombshell: he wanted voice-over narration during her wordless close-ups. Wald and Negulesco fought him on the point and won, but their victory was not without its costs: Warner fired Negulesco shortly thereafter, though the director did have the last laugh after *Johnny Belinda* brought an Academy Award to Jane Wyman and won nominations for Best Picture, Director, Screenplay, Actor, Supporting Actor, Supporting Actress, and Cinematography.[48]

While some filmmakers filled screens with victimized disabled civilians, others returned to the tradition of *Pride of the Marines*, *The Best Years of Our Lives*, and *Till the End of Time* by exploring the lives of veterans disabled by war. At the forefront of this second wave of vet movies were a producer, a screenwriter, and a director who initially worked together under the banner of an upstart film company called the Screen Plays Corporation.

"[Stanley] Kramer and I met in the Army, in the Signal Corps," remembered screenwriter Carl Foreman, "and we hit it off and found that we both had the same reservations about Hollywood now and the same frustrations about Hollywood, so he staggered me by telling me that he was thinking about going into independent production. I didn't even know what that meant, actually, but he explained to me it meant getting money from somebody and making your own films, and then you could get a release from somewhere. I thought that was pretty good."[49]

After producing several films in such a fashion, Kramer and Foreman and director Mark Robson created *Home of the Brave* (1949), in which an emotionally unstable black soldier and a physically disabled white soldier endure racist and ableist slurs. A rapidly produced film best remembered as Hollywood's breakthrough on postwar race relations, *Home of the Brave* tells the story of Peter Moss (James Edwards), a black private first class who serves as a member of an Army mapping unit in the South Pacific.[50] Others in the unit include Moss's boyhood friend Finch (Lloyd Bridges), hard-boiled Sergeant Mingo (Frank Lovejoy), and T.J. (Steve Brodie), a so-labeled "blue-plate special" who resents serving as a corporal in the low-paying Army and directs his anger primarily at Moss, the only black in the group. While surveying a Japanese-held island, the team is attacked. The assault leaves Finch dead, Mingo with a severe injury to his right arm, and Moss inexplicably paralyzed from the waist down. Believing Moss's disability psychosomatic, an Army psychiatrist (Jeff Corey) uses confrontational techniques to get him to talk about racial prejudice and the events on the mapping mission that led to his paralysis. With the medico's help, Moss snaps out of his hemiplegia.

As Mingo and Moss prepare for their return to the U.S. (Mingo because of the loss of his arm, Moss because of his mental health) during the film's final scene, the filmmakers attempted to draw a parallel between racism and ableism by having T.J., the same soldier who has baited Moss throughout the movie, verbally abuse Mingo as well. Afterwards, while waiting for a jeep to take them to the airfield, Mingo and Moss discuss T.J.'s prejudice against them:

MINGO: "He makes cracks about me, too."

MOSS: "Yeah, but those cracks . . . It's not the same, Mingo."

MINGO: "To *him* it's the same. To that crud and all cruds like him, it's the same thing. We're easy targets for him to take potshots at."

MOSS: "Yeah, but you and me . . ."

MINGO: "No, we're not the same. I am something special. I've got nothing in this sleeve but air, kiddo."

MOSS: "But, Mingo, you're . . ."

MINGO: "I'm what? Too tough? That's what I keep trying to tell myself."

As Mingo discusses his reactions to his injury, Moss comes to realize that the good feelings he had after his friend Finch was killed were not due to hatred of Finch for succumbing to racism (in a weak moment, Finch had started to call his boyhood friend a "nigger"), but the fact that he himself wasn't the one who got shot. Mingo undergoes a learning experience, too; he had been stressing his newly acquired difference from other people, but Moss notes the similarity of people underneath the surface. Drawn together by mutual understanding and buoyed by their new outlooks on life, Mingo and Moss decide to open a restaurant together after returning to the states.

Though the *Home of the Brave* filmmakers attempted to link Mingo and Moss as minority-group members who have suffered discrimination, the situation is not as simple as the film would have us believe. Moss has been the victim of discrimination all his life, while Mingo has had to experience it for only a few days. And, frankly, the prejudice he encounters from T.J. in the film is limited to a few random remarks, the most vicious of which is "Okay, I won't fight with a cripple." Insulting as they are, T.J.'s opinions of Mingo are considerably milder than his constant, outright baiting of Moss. Nevertheless, *Home of the Brave* remains commendable as yet another postwar film to raise the issue of discrimination directed toward people with physical disabilities.

Kramer, Foreman, and Robson split up with the director's departure following *Home of the Brave*, but it didn't take long for the three to conclude that a movie placing disabled vets at center stage would be a worthy follow-up to their famous 1949 film. For Kramer and Foreman, it was *The Men* (1950); for Robson, *Bright Victory* (1951).

"In *The Men*," wrote the movie's director, Fred Zinnemann, "we were dealing with the personal lives and problems of paraplegic veterans—young men paralyzed from the waist down and confined, without hope of recovery, to wheelchairs for life." *The Men* examines the story of Kenneth "Bud" Wilozek (Marlon Brando, in his film debut), a vet so paralyzed as a result of a bullet to the spine. Residing in a V.A. hospital's paraplegia ward headed by a medico known as "Bladder and Bowels" Brock (Everett Sloane, who played the mobility-impaired lawyer in *The Lady from Shanghai*), Bud has a difficult time containing his smoldering intensity—it's so strong that at the film's emotional high point it leads his wife Ellie (Teresa Wright) to acknowledge her doubts about their marriage—but the film, which faces wheelchair issues squarely, shows him gradually accepting his new life as a post-rehabilitative person.

Though Bud is the main focus of the movie, he is by no means the only wheelchair-user; numerous other vets with disabilities help this *primus inter pares* with his adjustment, and in general the film does a good job of showing "the men" pursuing a variety of interests and concerns that go beyond coping with life in a wheelchair. To the moviemakers' credit, they based *The Men* on the actual experiences of veterans disabled by the war. As Zinnemann acknowledged, "All of the situations and dialogue in the script of *The Men* were written by Carl Foreman from material he picked up from the men themselves while spending weeks with them at the hospital." Foreman, who as a youth was profoundly influenced by *All Quiet on the Western Front* ("It made me a pacifist, it made me hate war, and it made me realize what a powerful medium the motion picture was," said he), found the experience of *The Men* "emotionally very difficult, because of having to work with those wonderful guys who were paralyzed, and most of them were paralyzed because they were wonderful guys, because they had been in there fighting a war and the war had taken this terrible toll, and now you try to make a movie out of that, and you use them to make a movie. That's a heavy burden to carry."[51]

Zinnemann, a Vienna-born filmmaker who as a teenager had been deeply moved by *The Big Parade* and who emigrated to the U.S. in 1929 in time to serve as an extra (quite by coincidence) in *All Quiet on the Western Front*, had also demonstrated a sensitivity to disability issues. Known for choosing his projects with great care—he was called "the trouble maker" at MGM for rejecting so many scripts—Zinnemann like Harold Bucquet before him directed some of that studio's "Crime Does Not Pay" shorts as a means of working his way up through the ranks. In recognition of his emerging directorial talents, Dore Schary assigned him to direct 1942's insightful *Eyes in the Night*, one of his first feature films. Steeped in the documentary tradition and doubtless influenced by the success of *The Best Years of Our Lives*, Zinnemann added a strong degree of authenticity to *The Men* by shooting much of it in a V.A. hospital and recruiting forty-five veterans who actually used wheelchairs to act in the film. "When the work on the script of *The Men* had progressed far enough," he wrote, "both Producer Stanley Kramer and Writer Carl Foreman became very much interested in my suggestion to use actual paraplegic veterans from Birmingham Veterans Hospital in Van Nuys, Calif. My thought . . . was that if we could make these men play themselves, we could get far greater impact from them than from a group of actors, no matter how talented, who would have had only brief time for preparation. And to put an actor into a wheelchair on short notice and to tell him to act like a paraplegic seemed like a rather doubtful procedure."[52]

The veterans themselves seemed to appreciate the filmmakers' concepts and strategies, particularly Brando's "Method acting" idea of living with them in the paraplegia ward. The president of the Paraplegic Veterans' Association branch at the Birmingham hospital, Pat Grissom, thought Brando fit right in: "The guys were tired of the 'cheery' visits of celebrities or the deep-thought approach which viewed them as neurotics. Marlon had a natural approach . . . he saw us as human beings with problems. As a result, the guys accepted him more as a fellow paraplegic than as an actor."[53]

Despite the filmmakers' generally positive approach to their subject, *The Men* is not without its defects. The movie—particularly an early scene in which Brock lectures a group of women about their newly disabled loved ones—has a heavily didactic quality that makes it sag in places. In addition, several of the men speak in self-demeaning ways; Norm (Jack Webb) at one point says "It's not in the nature of the normal woman to be in love with one of us. Normal is normal and crippled is crippled and never the twain shall meet." Finally, the filmmakers highly fragmented the role of Bud's wife Ellie after they decided to exclude a subplot concerning her relationship with another man. As Brando biographer David Downing noted, "The actor hired to play this part was both talentless and the chief financial backer's son. He could not be replaced, so he ended up on the cutting-room floor with a large proportion of Teresa Wright's part."[54]

These faults notwithstanding, *The Men* works as a powerful, unromanticized account of newly disabled people and one of the most sensitive films to deal with physical disability issues. Though not a box office success (Zinnemann bitterly noted years later that "nobody gives a damn" about message pictures), *The Men* scored high marks with movie reviewers. The *New York Times*' Bosley

Crowther, who praised the "striking and authentic documentary quality [that] has been imparted to the whole film in every detail, attitude and word," spoke for the vast majority of critics: "Stern in its intimations of the terrible consequences of war, the film is a haunting and affecting, as well as a rewarding, drama to have at this time."[55]

As for Mark Robson, he followed *Home of the Brave*'s lead by directing another film that mixed issues of race and ability among veterans. *Bright Victory*, which tells the story of a blinded white veteran who hates blacks, carries the symbolic dimension of a disability even further than *Home of the Brave*; the blinded vet is unable to "see" beyond a fellow blinded vet's skin color, or the folly of his own racial intolerance, until the end of the film.

Bright Victory began its life as a 1945 novel by Baynard Kendrick, the same author whose mystery novels featuring blind sleuth Duncan Maclain had recently formed the basis for MGM's *Eyes in the Night* and *The Hidden Eye*. Officials at the Library of Congress had found his novels so realistic and attentive to detail that they recommended Kendrick to the War Department, which had been seeking writers who could ease the rehabilitation process for newly blinded veterans. Kendrick agreed to help and began writing a novel that dealt with a blinded vet and his eventual readjustment to civilian life. The result was the downbeat-titled *Lights Out*.

Having achieved some success with the Duncan Maclain movies, MGM authorized director Clarence Brown buy the screen rights to *Lights Out* for $10,000 shortly after the book's publication in 1945. Brown, a political conservative, found the book not to his liking and sold the rights for five times that amount to Robert Montgomery at Universal-International two years later. (Universal, famous for such wide-ranging disability fare as *All Quiet on the Western Front*, *Frankenstein*, and *Magnificent Obsession*, had merged with International Pictures in 1946.) The project stalled there as well—the book may have also proven too liberal-minded for Montgomery, who like Brown was a Hollywood conservative activist—and it remained on the U-I backburner until 1951 when the team of writer-producer Robert Buckner and director Mark Robson finally brought it to the screen.[56]

Buckner and Robson decided to add a greater note of veracity to their movie by filming it on location at the U.S. Army hospital in Valley Forge, Pennsylvania. As noted by Harry Niemeyer, a *New York Times* reporter who observed the production first-hand, the filmmakers "were convinced that they could turn out a more authentic job on the grounds of the institution where all the sections devoted to the rehabilitation of the blind were ready and waiting and furnished with the necessary and authentic 'props.'" Arthur Kennedy, the stage-trained actor chosen to play the film's central character, contributed further to the film's realistic veneer by following Jane Wyman's general approach to her role in *Johnny Belinda*; he received instruction from blinded veterans and wore opaque contact lenses that effectively rendered him sightless during the filming. Despite mishaps such as walking off a four-foot platform into thin air, Kennedy added a considerable degree of authenticity to his performance by wearing the lenses.[57]

Novelist Kendrick claimed no financial stake in the movie version of *Lights Out* but nevertheless proclaimed his delight with the way the yet-unreleased film was shaping up. In particular, he was quite pleased with the film's realism, its lack of melodrama, and Kennedy's performance. His enthusiasm is evident in this statement de-emphasizing the film's clinical qualities: "Don't use the word rehabilitation. That word might frighten people away from seeing the picture. *Lights Out* is not a story of the rehabilitation of the blinded war casualty in a clinical sense. It is a great emotional drama of how a man discovers a whole new life. It's a love story. . . . A very human drama. . . . Once people see the film they will enjoy a tremendous emotional experience."[58]

Retitled *Bright Victory* before its general release to suggest a more positive outlook, the film shows its lead character's disablement in a matter of minutes: Sgt. Larry Nevins (Kennedy), a white southerner, is serving in North Africa in 1943 when a Nazi bullet grazes his head, rendering him blind. Well after his return to the U.S. and initial adjustment to a new lifestyle without sight, his life is

Larry Nevins (Arthur Kennedy, standing left) and Joe Morgan (James Edwards, center) are among the enthusiastic participants in a bowling league for blinded veterans in Bright Victory. *Copyright © 1951 Universal Pictures Co.*

changed once again after he collides with a blinded black G.I. named Joe Morgan (James Edwards, the harassed Peter Moss from Robson's *Home of the Brave*) in a hospital corridor. He apologizes profusely, and after the vets get to know one another—and somehow remain unaware of each other's race—they develop a close friendship, which the filmmakers visualize in various scenes; they playfully dunk one another while swimming, outperform everyone in a blind bowling league, and play pinball before going to a USO dance. Back at the hospital after the dance, the buddies walk arm in arm and talk cheerfully until Larry notes that he has heard several "niggers" will soon be admitted to the hospital. He continues his rather matter-of-fact observation by saying he did not know niggers were allowed into that hospital.

Joe stops walking on hearing the first utterance of "niggers" while Larry continues walking as if nothing had happened. He momentarily asks, "Did you, Joe?" to which the latter solemnly notes, "Yeah, I've been here nearly seven months now." As Joe walks past Larry to get to his bunk, another blinded soldier remarks to the latter, "Maybe he thought you were colored, too."

Disturbed by his own lack of sensitivity toward a close friend of several months, Larry further alters his attitudes toward blacks after encountering discrimination while on a month-long furlough in his Florida hometown. He learns his fiancée's wealthy father plans to give him a job in his factory, but only because his daughter asked him to; he would never hire the vet otherwise, as his ableist opinions make clear: "Well, let's face it, Larry. You're no longer an able-bodied man. It's very pitiable, but it's true." Implying a similarity among racism and ableism (though significantly Larry would not have been denied a job because of his visual impairment), *Bright Victory* concludes by showing Larry eagerly making amends with Joe as the vets return from their separate furloughs.

Most critics praised *Bright Victory*'s handling of the readjustment issues faced by blinded veterans and, in particular, Arthur Kennedy's portrayal of Larry Nevins. *The Nation*'s Manny Farber wrote that "Kennedy contributes a solid, feverish, consistent characterization full of incredibly shrewd perceptions about both Southerners and the sightless," while *The New Republic*'s Robert Hatch, despite unfortunate language, urged "every man, woman and child who habitually patronizes the blind, treating them like helpless cripples or mental defectives" to see the film. Though awkward and contrived in its attempt to present an idealized world in which people can become truly "blind" to skin color (Hatch called the racial subplot "a tasteless and superficial effort to be progressive"), *Bright Victory* is right on course in its rendering of the lifestyles of newly blinded people.[59]

With such films as *Johnny Belinda*, many of Lionel Barrymore's post-disablement films, and particularly the disabled-vet films of the immediate post-WW II period, the Cinema of Isolation had reached an unprecedented level of sensitivity to issues of physical disability. Filmmakers had courageously broken away from the long history of disparaging imagery, often to create original stories based on the actual experiences of recently disabled people, and for a moment it seemed as if their movies would set the standard for future movies of physical disability to follow. Yet even as *Home of the Brave*, *The Men*, and *Bright Victory* were undergoing development at the end of the decade, a darkness that had been brewing for years had already begun enveloping Hollywood and would bring the progressive images to a virtual standstill.

6 / the path to apathy

In October 1947, a time when the Cold War was growing icier by the day, a handful of U.S. Congressmen constituting the House Committee on Un-American Activities, a group better known by its pejorative "HUAC" acronym, formally opened an investigation into the Hollywood industry. Led by New Jersey Republican J. Parnell Thomas, the committee sought to identify movie workers who may have associated themselves at some point with the Communist Party and in its opinion had tried to subvert the screen. In pursuit of that goal, the committee basically followed a double-pronged strategy: it danced with a number of Hollywood "friendly witnesses" quite willing to name names for whatever reasons (to express their own fundamental conservative beliefs, to preserve their sense of the movie industry, to settle old scores, or simply to save their own skins), and it sparred with those who had been so named—the "unfriendly witnesses." As chairman Thomas unhesitatingly gaveled the latter into silence whenever they began responding creatively to the question "Are you now or have you ever been a member of the Communist Party?" it was clear their fate had been determined before the hearings began. Thus was born the Hollywood blacklisting era, a period rife with political actions that were to have serious repercussions for the Cinema of Isolation.

As observed in the previous chapter, production executives had realized around the end of the war that a ready market existed for movies that dealt with the victims of society's ills and had courted screenwriters and directors known for their liberal views. For example, screenwriter Alvah Bessie noted that Jerry Wald of Warner Bros. had hired progressives "because these boys knew what society in general and fascism and the war in particular were all about and could create characters and situations that bore some resemblance to reality."[1] Dedicated to combatting various "isms"—fascism, racism, anti-Semitism, anti-Catholicism, and, most assuredly, ableism—these filmmakers of conscience had made considerable progress toward bettering the image of physically disabled people. During the late 1940s and early 1950s, however, many of these same artists found themselves under siege for their progressive views.

"How often do you go to the movies? Once a week?" queried Hollywood actor Joseph Cotten of the moviegoing public in 1948. "Chances are you have probably seen *Pride of the Marines*. And do you remember *Objective Burma*, *Kitty Foyle*, and *Thirty Seconds Over Tokyo*? And such great classics as *All Quiet on the Western Front*? Actors, directors, writers and producers who gave you those pictures have been attacked and smeared as Un-American for putting subversive propaganda into their pictures."[2] Among them were people who had given the Cinema of Isolation a generally positive spin during the 1940s and early 1950s but were blacklisted following the HUAC hearings of 1947 and 1951–52, their Hollywood careers cut short: John Garfield and Albert Maltz, star and screenwriter respectively of *Pride of the Marines*; Carl Foreman, screenwriter of *Home of the Brave* and *The Men*; Edward Dmytryk, director of *Till the End of Time*; Lillian Hellman, screenwriter of the prototypical *The Dark Angel*; Robert Rossen, screenwriter of *The Sea Wolf*; *Song of Russia* screenwriters Paul Jarrico and Richard Collins, the former of whom had also written a resonant portrait of a young blind woman in *The Face Behind the Mask* (1941); and Dalton Trumbo, screenwriter of *Thirty Seconds Over Tokyo* and author of an acclaimed 1939 anti-war novel about a severely disabled WW I vet called *Johnny Got His Gun*.

The committee hearings had other chilling effects. HUAC friendly witness Adolphe Menjou identified John Cromwell, director of the hardly revolutionary *Since You Went Away*, *The Enchanted Cottage*, and *Night Song*, as one of several acquaintances "who act an awful lot like Communists" and who "in his own house, said to me that capitalism in America was through." In partial response to this treatment, the stage-trained Cromwell returned to his theater environs in 1951 and did not resume his moviemaking career until 1958 at the age of 69. Robert Buckner and Mark Robson went over to England to make a number of films during the mid–1950s, while Stanley Kramer, a Rooseveltian Democrat and pragmatist at heart (according to Carl Foreman, Kramer begged him to keep his name out of the HUAC hearings for fear it would mark the end of his own Hollywood career), temporarily backed off from movies with progressive themes. In 1948, William Wyler observed that the HUAC members "are making decent people afraid to express their opinions. They are creating fear in Hollywood. Fear will result in self-censorship." To the chagrin of many, such concerns were coming true.[3]

Studio executives cooperated fully with HUAC for the most part. Perhaps the person who most vividly embodied the paranoia of the time was Warners production head Jack Warner, who flatly told the committee "anyone whom I thought was a Communist, or read in the papers that he was, I dismissed at the expiration of his contract." After Warner identified Albert Maltz as one of the writers he had let go, the committee chair asked, "Did Maltz get much [subversive material] into *Pride of the Marines*?" Warner responded that he tried and failed, but added: "Some of these lines [of dialogue] have innuendos and double meanings, and things like that, and you have to take eight or ten Harvard law courses to find out what they mean."[4]

Even the most sympathetic of the film executives did little to support the blacklistees. RKO production head Dore Schary, a liberal who like Jerry Wald had encouraged writers and directors to explore social themes, now found himself in the ironic position of having to inform the screenwriters' union that the studios via their infamous "Waldorf statement" of November 1947 had agreed to support HUAC in its investigations. Such cooperation, which Schary opposed but could do little about, included the firing of the unfriendliest of the "unfriendly witnesses"—the so-called "Hollywood Ten" who shortly went to prison for refusing to cooperate with the committee—and the blacklisting of all presumed subversives. To Schary's credit, he refused to fire RKO employees Edward Dmytryk and

Adrian Scott, two of the Hollywood Ten (that task fell to RKO president Peter Rathvon) but neither could he prevent their dismissal. As for Sam Goldwyn, the producer who had touched countless numbers of moviegoers with *The Best Years of Our Lives*, he voiced his opposition to the blacklist but nevertheless signed the Waldorf statement and pointedly refused William Wyler's request to hire one of the Hollywood Ten.[5]

The committee searched for subversive material with a zealotry that saw few bounds. Even *Best Years*, a much-honored film directed by a disabled veteran and scripted by a former Office of War Information executive, was not above reproach. The April 30, 1947 edition of *The Hollywood Reporter* contained an article by its publisher William Wilkerson listing movies "containing sizable doses of Communist propaganda," *Best Years* as well as *Pride of the Marines* among them, and the list fueled reactionary fires. According to blacklisted screenwriter Gordon Kahn, the Motion Picture Alliance for the Preservation of American Ideals, a group of Hollywood right-wingers subsidized by newspaper magnate William Randolph Hearst, "put the finger of subversion" on *Best Years*, piquing HUAC's interest. As Kahn further noted, "At one time Mr. Thomas' Committee thought they detected a few [subversive films] and contrived at an elaborate leak. They got as far as *Best Years of Our Lives* and *Margie* before they were laughed right out of the headlines." Some industry insiders like Gene Kelly were livid: "The House Un-American Committee has called on the carpet some of the people who have been making your favorite movies. Did you happen to see *The Best Years of Our Lives*, the picture that won seven Academy Awards? Did you like it? Were you subverted by it? Did it make you Un-American? Did you come out of the movie with the desire to overthrow the government?" Screenwriter Garrett Graham meant well when he wrote that "it's too bad the handless veteran featured in this picture can't be lent a fist to answer appropriately the slur on his patriotism." Wyler himself announced shortly after the first round of HUAC investigations that "I wouldn't be allowed to make *The Best Years of Our Lives* in Hollywood today. That is directly the result of the activities of the Un-American Activities Committee."[6]

In retrospect, the movies scripted, acted, directed, and produced by the progressives were hardly radical in their values. Paul Jarrico spoke for his peers when he remarked,

> We were anxious to have humanistic content. We weren't anxious to have revolutionary content. [We wanted our films] to have a kinder, more positive attitude towards women, towards minorities, towards people in general, towards poor people, and, insofar as we subverted the screen, that was about the extent of it.[7]

As if the HUAC inquisition and fall-out therefrom weren't traumatic enough, the movie industry had to contend with a series of debilitating blows to its economic base. In May 1948, the U.S. Supreme Court through its famous

"Paramount decision" found the the major Hollywood companies guilty of monopolistic business practices and among other things ordered MGM, Paramount, Warner Bros., Twentieth Century–Fox, and RKO to sell off their theater holdings and prohibited the other major companies from making restrictive exhibition arrangements. The industry faced problems with its overseas operations as well; that same month, the British government backed off from its tariff plans of the previous year (in which it had imposed a whopping 75 percent import duty on proceeds from American movies) to become the first of several European nations to place an annual limit on the earnings the Hollywood companies could take out of the country. The industry learned to adapt to the situation by making an increasing number of movies on foreign soil, thereby enabling it to tap into the "frozen" funds, but the practice didn't become widespread until well into the following decade.

The biggest concern of all, however, took the form of changing audience habits at home. Concerned about the 1947 slump in ticket sales from the all-time high of the previous year, movie executives had little inkling of the economic nightmare to follow; the annual decline in movie ticket sales from 1946 to 1962 would hover at a compounded rate of about 8 percent, translating into an overall drop-off of nearly 75 percent. They discovered to their chagrin that their erstwhile movie patrons had no trouble finding new ways of spending money and leisure time during the boom years of the postwar era, with the newly viable medium of television a chief attraction. Battered on all fronts by political and economic forces, the movie industry now found itself in the peculiar position of having to create inoffensive material, at least politically speaking, while simultaneously combatting the insipid new medium that was keeping would-be moviegoers at home.

The industry's political and economic woes had a powerful effect on the Cinema of Isolation. With so many filmmakers who had offered favorable treatments of physically disabled characters now either barred from Hollywood employment or in retreat, and with the industry itself preoccupied with creating bigger and splashier entertainments to lure audiences back into theaters, Hollywood abandoned the progressive road taken during the late 1930s and 1940s. Shortly after rival unionists clashed in front of his studio's gates Jack Warner declared he was through making movies about "the little man,"[8] and that pronouncement, uttered soon after the war's end, seemed to set the course for the rest of the industry. The path to apathy beckoned.

Though the social-issue cycle of films showed signs of decay by the early 1950s as a result of political and economic pressures, the industry still found eminently serviceable the victim-turned-hero formula and continued constructing characters "felled" by physical disabilities only to triumph over them. Very much a part of the new conservative age, the resulting movies emphasized civilians wealthy enough to pay their own bills (or at the very least fortunate enough to have a strong safety net of family and friends) and living in a world magically free of prejudice at the expense of disabled veterans dependent on government assistance and subject to ableist bias, however modestly depicted. In brief, disabled civilians began making a spectacular comeback in the movies while Noble Warriors—reminders of the old war and the new, unpopular one in Korea—were fast fading in popularity. With only a few exceptions, disabled veterans in movies of the mid–1950s appeared only in background roles or in situations that barely acknowledged their wartime service.

Postwar filmmakers evidently took Warner's statement about avoiding "little man" films to heart, for the civilians depicted in the new movies weren't at all average. Similar to the characters in *Night Song*, *The Lady from Shanghai*, *The Woman on the Beach*, and many of the prewar Civilian Superstar movies, they were world-class performers in such fields as politics, sports, and the arts—special enough, the studios hoped, to lure audiences away from the banal fare served up nightly on television. One of the studios, Twentieth Century–Fox, had attempted such a film during the wartime years—*Wilson* (1944), Darryl Zanuck's adulatory and sentimental biography of the nation's twenty-eighth president who used a wheelchair after a stroke—but it was clearly not the period for such movies; *Wilson* garnered all sorts of critical praise and won five Academy Awards, but audiences stayed away in droves and Zanuck lost millions on the film. Now, in a new political age dominated, it seemed, by television's celebration of the profoundly ordinary, the movie industry believed the time was right for creating tributes to larger-than-life heroes "overcoming" their disabilities.[9]

The resulting new generation of Civilian Superstar films went further than the prewar one by combining the latter's sense of the strong-willed individual with a pronounced concern for rehabilitation issues. (This latter attribute, common in the Noble Warrior films of the 1940s and 1950s, rarely if ever appeared in any movies made before World War II.) When their exceptional characters eventually triumph over the odds with the same kind of gumption that got them to the top of their profession (usually demonstrated in a climactic scene in which the Superstars, pursuing former greatness, perform while attempting to "pass" in some way), the average moviegoer, so the industry hoped, couldn't help but be inspired.

One of Hollywood's first filmmakers to make such a film during this new conservative period was Sam Wood. Unlike his progressive-minded peers, Wood had no problem finding work in postwar Hollywood; co-founder and first president of the Motion Picture Alliance for the Preservation of American Ideals, Wood was conspicuous in his contributions to the hysteria surrounding the 1947 HUAC hearings. "These Communists thump their chests and call themselves liberals, but if you drop their rompers you'll find a hammer and sickle on their rear ends," he opined.[10] As the industry headed towards its second showdown with HUAC, Wood was busy at work on a movie that would set the pattern for a number of other physical disability movies: *The Stratton Story* (1949).

Wood, who had made his mark at MGM during the 1930s before turning freelance in the 1940s (he had directed *Kings Row* for Warner Bros. during this latter period), returned to the studio later in the decade and found it the perfect home for his new project; MGM was, after all, the studio that had cultivated the Civilian Superstar image in such movies as *Young Tom Edison*, *Edison, the Man* (directed respectively by Wood's conservative friends Norman Taurog and Clarence Brown), the "Dr. Kildare" series, *Eyes in the Night*, and *The Hidden Eye*. In turn, the studio was delighted to have Wood direct this particular movie, for it had a sports theme and Wood was well-known for his mastery of the subject by virtue of his work on such films as *One Minute to Play* (1926) with Red Grange, *Huddle* (1932), *Navy Blue and Gold* (1937), *Stablemates* (1938), and, most significantly, his 1942 film on Lou Gehrig, *The Pride of the Yankees*.

Given a strong degree of control over the project by MGM producer Jack Cummings, Wood hired Douglas Morrow and Guy Trosper, two obscure writers with presumably impeccable conservative credentials, to base a script on the experiences of Monty Stratton, a Texas farmboy who rose to become an ace pitcher for the Chicago White Sox during the 1930s, lost a leg during a hunting accident in 1938, and showed that a disability did not necessarily signal the end of his baseball career. Wood and his writers worked closely with Stratton himself, who came to Hollywood in 1948 following two years of hurling in the Texas minor leagues. (In 1946, his first comeback year, he pitched in the Class C East Texas League and won eighteen games. The following year, he moved up to the Class B Big State League and won seven games before finally retiring from baseball.)

The Stratton Story starred James Stewart, who had insisted on Wood as director after having seen his *Pride of the Yankees*; June Allyson as Monty's wife Ethel; Frank Morgan as his friend and mentor Barney Wile; and Agnes Moorehead, less than two years older than Stewart, as Monty's mother. The movie goes into a fair amount of detail concerning Monty's life on the farm, his preparation for a baseball career and eventual breakthrough into the major leagues, and, shades of *Lifeboat*, his love of dancing. His life takes a major turn after he trips over a piece of fence during a rabbit-hunting expedition and accidently shoots himself in the leg. He is initially low-key about the amputation of his limb—in a line Stewart delivers in his classic understated way, Monty says, "Looks like I sorta gummed things up"—but soon becomes bitter and refuses to wear a prosthesis or do anything around the house. He manages to kill the joyful mood surrounding his year-old child's first steps when he says, "What's so wonderful about it? He's got two legs, hasn't he?" He's eventually brought around by his wife who says "I've made out much worse than you. You lost your leg, but I lost you," and with the help of his friend Barney he gets himself back into shape to play ball. Despite a few mishaps (he falls down between home plate and first base during a game and then elicits a laugh from his teammates by telling them he started his slide too early), Monty makes a successful return to professional baseball.

Critics generally applauded *The Stratton Story* for its restraint and sense of triumph that went beyond the world of sports. *Time*'s reviewer praised Stewart's performance and wrote that the movie "avoids the obvious temptations to jerk extra tears and belabor its moral," while *Commonweal*'s Philip Hartung, calling it "the success story supreme," stated that "whether you like baseball or not, you will like *The Stratton Story* because it is a well-made movie and is as honest as its theme of courage." Even Wood himself, pre-eminent figure that he was on cinematized athletics, downplayed the movie's sports angle. "The game itself," he said, "was merely a backdrop for the more important story of a man's faith in himself and a woman's faith in a man, plus the sympathetic understanding of his best friend." One of the first "inspiration to us all" kind of movies sans a military context (indeed, an offscreen narrator actually says that "he stands as an inspiration to all of us," the word "stands" taking on a particular resonance in this context), *The Stratton Story* remained true to its conservative heritage in a number of respects; it had Stratton avoid publicly funded rehabilitation in favor of sheer self-determination abetted by the support of family and friends, and it also had him encounter few if any difficulties related to prejudice or access.[11]

Wood didn't live long enough to develop other Civilian Superstar movies (he died of heart failure later that year at the age of 66), but other Hollywood filmmakers who shared his perspectives eventually took up the slack. Over at Twentieth

Monty Stratton and his coach (James Stewart, Frank Morgan) plot their strategy for winning the big one in 1949's The Stratton Story.

Century–Fox, screenwriter Lamar Trotti, who had won an Oscar for his *Wilson* script back in 1944, decided to retest the waters by creating another disabled Civilian Superstar. The resulting film—*With a Song in My Heart* (1952), which he wrote and produced with Walter Lang directing—demonstrated among other things Hollywood's de-emphasis of disabled veterans. The movie begins at an award ceremony in New York honoring Jane Froman (Susan Hayward) and through flashbacks shows how her career as a singer in nightclubs, stage musicals, movies, and on radio had been disrupted after a plane crash en route to a USO tour in London that left her with a leg almost severed below the knee. Numerous disabled veterans appear in the film after Jane has dealt with her personal struggles and gallantly resumed her USO tour, but unlike the Hollywood vets of the 1940s they distinctly play background roles. They are simply her fans, and she has no qualms about performing before them as a disabled person (she appears on crutches in front of the vets at one point). When singing before the general able-bodied public, however, she often hides her heavily encased leg under a long, flowing gown.

MGM's *Interrupted Melody* (1955) covered similar territory. Written by William Ludwig and Sonya Levien (the latter a screenwriter for RKO's *The Hunchback of Notre Dame*), directed by Curtis Bernhardt, and produced by *The Stratton Story*'s Jack Cummings, *Interrupted Melody* followed the story of Marjorie Lawrence King (Eleanor Parker), an Australian globe-trotting opera singer who contracts poliomyelitis at the peak of her career and becomes suicidally depressed. Her husband, an American M.D. named Thomas King (Glenn Ford), gamely tries to get her to follow various therapeutic techniques but she's extremely reluctant to participate. He tries to get her to walk, but she refuses to

Susan Hayward as Jane Froman serenades a shell-shocked paratrooper played by Robert Wagner in With a Song in My Heart. *Copyright © 1952 Warner Bros.–Seven Arts Inc.*

move off her couch. She says of her legs, "They're dead. Dead. Can anything be worse?" Her grief over the loss of the use of her legs reaches its lowest point when she says to her husband, "You're a doctor. Help me to die."

Thomas eventually persuades her that life remains worth living, but she's convinced her career is over. One day, an old friend of her husband, an Army doctor, asks Marjorie to sing for some of the "boys" at the local V.A. hospital, but she states flatly that she does not sing in public anymore. When the doctor queries, "But if your voice is okay, why not?," she responds by referring to her wheelchair: "Well, you see, I—I'm in this thing all the time." The doctor's scene-concluding response drips with poignancy: "So are a lot of the boys." Needless to say, she does perform in the hospital (she sings "Over the Rainbow" while wheeling through a ward full of disabled vets, many of whom also use wheelchairs), and she finds it such an uplifting experience that she does eventually resume her operatic career. It's interesting to note, however, that when she again reaches the professional stage she abandons the chair and sings while propping herself up against the scenery. The message, identical to the one in *With a Song in My Heart*, is clear: it is acceptable to be seen as disabled while performing among one's "own kind" (i.e., other disabled people, family, close friends, rehab professionals) but not in front of general able-bodied audiences. Only an attempt to "pass" as able-bodied will do.

Ludwig and Levien had little to go on when they began work on the *Interrupted Melody* screenplay. According to Ludwig, all they had was a "thin, badly ghosted autobiography, all sweetness and light, and [we were] ordered to whip up a credible script with plenty of laughs, tears and operatic arias." To flesh out the basic narrative framework, the writers worked extensively with Lawrence herself. As Levien explained, "We sat with her for months, questioning, digging, burrowing—we made her remember feelings she'd rather have forgotten—early polio therapy, for instance, two suicide attempts—we pulled out stops in her emotions that had all of us sobbing many an afternoon. But we finally worked a script out of it that we're proud of. Even Miss Lawrence likes it!"[12]

Though *The Stratton Story*, *With a Song in My Heart*, and *Interrupted Melody* were all based on true stories, filmmakers didn't limit their "inspirational" efforts to then-famous people who had actually gone through such experiences. Warner Bros. in collusion with International Artists began developing a fictional character seemingly appropriate for the new conservative age when they dredged up a property to which Warners already owned the screen rights—a play by Jules Eckert Goodman called *The Silent Voice*—and that eventually became known as *Sincerely Yours* (1955).

Produced by long-time Warners executive Henry Blanke, written by Irving Wallace years before hitting his stride as a novelist, and directed by Gordon Douglas, *Sincerely Yours* was the fourth in a series of films based on Goodman's 1914 play. (The first, a 1915 affair named after the play starring Francis X. Bushman, was followed by 1922 version called *The Man Who Played God* featuring

Broadway fixture George Arliss. Warners acquired the rights to the story and produced a sound remake in 1932, also called *The Man Who Played God* and starring Arliss.) Blanke conceived *Sincerely Yours* as a glossy first-time movie for Wladziu Valentino Liberace, a 36-year-old entertainer known simply by his surname to his throngs of adoring fans. Blanke undoubtedly saw a big return in the offing when he signed up the flamboyant pianist. At the peak of Liberace's popularity, Harry and Michael Medved have observed, "his weekly television show went out to some 30 million viewers on more than 200 stations, reaching even more people than the *I Love Lucy* series. 'Mr. Entertainment' won two Emmy awards and drew nearly 10,000 fan letters every week, most of them from the middle-aged matrons who made up his core audience."[13] To capitalize on his recognition, Blanke and Douglas had Liberace play nearly twenty songs on camera ranging from works by Tchaikovsky and Mozart to Gershwin to "Tea for Two" and "The Beer-Barrel Polka."

Liberace starred as Tony Warrin, a wealthy concert pianist whose career takes a turn when he develops deafness. In an attempt to have the audience "experience" the onset of his impairment, the filmmakers muffled the soundtrack while showing a close-up of him in concert (in which his face registers a sense of alarm) and then provided aural crystal clarity during a follow-up shot of his friends listening in the audience. The muffled sound returns in succeeding close-ups of Warrin's hands and face and grows fainter, forcing the pianist to cut the concert short.

Warrin later learns he has otosclerosis—a bony growth blocking the auditory nerves resulting in intermittent deafness—which an operation might cure but might also leave him permanently deaf. The pianist becomes exceedingly distraught and hides out in his lush penthouse apartment overlooking Central Park, but his "good nature" gets the better of him after he had learned to read lips with astonishing rapidity. Watching various sets of people converse in the park through high-powered binoculars, he senses their profound unhappiness and decides to perform good deeds. Among them, he finances an operation for an orthopedically impaired boy, takes an Irish woman on a clothes-shopping spree, and in a classic bit of ableist filmmaking "nobly" allows his fiancée Linda Curtis (Dorothy Malone) to break off their engagement. After he has returned to the ranks of the able-bodied via the operation, however, the filmmakers saw no reason to deny him marriage and had him become engaged to his adoring secretary, Marion Moore (Joanne Dru).

The critics had a field day lambasting the film's clichéd and schmaltzy qualities as well as Liberace's acting debut. The reviewer for *Films and Filming* suggested *Sincerely Yours* was "drenched in coy bathos to the point of embarrassment" while the *Los Angeles Times* reviewer found it "unintentionally hilarious." Bosley Crowther charitably described Liberace as "nobody's Barrymore. When he wears his black-sequined dinner jacket, he hits the peak of his acting skill."[14] Thrown off perhaps by the filmmakers' attempts to present the world from a disabled person's perspective, however, few of the reviewers picked up on the film's slurs aimed at deaf people, such as that illustrated by the pianist's lip-reading teacher: "You've overcome a great handicap, Mr. Warrin. From this day on you can live a normal existence, carry on conversation, be with friends, have a family. Yes, you're to be congratulated, because with lip-reading you can hear again." Fortunately, *Sincerely Yours* proved a major bomb within two weeks of its release and disappeared from theaters shortly thereafter.

The Civilian Superstar trend picked up a bit with *23 Paces to Baker Street* (1956), a Twentieth Century–Fox production written by Nigel Balchin from a novel by Philip MacDonald and directed by Henry Hathaway. Filmed in London presumably to gain access to frozen funds, the movie differed slightly from the earlier entries by having a later point of attack; the disablement of its recently blinded Superstar, successful playwright Phillip Hannon (Van Johnson, who had played a disabled vet in *Thirty Seconds Over Tokyo*), occurs before the movie begins. Embittered by the loss of his sight, he nevertheless works on a revision of a hit Broadway play for its London debut and is jolted out of his self-pity after overhearing what he believes is a kidnapping plot in the making while in a pub. Though the ensuing "detective story" is flimsy—Hannon perseveres on the basis of information that everyone else finds very sketchy and unconvincing—he like the Duncan Maclain character of *Eyes in the Night* and *The Hidden Eye* solves the crime by relying on information that sighted people might ordinarily overlook, such as the scent of a certain perfume. In addition, Hannon like other Civilian Superstars does attempt to pass (eschewing the use of a cane or a seeing-eye dog, he occasionally pretends to be sighted, such as by playing pinball, to throw off a person he's been tailing) and does gain back his self-esteem and renew his love for a doggedly supportive opposite-sex person in the process.

The Universal-International studio significantly altered the Civilian Superstar formula in 1957 when it produced and released a film about a show-biz performer who encounters and overcomes a crisis of a different sort: prejudice directed at him and his family because of his disabled parents. In *Man of a Thousand Faces*, a sentimental tribute to the old Universal's greatest star, Lon Chaney, James Cagney stars as the legendary Lon. Written by R. Wright Campbell, Ivan Goff, and Ben Roberts, produced by Robert Arthur, and directed by Joseph Pevney, the film begins with an ersatz Rod Serling introducing a theater audience to Chaney's story. Though ironically laced with ableist views, his comments reflect one of the movie's major themes: that Chaney's drive for success was strongly related to his childhood struggles against ableist intolerance. "He illuminated certain dark corners of the human spirit. He showed the world the souls of those people who were born different from the rest. To understand why he was destined for this, we would only have to go back to any day in his boyhood, in the town of Colorado Springs. Not a very easy boyhood, for his parents were different."

The filmmakers followed this monologue with a brief scene showing Lon as a boy coming home from a fight with other kids who had made fun of his deaf parents. The movie, which later shows Cagney recreating Chaney's character-building process in such films as *The Miracle Man* and *The Hunchback of Notre Dame*, reaches a critical juncture when Lon takes his pregnant wife Cleva (*Sincerely Yours'* Dorothy Malone) to meet his family. He has not told her about his parents' severe hearing loss, and when he finger-spells the introductions she is horrified and fears the child she's carrying may be deaf as well. "Ask them about my baby," she screams. "Will it be like them? It's in your blood. It could happen again." Though the Chaneys eventually learn their child Creighton (who later grew up to pursue his own movie acting career as "Lon Chaney, Jr.") can indeed hear, the damage done to their marriage is irreparable. Lon and Cleva divorce within a year or so after he has moved from a stage career to one in the movies, and by the time he remarries, this time to a woman who relates well to his parents, his years at Universal are well underway. An atypical Civilian Superstar film in several respects (not only does the main character remain able-bodied throughout but also the crisis he overcomes—ableist prejudice—was a topic seldom explored in other such films), *Man of a Thousand Faces* commendably shows Lon, his four hearing siblings, and their parents having a warm and loving family life during the movie's early going. By linking disability with the "dark corners of the human spirit" material and highly exaggerating Cleva's reactions to Lon's parents (nowhere in Robert Anderson's biography of Chaney does the author suggest that she reacted in such a way), however, the moviemakers vitiated their good intentions by perpetuating the very prejudice they seemed to be against.[15]

Though the cycle of Civilian Superstar movies hadn't yet run its course by the mid–1950s, a number of moviemakers did begin establishing disabled-vet characters as other than passive background material. The resulting movies, however, were in some ways quite different from those of the previous decade. Coming as they did on the heels of Korea, the first of America's "dirty wars," they were generally marked by an ambivalence ranging from indifference to intolerance. With the exception of a few biographical films based on the experiences of specific war heroes, the sympathy by which the Noble Warrior films had been conceived during the 1940s had practically vanished.

The year 1953 saw the creation of two movies that, on the surface, varied widely in their treatment of disabled veterans. Based on the popular 1951 Broadway play by Donald Bevan and Edmund Trzcinski (two former sergeants who had been held in a German prisoner of war camp for two years) and produced, directed, and co-written by Billy Wilder, *Stalag 17* followed the activities of Allied soldiers held in a German POW camp, one of whom is accused of being a Nazi spy. Among the many prisoners is a crutch-using guy named Steve, who has lost his left leg below the knee. In addition to helping deliver the mail, he smuggles various things in his empty pants leg: a radio for listening to BBC broadcasts, a tiny Christmas tree, even a lit smudge pot which he uses to create a literal smoke screen for his fellow POWs to rescue one of their own. To Wilder's credit, he did have the other soldiers treat him as an equal—during group scenes, for example, they do such things as rest their hands on his shoulders and give him slaps of approval—but nevertheless the gimmicky use of his leg makes him an equal with a difference. The fact that Wilder elected to have him speak not a single word in the film (presumably because the performer who played him, Jerry Singer, was a nonprofessional actor recruited only because he was so disabled) and referred to him in the credits not as Steve but as "The Crutch" only encouraged audiences then and now to regard him as not much more than a human novelty.

Another film that year, *Torch Song*, expressed filmmaker apathy in a noticeably different way. A high-gloss musical drama directed by Charles Walters, better known in Hollywood for his choreography skills, it starred Joan Crawford in one of her typical tough-woman roles: Jenny Stewart, an aging Broadway star anxious to revive her flagging career. Full of nervous energy and very critical of everyone she has to work with on her new Broadway show (including a klutzy dance partner played by Walters himself), she doesn't take long to clash with an exceptionally mild-mannered pianist named Ty Graham (Michael Wilding) who happens to be blind. An independent spirit whose ideas on the show's musical numbers are far different from Jenny's, the pipe-smoking Ty proves a major thorn in her side.

As a pianist whose talents are strong enough to land him in a Broadway musical, Ty certainly qualifies as a Civilian Superstar then popular with moviemakers. Unlike the others, however, he is also a disabled veteran, as revealed in this snippet of conversation between Jenny and her director, Joe Denner (Harry Morgan):

> JENNY: "Well, how can you work with a man who—who can't even see what you're doing? He doesn't even know what I look like. He has no business in this business."
> JOE: "Maybe he had no business being in the war."

This is the movie's sole reference to Ty's military service, a point made all the more interesting by the fact that the film's principal screenwriter, John Michael Hayes, was himself a disabled WW II veteran. A self-described "rock-ribbed conservative Republican" who acknowledged benefiting indirectly from the blacklisting era when his screenwriting career took off in 1952, Hayes had been laid up in a V.A. hospital for almost two years and walked with canes for a time thereafter. (These experiences, by the way, doubtless informed the screenplay for his most famous film: 1954's *Rear Window*, directed by Alfred Hitchcock.) Though he claimed to identify with the Ty Graham character and was unaware of any pressure to downplay disabled vets, he nevertheless de-emphasized the character's wartime service and rehabilitation issues related thereto while using a story by I.A.R. Wylie and an early script draft by Jan Lustig as his point of departure.[16]

Another, far starker example of how Hollywood attitudes toward disabled WW II veterans had changed around the time of the Korean War is MGM's *Bad Day at Black Rock* (1955), about a vet with one arm named John Macreedy

(Spencer Tracy) who visits an isolated hamlet in the Nevada desert on some mysterious purpose. The film reunited Tracy with long-time collaborator Dore Schary, the film's producer and former RKO production head who had come over to MGM in a similar capacity in 1948 following a dispute with RKO's new owner, archconservative Howard Hughes. A liberal caught in the middle during the blacklisting years, Schary had also produced *Till the End of Time* back in 1946; unlike the generally upbeat qualities of that film, however, *Bad Day* dwelled on the increasingly hostile actions of a xenophobic town toward the disabled stranger who has stirred things up.

To help with the lead character's authenticity, Schary hired two veterans for his directing and writing team. John Sturges, who was starting to make a name for himself as a director of action pictures, mainly Westerns, had directed and edited dozens of documentaries while serving in the Army Air Corps, most notably *Thunderbolt* (1945) which he co-directed with William Wyler. As for screenwriter Millard Kaufman, he had returned from the Marine Corps determined to pursue a career in the movies and landed his first job with the UPA animation studio, where among other duties he originated and developed the visually impaired Mr. Magoo cartoon character. He moved on to write the scripts for several feature-length live-action films during the late 40s and early 50s before signing on with Schary, who for this new project authorized him to base a screenplay on Howard Breslin's short story "Bad Time at Honda."[17]

Set several months after the end of World War II, *Bad Day at Black Rock* follows a Western structure by having a "good" outsider arrive in a sleepy western town only to find himself confronting villains. The outsider happens to be John Macreedy, a self-assured, goal-oriented fellow who piques the curiosity and resentment of the local townspeople. As Reno Smith (Robert Ryan) sagely notes to a crony: "I know those maimed guys. Their minds get twisted, they put on hairshirts, and act like martyrs. All of them are do-gooders, freaks, troublemakers." Refusing to tell them why he's come to their town, Macreedy finds himself the target of ableist aggression. It's verbal at first (one of the local yahoos, played by Lee Marvin, sees the one-armed Macreedy ascending the stairs to his hotel room and says tauntingly, "You look like you need a hand") but it quickly escalates into violence of various types, including attempted fisticuffs, which Macreedy expertly deflects through karate chops and a judo toss, and gunfire. The audience learns two things late in the film: that during the war several townspeople had murdered a farmer of Japanese descent and believed Macreedy was investigating the matter, and that Macreedy's sole purpose in visiting Black Rock was to find the farmer to give him a medal awarded posthumously to his son, who had died in Italy while saving Macreedy's life.

Though Schary, Sturges, and Kaufman followed the Breslin short story in its basic narrative flow, they deviated from it in a number of respects to stress Macreedy's difference from the other characters or to enhance his vulnerability. Attired in a dark suit for much of the movie, Macreedy stands out in sharp relief from the Black Rock denizens, virtually all of whom wear light-colored casual and work clothes. The filmmakers also underscored Macreedy's potential for victimization by casting an aging actor in the role; Tracy, a WW I veteran, was at 54 rather long in the tooth to be playing a recently discharged WW II enlisted man. Finally, and most importantly, they turned Breslin's explicitly able-bodied veteran into one with a missing arm. By pursuing such strategies, the filmmakers presumably wanted to increase the movie's tensions by stacking what they perceived as near-insurmountable odds against their courageous lead character, who in effect becomes "remasculinized" through his heroic deeds.

Though Schary and his crew provided a markedly different context for their disabled vet compared with the one surrounding the Perry Kincheloe character in Schary's *Till the End of Time* of nearly a decade before, both Kincheloe and Macreedy emerge as heroes who triumph over considerable adversities (mostly

A strange encounter with a nervous hotel clerk (John Ericson) turns out to be the least of the problems facing John Macreedy (Spencer Tracy) in 1955's Bad Day at Black Rock. *Someone at MGM must have found the prospect of featuring a one-armed character in its advertising somewhat unsettling, for both of Macreedy's hands are visible in this publicity still. Copyright © 1954 Loew's Inc.*

internal in Kincheloe's case, external in Macreedy's). It was an idea to which Schary would return shortly in one of his most heartfelt films.

While Schary was putting the finishing touches on *Bad Day at Black Rock*, his screenwriter for *Till the End of Time* was completing his own updated version of wartime disability: *The Eternal Sea* (1955), Republic Pictures' tribute to a charismatic true-life veteran of both World War II and Korea. A political moderate, Allen Rivkin had escaped the blacklisting era relatively unscathed and by the 1950s was writing movies for Republic, a studio awash in WW II-era profits that had begun supplementing its low-cost serialized movies and Westerns with prestigious movies, including Orson Welles's *Macbeth* (1948) and John Ford's *Rio Grande* (1950) and *The Quiet Man* (1952). Very much a part of this tradition, *The Eternal Sea* concentrated on John Hoskins (Sterling Hayden), an ambitious naval officer who loses a leg in a shipboard explosion during the engagement at Leyte Gulf but whose determination to succeed becomes if anything even stronger after his disablement.

As scripted by Rivkin and directed by John Auer, long a specialist in modestly budgeted war movies, *The Eternal Sea* exhibits a number of commendable qualities. For starters, Hoskins maintains a pretty good sense of humor about the loss of his leg. He informs his wife his athlete's-foot problem has now been cleared up, for example, and later tells Admiral Halsey all he has to worry about now are termites in his wooden leg. When the admiral asks him what he's going to do now, meaning after his presumed retirement, Hoskins says, "Oh, limp a little, I guess." Such self-directed quips might come across as slurs in a different context, but as delivered here (especially in Hayden's characteristic deadpan style), they are inoffensive and entirely consistent with the take-everything-in-stride Hoskins persona.

Despite these light touches, the filmmakers did not back off from readjustment issues, presenting his initial struggles and pain as he adjusts to the prosthesis (including a traumatic fall from a ladder while inspecting the construction of a ship). In general, however, the movie shows him to be quite matter-of-fact about his condition and his plans to return to active duty. At a hearing before a naval board, he disputes his physicians' conclusion that he should be retired: "I feel that they've erred in their personal fitness findings. They seem to be under the misapprehension that I have a physical disability." When reminded that he recently needed crutches, he responds: "That was two days ago. Sorry to see the Navy looking backwards." He does eventually take command of a new aircraft carrier, and, suitably remasculinized, he shakes up the Navy after the war's end by insisting that jets can and should be able to land on aircraft carriers and even volunteers to fly the lead jet to prove his point. Later, after he's been promoted to the rank of admiral, the Army recruits him and his jets to participate in the new war in Korea. After encountering several severely wounded veterans of the new conflict, Hoskins decides to dedicate himself to a new calling: working with disabled veterans to give them hope.

The Eternal Sea is marred by occasional able-biased indulgences (such as Auer's camera raking the lower half of Hoskins' body while he rests in a hospital bed) and a cornball ending in which a crosslike shadow falls on the floor while the Battle Hymn of the Republic—certainly an appropriate theme for this studio—fills the soundtrack, but perhaps its most serious drawback was and is its lack of availability. Most of Republic's "prestige" pictures performed poorly at the box office, appearing as they did during the industry-wide postwar slump, and *The Eternal Sea* was no exception. With his company in serious financial trouble by the time Auer finished the movie, Republic president Herbert J. Yates hustled *The Eternal Sea* in and out of theaters in rather short order. Though it remains an enigma to many—Jay Hyams's exemplary *War Movies*, encyclopedic in its range, makes no mention of it—this rarely screened film nevertheless is an outstanding visualization of a veteran's refusal to let a disabling circumstance and others' attitudes toward it stop him from pursuing a career.

A 1957 MGM film, *The Wings of Eagles*, presents a flamboyant hybrid of Noble Warrior and Civilian Superstar characteristics in the personage of Frank "Spig" Wead, a lieutenant commander in the Navy who became disabled in a non-military-related accident. A real-life WW I aviator who helped develop naval air power between the world wars, Wead also wrote short stories, novels, and the scripts for at least eighteen Hollywood movies, most of which dealt with military topics, up to the time of his death in 1947. John Ford, who shared his love of wartime action films and directed at least two productions from Wead scripts—*Air Mail* (1932) and *They Were Expendable* (1945)—sought to make a movie on his friend's life and had writers Frank Fenton and William Wister Haines develop a screenplay based on Wead's own writings, particularly his autobiographical *Wings for Men*. The resulting film, starring Ford's longtime collaborator John Wayne, is primarily an adulatory tribute to Wead's courage and resourcefulness.

The Wings of Eagles reaches a pivotal point about halfway through when Spig becomes paralyzed as a result of an accident. (As visualized in the film, he falls down a flight of stairs after responding to the cry of one of his young daughters in the middle of the night.) The movie thereafter spends considerable time examining Spig's rehabilitative process while sugar-coating Wead's relational difficulties with his wife Min (Maureen O'Hara) and their daughters. (As a example of this latter point, it shows Spig engaging in nostalgic reveries of his pre-disablement family life near the end as means of glossing over the Weads' estrangement.) It also dwells on his professional writing career, the highlights of which are his encounters with a John Ford-like director named "John Dodge," played by Ford regular Ward Bond.

Though its military context is highly conspicuous, *The Wings of Eagles* essentially follows a Civilian Superstar pattern, especially with regard to the way it shows Spig's extraordinary dual professions while concomitantly avoiding the typical problems of prejudice and access that wheelchair-users face daily. The film includes the near-mandatory scene of the Superstar walking a few climactic steps, and though to the filmmakers' credit they don't try to make him "pass" before a crowd of able-bodied onlookers (he walks those steps in a hospital with the support of crutches, leg braces, and friends) *The Wings of Eagles* does imply that he had to liberate himself from his wheelchair before he could leave the hospital and return to anything resembling a "normal" life. In addition, the film follows the frequent pattern of ascribing point-of-view shots to a disabled character mainly as a means of further isolating that character. Ford assigned two conspicuous "looks" to Spig while the latter gazes out a hospital window: a shot of people walking outside the facility, and a shot of a battleship with navy planes overhead. Spig seems rueful after both, since they remind him of two factors that for the moment seem insurmountable: his inability to walk and his disrupted naval career. Later, after Spig has in a sense returned to the ranks of the able-bodied (i.e., after he has walked a few steps and is back in uniform as a naval tactician following Pearl Harbor), Ford changed his visual strategy and endowed him with frequent POV shots, particularly as he looks through binoculars to see such things as planes landing and taking off, explosions, and ships sinking. Since Spig has by now been remasculinized, Ford returned to the usual Hollywood way of structuring narrative imagery.

An examination of the general tendencies by which mainstream filmmakers have depicted the disabled vets and their surrounding network of family and friends is perhaps a fitting way to conclude this discussion of mid–1950s Noble Warrior films. During the war, moviemakers more often than not stressed sentimental and patriotic qualities at the expense of fully fleshed-out characterizations, as in such films as *Song of Russia*, *Thirty Seconds Over Tokyo*, *Since You Went Away*, and *The Enchanted Cottage*. The first set of disabled-vet films to appear after the war—*Pride of the Marines*, *The Best Years of Our Lives*, *Till the End of Time*—contained more complex portrayals and emphasized the role of community, especially family, and the need of the disabled vet to return to it and be at one with it. As the mini-genre matured, however, fissures in the supporting network became more evident (e.g., the patronizing father-in-law in *Bright Victory*, the wife with second thoughts in *The Men*). By the time of *Stalag 17*, *Torch Song*, *Bad Day at Black Rock*, and *The Wings of Eagles*, the family had ruptured irreparably (despite the sentimentalized flashbacks of *The Wings of Eagles* noted above, the Wead family members remain estranged at film's end) if it was even present to begin with in the films' narrative framework. In the case of *Bad Day*, the community, far from welcoming the disabled vet, harasses him and tries to kill him. (*The Eternal Sea* remains a happy exception to this trend.) By eroding the disabled vets' supporting networks in this manner—in effect, re-isolating them— and by displacing or at least de-emphasizing the soldiers in favor of prominent disabled civilians (as in *With a Song in My Heart* and *Interrupted Melody*, which pushed the vets to the same kind of background status they "enjoyed" in the wartime *Since You Went Away*), moviemakers signaled a conclusion, if only a temporary one, to Noble Warrior films.

Though the new round of disabled-vet films sputtered within just a few years after it began, the Civilian Superstar trend continued into the 1960s with the appearance of *Sunrise at Campobello*, written and produced by Dore Schary and directed by Vincent Donehue. Schary, who had been fired from MGM as production head two years after *Bad Day at Black Rock*, decided to return to his east-coast roots and shortly thereafter began work on a play that examined a three-year period in the life of Franklin Roosevelt that commenced with the onset of his paralysis and ended triumphantly with his appearance before the 1924 Democratic national convention. The resulting play, *Sunrise at Campobello*, was a Broadway smash, winning five Tony awards and inspiring Schary to convert the drama into a film. Several people involved in the theatrical incarnation of *Campobello* also worked on the movie: Schary, who wrote the screenplay; Donehue, the director; Ralph Bellamy, who reprised his role as FDR (and had played a wheelchair-using character in the movies at least once before, in 1935's *Hands Across the Table*); and Alan Bunce, who replayed the part of New York governor Alfred Smith.

Stung by accusations that he had created propaganda on behalf of that year's Democratic national ticket, Schary tried to downplay the political significance of its mobility-impaired character by suggesting that *Campobello* was "a very simple, contained story about a man struck down by a crippling disease, and the effect it had upon his immediate family. He was a man who happened to be a political figure. . . . It could have been about any man; it happens to be the true story of the young Franklin Roosevelt." Like the other films of this trend, *Campobello* ends with its disabled main character returning to a former glory while concomitantly trying to "pass" for an able-bodied person. Schary saw FDR's lonely walk to the convention podium to nominate Al Smith for President as the film's climax: "At that moment, the entire convention broke loose. This was the moment that was to affect the entire world because this was the moment at which Roosevelt returned to politics." Yet, for Schary, the thing that defined the "moment" was not the speech itself (indeed, the movie ends before FDR gives it) but Roosevelt's emergence from his wheelchair to walk those ten long steps. Though FDR conducted much of his eventual presidency from a wheelchair, Schary found it necessary to conclude *Sunrise at Campobello* with the implication that he had to free himself from the vehicle in order to resume his career.[18]

Another "inspirational" film of the period that also had its basis in a hugely successful play was *The Miracle Worker* (1962), which examines the process by which Anne Sullivan (Anne Bancroft), an extraordinarily dedicated teacher, and Helen Keller (Patty Duke), a girl left deaf, blind, and speechless after contracting an infectious fever at the age of nineteen months, eventually break through communication barriers. Keller, whose later achievements included graduating cum laude from Radcliffe, lecturing throughout the world on such topics as blindness, deafness, socialism, and women's rights, and winning a roomful of awards for her tireless efforts on behalf of people with disabilities (Swedenborg Foundation executive director Darrell Ruhl spoke for many in suggesting that "her accomplishments in the face of unique difficulties have stirred our sense of the heroic"),[19] had also written numerous books. Playwright William Gibson used one of them—an autobiography of her early years called *The Story of My Life*—as the primary source material for *The Miracle Worker*, which ran on Broadway from 1959 to 1961. Even with the highly successful play still in production, its principals—Gibson, Bancroft, Duke, producer Fred Coe, and director Arthur Penn—started work on the movie adaptation.

Filming began in the summer of 1961, with interior scenes photographed in a Manhattan studio and exterior ones in Middletown, New Jersey. Penn and cinematographer Ernesto Caparos imbued the camerawork with "a very particular dark, moody look," in Duke's words, and often photographed Duke and Bancroft in the same shot. Their strategy of relying heavily on long and medium shots—often taken by cameras hand-held by operators riding in wheelchairs—took nothing away from the story's power, in Duke's opinion:

> One thing that characterized the look of *The Miracle Worker* was a lack of closeups. There was criticism at the time that this made the movie look too much like the play, but I don't agree. As I see it, Arthur concentrated on telling the story instead of punching it up every two minutes. Both as an actor and part of the audience, I never missed the closeups at all. There's so much action that to cut in is distracting. Also, there's so much going on psychologically between these two people that when you cut away to one or the other, you lose something of the dynamic. And boy, does it ever work when one of those rare closeups appears. You're so startled by it, you almost gasp.[20]

The Miracle Worker remains true to its theatrical heritage along another dimension by following the play closely in its narrative structure. Though the movie's ending is weaker in its emotional intensity than its Broadway counterpart, both movie and play focus on Sullivan, herself visually impaired, who has been given two weeks to "reach" the tantrum-throwing Keller on her own. She finger-spells constantly into Helen's hand, a strategy the girl perceives merely as game-playing. After frequent clashes of wills, culminating in the justly famous fight-for-authority dinnertime sequence, Anne and Helen finally achieve a major breakthrough; after Anne pulls the stubborn girl outside to a water pump, the latter remembers a babyhood term for water, "wah-wah," and finger-spells it to her teacher. The experience opens up a floodgate within Helen, who immediately and eagerly seeks out the names of everything and everyone around her.

The Miracle Worker differs from earlier Civilian Superstar movies in several respects. It divides its Civilian Superstar struggle-and-victory among two characters (indeed, much of the movie is about Anne, and Penn shot parts of it through filters to suggest her own impaired vision), and in neither case has the character reached major-league fame before her disablement. Nevertheless, the movie does resemble the others in the trend, particularly *Sunrise at Campobello*, in that the filmmakers treated the triumphs—Helen's utterance of her first word, FDR's walk to the podium—not only as hints of greatness to come but also as break-throughs toward an approximation of able-bodiedness. In an age when miracle cures had lost much of their vitality as narrative devices, these films seemed to say that the fulfillment of actions ordinarily associated with mainstream members is an acceptable symbolic substitute. In other words, the characters should start acting like majority members if they cannot be cured outright.

Despite the commercial and critical success of *The Miracle Worker* and its Academy Awards for Bancroft and Duke, the Civilian Superstar trend showed its age by taking a turn toward travesty two years later with the appearance of *Dr. Strangelove or: How I Learned to Stop Worrying and Love the Bomb*, a Columbia picture produced and directed by Stanley Kubrick. This dark satire on Cold War relations features Peter Sellers in three roles: a British colonel, an American presi-dent, and a German advisor to the president. The third of this trio, the film's title character, also happens to use a wheelchair and have a bionic arm prone to choking its owner or giving Nazi salutes during tense moments. Unlike most

Anne Sullivan and Helen Keller (Oscar-winners Anne Bancroft and Patty Duke) pump out a communication breakthrough in 1962's The Miracle Worker, *written by William Gibson and directed by Arthur Penn.*

other Civilian Superstars, Dr. Strangelove is disabled at the time the film introduces him, but like his peers he is an extraordinary person (an expert on international political affairs and weapons development, in his case) and does perform a "passing" act; while making plans with others for living underground in the post-Armageddon world, he rises out of his chair to take a few steps. "Mein Führer, I can walk!" he exclaims to the president, albeit mere seconds before a montage of thermonuclear bomb blasts concludes the film.

Dr. Strangelove got its start in 1961 when Kubrick discovered a 1958 Cold War novel by a former Royal Air Force lieutenant named Peter George. Recognizing its screen potential, he purchased the novel's screen rights for a paltry $3,000 and shortly thereafter began collaborating with George on the script. Kubrick originally envisioned the film as a weighty drama but changed his outlook as the writing progressed: "I was fascinated by the book—*Red Alert*, a serious suspense novel about what happens when one of the great powers pushes the wrong button. The film keeps the same suspense frame. But the more I worked on it, the more I was intrigued by the comic aspects—the façade of conventional reality being pierced."[21] To enhance the screenplay's sardonic comedy, he brought in humorist Terry Southern to work on it shortly before shooting began in early 1963.

The contributions of Kubrick, George, and Southern notwithstanding, Sellers was in many ways the main person responsible for developing the Strangelove character. Kubrick, who shot the movie in Great Britain mainly to accommodate the actor, allowed Sellers to improvise much of the Strangelove material—including the dramatic rise from a wheelchair—after jettisoning the film's original conclusion. (He had filmed and then rejected a pie fight of monumental proportions followed by the president and the Soviet ambassador, waist-deep in custard, feting Strangelove with a rendition of "For He's a Jolly Good Fellow.") For his part, Sellers was quite appreciative of the artistic license given him: "I especially enjoyed doing the mad scientist in *Dr. Strangelove* because Stanley Kubrick likes free improvisation that can be so stimulating. . . . Given a free hand, you can build, construct into the characterization. It's all any actor could ask for."[22] Despite its relatively brief screen time, his resulting creation remains a searing parody of the Civilian Superstar image.

The path to apathy during the 1950s and early 1960s was also strewn with relics of a bygone age: Sweet Innocents and Biblical characters cured of their disabilities. A British version of *A Christmas Carol* (1951) notwithstanding, adult women tended to dominate such movies during the first half of the 1950s while the latter portion of the decade and the first years of the next were a time for their more youthful counterparts, a rare adult male, and the recipients of Jesus Christ's faith healings.

Based on Tennessee Williams's greatest play, *The Glass Menagerie* (1950) set the stage for the industry's return to the adult Sweet Innocent. Adapted by Williams and Peter Berneis, directed by Irving Rapper, and released through Twentieth Century–Fox, the film reunited Jane Wyman and Jerry Wald, the actress and the producer who had worked together so successfully on *Johnny Belinda* two years before. Here Wyman played Laura Wingfield, the young St. Louis woman whom Williams had modeled after his own sister, Rose, turning the latter's reclusiveness and insanity into powerful shyness and a slight limp. Wyman played the character like a virginal, sweet young thing, a sheltered woman who blushes easily and often turns away. Broadway star Gertrude Lawrence made a rare movie appearance as her mother who cleaves to values of a bygone age, while Kirk Douglas played Jim O'Connor, the gentleman caller, and Arthur Kennedy, soon to appear in *Bright Victory*, played Laura's brother Tom.

With a famous play for its basis and a director with a strong theatrical background, *The Glass Menagerie* is hardly surprising in its talkiness, slow pace, and stagy feel. The filmmakers transferred most of Amanda and Laura's lengthy and demeaning discussions of disability to the screen intact, such as these samples from a representative conversation:

Peter Sellers in a publicity still for **Dr. Strangelove** *(1964). The photo hints at ideas never expressed in the final version of the film; the good doctor neither wields a pistol nor takes a spill out of his chair in the movie. Courtesy Movie Star News.*

LAURA: "But, Mother, I'm crippled."

AMANDA: "Don't use that word. How many times have I told you never, never to use that word? [pause] Well, you're not crippled. Just have a slight defect, that's all. Hardly noticeable. Laura, you don't even have to wear a brace anymore." [. . .]

LAURA: "But Mother, who would marry a . . .?"

AMANDA: "You're not crippled! Walk, Laura."

LAURA: "Walk?"

AMANDA: "Yes, walk. I want to see you walk. [Laura slowly gets up.] Walk around the room. Go on, walk! Walk around this room! You're not crippled. [Amanda begins to cry.] You're not crippled."

Rapper did give *The Glass Menagerie* some expressly cinematic touches here and there, but unfortunately they often suggested an ableist bias. As Laura, late for her typing exam, walks down a classroom aisle toward her seat, for example, Rapper's camera backtracks from her in close-up. Before she finally reaches her seat, he inserted a shot from her perspective as she walks forward, a shot designed to enhance Laura's isolation in conjunction with its use of sound: several other students turn to stare while the sounds of her uneven walking rhythm fill the soundtrack.

Faring not much better in its handling of disability issues, RKO's *Walk Softly, Stranger* (1950) tells the story of a card sharp and pathological crook named Chris Hale (Joseph Cotten) who arrives in a small Ohio town and works in a shoe factory with the intent of swindling the boss's daughter, Elaine Corelli (Alida Valli), a young woman who uses a wheelchair after an accident on the slopes of St. Moritz. Though director Robert Stevenson suggested a sense of the principals' perspectives by choosing camera angles corresponding roughly to their heights, he and writer Frank Fenton unfortunately bloated the movie with clichés and predictable events (most notably, that Chris falls for Elaine and allows himself to be reformed by her), including ableist manifestations. For example, when Chris suggests that "we're both failures—your legs and my life," Elaine, far from disputing him, responds with "Except that something can be done with your life."

RKO had actually completed *Walk Softly, Stranger* in 1948 but held it back until 1950 to capitalize on the presumed success of the upcoming British *The Third Man* (1949), which also starred Cotten and Valli. The strategy did nothing to improve the film's chances, however; *Walk Softly, Stranger* hardly left a footprint at the box office and indeed went on to become the studio's biggest money loser that year to the tune of more than a quarter of a million dollars. As it turned out, *Walk Softly, Stranger* was the final film overseen by Dore Schary for RKO before a dispute with Howard Hughes sent him packing to MGM. Fortunately for him, he got out before the film had a chance to detonate.[23]

The weakest of the 1950 films to depict an adult Sweet Innocent is unquestionably *Union Station*. With a screenplay by Sydney Boehm from a story by

Thomas Walsh and directed by Rudolph Maté, the Paramount movie starred William Holden as a police lieutenant on the trail of criminals who have abducted a young blind woman named Lorna Murchison (Allene Roberts) with the intent of squeezing ransom money out of her wealthy father. Though Lorna is by no means the main character of the film, it seems at first as if the filmmakers were going to treat her as a fully dimensional human being; once she's abducted, however, the other characters with one or two exceptions regard her merely as the human object in their deadly game, and the moviemakers limited her time on-screen to her father's pre-disablement home movies of her and scenes of her falling down, screaming, crying, and begging her kidnappers to kill her. Not only did the filmmakers make her out to be the picture of abject helplessness, but they devalued her further by indicating that her father never took any photographs or home movies of her after her blindness, as if she had ceased being a person worth photographing after her injury. Vague on some details and highly questionable on the others, *Union Station* exemplifies the Sweet Innocent kind of film at its worst.

RKO's *On Dangerous Ground*, which appeared the following year, represented a rare Hollywood film created by a person with a disability. Adapted from Gerald Butler's novel *Mad with Much Heart* and produced by John Houseman, *On Dangerous Ground* was directed and co-written by the celebrated film noir stylist Nicholas Ray, who lost the use of his right eye in a 1938 accident. (Classified 4-F during World War II, Ray honed his narrative skills by writing and directing radio programs for the Office of War Information.) The movie, which stars Robert Ryan as a cynical and stoic plainclothes cop named Jim Wilson, has the look of a classic *noir* at first with its urban setting, night scenes, and wet streets but takes an unexpected turn; Wilson, in danger of being thrown off the force for his above-the-law tactics, is assigned to a case seventy miles outside the city, where he helps a farmer (Ward Bond) track down his daughter's killer through rugged terrain.

Their efforts lead them to an isolated house in the mountains inhabited by a blind woman named Mary Mauldin (Ida Lupino). The men are not convinced of her blindness and in a gesture reminiscent of his actions in *The Woman on the Beach*, Ryan waves a lit cigarette lighter in front of her eyes. Drawing on his own experiences as a visually impaired person, Ray included a brief subjective shot that showing a flame against a blurry background to prove to the audience, if not to the men, that she is indeed blind. Such a visual tactic, however, was hardly sufficient to elevate her character beyond the usual helpless victim level. Ray portrays her as a stock Sweet Innocent: a "perfect" woman totally dedicated to and dependent on her younger brother, "blind" to his criminal activities. When the brother falls to his death after Wilson and the farmer trap him, she sadly notes that "he was my eyes" and Wilson, feeling guilty, allows pity and paternalism to win out again in the movies by taking his place.

The best known film of this trend during Hollywood's apathetic age remains *Magnificent Obsession* (1954), a remake of the 1935 Universal film of the same name directed by Douglas Sirk and produced by Ross Hunter for Universal-International. The Danish-born Sirk (né Detlef Sierck), whose peripatetic directorial career included stints in Germany and South Africa before he settled down in Hollywood in the mid–1940s, was interested in the premise ("I have always been intrigued by the problems of blindness," he said) but nevertheless had his doubts about the Lloyd Douglas material. "Ross Hunter gave me the book and I tried to read it, but I just couldn't," said Sirk. "It is the most confused book you can imagine, it is so abstract in many respects that I didn't see a picture in it. Then he showed me an outline he had had done of the old picture by John Stahl—a name that did not mean anything to me. (And, by the way, I did not see the Stahl picture.) I took the treatment home, and I read it. So far as I remember, the outline was quite different from the book. I had a feeling this could make a picture."[24]

Adaptor Wells Root and screenwriter Robert Blees worked directly from the original movie's script, and in Hunter and Sirk's hands the resulting movie, which cost only about $689,000 to produce, followed the basic structure of the original but deviated sharply in terms of its style and apparent attitudes toward the subject matter. In the earlier version Stahl used subtle humor to mock the story's patently absurd storyline, but Sirk and Hunter avoided that approach, choosing instead to amplify the storyline's soap opera-like qualities. In so doing they turned their film, in Betsy McLane's words, "into an operatic orgy of color, flowers, mirror shots, shadows, and process photography."[25]

The movie co-starred Rock Hudson as wealthy wastrel turned obsessed surgeon Bob Merrick. For the role of Helen Phillips (renamed from Helen Hudson to avoid overlap with the film's co-star), Hunter and Sirk selected Jane Wyman, who by virtue of her work in *Johnny Belinda* and *The Glass Menagerie* was fast becoming the queen of pan-disability roles. "In giving [the role of Helen] a new individuality I have, as with other characterization of handicapped persons, gone to considerable trouble to achieve two objectives: simplicity and authenticity," she wrote. "For *Johnny Belinda* I went to a school for the deaf, became friendly with several people who could neither speak nor hear and wore ear plugs throughout the portrayal which shut out all sound eight hours a day during shooting. To play the club-footed character of *The Glass Menagerie* I spent much time with a little crippled girl. I discovered then, even as I discovered from a blind companion who assisted me with technical advice on *Magnificent Obsession*, that my greatest problem would be the tendency to overact."[26]

A recently widowed woman on the verge of middle age, Helen Phillips represents a blend of the Sweet Innocent and Saintly Sage stereotypes; as critic David Rodowick has noted, she possesses "disturbing naïveté and apparent saintliness."[27] Sirk and Hunter played on such qualities in a memorable scene late in the film after a trio of European doctors has told her they think it unwise to attempt an operation to restore her sight. Alone in her hotel room with her friend Joyce (Barbara Rush) at night, she utters dialogue calculated to jerk tears from the driest of eyes: "It's funny, but nighttime is the worse time. It does get darker, you know.

And then when I finally do get to sleep, I—I know that when I wake up in the morning there won't be any dawn." As somber piano and string music plays on the soundtrack, Joyce cries on Helen's shoulder in a striking, shadowy two-shot of the women in which an offscreen light source illuminates Helen's profile from the left of the frame.

Closely following the original film, Hunter, Sirk, and their writers had Helen perceive herself a burden on Bob and run away. Meanwhile, Bob completes his training to become a surgeon and later tracks Helen down to a New Mexico hospital where he and the audience discover she has developed new symptoms and requires an immediate operation. Despite initial doubts Bob begins the surgical procedure, which, given the heavy-duty "oooooing" of an offscreen chorus and the presence of his spiritual mentor Ed Randolph (Otto Kruger) who through Russell Metty's cinematography appears to loom God-like above the operating room, takes on a quasi-religious quality of enormous proportions. Sirk's sudsy classic—"a combination of kitsch, and craziness, and trashiness," he called it—concludes with little doubt as to the fate of Helen's vision and relationship with her "magnificently obsessed" Bob.[28]

The Sweet Innocent trend took an unusual turn with *Porgy and Bess* (1959), Sam Goldwyn's $7 million widescreen musical extravaganza based on George and Ira Gershwin's 1935 "folk opera" of the same name which in turn had been based on a 1925 novel by DuBose Heyward and a play written two years later by Heyward and his wife Dorothy. A movie fraught with problems during its production (a fire of suspicious origin destroyed the set at Goldwyn's studio in July 1958, and later that month the producer fired director Rouben Mamoulian over "creative differences" and replaced him with Otto Preminger), *Porgy and Bess* is set during the years before WW I and focuses mainly on the impoverished, orthopedically impaired Porgy (Sidney Poitier) who lives in a black ghetto of Charleston, South Carolina, called Catfish Row and whose main form of transportation is a goat-drawn cart. Basically an easygoing fellow, Porgy is surrounded by amoral if not outright corrupt characters: the two-timing, heroin-imbibing Bess (Dorothy Dandridge), the dope-peddling Sportin' Life (Sammy Davis, Jr.), and the hot-blooded Crown (Brock Peters) who kills another man during a craps-game dispute near the film's beginning. After Crown leaves the community to avoid the police, his girlfriend Bess moves in with Porgy, but when he eventually reappears to claim her Porgy kills him during an ensuing struggle. Porgy goes into hiding,

Like so many advertisements for disability-related films, this one promoting 1954's Magnificent Obsession *hardly indicates a character's impaired status. In this instance, the ad's designers were far more "obsessed" with making the Jane Wyman character appear to gaze up at a higher authority and doctoring her décolletage.*

Magnificent Obsession

A story of Love...that will become one of the great emotional thrills of your lifetime!

Universal-International presents

JANE WYMAN
ROCK HUDSON
BARBARA RUSH

LLOYD C. DOUGLAS'

Magnificent Obsession

COLOR BY TECHNICOLOR

with AGNES MOOREHEAD · OTTO KRUGER · GREGG PALMER

Directed by Douglas Sirk · Screenplay by Robert Blees · Produced by Ross Hunter and while he does a hooked Bess decides to follow Sportin' Life up to New York City. When Porgy returns to Catfish Row and learns what happened, the movie ends with Porgy making plans to follow her.

Despite its downbeat ending (which one movie executive wanted changed by having Porgy rise up from his goat-cart and walk) and Porgy's killing of Crown, *Porgy and Bess* does contain vestiges of the Sweet Innocent type. Porgy is essentially an innocent character beset by evils of various sorts (in a review of the stage musical's 1976 revival, William Bender described the story as "simply a fable about man's innocence in a hard and corrupting world") and his impairment and use of a cart only enhance his presumed vulnerable qualities. A number of things do set him apart from the standard Sweet Innocent, however, and make for a more resonant character; he's an adult black male who conspicuously avoids the passivity so long associated with the stereotype. As *New York Times* correspondent Clifford Mason noted, Porgy is quick to take matters into his own hands: "Even though its Negroes are frankly stereotypes, at least we have a man, a real man, fighting for his woman and willing to follow her into the great unknown, the big city, poor boy from Catfish Row that he is." Whatever virtues the film may have by showing a disabled character refusing to be victimized, they are more than overwhelmed by the problem suggested in Mason's statement: namely, the black stereotypes. Goldwyn, who spent a hefty $650,000 to obtain the screen rights, endured considerable pressure from members of the African–American community before, during, and after the movie's production and initially had difficulty signing an actor willing to play Porgy. (Harry Belafonte, the only major black male star of the time, turned him down flat. Poitier agreed to play the part, thought better of it, and then had to be convinced by Goldwyn that the role and the movie would not do blacks a disservice.) The various disputes over the depiction of racial stereotypes in *Porgy and Bess* not only contributed indirectly to Goldwyn's retirement from the industry—at age 77, he had produced his last film with the money-losing *Porgy and Bess*—but also led to the production's current status as a rarely screened movie.[29]

Other members of the Sweet Innocent trend's second stage featured far more traditional and banal types: preadolescent Sweet Innocents and adults cured through the direct intervention of Jesus Christ. The kiddy pictures included such saccharine efforts as *The Leather Saint* (1956), Paramount's preposterous tale of an Episcopal priest (John Derek) who moonlights as a boxer to raise money for a bunch of unbelievably cute children who wear leg braces and use wheelchairs, and a couple of films—*The Littlest Hobo* (1958) and *Lad: A Dog* (1962)—that dealt with the therapeutic effects of their canine title characters on disabled youths. Overwhelming these B films in sheer dollar power was the Walt Disney entry into the disabled-child sweepstakes: *Pollyanna* (1960), a remake of the Mary Pickford silent. Written and directed by newcomer David Swift, *Pollyanna* starred an effervescent juvenile named Hayley Mills in the title role and Jane Wyman, taking a break from her frequent portrayals of disabled movie characters to play opposite one as the girl's Aunt Polly. Critics gave high marks to the film and Mills in particular, who won a special Oscar for her performance. For instance, A. H. Weiler of the *New York Times* wrote that "the blonde, pixieish Miss Mills gives a restrained, natural and gratifyingly mature performance. She is a likable youngster whose mannerisms and speech are unaffected and convincing." Swift changed the details of the girl's disabling accident—she's struck by a vehicle in the Eleanor Porter book and the Pickford film but falls out of a tree in this one—but like its forebears the Disney *Pollyanna* remains a vapidly optimistic treatment of a curable Sweet Innocent. As Weiler noted, "Only an unregenerate cynic with an abiding dislike of kids, good or bad, Technicolor, and a gentle legend spun in standard, obvious style, would rail at this picture-postcard remembrance of improbable things past. Like its sub-teen, 'Glad Girl' heroine, this visit with *Pollyanna* is pleasant and unlikely to hurt or excite even the small fry." [30]

Matching the Disney film in blandness were a pair of slow-moving, reverential accounts of the life of Christ that had facile faith healings among their narrative components: *King of Kings* (1961), an MGM "70 mm Super Technirama" spectacle directed by *On Dangerous Ground*'s Nicholas Ray from a script by Philip Yordan, and *The Greatest Story Ever Told* (1965), a United Artists release cowritten, produced, and directed in the Cinerama format by George Stevens. Mammoth in their scale, simplistic in their perspectives (the former film even had Christ, all shadows and blurred motion, wordlessly cure several people of their disabilities by merely casting his outline on them after narrator Orson Welles solemnly intones, "It was the time of miracles"), the movies represented the ultimate in apathy on disability issues.

The 1950s and early 1960s were also a time when filmmakers began reviving fears about disabled people by creating a disturbing number of films that returned to the ancient stereotype of the disabled villain. Amputees bore the brunt of such slurs, with the earliest of the films based on famous literature carrying seafaring themes.

The Disney company was one of the first studios to start making movies overseas as a means of getting at revenue accounts "frozen" by European governments. At the suggestion of Walt's brother Roy, Disney decided to make *Treasure Island* (1950) specifically in Great Britain for that purpose and put together a team consisting of producer Perce Pearce, writer Lawrence Edward Watkin, and director Byron Haskin to pull it off. Notable also as Disney's first feature-length film to contain no animation, *Treasure Island*, starring 13-year-old Bobby Driscoll as Jim Hawkins and Robert Newton in a memorable turn as Long John Silver, brought in fine critical reviews and a high margin of profit.[31]

Like the 1934 MGM version, *Treasure Island* initially objectifies Silver from Jim's perspective; Haskin first shows the pirate behind a counter after Squire Trelawney has just hired him as a cook, but seconds later the audience, sharing Jim's point of view, sees he's missing a leg. Unlike the earlier film, however,

Newton's Silver comes across as far less murderous a character than Wallace Beery's—due, no doubt, to a studio decision to trim the movie's more graphic scenes for its 1975 re-release. (This move likely affected the portrayal of the blind pirate Pew as well; he merely disappears in this version of the film.) It's thus difficult to determine the extent of violent behavior the filmmakers originally attributed to Silver, but even in the edited film there's no denying his lethal capabilities; after Squire Trelawney, Dr. Livesey, and Captain Smollett reject Silver's terms for peace and even refuse to help him up off the ground, he gets up by himself and swears they will be sorry. In a tight close-up of his ruddy mug, the pirate snarls, "Them that die will be the lucky ones."

Robert Newton pulled out all the stops in his portrayal of Long John Silver. Alternately pop-eyed and squinty, his charismatic Silver is loud, lying, and blustery, and an opportunist par excellence. If anything, Newton gave an even more overblown performance in the Australian-made sequel, *Long John Silver's Return to Treasure Island* (1954), written by Martin Rackin and produced by Joseph Kaufman, with Haskin again serving as director. Laden with shameless overacting by just about every actor concerned, this latter film, also known simply as *Long John Silver*, was a veritable ode to disabled villainy; the title character found himself competing with the likes of a murderous mutineer with one eye simply called "Patch" and Israel Hands, blinded by Jim Hawkins in the previous film and presumed dead, who now maniacally seeks revenge on the boy for the disablement.

While production on *Long John Silver's Return to Treasure Island* was underway, the Disney studio looked to ways of mixing disability, villainy, and the sea once again but in the form that had made it famous: animation. The studio had long been interested in the concept of an animated villainous amputee by virtue of its countless cartoons featuring Pegleg Pete, one of Disney's oldest recurring characters (an overweight, loud-mouthed, cigar-chomping feline dapper enough to wear spats on both his shoe and his prosthesis, Pete clashed with Mickey Mouse and friends in 1935's *Mickey's Service Station* and numerous other shorts).[32] Now, in the wake of *Treasure Island*'s success, the studio returned to the idea in one of its more famous animated features, *Peter Pan* (1953).

With Hans Conried, Kathryn Beaumont, and *Treasure Island*'s Bobby Driscoll providing the respective vocal characterizations for Captain Hook/Mr. Darling, Wendy, and the title character, *Peter Pan* was somewhat unusual for Disney in that the studio had to seek permission from another organization to make it. (Accustomed to using public-domain or original material for years, the studio had to secure the screen rights from London's Great Ormond Street Hospital for Sick Children, to which playwright James Barrie had assigned the copyright.) In addition, the studio head reportedly felt restrained by the familiarity of the play's characters and narrative structure; he believed he couldn't be as free to "Disneyfy" them as he could those of folk and fairy tales.[33] In most other respects, however, the film was a typical product of the assembly-line way of making cartoons that had become standard procedure at the studio by the early 1950s. No less than eight people were credited as story contributors, while three others—Hamilton Luske, Clyde Geronimi, and Wilfred Jackson—served as directors.

Critic and historian Richard Schickel has rightly asserted that "the Disney artists were never able to set the gentle wistfulness of *Peter Pan* on film. . . . By this time the studio style was so inflexibly realistic, so harsh and so obviously the product of a factory system, that it was incapable of catching more than the broad outlines of " the play. A vivid illustration of this point is the general characterization of Hook himself; all transparent craftiness and grating buffoonery, he comes across as far more lugubrious and manic than his predecessors in the play and Herbert Brenon's 1924 film of the same name. The filmmakers exaggerated everything about him as he single-mindedly seeks revenge on Peter Pan for cutting off his hand and feeding it to a crocodile. Instead of having their disabled creation merely try to poison Pan, for example, they provided a more visual dimension to his villainy by having him deliver a gift-wrapped bomb. (When Mr. Smee asks if it wouldn't be more humane to slit his throat, Hook while lowering the package on a rope into Pan's hideout replies with smirking relish, "Aye, that it would, Mr. Smee.

One of the most enduring of Obsessive Avengers, Captain Hook has appeared in at least three movies since James M. Barrie wrote his famous play near the turn of the century. Here he matches wits with the title sprite of Disney's Peter Pan. *Copyright © 1952 Walt Disney Productions.*

But I have given me word not to lay a finger, or a hook, on Peter Pan, and Captain Hook never breaks a promise.") Like their silent-film counterparts, however, the directors unfortunately accentuated Hook's prosthesis at every turn; indeed, there are very few shots of the captain in which the hook is *not* conspicuous, as he often uses to mete out punishment or simply brandishes it as a threat. By the time the crocodile—as obsessed with eating the rest of Hook as the latter is to gain revenge on Pan—pursues the hapless Avenger across the seas and into the sunset, about the only thing the movie leaves unanswered about Hook is his pre-disablement identity.[34]

A discussion of seafaring disability films of the 1950s would not be complete without *Moby Dick* (1956), John Huston's mammoth remake of the two Warner Bros. vehicles for John Barrymore. Huston, a liberal whose sympathies for HUAC-besieged filmmakers were well known (he, along with William Wyler and screenwriter Philip Dunne, had formed a group in 1947 called the Committee for the First Amendment to organize activities on the progressives' behalf), had been living and working in Ireland and Great Britain for several years when he began work on a dream delayed since 1942 to bring the novel back to the screen. "I must have read *Moby-Dick* eight or ten times without ever thinking of making a film," said he. "Then I did think of making a film of it and wrote a script and put it away and gave up the idea. It was several years after that that I returned to it. The material fascinated me, and it was a preoccupation—how to get it on the screen, and, indeed, how to define it."[35]

Huston spared little expense in pursuit of that quest. After setting himself up as the film's producer, director, and co-screenwriter (the other writer, Ray Bradbury, later complained bitterly about Huston receiving a writing credit) and striking a deal with Warners to distribute and help bankroll the film, he assembled an international cast that included Gregory Peck as Ahab, Richard Basehart as Ishmael, Leo Genn as Starbuck, Friedrich Ledebur as Queequeg, and Orson Welles as Father Mapple. Huston chose the southeastern Irish port of Youghal for its strong resemblance to New Bedford of the 1840s and shot much of the movie there as well as in London, Wales, Portugal, the Canary Islands, and the Irish Sea. His obsession with faithfulness to the novel led him to modify a century-old ship, which coincidentally had served as the *Hispaniola* in Disney's *Treasure Island*, to match Melville's description of the *Pequod* and insist on having Ahab's fabled prosthesis be made of genuine whalebone. Huston did interject a scene that had no direct equivalent in Melville's work, but as far as he was concerned it clarified a major unstated element of the novel:

> I finally perceived at least to my own satisfaction, what the point of the book was—a blasphemy—and there, by the way, was the most difficult problem in writing the screenplay: the realization on the part of the mate, the second mate, and the crew of the *Pequod* that they were engaged in an unholy undertaking. The whole script was right except for a scene that would point this up. . . .

What turned the trick was my realization one day—a ray of light hit me—that they were not doing what they were supposed to do: to furnish oil for the lamps of the world, light. In this they were committing, according to the Quaker mentality, a sin; and it was then the realization hit that they were engaged in something devilish. . . . The scene was in Ahab's cabin when Starbuck confronts him. That was really the heart of the picture and not in *Moby-Dick*, not in the book. I think Melville would have approved.[36]

In addition to stressing the diabolic side of Ahab and his aim, Huston emphasized the captain's isolated and objectified qualities. Unlike the Barrymore movies which turn Melville's Ahab into a highly sociable and able-bodied person for much of their running-time, Huston's movie immediately presents him as an outsider and defines him in terms of his disability; all conversation and music stop in a boisterous New Bedford tavern during a rainy evening when its occupants detect an odd tapping sound and stare out a window (as does the audience) to see the lower half of Ahab walk by, his whalebone prosthesis prominent. Huston preserved the captain's objectified quality throughout the movie—indeed, the distinctive sound of Ahab's walk becomes kind of a motif—and, abetted by Peck's wooden performance, the enigmatic character comes across as not much more than a basic Obsessive Avenger but with a distinctly demoniacal twist.

Though movies of the sea most strongly reflected Hollywood's renewed interest in linking villainy with disability during the 1950s, they weren't the only ones to do so. Warner Bros., never hesitant to authorize remakes of earlier successes, dusted off *Mystery of the Wax Museum* to serve as the basis for a prominent contribution to the 3-D craze: *House of Wax* (1953). Directed by the visually impaired André de Toth,[37] the film features Vincent Price as a sculptor burned in a fire whose orthopedic impairments, visualized as a conspicuous stoop and limp and scarred body quickly come to emblemize his evil ways, and Charles Bronson (né Buchinski) as Igor, a prelingual deaf assistant modeled after Matthew Betz's Hugo in the earlier film but given much more screen time to serve his demented employer. As for the director of the film's original incarnation, Michael Curtiz continued his long history of creating villains for the Cinema of Isolation with *The Proud Rebel* (1958), about a Civil War veteran (Alan Ladd) and his attempts to help his speech-impaired son (Ladd's real-life son David) between wranglings with a villainous one-armed sheep rancher (Dean Jagger) over the family dog. Produced by Samuel Goldwyn, Jr., son of the pioneer who had enlightened the screen with the *Dark Angel* films and *The Best Years of Our Lives*, *The Proud Rebel* demonstrates little of his father's philosophy. As with so many other disability dramas, it shows the villain as having absolutely nothing redeeming about him, his missing arm signifying a missing morality, while the dog-loving child (mostly the creation of screenwriter Lillie Hayward, who as principal writer for 1962's *Lad: A Dog* was to design a similar character) exhibits the usual sense of sweetness and innocence.

Hollywood's rediscovery of disabled villainy continued unabated into the early 1960s. It took a subtler form in *What Ever Happened to Baby Jane?* (1962), based by Lukas Heller on Henry Farrell's novel, produced and directed by Robert Aldrich, and released through Warners. In this famous shocker about two middle-aged show-biz sisters, the audience and just about everyone in the film are led to believe that, years ago, Baby Jane Hudson (Bette Davis) accidently hit her sister Blanche (Joan Crawford) with a car while in a drunken stupor, forcing the latter character to use a wheelchair the rest of her life. The film reveals much later that the circumstances surrounding Blanche's disabling accident were far different from the generally believed version of them; it was Blanche, humiliated by her sister at a party only moments before, who tried to run down Baby Jane but missed her target and struck a stone gate instead, the force of which snapped her spine. She was still able to gain revenge on her sister by keeping her awash in endless waves of guilt, but her scheme comes back to haunt her when Baby Jane learns the truth twenty-five years later and torments the wheelchair user with unbelievably macabre acts.

Filmed quickly on numerous improvised interiors and exteriors at a bargain-basement cost of $825,000, *Baby Jane* featured among other things the historic teaming of Bette Davis and Joan Crawford, both of whom had a history of playing opposite physically disabled characters in the movies. (For Davis, it was as early as *Of Human Bondage* and as recently as the previous year's *Pocketful of Miracles*; for Crawford, such productions as *The Unknown*, *Torch Song* and the 1957 British *The Story of Esther Costello*.)[38] Philosophical about Davis getting to play the juicier role, Crawford nevertheless expressed her perspectives in an unfortunate way: "I didn't go in blind, mind you. I knew that Bette had the best scenes, that she could top me all along the way. I was a cripple, physically, and she was demented, mentally, and the mental always wins out on the screen." She, Aldrich, and Heller ascribed a pronounced helpless quality to her character, presumably to obscure Blanche's dark secret, but as far as *New York Times* critic Bosley Crowther was concerned the strategy backfired: "As a poor thing stuck in a wheelchair . . . she might earn one's gentle compassion. But she is such a sweetly smiling fraud, such an artlessly helpless ninny, that one feels virtually nothing for her. No wonder her crazy sister finds her a deadly bore." Despite critical drubbings, *What Ever Happened to Baby Jane?* brought in almost double its production cost in less than two weeks and eventually grossed about $10 million.[39]

Baby Jane proved a low budget was no detriment in the fight against the ever-expanding influence of television during the early 1960s, but other moviemakers, convinced big money was the key to lure audiences back into theaters, placed their bets on wide-screen processes, color, and exotic locations for their productions. These latter films, several of which featured a return to the notion of evil males with amputated limbs, resulted in widely varying returns at the box office.

Among the first was 1962's *Taras Bulba*, a $7 million production adapted from Nikolai Gogol's novel by Karl Tunberg and former blacklistee Waldo Salt, directed by J. Lee Thompson, and produced by Harold Hecht for distribution through United Artists. Set in sixteenth century Ukraine but photographed on the sweeping pampas of Argentina with hundreds of Argentine soldiers recruited as extras, this costumer begins with the formation of an uneasy alliance of Cossacks and Poles led respectively by Taras Bulba and Prince Grigory (Yul Brynner and Guy Rolfe) against forces of the Ottoman empire. Immediately after their victory over the Turks, Grigory, ordinarily a smooth and crafty sort, badly misjudges the temperament of the Cossacks by stating the latter are mere stooges under the control of Poland. This verbal power gesture is met by a shocking physical one; an enraged Taras reaches over and slices off the prince's right hand with his saber. Grigory does not reappear until some twenty years later into the story, when he clashes with Taras' hot-blooded son Andrei (Tony Curtis). When the latter attempts to make a deal, Grigory snarls, "You ask me to accept your word, the handclasp of a Cossack? I extended my hand to a Cossack once." As he wields a saber above Andrei's own wrist while saying, "We take our hands too much for granted," Grigory almost pays back the house of Bulba for his disability but thinks better of it and later uses Andrei in a scheme involving a full-scale assault on the Cossack forces. In general, Grigory is a classic disabled villain: treacherous at every turn, completely transparent, and distressingly one-dimensional. When Taras later slays him during a "cast of thousands" battle scene, he elicits as much remorse as might a cardboard cutout being knocked over.

Taras Bulba mustered only scant praise and performed miserably at the ticket window (it ended up $3 million in the red)[40] but such was hardly the fate of another big-budgeted 1962 film with a villainous amputee: the British *Dr. No*, the first of the long-running James Bond movie series produced by Americans Harry Saltzman and Albert Broccoli. Richard Maibaum, who was to write most of the subsequent Bond scripts, served as the primary screenwriter of this loose adaptation of Ian Fleming's novel, with Terence Young directing. Saltzman and Broccoli narrowed a broad field of candidates to play the film's secret-agent protagonist down to an obscure Scots actor named Sean Connery, who had broken into British movies in 1956 playing a jewel thief in the bleak little disability-related drama *No Road Back*. As for the title character, an evil genius with mechanical claw-like appendages for hands, the producers settled on a native Montrealer named Joseph Wiseman after Noel Coward, their first choice, gave them "no" for an answer.

Filmed in Jamaica and London, *Dr. No* eventually reveals its mysterious disabled antagonist to be the bastard offspring of a German missionary and a Chinese woman who runs a multimillion-dollar atomic facility on a small island near Jamaica. His tinkering with the volatile fuel has had its consequences, as he matter-of-factly tells the British agent: "My work has given me a unique knowledge of radioactivity. But not without costs [raises his right prosthesis] as you see." As with all the Bond villains to come, No's nefarious plans carry global implications; spurned by both the eastern and western powers, he now works for the

SPECTRE terrorist organization and plots to upend a Mercury spacecraft at Cape Canaveral with a radio beam. Bond, who baits the scientist out of frustration (after No foils the agent's attempt to hide a knife, Bond says sarcastically, "Well, we can't all be geniuses, can we? Tell me, does the toppling of American missiles really compensate for having no hands?"), eventually escapes and throws No's facility into chaos. The scientist soon meets his death in classic fashion shortly after wrestling with Bond atop a core-element platform in the middle of a water coolant tank; as the platform lowers into the bubbling water, Bond pulls himself up but No, his mechanical "fingers" failing him, cannot and goes under with the nuclear core. Impassive, murderous, devoid of emotion, Dr. No helped make his namesake a heavyweight at the box office and set the pattern for a long line of assorted lethal oddities that passed for humans in the Bond movies to follow.

Moviemakers raised fears of amputees again in a 1963 effort that portrayed a disabled WW II veteran in the worst possible way: *Charade*, scripted by Peter Stone from his co-authored novel *The Unsuspecting Wife*, and produced and directed by Stanley Donen for Universal. Filmed amid picturesque French locations, *Charade* had among its lesser characters a sinister vet named Herman Scoby (George Kennedy), outfitted with a prosthesis on his right arm and one of a trio of villains after a fortune. The film eventually reveals him to have lost his hand to a Nazi machine-gun blast after he and his cronies had just stashed $250,000 in gold originally earmarked for the French resistance with the intent of retrieving it after the war. As the movie frequently demonstrates, Herman viciously wields his claw-like appliance against anyone who gets in his way, notably the movie's main characters played by Cary Grant and Audrey Hepburn. (Among the movie's more

The actor who said "yes" to No: Joseph Wiseman as Dr. No's *pernicious title character, the first in a line of disabled villains to battle British secret agent James Bond.*

vivid moments are Herman's rooftop struggle with the Grant hero—claw aimed at the latter's face—and his stalking of the Hepburn heroine, which Donen visualized by photographing him from a very low angle with a backtracking camera as he verbally and prosthetically threatens her.) Donen accentuated Herman's claw right up through the time when his cohorts come across his drowned body in a bathtub; they and the audience see Herman's prosthesis sticking up out of the water. Shockingly underwhelmed by his death, the gang leader (James Coburn) eulogizes him in the following terms: "Poor old Herman. Seems like him and good luck always *was* strangers. Well, maybe now he'll meet up with his other hand someplace." A far cry from the disabled-vet films of the 1940s and early 1950s, *Charade* aptly illustrates just how low the Cinema of Isolation had sunk.

Assessing the impact of this decidedly mixed bag of 1950s and early 1960s movies on able-bodied attitudes and on disabled people's self-esteem is a problem-fraught affair at best. According to Jane Wyman, who received considerable mail on her various portrayals, some of the movies had a positive influence. "Occasionally during the eternal job of reading manuscripts one comes along in which the leading character is a handicapped person," she wrote. "To me this becomes not only a great source of inspiration when the story is good but also a tremendous incentive to action. Such stories invariably have more spiritual value than others and my mail indicates that authentic creations of such characters on the screen do much good for the afflicted themselves. . . . My correspondents tell me that a good portrayal of such a role aids millions of people in understanding the problem of the handicapped and simultaneously to treat them as human beings rather than freaks of nature. An actress could ask no greater satisfaction from her work than this."[41]

Yet the "spiritual value" to which Wyman alluded remains a highly questionable dimension of the movies, especially with its strong ties to the longstanding stereotypes of the Sweet Innocent and the Saintly Sage. Particularly problematic were and are the "inspirational" Civilian Superstar movies, designed along what their creators undoubtedly believed were positive lines. Unlike the Noble Warrior films, which made at least a tentative effort to confront prejudice toward people with physical disabilities and questions of access, the Civilian Superstar films typically skimmed right over such problems. Discrimination seldom raised its ugly head in these movies, and in addition they carried implicit negative messages that audience members with physical disabilities could not help but perceive: that the only physically disabled people worth depicting are larger-than-life types (apart from the stereotypical extremes of innocents and villains, of course, with a few veterans tossed in for good measure), and that any disabled person who does not stage a dramatic professional comeback—including a virtually mandatory attempt to pass—is a failure. Consider the words of Irving Kenneth Zola, a disabled person who has found fault with the type of heroic images posed in these movies and other media:

In almost all the success stories that get to the public, there is a dual message. The first one is very important—that just because we have polio, cancer, or multiple sclerosis or have limited use of our eyes, ears, mouth, and limbs, our lives are *not* over. We can still learn, be happy, be lovers, spouses, parents, and even achieve great deeds. It is the second message which I have recently begun to abhor. It states that if a Franklin Delano Roosevelt or a Wilma Rudolph could OVERCOME their handicap, so could and should all the disabled. And if we fail, it's *our* problem, *our* personality, *our* weakness. And all this further masks what chronic illness is all about. For our lives and even our adaptations do not center around one single activity or physical achievement but around many individual and complex ones. Our daily living is not filled with dramatic accomplishments but with mundane ones. And most of all, our physical difficulties are not temporary ones to be overcome once-and-for-all but ones we must face again and again for the rest of our lives.[42]

Guided by conservative forces in the industry, Hollywood's limited approach to issues of physical disability during the 1950s and early 1960s belied the country's renewed interest in improving the lives of people with physical disabilities. In 1954, Congress added amendments to legislation originally passed during the WW I era and 1943 that expanded the government's rehabilitation program to include research, training, and facility support that weren't tied specifically to vocational objectives. For the first time, the federal rehabilitation program was not exclusively job-oriented in its goals. Except for failed attempts in 1959 and 1961 to pass legislation aimed at providing Independent Living services to people without reference to their employability, the U.S. government's rehabilitation program was for all intents and purposes comprehensive and, for the time, one of the largest social programs that it funded.[43]

As the country entered a new era of social commitment during the 1960s, further changes that would better the lives of people with disabilities were already underway. Disability-rights activists continued putting pressure on the government to enact favorable legislation, and the Independent Living movement, long stifled in the halls of Congress, was gaining renewed momentum. A new attitude was taking root in society, one that eventually led the movie industry—only then emerging from its disastrous postwar slump and undergoing major changes in the way it did business—to alter its notions about the type of characters and lifestyles it could portray. Hollywood's movement toward the mainstream, hesitant as it was, had begun.

7 / moving toward
the mainstream

By the early 1960s, there was little doubt the movie industry had experienced massive upheavals, its ways of doing business forever changed. In the wake of catastrophically declining ticket sales and other pressures, the traditional studio system and its assembly-line way of making movies had given way to a more cost-effective process by which smaller independent production companies made contractual arrangements with the old-line studios. The latter concerns, wielding considerable influence through their vast distribution networks and newly acquired financial clout (the latter a result of the conglomerate buy-outs that commenced with the Music Corporation of America's purchase of Universal in 1962), in turn helped bankroll many of the contracted films. In a sense, the situation had become a reversal of the studio years; independent producers such as Sam Goldwyn, Walt Disney, and David Selznick had done well for themselves during the Golden Age but created only a small fraction of Hollywood's total output, and even by 1949 they accounted for only about 20 percent. By the early 1960s, however, independents were responsible for an estimated 80 percent of the movies released through the old companies. *The Miracle Worker*'s Arthur Penn embodied the spirit of the times when he declared, "Everything I do from now on will be independent, on my own terms. You've got to have the ideas and the guts to carry them out. I won't touch anything I can't control to the end."[1]

Among the manifold results, the industry was now creating movies that no longer bore the stamp of a particular studio style in terms of such things as stars, genres, production value, and general "look." The process of creating movies at a typical one-a-week pace with interchangeable writers, directors, and other personnel had become extinct; in its place, the new independent companies were crafting their movies on a case-by-case basis. Critics and other industry watchers seldom referred to "MGM films" or "Paramount films" or "Warner Bros. films" anymore; very much influenced by the recent French-based auteurist theory that elevated the director to the status of "author," they began calling them "Preminger films" or "Hitchcock films" or "Capra films" instead.

The rise of independent filmmaking affected the Cinema of Isolation in a number of significant ways. For starters, the new producers weren't as concerned as had been the old studio bosses about their co-workers' past political affiliations and during the early 1960s began making job offers to blacklistees, often with the sole provision that the latter sign statements saying they were no longer Communists. At least five blacklisted writers returned to the Cinema of Isolation under such conditions during the 1960s and early 1970s, if with widely varying films.

In addition, the strength of the Production Code had eroded to such an extent that by the early 1960s filmmakers were paying minimal attention to the longstanding set of guidelines, particularly after learning they could not only flout the code with impunity but also make money doing it. Moviemakers dealing with physical disability were very much among the legions of independents now endowing their films with a grittier, earthier quality as the code's authority continued to weaken.

Finally, and perhaps most significantly, a number of moviemakers by the latter part of the decade were championing a new kind of Hollywood cinema that happened to be particularly well-suited to representing issues of physical disability: literate, nonformulaic movies that didn't reach for the lowest common denominator among audiences. These films were often relatively low-budgeted, an issue their makers didn't perceive as necessarily detrimental to their work. Luther Davis, an independent writer-producer who released his movies though Paramount, is a case in point; his ability to exert a strong degree of control over *Lady in a Cage*— a 1964 thriller about a temporarily mobility-impaired woman beset by youthful hoodlums, one of whom she blinds—was directly related to his decision to keep costs down by hiring mostly no-name actors. "Once you're saddled with the big stars and the big budget, suddenly you find the studios breathing down your neck to rewrite the scripts down to the level of the 12-year-old mind so as to protect their investment," he noted.[2] Serious-minded small movies, popular in Europe for years, were slow to take hold in the United States because of Hollywood's traditional "blockbuster" mentality, but gradually such movies, with costs typically ranging between $500,000 and $1.5 million, began forming a significant part the American commercial cinema.

The same years were marked by conspicuous achievements by and on behalf of people with physical disabilities in American society. The 1960s and early 1970s were a time when a number of socially disadvantaged subgroups accelerated their civil-rights activism, and among them were people with disabilities whose actions and those of rehabilitation professionals led Congress to pass important pieces of legislation, including the Architectural Barriers Act of 1968 and the Rehabilitation Act of 1973. The Independent Living movement did suffer a setback in 1972 when President Richard Nixon vetoed legislation passed by Congress that would have given federally funded rehabilitation programs a more pronounced nonvocational quality, thus impeding the lifestyles of those people for whom jobs were not an objective. Despite such resistance, however, a number of private and public groups made history during the early 1970s by establishing grassroots-level Independent Living centers, the most prominent of which were the Centers for Independent Living in Berkeley and Boston, the New Options program in Houston, and the Timbers in Wichita. The centers, dedicated to helping people with disabilities reclaim control over their lives, continue to serve important functions, as Patricia Wright has noted: "These centers are service agencies run by disabled people for disabled people. They coordinate the kinds of services—attendant care, blind services, interpreting for the deaf, peer counseling and advocacy—that help disabled people get and do what they want, as opposed to what someone else may think is good for them."[3]

Many independent filmmakers that dealt with physical disability from the mid–1960s to the early 1970s reflected a sense of the progressiveness of the times by giving more of an incidental treatment to their disabled characters. In other words, they made disability very much a part of the characters' lives but spent little if any time having them "overcome" physical and psychological difficulties. They were starting to treat the characters like people who simply happened to have disabilities, and the conflicts they introduced in their narratives were usually related more to others' prejudice or to issues that transcended disability than to the disabled characters' rehabilitation or internal conflicts. In a tale of a right-wing Louisiana radio station called *WUSA* (1970), for example, a minor character named Filomena (Cloris Leachman), a fount of expository information for the audience, happens to walk with metal canes and leg braces; the filmmakers refused to make an issue of her disability. In some cases, the characters were updated versions of the old stereotypes, but in revising the stereotypes the filmmakers often treated the disabilities in incidental ways. In Alfred Hitchcock's *Topaz* (1969), a civilian member of NATO, Henri Jarré (Philippe Noiret), is, like *WUSA*'s Filomena, orthopedically disabled. Though the film later reveals him to be working for the Soviets, his impaired mobility seems more an ordinary attribute than an effort by Hitchcock and his writer Samuel Taylor to suggest a link between disability and villainous behavior.[4] The moviemakers' efforts were far from perfect, but as they rethought their perspectives and adopted the general posture suggested above they set into motion their own version of the mainstreaming process.

Among the forefront of the "new" filmmakers who advocated small-budgeted serious productions was a fellow who ironically had been one of the old-line production heads: Pandro Berman, who while at RKO oversaw such films as *Of Human Bondage* and *The Hunchback of Notre Dame* before moving over to MGM in 1940, and whose moviemaking career would eventually span about forty years. Even while working in the old Hollywood, he felt uncomfortable with the factory way of making movies and sought to delegate more creative control to his underlings than did his peers. "I always believed that a picture should be the result of one man's feeling and thinking, whether he be a writer or a director or a producer," he said. "I never believed that it should be messed up by too many people having too much to say. If you had a director who really had a concept, then I believed in letting him carry that concept out."[5]

Still associated with MGM late in his career, Berman began developing a low-budget project with British writer-director Guy Green based on Elizabeth Kata's *Be Ready with Bells and Drums* that explored the situation of a young blind woman who lives in squalor with her abusive mother and grandfather. In attempting to obtain financing for the project, Berman discovered MGM was hesitant to bankroll the film because he and Green had conceived it as a small production with lesser-known actors. As Berman sourly noted during the film's production, "The financial minds in the movie industry can only think in terms of stars, not stories, and big stars mean big budgets."[6] After securing the talents of Sidney Poitier, a veteran of more than twenty Hollywood films including *Porgy and Bess*, and Shelley Winters, a movie actress since the early 1940s who won an Oscar for her role in *The Diary of Anne Frank* in 1959, Berman eventually brought the project, titled *A Patch of Blue*, to the screen in 1965.

"The decade of the 1960s reflected an extraordinary concern at the national political level for the poor and the economically disadvantaged, not evidenced since the depression," noted Richard Verville in his brief history of the relationship between the Independent Living movement and federal legislation,[7] and *A Patch of Blue* was one of the first films to exhibit a similar awareness. The movie focuses on Selina D'Arcey (movie newcomer Elizabeth Hartman), an impoverished young blind woman who strings beads for a living and lives with a couple of gin-guzzling relatives: her vile, hot-tempered mother Rose-Ann (Winters, who won a Best Supporting Actress Oscar for her performance) and her only slightly more sympathetic grandfather, "Ole Pa" (Wallace Ford, a Hollywood old-timer who had played an able-bodied clown in *Freaks* way back when). Selina eventually develops a friendship with Gordon Ralfe (Poitier), a black journalist appalled by her lack of education and the other dismal conditions of her life and who helps her break out of them.

Shortly after the audience learns Selina lost her vision during a youthful accident, the film reflects several efforts by Green and Berman to endow their disabled character with the look. As she sits beneath a tree in a park about to string beads, a daydream scene begins via a dissolve from a close-up showing her clouded corneas to another showing clear ones. She smiles and momentarily dances wordlessly through photographically overexposed woods and meadows. The reverie concludes by dissolving back to a close-up of her face that shows the obscured corneas once again. She re-achieves the look again moments thereafter when she explains to her new-found friend Gordon how she lost her vision. She was five years old when her sailor father returned home unexpectedly, found Rose-Ann with another man, and attacked him. Rose-Ann threw a bottle of acid at her husband, but he ducked and it hit Selina in the face. Her recollection ends with a visualization of the actual disablement from her perspective: a subjective shot of Rose-Ann as lightning-like bursts of light flash across the screen, turning it white for a split second before it goes black. Such moments unquestionably smack of the manipulative and the sensational (particularly the latter scene, which suggests punishment for seeing), but they do serve the greater purposes of signaling to the audience that she is indeed the main focus of the film and helping define her character along dimensions that simple verbiage could never achieve.

A Patch of Blue brought in notably mixed comments from the press. The *Newsweek* reviewer considered the movie a "monument to bad taste" that "combined the quintessential worst of such classics as *City Lights* [and] *The Miracle Worker*" and "managed simultaneously to insult the Negroes and the blind." The movie carried echoes of *Bright Victory* in the sense that a blind person is able to go beyond skin color to "see" the person underneath, but the reviewer even found fault over that point: "Undoubtedly the people who made this movie thought they were saying something significant about race relations, like how a blind girl can see a man more clearly than a sighted bigot can. But significant statements about the real world require real people and mature observation. *A Patch of Blue* has neither. The girl with her infinite tolerance and the boy with his flawless devotion [Hartman and Poitier were respectively 23 and 41 at the time] are only contemporary variations on contemptible old stereotypes." Matching the *Newsweek* critic in venom was Clifford Mason, who in a *New York Times* article called *A Patch of Blue* "probably the most ridiculous film Poitier ever made" and concluded his comments on it by posing several rhetorical questions, one of which compared visually impaired people to animals: "Why does he go to the park day after day and sit with her and string her beads and buy her lunch? Because he's running his private branch of the ASPCA, the Black Society for the Prevention of Cruelty to Blind White Girls, the BSPCBWG?"[8]

Several other writers, however, were more sensitive—and less ableist, sexist, and racist—in their judgments. *Commonweal*'s Philip Hartung called *A Patch of Blue* a film "of high quality" and suggested Green "was successful in keeping this tender tale from becoming soupy," criticizing it only for its lengthiness, occasional repetitiveness, and Winters' overblown performance. The *Time* reviewer also commended the writer-director, stating he "has a knack for sustaining the sort of idea that in lesser hands might easily slip from pathos into bathos. Green's style is simple, forceful and true, and he habitually activates a performer's most astonishing inner resources." The writer had particular praise for Hartman: "Spindly and coltish as Selina, with a plain-pretty face that can erupt unexpectedly into electric beauty, she wins genuine sympathy by playing up the spunk in her role, playing against the saccharine. She is achingly real without ever being soppy, whether cursing her fate, dodging flatware during a pitched battle between Winters and Ford, or unemotionally explaining to Poitier that she is 'experienced' with men because of a brutal encounter with one of her mother's drunken beaus."[9] Though Green and Berman may have been guilty of leaning too heavily on the Sweet Innocent type in emphasizing Selina's passivity, they also confronted the topic of prejudice head-on by showing that negative social attitudes, not her disability, were the main factors holding her back and keeping her isolated.

A Patch of Blue's appearance in late 1965 coincided with preparations for a Broadway play that would feature another isolated heroine with a visual impairment: *Wait Until Dark*, Frederick Knott's thriller about a recently blinded woman beset by crooks looking for heroin hidden in her apartment. Directed by Arthur Penn, *Wait Until Dark* with Lee Remick and Robert Duvall in the leads drew much critical praise when it hit the boards in early 1966 and immediately went into development as a movie. Itinerant actor and occasional director Mel Ferrer had recently begun wearing a producer's hat and perceived the play as a suitable vehicle for his wife Audrey Hepburn and Alan Arkin, currently in demand as a result of his work in his debut film, *The Russians Are Coming! The Russians Are Coming!* (1966). Ferrer lined up Warners to distribute the film and hired the husband-and-wife screenwriting team of Robert and Jane-Howard Carrington to adapt Knott's play. With the unavailability of Penn, who had already committed himself to several other projects (including the disability-related *Little Big Man* that would reach the screen in 1970),[10] however, Ferrer turned to an unlikely candidate to direct: Terence Young, a Briton better known for expensive action-adventure films than for modestly budgeted character-driven productions.

Though Young seemed fully "bonded" after having piloted such movies as *Dr. No*, *From Russia with Love* (1963), and *Thunderball* (1965), he proved a reasonably effective director for this smaller scaled production which appeared on screens in 1967. In a distinct turnabout from *Dr. No*, *Wait Until Dark* goes out of its way to present a sympathetic portrait of its disabled character. Too much so, in fact: the elfin-coiffed Susy Hendrix (Hepburn) with her almost perpetually upbeat and happy demeanor works a little too hard at being warm and fuzzy. She's obsessed with becoming, in her words, the "world's champion blind lady" and turns overly apologetic when she is less than perfect. Apart from these Sweetly Innocent qualities and her wealth-suggesting aristocratic manner (a throwback of sorts to the conservative films of Hollywood's apathetic age), Susy represents a step forward in the Cinema of Isolation. Granted, she is as much a victim as any Sweet Innocent and the director couldn't resist giving her isolation a prison-like quality by photographing her behind a staircase bannister after she learns her phone line's been cut, but unlike most other characters in the Sweet Innocent tradition Susy is tough, resilient, and resourceful in her fight against the criminals who have misrepresented themselves to her and have broken into her apartment.

The majority of critics who found fault with *Wait Until Dark* tended to dwell on the gaping holes in the narrative. *Newsweek* reviewer Joseph Morgenstern's comments were typical: "Many plot details cannot withstand scrutiny in this exciting, compelling and fundamentally unintelligent entertainment. The most notorious lapse, her failure to telephone the cops immediately instead of sending a friend out to look for her husband, was spotted by at least one critic when the show opened on Broadway. The screenwriters still did not see fit to repair the defect, and only the Teamsters Union could be happy with the continued presence of a hole big enough to drive trucks through."[11] Nevertheless, most reviewers gave high marks to Hepburn for her sensitive and refreshing portrayal of Susy Hendrix.

The representation of blindness took a bizarre turn the following year in *Barbarella*, a movie that would seem to epitomize Hollywood's apathetic era except that it was actually a French-Italian co-production that later gained some notoriety in the U.S. as a cult film. Based on a popular French comic strip and set twenty centuries into the future, *Barbarella* was filmed in Rome by French director Roger Vadim, written by Vadim and *Dr. Strangelove*'s Terry Southern, and produced by Italian schlockmeister Dino de Laurentiis, who made certain it enjoyed frequent American screenings through a distribution deal with Paramount.

Sporting a multinational cast, cheesy special effects, and an atrocious musical score, *Barbarella* tells the story of the sensual, planet-hopping title character (played by Vadim's then-spouse, Jane Fonda) who flies her pink, fur-lined space-ship on a mission to preserve intergalactic peace. After crash-landing on another world, she encounters a half-naked winged being named Pygar (a blond-wigged John Philip Law) who's been blinded and left to die in a mysterious labyrinth and who's lost his will to fly. Fortunately for all concerned, he regains his aeronautical abilities after having sex with Barbarella in his nest. An eternally victimized Sweet Innocent (he's even "crucified" by nasties at one point), the remasculinized Pygar eventually rescues not only Barbarella but also the evil Black Queen (Anita Pallenberg) who has been the main source of all his trouble, including his dis-ablement. When Barbarella asks him why he is saving the latter woman, he re-sponds with "An angel has no memory," a bland rejoinder that concludes an equally bland film.

If *A Patch of Blue*, *Wait Until Dark*, and *Barbarella* represent modernized if widely varying versions of the Sweet Innocent, *The Heart Is a Lonely Hunter* (1968) features an updated view of the Saintly Sage. Filmmakers had been inter-ested as early as 1950 in adapting Carson McCullers' 1940 novel of a Southern

Cut off from the outside world by crooks who severed her phone line, Susy Hendrix (Audrey Hepburn) awaits unknown dangers in Wait Until Dark. *Copyright © 1967 Warner Bros.–Seven Arts Inc.*

deaf man who touches the lives of so many people, but for various reasons the project kept falling through; no less than five production teams involving such people as Zero Mostel, Gavin Lambert, Sidney Meyers, and José Quintero had labored on it but it remained unrealized. Among the frustrated moviemakers was screenwriter Thomas C. Ryan, who had been intrigued by the novel for years. "I wrote the script about five years ago. And the book was something I deeply believed in long before that," he said in 1967. "The story of five people driven together by loneliness and various desperate needs, some of which are resolved while others are not, is a thing of beauty and truth." [12]

The film became something of an obsession for Ryan, who, like his predecessors, faced difficulties getting the project produced. "I closed the book on January 11, 1962 and wrote the movie," he said. "In August of 1963 I went to Carson McCullers' home in Nyack and read it to her. She loved it. Sidney Lumet was supposed to direct with Monty Clift as the mute. Then we couldn't get any insurance on Monty and it fell through. David Susskind optioned it. Ely Landau optioned it. But we got nowhere. The rights reverted back to me and I was right back where I started. I couldn't interest people by telling them 'Well, it's about this deaf mute . . .' Everybody said 'It's absolutely beautiful and I wouldn't touch it with a barge pole.'" [13]

When things looked their bleakest, two people helped invigorate the moribund project: producer Marc Merson and actor Alan Arkin. Merson became coproducer of the film with Ryan after his Brownstone Productions company acquired the rights to the novel in early 1967. "I'd heard of Ryan's script some time ago, and I was well aware how difficult it could be to translate into screen terms," he said. "But I was taken with it when I read it and we made the deal. And then Arkin jumped at the chance to play Singer." Arkin, interested in the role of the deaf John Singer for years, had been following the unproduced project's tortuous route and contacted Ryan after he hit it big with *The Russians Are Coming* and *Wait Until Dark*: "You gotta give me the part now," he told the writer. "I've gone to all the trouble of becoming a star just so I could play it." [14]

With a script in hand and a star lined up, Ryan and Merson contracted with Warner Bros.–Seven Arts to distribute and co-finance the film (Ryan noted with some astonishment that one of the Warners executives had said, "Some pictures you just have to make whether they make money or not") and signed up Joseph Strick to direct. Shooting was about to begin in September of 1967 when the bugaboo known as "creative differences" developed between Strick and Ryan; they clashed over the director's desire to turn the relationship of Singer and another man into a gay one and to emphasize the story's downbeat and depressing qualities. Strick quit the project, and Ryan and Merson hurriedly recruited Robert Ellis Miller, a director better known for his television work, to take his place. For his part, Miller was delighted to participate in the adaptation of the McCullers novel. "I read it in college and I always wanted to direct it," he said. "I had just finished *Sweet November* with Sandy Dennis and was getting ready to rest on the beach when the offer came through. I jumped at the chance." Filming finally took place during the fall and winter of 1967 on location in Selma, Alabama, with Warner Bros.–Seven Arts releasing the film the following year.[15]

The Heart Is a Lonely Hunter is unusual in having multiple disabled characters: chiefly John Singer and Spiros Antonapoulos (the latter played by Chuck McCann), both of whom are deaf. Antonapoulos is also mentally impaired—the film presents him not unlike a jolly fat child who does such things as breaking a store's windows to get at some bakery items, blithely unaware of the consequences—and when his cousin in exasperation turns him over to a state hospital, Singer, a generally unassuming fellow, quits his job in a jewelry store and moves to the small Southern city of Jefferson to be closer to his friend.

While living in Jefferson, Singer interacts with a number of down-on-their-luck types who come away enriched from the experience: among them, Mick Kelly (Sondra Locke, in her debut), a young woman initially resentful of Singer for renting a room in her parents' house that used to be hers; Jake (Stacy Keach),

A rare movie presenting more than one deaf character, The Heart Is a Lonely Hunter *starred Alan Arkin (left) and Chuck McCann as John Singer and Spiros Antonapoulos. Copyright © 1968 Warner Bros.–Seven Arts Inc.*

carnival roustabout and alcoholic ne'er-do-well; and Copeland (Percy Rodrigues), a black physician who is estranged from his daughter and refuses to treat whites for fear of being perceived as "uppity." Not unlike the classic Saintly Sages who flourished during the 1930s and 1940s, Singer is a gentle, asexual, and spiritual sort who perceives things that others do not. Though he's deaf, relatively young, and a main character—qualities that set him apart from the more traditional Sages—he does embody the same kind of irony; just as the blind characters of the earlier films were the only characters who could "see," the deaf Singer is the only one who "listens." In fact, he becomes a rather Christ-like character who takes on others' burdens while asking for nothing in return, and, when Singer, alone in his grief, commits suicide after learning that his friend Antonapoulos has died in the hospital, the people whom he helped finally acknowledge their debt to him. "None of us ever knew him, not really," Copeland notes to Mick at Singer's grave. "We all brought our troubles to him, never stopping to think he may have troubles of his own."

For all the moviemakers' good intentions, *The Heart Is a Lonely Hunter* emerges as very disjointed and unfocused, lacking the power of a carefully structured film and flawed in a number of other key respects. By making Singer almost completely voiceless (the filmmakers undoubtedly thought they were making a statement of some sort by creating a "singer" without a voice) and having the other characters constantly refer to him as a "dummy," the film perpetuates one of the most insidious of the deaf stereotypes while seemingly posing a critique of it. In addition, Singer seems forever isolated not only because of the other characters' lack of responsiveness to his needs but also because the filmmakers refused to make his signed conversations accessible to audiences unacquainted with American Sign Language.

Audiences familiar with ASL perceived problems of a different sort; as John Schuchman has observed, anyone who knows the language can readily tell when the hearing actors who play deaf characters are basically fumbling their way through it, Arkin's braggadocio to the contrary. ("The sign language was the easiest thing to learn," he said. "I got it in a day or two.") A scene in which Singer interacts with a black deaf person played by Horace Oats, who truly was deaf and knew the language well, only accentuated Arkin's lack of facility with the language and underscored the impropriety of casting a hearing actor in such a role.[16]

To be fair to Arkin, he did claim to have an enlightening experience while working on the film. "I visited a school for deaf-mutes in Montgomery and I learned that they are not freaks." he said. "Stereotyped in my mind, they were always people who were not terribly bright, wildly animated at all times in trying to express themselves, and undisciplined emotionally. I guess I got that from watching Patty Duke in *The Miracle Worker*. Then I met them and found an infinite variety in character, personality and intelligence." Yet the actor, who also admitted "this character remains a million miles away from me," indicated he still had a lot to learn at least as far as sensitivity was concerned: "This is the hardest role I've ever played, but as far as playing the mute as a freak, that's out. I've learned that the only difference between them and us is that when they make love they're much quieter about it." [17]

While Arkin congratulated himself on his keen awareness of the deaf experience, a fellow actor was about to resume his movie career with insights of a different sort. Jay C. Flippen, a veteran Broadway performer who began his Hollywood career in the mid–1930s with a specialization in Westerns and other action fare, was at work on the comic Western *Cat Ballou* in 1964 when his right leg developed an infection and had to be amputated shortly thereafter. The 64-year-old Flippen began using a wheelchair and like Lionel Barrymore before him carried on with his profession until his death in 1971. In addition to acting in several television programs, Flippen played supporting roles in a trio of movies: the James Stewart–Henry Fonda Western *Firecreek* (1968), a saga of oil well firefighters called *The Hellfighters* (1969), and *The Seven Minutes* (1971), a Russ Meyer adaptation of Irving Wallace's bestselling account of a pornography trial. In all three movies his impaired mobility was incidental to the characters he played.

Disability-informed roles also became a forte of sorts for one of Flippen's colleagues on *The Hellfighters*, John Wayne. Having essayed disabled screenwriter Spig Wead in *The Wings of Eagles* and a professional gunfighter who experiences ever-lengthening bouts of paralysis as a result of a bullet near his spine in *El Dorado* (1967), Wayne negotiated his way into *True Grit* (1969), a Western about a 14-year-old girl named Mattie Ross (Kim Darby) who recruits visually impaired U.S. Marshal Reuben J. "Rooster" Cogburn to help her hunt down the outlaw who killed her father. The Cogburn role would prove the peak of Wayne's career.

The *True Grit* filmmakers took their inspiration from a namesake novel by Charles Portis first published in serialized form in the *Saturday Evening Post* and then as a 1968 hardback book. The production team included director Henry Hathaway, who had dealt with physical disability intermittently over several decades (among his many films were 1947's *Kiss of Death* and 1956's *23 Paces to Baker Street*); veteran producer Hal Wallis, who had overseen such varied films as *Mystery of the Wax Museum*, *The Sea Wolf*, and *Kings Row* for Warner Bros. before turning independent in 1944; and screenwriter Marguerite Roberts, who had been blacklisted since 1951 after her refusal to cooperate with HUAC and had only recently returned to working in Hollywood. [18]

True Grit, which eventually brought in more than $15 million at the box office—making it one of the biggest money-making Westerns ever—and led to an inferior 1975 sequel called *Rooster Cogburn*, illustrated among other things the growing "chumminess" between Hollywood and other cultural industries. Portis wrote his novel with the aging Wayne in mind for the Cogburn role (even though Mattie, who calls him "an old one-eyed jasper that was built along the lines of Grover Cleveland," refers to him in the next breath as about 40 years old) and mailed him galleys of the unpublished novel in attempting to enlist his clout and get the book produced as a movie. The "Duke" immediately recognized its potential and offered $300,000 for the screen rights while planning to direct the film himself, but he lost out to producer Wallis who with his distributor Paramount had made a more lucrative offer: $500,000, with Simon and Schuster—a company that like Paramount had recently been acquired by the giant conglomerate Gulf + Western—slated to publish the book.

Roberts followed the general narrative structure of the novel in her screenplay but did scrap a few things along the way. Portis had made Mattie the central character of his book, even writing it from her perspective as an old woman looking back on her life, but Roberts, no doubt recognizing that "remembrances" often don't work well in the movies and that Cogburn would probably dominate the movie version by virtue of the sheer strength of Wayne's screen persona, avoided that approach in favor of a more straightforward unfolding of events.

Another difference concerned the film's ending. In the original narrative, Mattie breaks her arm after the recoil from a large pistol propels her into a snake pit, and she loses the limb shortly thereafter (with characteristic lack of sentimentality Mattie refers to herself in later years as "a woman with brains and a frank tongue and one sleeve pinned up"). This development proved too depressing for Roberts and she changed it, as Wayne himself noted: "In the book Mattie loses her hand from the snakebite, and I die, and the last scene in the book has her looking at my grave. But the way Marguerite Roberts wrote the screenplay, she gave it an uplift. Mattie and Rooster both go to visit her family plot, after she gets cured of the snakebite. By now it's winter. And she offers to let Rooster be buried there some day, seeing as how he has no family of his own. Rooster's happy to accept, long as he doesn't have to take her up on it too quick. So then he gets on his horse and says, 'Come and see a fat old man some time.' And then he spurs the horse and jumps a fence, just to show he still can." [19]

Despite this retreat from one of the novel's disability issues, Roberts and the other filmmakers did remain true to its main one: Cogburn's impaired vision. Both the movie and the novel showed that the loss of his eye—a Civil War wound, it turns out—and his advancing age did not unduly hinder him in his work, and Wayne was so taken by this aspect of his character that when he accepted the Academy Award for Best Actor he said, "If I'd have known that, I'd have put on a patch thirty-five years earlier."

Marguerite Roberts wasn't the only formerly blacklisted writer to stage a major comeback in 1969; the year was also auspicious for Waldo Salt, who won a Best Screenplay Oscar for a movie that also happened to deal with physical disability, albeit in a highly divergent way: *Midnight Cowboy*. Blacklisted from 1951 to 1962, Salt had come back as the principal screenwriter of the misbegotten *Taras Bulba*, a movie he'd just as soon forget. "United Artists decided that they didn't want to be caught hiring a blacklisted writer, so they decided to give me credit on it," he remembered. "I wish they hadn't. I figure it did more harm to my career than the blacklist." [20] Salt hit his nadir after writing the scripts for two other early–1960s misfires and returned to New York to resume the television-writing career he had taken up during the blacklist years, leaving his family behind in California. Salt later learned that plans were underway to make a movie based on James Leo Herlihy's 1965 novel *Midnight Cowboy*, but that the principals involved—producer Jerome Hellman and director John Schlesinger—were having difficulties finding someone who could help them develop a workable script. Based on the strength of an unproduced screenplay Salt had written in 1967 called "The Artful Dodger," Hellman and Schlesinger hired him to write the script for their film.

The novel and subsequent screenplay and film told the story of Joe Buck, a naïve young Texan who travels to Manhattan in the hope of becoming a high-priced stud, and Ratso Rizzo, a seedy, orthopedically impaired New Yorker who befriends him. Following Herlihy's lead, the filmmakers, like their *A Patch of Blue* counterparts, constructed their disabled character as impoverished; Rizzo, a pimp and a thief, lives in a condemned tenement building and survives mainly on wits honed by years of living on the streets. Tuberculosis is catching up with him, however, as a persistent hacking cough reveals.

In adapting Herlihy's novel, Salt based Rizzo on some of his own New York experiences. Schlesinger noted that "Waldo's experience in life, both good and bad" contributed to the shaping of the film, and Salt's daughter Deborah, recalling a visit she paid him while he was trying to revive his career as a TV writer and living in a fleabag hotel, offered a vivid illustration of this point: "He's sick and I bring him some soup, and he's in this little room that's cold and he's in this little bed that's really narrow," she said. "He's pale and coughing and he's got pneumonia, and he's really upset and he's in a life crisis."[21]

With Salt's script in hand, Hellman and Schlesinger began filming during the spring of 1968 on location in New York City, Texas, and Florida with Dustin Hoffman, just coming off his overwhelming success in *The Graduate* (1967), as Rizzo and a little-known actor named Jon Voight as Joe Buck. The resulting production stunned both the movie industry (its newly created rating board nervously slapped an "X" on it for its sexual kinkiness, a rating later reduced to an "R") and the critics. A few of the latter were put off by Schlesinger's fragmentary style, particularly in his handling of Joe's Texas flashbacks, but in general the community of critics was united in its praise for the film and in particular for Hoffman's performance as Ratso Rizzo. *The New Republic*'s Stanley Kauffmann, who described Rizzo as "a crippled guttersnipe, tricky but winning, who has green teeth and lank dirty hair, and who, to top it all, is dying of consumption—an actor's dream," spoke for the majority of reviewers when he opined that Hoffman "has a central vision of Ratso which he has worked out, as he always does, to the last small physical habit. . . . The light in his eyes is true weasel light; his discovery of brotherhood is grudgingly real; and the key moments, far beyond the reach of any night-club mimic, are beautiful. I won't easily forget Hoffman shivering on the cot in their dingy room, saying fearfully to Joe, 'Hey, don't get sore . . . but I don't think I can walk anymore.'"[22]

In addition to the critical acclaim, *Midnight Cowboy* won Best Picture, Director, and Screenplay Oscars (Hoffman and Voight, both nominated for Best Actor, lost out to John Wayne for his *True Grit* performance and arguably for his life's work), and it re-established Salt's screenwriting career. He never forgot the experience, and after writing or co-writing the scripts for several other notable films, including *Serpico* (1973) and *The Day of the Locust* (1975), he would return to the Cinema of Isolation with the screenplay for one of the most sensitive Hollywood movies ever made on issues of physical disability.

In the meantime, other filmmakers continued exploring various aspects of the physically disabled lifestyle. The theme of poverty that Salt and his fellow filmmakers examined also found expression, if in a less dramatic fashion, in another disability film of the period: *Tell Me That You Love Me, Junie Moon* (1970). Written by Marjorie Kellogg from her novel, and produced and directed by Otto Preminger, the movie actually deals with the topics of deinstitutionalization and independent living, offers an exceptionally rare portrait of a person with epilepsy, and like several progressive films before it (principally *Home of the Brave* and *Bright Victory*) establishes a link between ableism and racism.[23]

Junie Moon begins with a doctor who leads a flock of interns around a hospital and uses his most impersonal tones to describe a number of patients, including the

Midnight Cowboy, *starring Jon Voight and Dustin Hoffman, represented a major turning point in the career of screenwriter Waldo Salt, who later served as the principal writer for* Coming Home. *Copyright © 1969 United Artists Corp.*

three young people who emerge as the film's main characters: Junie Moon (Liza Minnelli), a woman who suffered third-degree burns on her left arm and most of her face; Arthur (Ken Howard), prone to epileptic seizures; and Warren Palmer (Robert Moore), a wheelchair-using gay man who blithely talks of suicide. Upon their release from the hospital the three decide to live together and "pool our disabilities," in Warren's words. As he tells a social worker, "We would have, among the three of us, one good pair of hands, one good pair of legs, three good livers, three warm hearts, and three functioning brains." They move into a dilapidated house, unoccupied for fifteen years but furnished, which Arthur equips with a ramp for Warren.

The house becomes the site for considerable commentary on issues concerning the disabled experience. As the threesome explore their new surroundings, for example, Warren refers to the architectural problems facing so many people by sarcastically noting that every bathroom doorway in the country is a half inch too narrow. He later becomes the object of ableist and homophobic slurs (offered unfortunately by another disabled person) when during a squabble the psychologically disturbed Arthur boils over with "I'll tell you one thing: Junie Moon and I do all the work around here. You—you sit in that—that—that—that little throne of a wheelchair and give out orders like some damn queen."

Junie Moon's linking of racist with ableist views occurs, in one instance, when the trio takes in a friend from the hospital, a black woman who has only a few weeks to live; a neighbor says disgustedly to her husband, "That new one is black," to which he responds, "They're *all* black as far as I'm concerned." Warren's black lover, a muscular sort known only as "Beach Boy" (Fred Williamson), also recognizes the kinship of the two forms of prejudice—albeit from a different perspective—when he refers to himself and Warren by saying, "Us blacks got to stick together."

Despite its progressiveness and insight on certain issues, *Junie Moon* is a most bothersome film on others. Wanting to cure Warren of something but recognizing how untenable curable disabilities had become in the movies, Kellogg and Preminger added a strange twist to their story by having a woman "cure" him of his homosexuality during an overnight encounter on the beach. The filmmakers' treatment of the epileptic Arthur is particularly problematic; not only did they have him toss around ableist notions during a weak moment but by making him suffer through a number of vivid and exceptionally disconcerting dreams they also tried to connect epilepsy with mental instability. Add to this the unsettling image of Beach Boy carrying a fully cooperative Warren over his shoulder like a sack of potatoes at a party and elsewhere, and the audience cannot help but concur with Lauri Klobas that this movie, generally a poorly received one, is among "the most bizarre representations of disability ever filmed." [24]

While such mixed-message movies were playing in theaters, a trend that temporarily undermined this period of good intentions began making its presence felt. It began rather surreptitiously with humor in the shape of *Little Big Man* (1970), *Start the Revolution Without Me* (1970), and the British-made *A Clockwork Orange* (1971). The first, a sprawling saga directed by Arthur Penn about a 121-year-old claiming to be the sole survivor of Custer's last stand, does present a compassionate updating of the Saintly Sage—Oscar nominee Dan George as Old Lodge Skins, a recently blinded Cheyenne chief who offers insights such as "My eyes still see, but my heart no longer receives it" and much wisdom to the title character—but it also features the comically villainous character of Allardyce T. Meriweather (Martin Balsam), a con man who when introduced is missing an ear and a hand and who later loses an eye and a leg, all related to his chicanery. As the film's central character Jack Crabb (*Midnight Cowboy*'s Dustin Hoffman) duly notes, "Deception was his life's blood, even if it caused him to get whittled down, kinda gradual-like." *Start the Revolution* had among its minor characters a blind man (Murray Melvin) who serves as a lookout for his fellow French revolutionaries and later finds himself dueling with a statue during the film's climactic scene in which the peasants storm the palace of Louis XVI. As for Stanley Kubrick's *A Clockwork Orange*, the most infamous of its sequences concerns a young hoodlum named Alex (Malcolm McDowell) who with his fellow "droogs" assault a couple to the tune of "Singin' in the Rain," leaving the woman dead and the man permanently paralyzed. The man, a prominent writer named Alexander (Patrick Magee) who now uses a wheelchair and ostensibly represents Alex's civilized half, later turns maniacal himself after he accidently encounters the youth again and carries out a bizarre music-based form of revenge.

These films, all with excessively violent contexts, were at the forefront of a quickly escalating phase that overshadowed, however briefly, Hollywood's shaky move toward the mainstream: the creation of malignant images that were so simplistic for the most part that they invited immediate parody. The late 1960s and early 1970s were a time when Americans were seeing nightly televised violence in the form of network news reports on the Vietnam War, and a number of moviemakers, perceiving the carnage as symptomatic of the profound moral uncertainties of the period, created works that either critiqued the senselessness of excessive violence or wallowed in it or both. War-related films and Westerns made up the bulk of this short-lived trend.

Hollywood filmmakers who held pessimistic outlooks on the Vietnam War in particular and war issues in general often hid their sentiments by creating movies with non-Vietnam contexts. The more familiar of these movies—*Catch-22* (1970) and *M*A*S*H* (1970) with their respective World War II and Korean War settings—tempered their bleak perspectives with strong doses of dark humor, but two other films in this tradition, ones that happened to have disabled veterans at their center, were unrelentingly grim: the Civil War-based *The Beguiled* (1971) and the WW I–era *Johnny Got His Gun* (1971).

Produced and directed by Don Siegel through Clint Eastwood's Malpaso production company and distributed through Universal, *The Beguiled* starred

Eastwood as John McBurney, a solitary Union corporal who comes off a battle-field with a badly broken leg. A 12-year-old Southern girl (Pamelyn Ferdin) dis-covers the semi-conscious McBurney and eventually leads him to a cloistered school in the woods where she and a handful of young women study such things as French and crocheting even as the war rages around them. The head of the school, Martha Farnsworth (Geraldine Page), invites him to stay and recuperate, much to the concern of the others who are uncomfortable with having "the enemy" in their midst. As the only male in a building full of sexually repressed women, McBurney soon stirs up jealousies and finds himself in an emotional hotbed, and a series of hot beds, that lead to his downfall. Judith Kass described the film in these terms: "*The Beguiled* depicts Eastwood, like the only rooster in the henhouse, flaunting his sexuality in the faces of several frustrated women who eventually pay him back, first by confining him behind boarded windows, then by amputating his leg, and lastly by killing him."[25]

Though this moody, slow-moving character study presents McBurney as very much a victimized person (while oblivious to many things, even he recognizes that Martha amputated his leg because, in his words, "I didn't go to your bed," and indeed the movie darkly equates amputation with castration on several occa-sions), he is hardly in the mold of the Sweet Innocent; he's unquestionably a liar and an opportunist of the worst sort, and Siegel exploited his overwhelming van-ity and relative lack of mobility to leave him vulnerable to various assaults. As Kass further noted: "Eastwood's spatial limitations, combined with his physical disability and pride, are his undoing. Given more elbow room, he might have ma-noeuvered to a position of escape, psychic or actual. He could have realised that the women's mood had changed, that they were massing—consciously or not—to attack. . . . In this, the most negative of Don Siegel's movies, the pessimism is infinite. No one is untainted; all are guilty."[26]

It's worth noting that the original screenwriter for *The Beguiled* was Albert Maltz, who had dealt with wartime disability before in *Pride of the Marines* and as one of the Hollywood Ten served time in a federal penitentiary for refusing to cooperate with the House Committee on Un-American Activities. Having re-ceived no screen credits since 1948, Maltz finally found work under his own name as the writer for a Universal film starring Eastwood and directed by Siegel called *Two Mules for Sister Sara* (1970), and even before they finished that film he had concluded a script draft for *The Beguiled* based on Thomas Cullinan's book, complete with a map of the school grounds and other illustrations. He had envisioned the film as more of a restrained antiwar tract, a perspective that did not coincide with the director's. (Several weeks after Maltz completed his draft, Siegel complained to Eastwood that "he wrote it in a mid-Victorian style, the dia-logue at times quite stilted. There's not near enough excitement, suspense, terror. It must be macabre, horrific in its intensity.") Unknown writers John Sherry and Grimes Grice along with Siegel revised Maltz's screenplay to such an extent that he ended up receiving no credit for his work.[27]

Siegel saw the movie as something special—*"The Beguiled* is the best film I have done, and possibly the best I will ever do," he said in a 1972 interview—but was frustrated with its marketing strategy. He wanted Universal to submit it to film festivals and arrange for its exhibition in smaller art-house theaters, but the studio, for whom "Clint Eastwood" and "moody, slow-moving character study" were mutually exclusive terms, treated it mainly as a mass-market film and it wound up receiving minimal profit or artistic recognition.[28]

Surpassing *The Beguiled* in sheer morbidity was *Johnny Got His Gun*, about a World War I veteran who has lost just about all but his consciousness and conscience. *Newsweek*'s Arthur Cooper effectively illustrated the film's difference from other antiwar movies of the period when he wrote that "*Catch-22* and *M*A*S*H* deftly scored their points with satire and black humor. They evoked uneasy laughter at the grisly horror of war they portray. *Johnny Got His Gun* hits squarely in the guts with the impact of a recoiling howitzer." The film's visceral effect was hardly accidental, as writer-director Dalton Trumbo himself noted: "The intellectual attack on war has been going on for a couple of thousand years and has failed. I decided one should try an emotional attack, and that is what I attempted to do." Trumbo, who like Albert Maltz was one of the Hollywood Ten who had written about wartime disablement decades before (the sentimental *Thirty Seconds Over Tokyo*, in Trumbo's case), had been blacklisted from 1947 to the early 1960s. *Johnny Got His Gun* represented the fulfillment of a long-delayed dream to bring his like-titled 1939 novel to the screen.[29]

Trumbo was inspired to write his antiwar book during the 1930s after learning about two severely injured WW I veterans: a British major who had been so mutilated that the army reported him missing in action to his family, and a Canadian soldier left dismembered, blinded, deafened, and tube-fed by the conflict. As Trumbo described the latter's story: "In the mid-thirties, the Prince of Wales visited a military hospital in Canada. At the end of a hallway, there was a door marked 'No Admittance.' 'What's in there?' he asked. 'We'd rather you not go in there,' they told him. But the Prince of Wales insisted, and when he came out of the room, he was weeping. 'The only way I could salute, the only way I could communicate with that man,' he said, 'was to kiss his cheek.' "[30]

Among the novel's appreciative readers was the famous Spanish surrealist Luis Buñuel, who had a long history of representing disability issues in his movies and who claimed the book "struck me like a bolt of lightning." He found its mixture of disability, antiwar qualities, dreams, and memories irresistible and worked with Trumbo to create a film version of it during the early 1960s with the intent of directing the movie himself in 1965. The funding for that project fell through, however, and what followed was a long line of rejections; no less than seventeen Hollywood companies turned it down as "too depressing," in Trumbo's words. "I'd be happy to think they rejected it because of my political past, but I fear otherwise," he said. The movie finally got off the ground in 1970 after Simon Lazarus, a long-time friend of former blacklistees, raised $750,000 for the film's production, and to keep costs down Trumbo decided to direct it himself. With the guidance of producer Bruce Campbell, *Johnny Got His Gun* began playing in movie theaters the following year.[31]

The focus of the film is Joe Bonham (Timothy Bottoms, in his first movie), who before the movie begins has been hit by an artillery shell on the last day of World War I. As Joe and the audience gradually realize, the injury has left him legless, armless, and faceless, his abilities to see, hear, and speak destroyed. Though his doctors consider him "completely decerebrated" and as "unthinking as the dead," Joe is far from a vegetable; he provides constant voice-over narration that informs the audience of his thoughts. In addition, Trumbo shot most of the movie from Joe's perspective, using color cinematography to represent Joe's memories and fantasies (populated mainly by his girlfriend, late father, and Jesus Christ, played respectively by Kathy Fields, Jason Robards, and Donald Sutherland) that show Joe before his disablement and monochrome for his present situation in the hospital, with doctors and nurses frequently huddling over a very low-angle camera suggesting the vet's point of view.

After Joe "converses" with the dream and fantasy characters, he figures out a way to communicate with his medical attendants; he taps out SOS messages in Morse code with his head on his pillow. Most of the doctors regard his movements as simple muscle spasms, but a sympathetic nurse (Diane Varsi, identified in the credits simply as "Fourth Nurse") finally understands and shares her knowledge with the doctors. Joe communicates through his head-tapping that he wants the army to put him on display in carnivals to show everyone the terrible cost of war, a request the army of course denies. Following that, Joe pleads to be killed and to his chagrin that request is denied as well.

Johnny Got His Gun won three awards at the Cannes Film Festival, including the Special Jury Prize, and critical kudos aplenty. Though the film's reputation has waned over the years (Leonard Maltin suggested it has a "moving opening and climax, but everything in the middle is either talky, pretentious, or amateurish," while Judith Crist wrote that its "intentions . . . and the intensity of its message are praiseworthy, but for this viewer it is so cloddish and naïve in its execution, so simplistic and self-consciously righteous that it vitiates its virtues"), *Johnny Got His Gun* remains a stark and effective reminder of the horrific effects of war.[32]

If *Johnny Got His Gun* presents its disabled vet as ultimate victim, another film produced that year but not appearing in the U.S. until the next shows him as consummate sadist. British director George Bloomfield, working without the political restraints facing his Hollywood counterparts, created one of the first films with a disabled Vietnam veteran in a major role: the highly disturbing *To Kill a Clown* (1972), a low-budget affair produced by Teddy Sills for London-based Palomar Pictures. Filmed on location in the American northeast, it stars Alan Alda as Evelyn Ritchie, an unhinged ex-Army major whose knees were destroyed in Vietnam and who now lives in isolation along a New England beach. He rents out a cottage to Timothy and Lily Frischer (Heath Lamberts and Blythe Danner), a couple of free-spirited potheads whom he eventually terrorizes with two Doberman pinschers after a friendly contest between Ritchie and Timothy (the "clown" of the title) escalates into a "Most Dangerous Game" kind of competition. "Femininized" by his disability (if not earlier in life by his first name), Ritchie develops an obsessive desire to reclaim his manhood by imposing a military-discipline mentality on Timothy and to a lesser extent Lily, and as the movie amply demonstrates, that mentality knows few if any bounds. Though the Frischers aren't particularly sympathetic, Ritchie's actions against them are wholly unjustified. About the only noteworthy aspect of this rather obscure film is a troubling one: it was among the first of a generation of movies to feature deranged Vietnam vets.

To Kill a Clown was hardly alone in its linkage of disability and sadistic villainy. The Western genre also exhibited a similar backlash by way of two entries that hastened the genre's temporary decline: *The McMasters* (1970) and *The Deadly Trackers* (1973), graphic low-budget efforts that followed in the spirit of *The Proud Rebel* and countless other movies dating back at least as early as *Hook and Hand* by including amputees among their villains.

   The McMasters tells the tale of Benjy McMasters (Brock Peters), a freed slave whose return from four years of service in the Civil War is so recent that he still wears his Union uniform as he rolls into town at the beginning of the film. His sympathetic former owner, Neil McMasters (Burl Ives), signs an agreement to split his ranch fifty-fifty with him, much to the ire of local racists who dedicate themselves to buying out the McMasters or, if that fails, burning them out. Despite the moviemakers' efforts to be progressive in their portrayals of blacks and native Americans, the lone disabled character is about as one-dimensionally villainous as they come: a one-armed ex-Confederate officer named Kolby (played in overblown style by Jack Palance), who proudly wears his rebel uniform despite the outcome at Appomattox and is so rabid in his racist views that he makes the Ku Klux Klan look like a paragon of moderation. Director Alf Kjellin and writer Harold Jacob Smith were ambivalent not only on the issue of minorities but also on how to end their film; they released the film to theaters in two different versions—one in which the good guys win, the other in which the baddies led by Kolby win—but in neither case did the film suggest any mastery of disability issues.

   Distributed by Warner Bros., *The Deadly Trackers* was a paint-by-numbers Western, high on violence and exceptionally low on humanity. Loaded with inexplicable circumstances and cartoon-like characters masquerading as human beings, *The Deadly Trackers* was the brain child of cult-film favorite Sam Fuller. He wrote its original story, called "Riata," and had begun directing the film but for unclear reasons Warners pulled the plug on the project after the celebrated high-priest of nihilistic values had already spent more than a million shooting the film in Spain. Warners then teamed up with Fouad Said's Cine Film Company to revive the film, and among the new producer's first acts was to move the production to Mexico and replace Fuller with the deservedly obscure director Barry Shear and the German-born screenwriter Lukas Heller, hoping the latter could work the same kind of magic that had led to the success of *What Ever Happened to Baby Jane?* a decade before. (For his part, Heller later asked Warner Bros. to remove his name from the credits.)[33] Richard Harris starred as Sean Kilpatrick, an Irish sheriff of a Texas town who pursues a gang of thugs into Mexico after they killed his wife and son. One gang member, known only as "Choo Choo" (Neville Brand), has in place of one of his hands a foot-long piece of iron rail, a momento from a childhood train accident that the filmmakers used as his characterization's centerpiece. Choo Choo elicits hearty guffaws from his cohorts by suggesting they go after someone who had wronged them "and give him a taste of my rail," and later the filmmakers indeed showed him using it to smash watermelons and people's heads with equal abandon. His demise comes when Kilpatrick knocks him with a rifle butt into a quicksand pool, and even as he goes under the filmmakers couldn't resist highlighting the bizarre prosthesis; the laws of physics to the contrary, the last bit of him to disappear in the muck is that heavy chunk of iron.

An actor who often essayed bad-guy roles, Jack Palance chewed the reins and much of the scenery as the villainous Kolby in 1970's The McMasters.

Disabled villains also appeared in movies that resembled Westerns either in trappings or structure. The normally sensible Kirk Douglas directed and starred in an atrocity called *Scalawag* (1973), a weird land-based adaptation of *Treasure Island* filmed in Yugoslavia that might best be labeled a Western-pirate-musical-comedy. Among the movie's lowlights, and there are many, are recurring unfunny gags about the Douglas character—"Captain Peg"—and his wooden prosthesis. For example, when a bullet strikes his wooden leg and a crewman asks if he's hurt, he responds, "Naaah, only a flesh wound." Making this hammily acted, cliché-driven movie all the harder to swallow is the knowledge that Albert Maltz, who had scripted *Pride of the Marines* and worked uncredited on *The Beguiled*, was its primary writer.

That same year saw the appearance of a Western in structure if not in look, *Enter the Dragon*, a co-production of Warner Bros. and Concord Productions filmed in the U.S. and Hong Kong. In his last movie role, the San Francisco-born Bruce Lee played a character creatively named Lee who enters a martial arts tournament as a means of infiltrating the island fortress of the one-handed Han (Shih

Neville Brand played a sadistic killer named "Choo Choo" in The Deadly Trackers. *The filmmakers who decided to give him a chunk of an iron rail for an artificial hand obviously had loco motives. Copyright © 1973 Warner Bros. Inc.*

Kien), a renegade monk now well-off after years of trafficking in drugs and female slavery. After Lee, a classic do-gooding outsider, learns his own sister had committed suicide after Han's men had assaulted her, the stage is set for numerous kung fu confrontations between Lee, Han, and the latter's goons. Though Han is equipped with an assortment of lethal prostheses (one has six-inch knife blades for fingers, for example) he ultimately proves no match for kicking, chopping, and evil-eye giving Lee. The totally flat characterizations and general mindlessness of the film notwithstanding, *Enter the Dragon* entered a stratospheric level of box-office business as a result of its mind-boggling action sequences.

Other disabled villains made appearances in different genres, almost always in low-budget movies. In *Frogs* (1972), Ray Milland played a thoroughly unpleasant wheelchair-using patriarch of a wealthy Southern family who has been fouling the environment in the name of corporate greed and who receives his comeuppance at the hands (or, more appropriately, the webbed feet) of hundreds of mutant amphibians. In 1973, Milland along with a host of other veteran performers who should have known better (among them Elsa Lanchester, Maurice Evans,

Archvillain Han and ultimate good guy Lee (Shih Kien, Bruce Lee) chop, kick, and slash their way through Enter the Dragon *(1973).*

John Carradine, Louis Hayward, and Broderick Crawford) appeared in a piece of debris called *Terror in the Wax Museum*, which had among its characters the obligatory disabled assistant: a cut-rate Quasimodo named Karkov (Steven Marlo), whose array of impairments include a twisted spine, a withered arm, a blind eye, deafness, and an inability to speak. Though Karkov turns out to be innocent of any crime, the moviemakers made him the prime murder suspect for about 98 percent of the movie and dispatched him in graphic fashion by having him crash through a railing and fall into a vat of molten wax. In *Massacre at Central High* (1976), three high-school hoods disable a new boy named David (Derrel Maury) by allowing a car to crush his leg, and in revenge David plots various schemes that result in his tormentors expiring in hideously vivid ways. Having accomplished those grisly deeds, David strangely begins assaulting students who had nothing to do with his disablement and is eventually blown to atoms by one of his own planted bombs.

By the time *Massacre* appeared, however, the renewed tradition of associating disability with villainy had already gone into sharp decline, with only *Enter the Dragon* having brought in respectable earnings. The dropoff may have been attributable to audience dissatisfaction with the high number of antiheroes in these and other films, as a *Variety* writer suggested in 1973: "Only a year ago extreme violence seemed a commercial sine qua non, but most gross-scanning execs overlooked that these recent b.o. [box office] hits had used violence as a protagonist's tool for achieving some measure of control over a highly bureaucratized environment. The 1973 crop of sadistic entries has spotlighted unpleasant 'heroes' with whom audience identification is near-impossible, and the commercial results have been dull. It just isn't wise to throw out the baby and keep the bathwater."[34]

A film that marked the transition from the villainous images back to the more fleshed-out characterizations is a strange concoction of comedy, pathos, and drama called *Fuzz* (1972), a Filmways co-production overseen by executive producer Edward S. Feldman. Evan Hunter, who under his "Ed McBain" pseudonym had published a number of "87th Precinct" tales featuring Boston police officer Steve Carella and his deaf wife Teddy, had seen his work adapted for television at least once (a 1961 NBC production simply called *87th Precinct* starring Robert Lansing and Gena Rowlands) and was ready to move to the big screen. Serving as screenwriter, he adapted one of his books and along with producer Jack Farren and director Richard Colla focused their black-humored film on Carella (Burt Reynolds) and his attempts to bring to justice a criminal known simply as the "Deaf Man" (Yul Brynner) in their hope of doing for police work what the *M*A*S*H* creators did for warfare. The Deaf Man, who occasionally uses the alias of "Sordo" (Spanish for "deaf"), is a high-living murderer and extortionist who surrounds himself with quirky underlings and whose latest scheme is the abduction of a wealthy man's wife and daughter. In addition to the ancient tendency of defining the character in terms of his difference, *Fuzz* like so many other films that associate villainy with disability places undue emphasis on the person's prosthetic device. Not only do other characters frequently mention it ("the bald guy with the hearing aid" becomes a virtual refrain in the film) but the film's final shot, after the Deaf Man has ended up in Boston Harbor, consists of the hearing aid floating on the water. Hoping *Fuzz* would be popular enough to justify a sequel, the filmmakers left a narrative loose end by showing the Deaf Man's hand coming up out of the water and grabbing the device within the same shot. The frame freezes, the credits roll, and Dinah Shore sings "I'll Be Seeing You" on the soundtrack.

Despite the Deaf Man's one-dimensional characterization, *Fuzz* also includes a far more incidental treatment of disability in the form of Carella's deaf wife, played by Neile Adams. A tender scene early in the film in which Teddy comforts her husband in the hospital helps establish her character, and Carella's partner Meyer Meyer (Jack Weston) can't help but remark on the coincidence of two deaf people looming large in his friend's life. In a reflective, almost somber tone, Carella responds simply by saying, "I just never think about her [pause] that way."

Yul Brynner as "The Deaf Man" lies wounded in the streets, abandoned by his criminal henchmen, in Fuzz. *Copyright © 1972 United Artists Corp.*

The filmmakers dropped the issue almost as quickly as they brought it up, but nevertheless *Fuzz* with its sharply contrasting images of deaf people suggests a sense of a changing Hollywood agenda.

Other moviemakers of the period who traveled the incidental route started giving greater prominence to disabled characters in their works. The producer-director team of Mike J. Frankovich and Milton Katselas was responsible for several such films, including the Columbia release *Butterflies Are Free* (1972) which screenwriter Leonard Gershe adapted from his 1969 Broadway hit also directed by Katselas. Gershe's inspiration for both the play and the movie was a remarkable person named Harold Krents, who despite severely impaired vision graduated cum laude from Harvard Law School. Krents was so proficient at adapting to his environment that a draft board thought he was faking his blindness and classified him 1-A. Therein, Gershe thought, lay the basis for a story.[35]

Butterflies Are Free is essentially a tale of three characters: Don Baker (Edward Albert), a young man blind since birth who desires the independent life; Jill Tanner (Goldie Hawn), his giggly next-door neighbor; and Florence Baker (Oscar winner Eileen Heckart, who also essayed the role on Broadway), Don's wealthy mother who threatens to smother him with overprotectiveness. In transforming the play into a movie, Katselas, Gershe, and Frankovich shifted the focus from Don to Jill, an unsurprising development in light of the fact that Frankovich had produced a string of other Hawn vehicles, including 1969's *Cactus Flower*, 1970's *There's a Girl in My Soup*, and 1972's *$*, a.k.a. *Dollars*. The readjustment is most evident during the film's early going, after Jill has just moved into a run-down San Francisco apartment that happens to adjoin his and becomes annoyed when she sees him apparently staring at her through the apartments' windows. At this point Katselas made him simply an object for her to contemplate. Yet once Jill and the audience have gotten to know Don (and, harkening back to that draft board's encounter with Harold Krents, she does take a while to realize he's blind), the director abandoned the strategy of restricting the movie to her point of view in favor of more conventional crosscutting that includes Don's perspective.

Though the filmmakers based their film on a person who seemed tailor-made for the Civilian Superstar treatment, *Butterflies Are Free* actually poses a modest critique of that 1950s stereotype. Don tells Jill that when he was a child his mother wrote several kid books about "Little Donny Dark," an extraordinary blind boy with whom he seldom identified. "I guess they were a projection of what she hoped I'd be." he says. "Sort of a sightless Superman." The problems he contends with aren't the usual ones 1950s moviemakers manufactured for their Superstars—self-pity, rehabilitation struggles, the uphill return to former glory—but instead are related mostly to others' attitudes, mainly his mother's. Except for a brief moment when Don erupts in front of Jill with a "thanks a lot but don't patronize me" harangue, which as Lauri Klobas has suggested seems out of place and more a concession to the old stereotypes, he spends most of his conflict-resolving energy puncturing people's misconceptions about blind people, often with gentle self-directed humor. A generally well-received movie, *Butterflies Are Free* commendably shows its disabled character to be an appealing, talented, intelligent fellow, independent, strong-willed (when it appears Jill is about to move in with another man, he almost succumbs to the idea of moving back with his mother but reconsiders), and content with his life.[36]

Frankovich and Katselas returned to the Cinema of Isolation with the 1975 production of *Report to the Commissioner*, a drama written by Abby Mann and Ernest Tidyman that takes on the issue of police corruption after detective Bo Lockley (Michael Moriarty) accidently kills an undercover cop who had infiltrated the domain of a big-time drug dealer and his department tries to hush it up. Rising above the movie's mostly banal characters is a legless, impoverished streetperson named Joey Egan (Robert Balaban). Reduced to selling pencils from his cart, Joey is both verbally and physically abusive—he thinks nothing of biting a police officer who's been giving him a hard time, for instance—but turns out to have a streak of tenacious loyalty. After Lockley retrieves his cart from a dumpster after another cop had pulled him off it and tossed it there, Joey returns the

Robert Balaban played Joey Egan, a streetperson who at high personal risk pursues a criminal through traffic-clogged New York thoroughfares in Report to the Commissioner. *Copyright © 1975 United Artists Corp.*

favor and then some by pursuing the drug dealer through the streets of Manhattan. After dodging traffic, he latches on to the rear bumper of the dealer's taxi and manages to hang on long enough to discover where the dealer was heading and leave his friend a message.

More salient than their establishment of Joey as a hero was the way the filmmakers represented him and his perspectives. Katselas often took special pains to have cinematographer Mario Tosi bring the camera to Joey's eye level when he photographed him to avoid high-angle shots and the sense of helplessness they usually connote. In addition, Joey wields the look during much of the hair-raising pursuit scene; the shots alternate between backtracking close-ups of him and forward-tracking shots showing what he sees (occasionally the latter were over-the-shoulder shots with the camera on the platform behind the actor) before Joey crashes into a pile of trashcans and then observes the location of the drug dealer. Despite the masochistic quality of this narrative unit—the disabled character sees and then is punished—and the brevity of his screen time, Joey shines like a beacon in a world of moral murkiness.

Other movies of the time took a less conspicuous approach to disability by featuring hearing-impaired children in background roles. One was *Nashville* (1975), a patchwork quilt of several dozen character studies designed by writer Joan Tewkesbury and producer-director Robert Altman to connect to a Nashville political rally on behalf of an enigmatic third-party presidential candidate. Among the characters in this Paramount release is Opal (Geraldine Chaplin), a flaky BBC reporter who interviews many other *Nashville* figures, including Linnea Reese (Lily Tomlin), married to the candidate's seedy campaign manager. During the interview, Opal learns Linnea is the mother of two preadolescents born deaf and responds by saying how awful that must be. Linnea immediately replies that the situation is not awful at all, and Altman later underscored her statement by showing Linnea and her children Jimmy and Donna (played by the hearing-impaired James Dan Calvert and Donna Denton) as they sit around a table singing and signing "Sing a Song," a bouncy tune composed by Joe Raposo made popular during the 1970s by the Carpenters. Though very brief, it is one of the movie's privileged moments.

Altman denied putting any message into this film. As he rather ingenuously put it, "I don't have anything that I'm trying to say. I have no philosophy that I'm trying to put across. I'm not saying, 'This is what I think things should be.' All I'm trying to show you is the way I see and think things are." While shooting *Nashville* he said he identified with Opal—"In a way, she's me in the film"—and, perhaps like this character from another culture seeking answers, he had regarded deafness as something of a tragedy. Knowing how heavily Altman has depended on his actors to bring their own life-experiences to their roles, however, one can't help but think he found working with the Calvert and Denton children, who essentially play themselves and even use their real first names, a moving and enlightening experience.[37]

Deaf children also play background roles in *Looking for Mr. Goodbar* (1977), a Freddie Fields production based on Judith Rossner's novel and distributed through Paramount. *Goodbar* dwells on Theresa Dunn (Diane Keaton), a young woman who has just begun a career as a teacher but also has a penchant for cruising bars after hours. Her sister characterizes her best by suggesting she is "St. Theresa by day and swinging Terry by night." Critic Robin Wood has rightly observed that the movie stresses her teaching much more than does the novel,[38] a point that has considerable bearing on disability issues. Rossner's book poses Theresa simply as a teacher and only occasionally alludes to her work, but writer-director Richard Brooks, who wanted to sharpen the distinction between the two halves of her life, enhanced her daytime "saintliness" by making her a teacher of specifically deaf children. He made his views clear during an early scene in which Theresa attends a slide-tape lecture on teaching deaf children; the speaker concludes the presentation with "If you can teach a deaf child, you have touched God," a line Theresa later repeats to other teachers of deaf kids. Brooks devoted considerable screen time to showing her interacting with a racially mixed class of about a half-dozen hearing-impaired children and paid particular attention to a subplot about a destitute girl in need of a hearing aid and Theresa's efforts to get her one. Though Brooks may have constructed the children as deaf mainly because of the ulterior motive suggested above (and in spite of a pointless scene in which they inexplicably turn hostile the first time Theresa shows up late for class), *Looking for Mr. Goodbar* does contain some truly touching moments between the pupils and their teacher.

A major trend within Hollywood's shaky movement toward the mainstream had a decidedly familiar quality. The 1970s, particularly the latter part of the decade, witnessed a return to Civilian Superstar movies, though among nonsports-related films the extraordinary characters' impairments reflected a mostly incidental, low-key treatment. One such example is *Julia* (1977), a Twentieth Century–Fox production that Oscar-winning screenwriter Alvin Sargent based on a story in Lillian Hellman's 1973 *Pentimento* memoirs about her relationship with a courageous friend dedicated to fighting fascism in pre–World War II Europe. Jane Fonda, her *Barbarella* days well behind her, played Hellman and Vanessa Redgrave won an Academy Award for her work as the exuberant title character, a woman from a wealthy background who persuades her to smuggle $50,000 of Julia's own money into Germany to help her and the underground free hundreds of Jews and others persecuted by the Nazis. The moviemakers told much of *Julia* from Lillian's perspective, so that after the two women meet in a restaurant after months of separation the audience shares in her surprise when she learns Julia had lost a leg during a violent confrontation between fascists and students in Vienna. (An objectifying, high-angle shot looking down on Julia's lower limbs reveals a wooden leg.) Lillian is overwhelmed by the news of her friend's disablement, but Julia is most matter-of-fact about it—"No tears, Lilly," she says simply—and notes that she'll soon have to curtail her antifascist work only because "the crutches make me too noticeable." Though Julia remains an enigmatic figure, the movie's understated attention to the details of her orthopedic impairment only enhances her heroic qualities. Fittingly, the main person who provided it was Fred Zinnemann, the same director responsible for the no-nonsense yet sympathetic treatment of paralyzed vets in *The Men* more than a quarter of a century before.

A film of similar vintage, *The Betsy* (1978), co-written by one-time blacklistee Walter Bernstein from Harold Robbins' bestseller, likewise took the incidental route in its story about the conflicts among several generations of a car-manufacturing family. Head of the clan is Loren Hardeman (Laurence Olivier), a wheelchair-using man of 86 known to most of his family and associates as "Number One." He founded Bethlehem Motors decades before but now threatens to buck the corporation in an effort to produce an affordable car with extremely efficient gas mileage—the title vehicle—and recruits a young race car driver named Angelo Perino (Tommy Lee Jones) to help him develop it. The moviemakers loaded their film with inanities (principally the casting of Robert Duvall as Number One's grandson—Olivier's twenty-four years over Duvall must have been long ones indeed—

Loren "Number One" Hardeman and Angelo Perino (Laurence Olivier, Tommy Lee Jones) size up Hardeman's new gas-turbine engine, and each other, in The Betsy. *Copyright © 1978 Allied Artists Pictures Corp.*

and having the 71-year-old British actor play Hardeman in flashbacks when the character would have been in his early 40s) and seemed interested mainly in having Number One use a wheelchair to help distinguish the flashback scenes (which reveal him able-bodied) from the present-day ones. They took the easy way out by refusing to show him encountering any architectural or attitudinal difficulties, his enormous wealth no doubt responsible for eradicating both sets of potential problems.

Despite these issues, *The Betsy* like *Julia* does feature a relatively incidental treatment of its character's impaired mobility. Angelo's query to Betsy—"How's the old man doing? Still running the world from his wheelchair?"—is one of the very few times a character refers to it. Though director Daniel Petrie occasionally objectified Number One, the character does share in the power of the look with the others, principally his daughter Sally (Katharine Ross), his great-granddaughter Betsy (Kathleen Beller), Angelo, and Loren III (Duvall). In addition, Petrie's cinematographer Mario Tosi often photographed Number One at the character's eye level—a visual strategy he had also pursued in *Report to the Commissioner* several years before—to minimize the effect of the audience "looking down" on the disabled character.

The sports films of the 1970s were a different matter. Ushered in by *Brian's Song* (1971), an Emmy-winning made-for-TV movie about Chicago Bears running back Brian Piccolo who died of cancer the previous year, a number of movies followed the direction of *The Stratton Story* by examining world-class sports figures whose lives and careers are forever altered by a disabling circumstance. The films differed significantly from the previous Civilian Superstar films in that they didn't usually try to show the athletes reaching former greatness or attempting to "pass."

Maurie (1973), later known as *Big Mo*, told the true story of Maurice Stokes, who played basketball for the Cincinnati Royals during the 1950s until a head injury left him paralyzed for the remaining ten years of his life. A movie based on Stokes's experiences went into development shortly after his death in 1970, with recently retired Los Angeles Rams wide receiver Bernie Casey signed as the title character and Bo Svenson as Jack Twyman, a teammate who spent years raising thousands of dollars to help with his friend's rehabilitation. With its emphasis on a professional sports figure "struck down" by a disabling accident, the Daniel Mann-directed *Maurie* followed conspicuously in the tradition of *The Stratton Story*. It was hardly a coincidence; its screenwriter and co-producer, Douglas Morrow, happened to be *The Stratton Story*'s chief writer and had won an Academy Award for that film. Morrow, who like Sam Wood had developed a reputation for sports movies (among other films he had written was 1951's *Jim Thorpe—All American*, about the trials of the famous native American athlete), tried weaving the same kind of tale of courage here but only managed to set off the majority of the critics, who praised the overall level of acting but berated the script's manipulative qualities. A. H. Weiler of the *New York Times* stated that although Svenson "is sincere and stalwart in his devotion as Stokes's official guardian and

Bernie Casey is dignified as the stricken Stokes" the movie "is, unfortunately, rarely moving as drama [and] evolves on screen with largely soap-opera effects." The *Variety* reviewer likened it to "a bad Sunday morning inspirational television drama." Latter-day critics Jay Nash and Stanley Ross agreed, noting that "the script is so laden with obtuse sentimentalism that all the work by Mann and his actors seems totally wasted."[39]

Other sports-minded disability dramas also followed the teary-eyed route, with the most famous, *The Other Side of the Mountain*, appearing in 1975. Financed and distributed by Universal, the film detailed the life of Olympic contender Jill Kinmont before and after a 1955 skiing accident left her paralyzed from the shoulders down. Despite the stated intentions of Kinmont and director Larry Peerce to avoid the Superstar treatment, *Other Side* emerged as a film well-informed by that tradition.[40]

The person who got the project off the ground was producer Ed Feldman, who while taking time out from his Filmways company's 1972 production of *Fuzz* came across a *Life* magazine story about Kinmont. The article was actually a follow-up to a 1964 fourteen-page *Life* photo essay that had also led to the publication of her lifestory, *A Long Way Up*, in 1966 and an aborted film in 1968. (The

Maurice Stokes and nurse Rosie Saunders (Bernie Casey, Paulene Myers) share a laugh in the sports-related melodrama Maurie *(1973).*

book, retitled *The Other Side of the Mountain* and reprinted in 1975 to coincide with the movie's release, would go through twelve printings that year.) Feldman, who already knew something about Kinmont from her work as a teacher at the Beverly Hills school his children attended, contacted her with a proposal to make film about her life, tentatively titled *The Jill Kinmont Story*. Kinmont agreed to the project and signed on as one of its technical advisors.

Writer David Seltzer completed a script draft in 1973 after holding frequent discussions with Kinmont and poring over her notebooks and scrapbooks. Though in some ways he seemed an ideal choice to write the screenplay—he was already familiar with disability as a result of his own brother's bout with polio—Seltzer had unfortunately let misconceptions guide the construction of the first draft. "When I read it, I cried four times," Kinmont said. "I thought, oh that poor girl, what a tragic life. But I never thought about her as me." Despite Kinmont's claim that she never went through a deep depression following her accident because of her family's strong support, Seltzer insisted otherwise—"With that terrible handicap, you had to have been depressed," he told her—and fabricated such a mental state to make the movie seem more believable. As Kinmont sarcastically confided to a friend, Seltzer "knows that *all* paraplegics become hopelessly despondent before they dramatically save themselves." In addition, he bestowed an isolated quality on her by only rarely acknowledging the supporting role of the people close to her. She later met with Seltzer, Feldman, and Peerce with a list of more than a hundred suggested script changes and found the writer receptive: "David took me very seriously, was hurt at some times and elated at others because I didn't want to change something. He did make many changes in the script, and I felt good about our meeting."[41]

With script adjustments underway, Feldman and Peerce began working on other aspects of the production. For the role of Jill, they chose Marilyn Hassett, a 26-year-old with minimal acting experience but who had had a brush with paralysis in 1969 after an elephant had stepped on her during the making of a television commercial, fracturing her pelvis and damaging nerves in her legs (she was bedridden for five months and used a wheelchair for months thereafter). Hassett also exuded, in Peerce's words, "a certain fragility" and attractiveness, qualities the producer also found important. "We wanted a pretty girl," explained Feldman, who with more than a touch of ableism added that "it is my belief that people relate to pretty things that are broken." With other casting decisions set—among them, Beau Bridges as her suitor Dick Buek, Belinda Montgomery as her friend Audra Jo Nicholson, Nan Martin as her mother, and Dabney Coleman as her coach Dave McCoy—filming began on location in Bishop, California, and the Sierra Nevada mountains in April 1974, with Kinmont and her family helping supervise the production.[42]

Despite Kinmont's continuing misgivings on the set (she perceived the hospital scenes to be chillingly accurate but remained quite concerned about inaccuracies in the movie's representation of the people surrounding her and the accident itself) and the widely varying critical reactions to the finished product, *The Other Side of the Mountain* and its tie-in book were financially very successful, and Peerce and Feldman immediately made plans to do a sequel. Kinmont resisted at first but was swayed by family members, most notably her mother, who offered compelling reasons that tapped into Kinmont's interest in a more incidental treatment. "You know how many people have told us the first film stopped at what was really the beginning," June Kinmont said. "They wanted to know *how* a quadriplegic could become independent. There are so many people who want to know more. And people want to know about your teaching career, which was barely touched upon in the first movie." Hoping the proposed movie would dwell at some length on her work as a teacher, of which she was very proud, Kinmont agreed in 1976 to participate. In the hands of Peerce and new screenwriter Douglas Day Stewart, however, *The Other Side of the Mountain Part II* (1978) evolved mainly into a soppy love story involving Kinmont and new beau John Boothe (Timothy Bottoms, the star of Dalton Trumbo's *Johnny Got His Gun*), with the frequently back-lit Hassett looking like she just rolled out of a shampoo commercial.[43]

The *Other Side* movies unquestionably bear a strong resemblance to the classic Civilian Superstar films of more than twenty years before. (*Other Side II* even

Olympic skiing hopeful Jill Kinmont (Marilyn Hassett) shortly before her accident in The Other Side of the Mountain. *Copyright © 1975 Universal Pictures Co.*

begins with Kinmont about to accept the city of Los Angeles' Woman of the Year award for her work as an educator, reminiscent of Jane Froman's Courageous Performer of the Year ceremony that starts *With a Song in My Heart*.) Yet some significant differences are apparent beneath their regressive trappings. In addition to avoiding the idea of having their disabled character trying to return to Olympic-level greatness, the *Other Side* films do show her encountering ableist prejudice—an issue that moviemakers often raised in the post–World War II Noble Warrior films but rarely in the follow-up Civilian Superstar films. A boyfriend in *Other Side* practically evaporates after he sees the extent of her paralysis, for example,[44] while a school administrator tells her he won't allow her to study for a teaching certificate. "At this moment in my life, my only handicap is you!" she tells him. The *Other Side* films thus embody a curious paradox; they are an indictment of the "inspiration to us all" type of film (indeed, this is the very phrase Kinmont and her friend predict the administrator will use as a prelude to turning her down, which he does) and yet, with all of their notorious tearjerking qualities, are very much a part of it.

In a similar vein, *Ice Castles* (1979) told the wafer-thin story of an Iowa farm-girl whose hopes for a big-time skating career are impeded only slightly by a blindness-causing accident. Directed and co-scripted by Donald Wrye, *Ice Castles* starred Robbie Benson and erstwhile Ice Capades performer Lynn-Holly Johnson as Nick Peterson and Lexie Winston, teenaged lovers who suffer from a terminal case of the cutes but whose relationship hits the skids after she starts receiving much attention for her potentially world-class skating abilities.

Lexie's life takes a turn after she crashes into tables and chairs set up on a badly lit ice rink during a solo practice and develops a blood clot in her brain that impairs her vision. She can only see light and dark patches, as Wrye's subjective camerawork reveals. Her father and her coach try to pull her out of her depression (which the filmmakers visualized by having Lexie hide in her attic and try on her dead mother's clothes) by encouraging her to start skating again, to little avail. Only after she smooths out her rocky relationship with Nick do she and her boyfriend work on practice sessions to get her back into competition.

After weeks of training, Lexie is ready for the midwestern regionals. Not unlike her counterparts in the 1950s–era Civilian Superstar movies, she insists on "passing"; she doesn't want her skating rivals to know of her impairment for fear they will feel sorry for her. After performing incredibly complex maneuvers with ease, she receives a standing ovation and bouquets of roses from the audience, her moment of glory marred only by other roses thrown on the ice, which she trips over. The auditorium goes instantly silent, as the spectators watch Lexie on her hands and knees. Nick, astutely observing "We forgot about the flowers," walks over, helps her up, and gently leads her away. The silence turns into uproarious applause, and the movie ends on an upbeat note.

The slight critical attention *Ice Castles* drew was generally favorable, but the reviewers were quick to pick up on the movie's old-fashioned narrative structure.

As *Time*'s Richard Schickel observed, "Obviously the people responsible for this movie are fully aware of all the conventions governing stories about the rise, fall and eventual triumph of stars of sports and show biz (and figure skating is, of course, an intriguing blend of both disciplines). But the film makers do not abuse these conventions, which are for the most part understated, glanced off." The most conspicuous legacy of the 1950s-style Civilian Superstar movies—the character's attempt to pass while striving for greatness—was an aspect of *Ice Castles* that did not go unnoticed by *Newsweek*'s David Ansen, who wrote that the filmmakers erred in "asking us to believe the world wouldn't know that Lexie had gone blind—in this fairy tale, the media magically vanish after the accident." To the filmmakers' credit, they did try to suggest the experience of blindness through the subjective camerawork, but in general that approach was lost amid the movie's undistinguished acting, simplistic story, and amateurish, ham-handed script. In retrospect, it seems Wrye and company created *Ice Castles* mainly as an excuse to showcase Lynn-Holly Johnson's formidable ice-skating skills and Melissa Manchester's rendition of the Marvin Hamlisch-Carole Bayer Sager hit song, "Through the Eyes of Love."[45]

Paralleling the reborn trend of the Civilian Superstar was the rise of a particular kind of disability comedy. Filmmakers themselves seemed to recognize just how overblown and campy the negative images of the early 1970s were, for the mid-to-late years of the decade witnessed a surge of movies that lampooned moviedom's disabled villains, both recent and vintage, and in a kind of spillover effect satirized other classic stereotypes such as the Sweet Innocent, Saintly Sage, and Noble Warrior. More a burlesque on the old Hollywood imagery than an assault on disabled people (though the line between the two was often obscure), the films began appearing in 1974, after the excessively violent movies had mostly run their course.

The filmmaker at the forefront of such efforts was Mel Brooks, who in 1974 created not one but two such movies: *Blazing Saddles* and *Young Frankenstein*. The former film has several brief scenes involving a hangman named Morris, a minor character who in this Western parody is starkly and intentionally out of place: a one-eyed, hunchbacked, club-footed fellow dressed in medieval garb whose demeanor, British accent, and slithering tongue make him look and sound like a cross between Charles Laughton's Quasimodo and Boris Karloff's Mord. Brooks threw in another reference to a famous disabled character of the late 1930s when Morris shows public official Hedley Lamarr (Harvey Korman) he's about ready to hang a man in a wheelchair. "Yes," recalls Lamarr. "The Dr. Gillespie killings."

Young Frankenstein offers a more extended satire of Hollywood's Golden Age offerings with parodies of several disability-related images from the *Frankenstein* series: the villain with a twisted spine, the police inspector with a mechanical arm, and the Saintly Sage. A shamelessly mugging Marty Feldman played the most conspicuous of the threesome: Igor, a grave-robbing assistant to Dr. Frederick Frankenstein (Gene Wilder) and the source of a seemingly endless number of gags related to the villainous Fritz and Ygor of yore. Igor points to his back after describing one of his insights as a "hunch." Frankenstein, cordially slapping him on the back and eliciting a sound akin to knocking hollow wood, offers to help Igor with his hump, to which the latter replies "What hump?" The doctor later is about to comment on its mysterious migration from Igor's right shoulder to his left but thinks better of it, leaving Igor to grin at the camera in secret amusement. Never known for restraint, Brooks even resuscitated the hoariest of visual gags: while leading Frankenstein down a short flight of stairs Igor says "Walk this way," and of course the good doctor obediently bends over.

The other two characters shared less but equally vivid screen time. Kenneth Mars played Kemp, a one-armed inspector who wears a monocle over an eye patch. Modeled after Lionel Atwill's Inspector Krogh of *Son of Frankenstein*, Kemp leads the townspeople in search of the Monster (Peter Boyle) while saying, "A riot is an ugly thing, *und* I think that it is just about time that we had one!" The people in turn use him and his mechanical arm as a battering ram to gain access to the Frankenstein castle, and when he later shakes hands with the Monster the audience is treated to the sight of the latter pulling Kemp's arm out of its socket—a bizarre visualization of what supposedly happened to Krogh as a child in *Son of Frankenstein*.

The third of the trio is parodied in a four-minute sequence that begins with a blind hermit named Harold (Gene Hackman), robed and bearded like his *Bride of Frankenstein* predecessor, praying to God for a friend. The door to his hut bursts open to reveal the Monster, drawn to the hut by the violin music Harold had been playing on his phonograph. After humbly introducing himself, Harold tries to serve the Monster soup and wine, but, in a classic illustration of the comic character whose disability leads to others' suffering, he unwittingly dishes up disaster instead; he ladles the soup into the Monster's lap several times and then smashes the latter's wine-filled mug with his own in a toast. Finally, after Harold offers a cigar to the Monster and then accidently sets the latter's thumb on fire, the Monster gets up and crashes through the front door, leaving a downcast Harold ("I was going to make espresso") in his wake.

Despite such images, or perhaps because of them, *Young Frankenstein* was a hit and prompted its distributor, Twentieth Century–Fox, to try to duplicate its success by producing its own comedy with disability at its core. The result was *Fire Sale* (1977), a miserable, terminally unfunny movie about the bizarre Fikus family. Among its members is Sherman (Sid Caesar), a mentally and physically impaired World War II veteran who's been living in a V.A. hospital for over thirty years. Benny and Russel Fikus (Vincent Gardenia and Rob Reiner) come across Sherman in the hospital plant nursery and discover that he has removed his prosthesis from his left leg and inserted the stump into a box of earth. As he waters it, Sherman says that something must be wrong with the soil since his leg hasn't grown over an inch in a year. Sherman believes WW II is still underway and later escapes from the hospital. In full combat dress, he commandeers a motorized wheelchair and careens wildly down a highway while pursued by a motorcycle cop before setting his relatives' department store on fire. With the knowledge that Alan Arkin not only starred in this pit of a movie but also directed it, one can't help but think the view he held of deaf people a decade before—"not terribly bright, wildly animated at all times in trying to express themselves, and undisciplined emotionally"—far from being expunged by his *The Heart Is a Lonely Hunter* experiences, had come back in a grotesquely mutated form.

Even before *Fire Sale* torched the screen, another movie had taken on an old stereotype and come up with wildly uneven results: *Tommy* (1975), a comedy if only in its vicious parody of the Sweet Innocent and the miracle cure. British writer-director Ken Russell, who had portrayed disability most graphically in 1971's *The Devils* (Vanessa Redgrave had starred as a seventeenth-century French nun with a severely twisted spine who fantasizes about an immoral priest), pulled out all the stops in this adaptation of the 1969 rock opera of the same name about a deaf, blind, and speechless boy penned by Peter Townshend and performed by The Who. Russell, who initially proclaimed the opera "rubbish," later offered the singular opinion that "*Tommy* is greater than any painting, opera, piece of music, ballet, or dramatic work that this century has produced" and with the financial backing of music magnate Robert Stigwood and a U.S. distribution deal with Columbia created the film without a word of spoken dialogue (the soundtrack consists solely of songs, an instrumental score, and sound effects). The Who's lead singer Roger Daltrey played the title character, who as a youth loses his sight, hearing, and speech after witnessing his father's death. While Tommy and his mother (Ann-Margret) search for a miracle cure, he develops quite the talent for pinball—so much so in fact that as his fame increases an uncounted number of admirers begin worshipping him and even take to wearing dark glasses and ear and mouth plugs to emulate their messiah. Tommy, who communicates through bogus sign language, later regains his abilities only to be abandoned by his followers, but as *Saturday Review* critic Hollis Alpert wrote, "Not to worry. Tommy becomes God. And presumably all is well."[46]

Russell, who perceived a connection between the film and *Lourdes*, his 1958 edited-to-music documentary about the famous site of supposed miracle cures and "the pilgrims, the processions, the exploitation," argued *Tommy* was mainly about spirituality, not disability:

> It's very religious. It's a pilgrim's progress. It's about somebody trying to find answers, it's about masses trying to find answers and the fact that answers are often not to be found in externals, but mostly in internals. It's all to do with "put on your eyeshades, put in your earplugs, put a cork in your mouth, turn inward and play pinball." I mean, that's a very good metaphor, it seems to me.

Who wants to do that? Nobody. Very few people, anyway. It's about instant enlightenment, instant answers, an obvious solution and it's about the exploitation of religion.[47]

Despite Russell's declamations, *Tommy* left critics split over its merits. Awash in assorted absurdities, the movie bears little relationship to the physically disabled experience, but one of its more garish scenes is worth noting: a faith-healing ceremony to which Tommy's mother in desperation drags her son. A plaster statue of Marilyn Monroe in her famous billowing-skirt pose from *The Seven-Year Itch* serves as a religious icon for hundreds of disabled people in the ceremony presided over by high priest Eric Clapton who sings "Eyesight for the Blind." Russell almost had to scuttle his plans for the scene after a British Royal Marines officer, who had permitted Russell the use of the Marines' chapel in Portsmouth, tried to halt production after seeing that the director had filled the building with several hundred wheelchair-using people with actual disabilities. Filming eventually went on as scheduled, with Russell defending his hiring of the extras. "They're the happiest people you could ever hope to meet," he claimed. "They loved being in the movie."[48]

Moviemakers who created more conventional comedies such as *The Last Remake of Beau Geste* (1977), *The Kentucky Fried Movie* (1977), and *Movie, Movie* (1978) were so conscious of the fact they were spoofing Hollywood films that the very titles they chose suggested their productions' reflexivity. Fresh from a series of Mel Brooks movies, Marty Feldman decided to have a go himself with *The Last Remake of Beau Geste*, a film he starred in, co-wrote, and directed. In this parody of the thrice-filmed 1925 novel by P. C. Wren, Peter Ustinov played the tyrannical Sergeant Markov, whose missing leg and odd collection of prostheses formed the basis for a stream of gags of exceptionally poor taste. A strange character with sergeant's stripes tattooed on his arms and an assortment of false scars, Markov also claims among his possessions a teddy bear with a false leg and even rides a horse with a prosthesis. An allegedly comical scene shows Markov and his assistant Corporal Boldini (Roy Kinnear) attempting to attach the sergeant's "dress leg"; as a result of Boldini incorrectly screwing the leg on, Markov injures himself when he tries to click his heels together. Other bits of slapstick include Digby Geste (Feldman) upending Markov by bowling a ball at his leg, and the sergeant attempting to run Beau Geste (Michael York) through with a sword-bearing prosthesis while swinging from a rope (he misses, of course, and crashes into a barrel). Though *The Last Remake of Beau Geste* was certainly beholden in its imagery and storyline to a very specific set of movies, Sergeant Markov's disability curiously wasn't among them; the previous incarnations of the sadistic sergeant, played by Noah Beery in 1926, Brian Donlevy in 1939, and Telly Savalas in 1966, were able-bodied, but nevertheless Feldman saw fit to so endow and ridicule him.

The Kentucky Fried Movie also had a disabled villain among its ranks, but unlike *Last Remake* his creators, collectively known as the Kentucky Fried Theater, a Madison, Wisconsin satirical group, modeled him closely after a recent movie villain. Directed by John Landis and written by David Zucker, Jerry Zucker, and Jim Abrahams, *The Kentucky Fried Movie* consists of a series of discrete (if hardly discreet) comic sketches strung together. The highlight of the movie is a rather lengthy parody of *Enter the Dragon* called "A Fistful of Yen" featuring dozens of authentic martial-arts experts. A Bruce Lee lookalike named Loo (Evan Kim) is up against a one-handed villain named Klahn (Bong Soo Han), who early in "Fistful" replaces his prosthesis with a huge knife blade, decapitates one of his prisoners, and says "Now take him to be tortured." Among his other appliances are a hair dryer, an electric toothbrush, and a flamethrower. When Loo douses him with water as he wields the latter item, Klahn sizzles and melts à la *The Wizard of Oz*'s Wicked Witch of the West.

Far more refined in its comic treatment of disability was *Movie, Movie*, producer-director Stanley Donen's tribute to the classic double feature of Hollywood's Golden Age. A paean to the mixed metaphor and the mangled cliché, *Movie, Movie* is actually two mini-movies combined into one, with the first, "Dynamite Hands," a wonderful send-up of such films as *Kid Galahad* (1937), *Golden Boy* (1939), and of course *City Lights*. It focuses on a young man named Joey Popchik (Harry Hamlin) who turns to boxing to raise money so that his visually impaired kid sister Angie (*The Betsy*'s Kathleen Beller) can get an eye operation in Vienna. The need for the operation is pressing, as a doctor (Art Carney) makes clear: "Angela's eye muscles are extremely weak. They can barely hold up what she sees. If any part of the human body has a tendency to break down, I'm afraid the eyes have it." After languishing on the low-paying boxing circuit, Joey wants to move on to Madison Square Garden and the big time, but his trainer Gloves Malloy (George C. Scott) says he isn't ready yet:

GLOVES: "Joey, Gloves knows best."
JOEY: "Yeah, I'll tell Angie that. No eyes this week. Gloves knows best."
GLOVES: "Now, that ain't fair, kid. Your sister's eyes are below the belt."

After various machinations in and out of the ring, Joey does raise the money with the help of Johnny Danko (Barry Bostwick), a gangster gone straight who has fallen for Angie. Lest there be any doubt about the outcome, "Dynamite Hands" concludes with Angie returning from Vienna to exclaim, "I can see with one eye tied behind my back!"

Vivid though they may be, the comedies couldn't obscure the fact that Hollywood was on its way toward providing reasonably positive images of physically disabled people. America was undergoing major changes in the way it perceived and responded to the needs of its physically disabled minority, reflected to a large degree in the 1978 legislation passed by Congress and signed into law by President Jimmy Carter that recognized the importance of the Independent Living movement. Picking up on these and related concerns, particularly the country's painful coming to terms with Vietnam, the movie industry poised itself to enter the 1980s with depictions that with some notable lapses would resonate with power and sensitivity.

8 / high-tech heroics and other concerns

The late 1970s witnessed the birth of an era in American mainstream film-making marked by significant economic, technological, and philosophical changes. The industry's "blockbuster" approach to moviemaking, brewing earlier in the decade with such films as *The Godfather* (1972) and *Jaws* (1975), returned in full force after years of smaller budgeted and modestly profitable movies. An increasing number of companies discovered that at least one megahit per year could help keep other, potentially less profitable projects afloat and began aggressively developing such multi-million dollar productions. The new technologies available to filmmakers—the Steadicam and the smoothness it imparted to mobile camerawork, four-track stereo soundtracks Dolbyized to reduce noise, and of course computer-assisted special effects—also contributed to the new age, but more importantly a basic conservatism began informing the new movies; not only did Hollywood filmmakers strongly renew their medium's mythmaking capacities by creating heroes who triumph in situations where good and bad are clearly demarcated (e.g., the protagonists of 1977's *Star Wars*, 1978's *Superman*, and 1985's *Rambo*) but they also lavished attention on average people who simply want to fit in with the rest of society, often by striving to achieve some personal objective. As cinema historians Gerald Mast and Bruce Kawin have suggested, "The rebels, misfits, loners, and oddballs that dominated American films [from the mid–1960s up to the late 1970s] were replaced by more ordinary citizens who sought to find a meaningful place for themselves within conventional American society."[1]

This latter characteristic coincided with a renewed interest among Cinema of Isolation practitioners during the late 1970s and beyond in offering relatively incidental treatments of physical disability. Moviemakers concerned about disability issues returned to the idea of showing characters trying to live ordinary, post-rehabilitation lives often within the mainstream of American society. The characters may still face problems connected to their impairments (others' attitudes, mostly), but nevertheless they frequently pursue goals that go beyond basic rehabilitation issues if indeed they deal with the latter at all. Filmmakers not only began inserting such figures into background roles in movies as otherwise disparate as *Terror Train* (1979), *Nine to Five* (1980), *Marie* (1985), *To Live and Die in L.A.* (1985), and *The Milagro Beanfield War* (1988), but they also started nudging them into the limelight in various other films.

The factors that led to the more incidental portrayals were mixed, but the main catalysts were arguably the Vietnam War and its aftermath as personified by the veterans disabled by the conflict. These former military men helped raise the consciousness of the entire country, even Hollywood, by working closely with disabled civilians and rehab professionals to achieve not only the landmark legislation of the late 1960s and early 1970s noted in the previous chapter but also the historic Rehabilitation Amendments of 1978 that funded comprehensive Independent Living services. The country's favorable response to their efforts was hardly a lone circumstance; commenting on a pattern that has occurred several times during the twentieth century, historians Leonard Quart and Albert Auster noted that "the nation's concern over the returning [wounded vets] stimulated and focused attention on the world of the disabled." That concern would lead to, among other things, the creation of films that gave a more sympathetic treatment of people with disabilities.[2]

An early round of movies that presented this new treatment fittingly focused on Vietnam veterans themselves. By 1977, four years after the United States had disengaged its troops from Vietnam and two after the war itself had ended, a number of Hollywood filmmakers were readying projects that would give serious attention to the war's ramifications. "A time arrives for almost everything," said United Artists west coast production head Mike Medavoy, whose company bankrolled and distributed such films as *Coming Home* (1978), *Who'll Stop the Rain?* (a.k.a. *Dog Soldiers*, 1978), and *Apocalypse Now* (1979). "The Vietnam War caused an enormous wound in the American consciousness, and sooner or later you knew people were going to come back to these years." It's interesting to note that narrative moviemakers seldom depicted disabled Vietnam veterans while the war was still being fought (one of the very few was the character played by Alan Alda in the British-made *To Kill a Clown*, noted previously), but after the nation had several years to ponder the implications of the war they began including such figures in their works, occasionally building entire films around them, and for the most part treated them favorably. The situation was certainly not without paradox, for the new images ran counter to the movie industry's early and exceptionally durable characterization of Vietnam veterans as crazed, sadistic killers. As Quart and Auster further noted, "it has been the Vietnam vet, whose image was often that of madman, bomb thrower, and drug addict, who ironically began to evoke a more consistently honest and realistic portrayal of the disabled from Hollywood." Among the more conspicuous of the entries bearing such imagery was a quartet of films from the late 1970s and early 80s: *Coming Home*, *The Deer Hunter* (1978), *Modern Problems* (1981), and *Cutter's Way* (1981).[3]

Coming Home got its start when Jane Fonda formed her own production company, IPC (for Indochina Peace Campaign) Films, with Bruce Gilbert during the early 1970s. Looking for socially relevant film projects to develop, the neophyte producers paid an advance to screenwriting newcomer Nancy Dowd to develop a script based on her relationship with a paraplegic Vietnam vet whom she had met in California while participating in antiwar activities. Dowd responded by creating a 230-page script, "Buffalo Ghosts," that focused primarily on two military wives within a V.A. hospital setting. Sensing the need for a traditional romantic triangle to make the film appeal to a wide audience ("To get it financed we knew

Jane needed to play a pivotal character caught between two people," said Gilbert), Fonda and Gilbert pressed Dowd to make one of the wives, her military husband, and the wheelchair-using Vietnam vet the central characters. This insistence, along with proposed cuts in the massive screenplay, led to a feud between the producers and the writer that culminated in Dowd's departure (she ultimately received story credit but not screenplay credit in the film), leaving behind what the producers felt was an unusable script.[4]

Fonda and Gilbert realized they were now in over their heads as producers and went about recruiting new talent to help them see the project through. They eventually began working with the same team that had realized the award-winning *Midnight Cowboy* in 1969: producer Jerome Hellman, writer Waldo Salt, and director John Schlesinger. The two sets of filmmakers quickly began developing strategies to inject new life into the moribund project.

Hellman and Salt cast aside much of Dowd's work except for its central concept, and even then Salt was reluctant to acknowledge her contributions. As he remembered it, he worked from the ground up "starting with a very simple idea— there's debate on who had the idea first—of a woman whose husband goes overseas and she goes to a hospital and sees a paraplegic and falls in love or gets involved. That was the idea, and building on top of that . . . was a matter of just constant interviews."[5] In his quest to make *Coming Home* as authentic as possible, Salt spent more than a year and $50,000 of his own money interviewing hundreds of disabled Vietnam vets before he wrote his version of the *Coming Home* screenplay.

While Salt sifted through the resulting five thousand pages of transcripts and began writing a screenplay draft, he also found the time to work closely with one of his interview subjects: an erstwhile gung-ho soldier paralyzed from the mid-chest down named Ron Kovic. Something of a father figure for the antiwar veteran (he was then in his early 60s while Kovic was around 30), Salt helped him through a project that would soon become the latter's autobiographical *Born on the Fourth of July*. "Ron was floundering and looking for a way out of his own problems," noted Hellman. "He frequently stayed at Salt's suite at the Chateau Marmont [in Los Angeles] and got emotional as well as literary support from him."[6] Salt and Hellman had even lined up Kovic to act as a technical adviser for their film, but the vet had other plans; after finishing *Born on the Fourth of July* he sold its movie rights to Al Pacino, an actor coming off star turns in *Serpico* (1973), *The Godfather Part II* (1974), and *Dog Day Afternoon* (1975) and whose onscreen persona, by turns brooding and explosive, seemed well-suited to the literary self-portrait Kovic had developed.

In addition to losing Kovic's services as an adviser and pondering the potential competition that a movie based on his book might pose, Hellman had to face several other forms of unpleasantness. He needed to find a replacement for the increasingly unhappy Schlesinger who in the producer's words "asked to be excused" from the project (a Briton, he felt the material would be better handled by an American director) and eventually chose Hal Ashby, a Utah-born editor-turned-director whose credits included *The Last Detail* (1973), *Shampoo* (1975), and *Bound for Glory* (1976). He also had to find a way of giving his film an authentic quality while working around the Veterans Administration, which had refused to cooperate on the venture. Hellman eventually made arrangements to photograph much of the film at the Rancho Los Amigos Hospital in Downey, California, a rehabilitation center for civilians with spinal cord injuries.[7]

Complicating matters further, Salt became quite ill in late 1976 before finishing the screenplay. Ashby brought in Robert C. Jones, a film editor who had written part of the *Bound for Glory* script, to revise Salt's screenplay mere weeks before the cameras were slated to roll in January 1977. "We started before we were ready," stated the director. "We had three or four scripts, an ending that didn't work and the first thirty or forty pages weren't any good—it wandered off into a political thing where a bunch of guys took over the hospital. But the actors got more and more into their characters, and we rewrote as we went. We would improvise in rehearsal a lot, but since I wasn't sure of the construction, of where a scene was going or how it would juxtapose with the next scene, I didn't feel comfortable doing it."[8]

With a patched-together script and numerous improvised scenes, *Coming Home* eventually coalesced into a film that explored a ménage à trois formed by Sally Hyde (Jane Fonda), a bored military wife and V.A. hospital volunteer; Bob Hyde (Bruce Dern), her husband and a Marine captain who cannot wait to return to Vietnam; and Luke Martin (Jon Voight), a tempestuous Vietnam veteran paralyzed from the waist down. Each character undergoes a profound, if unnaturally abrupt, change during the course of the film.

Luke's transformation from a confused, volatile cynic to a thoughtful antiwar activist is foreshadowed in the very first sequence of *Coming Home*, which appears before the main credits. As a group of disabled Vietnam vets play pool and kibbitz at a V.A. hospital, they ask each other if they would return to Vietnam and if they did the right thing by going in the first place. The sequence concludes with a view of Luke, lying prostrate on a gurney, deep in thought. He has yet to utter a word. The camera slowly zooms in on him while other veterans speak offscreen: "I have to justify being paralyzed, I have to justify killing people, so I say [fighting in Vietnam] was OK. But how many guys you know can make the reality and say 'What I did was wrong, and what all this other shit was wrong, man?' And still be able to live with themselves 'cause they're crippled for the rest of their fuckin' life?"

This sequence adds an immediate ring of truth to the film, for the men with the exception of Voight were not professional actors but actual vets disabled by the war. With its dimly lit environment, extraneous sound, and overlapping dialogue, the sequence has the strong flavor of a cinéma vérité documentary. This quality is also present in later scenes that show the men engaging in activities ranging from basketball to frisbee throwing to football. The cinematographer for *Coming*

Home, Haskell Wexler, found working with the veterans the most fascinating part of the filmmaking process. "Of all the location shots we did for the film I think those done at [Rancho Los Amigos] in Downey were the most interesting," he said. "There we had the opportunity to be around people who know the value of life. These paraplegics have overcome all sorts of physical disabilities and have tremendous positive mental capabilities. You would expect working with a bunch of paraplegics to be a real downer. But I was actually inspired by these men. In retrospect, it was the most interesting and exciting part of the whole film." Concerned about the way he photographed the vets, Wexler devised a special camera dolly that placed the camera at the same height as the men in wheelchairs. He was thus able to film them in a straightaway fashion, thereby avoiding high camera angles and the powerlessness that they often ascribe to their subjects.[9]

The filmmakers skillfully intertwined the activities and portrayals of the actual disabled vets with those of Luke, whom the filmmakers made the prime figure within the disabled-vet group. At first, he is extremely bitter toward everyone and everything around him; after he accidently collides with Sally during her first day as a hospital volunteer, for instance, he begins thrashing a nearby table with one of his canes in a total rage before hospital staffers restrain him and inject him with thorazine. Luke later berates Sally when he discovers she is married to an officer, claiming that her work at the hospital "gives you something to talk about over martinis—how you're helping out the poor cripples." Yet when he learns that Sally has been trying to drum up support for the disabled vets through the base newsletter, Luke begins to mellow and even accepts a dinner invitation from her. Still a bit suspicious of her motives, however, Luke asks the nervous Sally several now-famous questions: "This isn't 'have-a-gimp-over-for-dinner night,' is it? You're not one of *those* weirdos?" After she reassures him, he gently says, "I know you're not. I'm just very glad to be here."

At this point *Coming Home* courageously takes on one of moviedom's hitherto undefined areas of the physically disabled experience: sexual expression. In detailing the affair between Luke and Sally (climaxing, as it were, with Sally's orgasm while the Beatles' "Strawberry Fields" plays in the background), the film was one of the first—if not *the* first—to deal explicitly with a physically disabled person's sexual encounters. Among its numerous positive effects, *Coming Home* convincingly affirmed that disabled people are indeed sexual beings and set the stage for movies of the 1980s and beyond to explore the concept further.

The moviemakers further demonstrated courage by turning its Noble Warrior into a distinct variation on the image: a disabled veteran who protests the war in which he had just participated. To the trenchant strains of Steppenwolf's "Born to Be Wild" and Jimi Hendrix's "Manic Depression," Luke arrives at a Marine Corps recruit depot and shackles himself to the front gates in a symbolic effort to prevent others from going to Vietnam. Though the filmmakers created a traditional sense of isolation by having him go it alone (as Leo Cawley noted, he "carries out a one-man antiwar protest at a time in United States history when this was normally a group activity"),[10] this scene and a later one involving an impassioned antiwar speech to a group of high school students amply demonstrate that Luke has gone beyond basic rehabilitation issues to become a hero of a different sort.

The filmmakers had to overcome their own fears while making *Coming Home*. "When I started to write *Coming Home*, I was scared shitless of even sitting down to talk to a paraplegic, because naturally I'm scared of being a paraplegic," recalled Salt. "We all are." Yet whatever uncertainties they had were quickly soothed by the response they received to the film. With rare dissentions, critics praised it (the *Chicago Sun-Times*' Roger Ebert spoke for the majority in opining that "for most of its length *Coming Home* is great filmmaking and great acting") and it later won Oscars for Fonda, Voight, and the unlikely trio of Dowd, Salt, and Jones. More importantly, the response of disabled audience members matched these mainstream accolades. As Hellman noted of the Rancho Los Amigos residents who attended the film's premiere: "Their reaction was marvelous. The recurrent theme of disabled people who've seen this movie is that it's the first time that someone suffering from a disability has been dealt with in films as a

Coming Home *(1978), starring Jon Voight and Jane Fonda, was one of the first films to deal directly with the issue of sexuality as a component of the disabled lifestyle.*

whole human being, with a complete repertory of feelings, emotions, visceral and sexual needs." [11]

Unlike *Coming Home*, where the entire story occurs after Luke has returned from Vietnam, *The Deer Hunter* pays considerable attention to its characters' lives before, during, and after their involvement in the Asian conflict. Two and a half years in the making and bankrolled to the tune of $15 million by the U.S. film division of EMI, the giant British-based entertainment corporation, *The Deer Hunter* examines a trio of young men from a western Pennsylvania steel town who go off to fight in Vietnam: Michael (Robert De Niro), Nick (Christopher Walken), and Stevie (John Savage), the latter of whom loses both legs and an arm after falling from a helicopter. "For me, it's a very personal film," said Michael Cimino, who directed it and contributed to its story. "I was attached to a Green Beret medical unit. My characters are portraits of people whom I knew. During the years of controversy over the war, the people who fought the war, whose lives were immediately affected and damaged and changed by the war, they were disparaged and isolated by the press. But they were common people who had an uncommon amount of courage." [12]

During the film's early going, Cimino and screenwriter Deric Washburn led the audience to believe that Stevie would be the main focus by dwelling in considerable detail on his elaborate, orthodox wedding. The charismatic Michael and the war-stunned Nick quickly overshadow him, however, and by the time he returns to Pennsylvania the filmmakers have relegated him to minor-character status. He's not ignored, though; several critical scenes late in the film do help the audience gain a sense of his new life as a severely disabled Vietnam vet.

A depressing bingo game at a V.A. hospital sets the stage for the audience's reintroduction to Stevie. The elderly game announcer mixes a running commentary on their lives with his bingo chatter ("G-47. But I'm still satisfied with what I've got. That wonderful life I've lived. Think it over, buddy boys, and I'll give you O-61"). Like most of the other disabled vets Stevie does not seem terribly interested in the game, and the announcer's words—especially their suggestions that the vets' lives are now in the past—have a hollow quality. After the game, Michael visits him in the hospital. They inarticulately but happily greet each other (their dialogue initially consists of a series of joyful "hey"s) and embrace warmly, but Stevie's first remark suggests readjustment problems; he does not want to go home. By the end of their conversation, Michael insists on taking him home over the latter's objections. Stevie says he will not fit in, but Michael begins pushing the wheelchair. He tries to anchor himself to his surroundings and shove Michael away, but by the sheer strength of able-bodied force Michael wins the clash of wills. As Michael wheels him away, Stevie says, "I'm sorry. You do as your heart tells you, man."

Leonard Quart and Albert Auster have described Stevie as "nothing but a helpless, dependent victim," a characterization that, based on the forgoing scene, might seem appropriate. [13] Yet the last moments of the movie show a different side of Stevie. After he and other home town people attend Nick's funeral, Stevie and a half dozen of the gang go to an old hangout for breakfast. The cook begins to sing "God Bless America," and the others join in one by one by either humming or singing softly; soon they are singing in unison. At the song's conclusion, the friends lift their glasses in a toast to Nick. The film ends on that note.

This final scene has been a source of controversy for the filmmakers in that it leaves their political stance in doubt. (As Cimino himself commented, "The war is really incidental to the development of the characters and their story. It's a part of their lives and just that, nothing more. I have no interest in making a 'Vietnam' film, no interest in making a direct political statement.")[14] One clear element of the scene, however, is Stevie's full reintegration into his society. His friends and the filmmakers treat him as the equal of anyone present. Sitting with the others around the table, Stevie contributes to the strong camaraderie of the scene by singing along with his friends and joining in the toast to Nick. He is completely within his element. When the filmmakers freeze on the glasses raised high to their fallen friend, Stevie seems far from a "helpless, dependent victim."

In contrast to *Coming Home* and *The Deer Hunter*, the comedic *Modern Problems* (1981) makes no visual reference to the rehabilitation process. Created by a trio of friends—actor Chevy Chase, co-producer Michael Shamberg, and writer-director Ken Shapiro—for Twentieth Century–Fox, it focuses mostly on Max Fiedler (Chase), a New York City air-traffic controller, yet does contain a refreshing portrayal of a disabled veteran.

As Max and his ex-wife Loraine (Mary Kay Place) stroll through Central Park, they run into Brian Stills (Brian Doyle-Murray), an old high school friend and Vietnam vet who rides in a wheelchair pushed by Dorita (Nell Carter), his Haitian attendant and housekeeper. The amiable Brian, who owns his own publishing house, invites them to a press party held that evening for one of his authors. At the party, Loraine seldom takes her eyes off Brian and smiles frequently and seductively at him. She is completely enchanted by him and impressed that he runs his own business. As she confides to her ex-husband, "He just rolled into my life like a ton of bricks."

The burgeoning relationship of Loraine and Brian soon takes a backseat to an unexpected and unnecessary turn in the story; Max develops psycho-kinetic abilities after a truck splashes him with nuclear waste, and his use and abuse of these new powers overwhelm everything else for the remainder of the film. In their haste to provide as much pandemonium as possible by the movie's conclusion, the filmmakers unfortunately abandoned their early interest in Brian, Loraine, and the close relationship they have developed. Brian's Vietnam legacy becomes lost in the tangle of several other "modern problems" that the filmmakers succeeded in trivializing.

Despite the silliness of its main storyline, *Modern Problems* does have at least one virtue: Brian's characterization, which is a breath of fresh air. Though critics almost completely ignored the character (they spent most of their verbiage rightly attacking the film's faulty premises and disjointed structure), Brian is loving and caring, self-sufficient with a positive attitude toward life, and a success in business. He is not unduly self-pitying or bitter, and he has a sense of humor (at one point, he refers to himself as "hell on wheels"). He is athletic, quite able to play one-on-one basketball with Max. His characterization does at times border on the pollyanna-ish, but the filmmakers counteracted the sugariness by having him note his problems and regrets. When Max and Brian enter the latter's den filled with high school basketball momentos, for example, Brian notes with a touch of bitterness that Vietnam ended any Olympic hopes for him. He then immediately states, however, that he came out of the conflict better than other vets. Later, when Max shares his fears about losing his new girlfriend, Brian claps him on the shoulder and paraphrases an old rhyme: "I cried about having no shoes, till I met a man that had no feet." Lightly jabbing his thigh with a letter opener for emphasis, Brian says his legs are now simply sixty pounds of dead meat, but Max never hears him complain. He then slaps Max in a friendly way and says, "Gimme a break." Though *Modern Problems* only minimally suggests Brian's struggles to reach this point in his life (by making him a highly successful publisher, the filmmakers conveniently skirted the issue of financial problems that plague so many disabled people), he emerges amid the film's inanities—and they are legion—as a fully dimensional character and wonderful role model for anyone.

Brian, Luke, and Stevie represent the many disabled vets who made peace with themselves following their rehabilitation. Not all vets adjusted to their new lifestyles as smoothly, however; many found it a daily struggle to contain their rage. At least one film examined such a character: the troubled and troubling *Cutter's Way*, which began its life as a Hollywood project when independent producer Paul R. Gurian purchased the rights to Newton Thornburg's critically acclaimed novel *Cutter and Bone*. Gurian was intrigued by the work's ingredients: part murder mystery, part character study, part evocation of the post-Vietnam American landscape and the cynicism and complacency that characterized it. He hired Jeffrey Alan Fiskin to write the screenplay and took the project to EMI for development with the hope of securing Robert Mulligan as director. The corporation initially agreed to the project, perhaps thinking this Vietnam-related film would duplicate the success of the multi-Oscar winning *Deer Hunter*, but the arrangement did not last long; when scheduling problems prevented Mulligan from casting Dustin Hoffman in the role of Alex Cutter, both he and EMI backed out of the project.

Their deal broken, Gurian and Fiskin searched for another home for the *Cutter and Bone* project and eventually found one at United Artists, a studio that had scored reasonably well at the box office during the 1979 summer season with *Apocalypse Now*, *The Black Stallion*, *La Cage aux Folles*, *Manhattan*, *Moonraker*, and *Rocky II*. With the support of UA's idealistic young co-production head David Field and production executive Claire Townsend, the movie version of *Cutter and Bone* took further shape.

One of the first tasks facing Gurian was to find a new director. After Mark Rydell refused the job, Gurian turned to Ivan Passer, a Czech screenwriter and director who fled to the United States after the Soviets crushed the 1968 Prague Spring. Gurian and Fiskin were impressed by his 1966 film *Intimate Lighting* and found that his experiences with the after-effects of war and his penchant for "difficult" subjects made him a promising candidate to direct the film. As Passer himself noted of the things that attracted him to the *Cutter and Bone* project:

One, nobody wanted to make it, because the odds are very much against making this kind of movie. I like to do things that are seemingly impossible. It keeps me getting out of bed in the morning. And the second, I was very familiar with this kind of disillusionment. I've seen quite a few people who, in one way or another, were the victims of violent experience, or products of violence. After the war, people were put in prisons in thousands for no reason whatsoever and some of them would come out damaged psychologically. And because of that I said, "Yeah, I can do this movie better than most people." [15]

Gurian and Fiskin cleared the initial hurdle of securing UA approval of Passer as director but other problems immediately ensued. A conflict over the budget arose as a result of Field having taken on the *Cutter and Bone* project in the face of considerable opposition. As recalled by Passer, Field "had to fight tooth and nail for *Cutter and Bone*, because nobody wanted to make the film. [Other UA executives] said, 'This is difficult, closed-in, claustrophobic, intelligent—why make this film?' And he said, 'Because once in a while, along with the Judith Krantz, you've got to publish one volume of poetry occasionally.'" As a compromise, Field could approve a budget of only $3 million, forcing the production team to start looking for ways of trimming an already lean budget. UA further exacerbated their budgetary woes by insisting on big-name actors and brandishing deal breakers to back up its demands. It initially wanted Richard Dreyfuss to play Alex Cutter, but after Passer balked ("I love Richard Dreyfuss, he's wonderful in some parts, but he's wrong for this part"), UA threatened to pull the plug on the project. The company eventually acquiesced on Passer's choice of the little-known John Heard for the part but then insisted Jeff Bridges, a performer with proven star value, play the other major role of Richard Bone. Considerable turmoil in the UA executive ranks was to mark the film's production period (both Claire Townsend and David Field resigned more than a year before the film opened), and though Gurian, Fiskin, and Passer did finish their film they found themselves having to answer to people whose understanding of it was minimal. [16]

The movie begins after its lead character has been released from a V.A. hospital and currently lives in Santa Barbara. Alex, who lost an eye, an arm, and a leg in the war, is alternately witty and foul-mouthed. He is self-destructive, as evidenced by his constant smoking, heavy drinking, and quickness to antagonize everyone around him. He thinks nothing of insulting several blacks in a bar early in the film, for example, who are about to jump him but then back off after his able-bodied friend Rich Bone intervenes by noting Alex's Vietnam-vet status. Alex later gets angry when Rich walks away from him in frustration. He throws his cane at him hard but misses, managing to knock out one of the bar's neon lighting fixtures in the process.

This scene is one of many that illustrates the stormy relationship of Alex and Rich. Alex is forever berating Rich, a tanned, athletic, preppy type who sells sailboats for a living. Alex tells Rich not to lecture him on morality, for instance, by pointing out that while Rich was getting laid in the Ivy League he was getting shot up in Vietnam.

Alex soon diverts his pent-up energy and rage to a larger purpose: helping Rich solve a young woman's murder, which Rich has been accused of committing. When Alex is sober (which is not often), he is very sharp and immediately begins putting the puzzle pieces together. Working with Rich and Valerie Duran (Ann Dusenberry), the dead woman's sister, he concludes that the probable

The actors may be backlit but the story's anything but. Rich Bone, Alex Cutter, and George Swanson confer on a grisly murder in their community in the morally murky Cutter's Way. *(Left to right: Jeff Bridges, John Heard, Arthur Rosenberg) Copyright © 1980 United Artists Corp.*

murderer is J. J. Cord (Stephen Elliott), a big oilman whose corporation owns the sailboat company for which Rich works.

Rich and Valerie's reasons for wanting to solve the murder are simple and straightforward: Rich wants to clear his name so that he can get back to his casual lifestyle while Valerie wants to see justice served. Alex's reasons are more complex and are really at the heart of the movie. First, he wants to be a hero, a status that has eluded him ever since his return from Vietnam; second, he wants to do something about the immorality of people in high positions of power. Alex insists Cord is not just responsible for the woman's death; he and other corporate bigwigs are also behind world problems that affect countless people but never the powermongers themselves. Alex does not specifically mention Vietnam in this context (indeed the Vietnam War *per se* receives minimal attention in the film), but the implication is clear.

Perhaps the most interesting thing about the Cutter character is his unusual embodiment of two stereotypes: the Noble Warrior, obviously, but also the Obsessive Avenger, an image that harkens back to the days of Tod Browning and Lon Chaney. The similarities are striking: a severely disabled man, his moral code violated, becomes fatally obsessed with the idea of "bringing down" another male even though the evidence against the latter is slight (the movie's proof of Cord's culpability is minimal and even Passer suggested he "probably isn't guilty" of the crime). It's not clear how aware the filmmakers were of the Browning–Chaney canon or the general Oedipal scenario at the heart of so many films but they certainly perceived the parallels between their character and an important literary antecedent for the Obsessive Avenger: Captain Ahab of *Moby Dick*. They acknowledged their debt to Melville's novel and the famous obsession that propels it by having Alex utter "Thar she blows" on seeing Cord's corporate headquarters and including other references, as critic Richard Jameson observed: "Cutter entered the film making a barbed joke about his unscarred buddy as an Ishmael who carries 'Moby Dick,' an exotic social disease; and more than Alex's poetically apt wounds qualify him to be a contemporary Ahab. Cord is Cutter's Leviathan, and the way Fiskin and Passer present him, he partakes of something akin to the whiteness of Melville's whale; he is a blank on which any idea can be projected."[17]

The movie's resolute refusal to be obvious about its concerns was a prime factor that led to its mishandling. The new people at United Artists in charge of distributing *Cutter and Bone* could make little sense of it and opened it with minimal fanfare in March 1981 (one wag suggested the film premiered "with all the advance publicity of a traffic accident"), its limp advertising slogan of "Bone saw the killer, Cutter knew the motive" barely suggesting the film's richness and complexity.[18]

The initial critical reaction to *Cutter and Bone* was devastating. The *New York Times'* Vincent Canby dismissed the UA film as "a peculiarly unfocused murder-mystery about some eccentric young Southern Californians who live on booze, drugs and their wits." He found the dialogue particularly problematic, describing it as "vivid without being informative or even amusing on any level." The reviewer for *Variety* was equally uncharitable, calling the film "something of a mess" and suggesting that Passer and Fiskin "never come close to shedding light on what, if anything, this picture is really about." The *Variety* reviewer also offered a prediction guaranteed to send a chill down any movie executive's spine: "The general confusion and rather abrupt, unsatisfying ending seem certain to spell boxoffice trouble for this United Artists release." The UA officials, still smarting from the critical and financial drubbing they had taken on the now-infamous *Heaven's Gate* only several months before, acted with uncommon haste and pulled *Cutter and Bone* from theaters less than a week after it opened.[19]

Yet *Cutter and Bone* refused to die. Highly favorable reviews began appearing within days after the film's closing, and they helped revive UA's interest in marketing it. The distributor assigned the film to its art-film subsidiary, United Artists Classics, which promptly renamed the film *Cutter's Way* ("People were not happy with the title," noted Passer. "They said it sounded like two surgeons") and designed a promotional campaign that included screenings at competitive film festivals. Though ultimately the film failed to become a major box-office draw, the strategy did have immediate short-term benefits; within weeks after United Artists had given up *Cutter and Bone* for dead, a newly resurrected *Cutter's Way* won numerous awards at the 1981 Houston International Film Festival, including those for best feature film, best director, best scriptwriter, and best actor (John Heard).[20]

Though *Coming Home* and *The Deer Hunter* had fared well on Oscar night and at the box office, Hollywood filmmakers doubtless found the limited appeal of *Modern Problems* and *Cutter's Way* disconcerting and backed off from the topic of disabled Vietnam veterans for several years. Even before these latter disabled-vet movies began playing in theaters, however, a number of other moviemakers were fashioning projects that would give some measure of sensitivity and dignity to the physically disabled experience in other than war-related contexts. Though the earliest of them got off to a shaky start, it was a time for the disabled civilian to take center stage.

Voices (1979) examines the problematic relationship of a profoundly deaf woman and a hearing man and the differing reactions to it by their families. Written and directed by newcomers John Herzfeld and Robert Markowitz, respectively, and produced by Joe Wizan for release through MGM, it starred Amy Irving as Rosemarie Lemon (one can only hope the filmmakers didn't chuckle too loudly over their choice of a surname), a deaf teacher who dreams of a career as a dancer, and Michael Ontkean as Drew Rothman, a hearing man who drives a truck for his family's dry cleaning business while striving for rock and roll stardom. As much as a clash of deaf and hearing cultures as socio-economic backgrounds (Rosemarie lives with her well-to-do mother who tries to convince her to drop her hearing suitor, while Drew comes from a relatively open-minded working-class family), *Voices* benefited from a number of authentic touches: deaf actor Richard Kendall played Rosemarie's fiancé; deaf NYU professor Martin Sternberg served as an advisor; Irving's sister, a teacher at the Maryland School for the Deaf, helped her learn sign language; and teachers and students from Newark's Bruce Street School for the Deaf fleshed out the background roles.[21]

These attributes, however, were not enough to lift *Voices* out of its essential mediocrity; it is at base a sappy, formulaic love story laden with unbelievable occurrences. Late in the film, for example, when Drew bursts into a dance audition and orders everyone around, instead of throwing him out, everyone in the room respectfully complies with his directions. The filmmakers also attempted a misbegotten effort to have the audience experience the lead character's deafness. Earlier during that same audition, they included several shots from Rosemarie's perspective accompanied by total silence as she fumbles her way through a dance routine; such a technique, however, failed to explain why she couldn't detect any vibrations and continued dancing after the music has ended (or why she couldn't see that her peers had stopped moving).

Believing they had created a film with enlightened views, Wizan, Herzfeld, and Markowitz were unprepared for the hostile reception that greeted it. MGM had

Drew learns the details of Rosemarie's humiliating dance audition in the 1979 release Voices. *Michael Ontkean and Amy Irving co-starred in this controversial film. Copyright © 1978 Metro-Goldwyn-Mayer Inc.*

run *Voices* on a limited basis in San Francisco before releasing it nationwide, but a number of bay-area deaf groups boycotted the film because it lacked captions and had a hearing actress in the lead. The filmmakers insisted their audition process failed to turn up any qualified deaf actresses who could also dance, an argument that left the activists unmoved, and MGM later ran a subtitled print of the film but withdrew it after only a week in the face of the continuing boycott. The deaf groups also attacked the movie for perpetuating stereotypes. Albert Walla, an Oakland-based deaf counselor who led the *Voices* protest called it "a lousy movie. Deaf people don't like to see movies where they are portrayed as unable to survive without the support and love of a hearing person." *Voices* hardly fared better with other deaf activists—for example, the Greater Los Angeles Council on Deafness (GLAD) led by Marcella Meyer protested the film on similar grounds—and its rejection represented a significant victory for the deaf community. Savoring the protest in retrospect, deaf activist and *Deaf Life* editor Linda Levitan noted that "theaters were picketed, and the film was a flop. Very few of us even remember it." [22]

The late 1970s witnessed other questionable movies, most notably the winding-down of the big-budgeted "disaster" movies that traditionally overflowed with famous (and often suitably embarrassed-looking) stars. The person chiefly responsible for such spectacles was producer and occasional director Irwin Allen, who began the trend with *The Poseidon Adventure* in 1972 and made certain to include disabled people among the assorted victims, presumably for the vulnerable or innocent qualities he hoped they would bring to the screen. *The Towering Inferno* (1974), an early entry, presented a deaf woman (Carol McEvoy) unaware that the 100-story glass tower she lives in has caught on fire, her heat-sensing, ocular, and olfactory abilities apparently impaired as well. *The Swarm* (1978) offered Henry Fonda as a wheelchair-using immunologist of worldwide repute who ludicrously, and fatally, injects himself with a supposed antidote to the stings of bees that have wiped out half of a nearby town. *Beyond the Poseidon Adventure* (1979) had among its cross-section of characters a blind novelist (Jack Warden) and his wife (Shirley Knight). After disaster strikes—the writer loses both his spouse and, more importantly, the only copy of his latest novel—the ship's head nurse (Shirley Jones) in a gesture that reeks of Hollywood's most coagulated schmaltz offers to be his new "eyes." Not to be outdone by the Master of Disaster, Universal producer Jennings Lang and director David Lowell Rich featured not one but two disabled people in *The Concorde—Airport '79* (1979): a little deaf girl on board the ill-fated title vehicle, and a wheelchair-using woman (Kathleen Maguire) who pleads with a recalcitrant homicide lieutenant to investigate the mysterious death of her husband who had blown the whistle on a corrupt industrialist. [23]

If the disabled-civilian films of the late 1970s succeeded mainly in raising more questions than they answered, their counterparts in the next decade suggested a sense of maturation. One film appearing in early 1980—*Joni*, a low-budget effort bankrolled by evangelist Billy Graham about a teenager left a quadriplegic after a Chesapeake Bay diving accident—came and went with virtually no notice,[24] but a host of movies that followed made it clear that physical disability issues were moving toward the forefront of Hollywood concerns and demanding greater attention. The years 1980 and 1981 in particular yielded a bumper crop of movies that explored the physically disabled experience, if in highly varying ways.

Inside Moves (1980), about a small group of men with physical disabilities who enjoy life despite prejudice and fixed incomes, is an example of a film that owes a significant part of its existence to Hollywood's recently revived blockbuster mentality. Its director, Richard Donner, had skippered such huge moneymakers as *The Omen* in 1976 and *Superman* two years later and as a result was able, along with first-time producers Mark Tanz and Bob Goodwin, to find the funding necessary to create this modest little film based on Todd Walton's similarly titled 1978 novel. At the center of the film is Roary (John Savage, who also played *The Deer Hunter*'s severely injured Stevie), a young man who becomes permanently disabled after a suicide attempt off a building. After recovering shortly thereafter he wanders into Max's Bar, an Oakland hangout for less-than-affluent people, and there meets "Blue" Lewis (Bill Henderson), a black who uses a wheelchair; "Stinky" (Bert Remsen), a pornography-loving blind man; and "Wings" (Harold Russell), a fellow with prostheses in place of hands. Behind the bar is Jerry (David Morse), a young man with an injured leg who dreams of playing pro basketball. He strikes up a friendship with Roary, thereby inadvertently helping with the latter's emotional rehabilitation, and in return Roary supports him in his athletic quest only to be betrayed after Jerry, having undergone an undisabling operation, dumps him as a friend and starts dating the waitress he had been seeing.

Screenwriters Barry Levinson and Valerie Curtin initially wanted the Blue, Stinky, and Wings characters to be youthful like their counterparts in Walton's book. Donner overruled them by casting aging actors in the roles, however, and in discussing his reasons for so doing he revealed a typical mainstream view: that disabled people remain bitter about their status until reaching the threshold of their twilight years. "If they were young men and crippled, they would have a right to be angry at that point of their lives," he argued, "whereas in the film, they have mellowed out in their lives, and into their lives comes this young piece of anger. It was playing off something. Eventually, reluctantly, Barry and Valerie agreed with me."[25]

The film's greatest failing, however, may well be its depoliticalization; novelist Walton explicitly made Roary a disabled Vietnam veteran, a status the moviemakers expunged in their production. ("I got hurt in Vietnam," the character notes point blank on the book's first page. "This land mine blew a hole in my upper back and destroyed some vertebrae and part of my spinal cord and part of my brain.") Donner felt uneasy about that aspect of the novel—"I didn't want to do another Nam story, really," he said—and while he went off to Great Britain to work on *Superman* Paramount's Robert Evans had Curtin and Levinson eliminate all reference to Vietnam in their adapted screenplay.[26]

Whatever their knowledge of this significant alteration, the critics gave mixed marks to *Inside Moves*. David Sterritt of the *Christian Science Monitor* wrote that "we're supposed to respond to the inner decency and shared humanity of these people, but the performances and the direction are so uneven that the story never holds together. It all seems tacky, somehow—with lots of heart, but very little art." The *Village Voice*'s Carrie Rickey echoed these sentiments, noting that "this movie has more soliloquys than Eugene O'Neill wrote in his lifetime" and "exploits every liberal tragic convention." On the other hand, Rob Edelman of *Films in Review* called it "a spirited, unpretentious little film with wonderful characterizations," while *Newsweek*'s Jack Kroll suggested that "the movie's final feeling is one of sweetness and gritty dignity." Despite its political hesitancy, *Inside Moves* remains a warm, touching, and insightful celebration of the human spirit. Harold Russell, who hadn't acted in movies since *The Best Years of Our Lives* in 1946 ("I love being back," he enthused. "I love this part"), echoed the point: "This picture is going to show that handicapped people can have dreams that come true. My own have come true—I have a wonderful daughter and an airline pilot son. But I want this movie to give hope to others."[27]

As Donner was quick to acknowledge, *Inside Moves* with its community of physically disabled characters was a difficult sell to able-bodied audiences. "They didn't realize that these characters had such a rich sense of humor," he lamented. "People did not want to see a man without arms [sic] and a blind man and somebody in a wheelchair and somebody going out a window and a guy with a bad leg."[28] Another film released that year had no such problem, presumably because its idea of a lone disabled character corresponded far more closely to mainstream tastes: *The Elephant Man*. A movie that generated an enormous amount of attention from the news media (with almost every account duly noting its non-relation to Bernard Pomerance's Broadway play of the same name that had opened the year before), *The Elephant Man* unveiled the story of John Merrick, a character based on accounts of an actual Victorian-era fellow named Joseph Merrick whose body was thought for decades to have been deformed by the genetic disorder neurofibromatosis. (In 1986, two Canadian physicians rediagnosed Merrick's condition as a manifestation of the extremely rare Proteus syndrome—an opinion that has received widespread support from the medical community.)[29] Studios weren't initially that interested in making a movie about a man whose multiple bony growths, withered right arm, obstructed vision, and distorted spine masked a gentle, inquisitive soul until an unlikely patron in the form of Mel Brooks, the king of Hollywood genre farces, read the script by Christopher DeVore and Eric Bergren and wanted to get involved. He eventually acquired the screenplay through his Brooksfilms company, set up a distribution deal with Paramount, and hired as director David Lynch, a young Montanan whose only other feature—the visually and thematically arresting *Eraserhead* (1978)—had impressed the producer. Lynch, who later shared screenplay credit with DeVore and Bergren, plunged ahead with a mostly British cast headed by Anthony Hopkins as Dr. Frederick Treves, John Hurt as Merrick, John Gielgud as Dr. F. C. Carr Gomm, Freddie Jones as Bytes, and Brooks's wife Anne Bancroft as Madge Kendal.

Since DeVore, Bergren, and Lynch drew much of the material for their screenplay from Treves's published memoirs, it's hardly surprising that much of the movie is from the able-bodied doctor's point of view and arguably as much as about him as Merrick. The audience learns about Merrick primarily through Treves; he is the one who discovers Merrick in a sideshow run by the crude Bytes, learns that the latter has been beating him, rescues him, ministers to him, and, like Bytes, most assuredly profits from him, though in a more sedate and refined context. Merrick unquestionably benefits from the physician's treatment (his few years of relative comfort at London Hospital under Treves's care contrast vividly with his hardships under Bytes, who reappears late in the film to shanghai his

Dr. Frederick Treves (Anthony Hopkins) counsels the title figure of 1980's The Elephant Man: *John Merrick (John Hurt), David Lynch's unusual blend of character traits.*

former meal ticket off to France) and with his help becomes the toast of England, but like so many dramas of physical disability both before and after it *The Elephant Man* reflects a longstanding ableist view: that the best way to attract audiences is to tell the story mainly from an able-bodied person's perspective, at least until the "shock value" of the disabled person's appearance had abated somewhat.

The Elephant Man demonstrates time-worn points of view in other ways. Though Lynch in a celebrated *Rolling Stone* interview acknowledged his identification with outsiders like Merrick and regarded his cinematic creation as a "regular human being," he also saw in him several aspects that link the character with some of the old stereotypes. He called Merrick all "innocence and wonder," a quality that combined with the character's pronounced spirituality (thought an imbecile by many, Merrick chooses a recitation of the twenty-third Psalm to demonstrate his intelligence) rings of the Sweet Innocent. This latter quality also links him with the Saintly Sage, and indeed when asked if he thought Merrick had something saintly about him Lynch responded: "I like to think that way. He's a person who teaches people lessons. He teaches people to be human, and yet he's a monster. Who's to say what it was really like in his time, or what he himself was really like? But what he's become, through Dr. Treves's stories and everybody's imagination, is a beautiful symbol, the perfect thing to bring out the good in people."[30]

Guided by such attitudes, *The Elephant Man* not unexpectedly deviates often from the historical accounts of Merrick.[31] Nevertheless, most critics found much to praise about the film: Freddie Francis' stunning black-and-white cinematography; Christopher Tucker's equally stunning make-up patterned from a plaster cast made after Merrick's death and actual photographs of him; its use of Merrick as a visual symbol of industrial-revolution ills (even though his disabilities had nothing to do with the machine age); and its sensitive acting, with several explicitly comparing Hurt's performance to the work of Lon Chaney. *Newsweek*'s David Ansen wrote that the movie "has great dignity, sweetness and compassion in this portrait of an unlucky monster who must fight to make other humans recognize his humanity" while *Time*'s Richard Corliss suggested that Hurt despite the burdensome make-up "captures Merrick's humanity through his eyes and his gestures, the way he reflexively straightens his tie when a nurse enters the room, the way his voice rises and falls in the fruity arpeggios of a Covent Garden tenor."[32] Virtually all the critics picked up on the film's prime ethical dimension—its meditation on the nature of exploitation—which, though offered in a sledgehammery fashion, does make *The Elephant Man* one of the few films to acknowledge and confront such concerns.

Ethical issues also come to the fore in *Whose Life Is It Anyway?* (1981), an MGM release adapted from Brian Clark's award-winning British play by the playwright and Reginald Rose. It starred Richard Dreyfuss as Ken Harrison, a Boston-area sculptor who wants to die after he learns that the injuries he sustained in a car accident have left him paralyzed from the neck down and dependent on daily dialysis. "As far as I am concerned I am dead already," he says "I cannot believe that this—this condition constitutes life in any real sense of the word." The film presents numerous clashes between Harrison and his doctors, principally the grimly resolute Michael Emerson (John Cassavetes), over the right-to-die issue and concludes with a hearing held at the hospital in which a judge (Ken McMillan) finally grants him a discharge.

The theatrical incarnation of *Whose Life* is quite static, with the Harrison character immobilized in bed throughout, so director John Badham, who had also directed the play with Dreyfuss in the lead at the Williamstown Theatre Festival about two years before, decided to open it up for the movie. With the assistance of Mario Tosi, fast becoming the cinematographer of choice for disability dramas (he had also photographed *Report to the Commissioner* and *The Betsy*), Badham included a number of shots and scenes outside the hospital, including Harrison and his girlfriend (Jane Eilber) in pre-disablement scenes, a meeting between the latter and a sympathetic doctor (Christine Lahti) at Harrison's apartment, and an ill-considered nude ballet fantasy sequence presented mostly from Harrison's perspective. In addition, he put his lead character into a wheelchair every time an opportunity suggested itself in the script (Harrison's excursion to and enjoyment of a reggae concert reeking of marijuana in the hospital's basement is a standout) which combined with Tosi's whooshing-about-the-corridors camerawork gave the film an energized sense completely lacking in the play. Though Badham treated the main characters in a commendably even-handed fashion through Tosi's visualizations (he freely rotated the gaze among Harrison and the able-bodied characters and generally avoided objectifying shots), he undercut the emotional arguments of the play by invigorating the film in such a pronounced manner.

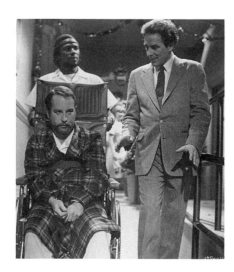

Richard Dreyfuss's performance as Ken Harrison, by turns cuddly and bustling, was at odds with his character's suicidal tendencies in Whose Life Is It Anyway?. *Copyright © 1981 MGM/United Artists Corp.*

Further weakening the play's philosophic basis was Dreyfuss' interpretation of the role. Critics admired his kinetic and engaging performance to such an extent that they found it hard to accept that his character wants to die. For example *Glamour*'s Stephen Schiff found Dreyfuss "so cuddly and witty and lovable that he defeats the movie's purpose" while *Time*'s Richard Schickel suggested the actor "seems to bustle while flat on his back, and it is almost impossible to believe that in the end he would not opt for life, however constricted it might be." Indeed, *Whose Life* engendered numerous debates about its heavily defeatist attitude: Harrison wishing to end it all because he can no longer do the things he loves. The film conveniently skirts some issues by making him out to have no family, and despite the fact that he spends the better part of a year in the hospital, he receives no professional or peer counseling (except for one pathetic attempt by an able-bodied woman whose philosophy seems to have been handed down from Pollyanna). Dreyfuss suggested that "what this film is really about is not living, it's about having a criterion of excellence about living," but by having Harrison hold such extremely high standards, *Whose Life* reduces the argument to an all or nothing proposition. Dreyfuss's compelling performance masks what is essentially a stick-figure character who has failed to consider the implications of his decisions.[33]

Whose Life Is It Anyway? raised so many questions about the physically disabled experience (as Dreyfuss himself noted, "I have never done a film where the points of view taken by people who have seen it have been so adamant and so opposed to one another") that it tended to eclipse the disability aspects of numerous other films that preceded it in 1981. The comedic *Bustin' Loose*, starring Richard Pryor as an ex-con who guides a busload of physically and emotionally disabled children through assorted misadventures (in a near-obligatory scene for comedies with blind characters, a severely visually impaired kid wants to drive and does so), fared poorly with reviewers but did well financially, earning back $7 million of its $11 million cost during one five-day period alone. The futuristic *Escape from New York*, directed and co-written by John Carpenter, presents Kurt Russell as a one-eyed war hero turned criminal named Snake Plissken recruited to rescue the U.S. president (inexplicably played by a British actor, Donald Pleasance) from a maximum security prison that takes up the whole of Manhattan island. *Choices* examines the tale of a teenager (Paul Carafotes) denied the chance to play football because of his impaired hearing, while the Disney film *Amy* presents a turn-of-the-century New England woman (Jenny Agutter) who teaches deaf children while promoting the supremacy of the oralist method. A hot young writer-director named Oliver Stone created the almost career-ending *The Hand*, a sorry blend of psychology and horror about a cartoonist (Michael Caine) whose drawing hand, severed in a car accident, begins murdering people all by itself. *Pennies from Heaven*, a revisionist look at the Depression featuring Steve Martin, has among its minor characters a pretty young blind woman who meets a far different fate than did her Sweet Innocent counterparts of an earlier age: not a miracle cure, but death. With *Whose Life*, the movies that appeared in 1981—by

coincidence, the International Year of Disabled Persons—offered an exceptionally varied composite of disabled images.[34]

The relatively incidental if somewhat problematic portrayals of disabled civilians continued apace during the mid–1980s with such films as *Something Wicked
This Way Comes* (1983), *Places in the Heart* (1984), *Just the Way You Are* (1984),
and *Children of a Lesser God* (1986). *Something Wicked*, about two small-town
boys who discover peculiar goings-on at a sinister traveling carnival, is based on
a number of Ray Bradbury literary vehicles dating back to a short story published
in *Weird Tales* in 1948 called "The Black Ferris." After several failed attempts to
bring it to the screen (various versions were to have been directed by such disparate directorial talents as Gene Kelly and Sam Peckinpah), the combination of
Walt Disney Productions and Kirk Douglas's Bryna Company finally succeeded,
with Bradbury himself serving as co-screenwriter and British filmmaker Jack
Clayton as director.[35]

Set during the early part of the twentieth century in a bit of Americana called
Green Town, Illinois, *Something Wicked This Way Comes* (the title is from one of
the witches' lines in reference to Shakespeare's Macbeth) contains a number of
minor characters who long for an idealized life and are "ripe for the carnival's
snares," in the words of critic Kevin Thomas. One of them is Ed the bartender
(James Stacy), a double amputee and one-time gridiron star who frequently revels
in his collegiate glory days. He wins a pass to the carnival's hall of illusions, a
place where he and the other characters learn that people can see themselves reflected as they want to see themselves; indeed, he stands before a mirror and
through the carnival's (and movie's) artifice sees his arm and leg restored. The audience later learns he has ridden the carnival's bizarre carousel that either adds or
subtracts a year off of each rider's life with every revolution, depending on which
direction it is going; he appears as a fully limbed child toting a football. Enjoying
only a few minutes of screen time and almost completely ignored by the critics, Ed
comes across as a rather flat character concerned only with the past. In that, he is
no different from many other characters in the film, however, and the moviemakers
treated his disability in a mostly incidental way. A noteworthy thing about the role
is that it was played by James Stacy, erstwhile star of TV's *Lancer* and several
low-budget movies who had lost an arm and a leg in a motorcycle accident.[36]

The following year saw the appearance of *Places in the Heart*, a Depression-
era tale close to writer-director Robert Benton's own heart; he set and filmed the
movie in his home town of Waxahachie, Texas, and modeled the lead character
after his great-grandmother. In this story of recently widowed Edna Spalding
(Sally Field), the audience quickly learns her late husband left her and their two
young children with only about $100 and a huge debt on their unprofitable farm.
To exacerbate matters, a black transient named Moze (Danny Glover) tries to run
off with the family silver and Edna's banker, knowing how beholden she is to his
institution, foists his brother-in-law on her as a boarder. The in-law, a blind World
War I veteran known simply as Mr. Will (John Malkovich), initially goes about

making brooms, caning chairs, and listening to recorded books in bitter isolation, but eventually he, Edna, and Moze, thrown together by circumstance, develop a mutual respect in the face of considerable external adversity and work closely to help Edna avoid defaulting on the mortgage.

To prepare himself for the role of Will, Malkovich went to the Lighthouse for the Blind organization and met a blind fellow who helped him learn how to make brooms and cane chairs. Benton observed that Malkovich "approaches a character the way a writer does more than any other actor I know. He does research, but he has a very good inner clock. When he has enough, he stops and creates that character in his mind and allows his instincts to work." The actor's preparation even extended to the way he held his facial muscles. Benton noted that Malkovich "said once, 'If I'm blind, I don't know what I look like in the mirror.' So his face had a slackness to it, the kind of repose that if you caught sight of it in a mirror you would compose it in some way." Critics joined Benton in appreciating Malkovich's approach. Writing in *Films in Review*, Kenneth Geist noted the actor "skillfully delineates the blind boarder's transformation from cranky isolation to devoted participation," for example, while Sheila Benson of the *Los Angeles Times* observed that his "slow humanizing of this intelligent, aloof and bitter man is without sentimentality" and added that the "stunning" actor gave a performance "so rich, intelligent and many-layered [it] can only be called triumphant." [37]

Critics were less charitable with *Just the Way You Are*, a lightweight romantic movie distributed by MGM and photographed on location in the French Alps. Written by *Mary Tyler Moore Show* alumnus Allan Burns and directed by Edouard Molinaro, who explored a different group of marginalized souls in *La Cage aux Folles*, *Just the Way You Are* contains echoes of the Civilian Superstar image: its main character, globe-trotting professional flutist Susan Berlanger (Kristy McNichol), wears a leg brace as a result of a childhood bout with polio. Though she is vivacious, charming, and has no problem attracting suitors, she harbors strong self-doubts because of her brace. While in European ski country on a series of concert tours, she tries to escape her minority status by convincing a reluctant physician to swap the brace for a knee-length cast in the hope others will think she had broken her leg in a skiing accident and is thereby only temporarily disabled. Unlike the old Civilian Superstars, she's motivated to pass not because she must perform professionally but because she wants to see what life for a mainstream type must be like. During her charades, she does learn a few lessons from François Rossignol (André Dussollier), a dynamic jet-set sort whose loss of a leg proves no detriment to a full life, and from her ski-lodge roommate Nicole (Catherine Salviat), who is attracted to François but to Susan's surprise cannot contain her negative feelings about his disability. When Susan finally finds the gumption to reveal the permanence of her impairment to a new beau (Michael Ontkean, who played a similar role in *Voices*) she makes the insipid discovery that being a disabled person isn't so bad after all.

The film's generally cheery exterior masked considerable turmoil on the set. Having recently been involved in several movie misfires, Kristy McNichol became overly concerned late in the movie's production period about the way the project, then titled *I Won't Dance*, was developing. "She was so afraid of the picture failing," said a production insider. "She worked hard, and would get very excited and hyper about what was happening." McNichol herself said she "was totally out of control [while trying] to please everybody all the time." Her misgivings combined with the stresses resulting from a manic-depressive disorder led her to leave the film with seventeen days of principal photography left. After about a year director Molinaro and producer Leo Fuchs were able to recall the cast and crew to finish the film, but the resulting *Just the Way You Are* seemed hardly worth the wait; most critics found it pleasant enough but flimsy. *Newsday*'s Leo Seligsohn stated "it's all rather bland, implausible stuff—a fairy tale that never quite knows how to shake the corn out of its gossamer wings," while Rex Reed writing for the *New York Post* called it "a smartly photographed but rather astonishingly dumb little romantic comedy." Lauri Klobas labeled it "a very superficial look at a difficult problem [in which] the old standby, devaluation, stepped in," while Sheila Benson perhaps put it best when she noted that "unfortunately, it is easier to admire the film makers' determination [to complete the film] than their fairy-tale presentation."[38]

Interability courtship also forms the basis for *Children of a Lesser God*, a film distributed by Paramount about a young deaf woman and her stormy relationship with a speech teacher. Written by Hesper Anderson and Mark Medoff, the latter of whom penned the Tony-winning play that served as the foundation for their script, *Lesser God* was directed by Randa Haines, who had written for ABC-TV's *Family* and later directed episodes of *Hill Street Blues* and the acclaimed made-for-TV movie *Something About Amelia* (1984). She assigned *Lesser God*'s female lead to a little-known performer named Marlee Matlin after seeing her in a videotaped recording of a Chicago production of Medoff's play, in which Matlin played a supporting character. Matlin, who had lost her hearing at the age of eighteen months after a severe case of baby measles, brought a certain energy and passion to the role that translated well on the screen. "Marlee is one of these people the camera loves," said Haines. "She has this radiance that we knew was there right away. We sensed her talent, but it was only after the filming started that we knew that it was there for sure."[39] Along with Matlin, established performers William Hurt and Piper Laurie headed a cast of sixteen main characters, ten of whom were played by deaf actors.

Set on a remote island off the coast of Maine, *Children of a Lesser God* revolves around the relationship of Sarah Norman (Matlin), a one-time honors student who remained at her school for hearing-impaired students to work as a janitor, and James Leeds (Hurt), an idealistic speech instructor new to the school who is given to such antics as falling down and standing on his head to reach his students. A feisty, independent person, Sarah refuses to read lips or speak and instead chooses to communicate primarily via American Sign Language. The oralist becomes intrigued ("You are the most mysterious, beautiful, angry person I have ever met," James tells her), and they eventually develop a passionate relationship. They never fully understand one another, however, and James' obsession with getting her to speak becomes a major obstacle between them.

To make the film more accessible to audiences unfamiliar with ASL, Haines and her collaborators employed a strategy that harkened back to *Johnny Belinda* almost forty years before: having a hearing person offer a running translation of the deaf person's dialogue. "The hurdle was getting through the first couple of scenes with that device," said Haines. "I thought that if something else could be happening it would help the audience over that bump so they would accept the convention. At first, talking to his class of deaf students, [James] says his signing is rusty. Later he has to deal with Sarah's hostility. We made him a character that talks to himself. He says, 'I'm a speech teacher—I like to hear my own voice.'"[40]

Though *Lesser God* fared reasonably well with mainstream critics (most found it a relatively conventional love story made palatable by the strong performances of the Oscar-winning Matlin and the Oscar-nominated Hurt), deaf audiences were split on a number of its qualities. Despite the movie's high number of deaf performers who sign, *Lesser God* is at times difficult to follow; many signings are cut off by the edges of the frame, executed in bad lighting, or obscured when the performer (Hurt, usually) turned away from the camera, and hearing characters would sometimes talk without signing. These problems were correctable through subtitling, but of the 215 theaters showing *Lesser God* in late 1986 only ten showed captioned versions, often only on early Saturday and Sunday mornings. One might have thought Paramount had learned something from MGM's *Voices* experience seven years before, but remarks by Paramount's distribution head Barry London indicate otherwise. "There is also a question of dealing with a market we know little about," said he. "We are really blazing new territory here with a movie about deafness."[41]

In addition to questioning the handling of basic communication issues, a number of deaf audience members objected to *Lesser God*'s depoliticalization. A good deal of Medoff's play focused on a deaf activist about to launch a lawsuit against the school for discriminatory hiring practices and on the political implications of hearing people acting on behalf of deaf people. The filmmakers reduced the activism at the play's core to the level of a subplot, with the romance of Sarah and James, which takes up only about half the play, consuming almost the entire movie. Their altering of the narrative becomes most apparent during Sarah's impassioned speech about the difficulty of achieving equitable relationships that allow people to respect each other as individuals. In the play she plans to convey it to a civil rights commission probing the school's employment procedures, but in the movie she delivers it to James in reference to their own relationship. Instead of confronting issues of discrimination, the makers of *Lesser God* were content to turn it into a love story—a highly charged one, but nevertheless a basic love story—complete with a traditional conclusion quite different from the play's ambiguous one and weighty dollops of symbolism (such as the heavily rustling curtains during the film's opening credits that suggest Sarah's inner turmoil followed immediately by tranquil harbor waters that foreshadow James' calming influence). For Haines, who saw the film as an advancement over the play due to its strong romantic angle, the very topic of deafness was interesting mostly for its figurative qualities. "It's difficult for any two people to really reach each other across the barriers that separate them," she said. "In this movie, the metaphor for what separates James and Sarah is her deafness. But, in some ways, he is also deaf."[42]

Such factors led most deaf audiences to perceive *Lesser God* as a film mainly for able-bodied viewers but yet having value for the deaf community. David Davis, a Harvard student born profoundly deaf, summarized the views of many when he suggested that "obviously, this is a movie for the hearing that was financed by a major studio that wants to make money, but the more exposure people have to the deafness on the screen, the sooner the worlds of the deaf and the hearing are going to be able to understand each other." Kevin Nolan, a

The political becomes the personal as Sarah Norman (Marlee Matlin) conveys her concerns about their relationship to James Leeds (William Hurt) in Children of a Lesser God. *Copyright © 1986 Paramount Pictures Corp.*

guidance counselor at the Clarke School for the Deaf in Northampton, Massachusetts, underscored this latter point: "The movie is still a very important work for the deaf because it educates the hearing. Hearing people still have so many misconceptions—like deaf people can't read or dance or cry or laugh. The movie shows that we have the same worries and feelings, abilities and aspirations as anyone else."[43]

Despite the growth of movies that offered relatively sympathetic and serious-minded treatments, assorted flaws notwithstanding, it would be a mistake to conclude that the old stereotypes had fallen into disuse. Perhaps wishing to exploit disabled people's ever-growing societal prominence, mainstream filmmakers in their typically divisive way continued to breathe new life into the ancient images and even began cultivating new ones associated with the 1970s and 1980s rise of high technology.

The concept of linking disability with comedy popped up with regularity during much of the 1980s. *Airplane!* (1980), created by many of the same people responsible for *The Kentucky Fried Movie*, featured a brief scene involving a man forced to remove his artificial arm and leg after setting off an airport metal detector. *Johnny Dangerously* (1984) contains numerous gags at the expense of disabled people, most notably a recurring bit about a blind newspaper vender (Ray Walston) who regains his vision after a bundle of newspapers hits him on the head only to lose his hearing after being struck by another. *All of Me* (1984) presented a blinded black musician (Jason Bernard) who helps a lawyer friend (Steve Martin) release the spirit of a woman from the latter's body, while Woody Allen took on one of the enduring stereotypes of the post-WW II era—the Civilian Superstar as embodied by *The Stratton Story*'s Monty Stratton—in *Radio Days* (1987), an affectionate look at life in Queens during the 1940s and the significance of radio for one family. Allen modeled one of the radio shows after the inspirational programs of Bill Stern, calling it "Bill Kern's Favorite Sports Legends" and focusing on a southpaw pitcher for the St. Louis Cardinals named Kirby Kyle whose story sounds suspiciously familiar. "Chasing a rabbit," says Kern, "he stumbled and his rifle went off." According to the announcer (and visualized by Allen), Kirby was back on the mound the following year though he had wounded himself in the leg and had it amputated two days later. Unfortunately, Kyle had another accident next winter that cost him his right arm, and the year after that his shotgun misfired, leaving him blind. Allen pushed the absurdity—a bizarre combination of Stratton and *Little Big Man*'s Allardyce T. Meriweather—to its limit by showing the multiply disabled Kyle continuing to pitch until, as Kern notes, a truck ran him over and killed him the following year. The announcer solemnly concludes the tale by noting that Kyle "won eighteen games in the big league in the sky" the next season.

At least two 1980s comedies elevated disabled figures to major-character status, both with highly uneven results. Writer Stuart Gillard and director Eric Till based their 1982 Canadian effort *If You Could See What I Hear* on the autobiography of blind singer turned TV newsman Tom Sullivan (played in the movie by Marc Singer) and documented the ease by which he skydives, wrestles, plays golf, drives a friend's car, and picks up women, among other activities, all accomplished with much mirthless humor. Critics berated the film for its endlessly precious qualities, with several picking up on its lack of a disabled person's perspective. *New York Times* critic Janet Maslin wrote that "the story of Mr. Sullivan, a television personality who was a consultant on the film, is told in a terribly cute manner—and it isn't told from Mr. Sullivan's point of view, though that would have helped immeasurably." Lawrence O'Toole of *Maclean's* called the film's perspective "a devastating problem," noting further that the movie "doesn't reflect a disabled sensibility; even the able-bodied viewer will not be entirely convinced he is seeing and hearing a blind person's account of what it is like to live in the world of the sighted." Though *If You Could See* incorporated actual events from Sullivan's life, its muddled point of view and generally shapeless narrative were no doubt the main factors that contributed to its failure on just about all counts.[44]

Overshadowing *If You Could See* in sheer bad taste was *See No Evil, Hear No Evil* (1989), starring Gene Wilder as Dave, a hearing-impaired former actor who runs a Manhattan newsstand with Wally, a black blind man (Richard Pryor), both

The blind Wally (Richard Pryor, left) and the deaf Dave (Gene Wilder) are almost as perplexed as the audience in See No Evil, Hear No Evil. *Copyright © 1989 Tri-Star Pictures Inc.*

of whom get mixed up with crooks after a woman murders a man in front of their stand. As directed by Arthur Hiller and written by a legion of screenwriters, Wilder among them, *See No Evil, Hear No Evil* is an unending series of slapstick gags that trade on the characters' disabilities. No doubt taking his cue from *Bustin' Loose* and its use of a blind kid who drives a bus, Pryor as Wally drives a commandeered police car onto a garbage barge and later has a shoot-out with a blind villain (Anthony Zerbe). In a strange parody of earlier films, particularly *23 Paces to Baker Street*, both characters attempt to pass while solving the crime; Wally pretends to read newspapers (upside down ones, of course) as he rides the subway while the lip-reading Dave tries to fulfill his side of conversations even while his back is turned. Created with astonishingly poor judgment, *See No Evil, Hear No Evil* does little beyond dredging up the old imagery of disabled people as Comic Misadventurers.

Hollywood filmmakers revived a few other stereotypes during the 1980s, but for the most part they did not enjoy much attention. Director Michael Chapman and screenwriter John Sayles constructed a Saintly Sage for a major role in *The Clan of the Cave Bear* (1986), a comic-book level adaptation of Jean Auel's novel of prehistoric times in which a one-eyed, one-armed elder with a limp named Creb (James Remar) dispenses medicine and wisdom in equal measure to members of his Neanderthal tribe and serves as surrogate father to a young Cro-Magnon woman (Daryl Hannah). Forsaking the sensitivity that had guided his depictions of Helen Keller and Old Lodge Skins in *The Miracle Worker* and *Little Big Man*, Arthur Penn created an evildoer with a disability in *Dead of Winter* (1987): Joseph Lewis (Jan Rubes), a wheelchair-using doctor who abducts an actress (Mary Steenburgen) for some nefarious scheme and holds her captive in his gloomy, snowbound mansion. The Tragic Victim surfaced briefly in 1980's *The Exterminator* and 1987's *The Hidden*, in which gang members permanently disable a black Vietnam vet and a speeding car mows down an anonymous wheelchair-using man, respectively. These latter films were related to a different kind of victimization that became popular during the late 1970s and 1980s in a certain type of movie: horror films that exploited the latest advances in movie-making techniques to present graphic disabling acts. In an effort to reach increasingly jaded audiences, filmmakers working in the horror genre seemed to think nothing of having some entity tear off a person's arm or leg to provide a transient shock effect. Inspired by the success, and excess, of *Jaws*, filmmakers treated audiences to casual dismemberment in such films as *Piranha* (1978), *Alligator* (1980), *Cat People* (1982), and *The Fly* (1986), in which several minor characters become forgotten almost as quickly as the title creatures maim them.

In addition to the reappearance of regressive imagery, the incidental treatment of people with physical disabilities gave rise to a new set of stereotypes tied to the growth of science and high technology during the 1970s and 1980s. Several movies informed by the science fiction, fantasy, and horror traditions include the images of people aided by scientific and technological advancements, particularly high-tech prostheses (inspired at least in part by the bionic extravagance of such 1970s television fare as *The Six Million Dollar Man* and *The Bionic Woman*, these films corresponded roughly with the development of actual if far less gimmicky prosthetic devices),[45] while other films present wheelchair-using males highly adept at using computers and other sophisticated electronic equipment.

Chief among the offending films possessing the first stereotype, an image we might call the "Techno Marvel," are the movies produced by George Lucas that make up the "Star Wars" trilogy. *Star Wars* (1977), *The Empire Strikes Back* (1980), and *Return of the Jedi* (1983) all present the character of Darth Vader as a warrior whose many battle injuries have transformed him into a walking wonderland of bionic effects. Indeed, one of the characters in the final film suggests that Vader is more machine than man. The filmmakers underscored the evil Vader's unnatural qualities by supplementing his commanding voice and black-robed presence (supplied respectively by James Earl Jones and David Prowse) with the sounds of labored breathing emanating from a mask-like respirator that looks out impassively from beneath a Nazi-esque helmet. The startling visage and aqualung style of breathing are the parts of Vader that soon come to represent the whole,

"A walking wonderland of bionic effects" : Darth Vader, the prime heavy and disabled Father figure of the "Star Wars" trilogy.

and it is clear he suffers from the parts-representing-the-whole syndrome afflicting so many other movie villains.

The saga's boyish hero Luke Skywalker (Mark Hamill) is another major character with a disability, and the circumstances under which he receives it carry distinct Oedipal overtones. Near the conclusion of *The Empire Strikes Back*, Skywalker and Vader have at each other in a laser-sword duel. At the climax of their protracted struggle, Vader slices off Skywalker's right hand at the wrist. Vader takes advantage of the situation by trying to talk Skywalker into joining forces with him on the dreaded Dark Side, but, when Skywalker rebuffs him, Vader drops an emotional bombshell: he reveals himself as Skywalker's father.

After considering the content and timing of Vader's revelation, it is easy to view the disabling blow as a symbolic castration arising out of a phallic-stage conflict between son and father (especially since it is Skywalker's "power appendage"—his sword-wielding right hand—that Vader cuts off). Yet in their desire to assure audiences that things are not as bad as they appear for the intrepid young hero, the filmmakers vitiated the power of this scene minutes later by showing a robot surgeon retrofitting Skywalker with a mechanical hand that responds just as well as his old one. The convalescing hero seems completely unmoved by the loss of his hand and adapts to his high-tech prosthesis with a rapidity that could be measured in nanoseconds. As the movie ends, we are left with the impression that this youthful Techno Marvel is about as distressed with his disability as one might be with a fleabite.

Throughout much of the follow-up *Return of the Jedi*, Skywalker's disability goes unacknowledged save for a black glove that he wears over the prosthesis. The filmmakers did return to the Oedipal power struggle between Vader and Skywalker, however, and made passing reference to the disabilities of both characters. It reaches its peak near the film's end, when the filmmakers revealed the extent of Vader's reliance on high-tech prostheses.

Vader and Skywalker slash away at each other during their final laser-sword confrontation. They are evenly matched until Vader makes the mistake of suggesting that if Skywalker does not turn to the Dark Side, perhaps Princess Leia, Skywalker's sister (and Mother figure), will. These words cause Skywalker to draw on an inner reserve, and in a rage he hacks Vader's hand off an already mechanical right arm. Vader goes down immediately after losing his hand, and the hooded, crusty old Emperor, who has been watching the conflict all along, tells Luke to finish the job. Luke silently responds by flexing his own mechanical right hand. In a close-up, Luke looks away from his fist to Vader, who is offscreen. A close-up of Vader's smoking right forearm shows wires and mechanical bits. We cut back to Luke, who turns off his laser-sword and tosses it aside, evidently believing the symbolic castration he has returned to his father is enough punishment. What occurs after the Emperor begins torturing the hapless Luke is worthy of any classic fairy tale.

The Star Wars saga provides all-too-easy answers concerning the physical dis-abilities of two of its leading characters. Specifically, the advanced technology enables the prostheses of Luke Skywalker and Darth Vader to respond as well as their original limbs, if not better; they clearly do not hinder the duo's swashbuck-ling abilities. These films and certain others that followed are throwbacks of sorts to an age when curable disabilities were the norm, with several important differ-ences: the replacement of divine intervention with technological achievement—an unseating that generally paralleled the relationship of religion and science during the twentieth century—and the fact that both villains and heroes could benefit from that replacement.

Another film that shows high technology coming to the rescue is *Blind Date*, a 1984 entry directed, produced, and co-written by the deservedly unheralded Nico Mastorakis, whose narrative depends heavily on coincidence to propel it. Joseph Bottoms plays Jonathon Ratcliff, a youthful advertising executive on a photo shoot in Athens. An encounter with a low-hanging branch leaves him blind, but a world-famous surgeon who just happens to be in Athens tells Ratcliff about a new form of technology that could help. Called Compuvision, it consists of a sonar-like device resembling a portable radio that can send signals to a computer chip implanted in the person's skull. The chip in turn sends electric impulses to the brain, which the latter converts into a synthetic vision. The good doctor warns Ratcliff that Compuvision has never been tested on humans, but Ratcliff, after thinking it over for a millisecond or two, agrees to the operation. Of course, no complications ensue and Ratcliff emerges from the skull drilling session with an ability to "see" objects and people in a rather unusual way: as white outlines set off against a black background.

Ratcliff adapts to his new sense with such effortlessness that he thinks nothing of taking up several causes fraught with extreme danger. Armed only with his white cane and synthetic vision, he metes out justice to three leather-clad hood-lums who had mugged him in a subway shortly after his injury. In addition, his ar-tificial vision's ability to play back events like a videotape recorder enables him to solve a string of grisly murders of young women, though his reasons for getting involved in such a risky venture go largely unexplained. Though artificial vision is very much within the realm of scientific possibilities,[46] the film's unrealistically facile and tensionless situations, undue reliance on coincidence, and several in-stances of cheated audience expectations add up to an unsatisfying experience. Though the end credits of *Blind Date* proclaim the eminent arrival of a sequel fea-turing the Ratcliff character, the filmmakers have not followed through with their threat as of this writing.

Wearing his executive-producer hat, Steven Spielberg unleashed a comedy/science-fiction hybrid called *Innerspace* three years later that presented as a minor character a muscular embodiment of utter ruthlessness named Igoe (Ver-non Wells). Not much more than a simplistic, high-tech variation on Captain

Hook, Igoe assists scientists trying to steal miniaturization technology by using an uncommonly versatile prosthetic arm to do such things as shoot bullets, drill holes, and throw out propane flames. In the tradition of such movies as *Dr. No*, *Fuzz*, and *The Deadly Trackers*, the film's final reference to its doomed Techno Marvel highlights the object that has come to represent him: his artificial limb, twitching on the ground.

Technology of a more down-to-earth sort in the form of a souped-up wheelchair comes to the aid of yet another young hero on a quest in the 1985 fantasy-horror film *Stephen King's Silver Bullet*. Horrormeister King initially planned to present the movie's story through an odd literary construction—a narrative calendar, more specifically a series of twelve vignettes that would correspond with a year's worth of monthly lunar phases—but eventually scrapped the idea in favor of a twelve-part novella called *Cycle of the Werewolf*. Reasonably pleased with the movies that producer Dino de Laurentiis had already based on his work, King sent him a copy of *Cycle* in 1984 as a proposed film. Not only did the Italian impresario agree to produce it but he also hired the novelist to write the screenplay.

Directed on location in North Carolina by Dan Attias and released through Paramount, *Silver Bullet* tells the tale of Marty Coslaw (Corey Haim), an 11-year-old who tools around one of King's celebrated small-town settings in a motorized wheelchair dubbed the "Silver Bullet." (In his introduction to the *Cycle of the Werewolf/Silver Bullet* screenplay combo published to coincide with the film's premiere, King gave no indication of his reasons for making the lead character a wheelchair-user; he merely noted in passing that "I started to write about this kid named Marty, who was stuck in a wheelchair.")[47] The film generally presents him as a high-spirited fellow who seldom allows his disability to interfere with life, but his lifestyle as a disabled person quickly takes a backseat to a more pressing concern: the discovery that a werewolf is running amuck in the community. The actions of local vigilantes prove fruitless against the beast, who has killed Marty's best friend as well as his girlfriend's father, among others. With assistance from his skeptical older sister Jane (Megan Follows) and their Uncle Red (Gary Busey), Marty discovers the identity of the werewolf. The latter character in human form almost succeeds in running Marty down with his car, but the youngster, riding in a vehicle created by his uncle that's more hot-rod than wheelchair, manages to elude him.

The conflict between Marty and the werewolf (which culminates in the boy's shooting of the beast with, yes, a custom-made silver bullet) becomes so overwhelming that it obscures many of the details about the film's characters and the views they hold. The audience learns from Jane, the film's occasional narrator, that relations between her and Marty are not that good; she refers to him as her cross to bear and later complains to her parents (who are virtual nonpresences in the film) that they always take Marty's side in sibling disputes "because he's crippled." Uncle Red is basically a good-hearted lout but occasionally has a hard time containing his ableism ("Sometimes I think your common sense got paralyzed along with your legs," he says to Marty at one point). The film never confronts the prejudice behind such utterances, and the attitude of Marty himself toward disability-related issues is limited largely to those times when his wheelchair is about ready to run out of gas.

Even an unusually poignant moment photographed from Marty's perspective—a scene near the end of the film in which he watches boys his age play baseball—carries ableist connotations. With the playground's wire fence separating Marty from the others, the film presents several close-ups of him intercut with shots of the boys filmed from his viewpoint, and significantly it shows the boys from the waist down as they run. King did not specify the scene to be shot that way (his script notation simply states "I think that here we are seeing a rare moment of depression in Marty—they can run and play ball. He can't"),[48] leading us to observe that a director has once again invited the audience to share a disabled character's perspective mainly to enhance that character's sense of isolation and punish him for seeing.

King praised his own work on *Silver Bullet* ("I like the screenplay a lot," he enthused) but was rather lukewarm on his working relationship with Attias. "*Silver Bullet* is his first feature," he wrote. "Dan and I worked hard on it, he giving a little here, I giving a little there. I think that things turned out as well as they ever do when you're spending ten to twelve million dollars on a piece of make-believe: we compromised when we had to and all ended up still friends." King also equivocated on the quality of the resulting film: "Is the picture any good? Man, I just

"This kid named Marty, who was stuck in a wheelchair" (Corey Haim), finds that werewolves don't discriminate in Stephen King's Silver Bullet. *Copyright © 1985 Famous Films B. V.*

can't tell. I'm writing without benefit of hindsight and from a deeply subjective point of view. You want that point of view? Okay. I think it's either very good indeed or a complete bust." Critics tended to concur with the latter opinion, but despite assorted problems and inanities *Silver Bullet* does provide a rather appealing portrayal of a mobility-impaired youngster.[49]

King's occasional colleague, George Romero, was responsible for another film from the same period featuring a wheelchair-using young man threatened by a beast. Romero, who soared to fame twenty years before with the low-budget shocker *Night of the Living Dead*, wrote and directed *Monkey Shines: An Experiment in Fear* (1988). Based on Michael Stewart's 1983 novel, the movie centers on Allan Mann (Jason Beghe), a law student who becomes a quadriplegic after being hit by a truck during the film's opening credits, and Ella, a capuchin monkey who's been trained to serve him. The two get along famously at first, with Ella doing such things as feeding and grooming him, fetching things, turning his textbook pages, even snuggling up to him while playing Peggy Lee tapes. Ella is no ordinary primate, however; Allan's best friend Geoffrey Fisher (John Pankow), a drugged-out medical student, has injected her with a dead woman's brain cells, and Allan quickly discovers a very odd bond developing between him and the monkey. She senses the anger and resentment he harbors toward others—his overprotective mother, an insensitive nurse, his wayward girlfriend, the surgeon who may have botched his operation—and murderously begins acting upon them. Allan, who reciprocates in a weird way by seeing things from her perspective while he dreams, eventually confronts his out-of-control helper in a terrifically suspenseful showdown.

Despite a conclusion hopelessly out of date for the 1980s—an undisabling operation for Allan, which producer Charles Evans had imposed on the movie over Romero's objections—reviewers took quite a shine to the movie. *People Weekly's* Peter Travers, while quick to separate the film's premise from the important work of Helping Hands: Simian Aides for the Disabled, a Boston-based organization that trains primates to assist mobility-impaired people ("This isn't real life, it's Romeroland," he wrote), nevertheless called it "a dazzling mix of mirth and menace." *Time's* Richard Corliss described *Monkey Shines* as "a horror movie with brains and guts" and found Beghe's performance particularly noteworthy: "Beghe must show all Allan's suicidal anxieties, homicidal anger and heroic resourcefulness while strapped in a wheelchair. His finger can hardly move, but his performance does, splendidly."[50]

The other stereotype related to developments in science and technology—the physically disabled person as "High-Tech Guru"— initially found expression in such prototypical films as *The Anderson Tapes* (1972), directed by Sidney Lumet, and *Three Days of the Condor* (1975), directed by Sydney Pollack. The former film shows a sharp-witted boy using a roomful of communications gear to notify police of burglars in his parents' townhouse, while the latter presents a CIA officer known simply as "the Major" who adroitly manipulates a communications console.

Both characters happen to use wheelchairs. With computers emerging as the technology of choice, the trend continued well into the 1980s with such movies as *Starman* (1984), *Power* (1986), *The Imagemaker* (1986), and *No Way Out* (1987), each presenting a wheelchair-using man in a supporting role as a technological whiz. Though the films certainly affirm their disabled characters' high level of intelligence, they unfortunately seldom if ever show the characters outside their electronic lairs. The films' common-denominator image—a wheelchair-using man who at the request of some able-bodied superior expertly manipulates the computers and associated paraphernalia surrounding him—creates the notion that the characters are all brains and no body, and that high technology coupled with high loyalty to an able-bodied boss are the only meaningful things in their lives. In addition, their wheelchairs start to take on a dehumanizing quality, in the sense that the vehicles and their users begin to mesh figuratively with the surrounding technology. The impression often left by these films is that the characters are eminently suited to operating the high-tech equipment because, by virtue of their wheelchair usage, they appear to be part machine themselves.

In addition to allowing filmmakers to play out their fantasies, the rash of movies combining physical disability with science and technology also temporarily displaced Hollywood's interest in disabled Vietnam veterans. A rather lengthy dry spell followed the initial flurry of interest in such characters during the late 1970s and early 1980s, as Hollywood filmmakers began following the same pattern of their 1950s peers by de-emphasizing disabled vets in subsequent movies. One of the first films to return to the concept of the Noble Warrior was *Suspect* (1987), directed on location in Washington D.C. by Peter Yates from a script by Eric Roth. Irish actor Liam Neeson played Carl Wayne Anderson, a homeless Vietnam vet who lost his hearing and speech during the war and is accused of killing a D.C. office worker. In preparation for the role, Neeson visited nearby Gallaudet University to meet with and learn from people with impaired hearing. "There were vets there that had suffered hearing loss in the war," said the actor. "I was particularly interested in talking to the ones that could hear before their sickness and had knowledge of the hearing world." To help him gain a sense of deafness, the university provided him with special earplugs to wear during the making of *Suspect* that rendered him 80 percent deaf.[51]

A major force behind the movie was Cher, who during the mid–1980s was making a name for herself in movies that featured disabled characters. (They include 1985's *Mask*, about a boy deformed by the rare disease craniodiaphyseal dysplasia and his romantic relationship with a blind Sweet Innocent, and 1987's *Moonstruck*, her Oscar-winning vehicle in which she played an Italian-American widow attracted to a younger man who happens to have an artificial hand.) In *Suspect* Cher starred as Kathleen Riley, the public defender assigned to the deafened vet's case. "A script has to mean something to me," she said. "I loved the idea that the story was about a homeless man, and I thought it said something about the condition of homelessness. And I felt like Kathleen and the homeless man, they're the same kind of character, people who are caught in the human condition doing the best they can." Despite Cher's pronouncements and the fact that he is the movie's title character, however, Anderson distinctly plays a supporting role to Cher's public defender and a smooth-talking jury member (Dennis Quaid) who illicitly work together to solve the crime of which the vet has been accused. Yates and Roth perceived the film primarily as a vehicle for Cher. As Roth noted, the movie pivots on her performance: "Others in *Suspect* are better actors, maybe, but it's her persona that shines through." Most critics ignored Neeson's performance or mentioned it only in passing. Sheila Benson of the *Los Angeles Times* was one of the more generous with this brief description: "Working entirely without dialogue, Neeson's tragic, homeless vet becomes a fully fleshed-out and powerful character."[52]

If moviemakers weren't exactly plumbing the depths of the disabled Vietnam vet experience during the mid–1980s, the topic made a roaring comeback in late 1989 in the form of the long-delayed *Born on the Fourth of July*. Ron Kovic, the paralyzed veteran who had completed a wrenching autobiography with the support of Waldo Salt and published it in 1976, had sold the book's screen rights to Al Pacino shortly thereafter in the hope that Oliver Stone, a scriptwriter and fellow Vietnam vet who had recovered from several severe war injuries, would help him turn his story into a film. With William Friedkin slated to direct, Stone to write, and Pacino to star, they were a mere four days away from the start of principal photography in 1978 when the funding for the film fell through. Though it seemed that Stone might be able to get the project moving again after a burst of attention in 1979 for his *Midnight Express* screenwriting Oscar, he hit a low point with the ill-fated *The Hand* two years later. ("I'd been hot, and all of a sudden I was cold," Stone said. "*The Hand* kind of buried me.") Only after he hit it big with *Platoon* (1986) and *Wall Street* (1987) did he gain the necessary clout to revive the Kovic project. "At the time, Oliver promised me, 'If I ever get the opportunity, if I'm ever able to break through as a director, I'll come back for you, Ronnie,'" remembered Kovic. "And he did."[53]

Having secured stable financing with co-producer A. Kitman Ho through a Universal distribution deal, Stone began working on a new screenplay with Kovic (the two eventually shared screenplay credit on the final film) and set about casting the newly reborn *Born on the Fourth of July*. For the central character, he hired a young actor who seemed an unlikely selection at first: Tom Cruise, prince of Hollywood glamor-boy roles. "I chose Tom because he was the closest to Ron Kovic in spirit," said Stone. "I sensed that they came from the same working-class Catholic background and had a similarly troubled family history. They certainly had the same drive, the same hunger to achieve, to be the best, to prove something. Like Ron too, Tom is wound real tight. And what's wrong with that?" Stone had Cruise work with a wheelchair on and off for a year in preparation for the part and found him quite willing to do almost anything to capture the essence of

Kovic's character. "I put a lot of pressure on Tom," he said. "Maybe too much. I wanted him to read more, visit more hospitals. I wanted him to spend time in that chair, to really feel it. He went to boot camp twice, and I didn't want his foxhole dug by his cousin. At one point I talked him into injecting himself with a solution that would have totally paralyzed him for two days. Then the insurance company—the killer of all experience—said no because there was a slight chance that Tom would have ended up permanently paralyzed. But the point is, he was willing to do it."[54]

Shot mostly around Dallas and in the Philippines, *Born on the Fourth of July* poignantly details the stages of Ron's life over a twenty-five year period: his youth in Massapequa, Long Island; his service in Vietnam that included an accidental killing of a fellow American and ended when a bullet severed his spine; a soul-shattering trip to Mexico; his rejection of U.S. policy in Vietnam and forcible ejection from the Republican National Convention in 1972; and his triumphant speech at the 1976 Democratic convention. Ron's transformation from hawkish superpatriot to impassioned war protestor, the movie's key narrative element, was a process that in real life took years. "Ron, when he came back from the war, was still very prowar," said Stone. "I mean, we didn't make it easy: that just because he got shot [and then used] a wheelchair that he changed overnight. It wasn't that easy. It took four, five years for him to deconstruct his mind, and to change the mind, to go from one bias to the other bias."[55] The filmmakers did offer a bit of foreshadowing, however, through a tip of the hat to another antiwar

Born on the Fourth of July *(1989), starring Tom Cruise, documents Ron Kovic's gradual conversion from Vietnam superhawk to antiwar activist.*

author and filmmaker; during the scene in which a doctor tells Ron he'll never walk again, Stone's camera glides over several books near the vet's bed, the most prominent of which is Dalton Trumbo's *Johnny Got His Gun*.

Though it does not shrink from such issues as the sexuality of paraplegics and prejudice against wheelchair users (Ron travels to a Mexican brothel that caters to injured veterans, for instance, while a security guard at the Republican convention dumps him out of his vehicle, an act that fails to diminish its user's resolve), *Born on the Fourth of July*, like its spiritual twin *Coming Home*, gradually de-emphasizes the lead character's impaired mobility in favor of other dimensions of his life, particularly his antiwar activities. Ron comes across as a complete human being, not one defined solely in terms of a disability, and it's a quality strongly enhanced by the work of Stone's cinematographer, Robert Richardson. Though the highly mobile, often dizzying camerawork does include a few brief objectifying shots of Ron (mainly from his mother's and girlfriend's perspectives), they are far outweighed by the numerous low camera angles from the vet's point of view, low-angle shots that bestow a sense of heroism on him, and frequent tight close-ups of his face. These shots strongly encourage the audience to identify with Ron and help it understand the range of his experiences and emotions.

The film's symbolic dimensions further inspire the audience to look beyond Ron's use of a wheelchair. He and the United States were coincidentally "born" on the same day, and the sense of Ron-as-America from the 1950s to the 1970s is central to both the autobiography and the movie. As Cruise pointed out, *Born on the Fourth of July* is more than a personal, coming-to-terms kind of story: "The film isn't about a man in a wheelchair. [It's about] the country, what it went through, was, became. You know, an invalid. . . . It was a crippling time for this country, and you had to get beyond this man and a chair."[56]

For Kovic, the film represented the chance to make people aware of the terrible legacy of Vietnam and the importance of never getting involved in something like that again. "When Oliver called me up and told me that we were going to do this film again, it was like being given a second life," he said. "I could never quite reconcile being in this wheelchair after Vietnam. I could never quite understand how my sacrifice could have any kind of meaning at all. Working on the script with Oliver was the first time that I began to understand that my sacrifice, my paralysis, the difficulties, the frustrations, the impossibilities of each and every day would now be for something very valuable, something that would help protect the young people of this country from having to go through what I went through."[57]

Though Born on the Fourth of July and earlier movies such as *Inside Moves*, *The Elephant Man*, and *Children of a Lesser God* suggested a generally positive direction (and I do emphasize the word "generally"), perhaps the clearest indication of a new-found sensitivity to disability issues during the decade was the arrival of several films that depicted what for the mainstream movie industry had long been an invisible disabling circumstance: cerebral palsy. Though the breakthrough was not without a few flaws, a trio of films based heavily on bio-graphical material—*Touched by Love* (1980), *Gaby—A True Story* (1987), and *My Left Foot—The Story of Christy Brown* (1989)—explored the CP experience with courage and conviction.

Written by *Lesser God*'s Hesper Anderson and directed by Gus Trikonis on lo-cation in the Canadian Rockies near Banff, Alberta, *Touched by Love* tells the story of Lena Canada (Deborah Raffin), a nurse's aide who spends a summer dur-ing the early 1960s at an isolated school for disabled children and finds herself drawn to one child in particular, a reticent young girl with CP named Karen (Diane Lane). Lena breaks through communication barriers and helps the wheelchair-using girl emerge from her shell by encouraging her to correspond with her idol, Elvis Presley. To the surprise of just about everyone except Karen, Presley does eventually write back, and the two share a lengthy pen-pal relationship until Karen's death.

Touched by Love, based on Canada's nonfiction book *To Elvis with Love* and fi-nanced by Presley's estate, left critics divided over its merits. Peter Mascuch of *Films in Review* described it as "one of those totally lifeless sob stories that audi-ences tend to laugh at derisively rather than cry with sorrowfully" and "light on genuine feelings we can identify with," while *Monthly Film Bulletin*'s Martyn Auty referred to "the overwhelming winsomeness of the saccharine script and dismayingly routine direction from Gus Trikonis." Others, however, were more impressed. While calling it a "tearduct workout," the *New York Post*'s Archer Winsten also praised it as "extraordinarily moving" and "a very special film . . . a very beautiful celebration of the power of love to heal and inspire. The sight of those incurables being lifted out of their depths is something that can lift and move an audience, too." The filmmakers were undeniably guilty of several things: basing Karen partially on the age-old stereotype of the Sweet Innocent (Lauri Klobas called her "forever innocent and full of shining, untarnished hope"), telling the story mainly from the able-bodied Lena's perspective, oversentimen-talizing their subject through frequent tearful scenes and such heavy-handed sym-bols as a wounded bird and a deer to represent Karen, and prettifying their film by casting Raffin and Lane in the leads. (Indeed, producer Michael Viner developed the project specifically for the glamorous Raffin, who happened to be his wife.) To his credit, however, Trikonis did elicit some fine performances from the ac-tresses—particularly Lane, who made her character's feelings clear through the various looks in her eyes—refused to go with a wispy happily-ever-after ending, and added a strong degree of authenticity to the film by surrounding the stars with actual disabled children.[58]

The Tri-Star release *Gaby—A True Story* returned to this rare movie topic by concentrating on a Mexican writer born with the disorder, Gabriela Brimmer, whose bestselling 1979 autobiography and extensive interviews with director Luis Mandoki formed the basis for the screenplay by Martin Salinas and Michael James Love. "I saw Gaby one time on television, and then I read the book," remembered Mandoki, a Mexican born of Hungarian immigrants. "Suddenly, the idea was reminding me that life is a gift that I take for granted. Gaby for me became a hope—a song to life." After meeting with Brimmer, Mandoki began pursuing a quest to make the movie that eventually extended over a period of more than six years due to limited contacts in the movie industry and availability of funds. When the movie finally came together in the mid–1980s, he was able to assemble an impressive cast that included Rachel Levin, a first-time film actress from New York whose recent bout with a paralyzing neuro-muscular disorder called Guillain–Barré syndrome allowed her to bring a certain authenticity to the role of Gaby. Liv Ullmann and Robert Loggia played her parents, well-to-do Austrian Jewish refugees who had settled in Mexico City in 1938, while Lawrence Monoson played her first love, Fernando, another person with CP.[59]

Gaby contains a number of touching moments while documenting Brimmer's life: her parents' discovery that their angelic-looking infant has cerebral palsy; their realization that they have been regarding Gaby as less than a human being ("We don't have a daughter; we have a problem," her father says. "If we want a daughter, for God's sake please let's start treating her like one"); and Gaby's eventual maturation into a youth determined to learn (Mandoki frequently employed shots of her left foot busily spelling out words on an alphabet board

Gaby—A True Story is one of a mere handful of narrative movies to depict the lifestyle of people with cerebral palsy. Rachel Levin (right) played the vivacious title character and Liv Ullmann her mother. Copyright © 1987 Tri-Star Pictures Inc.

attached to her wheelchair's footplate) and who believes her special-ed surroundings are holding her back. Both she and Fernando want to attend a regular public school, and in one of the movie's most powerful scenes Fernando actively rebels against the rehab school while Gaby refers to it as a "circus."

Critics praised the film, with Kevin Thomas of the *Los Angeles Times* writing for the majority in suggesting that "Levin's performance as Gaby Brimmer, a victim of cerebral palsy who became determined to live life as fully as possible, is so radiant that instead of pitying Gaby or shunning her, we are instead able to identify with her, to feel with her a common bond of humanity." Like *Coming Home*, *Gaby* refreshingly spends considerable time showing its disabled character in a variety of life activities, including sexual ones. (According to *New York Post* critic Jami Bernard, a love scene between Gaby and Fernando, "although sensitive, is so realistic it seems more voyeuristic than cinematic.") The film's main drawback is all too familiar: its point of view. Like *Touched by Love*, *Gaby* is told primarily from an able-bodied companion's perspective—in this case, the Brimmers' Mexican-Indian maid Florencia (Norma Aleandro), a woman of rather simple values who discovers that Gaby as a young child can control her left foot and teaches her how to communicate with it. Though the filmmakers vitiated *Gaby*'s potential power by unfolding the film this way, *Gaby* emerges as an eloquent, superbly acted plea for mainstreaming.[60]

A third take on cerebral palsy appeared two years later in the form of the Irish *My Left Foot*, guided by theater-turned-film director Jim Sheridan from a script he co-authored with Shane Connaughton. Budgeted at a mere $3 million and distributed by the upstart Miramax Films company, *My Left Foot* details the life of Christy Brown, an author and painter born with CP, who like Gabriela Brimmer could consistently control only his left foot. The tenth of twenty-two children born into an impoverished Dublin family, Christy is considered a "poor half-wit" for the first nine years of his life by just about everyone except his strongly supportive mother (Oscar-winner Brenda Fricker). After the youthful Christy (played at this point in the movie by Hugh O'Conor) astounds his family by writing the word "mother" with a piece of chalk that he holds with his foot, his father Paddy (Ray McAnally) is so taken that carries him over his shoulder like a bag of spuds to the local pub. "This is Christy Brown, my son," he says proudly. "Genius!" With the unswerving support of his family—his brothers even find a way to involve him in their soccer games—Christy develops into an adult intensely determined to succeed on a variety of levels. He learns to speak with the help of a therapist and his flinty, selfless mother, and though thwarted romantically at several turns (the film reaches an emotional high point when Christy in a drunken rage begins destroying a restaurant table over a woman who has rejected him) he does eventually marry. He also goes on to paint portraits and write an autobiography, novels, and books of poetry (the former, published in 1955 when Brown was 23, incidentally served as the basis for Sheridan and Connaughton's screenplay).

One of the things that elevates *My Left Foot* above the usual "inspirational" film is its unsentimental script. Sheridan and Connaughton were quite familiar with the Noble Warrior and Civilian Superstar movies of the post-World War II era and decided against portraying the requisite heroic rehabilitative struggle and the near-requisite suggestion that the character might be cured or must at least "pass" for able-bodied. "You could have had him stand and walk," Sheridan said, "and God, he did it. But it's a false trail. He doesn't get better—at the end of his life, when I met him, he was in a wheelchair. Most films about the handicapped are about overcoming physical disabilities. This is about an *emotionally* crippled person, and we're all crippled emotionally." As noted by Noel Pearson, the movie's producer and a close friend of Brown's, he "was a hero with massive [emotional] faults." Sheridan and Connaughton were also acutely aware of the dangers of sentimentalizing their subject because of the potentially strong feelings of pity the film might evoke. "The minute the audience reacted that way, I knew we would be finished," Sheridan said, "because then they are superior in a way they shouldn't be."[61]

Another major factor contributing to *My Left Foot*'s resonant qualities was Sheridan's inspired casting of Daniel Day-Lewis as the adult Christy. The British actor already knew something of the wheelchair-using experience—his late step-father had been paralyzed—and spent three months researching the role, which included observing children with CP at Dublin's Sandymount Clinic, studying a 1971 documentary made on Brown, and consulting extensively with Brown's family. The experiences helped him develop a fully fleshed-out conception of the role, and, like Brown, he even learned to write and paint with his left foot. "I felt that I had an understanding of to some extent his anger, his frustrations, his desire to create, his sense of impotence," he said. "Many different aspects of his life I felt I had an understanding of, and they didn't relate specifically in my mind to his disability at all." Day-Lewis gave a stunning performance as Christy and was a most worthy recipient of the Best Actor Oscar. The assessment by Richard Corliss was typical of the critical community's reaction: "Day-Lewis' triumph is nearly as spectacular as Christy's: to reveal the blind fury in his eyes and stunted gestures, to play him with a streak of fierce, black-Irish humor. Brilliantly, Day-Lewis shows a mind, and then a man, exploding from the slag heap of Christy's body." Sheridan abetted the actor's work by having cinematographer Jack Conroy film much of the movie from Christy's perspective and including relatively few objectifying shots, an approach similar to that followed by Oliver Stone and Robert Richardson in the concurrently produced *Born on the Fourth of July*. With much of the film unfolding from Christy's point of view, *My Left Foot* is most unlike the CP films, and indeed so many other disability-related movies, that preceded it.[62]

The generally positive quality of *My Left Foot* and the other CP films is doubtless related (and with no small irony) to their minimal association with Hollywood. Though all three received distribution from American companies, *My Left*

Foot is an Irish film, *Gaby* is Mexican, and *Touched by Love* has a conspicuously north-of-the-U.S.-border quality; adapted from a Canadian story (and written by someone calling herself Canada, no less), it was photographed entirely in Alberta and employed numerous children and teachers from Calgary's Gordon Townsend School as background characters. Since none of these three CP films is based on a U.S. story or has a U.S. setting, it is difficult to avoid concluding that, as of this writing, cerebral palsy remains a foreign experience in several senses for American moviemakers.

As I hope this chapter has shown, mainstream moviemakers of the late 1970s and 1980s created some relatively forward-moving images but still held deeply ambivalent views on physical disability. It seemed that almost every portrait no matter how worthy contained questionable elements, and that for every reasonably sensitive film they constructed one or two others revived an old stereotype or presented a new one. In addition, movies such as *Coming Home, Inside Moves,* and *Children of a Lesser God,* while compelling on their own terms, had undergone a toning-down process during their development, their political edges blunted. On this latter point in particular, the films contradicted a major phenomenon in U.S. society: the growing political strength of disability-rights activists. As the movement gathered renewed momentum at the end of the 1980s, culminating in the most important civil-rights legislation passed by Congress since 1964, Hollywood's equivocation would only increase.

conclusion /

reel life after the
americans with
disabilities act

Shortly after one-time movie actor Ronald Reagan took on the greatest role of his career in 1980, disability-rights advocates, aware that the conservative president though hearing-impaired was no friend to their cause, began working with civil-rights organizations in an effort to prevent his administration from dismantling the regulations they had devoted years to helping build and protect. Though they spent much of the 1980s resisting the Reagan administration's deregulatory efforts, the situation was not without some irony: the person Reagan had appointed to reduce or eliminate regulations as they related to disability issues, Vice President George Bush, turned out to be an unexpected ally. With one son dyslexic and another having undergone a colostomy, Bush was reasonably sympathetic to their concerns and as a presidential candidate in 1988 pledged to endorse legislation that extended civil rights to disabled people.

Sensing that a window of opportunity was opening during the twilight of the Reagan presidency, disability-rights activists had already begun seeking help from U.S. representatives and senators to enact legislation that would indeed provide full civil-rights protection. They worked particularly closely with lawmakers who were disabled themselves or who had disabled family members, including Senators Edward M. Kennedy, whose son Teddy Jr. had lost a leg to cancer; Lowell Weicker, the father of a Down's syndrome child and the person who initially introduced the legislation; and Tom Harkin, whose family members included a deaf brother and a quadriplegic nephew and who eventually became the chief sponsor of the bill.[1]

After almost a decade of defensive strategies topped by several years of offensive ones, the activists finally witnessed the Congressional passage of landmark legislation known as the Americans with Disabilities Act. Signed into law by then-President Bush in 1990 and phased in during the early 1990s, the ADA mandated accessibility to all forms of public transportation, accommodations, and telecommunication, and it also prohibited employers from discriminating against qualified applicants because of disabilities. Designed to have wide-ranging effects, the ADA, as Kennedy noted, "ensures that millions of men and women and children can look forward to the day when they will be judged by the strength of their abilities, not misconceptions about their disabilities."[2]

Despite its high significance, the ADA is only in its initial stages of implementation as of this writing and, in another example of lag, has yet to exert much noticeable influence on moviemakers; it is simply too early to assess its impact on the Hollywood community. Though it is true that a number of 1990s movies have presented minor characters with disabilities in a more or less incidental way, including *Fried Green Tomatoes* (1991), *The Fisher King* (1991), *The Player* (1992), and *Sommersby* (1993), they seem more indebted to (and indeed a continuation of) a movie pattern established about a dozen years earlier than to the ADA. Movies that placed such figures at their centers have proven particularly problematic; they have registered mostly regressive qualities with many of the old stereotypes still in force. If nothing else, these latter films amply demonstrated Hollywood's abiding ambivalence on issues of physical disability, as the following observations will no doubt suggest.

In 1991, the team responsible for such efforts as *The Kentucky Fried Movie* and *Airplane!*—Jim Abrahams, David Zucker, and Jerry Zucker—created *The Naked Gun 2 1/2: The Smell of Fear* which subjected a wheelchair-using scientist and his wicked double to seemingly interminable sight gags, while later that year Steven Spielberg, inspired perhaps by the evil Igoe character of his *Innerspace*, managed to incur the wrath of disability groups everywhere by resurrecting the twentieth century's most famous disabled villain: Captain Hook, now elevated to title character in a follow-up to Barrie's *Peter Pan* called *Hook*. (Given the missing word "Captain" and the prominence of the famous prosthesis in the movie's advertising and throughout the film, however, it's not clear if the movie's title refers to the person or the device.) Dustin Hoffman, who had starred in *Midnight Cowboy* and *Little Big Man* more than twenty years before and had recently played the mentally impaired Raymond of *Rain Man* (1988), essayed the Obsessive Avenger, modeling him partially after political commentator William F. Buckley, Jr. ("What interested me was [Hook's] combination of violence and effeteness," said Hoffman, "and Buckley came to mind—in a nice way. . . . He's bright and educated, but there's something scary there.") Hoffman along with Spielberg, who greatly appreciated the humor in the actor's approach, succeeded mainly in renewing fears of amputees under the guise of family entertainment.[3]

These Comic Misadventurer and Obsessive Avenger representations weren't the only clichéd images to appear. British writer-director Bruce Robinson created a modified Sweet Innocent in the form of Helena Robertson, a vulnerable young woman (and, as played by Uma Thurman, another in a long line of disabled women constructed as "pretty") who lives in a dilapidated institute for the blind and seems the next target of a serial killer in *Jennifer 8* (1992), for example, while John Sayles wrote and directed a film about a recently disabled woman that initially comes across as a profile in abject bitterness: *Passion Fish*. In this 1992 Miramax release, a soap-opera actress living in New York named May-Alice Colehaine (Mary McDonnell) loses the use of her legs after a cab strikes her. (In a perverse stroke that Alfred Hitchcock would doubtless have appreciated, Sayles had the disabling accident occur while she was on her way to a leg-waxing appointment.) Soured on life as a result, May-Alice isolates herself by moving to her ancestral homestead in Louisiana bayou country, keeping her distance from neighbors, and drinking heavily. She alienates a long line of caregivers with her sharply worded demands and comments, but the revolving door stops with the arrival of Chantelle (Alfre Woodard), a strong-willed African American with assorted problems of her own. Despite its early negative imagery, *Passion Fish* does eventually develop into an insightful female-buddy movie in which the women help each other, learn from each other, and grow to appreciate the world around them in a refreshingly understated way. Among the virtues of this thought-provoking film is its suggestion, noted by *Time*'s Richard Corliss, "that heroism is found not in the public victories we achieve but in the intimate truths we learn to accept."[4]

Passion Fish and its stress on the dynamics of basic human relationships, which Sayles may have developed in part to atone for his overindulgent *Piranha*, *Alligator*, and *The Clan of the Cave Bear* work-for-hire screenplays, grew out of things he had learned while working as an orderly in hospitals and nursing homes some twenty years before. "I had a lot of nurse friends who would moonlight as home-care companions," said he. "I got fascinated by the relationship between people who spent eight, ten, twenty hours at a time together, and yet don't necessarily have anything in common. They're stuck together; one needs the job and the other needs the care. Often it's a power relationship—one has the power to hire and fire and the other has the power of being physically able to get up and leave the room. And that balance of power might switch during the day."[5]

The substantial dollops of bitterness and anger that characterize *Passion Fish*'s early going (and indeed so many other films, from the first Obsessive Avenger films and *The Big Parade* through many of the classic Noble Warrior and Civilian Superstar films to *Whose Life Is It Anyway?* and *Children of a Lesser God*) were also defining qualities for *Scent of a Woman* (1992), written by Bo Goldman and directed by Martin Brest. Al Pacino, who had lost out on the opportunity to play a disabled Vietnam veteran in the aborted *Born on the Fourth of July* project in 1978, got a second chance by playing Lieutenant Colonel Frank Slade, an Army career officer accidently blinded in a stunt with a grenade after being passed over for promotion. The highly embittered vet, now staying in a shed behind his niece's home in New Hampshire, lives in the same kind of isolated, alcoholic, venomous "splendor" as May-Alice. Also like the latter character, the verbally abusive and suicidal Frank eventually encounters an able-bodied caretaker with problems of his own: Charlie Simms (Chris O'Donnell), a well-scrubbed prep-school student who faces possible expulsion and the loss of a Harvard scholarship if he doesn't inform on some classmates. The unlikely two become mutually helpful buddies, but not until after Frank tricks the youth into accompanying him to New York where he plans to rent an expensive hotel room, enjoy an extravagant meal, make love to a "top of the line" prostitute, and then kill himself. Another movie to showcase an able-bodied actor feigning disabled status en route to an Oscar and replete with questionable attributes (in a scene reminiscent of ones in *Bustin' Loose* and *See No Evil, Hear No Evil,* for example, Frank drives a sports car all over Manhattan), *Scent of a Woman* left disabled audience members extremely divided over its merits.[6]

Hollywood's deep equivocation on physical disability concerns found additional expression in several films of 1993 that happened to feature an able-bodied doctor at their centers: *Boxing Helena* and *The Fugitive.* The former film, starring Julian Sands and Sherilyn Fenn, pivots on a premise that ranks as one of the most repellent in movie history: an obsessive doctor amputates the limbs of the woman of his dreams. With a concept so perverse that such performers as Kim Basinger and Madonna backed out of agreements to star in the film, *Boxing Helena* was almost universally condemned by critics. Though directed by a woman (first-timer Jennifer Lynch, daughter of *The Elephant Man*'s David Lynch), it was also subjected to frequent protests for its misogynistic qualities and to virtually no one's regret departed theaters in rather short order.

The Fugitive, on the other hand, won wide praise from critics, though little of it had to do with its depiction of disability. With a suspenseful script by Jeb Stuart and David Twohy and taut direction by Andrew Davis, *The Fugitive* closely followed its namesake 1960s television program in its basic narrative premise: falsely accused of murdering his wife, Dr. Richard Kimble (Harrison Ford) spends most of his time eluding a Javert-like police officer while tracking down the real killer, a one-armed man (Andreas Katsulas). Unlike the TV show, however, *The Fugitive* spends a considerable amount of time inside a hospital's prosthetics and orthotics ward as Kimble, recalling the killer's specific type of prosthesis, uses the latest computer technology to match the device with its user. Despite its documentary-like representation of modern prosthetic and orthotic technologies, the fact remains that *The Fugitive,* like countless films before it (and indeed the TV program that prompted it), freely mixes disability and villainy. Though undeniably a well-crafted thriller, it serves as a yet another reminder that movies hadn't really come a long way in almost one hundred years' worth of disability depictions.

As if the movie images themselves weren't enough, other expressions of disparagement ranging in degrees of hurtfulness and trivialization have hindered progress during the 1990s. There is still the very real double problem facing actors with disabilities: members of the movie industry seldom consider them for roles that don't specify disabilities, and they often assign the parts that do to able-bodied performers. "Ideally, Hollywood should be a place where the best actor gets the part," said Ellen Stohl, a mobility-impaired actress. "I am not allowed to audition for roles that don't call for a wheelchair. It just doesn't happen. I can't get an agent that would send me out. I can't get a casting director to see me, and then when I go to audition for the roles that they [might] offer me, there are eight to ten able-bodied women there, and nine out of ten times the able-bodied person is cast for the disabled role." Negative attitudes continue to exist outside the industry as well. In a 1990 *U.S. News & World Report* essay titled "Our Hypersensitive Minorities," John Leo wrote that the disability rights movement "has a good argument, of course—physical disability is casually used as a symbol of evil in all sorts of fiction—but at the fringes oversensitivity runs rampant" and lamented that "the disability rights people are probably now strong and touchy enough to veto all disabled villains." *Time* critic Robert Hughes offered a vivid example when in a 1992 attack on political correctness he managed to insult the physical disability movement by noting that "the range of victims available ten years ago— blacks, Chicanos, Indians, women, homosexuals—has now expanded to include every permutation of the halt, the blind and the short, or, to put it correctly, the vertically challenged."[7]

Despite the insightful work by such filmmakers as Waldo Salt, Carl Foreman, and Fred Zinnemann over the years, it is evident that physically disabled people themselves will have to be the ones to effect the most meaningful changes in their movie portrayals, and it is happening, both inside the industry and out. A 1992 article in *Deaf Life* detailed the efforts of several deaf groups to get producer Penny Marshall and the others responsible for *Calendar Girl* (1993), a comedy about three Nevada boys who trek to Hollywood to meet Marilyn Monroe, to reconsider their decision to hire a hearing actor to play a minor character who is deaf. Though the activists lost that round, they refused to give up the battle and staged a series of protests during the film's opening. As Linda Levitan noted, the lessons they absorbed about Hollywood hardball would serve them well in future encounters with the industry. "The Deaf community has learned that it must take an assertive role in informing all casting directors that capable Deaf performers are here, ready, and willing," she wrote. "There will undoubtedly be a better-organized effort to provide extensive listings of such performers. That way, no studio will *ever* be able to say again in good faith: 'We made every effort to find them, and they weren't there, and the ones we did find weren't right for us.'"[8]

Disabled people working within the movie industry have been making inroads as well. "I'm extremely proud" of *Born on the Fourth of July*, noted screenwriter Ron Kovic. "I was able to see my story come out the way I wanted to see it and the way I felt it should come out," he said, adding that the able-bodied people with whom he worked "treated me with a great deal of respect." Ellen Stohl won a hard-fought struggle to land a leading role in a film tentatively titled *The Hooded Horseman*. "The director was very hesitant, my co-star was very hesitant," she said. "I had to fly myself out from L.A. to Austin to convince them that I was serious about the role, that I was a serious actor. I had to go over the script with them and say, 'Look, there aren't a lot of changes. I'm just a person, this is how I would do this,' and they took the chance."[9]

Perhaps the most significant development has been the elevation of a wheelchair-using screenwriter to the role of director. Neal Jimenez, author of the scripts for such movies as *River's Edge* (1986) and *For the Boys* (1991), wrote and co-directed a film based partially on his own experiences called *The Waterdance* (1992). Filmed largely on location at the Rancho Los Amigos Hospital, the same venue for much of *Coming Home*'s principal photography, and modestly bankrolled at $2.7 million by the Samuel Goldwyn company, *The Waterdance* examines the lives of three wheelchair-using young men—Joel Garcia (Eric Stoltz), Raymond Hill (Wesley Snipes), and Bloss (William Forsythe)—and their ways of grappling with issues of race and class. Jimenez, who was quick to point out the extent of the film's autobiographical qualities ("The film is about five months of my life that happened seven years ago," he said. "Maybe 20 percent is true. I expect people to recognize that Eric is playing me. He's a writer, he has a Mexican surname and doesn't really look Mexican . . . We're talking about me"), also noted *The Waterdance*'s orientation toward issues of masculinity: "It's very much about men, and men having to redefine their manhood when their physical being is entirely changed. The film, for me, is about three males who in some ways have to come to terms with who they are as men and what defines their sexuality." Marred only by crucified-Christ references in its early stages (photographed in a series of tight close-ups—a visual strategy the directors thereafter abandoned— and wearing a so-called "halo" head-and-neck brace resembling a crown of thorns complete with blood trickling from underneath it, the bearded and weary-eyed Joel is a dead ringer for Robert Powell's Christ in the 1977 film *Jesus of Nazareth*), *The Waterdance* is an unflinching look at the wide range of issues facing newly disabled males. The *New York Times*'s Vincent Canby gave it a very favorable review, noting that "though small in scale, it is big in feelings expressed with genuine passion and a lot of gutsy humor." *The Waterdance* also scored well with jurors at the Sundance Film Festival in January that year; its awards included the screenwriting prize (named incidentally for Waldo Salt, who had died in 1987) and another as the festival's most popular film.[10]

Through the combined efforts of activists outside Hollywood and people within the industry like Kovic, Stohl, and Jimenez working with open-minded, able-bodied peers (such as Spike Lee, who spoke of wanting to hired disabled people for his filmmaking crews),[11] the movie image of people with physical disabilities will undoubtedly reflect further refinements. It's an uphill struggle to be sure, but as their influence over the construction of Hollywood's social imagery continues to grow and as the Americans with Disabilities Act concomitantly brings people closer together, the day may not be that far off when the sense of isolation that has haunted people with physical disabilities in life and in the movies will become a thing of the past.

Where have we come in nearly a century's worth of physical disability movie depictions, and where do we seem to be going? More specifically, what challenges do post-ADA filmmakers face in light of this history as they commence work on new representations? Following the well-worn but still serviceable premise that we need to know where we have been if we are to know where we are going, I believe a brief reappraisal of the developments covered in this volume will help illustrate the most pressing concerns moviemakers must confront as they begin designing new disability-related films.

As I hope the preceding chapters have shown, the history of physical disability images in the movies has mostly been a history of distortion in the name of maintaining an ableist society. Since the images typically bear scant resemblance to actual people with physical disabilities, we are forced to ask not who but *what* these characters are supposed to represent. In a variation on feminist theorist Christine Gledhill's to-the-point observation about women in the movies—"Female figures in mainstream cinema do not represent women, but the needs of the patriarchal psyche"—we might argue that the movie industry has created physically disabled movie characters primarily to serve the needs of a society long committed to stifling and exploiting its disabled minority. As we have witnessed, this commitment has assumed various guises in the movies.[12]

Despite the negative nature of much of this imagery, the Cinema of Isolation has demonstrated a general sense of progress, a sense that will perhaps be more detectable if we divide the movie depictions into three general historical eras: the medium's origins to the late 1930s, the World War II years into the 1970s, and the 1970s through today. Films from the first period gravitated toward the highly exploitative, with their characters often not much more than comic stick-figures, freakish beasts, or pitiable objects. Films from the second frequently had an exploratory quality, in which the characters' disabilities and struggles to overcome them take center stage. The third tended to feature movies that dealt with disability in more of an incidental way, in which rehabilitation issues often take a back seat to other concerns such as fighting for social justice, sexually expressing one's self, and simply getting on with day-to-day life. Though this history has been marked by frequent slippage back to the older forms of expression, the general movement from exploitative treatments to exploratory to incidental does suggest a slowly developing enlightenment on issues of physical disability.

Progress has been particularly evident in independently produced and often modestly budgeted works such as *Inside Moves*, *My Left Foot*, and *The Waterdance*, with some, principally *Coming Home* and the prototypical *The Best Years of Our Lives*, becoming breakaway box-office hits. In addition, more positive depictions have surfaced in other mainstream media, particularly television commercials and print advertising.[13] As people with disabilities continue to make gains in our society (gains that the majority of U.S. citizens will learn of through mainstream news media, of course), their movie images will presumably begin to reflect the lives of people with physical disabilities with a greater degree of accuracy and sensitivity.

Despite some noteworthy achievements, it is clear that serious issues continue to restrain the cultivation of better-informed imagery. As a means of bringing our peregrinations through the Cinema of Isolation to a close, I would like to structure the stereotypes discussed in the foregoing chapters in terms of gender and age-related issues en route, I hope, to a better understanding of a highly pervasive and crushingly oppressive story structure that has guided (or, perhaps more appropriately, misguided) so many mainstream movies, disability-related and otherwise: the Oedipal scenario. Tania Modleski echoed many thinkers with her statement that "all traditional narratives re-enact the male Oedipal crisis,"[14] and, though in this book I have attempted to link the movie portrayals mainly to contemporaneous social phenomena and factors within the movie industry, Modleski's observation is strongly relevant here. Indeed, I would go so far as to argue that the Oedipal "plot" and its relationship to the construction and reception of movies may well be the biggest obstacle that filmmakers must overcome if they are to continue creating relatively fair-minded representations of the physically disabled experience.

As suggested in another essay and implied throughout this book, the stereotyping of physically disabled people is conspicuously linked to gender issues.[15] The deeply rooted forces that have created our patriarchal society are intimately related to the ones responsible for its ableist perspectives, as the following recapitulation of the three general movie eras and their stereotypes in light of psychosexual factors will reveal.

If we were to take the movie stereotypes that initially appeared during the first major stage of physical disability depictions (i.e., the 1890s up to the World War II years) and construct a spectrum based on age-related concerns, we would discover that the types on the extremes—Saintly Sages and preadolescent Sweet Innocents—typically do not have a gendered quality. In other words, moviemakers made only a minimal effort to inscribe these frequently marginal characters as male or female apart from their physical characteristics; there is little about their behavior that suggests gender differences. Except for the Elderly Dupes, silent-era stereotypes that share space with the Saintly Sages on one end of the spectrum and that do have more of a gender-specific quality (e.g., the blind mother of *The Man and the Woman*, the "Patriarch" of *The Miracle Man*), these reflections of ageist and ableist concerns are essentially nonsexed constructs.

Disabled characters who fall between these two poles, however, are another matter. With only scattered exceptions (e.g., the female Obsessive Avenger of *The Devil-Doll*, the adult male Sweet Innocent of *Of Human Bondage*), these stereotypes distinctly follow gender lines: adult Sweet Innocents are female while Comic Misadventurers, Tragic Victims, Noble Warriors, and Obsessive Avengers are male. The rigid sex-role stereotyping of these images, covering about forty years' worth of movie history, reveals a central paradox: though the movie industry seldom if ever constructed physically disabled people as sexual beings in its productions' surface stories, it exhibited a tremendous concern for sexual differences among such characters—differences that psychoanalytic theory can at least partially explain.

Though not commenting on images from this time-frame per se, feminist and disability-rights activist Anne Finger suggested a gender-related dichotomy in media imagery that happens to characterize this first period of movie images rather well: disabled women are asexual, disabled men are "filled with diseased lusts."[16] These general categories correspond closely to the two dominant stereotypes of the time: the Sweet Innocent and the image that eventually overwhelmed the male-inscribed others, the Obsessive Avenger.

Let's start with the Sweet Innocent, devised like so many other Hollywood female images to receive and be controlled by the desiring male gaze. Moviemakers almost always constructed nonelderly women with physical disabilities during this lengthy time-span as childlike objects requiring domination. These patriarchal images are among the most blatant examples of the mainstream culture's tendency to infantilize women. Such characters are not just ingénues; they are ultra-ingénues who by virtue of their femaleness and disabled status appear doubly disempowered. Filmmakers mitigated the women's two-fold "castration" somewhat by the type of disability they usually bestowed on them: blindness or, less frequently, deafness, either of which could support the illusion that the women's corporeal integrity remained intact (except for their "missing penises," of course). Not so coincidentally, the women are often pretty or at least pleasant in appearance (cf. Chaplin's insistence on an actress "who could look blind without detracting from her beauty" for *City Lights*) yet as sexless constructs were designed to harbor no desire of their own. They were and are the ultimate objects of the male gaze, as Linda Williams has argued: "In the classical narrative cinema, to see is to desire. It comes as no surprise, then, that many of the 'good girl' heroines of the silent screen were often figuratively, or even literally, blind. Blindness in this context signifies a perfect absence of desire, allowing the look of the male protagonist to regard the woman at the requisite safe distance necessary to the voyeur's pleasure, with no danger that she will return that look and in so doing express desires of her own."[17]

In other words, the adult Sweet Innocents are asexual yet are still subject to desiring/controlling looks from males within the movie's diegetic space as well as outside it. Not only does this reinforce the notion that women are perpetual children whose fate must be controlled by men (it is no accident that paternalistic figures do virtually all the curing in these early disability dramas) but it also raises what for some is a tantalizingly verboten topic: treating physically disabled people as objects of sexual desire. "All Freaks are perceived to one degree or another as erotic," wrote Leslie Fiedler. "Indeed, abnormality arouses in some 'normal' beholders a temptation to go beyond looking to *knowing* in the full carnal sense the ultimate other. That desire is itself felt as freaky, however, since it implies not only a longing for degradation but a dream of breaching the last taboo against miscegenation."[18]

Such a desire may also help explain the appeal of the Obsessive Avenger, a type that clearly suggests "diseased lusts" and that readily evokes the term "monster" and all larger-than-life appetites related thereto. Robert Bogdan and his associates noted in 1982 that "monster" was the standard medical term for a person with a deformity or disability not so long ago, and an understanding of the word's origins may well be the key to understanding the forces behind the Obsessive Avenger stereotype. Howard Chua-Eoan provided a succinct discussion of the term in an essay titled "The Uses of Monsters" in which he noted that etymologically "the word has few frills. It is related to *demonstrate* and to *remonstrate*, and ultimately comes from the Latin *monstrum*, an omen portending the will of the gods, which is itself linked to the verb *monere*, to warn. If a city sinned against heaven, heaven sent it a monster. . . . Monsters, therefore, were created to teach lessons. And they can still be pedagogical—even in an age that no longer believes in the gods or their messengers."[19]

Call him Cronk or Blizzard, Hook or Quasimodo, Dead Legs or Alonzo, the monstrous Obsessive Avenger represents above all else a warning issued by a major media institution on behalf of the dominant culture, and that warning is readily interpretable in terms of the classic Oedipal scenario. Consider the more salient aspects of this mythic structure so central to the maintenance of phallocentric society: under the threat of castration from the Father, the male child resolves his Oedipal crisis by repressing his desire for the Mother (whom he views as a castrated Other) and imitating the Father through introjection. He thus assumes a traditional male identity and, on a micro level, contributes to the continuation of patriarchal society. Films that feature Obsessive Avengers show what happens if the male refuses to control his desire for the Mother (and thereby bucks the patriarchal system) and is symbolically castrated. Disempowered and filled with revenge, he becomes a "monster" in his idiosyncratic quest to regain the phallus, and, since Oedipal transgressions seldom go unpunished, he almost always perishes. Viewed from this perspective, the warning posed in these tales is clear: males must resolve the Oedipal crisis in the "usual" way by repressing their sexual interest in the Mother under threat of castration from the Father and then identifying with that authority figure (and thus do their part to maintain the patriarchal order), or destruction inevitably follows.

For all their apparent differences, disabled male characters—particularly Obsessive Avengers—and female characters of either status have been constructed with a similar general purpose in mind: representing some force that able-bodied males find threatening, they are objectified, fetishized Others to be gazed at. Linda Williams, who as noted earlier observed only a minimal difference among objects of desire and horror as viewed by the male spectator, argued further that "the monster's power is one of sexual difference from the normal male. In this difference he is remarkably like the woman in the eyes of the traumatized male: a biological freak with impossible and threatening appetites that suggest a frightening potency precisely where the normal male would perceive a lack." Williams concluded by suggesting that the implied potency of the monster should perhaps "not be interpreted as an eruption of the normally repressed animal sexuality of the civilized male (the monster as double for the male viewer and characters in the film), but as the feared power and potency of a different kind of sexuality (the monster as double for the women)."[20]

Innocents and Avengers were a conspicuous part of the Hollywood norm during the medium's first four decades, but they began fading during the late 1930s and thereafter when a wave of movies featuring Civilian Superstars and refined Noble Warriors signaled the commencement of a second stage of physical disability depictions. The crude stereotypes were giving way to images of disabled people, mostly males, who frequently undergo rehabilitation, and, significantly, filmmakers were inscribing them with a heroic sense. Since the films containing these new images were essentially revised re-enactments of the Oedipal scenario, they embodied what for Hollywood was initially a paradoxical construct: symbolically castrated, "femininized" males simultaneously imbued with the heavily masculinized notion of heroism.

Film theorist Kaja Silverman explored this apparent contradiction in her article "Historical Trauma and Male Subjectivity." Paying particular attention to *The*

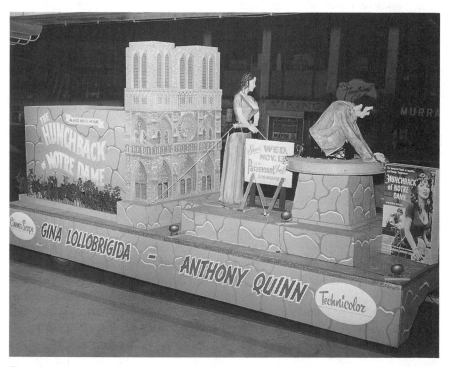

Fetishization of a different sort: the attributes of Esmeralda and Quasi-modo on display in a promotion for the 1957 version of The Hunchback of Notre Dame.

Best Years of Our Lives, a film she claimed "makes no effort to align male subjectivity with phallic values," Silverman argued that filmmakers were relinquishing traditional male points of view and indeed were representing males and their perspectives more like "women" than "men." Her comments in particular on the Homer Parrish character of *Best Years* echo Williams's observations on the similarity of women and male "monsters" in the movies: "Because Homer's lack is localized at the level of the body, and because it manifests itself in the guise of stunted limbs and physical helplessness, it also situates him in the position usually reserved for the female subject within classical cinema. Not only is he the object of a probing social gaze, obliged to account for his appearance to strangers at drugstore counters, but his undressing becomes the occasion for an intense erotic investment."[21]

Silverman invoked Freud's notion of a psychical "protective shield" as a means of explaining this general phenomenon. She suggested that a society develops myths as a means of defending itself from external forces, a process akin to a human psyche's development of a protective shield. Yet from time to time outside forces such as wars do rupture the shield, throwing the society into turmoil. "When this happens," wrote Silverman, "the social formation and its subjects are flooded with excitations which can neither be ignored nor assimilated, and which are conducive of a profound unpleasure." Such severe disruptions throw into question a society's myths, she argued, and a conspicuous symptom of the "major rifts between the dominant fiction and the larger social formation" that emerge is the erosion of sexual difference.[22]

Silverman's analysis, however, provides only a partial answer. Taking her observations a step further, we might argue that moviemakers felt the need to remasculinize the disabled veterans to show that patriarchal values had not been permanently weakened. In an earlier age, they would no doubt have resorted to miracle cures as a way of enabling the "good" disabled men to regain their phallic powers (even in *Pride of the Marines*, a relatively late film, this idea is implicit), but by the WW II years most had begun to realize that this approach was seldom viable any longer and started developing different strategies.

MGM's Mervyn LeRoy, Dalton Trumbo, and their colleagues attempted something relatively new in their wartime film *Thirty Seconds Over Tokyo*. The movie hints several times that Ted Lawson's loss of a leg is tantamount to sexual disempowerment (when friends awaken the newly injured Ted from a brief flashback that visualizes his wedding day, for example, he immediately shouts "Don't let them cut my leg off" several times), but it also shows his wife Ellen accepting everything about her now-disabled husband without question or remorse. Moments from the film's concluding scene—Ted and Ellen gazing lovingly at one another in a hospital corridor with the U.S. capitol dome clearly visible through a window behind him, Ted falling while trying to rise from his wheelchair—reinforce one of *Thirty Seconds Over Tokyo*'s more prominent messages: that Ellen's proper role is to act as a "repaternalizing" agent for her heroized, femininized husband.

Aware that the American people had long accepted Franklin Roosevelt as the country's prime paternalistic figure despite his use of a wheelchair, Dore Schary and his RKO associates provided a more striking example with their early postwar film *Till the End of Time*. In an action that on a subtextual level brims with incestuous intimations, the mother of the disabled veteran Perry Kincheloe remasculinizes her son by explicitly encouraging him to identify with the disabled father-figure of FDR. The resulting introjection is strikingly successful; not only does Perry avoid using his wheelchair for the rest of the film (his prostheses, hidden under his pants legs, help create the impression of a new wholeness) but he also punches out a few neo-fascists during a bar brawl.

Perhaps taking *Thirty Seconds* and *Till the End of Time* as their cue, subsequent filmmakers concerned with issues of male disability continued to subvert women's sexuality by suturing the classic madonna/whore dichotomy. In other words, movies such as *Best Years*, *The Men*, and *Bright Victory* demand that their female figures take on the duel role of mother-like nurturers and sexual partners for the disabled men. Asked to accommodate their men (and thus accept symbolic male castration), they must repress their sexual desires. This message, presented after World War I to some extent (the Renée Adorée character Melisande of *The Big Parade* is perhaps the most conspicuous madonna/whore combination of the time), loomed particularly large after World War II, a time when women had made significant political gains and then were called on to support and be subordinate to the returning males.

If the moviemakers did not provide female figures to accomplish this remasculinization, they at the very least offered female-like environments that allow the males to engage in heroic acts (e.g., the hostile landscape that John Macreedy penetrates in *Bad Day at Black Rock*, the womb-like hospital that continuously envelopes Leonard Gillespie in the Dr. Kildare films). *The Wings of Eagles*, in particular, strongly suggests the interchangeability of women and such environments (in this case, the maternal venue of the navy, the sea) in the resexualization process. After Pearl Harbor, Spig Wead tells his wife Min he will try to find out if the navy will have him in some capacity. "If they don't have you, Spig, I will," she says, to which he responds, "That's all I need." The navy does accept him, however, and as Spig heads into conflict on board a naval aircraft carrier, a longtime male friend who arguably represents the navy (if not part of a gay subtext) says to him, "Don't worry, I'll make a man out of you again."

While femininized men were being restored to wholeness and paternalistic authority at the expense of female sexuality or by means of associated imagery, their disabled female counterparts were receiving a more restricted treatment through the so-called "woman's film" then on the rise. A type of film designed by the movie industry for female consumption, the woman's film often centers on a female protagonist who is or becomes disabled or ill. Representatives of this genre, including *Johnny Belinda* and later works such as *The Glass Menagerie* and

Magnificent Obsession (all starring Jane Wyman, Hollywood's favorite "woman's disabled woman"), position spectators to view the characters not as erotic objects but as bearers of symptoms. As Mary Ann Doane has noted: "In the 'woman's film,' the erotic gaze becomes the medical gaze. The female body is located not so much as spectacle but as an element in the discourse of medicine, a manuscript to be read for the symptoms which betray her story, her identity. Hence the need, in these films, for the figure of the doctor as reader or interpreter, as the site of a knowledge which dominates and controls female subjectivity." [23] As a recipient of this low-level diagnostic seeing in which the spectators share the (typically male) physician's look, the female body has once again become the object of attention and control.

In a limited way, the treatment of women in these movies resembles that of the disabled war veterans; the latter, too, are subject to a probing gaze, though from both male and female spectators. The main difference, however, is that the males are remasculinized at the expense of women's sexuality or by penetrating gyne-comorphous environments en route to performing heroic deeds, while the females' physical/sexual restoration, if it occurs at all, is rigorously monitored and controlled by patriarchal authorities (male doctors or God). Disabled figures of either gender may become "de-fetishized" somewhat through these processes, but never completely so.

This same kind of dichotomy—"good" men are remasculinized, women are reduced to a set of symptoms—also characterizes the new round of Civilian Superstar films that appeared during the postwar era. Though these movies on a superficial level exhibit a sense of evenhandedness as to sex-based issues (i.e., the Superstar stereotype, unlike many others, is not tied to a specific gender), the women once again struggle to overcome their asexuality as their male "betters" preside over them while the men continue to pursue their Oedipal quest; embittered at first, they eventually become resexualized on their way to re-achieving superstardom. Monty Stratton's wife Ethel becomes pregnant shortly after remasculinizing him in *The Stratton Story*, for example, while in *Sincerely Yours* a lip-reading coach actually tells Tony Warrin he can now have a family (a standard Hollywood euphemism for having sex) after he has learned that particular reception process. His later undisabling operation would only improve his sexual prowess, no doubt.

The Oedipal structure continued to serve as the basis for movies as the industry began moving into a third phase of disability depictions, a phase that continues through today. As the disability-rights movement gathered momentum during the 1960s and 1970s and the country began grappling with the legacies of the Vietnam War, moviemakers began constructing more incidental treatments of physical disability. Though vestiges of the old stereotypes continued to find their way into the movies, filmmakers treated disability less like an all-defining and all-consuming factor and more like one of an array of human attributes. Jean

Seligmann's comments on *Born on the Fourth of July* and *My Left Foot*, two exemplars from the late 1980s, suggest this point: "Though very different from each other, the two new movies—and their success at the box office—seem to reflect new societal attitudes toward the disabled. The handicapped have come out of the closet, and audiences who might once have shunned movies that deal with catheters and drooling are now flocking to these. Viewers realize that such films are not *about* handicaps, but about the strength of character that allows two men to move beyond their physical limitations and get on with life."[24]

Despite the relative progressiveness of a number of these films (most notably, the construction of physically disabled characters as sexually active beings), Oedipal drama continued to serve as a major structuring factor for them and their more regressive and stereotype-prone counterparts, as a number of scholars have observed. Michael Selig made a convincing case for regarding *Coming Home* primarily as an Oedipal drama, its femininized appeal and antiwar stance notwithstanding, for instance, while Andrew Gordon offered a thorough examination of similar considerations in the "Star Wars" trilogy. Movies continued to depend heavily on the idea of women acting as remasculinizing agents to facilitate the protagonists' Oedipal adventures, particularly those featuring embittered veterans: *Coming Home*, *Born on the Fourth of July*, *Scent of a Woman*, and *Cutter's Way*, if in an obscured way in the case of the latter film. (The death of Alex's wife in a suspicious blaze propels him into his quest, and along the way he's assisted by a male able-bodied buddy against whom he had once hurled the epithet, "girl.") Like some of the post–World War II films, however, the newer movies did not always insist that women assume that function. As Carrie Rickey observed of the main female figure of *Inside Moves*, for example, "It's Louise who has to tearfully admit that for her the thought of sex with Roary is repulsive—a far cry from the Cathy O'Donnell saccharine acceptance of her war victim in *Best Years of Our Lives*." Instead, their rites-of-passage typically involved female-like environments akin to those found in *Bad Day at Black Rock* and *The Wings of Eagles* (representatives of the High-Tech Guru stereotype, for example, are almost exclusively visualized inside womb-like electronic dens) or, in the case of movies bearing the Techno Marvel image, advancements in science and technology in the form of highly potent prostheses.[25]

Though the Oedipal crisis cannot entirely account for the construction of movie images of physical disability, there is little question that the Cinema of Isolation—good films, bad, and everything in between—is heavily indebted to it. Movies such as *Coming Home*, *Cutter's Way*, *Born on the Fourth of July*, and going as far back as *The Sea Beast* and its 1930 remake are somewhat subversive in that their supposedly disempowered protagonists struggle against figures representing patriarchal authority and meet with success (a bittersweet success, in the case of *Cutter's Way*—the paternalistic figure dies but so does he), but nevertheless they still follow the classic pattern or at least conspicuous elements thereof.

Though the Cinema of Isolation has hinged so strongly on this retrograde male fantasy, it need not continue to do so. The Oedipal framework remains a formidable challenge to moviemakers wishing to represent the physically disabled experience with some measure of equity, but it is not insurmountable. If moviemakers, disabled and able-bodied alike, can break away from this narrative structure that has served as the foundation for the whole of mainstream narrative media (and indeed the whole of patriarchal society) and pursue alternative strategies for telling their stories, we may at long last see some real progress.

notes

Abbreviations

AFF	American Film Foundation, Santa Monica, California
Annals	*The Annals of the American Academy of Political and Social Science*
BR	Billy Rose Theatre Collection, Performing Arts Research Center, New York Public Library at Lincoln Center, New York City
ENHS	Edison National Historic Site, West Orange, New Jersey
FARC	Federal Archives and Records Center, Bayonne, New Jersey
FC	Frank Capra Collection, Wesleyan University Cinema Archives, Middletown, Connecticut
LACM	Los Angeles County Museum of Natural History
LAT	*Los Angeles Times*
LC	Library of Congress, Washington, D.C.
MH	Margaret Herrick Library, Academy of Motion Pictures Arts and Sciences, Los Angeles, California
MOMA	Museum of Modern Art, New York City
MPC	*Motion Picture Classic*
MPW	*Moving Picture World*
NYT	*New York Times*
RCB	*Rehabilitation Counseling Bulletin*

Preface and Acknowledgments

1 / Joseph Stubbins, "The Politics of Disability," in *Attitudes Toward Persons with Disabilities*, ed. Harold E. Yuker (New York: Springer, 1988), p. 22; E. Keith Byrd and Randolph B. Pipes, "Feature Films and Disability," *Journal of Rehabilitation* 47, no. 1 (Jan.–Mar. 1981): 80.

2 / Mary Ann Doane, Patricia Mellencamp, and Linda Williams, "Feminist Film Criticism: An Introduction," in *Re-vision: Essays in Feminist Film Criticism*, eds. Mary Ann Doane, Patricia Mellencamp, and Linda Williams (Frederick, Md.: University Publications of America, 1984), p. 6; Robert C. Allen and Douglas Gomery, *Film History: Theory and Practice* (New York: Alfred A. Knopf, 1985), p. 158.

3 / See Kovic's comments in Robert Seidenberg, "To Hell and Back," *American Film*, Jan. 1990, p. 56. See also E. Ann Kaplan, "Popular Culture, Politics, and the Canon: Cultural Literacy in the Postmodern Age," in *Cultural Power/Cultural Literacy*, ed. Bonnie Braendlin (Tallahassee: Florida State University Press, 1991), pp. 26–27.

4 / Kaplan, "Popular Culture," p. 20.

5 / Films that confront cerebral palsy and epilepsy constitute only a small minority of the works discussed in this book. As far as the majority of Hollywood filmmakers are concerned, they remain "invisible" disabling circumstances.

6 / For a study of how mainstream moviemakers have dealt with a major disabling disease—alcoholism—see Norman K. Denzin, *Hollywood Shot by Shot: Alcoholism in American Cinema* (Hawthorne, N.Y.: Aldine de Gruyter, 1991). Several works deal with the depiction of physical disability through other visual media. In addition to their obvious relevance to the subject matter at hand, *Hollywood Speaks: Deafness and the Film Entertainment Industry* (Urbana: University of Illinois Press, 1988) by John S. Schuchman and *Disability Drama in Television and Film* (Jefferson, N.C.: McFarland, 1988) by Lauri E.

Klobas also contain important discussions of television. For a study of the relationship between disability and still photography, see David Hevey, *The Creatures Time Forgot: Photography and Disability Imagery* (New York: Routledge, 1992).

7 / An overview of the language issue may be found in Andrew J. Grant and Frank G. Bowe, "Watch Your Language!," in *Handicapped Funding Directory*, 7th ed., ed. Richard M. Eckstein (Margate, Fla.: Research Grant Guides, 1990), pp. 5–7.

8 / For discussions of deaf culture, see Harlan Lane, *When the Mind Hears: A History of the Deaf* (New York: Random House, 1984); Barbara D. Hardaway, "Deafness: Explorations into a Community and Its Culture," Eastern Communication Association convention, Philadelphia, Mar. 1984; and Oliver Sacks, *Seeing Voices: A Journey into the World of the Deaf* (Berkeley: University of California Press, 1989). Amy M. Hamburger, "The Cripple and His Place in the Community," *Annals* 77, no. 166 (May 1918): 39.

9 / A commonly accepted label for prejudice or discrimination against people based on perceptions of their abilities has yet to emerge. "Handicappism" has its users but is too strongly tied to language of the past to be fully satisfactory. A more acceptable and precise expression might be "ability-ism," but it has a jarring, jerry-built quality. The term I have chosen for this book is the less awkward but still imperfect "ableism."

Introduction / Politics, Movies, and Physical Disability

1 / Leonard Quart and Albert Auster, "The Wounded Vet in Post-War Film," *Social Policy* 13, no. 2 (Fall 1982): 25.

2 / The fact that deaf audiences have long appreciated silent-era movies and subtitled foreign-language films is, I think, almost entirely incidental to the development of mainstream movie technology. For discussions of the descriptive services that enable visually impaired spectators to appreciate movies and TV programming more fully, see Francesca Riviere, "Movies for the Blind: Coppola and Frazier," *Premiere*, Dec. 1989, p. 68; and Steve Kline, "Television for the Blind," *TV Guide*, 13 June 1992, pp. 18–19.

3 / Moviemakers are hardly different from their literary predecessors on the general topic of perspectives. As Leslie Fiedler has observed, only a handful of pre–1900 writers (principally Victor Hugo and Mark Twain) ever constructed fiction that incorporated a disabled person's point of view. See Leslie A. Fiedler, *Freaks: Myths and Images of the Secret Self* (New York: Simon and Schuster, 1978), pp. 270–271.

4 / Grant and Bowe, "Watch Your Language!," p. 6; Paul K. Longmore, "Screening Stereotypes: Images of Disabled People," *Social Policy* 16, no. 1 (Summer 1985): 33.

5 / John J. McDermott, *Streams of Experience: Reflections on the History and Philosophy of American Culture* (Amherst: University of Massachusetts Press, 1986), p. 215.

6 / Stubbins, "Politics of Disability," p. 23; Gerald Mast and Bruce F. Kawin, *A Short History of the Movies*, 5th ed. (New York: Macmillan, 1992), p. 5.

7 / Klobas, *Disability Drama*, pp. xi–xii; Schuchman, *Hollywood Speaks*, p. ix.

8 / Longmore, "Screening Stereotypes," p. 34.

9 / *Variety*, 14 Oct. 1925, p. 43; Jim Gullo, "Oscaring the Handicaps," *Premiere*, Apr. 1991, p. 36. All the directors cited had impaired vision except Garnett, who suffered a severe leg injury during a World War I naval aviation accident, and Wyler, whose World War II service left him with significant hearing loss.

10 / Claire H. Liachowitz, *Disability as a Social Construct: Legislative Roots* (Philadelphia: University of Pennsylvania Press, 1988), p. 1.

11 / Syd Field, *Screenplay: The Foundations of Screenwriting*, expanded ed. (New York: Dell, 1982), p. 27. A similarly regressive view on physical disability may be found in

Ben Brady and Lance Lee, *The Understructure of Writing for Film and Television* (Austin: University of Texas Press, 1988), pp. 11–12.

12 / George Henderson and Willie V. Bryan, *Psychosocial Aspects of Disability* (Springfield, Ill.: Charles C. Thomas, 1984), p. 3. Fiedler's distinctions, murky at best, center around his belief that people with genetic disorders, "altered by forces we do not quite understand," have an unmatched awe-inspiring mystery about them. See Fiedler, *Freaks*, pp. 23–24.

13 / Fiedler, *Freaks*, pp. 251, 16; Linda Williams, "When the Woman Looks," in *Feminist Film Criticism*, ed. Doane, Mellencamp, and Williams, p. 88.

14 / Sigmund Freud, "The Uncanny," in *The Standard Edition of the Complete Works of Sigmund Freud*, Vol. 17 (1917–1919): *An Infantile Neurosis and Other Works*, ed. James Strachey (London: Hogarth Press, 1955), p. 231. See also Freud's "Some Points in a Comparative Study of Organic and Hysterical Paralysis" (1893) reprinted in his *Collected Papers*, Vol. 1, ed. Joan Reviere (New York: Basic Books, 1959), pp. 42–58.

15 / Henderson and Bryan, *Psychosocial Aspects*, pp. 4–5. See also Marsha Saxton, "Born and Unborn: The Implications of Reproductive Technologies for People with Disabilities," in *Test-Tube Women: What Future for Motherhood?*, eds. Rita Arditti, Renate Duelli Klein, and Shelley Minden (London: Pandora Press, 1984), pp. 302–303.

16 / For historical accounts of society's response to disabled veterans from earliest times through World War I, see Edward T. Devine, *Disabled Soldiers and Sailors: Pensions and Training*, Carnegie Endowment for International Peace, Preliminary Economic Studies of the War, no. 12 (New York: Oxford University Press, 1919), pp. 19–49; and Liachowitz, *Disability as a Social Construct*, pp. 19–44.

17 / Fiedler, *Freaks*, pp. 279–280; Nancy Weinberg and Carol Sebian, "The Bible and Disability," *RCB* 23, no. 4 (June 1980): 273, 281.

18 / Henderson and Bryan, *Psychosocial Aspects*, p. 8. A chilling reminder that such negative attitudes extended well into the twentieth century may be found in a 1949 article by Leo Alexander on Nazi atrocities against disabled people. Alexander, a physician attached to the Office of the Chief of Counsel for War Crimes in Nuremberg, wrote that "by 1936, extermination of the physically and socially unfit was so openly accepted that its practice was mentioned incidentally in an article published in an official German medical journal." A 1991 documentary film that examines Nazi propaganda promoting the state-mandated mass murder of people with disabilities provides disturbingly vivid corroboration; its narrator states bluntly that "during the Third Reich, some 200,000 mentally and physically disabled people were murdered by deliberate starvation, lethal medication, and toxic gas." See Leo Alexander, "Medical Science Under Dictatorship," *New England Journal of Medicine* 241, no. 2 (14 July 1949): 39ff; and *Selling Murder: The Killing Films of the Third Reich* (1991), a Domino Films production directed by Joanna Mack, written and researched by Michael Burleigh, and produced by Stewart Lansley.

19 / Marchette Chute, *Stories from Shakespeare* (New York: New American Library, 1956), p. 285. Though Chute does not mention it, Shakespeare relied heavily on the work of Tudor historians who clearly sought to vilify the Yorkist king. It's worth noting that a number of scholars have formed a "Richard III Society" with branches on both sides of the Atlantic specifically to undo the centuries' worth of damage done to his reputation. See Laura Blanchard, letter to the editor, *Time*, 13 Jan. 1992, p. 4.

20 / Richard K. Scotch, *From Good Will to Civil Rights: Transforming Federal Disability Policy* (Philadelphia: Temple University Press, 1984), p. 15.

21 / Jeffrey Klenotic, "Public Perception and Federal Policy: A Report on America's Response to Physical Disability," unpublished paper, University of Massachusetts/Amherst, 1990. See also Henderson and Bryan, *Psychosocial Aspects*, p. 7.

22 / Devine, *Disabled Soldiers and Sailors*, pp. 19–49; Scotch, *From Good Will to Civil Rights*, pp. 15–16.

23 / Fiedler, *Freaks*, p. 15; Leonard Kriegel, "The Wolf in the Pit in the Zoo," *Social Policy* 13, no. 2 (Fall 1982): 16–17.

24 / Saxton, "Born and Unborn," p. 303.

25 / Kaoru Yamamoto, "To Be Different," *RCB* 14, no. 3 (Mar. 1971): 186, 182. See also Hanoch Livneh, "On the Origins of Negative Attitudes Toward People with Disabilities," in *The Psychological and Social Impact of Physical Disability*, 2nd ed., eds. Robert P. Marinelli and Arthur E. Dell Orto (New York: Springer, 1984), pp. 167–184; and Roger G. Barker, Beatrice A. Wright, Lee Meyerson, and Mollie R. Gonick, *Adjustment to Physical Handicap and Illness: A Survey of the Social Psychology of Physique and Disability*, rev. ed. (New York: Social Science Research Council, 1953), pp. 76–77.

26 / Irving Kenneth Zola, "Communication Barriers Between 'the Able-Bodied' and 'the Handicapped,'" in *Psychological and Social Impact*, ed. Marinelli and Dell Orto, p. 144; Nancy Weinberg, "Another Perspective: Attitudes of People with Disabilities," in *Attitudes*, ed. Yuker, p. 141. See also Zola's *Missing Pieces: A Chronicle of Living with a Disability* (Philadelphia: Temple University Press, 1982).

27 / For an overview, see Teresa L. Thompson, "'You Can't Play Marbles—You Have a Wooden Hand': Communication with the Handicapped," *Communication Quarterly* 30, no. 2 (Spring 1982): 108. See also Yamamoto, "To Be Different," pp. 180–189.

28 / Longmore, "Screening Stereotypes," p. 32.

29 / Nancy Weinberg, "Modifying Social Stereotypes of the Physically Disabled," *RCB* 22, no. 2 (Dec. 1978): 123. For a compact survey-research study that includes such topics as disability demographics, work-related disabilities, levels of assistance, and medical conditions associated with disability, see *Disability in the United States: A Portrait from National Data*, eds. Susan Thompson-Hoffman and Inez Fitzgerald Storck (New York: Springer, 1991). For a splendid history of the disability rights movement from its origins to the passage and initial implementation of the Americans with Disabilities Act, see Joseph P. Shapiro, *No Pity: People with Disabilities Forging a New Civil Rights Movement* (New York: Times Books, 1993).

1 / Emergence of an Impoverished Image

1 / *NYT*, 29 Nov. 1895, p. 9.

2 / Kemp R. Niver, *Motion Pictures from the Library of Congress Paper Print Collection 1894–1912* (Berkeley: University of California Press, 1967), p. 183. Other descriptions of the film may be found in *Edison Films*, catalog no. 94, Mar. 1900, p. 36, LACM; and *Edison Films Complete Catalog*, no. 105, July 1901, p. 71, ENHS.

3 / For example, see Anthony Slide, *Aspects of American Film History Prior to 1920* (Metuchen, NJ: Scarecrow Press, 1978), p. 63; and Richard Schickel, *D. W. Griffith: An American Life* (New York: Simon and Schuster, 1984), p. 92.

4 / Sources for the Williamson, Hepworth, and Cooper films are Denis Gifford, *The British Film Catalog 1895–1985: A Reference Guide* (New York: Facts on File Publications, 1986), and Rachael Low and Roger Manvell, *The History of the British Film, 1896–1906* (London: George Allen & Unwin, 1948). See also *Complete Catalogue of Lubin's Films*, n.d., p. 45, MH Library.

5 / *Lubin's Films* catalog, Feb. 1906, n.p., MH Library; *MPW*, 1 June 1907, p. 203. The Lubin catalog also contains four stills from the film.

6 / Henri Bergson, "Laughter" (1900), reprinted in *Comedy*, ed. Wylie Sypher (Garden City, N.Y.: Doubleday, 1956), p. 93; Maurice Bardèche and Robert Brasillach, *The History of Motion Pictures*, trans. and ed. Iris Barry (New York: W. W. Norton, 1938), p. 87; Conlin cited in *NYT*, 21 Feb. 1896, p. 9; *NYT*, 23 Feb. 1896, p. 4.

7 / Mack Sennett, "The Psychology of Film Comedy," *MPC*, Nov. 1918, p. 37.

8 / Terry Ramsaye, *A Million and One Nights: A History of the Motion Picture* (New York: Simon and Schuster, 1926), pp. 324, 397; *American Mutoscope and Biograph Co. Picture Catalogue*, Nov. 1902, p. 225, MOMA. Three stills from the film are reproduced in an untitled, undated, and unpaginated Biograph photo catalog, vol. 4, film nos. 1503–2002, MOMA, and the film also exists in a reconstructed form in the LC paper print collection. Sources conflict on the film's length.

9 / Linda Arvidson Griffith, *When the Movies Were Young* (New York: Benjamin Blom, 1968; reprint of 1925 edition), p. 37; Ramsaye, *A Million and One Nights*, p. 422. For a more detailed description of this early chase film, see *Kleine Optical Co. Catalogue*, Nov. 1905, p. 238, as cited in George C. Pratt, *Spellbound in Darkness: A History of the Silent Film*, rev. ed. (Greenwich, Conn.: New York Graphic Society, 1973), p. 42.

10 / *American Mutoscope and Biograph Co. Bulletin*, no. 36, 26 Oct. 1904, n.p., ENHS. See also Joyce E. Jesionowski, *Thinking in Pictures: Dramatic Structure in D. W. Griffith's Biograph Films* (Berkeley: University of California Press, 1987), pp. 15, 61.

11 / See the Biograph catalog, Nov. 1902, p. 218, MOMA; *MPW*, 20 Mar. 1907, p. 62.

12 / *NYT*, 17 Jan. 1895, p. 2, and 23 Jan. 1896, p. 16; *MPW*, 10 Aug. 1907, p. 363.

13 / *MPW*, 22 June 1907, p. 253, and 11 Sept. 1909, p. 353; Lubin catalog, 26 Aug. 1909, n.p., MH Library; Ramsaye, *A Million and One Nights*, p. 427; *MPW*, 28 Sept. 1907, p. 473.

14 / *MPW*, 22 June 1907, p. 253. Another film in this tradition was Vitagraph's *The Marathon Craze* (1909), about a group of neighbors who catch the title fever and engage in long-distance running. Much to the chagrin of the able-bodied runners (and, presumably, to the delight of ableist audiences looking for a laugh), "a crippled old grandmother on crutches" wins the race. See *MPW*, 8 May 1909, p. 595.

15 / *MPW*, 29 May 1909, p. 723, and 5 June 1909, p. 753.

16 / *MPW*, 18 Apr. 1908, p. 352, and 3 Apr. 1909, p. 403.

17 / Cited in Bardèche and Brasillach, *History of Motion Pictures*, p. 13.

18 / The entire anecdote may be found in Frederick A. Talbot, *Moving Pictures: How They Are Made and Worked* (Philadelphia: J. B. Lippincott, 1914), pp. 211–213.

19 / *MPW*, 29 Feb. 1908, p. 172; *Variety*, 21 Nov. 1908, p. 13.

20 / *MPW*, 22 Jan. 1910, p. 103.

21 / *MPW*, 16 Apr. 1910, p. 613; *Variety*, 23 Apr. 1910, p. 16.

22 / The letter and Sargent's comments appear in Epes Winthrop Sargent, "The Photoplaywright," *MPW*, 29 Nov. 1913, p. 1001.

23 / "The Nickelodeons," *Variety*, 14 Dec. 1907, p. 33.

24 / *MPW*, 8 June 1907, p. 220.

25 / *MPW*, 21 Mar. 1908, p. 246. Envious of the financial rewards this film novelty gained for the Urban Trading Company and its American distributor George Kleine, the ever-imitative Lubin Company reeled off a markedly similar tune with *The Blind Musician* (1909), a six-scene film about a street-corner violinist whose young daughter, his daily guide to his performance venues, is struck and fatally injured by a car. The final graveside scene: "He bends down and kisses the stone. Then he plays the violin. Suddenly he reels, throws up his hands and falls dead over the little grave of the one he loved best." Also in 1909, the Chicago Film Exchange released an independently (and anonymously) produced film called *Blind Man's Daughter*. Judging from a description offered in *Moving Picture*

World, it is either a heavily plagiarized version of *His Daughter's Voice* or indeed the same film with a different title and distributor. See *MPW*, 30 Jan. 1909, p. 126; Lubin catalog, 4 Feb. 1909, n.p., MH Library; and *MPW*, 5 June 1909, p. 769.

26 / Charlene P. DeLoach, Ronnie D. Wilkins, and Guy W. Walker, *Independent Living: Philosophy, Process, and Services* (Baltimore, Md.: University Park Press, 1983), p. 15; Howard R. Heydon, "The Supremacy of the Spirit," *Annals* 80, no. 169 (Nov. 1918): 51. For a summary of the development of workers' compensation laws during this time, see James Weinstein, *The Corporate Ideal in the Liberal State: 1900–1918* (Boston: Beacon Press, 1968), pp. 40–61.

27 / James Bordley, "The Blind as Industrial Workers," *Annals* 80, no. 169 (Nov. 1918): 104.

28 / *MPW*, 20 June 1908, p. 534, and 3 Oct. 1908, p. 265.

29 / Longmore, "Screening Stereotypes," p. 32.

30 / *MPW*, 22 Feb. 1908, pp. 145–146; *Variety*, 29 Feb. 1908, p. 12.

31 / Curtis E. Lakeman, "The After-Care of Our Disabled Soldiers and Sailors," *Annals* 79, no. 168 (Sept. 1918): 121. See also Devine, *Disabled Soldiers and Sailors*, pp. 34–35, 47.

32 / *MPW*, 23 May 1908, p. 465, and 1 May 1909, p. 554.

33 / Though the founding of the Paris-based Film d'Art Company in 1908 officially marked the start of the movement, the interest in producing such films was hardly limited to one company or even one country. In France alone, no less than six other companies or programs within companies dedicated to producing such films were established. In addition to the output of the U.S.'s Vitagraph noted in the text, Italy's Ambrosio Company immediately started competing with the French concerns in 1908 by producing *The Last Days of Pompeii*, an adaptation of the Bulwer-Lytton novel directed by Luigi Mazzi and distributed by the Paris-based Raleigh & Robert Company that had among its characters the doomed blind woman Nydia. See Bardèche and Brasillach, *History of Motion Pictures*, pp. 43–44, 50; and *MPW*, 1 May 1909, p. 555.

34 / Bardèche and Brasillach, *History of Motion Pictures*, pp. 43, 46. The quote from the unnamed journal appears on p. 47.

35 / Joanmarie Kalter, "The Disabled Get More TV Exposure, but There's Still Too Much Stereotyping," *TV Guide*, 31 May 1986, p. 42.

36 / Robert Hamilton Ball, "Shakespeare in One Reel," *The Quarterly of Film, Radio, and Television* 8 (1953–54): 147; Ramsaye, *A Million and One Nights*, p. 442; Richard L. Stromgren, "The Moving Picture World of W. Stephen Bush," *Film History* 2 (1988): 17.

37 / Rachael Low, *The History of the British Film, 1906–1914* (London: George Allen & Unwin, 1949), pp. 225, 228. Her analysis and harsh criticism of the Benson *Richard III*, illustrated with nine stills from the film, appear on pp. 224–228. Richard of course plays a prominent role in Harrison Ainsworth's *The Tower of London*, the first movie version of which appeared in 1909. By coincidence, it was the final film of James Williamson, the British director and producer who early in his career created *The Fraudulent Beggars*, noted in the text.

38 / Kriegel, "The Wolf in the Pit," p. 18.

39 / Robert A. Nowlan and Gwendolyn Wright Nowlan, *Cinema Sequels and Remakes, 1903–1987* (Jefferson, N.C.: McFarland, 1989), p. 149; *MPW*, 5 Dec. 1908, pp. 458–459, and 1 Feb. 1908, p. 83; Low, *History of the British Film*, pp. 189, 277, 292; and Lubin catalog, Mar. 1908, n.p., MH Library. A photo from the 1908 production faces p. 201 of Talbot. The Zenith three-reeler was known simply as *Scrooge*.

40 / *MPW*, 12 Dec. 1908, p. 484.

41 / *MPW*, 4 Jan. 1908, p. 11.

42 / Ibid., p. 11–12. The same description also appears in Selig Polyscope's catalog supplement no. 75, Dec. 1907, n.p., MH Library.

43 / Edward Wagenknecht, *The Movies in the Age of Innocence* (Norman: University of Oklahoma Press, 1962), p. 51; *MPW*, 23 Sept. 1911, pp. 869–870.

44 / Teresa E. Levitin, "Deviants as Active Participants in the Labeling Process: The Visibly Handicapped," *Social Problems* 22, no. 4 (Apr. 1975): 549.

45 / *MPW*, 22 May 1909, p. 683, and 29 May 1909, p. 713. Information on the multi-part *Passion Play* remains sketchy at best. According to an 1899 catalog of the F. M. Prescott company, one of the film's twenty-eight episodes—"Christ Healing the Sick"—showed him curing a crutch-using man and a blind man in record time. (The episode was available in optional lengths of fifty seconds and about a minute and a half.) It's not clear, however, if *Passion Play* was made by Prescott, Edison, or some other enterprise. The Lubin Company listed an identical film in one of its own catalogs (even down to episode titles and descriptions, lifted verbatim out of the Prescott publication) but given that company's reputation for film pirating it was probably a replica. Muddying the waters further, neither *Passion Play* nor any of its installments appears in the LC copyright registration records. For descriptions of "Christ Healing the Sick," see F. M. Prescott Co. *Catalogue of New Films*, 1899, p. 41, FARC; and *Complete Catalogue of Lubin's Films*, n.d., p. 4, MH Library.

46 / *MPW*, 29 Aug. 1908, p. 164.

47 / Iris Barry, *D. W. Griffith: American Film Master*, with an annotated list of films by Eileen Bowser (New York: MOMA, 1965), p. 9; Ramsaye, *A Million and One Nights*, p. 455; "McCutcheon Rejoins Old Firm," *Variety*, 28 Jan. 1908, p. 11; Benjamin B. Hampton, *A History of the Movies* (New York: Covici, Friede, 1931), p. 40.

48 / D. W. Griffith, *A Fool and a Girl* manuscript, pp. 7, 18, MOMA.

49 / Cited in *Biograph Bulletins, 1908–1912*, comp. Eileen Bowser (New York: Octagon Books, 1973), p. 10.

50 / *MPW*, 6 Mar. 1909, p. 278, and 13 Mar. 1909, p. 304. Credits for Griffith's Biograph films may be found in Cooper C. Graham, Steven Higgins, Elaine Mancini, and João Luiz Vieira, *D. W. Griffith and the Biograph Company*, Filmmakers no. 10 (Metuchen, N.J.: Scarecrow Press, 1985).

51 / *MPW*, 6 Mar. 1909, p. 278, and 13 Mar. 1909, p. 304.

52 / Ibid.

53 / Schickel, *D. W. Griffith*, p. 42; Martin T. Williams, *Griffith: First Artist of the Movies* (New York: Oxford University Press, 1980), p. 5; Kalton C. Lahue and Terry Brewer, *Kops and Custards: The Legend of Keystone Films* (Norman: University of Oklahoma Press, 1968), p. 11.

54 / Cited in *Biograph Bulletins*, p. 96; *New York Dramatic Mirror*, 19 June 1909, p. 16; Kemp R. Niver, *D. W. Griffith, His Biograph Films in Perspective* (Los Angeles: Kemp R. Niver, 1974), p. 87.

55 / Robert M. Henderson, *D. W. Griffith: The Years at Biograph* (New York: Farrar, Straus and Giroux, 1970), p. 87; *MPW*, 27 Nov. 1909, p. 757; Klobas, *Disability Drama*, pp. xii–xiii and passim.

56 / Laura Mulvey, "Visual Pleasure and Narrative Cinema," *Screen* 16, no. 3 (Autumn 1975): 17.

57 / Jesionowski, *Thinking in Pictures*, pp. 38–41.

58 / MPPC films that dealt with the women's suffrage movement, for example, revealed similar sentiments; virtually without exception, they lampooned or belittled the women's struggle for social change. See Martin F. Norden, "'A Good Travesty Upon the Suffragette Movement': Women's Suffrage Films as Genre," *Journal of Popular Film & Television* 13, no. 3 (Winter 1986): 171–177.

59 / "Weekly Comments on the Shows," *MPW*, 20 Mar. 1909, p. 331.

60 / *MPW*, 17 Apr. 1909, p. 476.

2 / The Misbegotten Multi-Reelers

1 / Historians and critics agree that, except for its length and Bernhardt's presence, *Queen Elizabeth* is hardly a commendable film. Despite its four reels, the film has only twelve shots (by comparison, a contemporary Griffith one-reeler had sixty-eight shots), none of which were close-ups or medium shots. For a brief analysis of *Queen Elizabeth*, see Mast and Kawin, *A Short History*, pp. 46–47. An account of Bernhardt's disablement may be found in Joanna Richardson, *Sarah Bernhardt and Her World* (London: Weidenfeld and Nicolson, 1977), pp. 185 and 197–205.

2 / Uno Asplund, *Chaplin's Films: A Filmography*, trans. Paul Britten Austin (Newton Abbott, U.K.: David & Charles, 1973), p. 57. For further discussion of this film, see Martin F. Norden, "Reel Wheels: The Role of Wheelchairs in American Movies," in *Beyond the Stars III: The Material World in American Popular Film*, eds. Paul Loukides and Linda K. Fuller (Bowling Green, Ohio: Bowling Green State University Popular Press, 1993), pp. 188–189.

3 / Schickel, *D. W. Griffith*, p. 92; Hamburger, "The Cripple and His Place," p. 37.

4 / Several sources indicate that *Chelsea 7750* and *An Hour Before Dawn* were also released in a three-reel version. For reviews, see *MPW*, 27 Sept. 1913, p. 1398, and 25 Oct. 1913, p. 360; and *Variety*, 3 Apr. 1914, p. 21.

5 / *MPW*, 2 Sept. 1913, p. 1411. See also *MPW*, 12 Apr. 1913, p. 188, and 27 Sept. 1913, p. 1397.

6 / *MPW*, 29 Nov. 1913, p. 1017.

7 / One of the exceedingly few films that suggested "intermarriage" was *The Heritage of Hate* (1916), a Universal production that showed an able-bodied woman and a man with a distorted spine overcoming mutual misunderstandings and settling down to a happy life. See *The American Film Institute Catalog of Motion Pictures Produced in the United States: Feature Films 1911–1920* [hereafter, *AFI Catalog 1911–1920*], ed. Patricia King Hanson (Berkeley: University of California Press, 1988), p. 401.

8 / Ibid., pp. 105, 144.

9 / Ibid., pp. 113–114, 315, 569, 681, 702.

10 / Charles R. Doran, "The Kaiser's War Pictures," *Motion Picture Supplement*, Sept. 1915, pp. 45, 47; Ramsaye, *A Million and One Nights*, p. 781.

11 / Frank B. Gilbreth, "The Problem of the Crippled Soldier," *Scientific American Supplement* 80, no. 2086 (25 Dec. 1915): 402.

12 / Lakeman, "Aftercare," p. 123; Devine, *Disabled Soldiers and Sailors*, pp. 3–4; Harry E. Mock, "Reclamation of the Disabled from the Industrial Army," *Annals* 80, no. 169 (Nov. 1918): 129. The Surgeon General of the Army also oversaw at least one film with a disability theme: *The End of the Road* (1919), about a young woman who contracts syphilis. As a means of educating her about the disease, her doctor and nurse introduce her to people who bear its aftereffects, including a wheelchair-using woman and her blind son. See *AFI Catalog 1911–1920*, p. 241.

13 / Cited in Martyn Auty, *"The Big Parade,"* in *Movies of the Silent Years*, ed. Ann Lloyd (London: Orbis Publishing Ltd., 1984), p. 102. For descriptions of *For Valour, Too Fat to Fight*, and *Eyes of the Soul*, see *AFI Catalog 1911–1920*, pp. 255, 297, 941.

14 / A more explicit example was *The Greater Victory* (1919), produced with Elks Club money, which told the story of two disabled vets, one of whom immediately takes advantage of the government's vocational rehab program. The other does, too, but only after a nightmare about life without such training. Information on this film is extremely sketchy, however, and it is by no means clear if it was ever shown in theaters. See *AFI Catalog 1911–1920*, p. 353.

15 / Hamburger, "The Cripple and His Place," p. 36. See also John L. Todd, "The Meaning of Rehabilitation," *Annals* 80, no. 169 (Nov. 1918): 4. A brief history of Milbank's organization may be found in Howard A. Rush, " 'School of Another Chance' Is Leader in Rehabilitation," *NYT*, 19 Jan. 1947, p. 47.

16 / For sample articles, see *NYT*, 25 July 1915, sect. 2, p. 13; 2 Jan. 1916, sect. 2, p. 6; and 4 May 1918, p. 17. See in particular "What a Soldier Learned When He Was Blind," *Literary Digest*, 28 Dec. 1918, pp. 54, 57. The *Bit of Driftwood* anecdote appears in Thomas W. Bohn and Richard L. Stromgren, *Light and Shadows: A History of Motion Pictures*, 3rd ed. (Palo Alto, Calif.: Mayfield, 1987), p. 220. Lucy Wright, "Offsetting the Handicap of Blindness," *Annals* 77, no. 166 (May 1918): 31.

17 / Allan Nevins and Henry Steele Commager, *A Pocket History of the United States*, new enlarged ed. (New York: Washington Square Press, 1966), p. 424.

18 / *AFI Catalog 1911–1920*; *The American Film Institute Catalog of Motion Pictures Produced in the United States: Feature Films 1921–1930* [hereafter, *AFI Catalog 1921–1930*], ed. Kenneth W. Munden (New York: R. R. Bowker, 1971). The indexes of the AFI catalogs are not identical in terms of their categories but are reasonably consistent. The following represents a list of the total headings consulted: Amputation, Amputees, Blind persons, Blindness, Blindness—Temporary, Cripples, Deaf-mutes (spelled "Deafmutes" in the 1921–30 catalog), Deafness, Disabled persons, Hunchbacks, Invalids, Paralysis, Paralytics, and Paraplegia. I am reluctant to specify exact numbers of films based on the AFI data, as the volumes are not infallible in their reporting of disability topics. For example, one would not know from the AFI material that *The Strong Man*'s female lead is blind or that the WW I veteran at the center of *The Big Parade* lost a leg. The general numbers do give a reasonable sense of the trend, however.

19 / Hanson's AFI staff sifted through more than seventy trade and general-circulation periodicals in search of movie reviews, descriptions, and advertisements but in the case of *QAS* came up with only three references, two of which appeared in the same issue of *MPW*. See *AFI Catalog 1911–1920*, p. 751.

20 / Ramsaye, *A Million and One Nights*, p. 704.

21 / *The Two Orphans* pressbook, BR Collection.

22 / Ibid.

23 / Glendon Allvine, *The Greatest Fox of Them All* (New York: Lyle Stuart, 1969), p. 38.

24 / Cited in Upton Sinclair, *Upton Sinclair Presents William Fox* (Los Angeles: Upton Sinclair, 1933), p. 5.

25 / Gertrude Jobes, *Motion Picture Empire* (Hamden, Conn.: Archon Books, 1966), pp. 144–145. The information on Fox is summarized in Sinclair, pp. 21, 49.

26 / *Variety*, 6 Jan. 1922, p. 42.

27 / For a more detailed summary, see Roberta LeFeuvre, *"Orphans of the Storm,"* in *Magill's Survey of Cinema: Silent Films*, ed. Frank N. Magill (Englewood Cliffs, N.J.: Salem

Press, 1982), pp. 831–834. See also the breathless description in the *Orphans of the Storm* pressbook, MOMA. Many years later, Lillian Gish played another sighted woman who lives with a blind younger sister in *The Whales of August* (1987), a film otherwise unrelated to *Orphans* directed by Lindsay Anderson, written by David Berry, and co-starring Bette Davis.

28 / Williams, *Griffith*, p. 158.

29 / Janet Wasko, *Movies and Money: Financing the American Film Industry* (Norwood, N.J.: Ablex Publishing Corp., 1982), p. 28; Edward Wagenknecht and Anthony Slide, *The Films of D. W. Griffith* (New York: Crown Publishers, 1975), p. 182; Robert M. Henderson, *D. W. Griffith: His Life and Work* (New York: Oxford University Press, 1972), p. 230; William K. Everson, *American Silent Film* (New York: Oxford University Press, 1978), p. 179.

30 / Wasko, *Movies and Money*, p. 39; Hampton, *History of the Movies*, p. 339.

31 / *MPC*, Apr. 1918, p. 37.

32 / *MPW*, 9 Feb. 1918, p. 864; *Photoplay*, Apr. 1918, p. 70; *MPC*, Apr. 1918, p. 36; Kevin Brownlow, *The Parade's Gone By . . .* (New York: Ballantine Books, 1968), p. 138.

33 / Frances Marion, *Off with Their Heads!: A Serio-Comic Tale of Hollywood* (New York: Macmillan, 1972), pp. 66–67; Eleanor H. Porter, *Pollyanna* (New York: A. L. Burt, 1913), p. 26; *AFI Catalog 1911–1920*, p. 725; Everson, *American Silent Film*, p. 155.

34 / A summary of the film and Keller's sojourn to Hollywood may be found in Schuchman, *Hollywood Speaks*, pp. 30–31. For a contemporary review, see *Outlook*, 17 Sept. 1919, p. 83.

35 / Verneuil cited in A. R. Fulton, *Motion Pictures: The Development of an Art from Silent Films to the Age of Television* (Norman: University of Oklahoma Press, 1960), p. 70; Ramsaye, *A Million and One Nights*, p. 787. According to William Emboden, *Adrienne Lecouvreur* was also known as *Adrienne Lecouvreur, an Actress's Romance Under Louis XV, in Three Parts* and more economically as *An Actress's Romance*, while *Mères françaises* also went by such names as *Maids of France*, *Women of France*, and *Heroes of France*. For a fuller discussion of Bernhardt's film career, see Emboden's *Sarah Bernhardt* (London: Studio Vista, 1974), pp. 143–155.

36 / Brownlow, *The Parade's Gone By*, p. 530; Mast and Kawin, *A Short History*, p. 122. One of Hollywood's most closely guarded secrets was exposed years after Lloyd's death in 1971 when it became known that a stuntman named Harvey Parry doubled for Lloyd during the most hazardous stunts. See Frank Bies, "Hollywood's Oldest Working Stuntman," *TV Guide*, 2 July 1983, p. 31.

37 / Schuchman, *Hollywood Speaks*, pp. 23–28, 33, 34.

38 / Barrett C. Kiesling, "Lucrative Ugliness," *NYT*, 13 Sept. 1925, sect. 8, p. 5; De Mille cited in Kiesling, p. 5.

39 / Liam O'Leary, "Rex Ingram, Pageant-Master," in *Movies of the Silent Years*, ed. Lloyd, p. 136; Liam O'Leary, *Rex Ingram Master of the Silent Cinema* (New York: Harper & Row, 1980), pp. 47, 51, 73.

40 / Franklin C. Shontz, "Psychological Adjustment to Physical Disability: Trends in Theories," in *Psychological and Social Impact*, ed. Marinelli and Dell Orto, p. 120.

3 / Man of a Thousand Disabilities

1 / Arthur Lennig, *The Silent Voice: The Golden Age of the Cinema* (Albany: Faculty–Student Association of the State University of New York at Albany, 1966), p. 37.

2 / Hampton, *History of the Movies*, pp. 338–339.

3 / Though King based the film partially on his childhood experiences, the disabling of a relative wasn't among them. For his accounts, see Brownlow, *The Parade's Gone By*, pp. 122–124, and David Robinson, "The Enduring Craft of Henry King," in *Movies of the Silent Years*, ed. Lloyd, p. 213.

4 / Walter Coppedge, *Henry King's America*, Filmmakers no. 15 (Metuchen, N.J.: Scarecrow Press, 1986), p. 44. On p. 50, Coppedge noted a bizarre coincidence concerning Warner Richmond, the actor who played Allen. While filming a Western for the Monogram Company in 1939, Richmond was permanently paralyzed after being thrown from his horse.

5 / "'The Four Horsemen' Ride on the Screen," *Literary Digest*, 26 Mar. 1921, p. 28.

6 / Auty, *"The Big Parade,"* p. 102. For a summary of the film, see Anthony Slide, *"The Four Horsemen of the Apocalypse,"* in *Magill's Survey*, ed. Magill, pp. 450–453. Accounts of the film's making and reception may be found in Liam O'Leary, *Rex Ingram*, pp. 68–85; Ramsaye, *A Million and One Nights*, pp. 797–802; and Hampton, *History of the Movies*, p. 310.

7 / Sources conflict on the authorship of the play on which *The Dark Angel* was based. Both the AFI catalog for 1920s feature films and Goldwyn biographer Arthur Marx list H. N. Trevelyan, but latter-day Goldwyn biographer Scott Berg cites Guy Bolton. See *AFI Catalog 1921–1930*, p. 170; Arthur Marx, *Goldwyn: A Biography of the Man Behind the Myth* (New York: W. W. Norton, 1976), p. 147; and A. Scott Berg, *Goldwyn: A Biography* (New York: Alfred A. Knopf, 1989), p. 130. Swanson cited in Marion, *Off With Their Heads!*, p. x.

8 / *Variety*, 14 Oct. 1925, p. 42.

9 / Summaries of *The Dark Angel*'s reception may be found in Marx, *Goldwyn*, p. 147, and Berg, *Goldwyn*, pp. 149–151.

10 / In particular, *The Big Parade* had its Los Angeles premiere on September 10 but didn't go into general release until November 5, while *The Dark Angel* was released on September 27 after having been registered with the copyright office about two weeks before.

11 / Vidor cited in Auty, *"The Big Parade,"* p. 102; Tim Pulleine, "A Gentleman's Fate: The Career of John Gilbert," in *Movies of the Silent Years*, ed. Lloyd, p. 100; Jack Gilbert, "Jack Gilbert Writes His Own Story," *Photoplay*, Sept. 1928, p. 103.

12 / Hampton, *History of the Movies*, p. 341. For another view of the film's making and reception, see Michael T. Isenberg, "The Great War Viewed from the Twenties: *The Big Parade*," in *American History/American Film: Interpreting the Hollywood Image*, eds. John E. O'Connor and Martin A. Jackson (New York: Frederick Ungar, 1979), pp. 17–37.

13 / Frank Capra, *The Name Above the Title: An Autobiography* (New York: Macmillan, 1971), p. 67.

14 / *NYT*, 7 Sept. 1926, p. 44; *The New Yorker*, 18 Sept. 1926, p. 51.

15 / Capra, *Name Above the Title*, p. 67; Kathleen Walker, *"The Strong Man,"* *Cinema-Texas Program Notes* 8, no. 13 (3 Feb. 1975): 3.

16 / Cited in Joan Dickey, "A Maker of Mystery," *MPC*, Mar. 1928, p. 80.

17 / Cited in Maude S. Cheatham, "Meet 'The Frog,'" *MPC*, Mar. 1920, p. 81. Sources conflict on several aspects of this film. Robert Anderson called it a one-reeler directed by Edwin August, while Chaney referred to it a two-reeler and I. G. Edmonds identified Robert Z. Leonard as its director. See Robert G. Anderson, *Faces, Forms, Films: The Artistry of Lon Chaney* (New York: Castle Books, 1971), p. 166; and I. G. Edmonds, *Big U: Universal in the Silent Days* (South Brunswick, N.J.: A. S. Barnes, 1977), p. 70.

18 / These three films are discussed in greater detail in Edmonds, *Big U*, pp. 70–72.

19 / Akin to Famous Players' *An Hour Before Dawn*, which preceded it by about a month, this film had a disabled father help his daughter expose a vice ring by inventing a dictaphone by which the woman could record the gang leader's conversations.

20 / Bardèche and Brasillach, *History of Motion Pictures*, p. 201; Hampton, *History of the Movies*, pp. 216–218; *NYT*, 27 Aug. 1919, p. 9.

21 / Cited in Cheatham, "Meet 'The Frog,'" p. 38.

22 / Cited in Ruth Waterbury, "The True Life Story of Lon Chaney," *Photoplay*, Feb. 1928, pp. 94, 112.

23 / Cited in Edmonds, *Big U*, p. 97; Hampton, *History of the Movies*, p. 217.

24 / Maurice Tourneur, "Meeting the Public Demands" (1920), reprinted in *Hollywood Directors 1914–1940*, ed. Richard Koszarski (New York: Oxford University Press, 1976), p. 76. Edison's J. Searle Dawley took his crew to Bermuda to film *Treasure Island* in 1911, three years after the Vitagraph Company produced a one-reeler called *The Story of Treasure Island*. Brothers Chester and Sidney Franklin directed a feature-length version of Stevenson's novel for Fox, which appeared in January 1918. Tourneur's *Treasure Island* debuted just a little over two years later (April 1920).

25 / *MPW*, 21 Aug. 1920, p. 1069.

26 / *NYT*, 15 Nov. 1920, p. 12.

27 / In addition to Fox's *The Darling of Paris* already noted in the text, Alice Blaché wrote and directed *Esmeralda* for Gaumont in 1905 and Albert Capellani directed *Notre-Dame de Paris* for Pathé's Série d'Art in 1911. In addition, a British *Esmeralda* surfaced in 1906, followed by a French film called *Notre Dame* in 1913. See Nowlan and Nowlan, *Cinema Sequels*, pp. 344–346. Thalberg cited in Edmonds, *Big U*, p. 122.

28 / *Exceptional Photoplays*, Oct.–Nov. 1923, p. 4; Tay Garnett with Fredda Dudley Balling, *Light Your Torches and Pull Up Your Tights* (New Rochelle, N.Y.: Arlington House, 1973), p. 11.

29 / William Seabury, *The Public and the Motion Picture Industry* (New York: Macmillan, 1926), p. 127; *Life*, 24 Jan. 1924, p. 31.

30 / Mary Ann Doane, "The 'Woman's Film': Possession and Address," in *Feminist Film Criticism*, ed. Doane, Mellencamp, and Williams, p. 72. See also Williams, "When the Woman Looks," p. 85.

31 / Browning cited in Dickey, "Maker of Mystery," p. 80; Chaney cited in Waterbury, "Lon Chaney," p. 113.

32 / *NYT*, 1 Feb. 1926, p. 16.

33 / *NYT*, 29 June 1926, p. 21; Stuart Rosenthal and Judith Kass, *The Hollywood Professionals*, Vol. 4: *Tod Browning, Don Siegel* (New York: A. S. Barnes, 1975), p. 22.

34 / Further denigrating the film, Gilbert wrote, "I wanted to do *Lilliom*, but was denied the privilege of making that fine story. *The Show* was its illegitimate spew." See Gilbert, "Jack Gilbert," p. 105.

35 / Rosenthal and Kass, *Browning, Siegel*, p. 43.

36 / Chaney cited in Waterbury, "Lon Chaney," p. 113; Browning cited in Dickey, "Maker of Mystery," p. 80.

37 / Rosenthal and Kass, *Browning, Siegel*, p. 9.

38 / Ibid., p. 39.

39 / *Motion Picture News*, 27 Nov. 1920, p. 4155; *The Film Spectator*, 20 Aug. 1927, p. 7; Everson, *American Silent Film*, p. 221. For an authoritative study of Chaney and his life's work, see Michael F. Blake, *Lon Chaney: The Man Behind the Thousand Faces* (Vestal, N.Y.: Vestal Press, 1993).

40 / James M. Barrie, *The Plays of J. M. Barrie* (New York: Charles Scribner's Sons, 1928), p. 73; letter to Cynthia Asquith, 27 Dec. 1920, in *Letters of J. M. Barrie*, ed. Violet

Meynell (New York: Charles Scribner's Sons, 1947), pp. 187; ibid., letter to Cynthia Asquith, 14 Nov. 1924, p. 201.

41 / Jacqueline Rose, "Writing as Auto-Visualisation: Notes on a Scenario and Film of *Peter Pan*," *Screen* 16, no. 3 (Autumn 1975): 47.

42 / Barrymore cited in James Kotsilibas-Davis, *The Barrymores: The Royal Family in Hollywood* (New York: Crown Publishers, 1981), p. 99; John Barrymore [with Karl Schmidt], *Confessions of an Actor* (Indianapolis: Bobbs-Merrill, 1926), n.p. The quote appears on the book's final page.

43 / Cited in Gene Fowler, *Good Night, Sweet Prince: The Life and Times of John Barrymore* (New York: Viking Press, 1944), p. 194.

44 / Barrymore, *Confessions of an Actor*, n.p.

45 / Douglas Gomery, *The Hollywood Studio System* (London: Macmillan, 1986), p. 104; *Photoplay*, Mar. 1926, p. 55; *National Board of Review Magazine*, Mar.–Apr. 1926, p. 14. In an edition of *Moby Dick* published to coincide with *The Sea Beast*'s release, a Warners flack unconvincingly defended the movie's many departures from the novel. The statement is reprinted in Hollis Alpert, *The Barrymores* (New York: Dial Press, 1964), p. 260.

46 / By coincidence, one such setback had a bit of the Obsessive Avenger theme to it; a young man named Edward Bender lost a hand during the filming of Griffith's *America* (1924) when a cannon misfired, and he sued Griffith for $50,000. The judge ruled in his favor, awarding him $20,000. See Henderson, *D. W. Griffith: His Life and Work*, p. 267.

47 / Plays, paintings, operas, at least one symphonic poem, and a 1907 Vitagraph film produced by J. Stuart Blackton with Florence Turner in the title role were among its many artistic descendants over the centuries. See Wagenknecht and Slide, *Films of D. W. Griffith*, p. 230; and Anthony Slide, *The Big V: A History of the Vitagraph Company* (Metuchen, N.J.: Scarecrow Press, 1976), pp. 18–19. A sense of Griffith's strong appreciation for Barrymore's work may be found on pp. 89–90 of the former's untitled autobiographical account, MOMA.

48 / Oliver H. Evans, *George Henry Boker* (Boston: G. K. Hall, 1984), p. 79; Schickel, *D. W. Griffith*, p. 539. Evans's analysis of Boker's play centers on the inconsistencies in Lanciotto, and one of his prime arguments is that the playwright transformed Lanciotto into an amalgam of Shakespearean characters. Outwardly the character resembles Richard, but his indecisiveness, victimization, and suicidal qualities recall Hamlet, Macbeth, Lear, and Julius Caesar. See Evans, *George Henry Boker*, pp. 71–88 and 129–131.

49 / Everson, *American Silent Film*, p. 219. For a contemporary review, see *MPW*, 6 Nov. 1926, p. 41.

50 / Roland Barthes, *Mythologies*, trans. Annette Lavers (New York: Hill and Wang, 1972), p. 151; Robin Wood, *Hollywood from Vietnam to Reagan* (New York: Columbia University Press, 1986), p. 73.

51 / Molly Haskell, "Movies 1973," *The Massachusetts Review* 14, no. 4 (Autumn 1973): 815.

4 / Golden-Age Freakshows

1 / Following the early successes of its Vitaphone programs, Warner Bros. announced plans to outfit fifty seats in each of its theaters with headphones that would provide amplified sound to people with hearing losses and narrative commentary to those with visual impairments. As noble as these intentions sounded, the only notable thing about this brief experiment was the favorable attention it generated for the studio. See Harry M. Geduld,

The Birth of the Talkies (Bloomington: Indiana University Press, 1975), p. 145. See also John S. Schuchman, "Silent Movies and the Deaf Community," *Journal of Popular Culture* 14, no. 4 (Spring 1984): 58–78.

2 / Hampton, *History of the Movies*, p. 409. For an excellent financial overview of the period, see Wasko, *Movies and Money*, pp. 47–102.

3 / *The Film Spectator*, 10 May 1930, p. 7. Summaries of these films may be found in Jay Hyams, *War Movies* (New York: W. H. Smith, 1984), pp. 39–43.

4 / *All Quiet on the Western Front* souvenir program, MH Library; *Cinema*, June 1930, pp. 37–38; *The Film Spectator*, 10 May 1930, p. 7. The *All Quiet* script is reprinted in *Best American Screenplays*, ed. Sam Thomas (New York: Crown Publishers, 1986), pp. 13–72.

5 / *NYT*, 21 Nov. 1929, p. 24.

6 / John Kobler, *Damned in Paradise: The Life of John Barrymore* (New York: Atheneum, 1977), pp. 256–257.

7 / See Clarence A. Locan, "The Lon Chaney I Knew," *Photoplay*, Nov. 1930, pp. 58–64.

8 / Robert Bogdan, Douglas Biklen, Arthur Shapiro, and David Spelkoman, "The Disabled: Media's Monster," *Social Policy* 13, no. 2 (Fall 1982): 33.

9 / A compelling case for *The Magician*'s strong influence on the *Frankenstein* filmmakers, including the development of the Fritz character, may be found in Donald F. Glut, *The Frankenstein Legend: A Tribute to Mary Shelley and Boris Karloff* (Metuchen, N.J.: Scarecrow Press, 1973), pp. 82–83. One critic has gone as far as to suggest that Fritz symbolizes the evil side of Frankenstein himself, "an embodiment of his twisted emotions." See Martin Tropp, *The Story of Frankenstein* (Boston: Houghton Mifflin, 1976), p. 91.

10 / Cited in James Curtis, *James Whale*, Filmmakers no. 1 (Metuchen, N.J.: Scarecrow Press, 1982), p. 81.

11 / Cited in *No, but I Saw the Movie: The Best Short Stories Ever Made into Film*, ed. David Wheeler (New York: Penguin Books, 1989), p. 144.

12 / Fiedler, *Freaks*, p. 168; Budd Schulberg, *Moving Pictures: Memories of a Hollywood Prince* (New York: Stein and Day, 1981), p. 314.

13 / *Freaks* pressbook, BR Collection.

14 / For provocative studies of the movie, see Kristin Laskas, "*Freaks*," *CinemaTexas Program Notes* 10, no. 1 (29 Jan. 1976): 45–50; and Danny Peary, *Cult Movies: The Classics, the Sleepers, the Weird, and the Wonderful* (New York: Delacorte Press, 1981), pp. 107–110.

15 / John Brosnan, *The Horror People* (New York: St. Martin's Press, 1976), pp. 65–66.

16 / Marx and Vidor cited in *MGM: When the Lion Roars*, a 1992 Turner Pictures documentary produced by Joni Levin, directed by Frank Martin, and written by Frank Martin and Michael Henry Wilson. Marx's anecdote differs from a 1987 version of it, in which he claimed that the march on Thalberg's office was cut short by director Jack Conway, who said "Irving's right so often he's earned the right to be wrong." See Samuel Marx, *A Gaudy Spree* (New York: Franklin Watts, 1987), p. 132.

17 / Cited in Brosnan, *The Horror People*, p. 66.

18 / Cited in Samuel Marx, *Mayer and Thalberg: The Make-Believe Saints* (London: W. H. Allen, 1976), p. 180; Irving Thalberg and Hugh Weir, "Why Motion Pictures Cost So Much," *Saturday Evening Post*, 4 Nov. 1933, p. 10.

19 / Ephraim Katz, *The Film Encyclopedia* (New York: Thomas Y. Crowell, 1979), p. 98.

20 / Cited in Bob Thomas, *Thalberg: Life and Legend* (Garden City, N.Y.: Doubleday, 1969), p. 274.

21 / For accounts of the making of *Mutiny on the Bounty*, see Bosley Crowther, *The Lion's Share: The Story of an Entertainment Empire* (New York: E. P. Dutton, 1957), pp. 230–232; and Thomas, *Thalberg*, pp. 272–280.

22 / Charles Chaplin, "Pantomime and Comedy," *NYT*, 25 Jan. 1931, sect. 8, p. 6.

23 / For example, see Gerard Molyneaux, *Charlie Chaplin's 'City Lights'* (New York: Garland, 1983) and Charles J. Maland, *Chaplin and American Culture: The Evolution of a Star Image* (Princeton, N.J.: Princeton University Press, 1989), pp. 115–123.

24 / Charles Chaplin, *My Autobiography* (New York: Simon and Schuster, 1964), p. 325.

25 / Ibid., p. 326.

26 / Ibid.; Cherrill cited in *Unknown Chaplin*, a 1983 documentary produced by Kevin Brownlow and David Gill for Thames Television.

27 / Francis Fergusson, "A Month of the Theatre," *The Bookman*, Apr. 1931, p. 185; George Jean Nathan, *Passing Judgments* (New York: Alfred A. Knopf, 1935), p. 212; Chaplin, *My Autobiography*, pp. 382–383.

28 / *NYT*, 2 Nov. 1935, p. 13.

29 / Klobas, *Disability Drama*, p. 117.

30 / Laemmle cited in Curtis, *James Whale*, p. 118; Whale cited on pp. 102–103.

31 / Curtis, *James Whale*, p. x. See also Martin F. Norden, "Sexual References in James Whale's *Bride of Frankenstein*," in *Eros in the Mind's Eye: Sexuality and the Fantastic in Art and Film*, ed. Donald Palumbo (Westport, Conn.: Greenwood Press, 1986), pp. 141–150.

32 / *MPW*, 13 Nov. 1909, p. 696. This paragraph also appears in the journal's description of the film on p. 691 of the same issue.

33 / Perhaps silent-film audiences were relatively willing to accept the Elderly Dupe stereotype because they like the Dupe could not hear the voices that would have cleared up the misunderstandings.

34 / See Selznick's letter to Nicholas Schenck, June 1935, in *Memo from David O. Selznick*, ed. Rudy Behlmer (New York: Viking Press, 1972), p. 86.

35 / As John Schuchman has noted, the studio produced at least three movies around this time that dealt with deafness mostly to the side of their main stories: *Charlie Chan at the Olympics* (1936), *Sins of Man* (1936), and *The Story of Alexander Graham Bell* (1939). For his accounts, see *Hollywood Speaks*, pp. 114–115.

36 / See Dwan's comments in Eric Sherman, *Directing the Film: Film Directors on Their Art* (Los Angeles: Acrobat Books, 1976), p. 25.

37 / Betty Lasky, *RKO: The Biggest Little Major of Them All* (Englewood Cliffs, N.J.: Prentice-Hall, 1984), p. 110.

38 / Whitney Stine with Bette Davis, *Mother Goddam: The Story of the Career of Bette Davis* (New York: Berkley Medallion Books, 1974), p. 58.

39 / Betsy McLane, "Take One Stahl, Take Two Sirk: Genre Transpositions," Society for Cinema Studies conference, Pittsburgh, Pa., May 1983, p. 10.

40 / McLane, "Take One Stahl," pp. 11–12; Jean-Loup Bourget, "God Is Dead, or Through a Glass Darkly," *Bright Lights* 2, no. 6 (Winter 1977–78): 26.

41 / Thomson, "Man of a Thousand Faces," p. 125; Lasky, *RKO*, p. 156; Simon Callow, *Charles Laughton: A Difficult Actor* (London: Methuen, 1987), pp. 133–134.

42 / *NYT*, 1 Jan. 1940, p. 29; Dieterle cited in Callow, *Laughton*, p. 136. For a sense of how deeply the events in Europe affected the *Hunchback* cast and crew, see pp. 135–136.

43 / At least three other productions based on the Hugo novel have appeared since 1939: a 1957 French version directed by Jean Delannoy and starring Anthony Quinn, a British 1982 made-for-TV film directed by Michael Tuchner and starring Anthony Hopkins, and an American 1989 film called *Big Man on Campus*, directed by Jeremy Kagan and starring Allan Katz. The latter film, known throughout its nine-year development as *The Hunchback of UCLA* until the title school wisely refused the use of its name, was never released theatrically but went directly to video and pay-cable.

44 / Lugosi cited in Gregory Mank, *Karloff and Lugosi: The Story of a Haunting Collaboration* (Jefferson, N.C.: McFarland, 1990), p. 172. A detailed history of *Son of Frankenstein* may be found in on pp. 161–201.

45 / Donald Glut has noted that the initial *Ghost of Frankenstein* script, penned by Eric Taylor, called for a new Frankenstein assistant with a severely distorted spine, Theodor, to befriend Ygor. ("The two twisted men recognized a common bond and became friends," in Glut's words.) Theodor was to have played a pivotal role in *Ghost*, but W. Scott Darling, a writer brought in to revise the screenplay, doubtless realized how out of place such a character was by the 1940s and replaced him with the able-bodied Dr. Bohmer (played in the film by Lionel Atwill, who coincidentally had essayed the disabled police inspector in *Son of Frankenstein*). See Glut, *Frankenstein Legend*, pp. 153–155.

46 / Though Richard received much moviemaker attention during the medium's early years and again with *The Tower of London* in 1939, he didn't reappear until Laurence Olivier directed and starred in a lavish *Richard III* remake filmed in Great Britain in 1956.

47 / For a tongue-in-cheek review of Buell's oddity, see Harry Medved and Michael Medved, *The Golden Turkey Awards* (New York: Berkley Books, 1981), pp. 98–100; Raabe cited in Tom Collins, "AAL's Munchkin Is a Giant Success," *Correspondent*, Winter 1992–93, p. 6; *NYT*, 1 Jan. 1940, p. 29; see Marceline E. Jaques and Kathleen M. Patterson, "The Self-Help Group Model: A Review," *RCB* 18, no. 1 (1974): 48.

48 / In addition, Sidney Franklin's brother Chester, with whom he had co-directed numerous films such as 1918's *Treasure Island*, served in WW I and perhaps influenced his sibling's film. It's also worth noting that Goldwyn had originally hired Thornton Wilder to adapt *The Dark Angel* into a sound picture but eventually replaced him with British playwright Mordaunt Shairp and Hellman, the latter of whom referred to the film years later simply as "an old silly." For her account of the working methods of Franklin, Shairp, and herself on this film, see Lillian Hellman, *Three: An Unfinished Woman, Pentimento, Scoundrel Time* (Boston: Little, Brown, 1979), pp. 466–467. Summaries of the making and reception of *The Dark Angel* may be found in the biographies of Goldwyn by Marx, pp. 203–204, 213–214; and Berg, pp. 256–259.

5 / The Road to Rehabilitation

1 / Cited in *MGM: When the Lion Roars*.

2 / Capra, *Name Above the Title*, p. 242. The accident-and-arthritis combination is the most frequently cited cause of Barrymore's disablement, but as Margot Peters has pointed out the actual circumstances may never be known. Accounts from Barrymore's manager, the MGM and Columbia publicity departments, and Barrymore himself (a notoriously unreliable source) ranged from old hip and knee injuries to inflammatory rheumatism to syphilitic joint disease. It *is* known that Barrymore became addicted to morphine and cocaine after his disablement, and it's possible MGM supplied some of these drugs to keep its star working. If true, Barrymore and Mayer's mutual loyalty takes on a whole new dimension. See Peters, *The House of Barrymore* (New York: Alfred A. Knopf, 1990), pp. 437–439, 597.

3 / Letter to Merritt Hulburd, 23 Oct. 1938, in *Selznick*, ed. Behlmer, pp. 128–129.

4 / Capra, *Name Above the Title*, p. 377. The final draft of the script offers the following introduction: "Nearby, in a throne-like wheelchair, behind which stands the goon who furnishes the motive power, sits Henry F. Potter, his squarish derby hat on his head." See *It's a Wonderful Life* screenplay, 4 Mar. 1947, p. 12, FC Collection.

5 / *You Can't Take It with You* publicity brochure, FC Collection; *You Can't Take It with You* screenplay, 3rd draft, 17 Mar. 1938, p. 10, FC Collection.

6 / Barrymore cited in Ed Lawrence, "Hollywood's Jacks of All Trades," *NYT*, 17 Nov. 1940, sect. 9, p. 4. Bosley Crowther attributed the idea of turning Gillespie into a wheelchair-using character solely to Wilson, Ruskin, and Goldbeck, mysteriously excluding Barrymore and Bucquet. See Crowther, *The Lion's Share*, pp. 258–259.

7 / Ayres cited in *MGM: When the Lion Roars*; Barrymore cited in Kotsilibas-Davis, *The Barrymores*, p. 223

8 / Cited in J. Stuart Blackton, "Early History" (1929), reprinted in *Hollywood Directors*, ed. Koszarski, p. 15.

9 / Larry Swindell, *Spencer Tracy: A Biography* (New York: World Publishing, 1969), p. 166. Two years after *Edison, the Man*, Tracy and his wife Louise established the Los Angeles-based John Tracy Clinic, a speech and hearing facility that provided free assistance to all parents and children regardless of income. For more information on the clinic and the Tracys' son, see pp. 46–48, 57–58, 88–89, 185–187.

10 / See Thomas M. Pryor, "Happy, Happy Author," *NYT*, 28 Jan. 1951, sect. 2, p. 5.

11 / Edward G. Robinson with Leonard Spigelgass, *All My Yesterdays: An Autobiography* (New York: Hawthorn Books, 1973), p. 218; letter to Henry Blanke, 20 Nov. 1940, in *Inside Warner Bros. (1935–1951)*, ed. Rudy Behlmer (New York: Viking Penguin, 1985), p. 134; Philip Davies and Brian Neve, "Introduction," in *Cinema, Politics and Society in America*, ed. Philip Davies and Brian Neve (New York: St. Martin's Press, 1981), p. 8.

12 / Letter to Hal Wallis, 3 July 1940, in *Warner Bros.*, ed. Behlmer, p. 135.

13 / See the letters from Joseph Breen to Jack Warner, 22 Apr. 1941 and 24 Apr. 1941, in *Warner Bros.*, ed. Behlmer, pp. 136–139; *Time*, 2 Feb. 1942, p. 54.

14 / Ronald Reagan with Richard G. Hubler, *Where's the Rest of Me?* (New York: Duell, Sloan and Pearce, 1965), pp. 4–6; Steven Weisman, "Reagan Begins to Wear a Hearing Aid in Public," *NYT*, 8 Sept. 1983, p. 14.

15 / One of the more vocal opponents was Gerald Nye, a U.S. senator from North Dakota who accused the industry of making movies "to rouse the war fever in America and plunge this Nation to her destruction" mainly to protect its lucrative British market. See Gerald P. Nye, "Our Madness Increases as Our Emergency Shrinks," *Vital Speeches of the Day*, 15 Sept. 1941, pp. 720–723. See also Colin Shindler, *Hollywood Goes to War: Films and American Society 1939–1952* (London: Routledge & Kegan Paul, 1979), pp. 31–32.

16 / Katz, *The Film Encyclopedia*, p. 1174.

17 / See François Truffaut, *Hitchcock*, rev. ed. (New York: Simon and Schuster, 1984), p. 146.

18 / Though Hitchcock was not officially credited as one of the film's writers, Macgowan recalled that he contributed significantly to the movie's plot and dialogue. See Kenneth Macgowan, *Behind the Screen: The History and Techniques of the Motion Picture* (New York: Dell, 1965), p. 393.

19 / A *Lifeboat* photo-essay may be found in *Life*, 31 Jan. 1944, pp. 76–81. Hitchcock was notorious for planning everything in advance, but evidently the decision to show disembodied feet behind the newly disabled Gus came up during the shooting. He routinely gave his cinematographer sketches to illustrate the compositions he wanted, and the one for this particular shot, reproduced in Macgowan, shows people, not feet, behind the seaman. See Macgowan, *Behind the Screen*, p. 442.

20 / Richard E. Verville, "Federal Legislative History of Independent Living Programs," *Archives of Physical Medicine and Rehabilitation* 60 (Oct. 1979): 448.

21 / Ted W. Lawson, *Thirty Seconds Over Tokyo* (New York: Random House, 1943), p. 3. See also Clayton R. Koppes and Gregory D. Black, *Hollywood Goes to War: How Politics, Profits, and Propaganda Shaped World War II Movies* (New York: Free Press, 1987), pp. 266–267.

22 / Letter to Katharine Cornell, 6 May 1943, in *Selznick*, ed. Behlmer, p. 338.

23 / Ibid., letter to Jenia Reissar, 4 Oct. 1944, pp. 347–348; ibid., letter to George Gallup, 1 Feb. 1944, p. 343.

24 / *NYT*, 28 Apr. 1945, p. 19. In a 1943 "open letter," Marshall strongly assured movie actors in the armed forces that the industry and their audiences would welcome them once they returned from active duty. After acknowledging how his own career continued after his injury, he wrote with a liberal dose of idealism that "you will go on, too, just as before. Wounds make no difference." See Herbert Marshall with Drake Hunt, "An Open Letter to Hollywood's Fighting Men," *Hollywood*, Mar. 1943, pp. 28, 65.

25 / According to Maltz, the film premiered in twenty-eight cities "at Guadalcanal Day banquets under the auspices of the United States Marine Corps." Cited in Gordon Kahn, *Hollywood on Trial: The Story of the 10 Who Were Indicted* (New York: Boni & Gaer, 1948), p. 88.

26 / Thomas M. Pryor, "Jerry Wald, the Big Idea Man," *NYT*, 19 Jan. 1947, sect. 2, p. 5. Some confusion exists as to the authorship of the movie's script. In his critical examination of the work of the Hollywood Ten, Bernard Dick suggests that screenwriters Al Besserides and Alvah Bessie developed a treatment of twenty-six pages called "The Al Schmid Story" from a *Life* article given them by Wald in March 1943, but that for obscure reasons Maltz took over as sole screenwriter in September of that year. Dick makes no acknowledgment, however, of the contributions of Marvin Borowsky, listed in the film's credits as adaptor, or of Roger Butterfield, whose book provided the basis for Maltz's script. See Bernard F. Dick, *Radical Innocence: A Critical Study of the Hollywood Ten* (Lexington: University Press of Kentucky, 1989), pp. 91–92.

27 / Klobas, *Disability Drama*, p. 8.

28 / Dana B. Polan, "Blind Insights and Dark Passages: The Problem of Placement in Forties Films," *The Velvet Light Trap Review of Cinema*, no. 20 (Summer 1983): 29; Klobas, *Disability Drama*, p. 8.

29 / Busch briefly found himself at the center of the Cinema of Isolation, mostly by happenstance. That same year, Selznick used another Busch novel as the basis for *Duel in the Sun*, a movie that happened to feature two disabled actors, Lionel Barrymore and Herbert Marshall. In addition, and quite by coincidence, Busch was married to Teresa Wright, one of the stars of *The Best Years of Our Lives* who was soon to appear in another disabled-vet film, *The Men*. For an overview of his career, see David Thomson, "Niven Busch, Sportsman," *Film Comment*, July–Aug. 1985, pp. 40–49.

30 / Lasky, *RKO*, p. 194; letter to King Vidor and Joseph Bernhard, 11 Apr. 1952, in *Selznick*, ed. Behlmer, p. 408.

31 / Liberty Films biographical brochure, FC Collection; Wyler cited in Bernard R. Kantor, Irwin R. Blacker, and Anne Kramer, *Directors at Work: Interviews with American Film-Makers* (New York: Funk & Wagnalls, 1970), p. 414.

32 / Kantor, Blacker, and Kramer, *Directors at Work*, p. 410; William Wyler, "No Magic Wand," *The Screen Writer*, Feb. 1947, p. 6.

33 / Russell cited in Joseph C. Goulden, *The Best Years 1945–1950* (New York: Atheneum, 1976), p. 5; *Time*, 28 Oct. 1946, p. 3.

34 / Wyler, "No Magic Wand," p. 8.

35 / Robert Warshow's attack on the film remains the most notable, though he seriously undercut his arguments by insisting that the so-called "veterans' problem" of postwar

America did not really exist. See Robert Warshow, "The Anatomy of Falsehood," *Partisan Review* 14, no. 3 (May–June 1947): 305–309. See also Ralph Willett, "The Nation in Crisis: Hollywood's Response to the 1940s," in *Cinema, Politics and Society*, ed. Davies and Neve, pp. 72–73; and Martin A. Jackson, "The Uncertain Peace: *The Best Years of Our Lives*," in *American History/American Film*, ed. O'Connor and Jackson, pp. 147–165.

36 / Russell, the first actor in Hollywood history to receive two Oscars for the same role in a single film, was also the first to sell an Oscar at public auction; the statuette netted him about $55,000 in Aug. 1992, which he used to help pay for his wife's cataract operation and other expenses. For an article on Russell's pre– and post–*Best Years* life, see Dick Dietl, "He Cared," *Worklife*, Summer 1989, pp. 12–17.

37 / Cited in *Hollywood: The Golden Years*, a 1987 BBC Television Production in association with RKO Pictures, produced by Charles Chabot and Rosemary Wilton.

38 / George K. Pratt, *Soldier to Civilian: Problems of Readjustment* (New York: McGraw-Hill, 1944), p. 130.

39 / See Charles Hurd, *The Veterans' Program: A Complete Guide to Its Benefits, Rights and Options* (New York: McGraw-Hill, 1946), p. 31, 40–41. See also the May 1945 edition of *The Annals*, devoted entirely to issues related to disabled veterans.

40 / Eric F. Goldman, *The Crucial Decade—and After: America, 1945–1960* (New York: Vintage Books, 1960), p. 4; David A. Shannon, *Twentieth Century America*, Vol. 3: *World War II and Since*, 2nd ed. (Chicago: Rand-McNally, 1969), pp. 603–604; Martin F. Norden, "America and Its Fantasy Films: 1945–1951," *Film & History* 12, no. 1 (Feb. 1982): 1–11; Edward Dmytryk, *On Screen Writing* (Boston: Focal Press, 1985), p. 164.

41 / Letter to Spyros Skouras and Charles Schlaifer, 3 Jan. 1948, in *Memo from Darryl F. Zanuck: The Golden Years at Twentieth Century–Fox*, ed. Rudy Behlmer (New York: Grove Press, 1993), p. 150; Hathaway cited in Philip K. Scheuer, "Henry Hathaway," in *Directors in "Action,"* ed. Bob Thomas (Indianapolis: Bobbs-Merrill, 1973), p. 132.

42 / For production history details, see Frank Brady, *Citizen Welles: A Biography of Orson Welles* (New York: Anchor Books, 1989), pp. 394–404.

43 / Cited in Brady, *Citizen Welles*, p. 402.

44 / Cited in Raymond Durgnat, *Jean Renoir* (Berkeley: University of California Press, 1974), p. 261.

45 / Letter to Steve Trilling, 15 June 1946, in *Warner Bros.*, ed. Behlmer, pp. 271–272.

46 / Ibid., letter to Steve Trilling, 2 July 1947, pp. 300–301.

47 / Wyman cited in J. E. A. Bawden, "Jane Wyman: American Star Par Excellence," *Films in Review*, Apr. 1975, p. 198. For other details concerning the film's production and reception, see Schuchman, *Hollywood Speaks*, pp. 53–55.

48 / Jean Negulesco, *Things I Did . . . and Things I Think I Did* (New York: Linden Press, 1984), pp. 127–128. Wyman, who gave a very brief acceptance speech upon winning the Oscar for Best Actress ("I kept my mouth shut once," she said simply, "I think I'll do it again"), also received awards from the Latin American Consular Association and the Osaka Film Festival for her performance.

49 / Carl Foreman, transcript of 1981 interview, pp. 17–18, AFF.

50 / *Home of the Brave* began playing in theaters in mid–May 1949, well ahead of similar projects announced by other studios and a mere four months after Kramer and financier Robert Stillman set the project in motion by purchasing the screen rights to a play by Arthur Laurents on wartime discrimination. The film's production and distribution details may be found in Thomas F. Brady, "Crusade in Hollywood," *NYT*, 6 Mar. 1949, sect. 2, p. 5; Brady, "Hollywood Survey," *NYT*, 20 Mar. 1949, sect. 2, p. 5; Ezra Goodman, "'Champion' Producer," *NYT*, 10 Apr. 1949, sect. 2, p. 4; and Martin F. Norden, "The

Racism-Ableism Link in *Home of the Brave* and *Bright Victory*," *Film & History* 20, no. 2 (May 1990): 28–29.

51 / Foreman interview, pp. 14, 31.

52 / Fred Zinnemann, *A Life in the Movies: An Autobiography* (New York: Charles Scribner's Sons, 1992), p. 8; Murray Schumach, "Hollywood Tough," *NYT*, 31 May 1964, sect. 2, p. 7. All Zinnemann quotes are from Fred Zinnemann, "On Using Non-Actors in Pictures," *NYT*, 8 Jan. 1950, sect. 2, p. 7. Zinnemann helped photograph the Robert Siodmak–Edgar Ulmer documentary *Menschen am Sonntag* [*People on Sunday*] in 1929 and later assisted such prominent documentarists as Paul Strand and Robert Flaherty. He returned to the form in 1951 when executives of the Los Angeles Orthopedic Children's Hospital, impressed with his handling of *The Men*, recruited him to direct a factual film on their organization's behalf called *Benjy*. See Zinnemann, *A Life*, p. 111.

53 / Cited in Ron Offen, *Brando* (Chicago: Henry Regnery, 1973), p. 54. Zinnemann also admired Brando's work, if from a different perspective. When Kramer raised the possibility of Brando for the role of Bud, Zinnemann remembered that "we were in instant agreement about him; he was not only a great actor, but a shattering force of nature. He had a volcanic quality about him that seemed essential for 'our' hero." See Zinnemann, *A Life*, p. 82.

54 / David Downing, *Marlon Brando* (New York: Stein and Day, 1984), p. 28.

55 / Zinnemann cited in Sherman, *Directing the Film*, p. 324; *NYT*, 21 July 1950, p. 15. Calling *The Men* "a noble failure," Zinnemann attributed its initial lack of popularity to bad timing: the film opened two weeks after the outbreak of the Korean War. "Designed as a post-war picture it was suddenly facing a pre-war mentality. No wonder that people whose sons, husbands and fathers were going to fight could not bear to watch a movie such as ours. It folded in two weeks." Zinnemann, *A Life*, p. 85. For his detailed account of the making of *The Men*, see Zinnemann, *A Life*, pp. 77–85.

56 / Larry Ceplair and Steven Englund, *The Inquisition in Hollywood: Politics in the Film Community 1930–1960* (Garden City, N.Y.: Anchor Press, 1980), p. 210; Thomas F. Brady, "Hollywood Tackles the Facts of Life," *NYT*, 16 Mar. 1947, sect. 2, p. 5.

57 / Harry Niemeyer, "Hospital as Film Set," *NYT*, 3 Sept. 1950, sect. 2, p. 3; Mark Robson, "Plea for a Flock of Film Fledglings," *NYT*, 22 July 1951, sect. 2, p. 3.

58 / Cited in Pryor, "Happy, Happy Author," p. 5.

59 / *The Nation*, 11 Aug. 1951, p. 118; *The New Republic*, 27 Aug. 1951, p. 22. See also Norden, "The Racism–Ableism Link."

6 / The Path to Apathy

1 / Alvah Bessie, *Inquisition in Eden* (New York: Macmillan, 1965), p. 65.

2 / Cited in Kahn, *Hollywood on Trial*, p. 222.

3 / Menjou cited in Kahn, *Hollywood on Trial*, p. 49; Foreman interview, pp. 10–11; Wyler cited in Kahn, *Hollywood on Trial*, p. 221. For a more detailed discussion of Foreman and Kramer's problem-fraught relationship, see Victor S. Navasky, *Naming Names* (New York: Viking Press, 1980), pp. 156–165.

4 / See Kahn, *Hollywood on Trial*, pp. 10–18.

5 / Navasky, *Naming Names*, p. 150.

6 / Kahn, *Hollywood on Trial*, pp. 136, 2; Kelly cited in Kahn, *Hollywood on Trial*, p. 222; Garrett Graham, "Witch-Hunting in Hollywood," *The Screen Writer*, June 1947, p. 19; Wyler cited in Kahn, *Hollywood on Trial*, p. 221.

7 / Cited in *Waldo Salt: A Screenwriter's Journey*, a 1990 documentary film by Robert Hillmann and Eugene Corr.

8 / Cited in Kahn, *Hollywood on Trial*, p. 11.

9 / A sense of Zanuck's pre-release enthusiasm for *Wilson* and post-release chagrin may be found in *Zanuck*, ed. Behlmer, pp. 73–78.

10 / Cited in Lasky, *RKO*, p. 200.

11 / *Time*, 9 May 1949, p. 103; *Commonweal*, 20 May 1949, p. 150; Wood cited in Grady Johnson, "Force of Habit," *NYT*, 6 Feb. 1949, sect. 2, p. 4.

12 / Ludwig and Levien cited in Barbara Jamison, "Biography Boom," *NYT*, 8 May 1955, sect. 2, p. 5.

13 / Harry Medved and Michael Medved, *The Hollywood Hall of Shame: The Most Expensive Flops in Movie History* (New York: Perigee Books, 1984), p. 74.

14 / Cited in Medved and Medved, *Hollywood*, p. 77; *NYT*, 3 Nov. 1955, p. 37.

15 / See Anderson, *Faces, Forms, Films*, pp. 15–24. John Brosnan noted that Creighton Chaney, who had sold the rights to his father's story to U–I in 1955 but did not participate in the scriptwriting process, complained strenuously about the film's misrepresentations. See Brosnan, *The Horror People*, pp. 23–24.

16 / Interviews with the author, 4 Mar. 1992 and 13 Apr. 1992.

17 / For a discussion of Kaufman's development of the Magoo character, see Frederick Kaufman, "A Father's Anger," *NYT Magazine*, 15 Sept. 1985, p. 84. A brief account of the making of *Bad Day* may be found in Dore Schary, "Bad Day with Spencer Tracy," *American Film*, Nov. 1979, p. 54.

18 / Dore Schary, "Road to 'Campobello,'" *NYT*, 25 Sept. 1960, sect. 2, p. 9; Schary cited in Murray Schumach, "Democrats 'See' 1924 Convention," *NYT*, 21 Apr. 1960, p. 24. For a more detailed discussion of this film within its political context, see Martin F. Norden, "*Sunrise at Campobello* and 1960 Presidential Politics," *Film & History* 16, no. 1 (Feb. 1986): 2–8.

19 / Darrell Ruhl, discussion guide for *Helen Keller—The Light of Faith* (New York: Swedenborg Foundation, n.d.), p. 1.

20 / Patty Duke and Kenneth Turan, *Call Me Anna: The Autobiography of Patty Duke* (New York: Bantam Books, 1987), p. 100. A brief production history of *The Miracle Worker* may be found in Eugene Archer, "'Miracle' on Camera," *NYT*, 11 June 1961, sect. 2, p. 7; and Duke and Turan, *Call Me Anna*, pp. 98–104.

21 / Cited in Eugene Archer, "How to Learn to Love World Destruction," *NYT*, 26 Jan. 1964, sect. 2, p. 13.

22 / Peter Bull, "The Ending You Never Saw in 'Strangelove,'" *NYT*, 9 Jan. 1966, sect. 2, p. 9; Sellers cited in Howard Thompson, "Pause for Reflection with Peter Sellers," *NYT*, 25 Oct. 1964, sect. 2, p. 7. Richard Corliss, in his *Talking Pictures: Screenwriters in the American Cinema* (New York: Penguin Books, 1975), pp. 350–351, also attributes much of the Strangelove character to Sellers. Quite coincidentally, another studio released a "straight" version of a similar story later that year—*Fail Safe*, directed by Sidney Lumet and scripted by former blacklistee Walter Bernstein—that featured a disabled person in another high position of power: U.S. Defense Secretary Swenson (William Hansen), who walks with canes. For further discussions of Kubrick's film, see Thomas Allen Nelson, *Kubrick: Inside a Film Artist's Maze* (Bloomington: Indiana University Press, 1982), pp. 78–98; and Lawrence Suid, "The Pentagon and Hollywood: *Dr. Strangelove or: How I Learned to Stop Worrying and Love the Bomb*," in *American History/American Film*, ed. O'Connor and Jackson, pp. 219–235.

23 / *NYT*, 16 Oct. 1950, p. 30; Jay Robert Nash and Stanley Ralph Ross, *The Motion Picture Guide, 1927–1984* (Chicago: CineBooks, 1987), p. 3723.

24 / Cited in *Sirk on Sirk: Interviews with Jon Halliday*, ed. Jon Halliday (New York: Viking Press, 1972), pp. 97, 93.

25 / McLane, "Take One Stahl," p. 10. For insightful analyses of the film, see David Rodowick, *"Magnificent Obsession," CinemaTexas Program Notes* 12, no. 4 (4 Apr. 1977): 65–70; and Michael Stern, *Douglas Sirk* (Boston: Twayne Publishers, 1979), pp. 93–108.

26 / Jane Wyman, "The Lady's Not for Spurning Character Roles," *NYT*, 29 Nov. 1953, sect. 2, p. 5.

27 / Rodowick, *"Magnificent Obsession,"* p. 68.

28 / Cited in *Sirk on Sirk*, ed. Halliday, p. 96.

29 / Berg, *Goldwyn*, p. 487; William Bender, "The Return of *Porgy*," *Time*, 19 July 1976, p. 64; Clifford Mason, "Why Does White America Love Sidney Poitier So?," *NYT*, 10 Sept. 1967, sect. 2, p. 1. For further discussions of the film, see Berg, *Goldwyn*, pp. 478–489; and Daniel J. Leab, *From Sambo to Superspade: The Black Experience in Motion Pictures* (Boston: Houghton Mifflin, 1976), pp. 207–209.

30 / *NYT*, 20 May 1960, p. 26.

31 / Richard Schickel, *The Disney Version* (New York: Avon Books, 1968), p. 248.

32 / Pegleg Pete resurfaced in a number of mutated forms since the 1930s. He made a bizarre appearance in *The Eternal Sea* in the form of the symbol for John Hoskins that his pilots painted on their jets. Conspicuous among their modifications was the replacement of Pete's prosthesis with a blazing machine gun. He somehow regrew his foot years later in various Disney comic-book manifestations and saw his moniker change from Pegleg Pete to "Big Bad Pete."

33 / Schickel, *Disney*, p. 251.

34 / Ibid., pp. 251, 252. For a thorough analysis of the film, see Donald Crafton, "The Last Night in the Nursery: Walt Disney's *Peter Pan*," *The Velvet Light Trap Review of Cinema*, no. 24 (Fall 1989): 33–52. See in particular his Oedipal reading on pp. 38–40.

35 / Cited in Sherman, *Directing the Film*, p. 34.

36 / Ibid., pp. 34, 35. Notes on the production may be found in Charles Hamblett, "On Launching 'Moby Dick' in Eire," *NYT*, 15 Aug. 1954, sect. 2, p. 5; Stuart M. Kaminsky, *John Huston: Maker of Magic* (Boston: Houghton Mifflin, 1978), pp. 101–109; and John Huston, *An Open Book* (New York: Alfred A. Knopf, 1980), pp. 251–258. For Bradbury's accounts, see Arnold Kunert, "Ray Bradbury on Hitchcock, Huston and Other Magic of the Screen," *Take One*, May–June 1972 [published Sept. 1973], pp. 16–17; and Ray Bradbury, *Green Shadows, White Whale* (New York: Alfred A. Knopf, 1992).

37 / A rather pointed anecdote made the rounds in Hollywood concerning de Toth, who had one eye, and his ability to direct this 3-D film. Assuming he could not perceive depth the same way as those with binocular vision, someone once asked de Toth how he could have made such a movie. Legend has it that he replied, "Beethoven couldn't hear, could he?"

38 / Roy Newquist, *Conversations with Joan Crawford* (Secaucus, N.J.: Citadel Press, 1980), p. 105. *Pocketful of Miracles*, a Frank Capra production of a Damon Runyon story, is a sentimental comedy starring Davis as the head of a bunch of peddlers and panhandlers that includes an amputee, a blind man, a deaf woman, and a small-statured man. *The Story of Esther Costello* featured Crawford as a wealthy American who takes charge of the deaf-blind title character, an impoverished Irish girl. For further discussions of these films, see Schuchman, *Hollywood Speaks*, pp. 61–62, 64–65.

39 / Crawford cited in Newquist, *Conversations*, p. 108; *NYT*, 7 Nov. 1962, p. 48; Bette Davis with Michael Herskowitz, *This 'n That* (New York: Berkley Books, 1988), p. 107.

40 / Medved and Medved, *Hollywood*, p. 228.

41 / Wyman, "The Lady's Not for Spurning," p. 5.

42 / Zola, "Communication Barriers," pp. 142, 143.

43 / Verville, "Federal Legislative History," p. 448; Gerben DeJong, "Independent Living: From Social Movement to Analytic Paradigm," in *Psychological and Social Impact*, ed. Marinelli and Dell Orto, p. 44.

7 / *Moving toward the Mainstream*

1 / Murray Schumach, "Hollywood Maverick," *NYT*, 28 May 1961, sect. 2, p. 7; Wasko, *Movies and Money*, p. 107; Penn cited in Rex Reed, "Penn: Where Did All the Chase-ing Lead?," *NYT*, 13 Feb. 1966, sect. 2, p. 3.

2 / Cited in Peter Bart, "The 'Big' Little Picture," *NYT*, 11 Apr. 1965, sect. 2, p. 7.

3 / Patricia Wright, "Disabling Attitudes," *Contact*, Spring 1987, p. 6. See also Verville, "Federal Legislative History," pp. 448–450, and DeLoach et al., *Independent Living*, pp. 17–18.

4 / Though Jarré's use of a cane seems mostly incidental, Hitchcock on other occasions created minor characters with disabilities to make some point. Bruno Anthony (Robert Walker) of *Strangers on a Train* (1951) helps a blind man cross the street mere moments after strangling a woman in an amusement park, the juxtaposition of deadly and kindly deeds further underscoring his psychotic nature. In a Hitchcockian exercise designed to encourage audience identification with criminal behavior, the title character of 1965's *Marnie* (Tippi Hedren) fears she has drawn the attention of a cleaning woman while trying to break into a company safe after hours. Quite by coincidence the woman is deaf and doesn't notice, however, allowing Marnie and the audience to share a sigh of relief.

5 / Cited in Sherman, *Directing the Film*, pp. 18–19.

6 / Cited in Bart, "The 'Big' Little Picture," p. 7.

7 / Verville, "Federal Legislative History," p. 449.

8 / *Newsweek*, 27 Dec. 1965, p. 71; Mason, "Sidney Poitier," p. 1.

9 / *Commonweal*, 24 Dec. 1965, p. 376; *Time*, 17 Dec. 1965, p. 98.

10 / Reed, "Penn," p. 3.

11 / *Newsweek*, 6 Nov. 1967, p. 94.

12 / Cited in A. H. Weiler, "Arkin Is a Lonely Hunter," *NYT*, 26 Mar. 1967, sect. 2, p. 17.

13 / Cited in Rex Reed, "The Stars Fall on Alabama — Again," *NYT*, 10 Dec. 1967, sect. 2, pp. 19–20.

14 / Merson cited in Weiler, "Arkin," p. 17; Arkin cited in Reed, "The Stars," p. 20.

15 / The unnamed Warners executive cited in Reed, "The Stars," p. 20; Miller cited on p. 19.

16 / Schuchman, *Hollywood Speaks*, p. 69; Arkin cited in Reed, "The Stars," p. 19.

17 / Cited in Reed, "The Stars," p. 19.

18 / MGM had terminated her contract with twenty-one months left on it after she took the Fifth Amendment during the second round of HUAC hearings. See *NYT*, 23 Nov. 1951, p. 32.

19 / Cited in Roger Ebert, "Can That Fat Old Man Be John Wayne?," *NYT*, 29 June 1969, sect. 2, p. 15.

20 / Cited in *Waldo Salt*.

21 / Schlesinger and Salt cited in *Waldo Salt*.

22 / *The New Republic*, 7 June 1969, p. 20. Hoffman shared Kauffmann's "actor's dream" assessment of the role. "That kind of part, a real character role, really comes easiest to me," he said. "The *hard* thing for me is *not* to have a particular voice for a part, a particular gait. And I started to wonder if doing those roles isn't a cop-out, because they do come so easily." Cited in Tom Burke, "Dustin Hoffman Graduates," *Eye*, May 1969, p. 54.

23 / Hollywood moviemakers have long demonstrated a hesitancy to deal with epilepsy, and those that have tend to avoid the form characterized by *grand mal* seizures (i.e., convulsions). Among the few other epilepsy-related films are *Dr. Kildare's Crisis* (1940), one of the "Dr. Kildare" cycle of movies that featured Robert Young as a man affected by a nonhereditary variant; *Night Unto Night* (1949), a film directed by Don Siegel that starred Ronald Reagan as a biochemist with epilepsy and that unfortunately implies that the disorder is tantamount to a death sentence; and *The Brothers Karamazov* (1958), an adaptation of the Dostoyevsky novel written and directed by Richard Brooks that had among its four title characters a man with epilepsy played by Albert Salmi. These U.S. productions fade in stark contrast to an Italian black comedy called *I Pugni in Tasca* [*Fist in His Pocket*], a 1966 film directed by Marco Bellochio about an epileptic young man who plots to murder his blind mother, epileptic sister, and developmentally disabled younger brother to allow his older brother to lead more of a mainstream life.

24 / Klobas, *Disability Drama*, p. 414.

25 / Rosenthal and Kass, *Browning, Siegel,* pp. 80–81.

26 / Ibid., pp. 145–146.

27 / Cited in Stuart M. Kaminsky, *Don Siegel: Director* (New York: Curtis Books, 1974), p. 253. See also Dick, *Radical Innocence*, pp. 97–98.

28 / Cited in Stuart M. Kaminsky, "Don Siegel," *Take One*, Mar.–Apr. 1971 [published June 1972], p. 14.

29 / Arthur Cooper, "The Spoils of War," *Newsweek*, 9 Aug. 1971, p. 70; Trumbo cited on p. 72.

30 / Cited in Guy Flatley, "Thirty Years Later, Johnny Gets His Gun Again," *NYT*, 28 June 1970, sect. 2, p. 11.

31 / Luis Buñuel, *My Last Sigh*, trans. Abigail Israel (New York: Alfred A. Knopf, 1983), p. 193; Trumbo cited in "Trumbo's 'Johnny Got His Gun' Is Screened at Cannes Festival," *NYT*, 15 May 1971, p. 20. Ever since the famous blinding scene in *Un Chien Andalou* (1929), Buñuel demonstrated a fascination with disability issues and often included people with physical disabilities in his films. Among the many characters are a blind man and a legless man beset by youthful tormentors in *Los Olvidados* (1950), a classic Sweet Innocent in the form of a young deaf-mute woman in *La Muerte en este Jardin* (1956), the disabled beggars who participate in the infamous "Last Supper" scene in *Viridiana* (1961), and the young woman with an amputated leg in *Tristana* (1970). Buñuel is a problematic figure in the international Cinema of Isolation. Though hearing-impaired, he expressed his distaste for people with blindness on several occasions. See *My Last Sigh*, pp. 220–222, and Luis Buñuel, *The Exterminating Angel, Nazarin, Los Olvidados*, trans. Nicholas Fry (London: Lorrimer, 1972), p. 298.

32 / For a summary of the numerous positive reviews, see the *Johnny Got His Gun* pressbook, BR Collection. See also Leonard Maltin, *TV Movies and Video Guide* (New York: New American Library, 1988), p. 542; and Judith Crist, "This Week's Movies," *TV Guide*, 25 June 1983, p. A-5.

33 / *Variety*, 28 Nov. 1973, p. 14.

34 / Ibid.

35 / Krents, a disability rights activist who died in 1987 of a brain tumor at age 42, was also the focus of another production: *To Race the Wind* (1980), a CBS made-for-TV movie based on his autobiography that dealt mainly with his law-school years. Director Walter Grauman, who in 1964 had equated blindness with disempowerment in the highly unsettling shocker *Lady in a Cage*, presented the Krents character (Steve Guttenberg) in a notably sympathetic way.

36 / Klobas, *Disability Drama*, p. 29. For a sample positive review, see *Variety*, 5 July 1972, p. 16.

37 / Cited in Sherman, *Directing the Film*, p. 323, and in Wood, *Hollywood from Vietnam to Reagan*, p. 41. See also Giles Fowler, "Moviemaker Altman: Artist as Freewheeler," *Kansas City Star*, 3 Aug. 1975, sect. 4, pp. 1–2.

38 / Wood, *Hollywood from Vietnam to Reagan*, p. 57.

39 / NYT, 2 Aug. 1973, p. 31; *Variety*, 25 July 1973, p. 6; Nash and Ross, *The Motion Picture Guide*, p. 1905.

40 / Evans G. Valens, *The Other Side of the Mountain Part II* (New York: Warner Books, 1978), pp. 116, 120. A brief summary of Kinmont's post-disablement life may be found on pp. 16–17.

41 / Kinmont cited in Evans G. Valens, *The Other Side of the Mountain* (New York: Warner Books, 1975), pp. 296, 297, and in Valens, *Other Side II*, pp. 55–56; Seltzer cited, p. 47. See also p. 119.

42 / Peerce and Feldman cited in Valens, *Other Side*, p. 298.

43 / For a sense of Kinmont's concerns, see Valens, *Other Side II*, p. 153. In general, the critics either praised the film for its sensitivity or condemned it for its manipulative qualities. For excerpts from ten reviews, see pp. 165–169. June Kinmont cited on p. 185.

44 / Though, apparently, this scene was largely the invention of the filmmakers. See Valens, *Other Side II*, p. 151.

45 / Time, 5 Mar. 1979, pp. 74, 76; *Newsweek*, 5 Feb. 1979, p. 79.

46 / Cited in Patrick McGilligan and Janet Maslin, "Ken Russell Faces the Music," *Take One*, July-Aug. 1974 [published Dec. 1975], p. 20, and in Hollis Alpert, "Puzzles and Pop," *Saturday Review*, 3 May 1975, p. 35.

47 / Cited in McGilligan and Maslin, "Ken Russell," p. 20.

48 / Cited in Jay Cocks, "Tommy Rocks In," *Time*, 31 Mar. 1975, p. 57.

8 / High-Tech Heroics and Other Concerns

1 / Mast and Kawin, "A Short History," pp. 513–514.

2 / Kent Hull, *The Rights of Physically Handicapped People* (New York: Avon Books, 1979), p. 23; Quart and Auster, "The Wounded Vet," p. 25.

3 / Cited in "Hollywood Tackles Vietnam War," *NYT*, 2 Aug. 1977, p. 24; Quart and Auster, "The Wounded Vet," p. 25.

4 / Cited in Kirk Honeycutt, "The Five-Year Struggle to Make *Coming Home*," *NYT*, 19 Feb. 1978, sect. 2, p. 13. See also "Dialogue on Film: Jerome Hellman," *American Film*, June 1978, pp. 33–48; and Stephen Farber and Marc Green, *Hollywood Dynasties* (New York: Delilah, 1984), pp. 160–162.

5 / Cited in *Hollywood Screenwriters and Their Craft*, a three-part 1986 video series produced by Mark Schaubert Productions for the Institute for Communication and Professional Studies, California State University–Northridge.

6 / Cited in Peter Collier, *The Fondas: A Hollywood Dynasty* (New York: G. P. Putnam's Sons, 1991), p. 253.

7 / The V.A. political scene changed considerably during *Coming Home*'s filming after newly elected president Jimmy Carter appointed Max Cleland its executive director. Within weeks Cleland, who lost three limbs in Vietnam, offered Hellman and Schlesinger his assistance, but by that time the filmmakers had already completed their work at Rancho Los Amigos. See "Dialogue on Film: Jerome Hellman," p. 39.

8 / Cited in Honeycutt, *"Coming Home,"* p. 13. Ashby noted in a subsequent interview that he and a writer named Rudy Wurlitzer rewrote much of the script after shooting had begun, but that their restructuring of it "had a lot to do with some of the conversations I'd had with Waldo Salt. I think we accomplished most of the ideas he described and wanted to go toward." See "Dialogue on Film: Hal Ashby," *American Film*, May 1980, p. 55.

9 / Cited in David Keller, "Making *Coming Home*: An Interview with Haskell Wexler," *Filmmakers Newsletter*, Mar. 1978, p. 21.

10 / Leo Cawley, "The War About the War: Vietnam Films and American Myth," in *From Hanoi to Hollywood: The Vietnam War in American Film*, eds. Linda Dittmar and Gene Michaud (New Brunswick, N.J.: Rutgers University Press, 1990), p. 71.

11 / Salt cited in *Waldo Salt*; Ebert's 1978 review reprinted in Roger Ebert, *Roger Ebert's Movie Home Companion* (Kansas City, Mo.: Andrews, McMeel & Parker, 1988), p. 119; Hellman cited in Honeycutt, *"Coming Home,"* p. 13.

12 / Cited in Letitia Kent, "Ready for Vietnam? A Talk with Michael Cimino," *NYT*, 10 Dec. 1978, sect. 2, p. 23.

13 / Quart and Auster, "The Wounded Vet," p. 30.

14 / Cited in Roger Copeland, "A Vietnam Movie That Does Not Knock America," *NYT*, 7 Aug. 1977, p. 19.

15 / Cited in "Dialogue on Film: Ivan Passer," *American Film*, Nov. 1988, p. 16.

16 / Cited in Joe Leydon, "Ivan Passer and Jeffrey Alan Fiskin Interviewed by Joe Leydon," *Film Comment*, July–Aug. 1981, p. 22; and in "Dialogue on Film: Ivan Passer," p. 16.

17 / Cited in Richard T. Jameson, "Passer's Way," *Film Comment*, July–Aug. 1981, p. 21; Jameson, p. 19.

18 / Leydon, "Ivan Passer," p. 21.

19 / *NYT*, 20 Mar. 1981, sect. 3, p. 6; *Variety*, 18 Mar. 1981, p. 133.

20 / Cited in Chris Chase, "At the Movies," *NYT*, 29 May 1981, sect. 3, p. 8. For a more detailed discussion of *Cutter's Way* and its themes, see Martin F. Norden, "Portrait of a Disabled Vietnam Veteran: Alex Cutter of *Cutter's Way*," in *From Hanoi to Hollywood*, ed. Dittmar and Michaud, pp. 217–225.

21 / Stephen Farber, "Once in Love with Amy . . .," *Cosmopolitan*, Mar. 1985, p. 92.

22 / *Voices* pressbook, BR Collection; Walla cited in "Movie Captioned for the Deaf Closes," *NYT*, 7 June 1979, sect. 3, p. 17; Lee Grant, "Films of Deaf Not for Deaf," *LAT*, 14 Mar. 1979, sect. 4, pp. 1, 15, 16; Linda Levitan, "Faking It!" *Deaf Life*, Aug. 1992, p. 26. For a more thorough discussion of the film's content, see Schuchman, *Hollywood Speaks*, pp. 78–80.

23 / Over the objections of GLAD, *Concorde* producer Lang and director Rich used a hearing performer to play the deaf girl. According to Marcella Meyer, "We asked them to use a real deaf child. They told us no way. So we at least taught her sign language." See Grant, "Films of Deaf," p. 16.

24 / Audiences and critics shunned the $2 million *Joni*, which starred the wheelchair-using Joni Eareckson in her own life story, presumably because of the perception that it was religious propaganda on behalf of Graham's ministry. For a discussion of the movie's production, see Twila Knaack, "Picture of Courage," *Saturday Evening Post*, Mar. 1980, pp. 60–61, 81.

25 / Cited in "Dialogue on Film: Richard Donner," *American Film*, May 1981, p. 59.

26 / Ibid., p. 58.

27 / *Christian Science Monitor*, 5 Feb. 1981, p. 19; *Village Voice*, 24–30 Dec. 1980, p. 42; *Films in Review*, Feb. 1981, p. 119; *Newsweek*, 5 Jan. 1981, p. 55; Russell cited in "An Oscar Winner Makes Film Comeback After 33 Years," *NYT*, 15 Feb. 1980, sect. 2, p. 2.

28 / Cited in "Dialogue on Film: Richard Donner," p. 59.

29 / John A. R. Tibbles and M. Michael Cohen, Jr., "The Proteus Syndrome: The Elephant Man Diagnosed," *British Medical Journal* 293 (13 Sept. 1986): 683–685. See also "What the Elephant Man Really Had," *Newsweek*, 29 Feb. 1988, p. 64.

30 / Cited in Henry Bromell, "Visionary from Fringeland," *Rolling Stone*, 13 Nov. 1980, p. 16.

31 / As Robert Asahina pointed out in his review of *The Elephant Man*, a comparison of Michael Howell and Peter Ford's *The True Story of the Elephant Man* (New York: Penguin, 1980) with the film reveals numerous discrepancies. His summary may be found in *New Leader*, 22 Sept. 1980, p. 18. Peter W. Graham and Fritz H. Oehlschlaeger offered a compelling and richly detailed comparative analysis of the often contradictory literary, theatrical, and filmic representations of Merrick in their *Articulating the Elephant Man: Joseph Merrick and His Interpreters* (Baltimore: Johns Hopkins University Press, 1992).

32 / *Newsweek*, 6 Oct. 1980, p. 72; *Time*, 6 Oct. 1980, p. 93.

33 / *Glamour*, Feb. 1982, p. 82; *Time*, 14 Dec. 1981, p. 92; Dreyfuss cited in Leslie Bennetts, "Richard Dreyfuss—Reviled Heroes Fascinate Him," *NYT*, 27 Dec. 1981, sect. 2, p. 17.

34 / Cited in Bennetts, "Richard Dreyfuss," p. 17. See also Aljean Harmetz, "Pryor and Alda Proving Stars Still Sell Movies," *NYT*, 30 May 1981, p. 10; and Schuchman, *Hollywood Speaks*, pp. 80–82.

35 / John Mortimer, who rewrote about a third of the script, went uncredited. For a brief history of the film and its literary predecessors, see Mitch Tuchman, "Bradbury: Shooting Haiku in a Barrel," *Film Comment*, Nov.–Dec. 1982, p. 39.

36 / *LAT*, 29 Apr. 1983, sect. 6, p. 9. Stacy's post-disablement acting career received several boosts from Kirk Douglas; his Bryna company not only co-produced *Something Wicked* but also created *Posse* (1975), a Western that Douglas starred in, produced, and directed, and that featured Stacy in a supporting role. Stacy scored greater successes as a television actor, playing lead roles in such made-for-TV movies as *Just a Little Inconvenience* (1977) and *My Kidnapper, My Love* (1980), the latter of which he also produced. According to Lauri Klobas, his guest-starring work on a 1986 episode of *Cagney and Lacey* "generated an overwhelming amount of mail from viewers, *all* of it positive." See Klobas, *Disability Drama*, p. 309.

37 / Benton cited in Don Shewey, "True Midwest," *American Film*, Oct. 1985, p. 28; *Films in Review*, Oct. 1984, p. 495; *LAT*, 21 Sept. 1984, sect. 6, p. 16.

38 / The anonymous source cited in Michael Leahy, "'I Wasn't on Drugs,'" *TV Guide*, 5 Oct. 1985, pp. 15–16; McNichol cited in an Associated Press story published as "'Empty Nest' Star Talks About Her Breakdown," *Daily Hampshire Gazette* (Northampton, Mass.), 28 Mar. 1989, p. 27; Lorrie Lynch, "Who's News," *USA Weekend*, 8–10 Jan. 1993, p. 2; *Newsday*, 16 Nov. 1984, sect. 3, p. 3; *New York Post*, 16 Nov. 1984, p. 47; Klobas, *Disability Drama*, p. 433; *LAT*, 15 Nov. 1984, sect. 6, p. 6.

39 / Cited in Robert Garrett, "Why 'Children' Is a Hollywood Rarity," *Boston Globe*, 28 Sept. 1986, sect. 2, p. 38

40 / Cited in Nina Darnton, "At the Movies," *NYT*, 26 Sept. 1986, sect. 3, p. 6. Hurt incidentally spent three months learning ASL for the role.

41 / Cited in A. E. Hardie, "The Deaf Are Divided on the Film 'Lesser God,'" *NYT*, 16 Nov. 1986, p. 72.

42 / Cited in Lynn Minton, "What's Up This Week," *Parade*, 28 Sept. 1986, p. 19. See also Paul Attanasio, "Randa Haines' Inner Voice," *Washington Post*, 12 Oct. 1986, sect. 6, pp. 1, 5.

43 / Davis and Nolan cited in Hardie, "The Deaf Are Divided," p. 72.

44 / *NYT*, 23 Apr. 1982, sect. 3, p. 8; *Maclean's*, 10 May 1982, p. 63.

45 / As noted by Kirk Bauer, executive director of the National Handicapped Sports and Recreation Assn., "The top is literally being blown off of what we can do because of the new high-tech equipment." Cited in Anastasia Toufexis, "Breaking the 'Can't Do' Barrier," *Time*, 28 Nov. 1988, p. 100. This same article also provides a brief overview of several new prosthetic aids.

46 / Indeed, experiments by the National Institute of Health's Neural Prosthesis Program involved electronic devices and procedures not all that different from those depicted in *Blind Date*. See Richard Stone, "An Artificial Eye May Be Within Sight," *Washington Post*, 20 Aug. 1990, p. 3.

47 / Stephen King, *Silver Bullet* (New York: New American Library, 1985), p. 11.

48 / Ibid., p. 231.

49 / Ibid., p. 16.

50 / *People Weekly*, 1 Aug. 1988, p. 19; *Time*, 8 Aug. 1988, p. 68. A thorough synopsis and a discussion of Romero's troubles with Evans, including the writer-director's overridden ending, may be found in *The Motion Picture Guide 1989 Annual*, ed. William Leahy (Evanston, Ill.: CineBooks, 1989), pp. 113–114.

51 / Cited in an Associated Press story published as "Actor Plugs His Ears to Get Feel of Role," *Daily Hampshire Gazette*, 27 Oct. 1987, p. 26.

52 / Cher and Roth cited in Bruce Weber, "Cher's Next Act," *NYT Magazine*, 18 Oct. 1987, p. 56; *LAT*, 22 Oct. 1987, sect. 6, p. 9. For a brief article on *Mask*'s marketing, see Aljean Harmetz, "Deformity in 'Mask' Poses Publicity Problems," *NYT*, 27 Apr. 1985, p. 9.

53 / Oliver Stone, "My Brilliant Career," *Time*, 26 Jan. 1987, p. 60; Kovic cited in Seidenberg, "To Hell and Back," p. 56.

54 / Cited in Richard Corliss, "Tom Terrific," *Time*, 25 Dec. 1989, p. 79.

55 / Cited on *The Today Show*, NBC-TV, 22 Dec. 1989.

56 / Cited on *The Today Show*, NBC-TV, 19 Dec. 1989.

57 / Cited in Seidenberg, "To Hell and Back," p. 28. Though bedeviled by minor fact errors, Steve Lipkin's analysis of *Born on the Fourth of July* provides important insights into this provocative film. See his "The Object Realm of the Vietnam War Film," in *Beyond the Stars III*, ed. Loukides and Fuller, pp. 183–186.

58 / *Films in Review*, Jan. 1981, p. 58; *Monthly Film Bulletin*, Mar. 1981, p. 57; *New York Post*, 31 Oct. 1980, p. 41; Klobas, *Disability Drama*, p. 385.

59 / Cited in an Associated Press story published as "'Gaby' Was Six-Year Obsession for Director," *Daily Hampshire Gazette*, 5 Jan. 1988, p. 10.

60 / *LAT*, 13 Nov. 1987, sect. 6, p. 10; *New York Post*, 30 Oct. 1987, p. 33.

61 / Sheridan and Pearson cited in Anna McDonnell, "Director Jim Sheridan," *Premiere*, Dec. 1989, p. 73.

62 / Day-Lewis cited in an Associated Press story published as "Actor Wows Critics with Handicap Role," *Daily Hampshire Gazette*, 1 Dec. 1989, p. 18; *Time*, 6 Nov. 1989, p. 84. See also *Time*, 19 Feb. 1990, p. 93; Linda Joffee, "Special Night for a Dublin Family," *Christian Science Monitor*, 14 June 1990, p. 11; and Jean Seligmann, "Heroes with Handicaps," *Newsweek*, 15 Jan. 1990, pp. 59–60. For a discussion of *My Left Foot*'s marketing campaign, see Bruce Horovitz, "Targeting Movie Ads Without Sticking Your (Left) Foot in Your Mouth," *LAT*, 20 Mar. 1990, p. 6.

Conclusion / Reel Life after the ADA

1 / Susan F. Rasky, "How the Disabled Sold Congress on a New Bill of Rights," *NYT*, 17 Sept. 1989, sect. 4, p. 5.

2 / Cited in an Associated Press story published as "Rights Bill for Disabled Passes," *Daily Hampshire Gazette*, 13 July 1990, pp. 1, 8.

3 / Cited in Sean Mitchell, "No-Holds Hoffman," *USA Weekend*, 6–8 Dec. 1991, p. 4. A lightweight production history of the film may be found in Jeannie Park, "Ahoy! Neverland!" *People Weekly*, 23 Dec. 1991, pp. 92–102. One element of *Hook*'s merchandising strategy was a tie-in book adapted from James V. Hart and Malia Scotch Marmo's *Hook* screenplay and laden with stills from the film. See Justine Korman, *Hook: The Storybook Based on the Movie* (New York: Random House, 1991).

4 / *Time*, 25 Jan. 1993, p. 69.

5 / Cited in a syndicated article by Roger Ebert, published as "Interview with *Passion Fish* Director John Sayles," *The Valley Optimist* (Northampton, Mass.), 15 Feb. 1993, p. 20. See also Trevor Johnston, "Sayles Talk," *Sight and Sound*, Sept. 1993, pp. 26–29.

6 / A listing of such Oscar-winning performances up to 1991 may be found in Gullo, p. 36. For a sense of the varying reactions of disability activists to *Scent of a Woman*, see Betsy A. Lehman, "The Hurtful Stereotypes About the Disabled," *Boston Globe*, 5 Apr. 1993, pp. 29, 31.

7 / Stohl cited on *The Maury Povich Show*, 14 July 1992; John Leo, "Our Hypersensitive Minorities," *U.S. News & World Report*, 16 Apr. 1990, p. 17; Robert Hughes, "The Fraying of America," *Time*, 3 Feb. 1992, p. 45.

8 / Levitan, "Faking It!" p. 26.

9 / Kovic cited on *The Today Show*, NBC-TV, 21 Dec. 1989, and in Seidenberg, "To Hell and Back," p. 56; Stohl cited in *The Maury Povich Show*, 14 July 1992.

10 / Jimenez cited in Bernard Weinraub, "In This Director's Story, Men Are Linked by Broken Bodies," *NYT*, 10 May 1992, sect. 8, p. 19; *NYT*, 13 May 1992, sect. 3, p. 13.

11 / Jack Kroll, "Spiking a Fever," *Newsweek*, 10 June 1991, p. 47.

12 / Christine Gledhill, "The Melodramatic Field: An Investigation," in *Home Is Where the Heart Is: Studies in Melodrama and the Woman's Film*, ed. Christine Gledhill (London: BFI Publishing, 1987), p. 10.

13 / See Jonathan Rabinovitz, "Disabled People Gain Roles in Ads and on TV," *NYT*, 23 Sept. 1991, p. 14.

14 / Tania Modleski, "Never to Be Thirty-Six Years Old: *Rebecca* as Female Oedipal Drama," *Wide Angle* 5 (1982): 34.

15 / Martin F. Norden, "Movie Constructions of Gender and Physical Disability: Some Theoretical and Historical Intersections," University Film and Video Association conference, Philadelphia, Aug. 1993.

16 / Anne Finger, "Claiming *All* of Our Bodies: Reproductive Rights and Disability," in *Test-Tube Women*, ed. Arditti, Klein, and Minden, pp. 282, 291–292. See also *Women with Disabilities: Essays in Psychology, Culture and Politics*, ed. Michelle Fine and Adrienne Asch (Philadelphia: Temple University Press, 1988).

17 / Williams, "When the Woman Looks," p. 83.

18 / Fiedler, *Freaks*, p. 137.

19 / Bogdan et al., "The Disabled: Media's Monster," p. 32; Howard G. Chua-Eoan, "The Uses of Monsters," *Time*, 19 Aug. 1991, p. 66.

20 / Williams, "When the Woman Looks," pp. 87–88.

21 / Kaja Silverman, "Historical Trauma and Male Subjectivity," in *Psychoanalysis and Cinema*, ed. E. Ann Kaplan (New York: Routledge, 1990), pp. 118, 121.

22 / Ibid., pp. 114, 117. See also Silverman's *Male Subjectivity at the Margins* (New York: Routledge, 1992).

23 / Doane, "The 'Woman's Film,'" p. 59.

25 / Michael Selig, "Boys Will Be Men: Oedipal Drama in *Coming Home*," in *From Hanoi to Hollywood*, ed. Dittmar and Michaud, pp. 189–202; Andrew Gordon, "The Power of the Force: Sex in the *Star Wars* Trilogy," in *Eros in the Mind's Eye*, ed. Palumbo, pp. 193– 207; *Village Voice*, 24–30 Dec. 1980, p. 42.

selected bibliography

Books

Anderson, Robert G. *Faces, Forms, Films: The Artistry of Lon Chaney*. New York: Castle Books, 1971.

Bardèche, Maurice, and Robert Brasillach. *The History of Motion Pictures*. Translated and edited by Iris Barry. New York: W. W. Norton, 1938.

Barrie, James M. *The Plays of J. M. Barrie*. New York: Charles Scribner's Sons, 1928.

Barry, Iris. *D. W. Griffith: American Film Master*. With an annotated list of films by Eileen Bowser. New York: Museum of Modern Art, 1965.

Barrymore, John [with Karl Schmidt]. *Confessions of an Actor*. Indianapolis: Bobbs-Merrill, 1926.

Behlmer, Rudy, ed. *Inside Warner Bros. (1935–1951)*. New York: Viking Penguin, 1985.

———, ed. *Memo from Darryl F. Zanuck: The Golden Years at Twentieth Century–Fox*. New York: Grove Press, 1993.

———, ed. *Memo from David O. Selznick*. New York: Viking Press, 1972.

Berg, A. Scott. *Goldwyn: A Biography*. New York: Alfred A. Knopf, 1989.

Bohn, Thomas W., and Richard L. Stromgren. *Light and Shadows: A History of Motion Pictures*. 3rd edition. Palo Alto, Calif.: Mayfield Publishing Co., 1987.

Bowser, Eileen, comp. *Biograph Bulletins, 1908–1912*. New York: Octagon Books, 1973.

Brady, Frank. *Citizen Welles: A Biography of Orson Welles*. New York: Anchor Books, 1989.

Brosnan, John. *The Horror People*. New York: St. Martin's Press, 1976.

Brownlow, Kevin. *The Parade's Gone By . . ..* New York: Ballantine Books, 1968.

Callow, Simon. *Charles Laughton: A Difficult Actor*. London: Methuen, 1987.

Capra, Frank. *The Name Above the Title: An Autobiography*. New York: Macmillan, 1971.

Collier, Peter. *The Fondas: A Hollywood Dynasty*. New York: G. P. Putnam's Sons, 1991.

Coppedge, Walter. *Henry King's America*. Filmmakers no. 15. Metuchen, N.J.: Scarecrow Press, 1986.

Crowther, Bosley. *The Lion's Share: The Story of an Entertainment Empire*. New York: E. P. Dutton, 1957.

Curtis, James. *James Whale*. Filmmakers no. 1. Metuchen, N.J.: Scarecrow Press, 1982.

DeLoach, Charlene P., Ronnie D. Wilkins, and Guy W. Walker, *Independent Living: Philosophy, Process, and Services*. Baltimore: University Park Press, 1983.

Devine, Edward T. *Disabled Soldiers and Sailors: Pensions and Training*. Carnegie Endowment for International Peace, Preliminary Economic Studies of the War, no. 12. New York: Oxford University Press, 1919.

Dick, Bernard F. *Radical Innocence: A Critical Study of the Hollywood Ten*. Lexington: University Press of Kentucky, 1989.

Duke, Patty, and Kenneth Turan. *Call Me Anna: The Autobiography of Patty Duke*. New York: Bantam Books, 1987.

Eastman, John. *Retakes: Behind the Scenes of 500 Classic Movies*. New York: Ballantine Books, 1989.

Edmonds, I. G. *Big U: Universal in the Silent Days*. South Brunswick, N.J.: A. S. Barnes, 1977.

Erickson, Wendy, and Diane Wolfe, comps. *Images of Blind and Visually Impaired People in the Movies, 1913–1985: An Annotated Filmography with Notes*. New York: American Foundation for the Blind, 1985.

Everson, William K. *American Silent Film*. New York: Oxford University Press, 1978.

Fiedler, Leslie A. *Freaks: Myths and Images of the Secret Self*. New York: Simon and Schuster, 1978.

Fowler, Gene. *Good Night, Sweet Prince: The Life and Times of John Barrymore*. New York: Viking Press, 1944.

Fulton, A. R. *Motion Pictures: The Development of an Art from Silent Films to the Age of Television*. Norman: University of Oklahoma Press, 1960.

Gartner, Alan, and Tom Joe, eds. *Images of the Disabled, Disabling Images*. New York: Praeger Publishers, 1987.

Gifford, Denis. *The British Film Catalog, 1895–1985: A Reference Guide*. New York: Facts on File Publications, 1986.

Glut, Donald F. *The Frankenstein Legend: A Tribute to Mary Shelley and Boris Karloff*. Metuchen, N.J.: Scarecrow Press, 1973.

Gomery, Douglas. *The Hollywood Studio System*. London: Macmillan, 1986.

Goulden, Joseph C. *The Best Years 1945–1950*. New York: Atheneum, 1976.

Graham, Cooper C., Steven Higgins, Elaine Mancini, and João Luiz Vieira. *D. W. Griffith and the Biograph Company*. Filmmakers no. 10. Metuchen, N.J.: Scarecrow Press, 1985.

Halliday, Jon, ed. *Sirk on Sirk: Interviews with Jon Halliday*. New York: Viking Press, 1972.

Hampton, Benjamin B. *A History of the Movies*. New York: Covici, Friede, 1931.

Hanson, Patricia King, ed. *The American Film Institute Catalog of Motion Pictures Produced in the United States: Feature Films 1911–1920*. Berkeley: University of California Press, 1988.

Hellman, Lillian. *Three: An Unfinished Woman, Pentimento, Scoundrel Time*. Boston: Little, Brown, 1979.

Henderson, George, and Willie V. Bryan. *Psychosocial Aspects of Disability*. Springfield, Ill.: Charles C. Thomas, 1984.

Henderson, Robert M. *D. W. Griffith: His Life and Work*. New York: Oxford University Press, 1972.

———. *D. W. Griffith: The Years at Biograph*. New York: Farrar, Straus & Giroux, 1970.

Hyams, Jay. *War Movies*. New York: W. H. Smith Publishers, 1984.

Jesionowski, Joyce E. *Thinking in Pictures: Dramatic Structure in D. W. Griffith's Biograph Films*. Berkeley: University of California Press, 1987.

Jobes, Gertrude. *Motion Picture Empire*. Hamden, Conn.: Archon Books, 1966.

Kahn, Gordon. *Hollywood on Trial: The Story of the 10 Who Were Indicted*. New York: Boni & Gaer, 1948.

Katz, Ephraim. *The Film Encyclopedia*. New York: Thomas Y. Crowell, 1979.

King, Stephen. *Silver Bullet*. New York: New American Library, 1985.

Klobas, Lauri E. *Disability Drama in Television and Film*. Jefferson, N.C.: McFarland, 1988.

Kobler, John. *Damned in Paradise: The Life of John Barrymore*. New York: Atheneum, 1977.

Kotsilibas–Davis, James. *The Barrymores: The Royal Family in Hollywood*. New York: Crown Publishers, 1981.

Lasky, Betty. *RKO: The Biggest Little Major of Them All*. Englewood Cliffs, N.J.: Prentice-Hall, 1984.

Lennig, Arthur. *The Silent Voice: The Golden Age of the Cinema*. Albany: Faculty-Student Association of the State University of New York at Albany, 1966.

Liachowitz, Claire H. *Disability as a Social Construct: Legislative Roots*. Philadelphia: University of Pennsylvania Press, 1988.

Low, Rachael, and Roger Manvell. *The History of the British Film, 1896–1906*. London: George Allen & Unwin, 1948.

Low, Rachael. *The History of the British Film, 1906–1914*. London: George Allen & Unwin, 1949.

Maland, Charles J. *Chaplin and American Culture: The Evolution of a Star Image*. Princeton, N.J.: Princeton University Press, 1989.

Mank, Gregory. *Karloff and Lugosi: The Story of a Haunting Collaboration*. Jefferson, N.C.: McFarland, 1990.

Marion, Frances. *Off with Their Heads!: A Serio-Comic Tale of Hollywood*. New York: Macmillan, 1972.

Marx, Arthur. *Goldwyn: A Biography of the Man Behind the Myth*. New York: W. W. Norton, 1976.

Mast, Gerald, and Bruce F. Kawin. *A Short History of the Movies*. 5th ed. New York: Macmillan, 1992.

McDermott, John J. *Streams of Experience: Reflections on the History and Philosophy of American Culture*. Amherst: University of Massachusetts Press, 1986.

Meynell, Violet, ed. *Letters of J. M. Barrie*. New York: Charles Scribner's Sons, 1947.

Molyneaux, Gerard. *Charlie Chaplin's 'City Lights'*. New York: Garland, 1983.

Munden, Kenneth W., ed. *The American Film Institute Catalog of Motion Pictures Produced in the United States: Feature Films 1921–1930*. New York: R. R. Bowker, 1971.

Nash, Jay Robert, and Stanley Ralph Ross. *The Motion Picture Guide, 1927–1984*. Chicago: CineBooks, 1987.

Navasky, Victor S. *Naming Names*. New York: Viking Press, 1980.

Newquist, Roy. *Conversations with Joan Crawford*. Secaucus, N.J.: Citadel Press, 1980.

Niver, Kemp R. *D. W. Griffith, His Biograph Films in Perspective*. Los Angeles: Kemp R. Niver, 1974.

―――. *Motion Pictures from the Library of Congress Paper Print Collection 1894–1912*. Berkeley: University of California Press, 1967.

Nowlan, Robert A., and Gwendolyn Wright Nowlan. *Cinema Sequels and Remakes, 1903–1987*. Jefferson, N.C.: McFarland, 1989.

O'Leary, Liam. *Rex Ingram: Master of the Silent Cinema*. New York: Harper & Row, 1980.

Peters, Margot. *The House of Barrymore*. New York: Alfred A. Knopf, 1990.

Pratt, George C. *Spellbound in Darkness: A History of the Silent Film*. Revised edition. Greenwich, Conn.: New York Graphic Society, 1973.

Ramsaye, Terry. *A Million and One Nights: A History of the Motion Picture*. New York: Simon and Schuster, 1926.

Reagan, Ronald, with Richard G. Hubler. *Where's the Rest of Me?* New York: Duell, Sloan and Pearce, 1965.

Richardson, Joanna. *Sarah Bernhardt and Her World*. London: Weidenfeld and Nicolson, 1977.

Rosenthal, Stuart, and Judith M. Kass. *The Hollywood Professionals*. Vol. 4: *Tod Browning, Don Siegel*. New York: A. S. Barnes, 1975.

Schickel, Richard. *The Disney Version*. New York: Avon Books, 1968.

―――. *D. W. Griffith: An American Life*. New York: Simon and Schuster, 1984.

Schuchman, John S. *Hollywood Speaks: Deafness and the Film Entertainment Industry*. Urbana: University of Illinois Press, 1988.

Schulberg, Budd. *Moving Pictures: Memories of a Hollywood Prince.* New York: Stein and Day, 1981.

Sherman, Eric. *Directing the Film: Film Directors on Their Art.* Los Angeles: Acrobat Books, 1976.

Shindler, Colin. *Hollywood Goes to War: Films and American Society 1939–1952.* London: Routledge & Kegan Paul, 1979.

Sinclair, Upton. *Upton Sinclair Presents William Fox.* Los Angeles: Upton Sinclair, 1933.

Slide, Anthony. *Aspects of American Film History Prior to 1920.* Metuchen, N.J.: Scarecrow Press, 1978.

———. *The Big V: A History of the Vitagraph Company.* Metuchen, N.J.: Scarecrow Press, 1976.

Swindell, Larry. *Spencer Tracy: A Biography.* New York: World Publishing, 1969.

Talbot, Frederick A. *Motion Pictures: How They Are Made and Worked.* Philadelphia: J. B. Lippincott, 1914.

Thomas, Bob. *Thalberg: Life and Legend.* Garden City, N.Y.: Doubleday, 1969.

Truffaut, François. *Hitchcock.* Revised edition. New York: Simon and Schuster, 1984.

Valens, Evans G. *The Other Side of the Mountain.* New York: Warner Books, 1975.

———. *The Other Side of the Mountain Part II.* New York: Warner Books, 1978.

Wagenknecht, Edward. *The Movies in the Age of Innocence.* Norman: University of Oklahoma Press, 1962.

Wasko, Janet. *Movies and Money: Financing the American Film Industry.* Norwood, N.J.: Ablex Publishing Corp., 1982.

Wheeler, David, ed. *No, but I Saw the Movie: The Best Short Stories Ever Made into Film.* New York: Penguin Books, 1989.

Williams, Martin T. *Griffith: First Artist of the Movies.* New York: Oxford University Press, 1980.

Zinnemann, Fred. *A Life in the Movies: An Autobiography.* New York: Charles Scribner's Sons, 1992.

Articles

Auty, Martyn. "*The Big Parade.*" In *Movies of the Silent Years.* Edited by Ann Lloyd. London: Orbis Publishing Ltd., 1984, pp. 102–103.

Ball, Robert Hamilton. "Shakespeare in One Reel." *The Quarterly of Film, Radio, and Television* 8 (1953–54): 139–149.

Byrd, E. Keith, and Randolph B. Pipes. "Feature Films and Disability." *Journal of Rehabilitation* 47, no. 1 (Jan.–Mar. 1981): 51–53, 80.

Crafton, Donald. "The Last Night in the Nursery: Walt Disney's *Peter Pan.*" *The Velvet Light Trap Review of Cinema,* no. 24 (Fall 1989): 33–52.

DeJong, Gerben. "Independent Living: From Social Movement to Analytic Paradigm." In *The Psychological and Social Impact of Physical Disability.* Edited by Robert P. Marinelli and Arthur E. Dell Orto. 2nd edition. New York: Springer Publishing Co., 1984, pp. 39–63.

Doane, Mary Ann, Patricia Mellencamp, and Linda Williams. "Feminist Film Criticism: An Introduction." In *Re-vision: Essays in Feminist Film Criticism.* Edited by Mary Ann Doane, Patricia Mellencamp, and Linda Williams. Frederick, Md.: University Publications of America, 1984, pp. 1–17.

Doane, Mary Ann. "The 'Woman's Film': Possession and Address." In *Re-vision: Essays in Feminist Film Criticism*. Edited by Mary Ann Doane, Patricia Mellencamp, and Linda Williams. Frederick, Md.: University Publications of America, 1984, pp. 67–82.

Doran, Charles R. "The Kaiser's War Pictures." *Motion Picture Supplement*, Sept. 1915, pp. 45–47, 62.

Elliott, Timothy R., and E. Keith Byrd. "Media and Disability." *Rehabilitation Literature* 43, no. 11–12 (Nov.–Dec. 1982): 348–355.

Finger, Anne. "Claiming *All* of Our Bodies: Reproductive Rights and Disability." In *Test-Tube Women: What Future for Motherhood?*. Edited by Rita Arditti, Renate Duelli, and Shelley Minden. London: Pandora Press, 1984, pp. 281–297.

Gledhill, Christine. "The Melodramatic Field: An Investigation." in *Home Is Where the Heart Is: Studies in Melodrama and the Woman's Film*. Edited by Christine Gledhill. London: BFI Publishing, 1987, pp. 5–39.

Gordon, Andrew. "The Power of the Force: Sex in the *Star Wars* Trilogy." In *Eros in the Mind's Eye: Sexuality and the Fantastic in Art and Film*. Edited by Donald Palumbo. Westport, Conn.: Greenwood Press, 1986, pp. 193–207.

Grant, Andrew J., and Frank G. Bowe. "Watch Your Language!" In *Handicapped Funding Directory*. Edited by Richard M. Eckstein. 7th edition. Margate, Fla.: Research Grant Guides, 1990, pp. 5–7.

Gullo, Jim. "Oscaring the Handicaps." *Premiere*, April 1991, p. 36.

Hamburger, Amy M. "The Cripple and His Place in the Community." *The Annals of the American Academy of Political and Social Science* 77, no. 166 (May 1918): 36–44.

Kaplan, E. Ann. "Popular Culture, Politics, and the Canon: Cultural Literacy in the Post-modern Age." In *Cultural Power/Cultural Literacy*. Edited by Bonnie Braendlin. Tallahassee: Florida State University Press, 1991, pp. 12–31.

Kriegel, Leonard. "The Wolf in the Pit in the Zoo." *Social Policy* 13, no. 2 (Fall 1982): 16–23.

Levitan, Linda. "Faking It!" *Deaf Life*, August 1992, pp. 21–26.

Lipkin, Steve. "The Object Realm of the Vietnam War Film." In *Beyond the Stars III: The Material World in American Popular Film*. Edited by Paul Loukides and Linda K. Fuller. Bowling Green, Ohio: Bowling Green State University Popular Press, 1993, pp. 175–186.

Locan, Clarence A. "The Lon Chaney I Knew." *Photoplay*, November 1930, pp. 58–64.

Longmore, Paul K. "Screening Stereotypes: Images of Disabled People." *Social Policy* 16, no. 1 (Summer 1985): 31–37.

Mulvey, Laura. "Visual Pleasure and Narrative Cinema." *Screen* 16, no. 3 (Autumn 1975): 6–18.

Norden, Martin F. "Portrait of a Disabled Vietnam Veteran: Alex Cutter of *Cutter's Way*." In *From Hanoi to Hollywood: The Vietnam War in American Film*. Edited by Linda Dittmar and Gene Michaud. New Brunswick, N.J.: Rutgers University Press, 1990, pp. 217–225.

———. "The Racism-Ableism Link in *Home of the Brave* and *Bright Victory*." *Film & History* 20, no. 2 (May 1990): 26–36.

———. "Reel Wheels: The Role of Wheelchairs in American Movies." In *Beyond the Stars III: The Material World in American Popular Film*. Edited by Paul Loukides and Linda K. Fuller. Bowling Green, Ohio: Bowling Green State University Popular Press, 1993, pp. 187–204.

———. "*Sunrise at Campobello* and 1960 Presidential Politics." *Film & History* 16, no. 1 (February 1986): 2–8.

————. "Victims, Villains, Saints, and Heroes: Movie Portrayals of People with Physical Disabilities." In *Beyond the Stars: Stock Characters in American Popular Film.* Edited by Paul Loukides and Linda K. Fuller. Bowling Green, Ohio: Bowling Green State University Popular Press, 1990, pp. 222–233.

O'Leary, Liam. "Rex Ingram, Pageant-Master." In *Movies of the Silent Years.* Edited by Ann Lloyd. London: Orbis Publishing Ltd., 1984, pp. 136–139.

Polan, Dana B. "Blind Insights and Dark Passages: The Problem of Placement in Forties Film." *The Velvet Light Trap Review of Cinema,* no. 20 (Summer 1983): 27–33.

Pulleine, Tim. "A Gentleman's Fate: The Career of John Gilbert." In *Movies of the Silent Years.* Edited by Ann Lloyd. London: Orbis Publishing Ltd., 1984, pp. 98–101.

Quart, Leonard, and Albert Auster. "The Wounded Vet In Post-War Film." *Social Policy* 13, no. 2 (Fall 1982): 24–31.

Robinson, David. "The Enduring Craft of Henry King." In *Movies of the Silent Years.* Edited by Ann Lloyd. London: Orbis Publishing Ltd., 1984, pp. 212–214.

Rose, Jacqueline. "Writing as Auto-Visualisation: Notes on a Scenario and Film of *Peter Pan.*" *Screen* 16, no. 3 (Autumn 1975): 29–53.

Saxton, Marsha. "Born and Unborn: The Implications of Reproductive Technologies for People with Disabilities." In *Test-Tube Women: What Future for Motherhood?* Edited by Rita Arditti, Renate Duelli, and Shelley Minden. London: Pandora Press, 1984, pp. 298–312.

Schuchman, John S. "Silent Movies and the Deaf Community." *Journal of Popular Culture* 17, no. 4 (Spring 1984): 58–78.

Seidenberg, Robert. "To Hell and Back." *American Film,* January 1990, pp. 28–31, 56.

Selig, Michael. "Boys Will Be Men: Oedipal Drama in *Coming Home.*" In *From Hanoi to Hollywood: The Vietnam War in American Film.* Edited by Linda Dittmar and Gene Michaud. New Brunswick, N.J.: Rutgers University Press, 1990, pp. 189–202.

Seligmann, Jean. "Heroes with Handicaps." *Newsweek,* 15 Jan. 1990, pp. 59–60.

Shontz, Franklin C. "Psychological Adjustment to Physical Disability: Trends in Theories." In *The Psychological and Social Impact of Physical Disability.* Edited by Robert P. Marinelli and Arthur E. Dell Orto. 2nd edition. New York: Springer Publishing Co., 1984, pp. 119–126.

Silverman, Kaja. "Historical Trauma and Male Subjectivity." In *Psychoanalysis and Cinema.* Edited by E. Ann Kaplan. New York: Routledge, 1990, pp. 110–127.

Stromgren, Richard L. "The Moving Picture World of W. Stephen Bush." *Film History* 2 (1988): 13–22.

Stubbins, Joseph. "The Politics of Disability." In *Attitudes Toward Persons with Disabilities.* Edited by Harold E. Yuker. New York: Springer Publishing Co., 1988, pp. 22–32.

Thomson, David. "Lon Chaney—The Man of a Thousand Faces." In *Movies of the Silent Years.* Edited by Ann Lloyd. London: Orbis Publishing Ltd., 1984, pp. 124–126.

Verville, Richard E. "Federal Legislative History of Independent Living Programs." *Archives of Physical Medicine and Rehabilitation* 60 (October 1979): 447–451.

Weinberg, Nancy. "Another Perspective: Attitudes of Persons with Disabilities." In *Attitudes Toward Persons with Disabilities.* Edited by Harold E. Yuker. New York: Springer Publishing Co., 1988, pp. 141–153.

————, and Carol Sebian. "The Bible and Disability." *Rehabilitation Counseling Bulletin* 23, no. 4 (June 1980): 273–281.

Williams, Linda. "When the Woman Looks." In *Re-vision: Essays in Feminist Film Criticism.* Edited by Mary Ann Doane, Patricia Mellencamp, and Linda Williams. Frederick, Md.: University Publications of America, 1984, pp. 83–99.

Wyler, William. "No Magic Wand." *The Screen Writer*, February 1947, pp. 1–14.

Yamamoto, Kaoru. "To Be Different." *Rehabilitation Counseling Bulletin*, 14, no. 3 (March 1971): 180–189.

Zola, Irving Kenneth. "Communication Barriers Between 'the Able-Bodied' and 'the Handicapped.'" In *The Psychological and Social Impact of Physical Disability*. Edited by Robert P. Marinelli and Arthur E. Dell Orto. 2nd edition. New York: Springer Publishing Co., 1984, pp. 139–147.

general index

Italicized numbers indicate illustrations.

film index

Italicized numbers indicate illustrations. For television films and series, see the general index.

about the author

Martin F. Norden earned a Ph.D. in speech and dramatic art from the University of Missouri–Columbia in 1977 and is currently a professor of communication at the University of Massachusetts–Amherst. His articles on moving-image media have appeared in such periodicals as *Journal of Film and Video, Wide Angle, Film & History*, and *Journal of Popular Film and Television* and in numerous anthologies. He has participated in many radio, TV, film, and theater productions in various capacities since the early 1970s and is now at work on a biography of an actor who relished playing disabled characters in movies and on stage, John Barrymore.